Fodor's
COMPLETELY REVISED SECOND EDITION

D0834657

NATIONAL PARKS
OF THE
WEST

Fodor's Travel Publications, Inc.
New York • Toronto • London • Sydney • Auckland

ISBN 0–679–02580–4

Fodor's National Parks of the West

Editor: Paula Consolo

Editorial Assistant: Hannah Borgeson

Contributors: Steven K. Amsterdam, Robert Blake, Ron Butler, Deke Castleman, Andrew Collins, Pam Earing, Susan Farewell, Jonathan Gelber, Andrew Giarelli, William Hafford, Pamela Hegarty, Barbara Hodgin, Amy Hunter, Edie Jarolim, Bud Journey, Mimi Kmet, Jeff Kuechle, Andrea Lehman, David Low, Anita Marks, Candy Moulton, Denise Nolty, Peter Oliver, Matt Peters, Carolyn Price, Susan Prockop, Andres Puhvel, Linda K. Schmidt, Stephen Singular, M.T. Schwartzman, Kirby Warnock, Tom Wharton, Dick Willis

Art Director: Fabrizio La Rocca

Cartographer: Maryland Cartographics

Cover Photographs: Yosemite National Park, Jan Hubar/Image Bank; Monument Valley, Don Landwerhle/Image Bank; kayak, Michael Kevin Daly/The Stock Market; trees, Bill Ross/Westlight

Design: Tigist Getachew

Special Sales

MANUFACTURED IN THE UNITED STATES OF AMERICA
10 9 8 7 6 5 4 3 2 1

CONTENTS

ACKNOWLEDGMENTS

 e would like to thank those who helped ensure the accuracy of this book. Special thanks go to the following, who, unless stated otherwise, are employees of the U.S. National Park Service.

Arches: Noel Poe, Diane Allen. **Badlands:** Joe Zarki, Valerie Naylor. **Banff:** Staff (Canadian Parks Service). **Big Bend:** Betty Alex, Tom Alex, Roy Given, Jeff Selleck, Dennis Vasquez. **Black Hills:** Terry Reetz, Gene Singsaas (National Forest Service). **Bryce Canyon:** Lou Good, Susan Colclazer. **Canyon de Chelly:** Wilson Hunter, Lupita Johnson, Max King, Herbert Yazhe. **Canyonlands:** Linda Kuehne, Deb Nester, Saxon Sharpe, Larry Frederick. **Carlsbad:** Bob Crisman. **Crater Lake:** Kent Taylor. **Death Valley:** Karen Rosga, Ross Hopkins, Glenn Gossard. **Denali:** Bob Butterfield, Melanie Heacox, Kit Tangen (Alaska resident). **Glacier:** Joe Decker, Cindy Nielsen, Amy Vanderbilt. **Grand Canyon:** L. Greer Price. **Grand Teton:** Staff. **Jasper:** Maryse Blovin, Jim Todgham (Canadian Parks Service). **Joshua Tree:** Carol Peterson. **Kootenay:** Ken Fisher, John Pitcher (Canadian Parks Service). **Mount Rainier:** Glenn Baker, Cy Hentges, Carolyn Driedger (USGS). **Mount Rushmore:** James Popovich. **Olympic:** Hank Warren, Michael Smithson. **Point Reyes:** John Dell'Osso, Erin O'Bryan. **Redwood:** Staff. **Rocky Mountain:** James Mack, Jeff Maugans, Christy Metz. **Sequoia and Kings Canyon:** Malinee Crapsey, Deborah Mason. **Washington, D.C.:** Duncan Morrow. **Waterton:** Staff. **Yellowstone:** Marsha Karle, Cheryl Matthews. **Yoho:** Staff (Canadian Parks Service). **Yosemite:** Lisa Dapprich, Bob Clopine. **Zion:** Tim Manns, Andrea Bornemeier, Rich Fedorchak.

While every care has been taken to ensure the accuracy of the information in this guide, the passage of time will always bring change, and consequently, the publisher cannot accept responsibility for errors that may occur.

All prices and opening times quoted here are based on information supplied to us at press time. Hours and admission fees may change, however, and the prudent traveler will avoid inconvenience by calling ahead.

Fodor's wants to hear about your travel experiences, both pleasant and unpleasant. When a campground, hotel, or restaurant fails to live up to its billing, let us know and we will investigate the complaint and revise our entries where the facts warrant it. Write to Fodor's Travel Publications, 201 E. 50th St., New York, NY 10022.

Every year millions of people pack up their outdoor gear and head for the U.S. and Canadian national parks. They come from many backgrounds in search of many things, but they are all eager to take in the landscapes for which the parks are famous—the wide-open spaces, sky-skimming mountains, wilderness beaches, deserts, and giant sequoias. But although these travelers are familiar with the natural beauty preserved in our national parks, many don't fully understand what a national park is and why it has been set aside as such. Malinee Crapsey, a public information officer and former park ranger at Sequoia and Kings Canyon National Parks, explains:

"National parks are *internationally* significant. They are one of this country's greatest contributions to global culture. They preserve for everyone not only areas of great scenic beauty, but also areas whose scientific values are both known and not yet discovered. They hold a tremendous genetic resource and offer outstanding outdoor laboratories for researchers.

"In general, Americans are aware that laws protect our national parks, but they do not realize that long-term protection involves preserving the *processes* that create the landscape so that it will still be a natural environment when future generations venture here. That is why it is so important that visitors not pick flowers, feed bears (a big issue in these parks), or expect the environment to be otherwise manipulated for their comfort. Not only are the individual plants and animals affected, so are the processes of growth and life that are supposed to proceed unimpeded.

"For those reasons we encourage altruistic behaviors in visitors. Their enjoyment is extremely important, but of equal importance is the enjoyment of future generations. Rules and regulations are designed to support both ends; without the public's cooperation, neither can be fully achieved."

As you visit the parks, please keep in mind that these lands will not thrive without your care, will not last without your support.

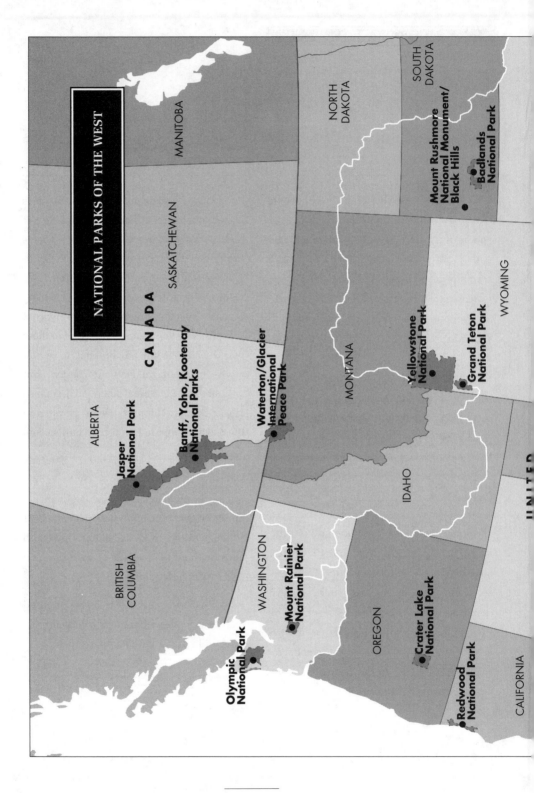

NATIONAL PARKS OF THE WEST

CANADA

MANITOBA

SASKATCHEWAN

ALBERTA

BRITISH COLUMBIA

Jasper National Park

Banff, Yoho, Kootenay National Parks

Waterton/Glacier International Peace Park

NORTH DAKOTA

SOUTH DAKOTA

Mount Rushmore National Monument/ Black Hills

Badlands National Park

MONTANA

IDAHO

WYOMING

Yellowstone National Park

Grand Teton National Park

WASHINGTON

Olympic National Park

Mount Rainier National Park

OREGON

Crater Lake National Park

Redwood National Park

CALIFORNIA

UNITED

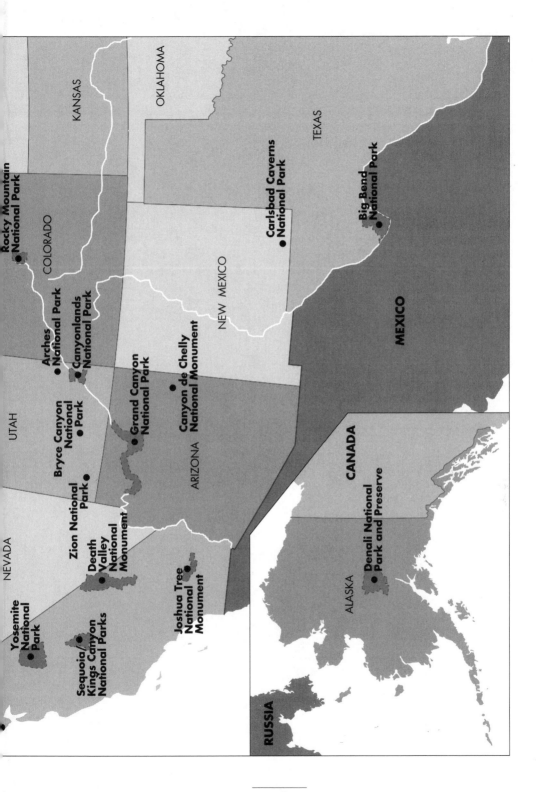

RUSSIA

ALASKA

Denali National
Park and Preserve

CANADA

NEVADA

Yosemite
National
Park

Sequoia/
Kings Canyon
National Parks

Death
Valley
National
Monument

Joshua Tree
National
Monument

Zion National
Park

Bryce Canyon
National
Park

UTAH

Grand Canyon
National Park

Arches
National Park

Canyonlands
National Park

Canyon de Chelly
National Monument

ARIZONA

Rocky Mountain
National Park

COLORADO

KANSAS

OKLAHOMA

NEW MEXICO

Carlsbad Caverns
National Park

TEXAS

Big Bend
National Park

MEXICO

Essential Information

By Susan Farewell

PLANNING YOUR TRIP

VISITOR INFORMATION For general information on the U.S. national park system, contact the Office of Public Inquiries, **National Park Service**, Box 37127, Washington, DC 20013, tel. 202/208–4747. For information on the Canadian park system, contact the **Canadian Parks Service,** Western Regional Office, Room 520, 220 4th Avenue SE, Box 2989, Station M, Calgary, Alberta T2P 3H8, tel. 403/292–4440. For detailed information on the individual parks (weather, special events, campsite availability), contact each park directly (*see* individual park chapters). In addition, the following regional offices of the U.S. National Park Service provide general information on parks in their areas.

Pacific Northwest region: Outdoor Recreation Information Center, 915 Second Ave., Suite 442, Seattle, WA 98174, tel. 206/220–7450.

Rocky Mountain region: National Park Service, Box 25287, 12795 West Alameda Parkway, Denver, CO 80225–0287, tel. 303/969–2000.

Southwest region: National Park Service, Box 728, 1100 Old Santa Fe Trail, Santa Fe, NM 87504–0728, tel. 505/988–6012.

Western region: National Park Service, Fort Mason Building 201, San Francisco, CA 94123, tel. 415/556–0560.

When you arrive at a park, stop by one of the visitor centers and pick up a free map and literature. Some visitor centers have exhibits, slide presentations, and brief films that will help you understand the area.

SPECIAL TOURS One way to visit the national parks is to go with an environmental tour group. A variety of associations offer naturalist-led tours that may include hiking, biking, camping, and/or canoeing. Some offer special educational programs, seminars, workshops, and field trips. These tours can be rugged and ambitious or relaxed and luxurious. Here's a sampling of what you'll find:

American Wilderness Experience (Box 1486, Boulder, CO 80306, tel. 303/444–2622 or 800/444–0099, fax 303/444–3999) leads a variety of wilderness tours in the national parks, from backpacking through the Canyonlands to horseback riding in Yellowstone.

Backroads Bicycle Touring (1516 5th St., Berkeley, CA 94710–1740, tel. 510/527–1555 or 800/462–2848, fax 510/527–1444) runs cycling tours to several of the western national parks.

Canyonlands Field Institute (Box 68, Moab, UT 84532, tel. 801/259–7750) schedules seminars designed to educate people about the Colorado Plateau. These range from one-day field hikes to week-long canoe and river-rafting trips.

National Audubon Society (National Environmental Education Center, 613 Riversville Rd., Greenwich, CT 06831, tel. 203/869–2017) hosts a variety of natural-history camps and workshops in the national parks, including an ecology workshop in Death Valley, a winter-ecology and nature-photography workshop in Yellowstone, and a trip to study the ecology of the Grand Canyon.

National Wildlife Federation (1400 16th St. NW, Washington, DC 20036, tel. 703/790–4363 or 800/432–6564) runs a series of week-long seminars in the national parks that include nature hikes, classes, and workshops.

Pacific Northwest Field Seminars (83 S. King St., Seattle, WA 98104, tel. 206/553–2636) offers an array of naturalist-led field trips in the national parks of Washington and Oregon. These include bird-watching on Mount Rainier, hiking through volcanic landscapes, and exploring the great glaciers of the Pacific Northwest.

Questers Worldwide Nature Tours (257 Park Ave. S, New York, NY 10010, tel. 212/673–3120 or 800/468–8668) pampers participants on its naturalist-led luxury tours to some of the western national parks.

The **Sierra Club** (730 Polk St., San Francisco, CA 94109, tel. 415/776–2211) will take you backpacking and put you to work. The group runs trips in which participants work to help preserve the environment in several of the national parks.

Wild Horizons Expeditions (West Fork Rd., Darby, MT 59829, tel. 406/821–3747), a guide and outfitter that is licensed by the National Park Service, offers more than a dozen wilderness trips every year within the various national parks.

Womantrek (Box 20643, Seattle, WA 98102, tel. 206/325–4772 or 800/477–TREK) leads women on biking, hiking, and rafting trips in some of the western national parks.

Yellowstone Institute (Box 117, Yellowstone National Park, WY 82190, tel. 307/344–7381, ext. 2384) teaches participants about the natural environment of the park in a series of two- to six-day classes and workshops. Among the activities are llama packing, fly-fishing, and bird-watching.

Yosemite Association (Box 230, El Portal, CA 95318, tel. 209/379–2646, fax 209/379–2486) offers various seminars: One combines skiing with lessons on winter ecology; another turns hiking into an exploration of wildflowers. There are also geology treks and natural-history workshops. Call for a course catalog.

SEASONAL EVENTS Powwows, agricultural fairs, rodeos, parades: There's almost always something going on in and around the western national parks, especially in summer. When you arrive at your destination, scan local newspaper listings, read flyers, and keep your eyes open for colorful banners stretched across the main streets of small towns. To get you started, here are some events you may want to keep in mind while planning your trip. For additional details, call the number listed for each.

January: In the Victorian seaport of Port Townsend, Washington, near Olympic National Park, a widely praised **Chamber Music**

Festival (tel. 206/385–2722), with artists from around the county, takes place the fourth weekend of January (Friday and Saturday nights).

February: On various weekends throughout the month, winter carnivals take place near some of the western national parks. The **Teton Winterfest** (tel. 307/733–4417), in Jackson Hole, Wyoming, near Grand Teton National Park, is highlighted by a sled-dog race and a softball game in the snow. In Whitefish, Montana, near Glacier National Park, the **Annual Whitefish Winter Carnival** (tel. 406/862–3501) includes the crowning of a king and queen, all sorts of outdoor games, ice sculptures, and a parade. Ski races, exhibits, food booths, and an all-around party atmosphere prevail at West Yellowstone's **Winter Festival** (tel. 406/646–7701), in Montana, close to Yellowstone National Park.

March: St. Patrick's Day (tel. 602/282–7722) is celebrated with a parade, a barbecue, and lots of partying in Sedona, Arizona, near Grand Canyon National Park.

April: Parades, art exhibits, musical productions, and a carnival are all part of the **Washington State Apple Blossom Festival** (tel. 509/662–3616) in Wenatchee, Washington, near Mt. Rainier National Park.

May: Near Grand Canyon National Park, the **Cinco de Mayo Festival** (tel. 602/282–7722) in Sedona, Arizona, is a wonderful Mexican extravaganza with contests, foods, and dancing. A rodeo, Native American dancing, and a cowboy-poetry gathering are only a handful of the events that take place every Memorial Day weekend, during **Old West Days** (tel. 307/733–3316), in Jackson Hole, Wyoming, near Grand Teton National Park.

Mid-May to September: Ashland, Oregon, is the site of the annual **Oregon Shakespeare Festival** (about 2 hours from Crater Lake National Park, tel. 503/482–4331), in which a nationally known repertory company performs classic and contemporary dramas.

June to August: Musicians from around the world perform at the **Grand Teton Music Festival** (tel. 307/733–3050), a summer music festival that includes chamber and orchestral concerts.

July to September: Throughout the summer, Shakespeare is presented on an outdoor stage at the **Utah Shakespearean Festival** (tel. 801/586–1970), in Cedar City, Utah, near Zion National Park.

August: The arts—both visual and performing—are celebrated annually at the **Sierra Summer Festival** (tel. 619/934–2712), in Mammoth Lakes, California, close to Yosemite National Park. Come to hear jazz, blues, classical, folk, bluegrass, and pop music.

September: At the **Wooden Boat Festival** (tel. 206/385–2722), in Port Townsend, Washington, near Olympic National Park, there are races, rides, crafts shows, and sing-alongs.

October: The third Saturday in October is reserved for **International Good Neighbor Day** (tel. 915/477–2252) in Rio Grande Village, Texas, near Big Bend National Park. The day is one big open-air party with musicians, craftspeople, and cooks from the United States and Mexico.

November: New York has its Macy's Thanksgiving Day parade, but in Santa Clara, Utah, near Zion National Park, there's a Western-style tradition—the **Annual Thanksgiving Day Rodeo** (tel. 801/673–4555).

December: The **Festival of Lights at Tlaquepaque** (tel. 602/282–7722) takes place annually in Sedona, Arizona, near Grand Canyon National Park, with caroling and a Christmas candlelight procession.

If you'd like to find out about events taking place along your driving route, get a copy of the American Bus Association's booklet "Top 100 Events in North America." It lists major festivals, state fairs, and other significant events across the country. For the latest edition, contact the **American Bus Association,** 1015 15th Street NW, Suite 250, Washington, DC 20005, or call 202/842–1645. It's free.

WHEN TO GO Summer is without question the busiest time of the year to visit most of the national parks, so be prepared to deal with full parking lots and traffic jams. If you must travel during summer, go early or late in the season to avoid the mid-season peak. Be aware, however, that in desert parks summer's heat keeps the crowds away. Spring and fall are good times of the year to visit most of the western parks. During winter, some parks close certain roads because of heavy snowfall. Others have just as much going on during the winter as they do during the summer: In Yosemite and Mount Rainier, for example, hiking paths become cross-country ski trails and rangers conduct snowshoe walks. In such desert parks as Death Valley and Big Bend, winter is the busiest time of year.

Keep in mind that even during summer the weather can vary—especially in the mountainous parks. In Yellowstone temperatures can rise into the 90s during the day and drop into the teens or lower at night. Also, the climate often changes with elevation. Within a matter of minutes, a blue sky and brilliant sunshine can erupt into an extravaganza of hail and lightning. The key to enjoying your time in the parks is always to have warm clothing and rain gear handy, no matter how promising the day.

OPENING AND CLOSING TIMES The buildings within national parks, including visitor centers, are generally open daily from 9 to 5, but these times do vary from park to park and season to season. Most park buildings are open every day of the year except Christmas. Natural areas of the parks are usually open 24 hours a day, 365 days a year, but fees are generally collected only during peak seasons and hours. If the fee station is closed you may enter free, but consider making a donation to help maintain the park.

CAR RENTALS Renting a car to drive to and around the national parks is easy, provided you are over 21 (25 in some states) and have a valid driver's license and a major credit card. Rates vary from state to state as well as from company to company and season to season. Generally, the smaller the car, the lower the rate, but ask about temporary rental promotions, which can mean substantial sav-

ings. Be aware that over-the-phone quotes do not include the collision damage waiver (CDW), personal accident insurance, or tax. To save money, check with your insurance agent to see whether your personal coverage includes rental cars, and find out if your credit card company insures car rentals that are charged to your card. The CDW covers travel in all U.S. states but not necessarily in Mexico and Canada. If you plan to cross borders ask the agency if you will be covered. If you want to leave the car at a location different from the one where you picked it up, you will most likely have to pay an additional drop-off charge, which can be a couple of hundred dollars, depending on your route. Always ask in advance.

Many companies charge a flat daily or weekly rate with unlimited mileage; others charge by the mile over a certain number of miles. The rates for a subcompact vehicle with unlimited mileage start at about $35 a day and about $195 a week.

Once you find the best rate, make a reservation over the phone. If you're picking the car up at an airport, have your arrival time handy when you call. Record the reservation number, the name of the agent to whom you spoke, and the time and date of your call. Be sure to verify that the company will honor your credit card.

Among the major national car-rental firms are: **Alamo** (tel. 800/327–9633), **Avis** (tel. 800/331–1212), **Budget** (tel. 800/527–0700), **Dollar** (tel. 800/421–6868), **Hertz** (tel. 800/654–3131; in OK, 800/755–4400), and **National** (tel. 800/227–7368).

RV RENTALS The same rules for renting a car apply when you rent an RV: You must be over 21 (25 in some states) and have a valid driver's license and a credit card. No special license or driving skills are required. In fact, driving an RV is much like driving a car, thanks to automatic transmissions and power brakes. The difficult part is handling a vehicle of that size (a motorhome can be anywhere from 20 to 34 feet long), especially getting in and out of parking spaces and backing up. Many veteran RVers avoid having to go in reverse as much as possible. Most rental agencies provide a brief (30-minute to one-hour) familiarization course in which drivers can get acquainted with the operation of the RV. All the technical equipment—the propane system for heating and cooking, the water tanks, the waste-disposal system, and the generator—is fully explained when you arrive at the rental office. Once you're on your way, stay in the slow lane, and go easy when braking and accelerating. Try to avoid driving at night.

You must reserve far in advance if you plan to rent an RV in summer. Also, prices are at their highest during these months.

Depending on the size of the vehicle you rent, you will be charged $75 to $150 a day during high season. That may include unlimited mileage, or it may include a set number of free miles, and you will have to pay more for each additional mile. Most RVs use regular, unleaded gasoline, and it can be expensive: The gas tanks usually hold 40 to 79 gallons, but RVs only get 8 to 9 miles to the gallon. Add to that the campground fees—roughly $15 to $20 per night—and an RV vacation may not be as inexpensive as you had hoped.

First-time motor home renters should get a copy of "Rental Ventures," a $5 guide published annually by the **Recreation Vehicle Rental Association** (tel. 703/591–7130 or 800/336–0355). It includes information on campgrounds, safety, and the types of motorhomes available and their features and accessories. Another RV-vacation planner is available free by calling **Go Camping America** (tel. 800/477–8669). It includes information on RV campgrounds and events.

To locate a rental agency, look under "Recreation Vehicles—Renting and Leasing" in the yellow pages for the dealer nearest you. You can also order a directory of RV-rental agencies called *Who's Who in RV Rentals,* published by the **Recreation Vehicle Dealers Association** (tel. 703/591–7130 or 800/ 336–0355). It costs $7.50, including first-class delivery. One nationwide RV-rental firm is **Cruise America** (tel. 800/327–7778).

DRIVING Before setting out on any driving trip, it's important to make sure your vehicle is in top condition. It is best to have a complete tune-up before setting out; at the very least, you should make the following checks:

See that all lights are working, including brake lights, backup lights, and emergency lights; make sure tires are in good shape (including the spare); check the oil; check the engine coolant; fill the windshield-washer bottle, and make sure the blades are in good condition; and make sure brakes are in good condition, too.

For emergencies, take along flares or reflector triangles, jumper cables, an empty gas can, a fire extinguisher, a flashlight, a plastic tarp, blankets, and coins for phone calls. If you're traveling in winter, be sure to have a collapsible shovel, an ice scraper, traction mats, sand, and antifreeze. Chains are a good idea.

Many roads in western national parks are narrow and winding. Some have restrictions on large vehicles. If you are driving a large RV or pulling a trailer, be sure to call the park in advance of your trip to find out about road restrictions.

COSTS Almost all the national parks have an entrance fee, ranging from $3 to $10 per vehicle and good for seven consecutive days. Senior travelers, disabled travelers, and frequent park goers can take advantage of the **Federal Recreation Passport Program,** which includes a number of passes that waive entrance fees for the card holder and an accompanying carload of passengers.

For travelers 62 years and older, the **Golden Age Passport** now costs $10 but is good for life. It is available at national parks upon arrival. You must have proof of your age and U.S. citizenship or permanent residency status; a drivers' license or birth certificate is fine. In addition to free admission to the parks, the pass gives the holder a 50% discount on park facilities and services (excluding those run by private concessionaires).

The **Golden Access Passport** is free and available to those who are permanently disabled.

The passport can be obtained at a park entrance with proper proof of a disability; it is good for life. Holders of this pass also receive a 50% discount on all park facilities and services (excluding those run by private concessionaires).

The **Golden Eagle Pass** costs $25 and entitles the card holder and an accompanying party to free admission to all parks for the calendar year. It is neither refundable nor transferable and does not cover such additional park fees as those for camping and parking. The Golden Eagle Pass can be purchased in person or by mail, by sending $25 to any of the National Park Service headquarters or regional offices (*see* Visitor Information, *above*).

For those planning to visit one specific park repeatedly, a **Park Pass** is available for $10 or $15, depending on the park. It gives the pass holder and accompanying party free admission to that park for the calendar year (January 1 through December 31). The pass can be purchased in person or by mail from the specific national park at which it will be honored. It is neither transferable nor refundable.

In addition to entry fees, most of the national parks charge fees at their drive-in campgrounds. These fees range from $5 a night for tenters to $12 a night for RVs.

The U.S. Fish and Wildlife Service's **Duck Stamp** pass is also honored for entry to national parks.

PETS Generally, pets are allowed only in developed areas of the national parks, including drive-in campgrounds and picnic areas, but they must be kept on a leash at all times. With the exception of guide dogs, pets are not allowed inside buildings, on most trails, on beaches, or in the backcountry. They also may be prohibited in areas controlled by concessionaires. Some of the parks have kennels, which charge about $6 a day, but before you decide to bring a pet to a national park, call to find out about specific restrictions.

FURTHER READING Many of the national parks have book stores, which sell field guides, maps, and other publications on the history, geology, plants, and wildlife of their specific area. The National Park Service once published a handy guide for campers, called *The National Parks: Camping Guide* ($3.50), and a guide for people with disabilities, called *Access National Parks: A Guide for Handicapped Visitors* ($6.50). Both are out of print, but some parks may still have copies.

Two bibles for identifying plant and animal life are the Peterson Field Guide series, which includes guides to *Western Birds, Rocky Mountain Wildflowers,* and *Western Butterflies;* and the Audubon Society Field Guide series (Alfred A. Knopf), with books on *Western Birds, Western Trees,* and *Western Wildflowers.* Two other good sources of information are *Wild Plants of America: A Select Guide for the Naturalist and Traveler* (John Wiley & Sons), by Richard M. Smith; and *The Traveling Birder* (Doubleday), by Clive Goodwin.

The most detailed topographical maps of the national parks are those published by the **United States Geological Survey (USGS)** (Box 25286, Denver Federal Center, Denver, CO 80225, tel. 303/236–7477). Printed on plastic, USGS maps are waterproof and tearproof—ideal for hiking trips. **Trails Illustrated** (Box 3610, Evergreen, CO 80439–3425, tel. 303/670–3457) also offers a line of topographical maps printed on plastic.

The **National Parks and Conservation Association** (tel. 800/PARK–KIT, ext. 89) sells "National Park Vacation Kits" for many western parks. These kits include a 60-minute audio tape, fact book, topographical map, National Park Service handbook, trail guides, and campground information, and each one costs $39.95.

VISITING THE PARKS

STAYING HEALTHY AND SAFE The three leading causes of death in the parks are, in order, motor-vehicle accidents, drownings, and falls. Accidents often occur when drivers take their eyes off the road to look at wildlife and scenery. Experienced swimmers are often the people who drown; they don't understand that cold water and swift currents make swimming in parks far more difficult (and treacherous) than swimming in pools. People fall off cliffs when they get too close to the unstable edge, and rock climbers fall when they use frayed or weathered ropes. It is important that when visiting the parks you make it a point to learn the rules. Pay attention to signs warning of potential dangers, stay on the trails, and, when in doubt, don't do it. Chances are you will have a safe and fulfilling park experience. Following, however, are a number of problems you should know how to deal with.

Foot Care. If you're planning to do a lot of hiking, by all means, do not start your trip with a new pair of shoes or boots: Break them in before you leave home. Wear boots that have good ankle support. Once you're out and about in the wilderness, it's important to always watch your step. Sprains can happen easily, especially on loose rocks and slippery paths.

Sun Protection. Take great care in protecting yourself from the sun—even when it's cloudy or there's snow on the ground. Keep in mind that at higher altitudes, where the air is thinner, you will burn more easily, and that sun reflected off the snow, off sand, and off water can be especially strong. Apply sunscreen liberally before you go out, and wear a visored cap or sunglasses. Many scientists fear that overexposure to UV light increases the rate of skin cancer and cataracts.

If you are exposed to extreme heat for a prolonged period, you run the risk of heat stroke (also known as sunstroke), a serious medical condition. It begins quite suddenly with a headache, dizziness, and fatigue, but can quickly escalate into convulsions, unconsciousness, or death. If someone in your party develops any of these symptoms, have one person go for emergency help; meanwhile, move the victim to a shady place, wrap her in wet clothing or bedding, and try to cool her down with water or ice.

Lyme Disease. When walking in woods, brush, or through fields in areas where lyme disease has been found, wear tick repellent and long pants tucked into socks. When you undress, search carefully for deer ticks, which are not much bigger than the period at the end of this sentence. If you should find one attached to the skin, remove it with rubbing alcohol and tweezers. Watch the area for several weeks. If you spot a rash or develop flulike symptoms, see your physician immediately. Lyme disease can be treated with antibiotics if caught early enough.

Snake Bites. Snakes will do everything to avoid you, but in the event you have a run-in and are bitten, it's necessary to act quickly. If it's a harmless snake, ordinary first aid for puncture wounds should be given. If it is poisonous, the victim should remain as still as possible, so as not to spread the venom through the body. He should lie down, keeping the wound area below the rest of the body, and another person should seek medical help immediately.

Animal Bites. Some animals, especially rodents, carry dangerous diseases. Pneumonic plague (which becomes bubonic plague in humans) is carried by animals throughout the west. If you see several dead animals in a small area, beware: This may be a sign of the plague. If you are bitten by a wild animal, it's important to see a doctor as soon as you possibly can. Many animal bites require a tetanus shot and, if the animal is rabid, a rabies shot.

Frostbite. Caused by exposure to extreme cold for a prolonged period of time, frostbite is marked by the numbing of ears, nose, fingers, or toes. A sure sign that you aren't simply cold is when the skin turns white or grayish yellow. The victim should be taken into a warm place as soon as possible, and wet clothing in the affected area should be removed. The area should then be immersed in warm—not hot—water or wrapped in a warm blanket. When the area begins to thaw, the victim should exercise it, to stimulate blood circulation. If bleeding or other complications develop, it's important to get to a doctor as soon as possible.

Hypothermia. It does not have to be below freezing for you to get hypothermia: If you're not dressed warmly enough for the outdoor temperature, you're at risk. A person with hypothermia will at first feel chilly and tired and will then suddenly begin shivering uncontrollably and acting irrationally. The minute these signs are spotted, get the victim to shelter of some kind and wrap her in warm blankets or a sleeping bag. If the sleeping bag is cold, another member of the party should warm it up by getting into it first; it may even be wise for that person to remain in the sleeping bag with the victim. If practical, it's best for both people to be unclothed, but if clothing remains on, it must be dry.

Plant Poisons. If you touch poison ivy, poison oak, or poison sumac, wash the area immediately with soap and water and then with rubbing alcohol. Later, apply Calamine lotion to relieve itching.

Safe Water for Drinking. It is best to carry bottled water for day trips, and drinking water is available at many campgrounds. But if you're hiking into the backcountry you may not be able to carry enough water, so you will have to purify spring or stream water for drinking. Do this no matter how crystal clear the water looks: You can't see giardia, but these tiny organisms can turn your stomach inside out. The easiest way to purify water is to add a water-purification tablet to it. These come in packages with directions. The most widely used brand is Potable Aqua, which is made by Wisconsin Pharmacal and sells for about $5.50 for 50 tablets (good for 50 quarts of water). You can also purify water by filtering it through a water-purification pump available at camping equipment stores. Boiling water is the least favorite method since it takes time and uses fuel, but, if it is the only method available to you, use it; bring the water to a boil for at least 15 minutes.

First Aid. Packing a complete first-aid kit is essential for all trips in the great outdoors. Be sure to have a first-aid manual, any necessary prescriptions for allergies or pre-existing diseases or disorders, aspirin, adhesive bandages, butterfly bandages, sterile gauze pads (2″ x 2″ and 4″ x 4″), 1″-wide adhesive tape, an elastic bandage, antibiotic ointment, antiseptic cream, antihistamines, razor blades, tweezers, a needle, scissors, insect repellent, Calamine lotion, and sunscreen.

MEDICAL EMERGENCIES The best way to deal with medical emergencies is to avoid them. Never hike alone in the national parks—especially not into the backcountry. Ideally, you should hike with at least two other people. That way, if one person is injured, a companion can stay with the injured person while the other goes to get help. Fortunately, in the national parks, rangers and other hikers are usually close by—especially during July and August. If you find yourself in an emergency situation, you can call 911 from telephone booths at visitor centers and other locations throughout the parks. Some of the parks have their own emergency numbers, as well.

If you break a leg or arm on the trail, it is best to keep the broken area as still as possible and elevated, while someone goes for help. If help is far away, make a splint from a branch, and strap it on with a bandana or article of clothing.

For information on specific health and safety hazards, *see* Staying Healthy and Safe, *above*.

PROTECTING THE ENVIRONMENT More than ever, our national parks are being discovered and rediscovered by travelers who want to spend their vacations appreciating nature, watching wildlife, and taking adventure trips. But as the number of visitors to the parks increases, so does stress on wildlife and plant life. Tourism can drum up concern for the environment, but it can also cause great physical damage to parks. Many of the trails and roadways in our national parks are overused and abused.

Take great care as you explore the parks. Have respect for the animals you encounter: never sneak up on them, don't disturb nests and other habitats, don't touch animals or try to remove them from their habitat for the sake of a photograph, don't stand between animal parents and their young, and never surround an animal or group of animals. You can also help to protect endangered species by reporting any sightings. (For more information on endangered species in the national parks, write: Chief, Wildlife and Vegetation Division, National Park Service, Box 37127, Washington, DC 20013.)

Respect the environment. Do not leave garbage on the trails or in campgrounds. If you hike into the backcountry, carry your trash out with you. Bury human waste at least 100 feet from any trail, campsite, or backcountry water source. Some parks and many environmental organizations are starting to advocate packing out even human waste. Do not wash dishes or clothing in lakes and streams. If you must use soap, make sure it is biodegradable, and carry water in clean containers 100 feet away from its source before using it for cleaning.

A free brochure titled "Leave No Trace" supplies more information on protecting the environment; to get a copy call 800/332–4100.

Many of the national parks—including Yellowstone, Yosemite, and the Grand Canyon—are threatened by serious problems, including air pollution, acid rain, wildlife poaching, understaffing of rangers, and encroaching development. These problems are being addressed by the National Park Service, but you can play a role by donating time or money. The National Park Service's Volunteers in the Parks program welcomes volunteers to do anything from paperwork to lecturing on environmental issues. To participate, you must apply to the park where you would like to work.

To make financial contributions to the parks, contact the **National Park Service,** Budget Division, Box 37127, Washington, DC 20013; or the **National Parks Preservation Fund,** 1101 17th Street NW, Washington, DC 20036. The latter is a nonprofit organization that supports the park service with supplementary assistance programs.

FIRE PRECAUTIONS When it comes to fire, never take a chance. Keep these pointers in mind: Don't build fires when you're alone. Build small fires. Always build campfires in a safe place (away from tinder of any kind). Use a fireplace or fire grate if one is available. Clear the ground around the fireplace so that wind cannot blow sparks into dry leaves or grass. Throw used matches into the fire. Never leave a fire unattended. Always have a pot of water or sand next to a campfire or stove. When finished, be sure the fire is out cold (meaning you can touch it with your bare hands). Never cook in your tent or a poorly ventilated space.

HIKING Three things should be taken into consideration when choosing hiking trails suitable to your physical condition and the amount of weight you plan to carry: 1) How long is the trail? 2) How steep is it and how quickly does the elevation increase? 3) How acclimated are you to the altitude at the start and finish?

One of the most common problems for hikers is altitude sickness, which results when a hiker ascends to heights over 8,500 feet without being properly acclimated. The symptoms include headache, nausea, vomiting, shortness of breath, weakness, and sleep disturbance. If any of these occur, it's important to retreat to a lower altitude. Altitude sickness can develop into high-altitude pulmonary edema (HAPE) and high-altitude cerebral edema (HACE). Both can be permanently debilitating or fatal. If you have a history of heart or circulatory problems, talk to your doctor before planning a visit to areas at high altitudes.

CAMPING Most automobile campsites in the national parks are offered on a first-come, first-served basis. If you are traveling during the peak summer months, be sure to arrive as early in the day as possible or make reservations at a nearby privately owned campground. At some campgrounds in some parks (Death Valley, Joshua Tree, Grand Canyon, Rocky Mountain, Sequoia and Kings Canyon, Yellowstone, and Yosemite) you can make camping reservations prior to your visit through Mistix (tel. 800/365–2267). At some National Forest Service campgrounds you can make reservations through the U.S. Forest Reservations (tel. 800/280–2267).

Tips on Camp Cooking. How fancy your food preparation can be will depend on whether you are traveling on foot or by car and how long your trip is. If you're traveling with a group, take time to coordinate in advance who should pack what. Some staples that travel well: cheese (for summer backpacking, take hard cheeses that don't have to be refrigerated), dry milk, seeds and nuts, dried fruits, powdered eggs, pasta, bagels, rice, flour, baking soda, popcorn, instant soups, instant drinks, honey, cooking oil, lentils, split peas, oatmeal and other cereals, coffee, tea, and freeze-dried foods.

If you're traveling on foot, it is best to carry food in a large drawstring sack inside your pack. Be sure to bring a long, strong cord so you can hang your food out of reach of animals at night. Tie a rock to one end of the cord and the sack to the other and throw it up over a branch, about 10 feet off the ground. If you're traveling in summer and have food that should be kept cool, once you arrive in your camp, put the food in a waterproof container and submerge it in a stream. This is especially effective at high altitudes, because the water usually remains icy cold even during the hottest months. Although this is a good way to keep food cold, it is not a good way to keep it safe from bears and raccoons.

When packing for camping trips, be sure to include the following supplies: a stove and a supply of fuel, matches in a waterproof case or lighter, a cookset, pot holders, spoons, forks, knives, cups, plates, a water bottle, a can opener, a cooking spoon, a spatula, salt, pepper, sugar, aluminum foil, plastic wrap, trash bags, a scouring pad, a sponge, and a lantern (optional).

Sample Recipes. Cooking outdoors can be something of a challenge when you consider the shortage of pots and pans, the weather conditions, and, usually, the limited ingredients. Your best bet is to stick with familiar or very easy recipes. A lot of campers prepare dishes ahead of time, such as cold pasta salads, hearty soups, chili, ratatouille, and fried chicken. One excellent method of preparing food is to use aluminum foil to wrap the ingredients and then place the bundle on hot coals to steam cook the food. Salt, pepper, and other spices can make an otherwise bland meal tasty. Potatoes cook well in foil, although they are heavy to carry, and you can steam corn on the cob directly on your campfire without removing the husks.

Here are two easy camp-dinner dishes:

Baked Fish in Foil. *Ingredients:* fresh-caught fish (perch, trout), salt, pepper, butter. *Preparation:* Clean the fish completely. Sprinkle with salt and pepper. Add a dollop of butter. Wrap fish individually and tightly in aluminum foil, so steam cannot escape. Place the package on red-hot wood (not in flames) and turn it a couple of times. When cooked (at least 20 minutes), the foil is your plate.

Couscous with Steamed Vegetables. *Ingredients:* couscous, butter, water, broccoli, carrots, snow peas (or any vegetables that steam well). *Preparation:* Prepare couscous according to instructions on box (takes about 5 minutes). While cooking, steam vegetables. Spread vegetables on couscous.

HIKING AND CAMPING EQUIPMENT Before you pack, do yourself a big favor and write a checklist, using the following list as a starting point:

Clothing and footwear (warm weather): cotton T-shirt, shorts, cotton or cotton-blend long pants, long-sleeve cotton shirt, swimsuit, lightweight long-sleeve wool shirt or sweater, cotton briefs, insulated underwear (for cold nights), inner socks, two pairs wool socks, rain gear (hooded parka and pants), visored cap or rain hat, hiking boots, sneakers.

Clothing and footwear (cold weather): cotton T-shirt, lightweight long-sleeve wool shirt, wool pants, cotton briefs, insulated underwear, inner socks, two pairs wool socks, insulated vest or wool sweater, down or polyester-insulated parka, rain gear (hooded parka and pants), wool cap, wool or insulated gloves or mittens, insulated hiking boots, sneakers. Down bootees are a comforting nicety.

Personal gear: belt, bandana, eyeglasses, sunglasses, toothbrush, toothpaste, soap and other toiletries, toilet paper, lip balm, sunscreen, insect repellent, first-aid kit (*see* Staying Healthy and Safe, *above*), watch, compass, maps, multipurpose pocketknife, small flashlight, extra batteries, binoculars, water bottle, field guide.

Equipment: tent, ground cloth, sleeping bag, sleeping pad, backpack, day pack or fanny pack for day trips.

DINING The restaurants you are most apt to find in or near the national parks are casual places serving everything from pizza, sandwiches, and burgers to pasta, steak, and fish. America's move toward healthy diets has certainly affected restaurants throughout the West (some say the idea started here), with salad bars and low-cholesterol entrées found in every state, but this is still cattle country, where some of the finest beef can be had at moderate prices. Meals here tend to be hearty—enough to satisfy any hungry hiker. Mexican food makes an appearance on many menus, especially in the Southwest, and your craving for Chinese or Italian cuisine can often be satisfied in larger cities outside the parks (although you may have to drive 50 miles or more to get there). Fast-food chains are present near some parks but are nowhere to be found around others.

Within the parks themselves there are plenty of picnic areas complete with tables and fire grates.

Prices for meals (per person, excluding drinks and taxes) at restaurants listed in this book are as follows: **Expensive,** over $25; **Moderate,** $10 to $25; **Inexpensive,** under $10.

LODGING In addition to campgrounds in and near the national parks, you can choose from a range of accommodations, from chain hotels and motels with modern appliances to rough and rugged wilderness camps with kerosene lamps instead of electricity. Cabins with housekeeping facilities are one of the most popular types of lodging. There are also small, family-owned bed-and-breakfasts and grand old established hotels.

If you're traveling during the high season—roughly between Memorial Day and Labor Day—it's advisable to make reservations three or four months in advance. At some of the most desirable hostelries, such as the Jenny Lake Lodge in Grand Teton National Park and El Tovar in Grand Canyon National Park, guests are known to make reservations for the next summer as they check out.

Also, bear in mind that prices are higher in summer. In fact, they sometimes drop as much as 25% when the season comes to a close.

Prices for lodgings (for two people in a double room) listed in this book are as follows: **Expensive,** over $70; **Moderate,** $40 to $70; **Inexpensive,** under $40.

CREDIT CARDS The following credit-card abbreviations are used throughout this guide: AE, American Express; D, Discover; DC, Diners Club; MC, MasterCard; V, Visa.

GETTING MONEY Carry credit cards, traveler's checks, and some cash when visiting the national parks. Many hotels and restaurants take all major-bank traveler's checks, and major credit cards—American Express, Mastercard, Visa—are honored at car-rental agencies, most hotels, and some restaurants.

If you need cash quickly, you will probably have to drive into the nearest town or city to find an automated-teller machine (ATM). Cirrus and Plus cards are widely accepted. Before you leave home, check with your credit-card company or bank to find out where there is an ATM near your destination that will accept your card. Also ask what the fee is for obtaining cash from a machine (it varies from bank to bank).

TRAVELING WITH CHILDREN Packing. When traveling into the national parks with children, it's important to be as self-sufficient as possible. Bring diapers, formula, and any special foods your child may require. Consider packing airtight fresh milk cartons, which don't need refrigeration, or powdered milk and distilled water. Be sure your first-aid kit is complete: You can't expect to easily run to the pharmacy to have prescriptions filled. And always carry your pediatrician's phone number.

If you're planning to rent a car, take along your child's own safety seat. Chances are, you will spend a lot of time in the car, whether getting to and from the national parks or traveling within them. You might also have your children pack their own "car bags" (preferably kiddie knapsacks), with crayons, coloring books, and toys to play with en route. Older kids may want to take along tape players with cassettes and extra batteries. For snacking along the way, stock up on finger foods (raisins, cereal, anything not sticky) and juice pouches (with straws).

Getting there. If you're flying with children to one of the national parks, keep these pointers in mind when making your travel arrangements: 1) Don't go with the most economical flight; look for the quickest, easiest way to reach your destination. 2) If getting on a direct flight means shifting your vacation a day or two, do it. 3) For in-flight meals, order a child's meal ahead of time. 4) Request bulkhead seats for more space.

Park activities. As a family you will find many trails to follow, lakes to swim in, routes to bicycle on, and all sorts of animals and birds and geologic wonders to look at. In addition, some parks offer guided horseback rides, campfire programs, and ranger-led naturalist walks that are geared to children. Some of them have special child-care programs in which parents leave their children for the day.

To help your child get the most out of the trip, you might want to encourage him or her to keep a travel log. Start little ones off with a large sketch book, so they can draw what they see. Encourage older children to take pictures with an instamatic camera so that they can make their own photo albums.

Never let children play unattended, particularly near streams or lakes.

Staying overnight. When setting up camp, it's important that all children have their own jobs or duties. Before arriving at your campsite, determine who will do what. For example, one child may be responsible for helping put up the tent, another may be expected to unload the kitchen gear. That way, when you arrive after a long day of driving and the kids are cranky, everyone will have to get busy with his own chore.

Most of the motels, hotels, and lodges near the national parks are child-friendly; in fact, they cater predominately to families. Try to stay where guest rooms have kitchenettes or refrigerators (for milk and snacks) and the dining room has a children's menu. If you have a small child, request a room on the first floor. Terraces and balconies are potential hazards, and it can be tiresome carrying your child and paraphernalia up and down stairs.

To find out more about traveling with children contact the following agencies:

Rascals in Paradise (650 5th St., Suite 505, San Francisco, CA 94107, tel. 415/978–9800 or 800/872–7225), a full-service travel agency, prides itself on taking care of all the details of traveling with children, everything from getting bumper pads for cribs to arranging for distilled water for breast-feeding moms.

Family Travel Times is a newsletter published 10 times a year by Travel With Your Children (TWYCH, 45 W. 18th St., 7th floor, New York, NY 10011, tel. 212/206–0688). A one-year subscription costs $55.

HINTS FOR TRAVELERS WITH DISABILITIES The parks are meticulously accommodating to the handicapped traveler. Visitor centers provide information in braille, large print, and tape-recorded formats. In some visitor centers and park museums, free wheelchairs are available; and ramps are strategically placed throughout the parks. The **Golden Access Passport** entitles those who are permanently disabled to free access to all U.S. national parks (*see* Costs, *above*).

A handful of nonprofit organizations take mixed-ability groups on guided adventure trips to some of the parks. These include **Wilderness Inquiry** (1313 5th St. SE, Minneapolis, MN 55414, tel. 612/379–3858), **All Outdoors** (42 N.W. Greeley, Bend, OR 97701, tel. 503/388–8103), **Cooperative Wilderness Handicapped Outdoor Group** (Idaho State University, Box 8118, Pocatello, ID 83209, tel. 208/236–3912), and **Environmental Traveling Companions** (Building C, Fort Mason Center, San Francisco, CA 94123, tel. 415/474–7662).

The following organizations provide travel advice and services for travelers with disabilities:

The **Information Center for Individuals with Disabilities** (Fort Point Pl., 1st floor, 27–43 Wormwood St., Boston, MA 02210, tel. 617/727–5540 or 800/462–5015 in MA between 11 and 4, or leave message; TDD/TTY tel. 617/345–9743) provides a list of travel agents who specialize in tours for the disabled.

Moss Rehabilitation Hospital Travel Information Service (1200 W. Tabor Rd., Philadelphia, PA 19141–3009, tel. 215/456–9603,

TDD 215/456–9602) provides travel information for people with special needs. A small fee is charged.

HINTS FOR OLDER TRAVELERS If you have any special dietary or medicinal needs, be sure to carry your own supply when visiting the national parks. The **Golden Age Passport** entitles those over 62 to free admission to all U.S. national parks (*see* Costs, *above*).

The **American Association of Retired Persons** (601 E St. NW, Washington, DC 20049, tel. 202/434–2277) offers several cost-cutting programs for the older traveler, including discounts on hotels, airfares, car and RV rentals, and sightseeing attractions.

Mature Outlook (6001 N. Clark St., Chicago, IL 60660, tel. 800/336–6330), a travel club for people over 50, offers hotel and motel discounts and a bimonthly newsletter. Annual membership is $9.95 (covers a single person or a couple).

National Council of Senior Citizens (1331 F St. NW, Washington, DC 20004, tel. 202/347–8800) is a nonprofit group that offers members a multitude of travel discounts. Annual membership is $12 per person or per couple.

Arches and Canyonlands National Parks

Utah

By Tom Wharton

n the first place you can't see *anything* from a car; you've got to get out . . . and walk, better yet crawl, on hands and knees, over the sandstone and through the thornbush and cactus. When traces of blood begin to mark your trail you'll see something, maybe." Thus wrote Edward Abbey of southern Utah's canyonlands country in his 1967 introduction to *Desert Solitaire,* a book inspired by his experiences as a seasonal park ranger at Arches National Park.

Although Abbey probably would be dismayed by today's development in southeastern Utah's national parks, to a large degree Arches and Canyonlands remain wild, inhospitable, and deeply beautiful lands that no humans can tame. With little in the way of amenities, they are certainly among the most difficult national parks to visit. In fact, until 30 years ago, only a few hardy souls—Native Americans, cowboys, such notorious outlaws as Butch Cassidy, and, most recently, ura-nium prospectors—had penetrated the canyonlands.

Rushing waters carved out this desolate region of arches, box canyons, balanced rocks, and narrow sandstone canyons whose colors change with the season and with the time of day. In Arches National Park you will find nature's sculpture garden: here, the world's greatest concentration of natural arches combines with an array of other intricate formations. In nearby Canyonlands National Park, the surging Colorado and Green rivers and the rugged canyon roads make up one of the United States' ultimate adventure terrains.

Of the two parks, Arches is unquestionably the easier to see. It is ideal for people who enjoy relatively effortless hikes of 1 to 5 miles starting from trailheads along the main park road. Canyonlands, on the other hand, demands more of its visitors. There are only two paved roads in the park, one leading into the Island in the Sky district, north of Moab, and the other to the Needles area, northwest of Monticello. The Maze district, on the west side of the Green and Colorado rivers, can only be reached on foot or with a four-wheel-drive vehicle. To get to the Colorado and Green rivers, you must take a long, difficult hike or a raft trip.

Adventure-sports enthusiasts flock to Canyonlands. The park's dirt roads are heaven for mountain bikers, and people with four-wheel-drive vehicles love to challenge their driving skills and the capabilities of their machines by tackling Elephant Hill or the Flint Trail. Rafters roar through the surging rapids of Cataract Canyon. In addition, there are commercial tours by horseback, by airplane, and even by llama.

The small town of Moab serves as the hub for this region, and since you won't find much in the way of food and lodging in the parks, Moab will come to look like civilization. But even with the advent of tourism, this old mining town has retained an authentic southern Utah gruffness.

Arches was made a national monument in 1929. Over the years its boundaries were stretched, and in 1971 it was made into a national park. Canyonlands was proclaimed a national park in 1964.

ESSENTIAL INFORMATION

VISITOR INFORMATION For information on Arches, contact the Superintendent, **Arches National Park,** Box 907, Moab, UT 84532, tel. 801/259–8161, TDD 801/259–5279. For information on Canyonlands National Park, write to: Superintendent, **Canyonlands National Park,** 125 West 200 South, Moab, UT 84532; or call 801/259–7164. New to Moab is the **Moab Information Center** (Main and Center Sts., Moab, UT 84532, tel. 800/635–6622), manned by five agencies—the U.S. Park Service, the U.S. Forest Service, the Bureau of Land Management, the Grand County Travel Council, and the Canyonlands Natural History Association. The center is open to visitors daily from 8 AM to 9 PM.

A free permit is required if you plan on spending the night in the backcountry at either Arches or Canyonlands. This can be picked up at the Arches visitor center, the visitor centers near the entrances of the Island in the Sky and Needles districts of Canyonlands, and the Hans Flat Ranger Station near the Maze district of Canyonlands.

In Canyonlands, permits are also required for rock climbing and for boating, rafting, canoeing, and kayaking on the Green and Colorado rivers. Only experienced boaters should attempt Cataract Canyon; if you plan to take a noncommercial river trip through Cataract Canyon, you must obtain a noncommercial boating permit in lieu of a backcountry permit by contacting the park well ahead of your trip. More detailed information on where and when to boat in the Canyonlands area may be found in the "Canyonland River Recreation" and "Calm Water Float Trips" brochures, which are available free from the **Grand County Travel Council** (tel. 801/259–8825 or 800/635–6622).

FEES The entrance fee is $4 per vehicle for a seven-day pass. Fees are charged at the Needles and Island in the Sky districts of Canyonlands and at Arches. Passes purchased at Arches cannot be used at Canyonlands or vice versa, but if you plan to visit often, you might want to purchase a $10 annual pass, which is valid at both parks for the calendar year. A $2 individual fee is charged for bicyclists, motorcyclists, walkers, and bus passengers.

PUBLICATIONS The classic book on this area is Edward Abbey's *Desert Solitaire,* which ranks among the greatest philosophy/natural-history books ever written. Read this book and chances are you won't be able to resist the temptation to visit canyonlands country.

Books, maps, videos, river guides, posters, and slides on both Arches and Canyonlands national parks can be purchased at the visitor centers or obtained from the **Canyonlands Natural History Association** (30 South 100 East, Moab, UT 84532, tel. 801/259–6003). **Back of Beyond** (83 N. Main St., Moab, UT 84532, tel. 801/259–5154), a well-stocked bookstore, also sells many of the publications listed here.

Hikers should consider buying Sandra Hinchman's *Hiking the Southwest's Canyon Country,* published by the Mountaineers. *Canyon Country Hiking and Natural History,* by F. A. Barnes, is another good guide to trails in Arches and Canyonlands. Many of Barnes's other guidebooks are standard resources on canyonlands country, including *Canyon Country Exploring, Canyon Country Highway Touring, Canyon Country Arches and Bridges, Utah Canyon Country, Canyon Country Geology,* and *Canyon Country Off-Road Vehicle Trails* (three volumes).

To get your kids excited about Utah's parks, pick up the Canyonlands Natural History Association's "Buffalo Collection," a combination coloring book/notebook guide for kids, covering such places as Arches, Canyonlands, Zion, and other area attractions. Each page is pre-punched for a three-hole notebook and costs 25¢.

Geologic maps of Arches ($6.50) and Canyonlands ($10) and the more detailed United States Geological Survey (U.S.G.S.) maps are also available from the Canyonlands Natural History Association. **Trails Illustrated** (tel. 303/670–3457), based in Evergreen, Colorado, offers detailed maps of the area for $8 each.

GEOLOGY AND TERRAIN Deep beneath Arches and Canyonlands lies a thick bed of salt deposited more than 300 million years ago, when the sea that once flowed over southern Utah evaporated. This fragile and unsteady salt foundation has caused the land above it to fold, buckle, break, and bend into formations later to be refined by the artistry of water.

The more than 1,500 sandstone arches that crowd Arches National Park represent the greatest concentration of natural arches in the world. These arches are found in narrow walls of sandstone called fins, which are a result of the upthrusting and faulting of the earth. The arches are formed by water, which freezes and expands in cracks in the fins, thus putting pressure on the sandstone until a chunk of it falls out. Other formations resulting from this strenuous environmental wear and tear are spires and balanced rocks. Natural bridges differ from natural arches in that they are carved mainly by flowing water, not the freezing action of water. There are few natural bridges in Arches and Canyonlands; to see three outstanding ones you'll have to travel to Natural Bridges National Monument, west of Blanding and south of Canyonlands National Park.

Canyonlands, with 337,570 acres of land as compared to Arches' 73,379 acres, comprises an even wider selection of geological formations. The Colorado and Green rivers meet here, thus dividing the park neatly into three distinct districts: the Island in the Sky, a high-level mesa in the northern part of the park; the Needles, an assemblage of wind-sculpted formations in the southeast, including arches, potholes, spires, and grabens; and the remote Maze, with its truly labyrinthine box canyons. Then there are the rivers themselves, carving out canyons and meanders and roaring with rapids—particularly in Cataract Canyon.

The reddish Kayenta, crumbly Chinle, and light-colored, erosion-resistant White Rim sandstones in Canyonlands are slightly older than the Entrada and Navajo varieties found at Arches. (Navajo sandstone is also found at Canyonlands, on top of the Kayenta in the Island in the Sky district.) White Rim sandstone forms benches and rims at the heads of canyons and can be seen on the eponymous White Rim Road in the Island in the Sky district. The white Cedar Mesa sandstone prevalent in the Needles and Maze districts tends to be easily eroded into potholes. A kind of desert catch basin, a pothole is a depression in the stone caused by erosion. Slickrock (large expanses of sandstone where little or no vegetation can grow) is found throughout both parks.

Traveling on the entrance road to the Needles district visitors will see Canyonlands' most prominent example of desert varnish, which looks like dark paint splashed over the rocks.

In actuality, desert varnish's color can range from red to black and is directly related to the amount of manganese and iron in its composition. Also composed of clay minerals, grains of sand, and other trace elements, rock varnish is cemented to rock surfaces by microorganisms living on the rock. These microorganisms take manganese out of the environment—from airborne dust and run-off—oxidize it, and imbed it in the rock. In the course of thousands of years, the 300- to 700-foot Wingate cliffs have been covered by a thin layer of the dark brown to black "varnish." Where sections of the cliff have recently chipped off, the difference in color is particularly dramatic.

For more information on geology, see *CanyonLands Country: Geology of Arches and Canyonlands National Parks,* by Donald L. Baars, or F. A. Barnes's *Canyon Country Geology.*

FLORA AND FAUNA The sparse rainfall and dry desert climate of Arches and Canyonlands limit the number of plants and animals that can survive here. But from mid-April to mid-June, desert wildflowers bloom in the canyons and the meadows. Particularly after a year of heavier-than-usual rainfall, expect to see the brilliant blooms of prickly poppy, evening primrose, Indian paintbrush, jimson-weed (late summer), and rabbitbrush (fall). From April through October, the Arboretum of Utah provides a "wildflower hotline" (tel. 801/581–4747), which gives information about which flowers and plants are blooming; in September and October it tells about the fall foliage.

"Pygmy forests" of piñon and juniper trees dominate the landscape. The trees (both piñon and juniper) are described as "pygmy" because of their short stature. Large, stately cottonwood trees grow in washes or near the few flowing streams and rivers. Exotic tamarisk chokes the sides of the banks of both the Green and Colorado rivers and some washes. Such common desert plants as the yucca, sagebrush, Mormon tea, prickly pear cactus, and buffalo berry can be viewed on most hikes. Signs on an easy self-guided nature trail near the entrance to the Arches visitor center introduce some common local plant species. Brochures on the park's plantlife are available at the center.

The Canyonlands Natural History Association sells bird, plant, and reptile/amphibian lists (24¢ each) covering the species found in the area.

When visiting Canyonlands or Arches, you will be reminded by rangers not to step on the cryptobiotic crust. A delicate, dark crust made up of various fungi, algae, lichens, and mosses, it covers untrammeled desert regions. This substance requires years to grow and is as fragile as it is necessary to the desert ecosystem. It acts as a natural shield, helping to prevent erosion and to keep in moisture needed for plants to grow. So watch your step: Walk on bare rock or in sandy washes.

Wildlife does not thrive in great numbers in the inhospitable climate of canyonlands country. Nonetheless, some mammals and reptiles can be viewed easily. Sightings of mule deer and jackrabbits around campgrounds are common. Lizards sun themselves on rocks along the trails. Resident birds include golden eagles, red-tailed hawks, turkey vultures, and pinyon jays. Glimpses of coyotes, ringtail cats, foxes, and even cougars are rare, but memorable. If you are taking a river trip down Cataract Canyon, search the sides of canyons for rare desert bighorn sheep. In the winter, visitors might also spot an occasional bald eagle or peregrine falcon.

WHEN TO GO The best times to visit Arches and Canyonlands national parks are in the spring and fall, when temperatures are most conducive to hiking and mountain biking. During a warm spring rainstorm, hikers are delighted by the waterfalls that miraculously appear. River trips down the Colorado and Green rivers, however, are best in the summer, when rafters can beat the heat by plunging into the cool, muddy waters.

Crowds disappear from the parks in the winter months, and even the most popular trails and overlooks are left all but deserted. Imagine gazing out at the snow-capped peaks of the Henry, La Sal, and Abajo mountains on a January afternoon just after a flurry has dusted snow over the red rock canyons.

The climate in this area is dry year-round, with the humidity seldom climbing above 10%. Temperatures fluctuate quite a bit even in winter months. In January, record highs of 66°F and record lows of -18°F have been recorded at Arches, but the average high is 41°F and the average low, 18°F. In April and October, expect temperatures to reach into the 70s and drop to the low 40s at night. The hottest month of the year is July, when the maximum temperature hovers around 99°F in Arches and 92°F in Canyonlands, and the minimum is about 65°F in Arches and 62°F in Canyonlands. October is the rainiest month at Arches, and surprisingly, August, with its sudden, spectacular thunderstorms, is the second-wettest. In Canyonlands, July is the wettest month.

SEASONAL EVENTS Week before Easter: More than 1,000 jeeps from all over the country and the world sign up for the **Moab Jeep Safari.** Guides take groups of jeepers, from beginner to expert, along four-wheel-drive roads on Bureau of Land Management land. For more information, call 800/635–6622. **Second week in June: Butch Cassidy Days** (tel. 800/635–6622) in Moab include a professional rodeo, barbecue, shootouts, dances, and live entertainment. **Halloween Week:** The **Fat Tire Festival** (tel. 800/635–6622) is a mountain-bike gala with bicycle polo, a bicycle rodeo, guided rides, dances, and entertainment; it concludes with a costume ball.

WHAT TO PACK Canyonlands and Arches are short on creature comforts: Drinking water, food, gasoline, stores, and lodgings are not available within the park (with the exception of a seasonal water supply at Squaw Flat Campground in the Needles district of Canyonlands and Devils Garden Campground in Arches). Heat can be extreme in the summer.

For any trip into Canyonlands and Arches, and especially for overnight stays and travel into remote areas, it is imperative to bring along a good supply of food, enough water bottles to carry an adequate amount of water

(a gallon per person per day), a map, sunscreen and sun hat, good hiking boots, and tools (if you're driving).

If you go on a guided river trip, chances are your guide will provide you with waterproof bags and equipment, but be sure to ask—the rapids are a drenching experience.

GENERAL STORES No stores are located inside Canyonlands or Arches. Stopping for supplies in town—Moab, Green River, Monticello, or Blanding—is a must. All four towns have 24-hour service stations that can provide the basics. The **City Market** (tel. 801/259–5181) on Moab's Main Street at the southern end of town is the largest full-service grocery and drugstore in the area. Open 24 hours a day, every day of the year except Christmas, it carries just about any supply you might need. The small and expensive **Needles Outpost** (tel. 801/259–2032), located near the Needles entrance to Canyonlands, sells some camping supplies, gasoline, and food. It is open from about March 15 to the end of October, 8 to 7 daily.

ARRIVING AND DEPARTING The best way to get to Canyonlands and Arches is by automobile. Although some public transportation is available to Moab, getting around inside the parks requires a car. If you take a guided river, mountain bike, or four-wheel-drive trip, however, the outfitters will usually arrange for your transportation from Moab to the park.

By Plane. Alpine Air (tel. 801/373–1508 or 800/253–5678), a small commuter airline, provides daily service to Moab from Salt Lake City. Flights leave Salt Lake City at 7 AM and arrive at 8:25 AM. The Moab airport is 17 miles from downtown, so plan on using the local shuttle service run by **KJ Cab** (tel. 801/259–8294); it costs $22.50 for up to three people. The closest major airport to Arches and Canyonlands is in Grand Junction, Colorado, 125 miles away. From there you can rent a car through **Avis** (tel. 800/331–1212), **Hertz** (tel. 800/654–3131), **Thrifty** (tel. 800/367–2277), or **Budget** (tel. 800/527–0700).

By Car and RV. The town of Moab, the main access point into Arches National Park and Canyonlands' Island in the Sky and Needles districts, lies on Highway 191, which links I–70 in Utah to I–40 in Arizona. Plan on a driving time of just under five hours for the 236-mile trip between Salt Lake City and Moab. Traveling on I–70 from Denver to Arches, plan on a 380-mile trip taking just under seven hours. The North Rim of the Grand Canyon is 402 miles and eight hours away; Zion National Park is a 325-mile, 6¹/₂-hour drive.

To reach Highway 191 from Salt Lake, travel south on I–15 to Spanish Fork. Take the Price–Manti exit to Highway 6. Stay on that road through the towns of Price and Wellington until reaching I–70. Go 17 miles east on I–70 to Crescent Junction and turn off for Highway 191.

The only entrance to Arches is in the south of the park, just off Highway 191 and about 5 miles north of Moab. There are three entrances to Canyonlands but only two paved routes, both of which are accessible from Highway 191. One paved route is along Highway 313 to the Island in the Sky district; the other follows Highway 211 into the Needles district. The Island in the Sky district is only 35 miles from Moab. The Needles district is 80 miles from Moab and 50 miles northwest of the town of Monticello, where the nearest motels are located.

Entering Canyonlands through the Maze district is not recommended without a four-wheel-drive vehicle. To reach this entrance, take I–70 to Highway 24 and drive south 24 miles until the turnoff near Goblin Valley State Park, 20 miles north of Hanksville. Then plan on a long, dusty, and often rugged trip to the Maze along an 80-mile dirt road, which includes the challenging switchbacks of the Flint Trail Road. The small Horseshoe Canyon Unit of Canyonlands, which is separated from the main part of the park by Bureau of Land Management lands, is accessible by passenger car, but only in dry weather. To get to Horseshoe Canyon, follow the directions above, but after traveling 25 miles on the dirt

road, turn left and continue for 5 miles to the canyon rim.

By Train. The **Amtrak** station (tel. 800/872–7245) nearest to Moab is in the tiny hamlet of Thompson, about 32 miles north of town. **Thrifty Rent-a-Car** (tel. 801/259–7317) in Moab will leave a car for you at the station if prior arrangements are made.

By Bus. **Greyhound** buses stop at Crescent Junction, about 27 miles north of Moab. You can arrange to have Thrifty Rent-a-Car (*see above*) deliver a car there or have the **Moab taxi service** (tel. 801/259–8294) pick you up.

EXPLORING

Canyonlands. The difficulty of exploring Canyonlands is part of its charm. Most visitors drive through the park, taking short hikes off the main roads. Those roads, however, are limited, so if you want to truly penetrate the park, you should choose a longer hike or a rafting, mountain biking, or four-wheel-drive adventure in the backcountry. If you are a newcomer to the area, consider one of the many excellent guided tours (*see* Guided Tours, *below*). Plan on spending at least one day in the Island of the Sky district and one day in the Needles district; to understand what the park is all about, you'll have to take one more day to go rafting down one of the rivers that formed the canyons.

Of Canyonlands' three districts, Island in the Sky is the most accessible. A paved road leads to several dramatic viewpoints—Grand View Point, Green River Overlook, and the Upheaval Dome are the best—and to trailheads for some short hikes. Here you will also find the mountain bikers' favorite route, the White Rim Road.

The Needles district to the south is more remote. A paved road leads to the entrance, but it runs only slightly more than 8 miles into the park. Elephant Hill, the consummate four-wheel-drive challenge, and the hikers' favorite, Joint Trail near Chesler Park, are both located in Needles.

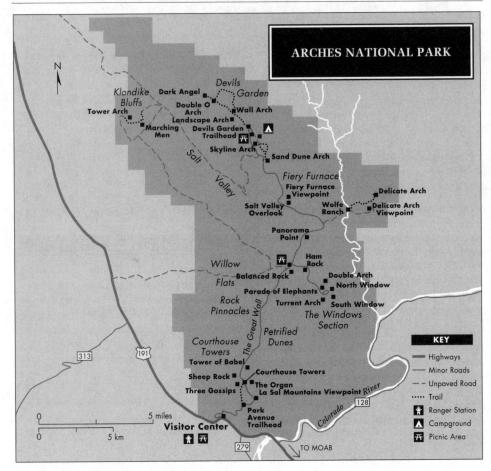

The third district of Canyonlands, the Maze, may be the hardest national park area to reach in the lower 48 states. There are no paved roads in the Maze, so you must either hike in (it takes a full day) or have a four-wheel-drive vehicle and at least two days if you want to visit this region. Only the Horseshoe Canyon Unit of the Maze is even close to accessible by passenger car (*see* Arriving and Departing, *above*). It is also the most visited area in the Maze district.

Arches. In contrast to Canyonlands, Arches can easily be explored by car on a 20-mile paved road. You will not, however, want to stay in your car and miss two of the greatest hikes in Utah, Fiery Furnace and Delicate Arch. Mountain biking is highly regulated in

Arches; it's restricted to the paved road, which is somewhat narrow, and a few dirt roads. You'll need at least one full day here.

THE BEST IN ONE DAY It is possible to see both Arches and the Island in the Sky district of Canyonlands in one day, but it wouldn't be much fun. This is a land of great expanses, and unless you want to spend the whole day driving, you would do best to visit just one park. First-time travelers to this region should opt for Arches.

Arches. No visit to Arches would be complete without doing the Fiery Furnace and the Delicate Arch hikes (*see* Longer Hikes, *below*). The strenuous jaunt around Fiery Furnace is so convoluted that rangers must lead you

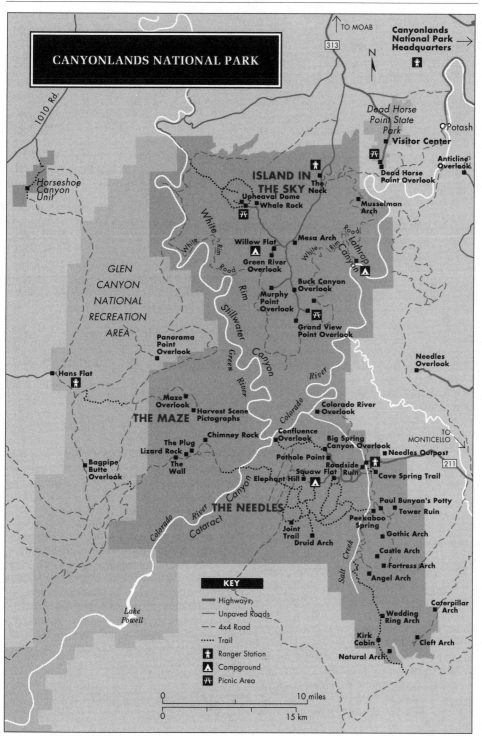

CANYONLANDS NATIONAL PARK

TO MOAB

Canyonlands
National Park
Headquarters

313

N

1010 Rd.

Dead Horse
Point State
Park

Potash

Horseshoe
Canyon
Unit

Visitor Center

Anticline
Overlook

Dead Horse
Point Overlook

ISLAND IN
THE SKY

The
Neck

Musselman
Arch

Upheaval Dome
Whale Rock

White Rim Road

Willow Flat

Mesa Arch

Lathrop Canyon

GLEN
CANYON
NATIONAL
RECREATION
AREA

Green River
Overlook

White Rim Road

Buck Canyon
Overlook

Murphy
Point
Overlook

Grand View
Point Overlook

Stillwater Canyon

Green River

Panorama
Point
Overlook

Needles
Overlook

Hans Flat

Maze
Overlook

Harvest Scene
Pictographs

Colorado River

River

Colorado River
Overlook

THE MAZE

Confluence
Overlook

Big Spring
Canyon Overlook

TO
MONTICELLO

Chimney Rock

The Plug
Lizard Rock

Pothole Point

Needles Outpost

211

The
Wall

Roadside
Ruin

Squaw Flat

Cave Spring Trail

Bagpipe
Butte
Overlook

Elephant Hill

Paul Bunyan's Potty

Tower Ruin

Colorado River

THE NEEDLES

Peekaboo
Spring

Gothic Arch

Cataract Canyon

Joint
Trail

Druid Arch

Castle Arch

Fortress Arch

Angel Arch

Salt Creek

Caterpillar
Arch

Lake
Powell

Wedding
Ring Arch

Kirk
Cabin

Cleft Arch

Natural Arch

KEY

Highways

Unpaved Roads

4x4 Road

Trail

Ranger Station

Campground

Picnic Area

0   10 miles

0   15 km

through. First thing in the morning, stop at the visitor center and sign up for this walk. Since the required reservations can be made up to 48 hours in advance, you'll be lucky to get a spot. If possible, sign up for an afternoon tour. Then, head out to the Wolfe Ranch (*see* Historic Buildings and Sites, *below*) and the trailhead for Delicate Arch. The walk out to Delicate Arch is perhaps one of the best hikes in the state. Since this trail is quite exposed, you will enjoy it much more in the cooler hours of the day. Plan to spend the entire morning here. Bring lunch to eat out on the trail, and carry plenty of water.

Continue on to the meeting place for the Fiery Furnace hike. Despite its name, this is the best place to be in the heat of the day, because you will be walking in shade cast by sandstone fins. After 2¹/₂ hours of walking, drive out to the Balanced Rock and the famed Windows section, where scenes from *Indiana Jones and the Last Crusade* were filmed (*see* Nature Trails and Short Walks, *below*). Take plenty of photos in the late afternoon light.

As you work your way back toward the visitor center and the entrance to the park, drop some members of your party off at the Courthouse Towers viewpoint. Here they can begin the 1-mile one-way stroll up Park Avenue to see its sandstone skyscrapers. Pick them up at the Park Avenue Trailhead and exit the park where you entered in the morning.

Canyonlands. A day's itinerary in Canyonlands will entail more driving than walking. Island in the Sky is the easiest part of Canyonlands to see in a short amount of time. Leaving Moab, take Route 313 to Dead Horse Point State Park for a vista over the Colorado River and the Island in the Sky district (*see* Scenic Drives and Views, *below*). You'll have to backtrack to reach the juncture where Route 313 meets the road that enters Canyonlands. Your first stop in the park should be the ranger station at the Neck. There you can ask questions and pick up a map and brochures. From the Neck it is best to drive straight through to Grand View Point Overlook and walk the Grand View Trail (*see* Nature Hikes and Short Walks, *below*). Driv-

ing back toward the Neck, you should stop first at the Buck Canyon Overlook, then continue on and take the unpaved spur road to the Murphy Point Overlook. Return to the main road going north; at the fork, turn left to reach the Green River and Upheaval Dome overlooks. Upheaval Dome is a mound of earth in the center of a large crater. You can't get to the dome without taking a long hike, but from the parking area a 1-mile round-trip trail leads to Crater View Overlook, from which you can see Upheaval Dome jutting out of the center of the crater.

Head back toward the Neck and stop to hike out to the Mesa Arch (*see* Nature Trails and Short Walks, *below*). The La Sal Mountains in the afternoon light provide great pictures. Before exiting the park, stop near the Shafer Trail to watch the antics of the four-wheel-drive enthusiasts on the treacherous switchbacks.

Arches and Canyonlands. If you insist on seeing both Canyonlands and Arches in the same day, get an early start and head to the Island in the Sky district southwest of Moab, where you should plan to spend about four to five hours. Do not miss the view from Dead Horse Point State Park, Grand View Point, and Crater View Overlook/Upheaval Dome. Take the short hike to Mesa Arch. After breaking for lunch, head into Arches for a late afternoon drive and take a sunset hike to the Delicate Arch or to the Double Arch in the Windows section.

ORIENTATION PROGRAMS Visitor centers at the entrance to Arches and to the Island in the Sky and Needles districts of Canyonlands provide information about the geology and human history of the area, and sell books, maps, and posters. Park rangers coordinate interpretive activities and guided hikes from these centers. An interesting slide show is shown at Arches, and there is a short, self-guided nature walk at the front of the visitor center. This walk provides an introduction to the plant life of the park.

GUIDED TOURS Moab, with a population of less than 6,000, may offer more guided tours than any town its size in the country. You can choose from a multitude of river trips, horseback excursions, mountain bike tours, airplane flights, and four-wheel-drive expeditions through Canyonlands. The guide business in Moab is extremely competitive so most guides and tour operators offer the same excellent service. When you sign up with a Moab guide, expect to be pampered—high-quality meals, first-class equipment, and hair-raising campfire tales await you. You will pay about $100 to $125 per person per day for a guided trip, which can be as short as half a day and as long as a week or 10 days. Contact the **Utah Travel Council** (Council Hall/Capitol Hill, Salt Lake City, UT 84114, tel. 801/538–1030) for a free brochure, "Utah Tour Guide," which lists all of the state's guide services. A list of tour operators licensed to operate in Arches and Canyonlands national parks is available through both parks (*see* Visitor Information, *above*).

Visitors who expect to tour the parks by bus may be disappointed. Because of the area's sparse population and dearth of large hotels, bus tours are not regularly scheduled. Special bus trips, however, can be arranged out of Salt Lake City. Try **On the Town Tours** (Box 510541, Salt Lake City, UT 84151, tel. 801/575–6040) or **Western Leisure** (1172 Brickyard Rd., Suite 200, Salt Lake City, UT 84106, tel. 801/467–6100 or 800/532–2113).

In addition, **Off the Beaten Track** (Box 235, La Sal, UT 84530, tel. 801/686–2304, fax 801/467–7301) sponsors wildflower and nature tours via four-wheel-drive vehicle in Canyonlands and Arches. The day-long tours cost $75 per person and are limited to three guests.

On the more upscale side, **High Desert Adventures** (5500 Amelia Earhart Dr., Salt Lake City, UT 84116 tel. 801/483–6165 or 800/345–RAFT) offers the 10-day-long, $1,350 "Utah Odyssey," which includes hiking in Arches; a stay at the Pack Creek Ranch; biking in Canyonlands; a river trip down the Colorado; hiking in Capitol Reef, Bryce, and Canyonlands national parks and the Escalante Petrified Forest State Park; as well as climbing, hiking, and canyoneering in Zion National Park.

Canyonlands Field Institute (Box 68, Moab, UT 84532, tel. 801/259–7750) runs educational trips ranging from archaeological digs and biological field trips to writers' workshops.

SCENIC DRIVES AND VIEWS It's difficult to select a drive in the Canyonlands area that isn't scenic and doesn't lead to spectacular views. But a few are especially noteworthy.

The best of these is the 50-mile drive north from Moab along **Highway 191 to Route 313** and across the narrow mesa of the Canyonland's Island in the Sky district, with a detour into Dead Horse Point State Park. Plan on five hours for this journey so that you'll have plenty of time to enjoy the views at Dead Horse Point, the Grand View Point, and the Upheaval Dome. True to its name, the Grand View Point provides the best overall vista of Canyonlands National Park, including the Maze, the Needles, and the Henry, La Sal, and Abajo (known locally as Blue) mountain ranges looming in the distance like islands.

The popular 41-mile round-trip drive on the main road and one spur road through **Arches National Park** leads to a half-dozen short hikes (*see* Nature Trails and Short Walks, *below*), balanced rocks, and views of many arches. In the Windows area alone, visitors can see five arches from their cars and take short, easy hikes, all of which are less than a mile, to the bases of the formations.

A drive many visitors wrongly ignore originates about 30 miles south of Moab, just south of the Wilson Arch, on Highway 191. The road travels west off the highway and leads through Canyon Rims Recreation Area to the Bureau of Land Management's Windwhistle Campground and the **Needles Overlook.** Although the approximately 25-mile one-way drive does not actually pass through the borders of Canyonlands National Park, it affords an impressive view of the Needles section of the park. The road is paved and on most days can be experienced in relative solitude.

HISTORIC BUILDINGS AND SITES Few humans have succeeded in leaving their mark on these rugged lands. Aside from some Native American ruins and restored pioneer buildings, few man-made artifacts exist in Arches and Canyonlands.

The **Wolfe Ranch** in Arches National Park was originally built in 1888 by Civil War veteran John Wesley Wolfe and later restored. Found at the trailhead to the Delicate Arch, this ranch offers visitors a glimpse of early pioneer life. A brochure available at the cabin describes what life was like here in the late 19th century.

In the Needles district of Canyonlands National Park, the Cave Spring Trail, which originates near the Salt Creek four-wheel-drive road, leads to an authentic **cowboy line camp** dating to the late 1800s. A short hike from the trailhead just past the Needles visitor center takes you to **Roadside Ruin,** an Anasazi granary once used to store corn, seeds, and nuts. **Tower Ruin** in the Needles' Horse Canyon is an example of an Anasazi cliff dwelling. Better-preserved Anasazi buildings can be seen at nearby Hovenweep National Monument, Edge of the Cedars State Park in Blanding, and Mesa Verde National Park in Colorado.

NATURE TRAILS AND SHORT WALKS Despite the rough terrain and great size of Arches and Canyonlands, both parks offer a number of short hikes.

Arches. First-time visitors will enjoy the short **Arches Desert Nature Trail,** near the visitor center, which introduces the various indigenous plants. One of the most popular hikes for kids is the 1/2-mile round-trip walk through an extremely narrow canyon to **Sand Dune Arch,** a shaded rock formation guarding a sand dune. Kids love to play in the fine, pink sand. The parking area at the trailhead is found just before reaching the campground.

Another short hike in Arches leads around the **Balanced Rock** (1/2-mile round-trip). In the nearby **Windows** section, you can stroll on one or more of the mostly flat trails to the North and South Windows, Turret Arch, and/or Double Arch, which was featured in *Indiana Jones and the Last Crusade*. Visible from your car, these formations are just short walks from the road.

Canyonlands. There are three relatively easy hikes with self-guiding trail brochures in the Needles district of Canyonlands. The 1/4-mile round-trip **Roadside Ruin** hike leads to a small Anasazi granary (*see* Historic Buildings and Sites, *above*). The 1/2-mile round-trip **Pothole Point** trail, off the road to Big Spring Canyon Overlook, leads to sandstone potholes, often filled with water, and fairy and tadpole shrimp. In fact, these tiny potholes harbor myriad creatures that form a fragile ecosystem. Hikers should not disturb them— not even by splashing in the water. The oils from your skin can change the pH of the water enough to kill or damage the desert dwellers. These potholes are also the only water source for wildlife, so only take a drink from them in an emergency. And if you do, use a clean cup or pot to dip the water out, and be sure to boil or treat it before you gulp it down. Finally, the **Cave Spring Trail,** a 1/2-mile loop, takes you into an authentic cowboy line camp and then under a giant alcove.

The best easy walk in the Island in the Sky district is the 1/2-mile round-trip loop trail through a piñon-juniper forest to **Mesa Arch.** Take along a camera with a wide-angle lens so you can frame the small arch and the La Sal Mountains in the distance. The brochure available on the 1-mile round-trip hike to the Crater View of **Upheaval Dome** raises questions about how this unusual dome was formed—one theory is that a meteor crashed to earth here. The flat 1 1/2-mile round-trip walk along the edge of **Grand View Point** provides some of the best views of the canyon country, as well as of three major mountain ranges, the Henry, La Sals, and Abajos.

LONGER HIKES **Arches.** Do not come to Arches and miss the 3-mile round-trip trek to the **Delicate Arch.** Though the 480-foot ascent can be grueling on a hot summer day, the reward of seeing this 45-foot-high and 33-foot-wide arch, one of nature's most fantastic creations, is well worth the work. The trail is designed so that the arch does not become visible until the last possible second. Take time to sit on the warm red rock of the natural amphitheater surrounding the arch to contemplate the forces that created it. Bring plenty of water.

Another exceptional hike in Arches is the strenuous 2-mile round-trip **Fiery Furnace** hike, which takes 2½ hours to complete. This labyrinth of narrow canyons, twisted passageways, and hidden arches is so confusing that you'll have to go through with a ranger. Within minutes of entering the Fiery Furnace, you're likely to lose all sense of direction. Reservations are required for this hike and must be made at the Arches Visitor Center in person, up to 48 hours in advance. Rangers lead the hike twice daily, March through October.

A pleasant day can be spent exploring the **Devils Garden** area, near the Arches Campground, at the north end of the park road. The Devils Garden trail leads up to seven arches—including the famous Landscape Arch, with its 306-foot span the longest in the park—and provides views of several more. The world seems to drop away beyond the Double O Arch. Allow at least three hours for this moderately strenuous 5-mile round-trip hike, but plan on more time if it's a hot day. Hikers can take side trips from here.

Canyonlands. One of the most rewarding hikes in Canyonlands is the 6½-mile round-trip trek into the **Great Gallery**, in the Horseshoe Canyon Unit of the park. Since there is no drinking water available there, bring plenty of your own. Reaching the trailhead often requires driving on rough dirt roads, but can be done in a two-wheel-drive vehicle unless the weather turns bad. To reach the trailhead, drive north from Hanksville on Highway 24 until you see the turnoff to the Maze district, across and south of the road from the Goblin Valley State Park turnoff. Follow the signs for just over 30 miles to reach the trailhead. From there, you will descend about 800 feet into the bottom of the canyon, then walk upstream almost 2 miles

more until you see a haunting prehistoric Native American rock art panel, the 100-foot Great Gallery, which includes the Ghost King. On the walk, watch for Native American ruins and other examples of rock art along the way.

Hiking into the **Maze** can be exciting, but it can also be frightening and potentially dangerous because of the many box canyons, which seem to lead to one dead end after another. The main drainages in this area are quite obvious, but once you are down inside one of the side canyons, finding your way back out can be difficult. Make sure you bring a map, compass, and guidebook (that you know how to use!) before hiking in this seldom-visited area.

There are several fine, long hikes in the Needles district of the Canyonlands, many of which are excellent for backpacking. One of the best, the 6-mile round-trip **Joint Trail**, leads to Chesler Park through narrow cracks or joints in the rock, past potholes, and up to points with sweeping vistas. Other hikes in the **Needles district** include the one-way trek of almost 6¾ miles to a point overlooking the confluence of the Green and Colorado rivers; the 5½-mile one-way hike to Druid Arch; the 10-mile one-way hike from the Big Spring Canyon Overlook to the Colorado River Overlook; the 5½-mile one-way trek to Peekaboo Spring; and the nearly 8¾-mile loop through Squaw and Lost canyons. Most of these hikes originate at Squaw Flat.

Longer hikes in the **Island in the Sky district** are more difficult; you must be prepared to hike back up after hiking down into the canyons. Rangers at the visitor center can offer suggestions on routes through this area. Serious hikers should consider purchasing guides with more detailed descriptions of trails (*see* Publications, *above*).

OTHER ACTIVITIES Back-Road Driving. Some of the nation's premier four-wheel-drive roads are in Canyonlands National Park. People come from all over the world to tackle **Elephant Hill** in Needles District. At one point, the trail is so narrow that the driver has to back up to the edge of a steep cliff in order to make a turn. If you would like to view the towering canyons from a lower vantage point, try the less-dizzying route along the **Salt Creek** wash to **Angel Arch** in Needles District.

The greatest driving challenge in the Maze district is the **Flint Trail.** Four-wheel-drive and high clearance are required to make the steep, twisting trip up to the Maze Overlook. Bring plenty of water and extra gasoline on this journey as service stations and stores are miles away.

The trips to **Gemini Bridges,** outside the parks, and the **White Rim Road** in Canyon-lands' Island in the Sky district provide beautiful views over the canyons.

Although less well known, the few jeep trails in Arches National Park, such as **Klondike Bluffs** and **Willow Flats,** are enjoyable.

A good way to discover the best four-wheel-drive roads in the area is to join the annual **Moab Jeep Safari,** an event that takes place the week before Easter (*see* Seasonal Events, *above*) outside the parks.

Although not quite as popular as river trips, guided four-wheel-drive expeditions through Canyonlands offer yet another adventure available in few U.S. national parks. One of the best four-wheel-drive tour operators into Canyonlands and Arches national parks is **Tag-A-Long Expeditions** (452 N. Main St., Moab, UT 84532, tel. 801/259–8946 or 800/453–3292). Another reputable operator is **Lin Ottinger Tours** (600 N. Main St., Moab, UT 84532, tel. 801/259–7312).

You can rent a four-wheel-drive vehicle from **Tag-A-Long Expeditions** (*see above*), **Certified Ford-Mercury** (500 S. Main St., Moab, UT 84532, tel. 801/259–6107), and **Farabee Rentals** (550 N. Main St., Moab, UT 84532, tel. 801/259–7494).

Bird-Watching. Spring is the best time to go birding in Canyonlands and Arches national parks. During the summer heat, the prime bird-viewing times are before sunset and around sunrise. Concentrate your efforts on the river washes or around cottonwood trees.

Canyonlands birds include flickers, scrub and pinyon jays, grosbeaks, canyon wrens, swallows, hummingbirds, and many different types of raptors, such as red-tailed hawks and even peregrine falcons. A bird list published by the Canyonlands Natural History Association is available at the visitor centers at Arches and Canyonlands.

Boating and Rafting. If you want to challenge the wildest rapids this side of the Grand Canyon, take a river trip through **Cataract Canyon** on the Colorado River in Canyon-lands. The rapids reach their raging peak in June and taper off through the summer. Plan to spend from three to six days on the river and from $400 to $800, depending on the type of trip you take. High-water trips must be booked six months in advance, but during August and September, when the waters run low, it is possible to make arrangements with just a week's notice.

For those who want a smaller taste of the waters, there are half-day trips on the Colorado near Moab for as little as $25. These can be arranged with one day's notice.

The best-known of the river guide companies offering safe trips with well-trained guides include **Griffith River Expeditions** (Box 1324, Moab, UT 84532, tel. 800/332–2439), **Holiday River and Bike Expeditions** (544 East 3900 South, Salt Lake City, UT 84107, tel. 800/624–6323), **Moki Mac River Expeditions** (Box 21242, Salt Lake City, UT 84121-0242, tel. 800/284–7280), **Tag-A-Long Expeditions** (*see above*), **Tex's Canyonland River Expeditions** (Box 336, Moab, UT 84532, tel. 800/232–7247), **Western River Expeditions** (7258 Racquet Club Dr., Salt Lake City, UT 84121, tel. 800/453–7450), and **World Wide Expeditions** (942 East 7145 South, Midvale, UT 84047, tel. 800/231–2769).

Some calm-water trips on both the Colorado and Green rivers can also be enjoyed. The best of them runs from the Ruby Ranch on the Green River to Mineral Canyon. This is especially good in canoes during the late summer months.

Private rafting trips are allowed through sometimes-dangerous Cataract Canyon, but you must have a permit in advance to run these rapids. Although the permits are free, in order to get one, you must convince the ranger in charge that you are an experienced rafter. For information on permits, write to the superintendent of Canyonlands National Park (see Essential Information, above). Free brochures on river recreation in the area are available through the Grand County Travel Council (805 N. Main St., Moab, UT 84532, tel. 800/635–6622).

Raft and canoe rentals are available from **Holiday River and Bike Expeditions** (see above), **Moki Mac River Expeditions** (see above), **Rental Rafts** (105 Thompson, Green River, UT 84525, tel. 801/564–3322), **Tag-A-Long Expeditions** (see above), and **Western River Expeditions** (see above).

Fishing. Anglers are out of luck at Arches; fishing within the park is essentially nonexistent. And, while a few catfish may be caught in the Colorado and Green rivers, fishing within Canyonlands is generally poor and river access extremely limited. For trout fishing in the area, try Ken's Lake or the La Sal Mountain lakes near Moab. Warm-water fishing is best in Lake Powell. Licenses, available in Moab grocery and outdoors stores, cost $40 per season for nonresidents, $18 for residents; five-day licenses cost $15, and one-day licenses are $5.

Flight-Seeing. Flying over the canyonlands is an exhilarating and relatively inexpensive way to get a feel for the immensity of this landscape and an overview of its complex geology. Ideal for people in a hurry, flights can be as brief as half an hour and take off from Moab, Blanding, Price, and Monticello airports. An hour in the air costs about $40. Flying from the tiny airport at Hite Marina in the Glen Canyon National Recreation Area back to Moab after a Cataract Canyon river trip can be almost as much fun as the river trip itself. But be warned: The landing strip at Hite is one of the scariest around. The 500-foot cliff at the edge of the runway makes for very dramatic takeoffs.

Airplane operators offering tours over the canyonlands include **Castle Valley Aviation** (Box 1070, Huntington, UT 84528, tel. 801/687–9981), **Lake Powell Air Service** (Box 1385–901 N. Sage Navajo, Page, AZ 86040, tel. 800/245–8668), **Needles Outpost** (Box 1107, Monticello, UT 84535, tel. 801/259–2032), **Redtail Aviation** (Box 515, Moab, UT 84532, tel. 801/259–7421), and **Scenic Aviation** (Box 67, Blanding, UT 84511, tel. 801/678–3222).

Horseback Riding. The **Pack Creek Ranch** (Box 1270, Moab, UT 84532, tel. 801/259–5505), one of Utah's premier dude ranches, offers outstanding pack trips into Arches and nearby national forests. You do not have to be an overnight guest at the ranch to take one of these trips. Trail ride rates are $10 the first hour and $7.50 for each additional hour. A two-hour ride into Arches costs $25. Pack trips run from $125 to $200 per person per day. **Canyonlands Llamas** (Castle Valley Star Rte. 1911, Moab, UT, 84532, tel. 801/259–5739) runs horse-pack tours just outside the parks in Mill Creek Canyon, Castle Valley, and the La Sal Mountains.

Llama Riding. One of the more unusual ways to see the backcountry is on a llama tour available through **Canyonlands Llamas** (see above). While you hike, llamas carry your water, snacks, and gourmet meals.

Mountain Biking. The most rugged way to see Canyonlands short of a major backpacking trip is on a mountain bike tour along jeep roads, such as the **White Rim Road,** which runs from the top of the Island in the Sky district to the White Rim, 1,200 feet below the top of the mesa. Mountain biking expeditions from half-day to seven days are offered by several operators.

White Rim is perhaps the most popular route, but jeep trails through the Maze and Needles districts also make for great rides. Bikers must keep to the road and stay off the hiking trails. This is critical to protect the fragile cryptobiotic crust, which helps hold the loose desert sands together.

Bicycle rentals are available from **Adrift Adventures** (Box 577, 378 N. Main St., Moab, UT 84532, tel. 801/259–8594 or 800/874–4483), **Nichols Expeditions** (497 N. Main St., Moab, UT 84532, tel. 801/259–7882 or 800/635–1792), **Western Spirit Cyclery** (Box 411, 38 South 100 West, Moab, UT 84532, tel. 801/259–8732 or 800/845–BIKE, fax 801/259–2736); **Tag-A-Long Expeditions** (*see above*), and **Rim Cyclery** (94 West 100 North, Moab, UT 84532, tel. 801/259–5333).

Adrift Adventures (*see above*) offers combination mountain biking/river trips, and **Scenic Byways Bicycle Touring** (942 East 7145 South, Midvale, UT 84047, tel. 800/231–2769) leads mountain biking/hiking trips in the Maze area.

Other good bicycle tour operators are **Slickrock Adventures** (Box 1400, Moab, UT 84532, tel. 801/259–6996) and **Western Spirit Cycling** (*see above*).

KJ Cab (174 East 200 North, Moab, UT 84532, tel. 801/259–8294) provides shuttle services within the park for independent cyclists.

Rock Climbing. Free climbing permits, which are available at the visitor centers, are required at Canyonlands National Park. In Arches, you are not allowed to climb on arches named on the U.S.G.S. map. A good book on rock climbing in the area is Mark Hesse's *Desert Towers* (Chockstone Press, Box 3505, Evergreen, CO 80439, tel. 303/674–6888), which describes more than 100 climbs in the parks and surrounding areas.

Ski Touring. Warm weather restricts ski touring in Arches and Canyonlands, but during heavy snow years, it is not just possible—it's dazzling. The dry crystal snow sparkling on the bright orange rocks creates a striking tableau. If you're lucky, you might spot a coyote. The nearby La Sal Mountains provide the best ski touring in the area. Rentals are available through **Rim Cyclery** (94 West 100 North, Moab, UT 84532, tel. 801/259–5333) and **Global Expeditions** (3075 Hwy. 191, Moab, UT 84532, tel. 801/259–6604, fax 801/259–8069).

Swimming. The Colorado River with its often fast and powerful currents is not the best place to swim. Lake Powell, southwest of Canyonlands park, is a popular alternative, but be careful when diving there—dangerous rock formations lie beneath the water. In Moab, swimming is limited to motel pools and a public pool, which is open in the summer. Many backpackers use the showers at the Moab city pool.

CHILDREN'S PROGRAMS Arches has a Junior Ranger program for children ages 6–12, with some hands-on nature activities and special interpretative hikes geared to children. The visitor centers at both parks sell publications for kids. Some river guide companies sponsor family raft trips on the Colorado. For babysitting services, check with the Grand County Travel Council (805 N. Main St., Moab, UT 84532, tel. 800/635–6622).

EVENING ACTIVITIES **Arches.** Arches offers a standard evening program each night just after sunset at an amphitheater in the Devils Garden Campground. This amphitheater, however, is far from standard. Located underneath Skyline Arch, it is one of the most dramatic theater settings in the National Park Service system. Evening programs usually begin before Easter weekend and run into October, depending on staff. Check at the visitor center for the program being offered.

Canyonlands. Evening programs are held at the Squaw Flat Campground in the Needles district, in the Island in the Sky district at the Willow Flat Campground, and at nearby Dead Horse State Park. From April through October these programs are offered at least three times a week, but check with the park for a schedule.

"Canyon's Edge," a multimedia presentation featuring the landscape, people, and ancient stories of the Colorado Plateau, plays nightly at the Moab Information Center April–October.

DINING

Since there are no lodges in either Canyonlands or Arches, you will have to venture outside the park to find a restaurant. The towns of Green River and Monticello have a few restaurants, but Moab offers the greatest selection of cuisines and particularly good Mexican fare. Authentic 1950s diners also abound in this area; they are great places to find inexpensive food, a powerful cup of coffee, and plenty of colorful local characters. Dress is always casual. If you expect to have a drink with your dinner, make sure the restaurant you choose serves alcoholic beverages; lots of restaurants in Utah do not.

Mi Vida. Once the home of uranium magnate Charlie Steen, this restaurant is a Moab landmark. Mi Vida was the name he gave to his lifelong project: a patent for a uranium mine. Built high on a cliff overlooking town, Mi Vida unfortunately does not serve food to compete with its spectacular view. The specialties here are mesquite-broiled steak and seafood. *900 N. Hwy. 191, Moab, UT, tel. 801/259-7146. Reservations advised. AE, DC, MC, V. Expensive.*

Pack Creek Ranch. Located 16 miles southeast of downtown Moab, this rustic dude ranch rivals the Sundowner (*see below*) for the best food in town. Fresh fruit and salad bar, barbecue specialties, French pepper steak, and seafood are served in the spacious dining room with a large stone fireplace, but the ranch does not have a state liquor license. To get to the Pack Creek from Moab, take Highway 191S to the Ken's Lake/La Sal Mountain Loop turnoff, and follow the sign to the Forest Service's Pack Creek Picnic Area. *La Sal Mountain Loop Rd., Box 1270, Moab, UT, tel. 801/259-5505. Reservations advised. AE, MC, V. Closed Nov.-Dec. Expensive.*

Grand Old Ranch House. Located in a two-story brick building listed on the National Register of Historic Places, this restaurant brings back memories of grandma. Sadly, the food, which consists of German dishes, prime rib, seafood, and steaks, does not rival hers. *N. Hwy. 191, Moab, UT, tel. 801/259-5753. Reservations advised. AE, DC, V. Generally closed mid-Dec.-Feb. No lunch. Moderate-Expensive.*

Sundowner Restaurant. This longtime Moab favorite is the best bet in town. West German chef Uve Weber serves up hearty German fare side by side with pastas, fajitas, steaks, and prime rib. The wiener schnitzel is worthy of Deutschland, and the salad bar is terrific. Originally built for a movie set, the Sundowner looks like a Western fort from the outside. You'll be surprised, however, by the more urbane setting inside, complete with linen tablecloths, chandeliers, wood paneling, and even stained-glass windows. *N. Hwy. 191, Moab, UT, tel. 801/259-5201. Reservations advised. AE, MC, V. No lunch. Moderate-Expensive.*

Bar M Chuckwagon Suppers. A popular stop for bus tours, this open-air restaurant attempts to capture the feel of an old cowboy camp. There's even a small western theme park on the property with a log-cabin gift shop, Native American teepee (somewhat out of place in a cowboy camp), and shooting gallery. Barbecued beef and chicken, baked beans, sourdough biscuits, and peach cobbler are served to guests seated around picnic tables. Nightly entertainment can include such western favorites as clogging and cowboy singing. Inclusive dinner price is $12. Beer and wine coolers are served. *400 East 541 South on Mulberry La., Moab, UT, tel. 801/259-2276. Reservations advised, especially for groups. MC, V. Closed Oct.-Mar. No lunch. Moderate.*

Dos Amigos Mexican Cantina. Festive Mexican piñatas and puppets hang from the walls of this popular, reasonably priced restaurant. The $3.99 all-you-can-eat daily lunch taco bar is a good deal, especially if you're hungry. *56 East 300 South, Moab, UT, tel. 801/259-7903. Reservations advised. AE, MC, V. Moderate.*

Eddie McStiff's Brew Pub & Restaurant. After a tough, dusty day of mountain biking, this pub is a great place to unwind. Five different types of ales are brewed regularly right on the premises, and special brews are sometimes made. You can sit by the huge brewing vats inside and watch the beer-making process from start to finish. The specialties here are the New York– and Chicago-style pizzas, but the menu also offers pastas, sandwiches, salads, steaks, and charbroiled burgers. *57 S. Main St., Western Plaza, Moab, UT, tel. 801/259–2337. Reservations advised for large parties. MC, V. Moderate.*

Honest Ozzie's Café and Desert Oasis. A play on the word *Anasazi,* Honest Ozzie's is a haven for vegetarians in this land of steak lovers. Natural foods and seafood are the specialties. Two popular dishes are the breakfast waffles and Ozzie's Oriental, a vegetable stir-fry. Outdoor seating in a garden is available. *60 North 1st West, Moab, UT, tel. 801/259–8442. Reservations not accepted. No credit cards. No lunch. Moderate.*

La Hacienda. This Mexican restaurant adjacent to a motel feels like a franchise, but the large portions of fine food more than make up for any lack of ambience. La Hacienda serves delicious Mexican breakfasts, including huevos rancheros. Beer is the only alcohol served. *574 N. Main St., Moab, UT, tel. 801/259–6319. Reservations not accepted. MC, V. Moderate.*

Milt's Stop and Eat. This little drive-in has only about eight stools around its lunch counter and is still serving the same good food it was back in the 1950s, when it first opened. Chili and chili-cheeseburgers are specialties. Milt's is an especially good place for breakfasts—most are under $3. *356 Millcreek, Moab, UT, tel. 801/259–7424. No credit cards. Closed Sun. Inexpensive.*

Rumours Gourmet Cafe. Formerly a drive-in, this restaurant isn't much to look at, but the food's great and cheap. The menu includes gourmet burgers, vegetarian sandwiches, espresso, cappuccino, and old-fashioned shakes, malts, and sodas. *606 S. Main St., Moab, UT, tel. 801/259–5908. Reservations not necessary. No credit cards. Closed Sun. Inexpensive.*

Westerner Grill. Signs bearing words of wisdom plaster the walls of this funky '50s diner where locals grumble about the government and cooks chat with the customers. In addition to serving a full line of diner standards, the Westerner has the distinction of brewing the best cup of coffee in southeastern Utah. *331 N. Main St., Moab, UT, tel. 801/259–9918. No credit cards. Inexpensive.*

PICNIC SPOTS Picnic areas are limited in both Arches and Canyonlands. Since there are no stores inside either park, make sure you bring your own supplies and plenty of water. Picnic areas with tables and fire grates in Arches are found at the **visitor center,** near **Devils Garden Trailhead,** and at the turnoff to **Balanced Rock.** Picnic tables are provided at **Upheaval Dome** and near the **Grand View Point Overlook** in the Island in the Sky district of Canyonlands.

LODGING

There are no overnight accommodations in Arches or Canyonlands national parks. Motels in the towns of Moab, Green River, Hanksville, and Monticello are fairly standard. The best of the chain motels are: **Best Western Canyonlands** (16 S. Main St., Moab, UT 84532, tel. 801/259–2300), **Best Western Greenwell** (105 S. Main St., Moab, UT 84532, tel. 801/259–6151 or 800/528–1234), **Comfort Suites** (800 S. Main St., Moab, UT 84532, tel. 801/259–5252), **Ramada Inn** (182 S. Main St., Moab, UT 84532, tel. 801/259–7141), and **Super 8** (889 N. Main St., Moab, UT 84532, tel. 801/259–8868). If you can afford it, the nicest and most authentic place to stay in southeastern Utah is the Pack Creek Ranch (*see below*).

For a complete list of lodges and campgrounds in Moab and Green River, contact the Moab Visitor Center (805 N. Main St., Moab, UT, 84532, tel. 801/259–8825 or 800/635–6622). Make reservations well ahead of time if you plan to visit Moab between Easter weekend and the end of October. If you plan to bring your children with you to a bed-and-breakfast, consult with the proprietors in advance.

Castle Valley Inn. The best thing about this inn is the hot tub, with its great views of the red rock cliffs that rise 2,000 feet overhead. Castle Valley is located a half-hour drive from Moab on a serene 11-acre property. Filipino baskets, African masks, and carpets from southern Mexico decorate the rooms, reflecting the proprietors' penchant for international travel. To get here, follow the Colorado River to Fisher Towers and then follow the signs. *424 Amber La., Castle Valley, Moab, UT 84532, tel. 801/259–6012. Reservations: Castle Valley Star Route, Box 2602, Moab, UT 84532. 8 rooms with bath. MC, V. Breakfast included. No pets. Closed Jan. Expensive.*

Pack Creek Ranch. In the foothills of the La Sal Mountains, this dude ranch is a southern Utah institution and among the best lodgings the state has to offer. You won't find phones or televisions in the rooms, which are located in individual cabins, but you will enjoy comfortable chairs, wood-burning fireplaces, well-stocked bookshelves, and some of the best views in the state—over the Moab Rim and the La Sal Mountains. The cowboy-western feel of Pack Creek could not be more authentic; the life of Ken Sleight, the ranch's owner, was the inspiration for the polygamist river runner Seldom Seen Smith in Edward Abbey's book *The Monkey Wrench Gang*. The Pack Creek Ranch is located 15 miles southeast of Moab (for directions, *see* Dining, *above*). Breakfast is included with the room rate. *Box 1270, Moab, UT 84532, tel. 801/259–5505, fax 801/259–8879. 11 rooms with bath. Facilities: restaurant. AE, MC, V. Expensive.*

Sunflower Hill. This B&B is located in a 100-year-old farmhouse with adobe walls. The colorful barnyard signs and painted objects scattered around the rooms are the handiwork of the owner's daughter. *185 North 300 East, Moab, UT 84532, tel. 801/259–2974. 3 rooms, 1 with bath; 1 suite. MC, V. Breakfast included. Moderate.*

Lazy Lizard International Hostel. Popular with mountain bikers, this hostel is not fancy, but the $6 to $10 a night price range makes it almost as inexpensive as camping. The hostel offers dorm-style accommodations, a picnic area, and weekly and group rates. The Lazy Lizard belongs to the American Association of International Hostels (AAIH), but you do not need a hostel card to stay here. Showers are available to nonguests for $2. *1213 S. Hwy. 191, Moab, UT 84532, tel. 801/259–6057. 5 doubles and 5 rooms for 4 to 7 people share 6 baths. Facilities: hot tub, kitchen, laundry. No credit cards. Inexpensive.*

CAMPING

Very few sites can be reserved at campgrounds in Arches and Canyonlands national parks, unless you are part of a large group. If you plan to visit these parks in high season, it is a good idea to make reservations at nearby public campgrounds where they are accepted. Try Dead Horse Point State Park or Bureau of Land Management land. The generally unattractive private campgrounds near Moab are incongruous sights in this beautiful country.

Many people choose to camp out freelance along the Colorado River up- and downriver from Moab. Check with the Bureau of Land Management (tel. 801/259–8193) for regulations.

INSIDE THE PARKS You will have to get up very early in the morning to get a campsite at **Devils Garden Campground** (flush toilets, drinking water, fire grates), the only campground in Arches. It begins filling in early March and stays full until the end of October. Set against a backdrop of red slickrock and surrounded by the park's famous arches, it is justly popular. There are 54 sites here, for both RVs (no hookups) and tents, as well as two group sites where up to 50 people can stay. Pit toilets are used during the winter, and there is no water here from November through mid-March. Sites cost $7 per night, but are free when the water is turned off. Check at the entrance station or visitor center for the availability of campsites.

There are 26 tent and RV sites in **Squaw Flat** (vault toilets, fire grates, drinking water), in the Needles section of Canyonlands. These are a good distance from one another and are

ARCHES AND CANYONLANDS CAMPGROUNDS

	INSIDE ARCHES	INSIDE CANYONLANDS		NEAR THE PARKS									
	Devils Garden	Squaw Flat	Willow Flat	Dead Horse Point State Park	Hatch Point (BLM)	Windwhistle (BLM)	Oowah Lake (National Forest)	Warner Lake (National Forest)	Needles Outpost	Moab KOA	Slickrock Country	Up the Creek
Total number of sites	54	26	12	21	10	19	6	20	46	78	198	18
Sites suitable for RVs	54	20	2	21	10	19	6	20	20	60	148	0
Number of hookups	0	0	0	0	0	0	0	0	0	38	103	0
Drive to sites	●	●	●	●	●	●	●	●	●	●	●	●
Hike to sites												
Flush toilets	●			●					●	●	●	●
Pit/chemical toilets		●	●	●	●	●	●	●				
Drinking water	●	●		●	●	●		●		●	●	●
Showers									●	●	●	●
Fire grates	●	●	●	●	●	●		●			●	
Swimming										●	●	
Boat access												
Playground										●		
Disposal station				●						●		
Ranger station				●								
Public telephone				●						●	●	
Reservation possible				●**					●	●	●	
Daily fee per site	$7*	$6*	free	$7–$8	$5*	$5*	free	$5	$10	$12–$18	$12–$22	$12
Dates open	year-round	year-round	year-round	late Mar.–late Oct.	year-round	year-round	June–late Sept.	mid-May–Oct.	mid-Mar.–late Oct.	mid-Feb.–mid-Nov.	year-round	Mar.–mid-Nov.

*Fee charged only when water is available. **Reservation fee charged.

nestled in little rock coves. The water is turned off from October through mid-March, but the campground remains open. Sites cost $6 from March through October; the rest of the year you can camp free of charge.

Located atop a mesa and accessible by a 1-mile dirt road from the main paved road is **Willow Flat,** a primitive camper's delight in the Island in the Sky district of Canyonlands. The 10 sites for tents and 2 for RVs (no hookups) are shaded by a few trees, but the ubiquitous gnats detract from the scenic grandeur a good part of the summer. Sites are spaced 30 to 50 feet apart and will accommodate a 22-foot RV. There are vault toilets and fire grates here but no water, and year-round you can set up camp for up to seven days without paying a fee.

Canyonlands has a number of four-wheel-drive campsites in the Island in the Sky, Needles, and Maze districts. In Island in the Sky District these are along the popular White Rim Road and can be reserved by mail or by phone with Mastercard or Visa. In the Needles and Maze districts, backcountry permits are required for four-wheel-drive campsites, but it is not possible to make reservations.

Camping with any vehicle (bikes are considered vehicles) within the park boundaries requires a designated campsite. The Willow Flat and Squaw Flat campgrounds can accommodate passenger cars, but they are small and have very limited facilities. No reservations are taken, and these campgrounds may fill up by early morning from March through June and mid-September to October.

Camping is permited in the backcountry at both Arches and Canyonlands, but in both parks you must obtain a free backcountry permit from a visitor center or ranger station. You can set up camp in areas that are more than 1 mile from any road and 1/2 mile from any park trail—and out of view. Gathering firewood is not permitted in either park. Campers in frontcountry sites and designated four-wheel-drive sites can bring in their own wood or charcoal, but backpackers cannot have fires.

NEAR THE PARK If the Devils Garden Campground in Arches is full, the public camping area at **Dead Horse Point State Park** (Box 609, Moab, UT 84532, tel. 801/259–6511) near Canyonlands is a good second choice; it often fills a few hours later than Arches. Impressively set near the edge of a 2,000-foot cliff above the Colorado River, this facility has 21 RV and tent sites. Picnic tables are covered and have windbreaks. Although the rest rooms have no showers, they do have flush toilets and hot and cold running water. There is a disposal station here as well as a ranger station and a public phone. Sites cost $7 per night Sun.–Thurs., $8 Fri. and Sat., and reservations may be made for a $5 fee by calling 800/322–3770.

The Bureau of Land Management's (tel. 801/259–8193) two campgrounds along the eastern border of Canyonlands, **Hatch Point** and **Windwhistle,** are less crowded and more primitive than most of the campgrounds in this area. Both have drinking water, pit toilets, and fire grates. Hatch Point is near the Anticline Overlook and has 10 RV and tent sites; Windwhistle is on the road to the Needles Overlook and has 19 RV and tent sites. To get to these campgrounds from Moab, take Highway 191 south 32 miles and then go west 5 miles for Windwhistle, and west and north 25 miles for Hatch Point. These campgrounds are open year-round, but the water is on only from April 1 through October. Sites cost $5 per night when there's water.

High in the La Sal Mountains are two other public campgrounds, **Oowah Lake,** with 6 tent and RV sites, and **Warner Lake,** with 20 tent and RV sites. Both have pit toilets, but only Warner Lake has drinking water. Oowah is open from June through the end of September; Warner Lake, from mid-May to October. Call the U.S. Forest Service (tel. 801/259–7155) for more information.

The best private facility in the Canyonlands area is the **Needles Outpost** (Box 1107, Monticello, UT 84535, tel. 801/259–2032), located at the entrance to the Needles district on Highway 211. A good alternative when the Squaw Flat campground inside the park is full, this facility has 26 sites for tents and 20 for RVs (no hookups), flush toilets, a snack bar, and the only showers within miles. Sites cost $10 per day.

In the Moab area, there are eight private campgrounds, none of which are outstanding. The best of these is the **Moab KOA** (tel. 801/259–6682), 4 miles south of Moab on Highway 191, which has a view of the Moab Rim, the cliffs surrounding town, and the farming area of Spanish Valley. This facility has 60 RV sites (38 with complete hookups), 18 tent sites, drinking water, flush toilets, showers, and a disposal station. In addition, it has a grocery store, snack bar, pay phone, swimming pool, and playground. Sites cost $12 to $18 per day. Overlooking the portal of the Colorado River at the other end of town, **Slickrock Country Campground** (1301½ N. Hwy. 191, Moab, UT 84532, tel. 801/259–7660) is another okay choice. It has 198 sites, including cabins, full and partial hookups, and cleared areas for tents. Open year-round, Slickrock has flush toilets, showers, drinking water, swimming, and fire grates. For two people expect to pay $12 for tent sites, $17.50 for full hookups, $15 for water/electric, and $22 for cabins. The small **Up the Creek** campground (210 East 300 South, Moab, UT 84532, tel. 801/259–2213), three blocks off Main Street in a residential neighborhood, is for tenters only, with just 18 sites that cost about $12 per day. The campground has flush toilets, drinking water, and showers. It's open from March to mid-November.

The other Moab private campgrounds include: **Canyonlands Campark** (555 S. Main St., Moab, UT 84532, tel. 801/259–6848), with 108 RV sites, 60 of which have complete hookups, and 60 tent sites, flush toilets, showers, drinking water, swimming pool, disposal station, and public phone; the **Holiday Haven RV Park** (400 North 5th West, Moab, UT 84532, tel. 801/259–8526), with 60 RV sites with complete hookups and 40 tent sites, flush toilets, showers, drinking water, fire grates, playground, swimming pool, disposal station, and public phone, and open from March through October; the **Pack Creek Mobile Home Estate and Campground** (1520 Murphy La., Moab, UT 84532, tel. 801/259–2982), with 18 RV sites without hookups and 60 tent sites, drinking water, and a disposal station; and the **Tumbleweed RV Kampark** (3282 S. Hwy. 191, Moab, UT 84532, tel. 801/259–2988), which has 57 RV sites, 20 of which have complete hookups, and 31 tent sites, flush toilets, drinking water, showers, and a disposal station.

The Badlands, Mount Rushmore, and the Black Hills

South Dakota

By Dick Hoyt Willis

he 244,000 acres of sheer cliffs and buttes at Badlands National Park are dramatic and eerie: The landscape is stark, almost lunar, and it is easy to see why the French Canadian trappers who visited in the 18th century would label the area "bad lands to travel across," thereby awarding it its foreboding name. Things have changed since the days of those grizzled mountain men, however, and visitors today will find easy driving, scenic overlooks, well-marked hiking trails, and the chance to safely experience the most desolate terrain of the Great Plains.

Adding to the attraction of the Badlands, but in sharp contrast to it, are Mt. Rushmore and the surrounding pine tree–blanketed hills, just two hours to the west. Set against the rugged natural beauty of the Black Hills, the carvings of George Washington, Thomas Jefferson, Theodore Roosevelt, and Abraham Lincoln on the granite face of Mt. Rushmore strike a curious note: one immense, man-made symbol carved into and surrounded by nature's spectacle. Work on this huge tribute to democracy, located 23 miles southwest of Rapid City, South Dakota, began in 1927 under the supervision of artist Gutzon Borglum. He employed jackhammers and dynamite to coax the presidents' images from the stone, and although the carving was completed 14 years later, in 1941, maintenance to protect the memorial from the ravages of the elements is an ongoing project. As the crown jewel of the Black Hills tourism industry, Mt. Rushmore National Memorial hosts 2.5 million visitors each year.

Most of these tourists pass through the area quickly, on their way to Yellowstone or the Tetons, leaving more thorough exploration to the hikers and naturalists. The well-traveled route between Rapid City and the memorial has become a home to roadside video arcades, giant water slides, and an assortment of other capitalist ventures.

But since relatively few of these visitors stray off the beaten path into the forested back-country, much of the Black Hills remains an unspoiled playground, secluded valleys thick with pine and aspen. It is only after you watch mountain goats graze in the forests of the Black Hills and feel the energy of an afternoon thunderstorm over the rocky cliffs of the Badlands, that you truly can understand why many Sioux and Cheyenne believe there is power in these mountains and still consider these lands sacred.

The Badlands was designated a national monument in 1939, but it wasn't until 1978 that it became a national park.

ESSENTIAL INFORMATION

VISITOR INFORMATION If you are interested in visiting the Badlands, contact **Badlands National Park** or **Badlands Natural History Association** (Box 6, Interior, SD 57750, tel. 605/433–5361, for both). Rangers at the Badlands' **Ben Reifel Visitor Center** (formerly called Cedar Pass Visitor Center) can answer many of your questions.

There are a number of government offices and private organizations that can supply you with information on Mt. Rushmore and the Black Hills. Try **Mount Rushmore National Memorial** (Superintendent, Box 268, Keystone, SD 57751, tel. 605/574–2523); **Mount Rushmore National Memorial Society** (Box 1524, Rapid City, SD 57709, tel. 605/341–8883); **Black Hills National Forest** (Supervisor's Office, R.R. 2, Box 200, Custer, SD 57730, tel. 605/673–2251); and **Black Hills Parks and Forest Association** (Rte. 1, Box 190–WCNP, Wind Cave National Park, Hot Springs, SD 57747, tel. 605/745–4600).

For information on Rapid City, contact the **Rapid City Convention and Visitors Bureau** (Box 747, 444 Mt. Rushmore Rd. N, Rapid City, SD 57709, tel. 605/343–1744); the **South Dakota Department of Tourism** (Capital Lake Plaza, Pierre, SD 57501, tel. 605/773–3301, 800/843–1930, or in SD, 800/952–2217) covers the entire state. You may also want to contact nearby **Custer State Park** (HC83, Box 70, Custer, SD 57730, tel. 605/255–4515).

A backcountry permit isn't required for hiking or camping in Badlands National Park, but it is a good idea to check in at park headquarters before setting out on a backcountry journey. Backpackers may set up camps anywhere except within a half mile of roads. At Mt. Rushmore, visitors must stay on developed trails in the area of the memorial. No permits are needed to hike or camp in nearby Black Hills National Forest and Black Elk Wilderness.

FEES Entrance to Mt. Rushmore is free, but from May through September Badlands National Park charges $5 per car and $3 per person on a motorcycle, in a bus, or on foot.

PUBLICATIONS **Mt. Rushmore and the Black Hills.** One excellent book on the area is *America's Shrine of Democracy: A Pictorial History,* available from the Mt. Rushmore National Memorial Society (*see* Visitor Information, *above*). The society also sells *Mount Rushmore: The Shrine,* a 20-minute videotape showing historic footage of the construction of the memorial. The most comprehensive map of the Black Hills is the *Black Hills National Forest Recreation Map,* available from the Black Hills National Forest (*see* Visitor Information, *above*). The Sierra Club's *Hiking Map of the Norbeck Wildlife Preserve* includes the Black Elk Wilderness and gives more detail on these areas than the national forest's recreation map. It's available from the Black Hills Group of the Sierra Club (tel. 605/348–1351).

The **Geology Department, South Dakota School of Mines and Technology** (Room 307, Mineral Industries Bldg., Rapid City, SD 57701, tel. 605/394–2461) sells USGS maps and publications, as well as a limited number of books. *An Introduction to Custer State Park,* a basic, inexpensive guide to the region's flora and fauna, is available from the Black Hills Parks and Forest Association (*see* Visitor Information, *above*).

The Badlands. *Badlands: Its Life and Landscape* can be purchased from the Badlands

Natural History Association (*see* Visitor Information, *above*). The same association publishes *A Curious Country: Badlands National Park,* which is a good introduction to the plants, animals, geology, and history of the Badlands. The association's 18-minute video, *Buried Fossils, Living Prairie,* is also for sale, as is its Badlands topographic map, which is useful for hiking.

GEOLOGY AND TERRAIN The unique terrain at both Mt. Rushmore and the Badlands is the result of 60 million years of geologic activity. The Black Hills began as a mountainous landscape covered with limestone and shale sedimentary rock, but this covering gradually eroded away, exposing a granite face. Much of the sedimentary rock that eroded from the Black Hills was deposited in the Badlands, along with ash from the volcanoes in the Yellowstone area. Water flowed over the landscape and carved out the huge buttes and cliffs—a process that continues to this day. The gradual erosion also exposed fossils of a host of extinct animals, including ancient horses, camels, rodents, turtles, alligators, giant pigs, and saber-toothed cats. One of the Badlands' most unusual finds is the *titanothere,* a large beast with horns on its face. The Sioux called them thunder-horses, claiming they fell from the sky during rainstorms. While many of the Badlands fossils are now on display at museums around the world, you'll find a good number of them at the Ben Reifel Visitor Center, along the Fossil Exhibit Trail in the park, and at the Museum of Geology at the South Dakota School of Mines and Technology (501 E. St. Joseph St., Rapid City, tel. 605/394–2467). The geology museum is open weekdays 8 to 6, Saturday 9 to 2, and Sunday 1 to 4 from Memorial Day to Labor Day; and Monday through Saturday 8 to 6 and Sunday noon to 6 the rest of the year. Admission is free.

FLORA AND FAUNA The lunar landscape of the Badlands seems barren at first, with its light-color buttes and cliffs and sparse greenery. But closer inspection will prove your first glance wrong: The short prairie grass supports antelope, mule deer, and white-tailed deer, which seek shelter under small clumps of juniper trees. Some 400 buffalo roam the park, and one of the country's largest populations of Rocky Mountain bighorn sheep occupies the steep buttes and cliffs. The bighorns are often spotted in the Pinnacles area, and during winter they sometimes even walk on Highway 240.

Prairie rattlesnakes thrive in the rocky terrain of the Badlands, blending in well with the light-color soil. The rattlers spend their winters underground in large dens, but during the summer they become very active, feeding on insects, mice, and eggs.

Meadowlarks, sharptail grouse, and mountain bluebirds are regularly seen, and visitors can often spot golden eagles, hawks, and turkey vultures soaring high above the park in the warm air currents. These birds eat prairie dogs, which are a common sight in the Badlands. In fact, there are so many prairie dogs in and around the park that this may be one of the first spots in the world where the endangered, prairie-dog–eating, black-footed ferret will be reintroduced.

The green mountainsides of the Black Hills are quite different from the Badlands. The hills around Mt. Rushmore are dotted with ponderosa pine trees, while in the cooler, higher elevations spruce thrive. Stands of aspen and birch grow near the many streams, particularly in the northern part of the Black Hills.

Nature lovers will find that it's easy to spot mountain goats around Mt. Rushmore, especially in the big rock formations on Highway 244. Mule deer and white-tailed deer are also common in the area surrounding the memorial, and observers with sharp eyes should be able to spot porcupines, pine squirrels, wild turkeys, and elk in the forest. Around the park concession are a number of chipmunks that are very accustomed to the presence of human beings.

WHEN TO GO Both Mt. Rushmore and the Badlands are open year-round, but the peak tourist season falls between Memorial Day and Labor Day, when daytime temperatures around Mt. Rushmore hover in the 80s and are even higher in the Badlands. Relief from the heat can be found at higher elevations in the Black Hills. About 20,000 people pass through Mt. Rushmore on a typical summer day, but the biggest crowds arrive during early August for the Sturgis Motorcycle Classic, when thousands of bikers roar through the Black Hills on Harley-Davidsons. The autumn weather is sunny and warm, with temperatures usually in the 60s or 70s, although by October the thermometer may fall below freezing and there may be some snow. Many consider fall to be the best time to visit, since the temperatures are cooler and the crowds thin out. Spring is often wet, cold, and unpredictable, with surprise snowstorms as late as April.

SEASONAL EVENTS **Easter:** A nondenominational **Easter sunrise service** takes place on Mt. Rushmore's main view terrace at the visitor center (tel. 605/574–2523). **July 4: Independence Day** is always a big event at Mt. Rushmore. For a schedule of events contact the visitor center. **June to August:** Throughout summer, bands and choruses from across the country perform free concerts at the Mt. Rushmore amphitheater. Contact the visitor center for a schedule of related events. **August 10:** Speeches and a concert are held on **Gutzon Borglum Day** to commemorate the artist who oversaw the creation of Mt. Rushmore. **Mid-September: On POW/MIA Day** patriotic speeches and a band help to commemorate imprisoned and missing wartime servicemen and women.

WHAT TO PACK Hikers and campers should be prepared for abrupt changes in weather at any time of the year in the Black Hills. Rain gear can come in handy during those unexpected thunderstorms, particularly during the spring and fall, and long underwear can be a blessing at night when the temperature drops in the mountains. If you are hiking or camping during the summer, especially in the hot, arid Badlands, bring plenty of cool cotton clothing, a hat, and sunscreen.

GENERAL STORES The **Rushmore Mall** (exit 58 or 59 off I–90, Rapid City, tel. 605/348–3378) has 120 stores selling virtually every-

thing but groceries. It's open weekdays 10 to 9, Saturday 10 to 6, and Sunday noon to 5. **Mighty Mart** (Hwy. 16/385, Hill City, tel. 605/574–2717), 1 mile east of Hill City's town center, sells groceries and general camping accessories, such as gloves, caps, and camp stove fuel. It's open Monday through Thursday 7 AM to 8 PM, Friday and Saturday 7 AM to 9 PM, and Sunday 8 to 6. **Badlands Grocery** (Main St., Interior, tel. 605/433–5445) is 2 miles south of the Ben Reifel Visitor Center and is open daily 7 AM to 8 PM in summer and 8 to 4:30 in winter. TW Recreational Services (Mt. Rushmore, tel. 605/574–2515), at the memorial, has a snack bar, dining room, and gift shop. Daily summer hours are 7 AM to 10:30 PM; winter hours are 8:30 to 5. **Wall Drug** (510 Main St., Wall, tel. 605/279–2175) has a restaurant and carries a huge assortment of gift items, but its claim to fame since 1931 has always been free ice water and a 5¢ cup of coffee. Wall Drug is open daily in summer 6 AM to 10 PM and in winter 6:30 to 5. **Cedar Pass Lodge** (Cedar Pass, tel. 605/433–5460), near Ben Reifel Visitor Center in Badlands National Park, sells gift items and has a restaurant. It's open daily 7 AM to 9 PM in summer, 8 to 6 in fall, and is closed from mid-December through March.

ARRIVING AND DEPARTING The most practical way to reach Mt. Rushmore or the Badlands is by car. There is a bus station in Rapid City, as well as an airport outside the city, but unless you are planning to make a day-trip with a bus tour, you'll have to drive yourself. It is more than 23 miles from the memorial to Rapid City and another 50 miles or so to the Pinnacles entrance of the Badlands.

By Plane. Rapid City Regional Airport (tel. 605/394–4195) lies 10 miles southeast of Rapid City, off Highway 44. **Airport Limousine Service** (8403 Okpealuk St., Rapid City, tel. 605/343–5358) meets every flight at the airport baggage counter and provides shuttle service to anywhere in Rapid City for $9 per person or $13 for a couple. The limo service will take you just about anywhere you want to go for about $1 per mile. You can rent a car at the airport from **Avis** (tel. 605/393–0740), **Budget** (tel. 605/393–0488), **Hertz** (tel.

605/393–0160), **National** (tel. 605/393–2664), and **Thrifty** (tel. 605/393–0663).

By Car and RV. I–90 is the most direct route into the Badlands and Mt. Rushmore by car. Free state highway maps are available from the South Dakota Department of Tourism (*see* Visitor Information, *above*), and free maps for the Badlands are available from Badlands National Park (*see* Visitor Information, *above*).

To reach the Badlands, drive from Rapid City east on I–90 for 50 miles. You can pick up scenic Highway 240 to go through the park via the Pinnacles entrance (take exit 110 at Wall) or travel another 20 miles on I–90 to the other end of Highway 240 and enter the park at the Northeast entrance (take exit 131 at Cactus Flat). If you choose exit 110 you will find yourself closer to the Sage Creek Wilderness Area, and if you choose exit 131 you will be only a few miles from the Ben Reifel Visitor Center.

To reach Mt. Rushmore National Memorial from Rapid City, follow Mt. Rushmore Road (Highway 16) southwest for 23 miles. If coming in from I–90, take exit 57 to Mt. Rushmore Road and continue to the memorial. Yellowstone is a nine-hour, 440-mile drive west of Rapid City. Grand Teton National Park is another hour south of Yellowstone.

By Train. The nearest train stations are in Williston, North Dakota, and Denver, Colorado—both more than seven hours from the park. There are no bus or plane connections from Williston to the Badlands, and it is neither cost-effective nor quick to take a plane or bus from Denver's train station.

By Bus. The **bus station** (333 6th St., tel. 605/348–3300) in downtown Rapid City serves Jackrabbit and Powder River regional bus lines, both of which make connections with Greyhound Lines elsewhere but neither of which goes to the parks. Bus service into the parks is available with several of the tour companies in the area throughout summer (*see* Guided Tours, *below*), but if you are planning to stay in the parks for longer than a day, you'll have to negotiate prices with the company. Both **Budget** (in the Holiday Inn, 505 N. 5th St., tel. 605/343–8499) and **Economy Car Rental** (1017 Farlow Ave., tel. 605/343–5615) have offices within walking distance of the bus station. Economy has a free pick-up service.

EXPLORING

Mt. Rushmore National Memorial, to the southwest of Rapid City, and Badlands National Park, to the southeast, are only a two-hour drive from each other. Travelers with a time restriction can see both in one day, but in order to really appreciate the natural beauty of the area visitors should set aside at least three or four days to make a few side trips into the wilderness. The best way to explore the area is in your own car.

Mt. Rushmore is a must-see, naturally. Try to visit in the early morning, when the natural lighting is most dramatic, or at sunset, in order to see the nightly lighting ceremony. Also head south to Custer State Park, with its 1,400 head of buffalo, and farther south to Wind Cave or west to Jewel Cave, a spelunker's dream come true.

For a good overview of the Badlands follow Highway 240 through the park, stopping at the 13 scenic overlooks along the way. The Ben Reifel Visitor Center provides informative brochures on the park's many hiking trails—you really ought to leave the car behind and head out into the backcountry on foot. Visitors who remain in their cars can see the most popular Badlands sights in about four hours, but if you're going to do any hiking, allow a full day.

THE BEST IN ONE DAY The 100-mile trip between Badlands National Park headquarters and Mt. Rushmore National Memorial can be driven in two hours, so you can visit both places in one day if you start out early and make a quick tour through each one. Coming from the east on I–90, take exit 131 at Cactus Flat in the Badlands, and head south on Highway 240 for 30 minutes until you reach the Ben Reifel Visitor Center, a good place to stop, stretch your legs, and eat breakfast. You can

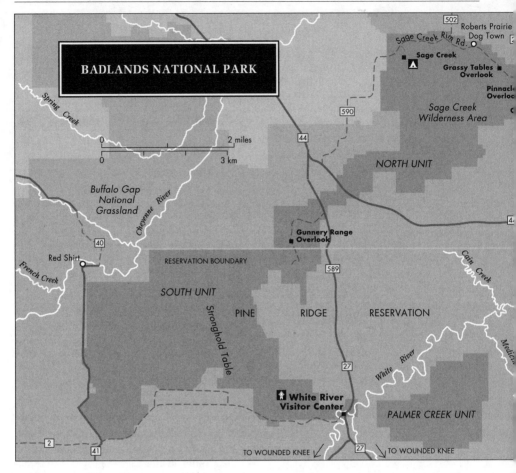

also take a short stroll along one of the hiking trails near the visitor center.

When you leave Cedar Pass follow Badlands National Park Highway 240 west, stopping at the scenic overlooks along the way. Shortly after the Pinnacles Overlook head north to I–90 to leave the park. Take I–90 through Rapid City, and then exit 57 to Mt. Rushmore Road (Highway 16). Follow that south, straight to the memorial. This route is lined with diversions: a water slide; reptile gardens; an aquarium; and Bear Country U.S.A., a wildlife park (*see* Children's Programs, *below*).

When you reach the memorial, continue past it heading south on the Iron Mountain Road (*see* Scenic Drives and Views, *below*). You can double back to the memorial later in the day, in time to see the lighting ceremony. Iron Mountain Road connects Mt. Rushmore with Custer State Park in the southern hills. The park's Wildlife Loop Road takes about an hour to drive.

If time permits, leave the Wildlife Loop Road at Route 6 and continue south into Wind Cave National Park (Hot Springs, tel. 605/745–4600), which contains the third-longest cave in the country (*see* Other Activities, *below*).

Later follow Highway 87 out of Wind Cave National Park, where it becomes the west end of the Wildlife Loop Road. Then continue northwest on Highway 87 through the Needles rock formations to Sylvan Lake. Go past the lake on Highway 87 until you reach High-

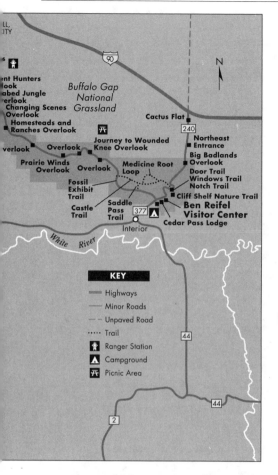

KEY

- ═══ Highways
- ─── Minor Roads
- ─ ─ Unpaved Road
- ····· Trail
- 👤 Ranger Station
- ⛺ Campground
- 🏕 Picnic Area

is illuminated for several hours beginning at sunset.

ORIENTATION PROGRAMS At the memorial's **Lincoln Borglum Visitor Center** (tel. 605/574–2523) you can learn how the mountain was carved. There are displays of the equipment that was used—including a pneumatic hammer and a chair that carvers sat in while being hoisted up and down the faces—and a 13-minute video runs continuously. In summer the center is open 8 AM to 10 PM; in the off-season, 8 to 5.

At the **Ben Reifel Visitor Center** (tel. 605/433–5361) in Badlands National Park, an 18-minute video about Badlands geology and wildlife runs every half-hour during summer. Exhibits about fossils, geology, wildlife, and the Sioux give visitors a basic understanding of the park.

GUIDED TOURS **Gray Line of the Black Hills** (1600 E. St. Patrick St., Rapid City, SD 57701, tel. 605/342–4461 or 800/456–4461) offers a variety of bus tours from Rapid City to Mt. Rushmore, Black Hills National Forest, Custer State Park, and Crazy Horse Monument, all ranging in price from $9 to $28. **Stagecoach West** (Box 264, Rapid City, SD 57709, tel. 605/343–3113) and **Golden Circle Tours** (40 5th St. N, Custer, SD 57730, tel. 605/673–4349) lead similar tours in the same price range, but Golden Circle Tours also offers a $25 tour out of Custer to more remote spots in the Black Hills, including visits to abandoned gold mines and a stop at Spring Creek, where guests can pan for gold and garnets.

Gray Line of the Black Hills runs a tour to the Black Hills Passion Play in Spearfish every Tuesday, Thursday, and Sunday from June through August. The bus trip with a ticket to this re-enactment of the last days of Christ costs $19. Gray Line also has a $13 "Wild West Evening" tour to Deadwood, where gambling is the big draw. Golden Circle can tailor its all-day mountain bike tour to the ability of the participants. Bikes, helmets, and a picnic lunch are included, and a shuttle van joins the group at various points along

way 16/385, which you must take north to Highway 244 east back toward Mt. Rushmore.

Mt. Rushmore National Memorial, the centerpiece of the Black Hills National Forest, can be explored on foot in just an hour or so. Visitors can stroll down the Avenue of Flags to the visitor center and watch a short video outlining the history of the memorial. During the summer you might be able to catch one of the many concerts held in the amphitheater below the huge carvings. The nightly lighting ceremony is preceded by a patriotic speech by one of the park rangers and a short film about the memorial. The time of the ceremony varies with the sunset in spring and fall, but it is at 9 PM during the summer. There is no ceremony in winter, but the mountain

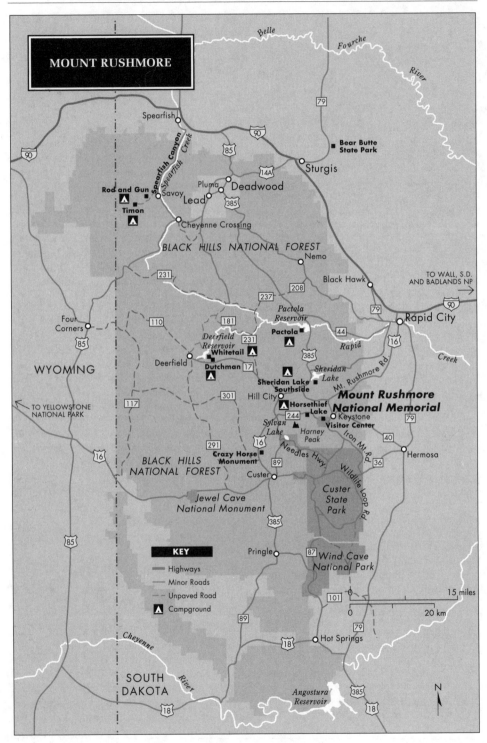

MOUNT RUSHMORE

Belle
Fourche
River

[79]

Spearfish

[90]

[85]

Bear Butte
State Park

Sturgis

[14A]

Spearfish Canyon
Spearfish Creek

Rod and Gun
Savoy
Timon

Pluma
Lead
Deadwood

[385]

Cheyenne Crossing

BLACK HILLS NATIONAL FOREST

Nemo

TO WALL, S.D.
AND BADLANDS NP

[231]

[208]

Black Hawk

[237]

[79]

Rapid City

[90]

[110]

[181]

*Deerfield
Reservoir*
Whitetail

[231]

*Pactola
Reservoir*

Pactola

[44]

Rapid

Four
Corners

[85]

WYOMING

Deerfield

Dutchman

17

[385]

Creek

[16]

Mt. Rushmore Rd.

TO YELLOWSTONE
NATIONAL PARK

[117]

[301]

Sheridan Lake
Southside

Hill City

*Sheridan
Lake*

**Mount Rushmore
National Memorial**

Horsethief
Lake

244

Keystone

Visitor Center

[79]

Iron Mt. Rd.

[16]

[291]

*Sylvan
Lake*

Harney
Peak

[40]

Hermosa

Crazy Horse
Monument

[89]

Needles Hwy.

[36]

Wildlife Loop Rd.

BLACK HILLS
NATIONAL FOREST

Custer

*Custer
State
Park*

Jewel Cave
National Monument

[385]

KEY

Highways
Minor Roads
Unpaved Road
Campground

Pringle

[87]

*Wind Cave
National Park*

[101]

15 miles

0   20 km

[85]

[89]

[79]

Cheyenne

[18]

Hot Springs

River

SOUTH
DAKOTA

[18]

*Angostura
Reservoir*

[385]

N

[18]

the route to pick up tired bikers. The cost varies depending on time and distance.

Airport Limousine Service (tel. 605/343–5358) provides a four-hour round-trip tour of the Badlands from Rapid City. The cost starts at $85 for one person, with each additional person paying up to $10. A two-hour trip to Mt. Rushmore, including a half-hour stay at the monument, costs $35 for one person and up to $10 for each additional person.

SCENIC DRIVES AND VIEWS **The Badlands.** There are 13 scenic overlooks along the 27 miles of **Highway 240** (Badlands Loop Road) in Badlands National Park. You can easily take two hours or more driving this route, stopping at overlooks along the way to admire the splendid landscapes. The **Sage Creek Rim Road,** in the northwest part of the Badlands, is gravel, but it is safe for all kinds of vehicles. To the south of this road lies the rugged Sage Creek Wilderness. A hike of even 50 yards or so into this rocky area will reward the visitor with a more genuine appreciation of the Badlands. Take a hike around the Roberts Prairie Dog Town on the north side of Sage Creek Rim Road, where you're likely to see some of these furry animals scampering about, constantly wary of the golden eagles that swoop down and snatch them in their powerful talons.

Mt. Rushmore and the Black Hills. One span of **Mt. Rushmore Road** (Highway 16), the route most used from Rapid City to the memorial, is plastered with commercial billboards, but once it enters the Black Hills National Forest, nature takes the lead with pine forests and clear mountain lakes. Mt. Rushmore Road meets **Iron Mountain Road** (Highway 16A), and the latter winds through some of the most rugged and dramatic sections of the Black Hills. This scenic road, part of the Peter Norbeck National Scenic Byway, was specially designed for sightseeing: As you follow it through mountain passes and over old wooden bridges, notice how tunnels along the route provide glimpses of Mt. Rushmore in the distance. The 17-mile drive from near the memorial to near the game lodge in Custer State Park takes more than half an hour.

Iron Mountain Road continues south into Custer State Park. A few buffalo can be spotted munching the prairie grass near the park's eastern entrance on Highway 36, and more are found along the **Wildlife Loop Road** in Custer State Park, where you'll often see them grazing at the side of the road or standing on the road itself. Don't attempt to shoo them away: These unpredictable animals can be extremely dangerous. Antelope, mule deer, coyotes, and eagles can also be spotted on the Wildlife Loop Road, particularly in the early morning and evening. The Loop takes an hour to drive if few stops are made.

From the northern stretch of the Wildlife Loop in Custer State Park, take **Highway 87** (Needles Highway), which is also part of the scenic byway, through the Needles rock formations. These impressive rock spires are popular with rock climbers. There are several tunnels along this section of road, and RVs have been known to lose their side mirrors and pieces of their aluminum siding as they try to squeeze through. Cars, however, will have no trouble. Farther along Highway 87 you'll find Sylvan Lake, the highest lake in the Black Hills. Several parking areas along the roadside make it easy for you to pull over and take in the view. Across the lake is the spot where hikers begin the uphill trek to the top of Harney Peak, the highest point between the Wyoming and Colorado Rockies and the Swiss Alps.

Continue north past Sylvan Lake to Hill City, and take **Deerfield Road** (Highway 17) past little Newton Lake up to Deerfield Reservoir in the Black Hills high country. From Deerfield, venture off onto any one of the many gravel and dirt roads leading into the wild and remote country in the northern and western Black Hills. Some of these roads, such as Forest Service Road 291 along Ditch Creek, are good gravel; others are old logging roads that now barely qualify as trails. The best way to navigate this country is with a Black Hills National Forest recreation map (*see* Publications, *above*): Without it you stand an excellent chance of getting lost.

From Hill City you might also opt to take the **Black Hills Parkway** (U.S. 385) north through the scenic central Hills up to Lead and Deadwood. Deadwood is an old mining town that has legalized gambling, with slot machines and poker, and a deliberate, commercialized Old West atmosphere. The huge underground Homestake gold mine sprawls under the town of Lead. A giant open pit gold mine can also be seen in the town. The road to Lead–Deadwood winds past the campground at Roubaix Lake (tel. 605/578–2744), a 10-acre lake stocked with trout; Custer Crossing Picnic Ground; and Strawberry Hill Campground (tel. 605/578–2744), which has excellent access for the disabled. The 37-mile route north from Hill City through the central Hills takes about 45 minutes with no stops.

If you're visiting during the fall you may want to continue past Lead–Deadwood up to **Spearfish Canyon** in the northern Hills. Here, along another scenic byway, the trees lining the banks of the creek put on a breathtakingly colorful show as their leaves change color. To reach Spearfish, follow U.S. 85 southwest from Lead–Deadwood to Cheyenne Crossing and take U.S. 14A north past Savoy to the canyon.

HISTORIC BUILDINGS AND SITES The creation of the **Mt. Rushmore National Memorial** began in 1927 under the supervision of artist Gutzon Borglum. Borglum died in 1941 after 14 years of work on the memorial, and his son Lincoln continued the project until funds ran out later that year. The faces of presidents Washington, Jefferson, Roosevelt, and Lincoln represent, respectively, independence, representation in government, leadership in world affairs, and equality and a strong union.

While at Mt. Rushmore, visit the **sculptor's studio,** which was built in 1939. It houses the working models of the memorial, as well as tools used for its construction. The studio is open to the public from mid-May through September. You can visit on your own or take a tour, conducted daily 9 to 6.

In the southern end of Badlands National Park is 3-mile-long **Stronghold Table,** a mesa that can be reached only by crossing one narrow land bridge just wide enough to let a wagon pass. It is on this mesa that one faction of the Sioux tribe gathered to perform the Ghost Dance, a ritual in which the Sioux wore white shirts that they believed would protect them from bullets. Some 600 Sioux danced here in 1890, praying for a future paradise where white men were gone and Native Americans once again dominated the Plains.

In December of 1890 the last Sioux left Stronghold Table to join Chief Big Foot and 350 other Sioux from the north in a trek to Pine Ridge, the headquarters of the Sioux reservation. They were planning to give up their fight for independence and submit to the U.S. government's authority, but when they reached Wounded Knee, they met with the U.S. 7th Cavalry in what was to be the last major military encounter beween the Sioux and the United States Army. It is estimated that some 200 Sioux men, women, and children and 30 cavalry troopers died. Part of the route taken by the Sioux can be seen at **Journey to Wounded Knee Overlook** along Highway 240 in the park.

NATURE TRAILS AND SHORT WALKS There are nature trails ranging in length from 1/4 mile to 12 miles that wind through Badlands National Park near the Ben Reifel Visitor Center. All are well marked, so there is no danger of getting lost. You can buy trail guides to the Door, Fossil, and Cliff Shelf trails for 50¢ each, or borrow them at the trailheads and return them when you're done.

Notch Trail goes 1 1/2 miles round-trip over moderately difficult terrain and includes a climb up a ladder. Winds at the notch can be fierce, but the view of the White River Valley and the Pine Ridge Indian Reservation are worth the effort. Fossils are displayed under glass along the 1/4-mile loop of the **Fossil Exhibit Trail,** which is a good choice for those in wheelchairs. Walking the 3/4-mile round-trip course of **Door Trail** will give visitors a sense of what the Badlands country is all about; fossil soils, ash layers, and erosion are evident. **Cliff Shelf Nature Trail** is an easy 1/2-mile loop that runs past a pond bordered by cattails. Red-winged blackbirds live in this wet environment. **Castle Trail** stretches for 5 1/2 miles one-way from the Fossil Exhibit Trailhead on Highway 240 to the parking area for the Door and Windows trails; hikers who choose to use the **Medicine Root Loop,** which detours off the Castle Trail, will add 1/2 mile to the trek. This is an easy hike, but since you'll be walking for two hours you should bring drinking water with you. **Saddle Pass Trail,** which connects Highway 240 to the middle of Castle Trail and the beginning of the Medicine Root Loop, is a steep 1/2-mile climb up the side of "The Wall," an impressive rock formation.

LONGER HIKES You can cut out across the wild range of the Badlands' 64,144-acre **Sage Creek Wilderness** and walk for miles and miles, but bring along a topographical map (*see* Publications, *above*) to help you find your way—there are no marked trails.

Even more remote are the **South Unit** and **Palmer Creek Unit** of the park: Again, there are no marked trails, and primitive conditions mean that hikers should bring their own water. Beware of parking along Highway 40 near Red Shirt Table, on the west side of the South Unit; vandals have been known to break into cars there. Stop at the White River Visitor Center and ask about back roads where vehicles can be parked out of sight.

Some of the finest hiking near Mt. Rushmore can be found just to the west, in the **Norbeck Wildlife Preserve** and the **Black Elk Wilderness**—both part of the Black Hills National Forest. The nearest trailhead (unmarked) starts just across Highway 244 from the Mt. Rushmore Memorial parking lot; it is a good place to start out on day hikes, but no overnight parking is permitted.

A trailhead that's easy to find is near **Horsethief Lake.** Go west of the memorial 2 miles on Highway 244 and make a left on the first gravel road, just before Horsethief Lake. The well-marked trailhead is a quarter-mile down the road. The trail wanders between rough boulders, and farther along,

large rock formations jut up into the sky. Farther still, a network of trails crosses through the Black Elk Wilderness. The Sierra Club Hiking Map of the Norbeck Wildlife Preserve (*see* Publications, *above*) is a handy companion for full-day trips.

There's another good access point 3 1/2 miles farther west on Highway 244. Take the Palmer Gulch turnoff, which skirts some huge aspen stands. The strenuous **Lost Cabin Trail** goes uphill more than a mile before entering the Black Elk Wilderness and continuing to Sylvan Lake or Harney Peak. The summit at Harney Peak is a difficult two-hour climb from the lake. From the Sylvan Lake Dam, the relatively easy **Sunday Gulch Trail** winds 1 1/2 miles through lush bottomland forest along a tiny, sparkling mountain stream.

The very level and easily hiked 15-mile round-trip **Flume Trail** runs along an old mining flume from Sheridan Lake to Coon Hollow. Pick up the trail at either end.

Ten miles northeast of I–90 is **Bear Butte State Park** (Box 688, Sturgis, SD 57785, tel. 605/347–5240), which rises up out of the Plains east of Sturgis. The Cheyenne, Sioux, and other Native Americans hold this mountain sacred and make pilgrimages to it. Hiking trails lead through the pines to the top, where visibility can be more than 50 miles on clear days. Admission is $2.

Another popular route is the 111 miles of **Centennial Trail** from Wind Cave National Park to Bear Butte State Park. The trail runs along the eastern edge of the Black Hills and through Custer State Park, Black Hills National Forest, and Fort Meade Recreation Area on its way.

OTHER ACTIVITIES Back-Road Driving. Driving off roads isn't allowed in Badlands National Park or Mt. Rushmore National Memorial. You can, however, drive on the many logging roads that wind through the Black Hills National Forest. To find those roads pick up a copy of the Black Hills National Forest recreation map (*see* Publications, *above*).

Bird-Watching. From high points in the Badlands during the summer, hawks and golden eagles floating along on the warm air currents are a common sight. In the Black Hills, some of the more interesting mountain birds include the Clark's nutcracker, dark-eyed junco, pine siskin, and various grosbeaks. Even if you're not a serious bird-watcher, bring along binoculars.

Fishing. In the Black Hills, Rapid Creek and Spearfish Creek are both popular spots to angle for wild brown trout, and all the headwater streams, including Grizzly Bear Creek behind Mt. Rushmore, have brook trout. Horsethief Lake below Mt. Rushmore is stocked with rainbow trout, as are other lakes in the Black Hills. Try Deerfield, Pactola, and Sheridan lakes in the Black Hills National Forest, and Center and Stockade lakes in Custer State Park. Nonresident fishing licenses are available at any sporting-goods store and many convenience stores; they cost $6 for 24 hours, $14 for five days, or $30 annually. In Keystone, **Panama Red's Outdoor Adventure Tours** (tel. 605/666–4949) gives fly-fishing classes.

Horseback Riding. Western horse-packing trips in Badlands National Park and the Black Hills are run by **Gunsel Horse Adventures** (Box 1575, Rapid City, SD 57709, tel. 605/343–7608) for about $150 a day. A six-day excursion covers some of the most secluded and scenic areas of the Badlands, and a 10-day trip treks 111 miles on the Centennial Trail, through pine forests and mountain meadows from Custer State Park, past Mt. Rushmore, to Bear Butte.

Mountain Biking. Old logging roads in the Black Hills National Forest are just the right terrain for mountain biking. Few of these roads are marked on the Black Hills National Forest map, but if you follow any gravel road into the forest, such as Deerfield Road west of Hill City, you'll be able to connect with a logging road into the woods. Street bikes can be rented for $10 a day at **Everybody's Bookstore** (515 6th St., tel. 605/341–3224) in Rapid City. Mountain bikes are available in Rapid City from **Mountain Mania Bicycles** (4242-B Canyon Lake Dr., tel. 605/343–6596) for $19.95 to $34.95 per day and at **Two Wheeler Dealer Cycle & Fitness** (100 E. Blvd. N, tel. 605/343–0524) for $26 to $30 per day. In Keystone, **Panama Red's Outdoor Adventure Tours** (Keystone Mall, Hwy. 16, tel. 605/666–4949) rents bikes for $35 to $45 per day.

Rock Climbing. Rock climbing is growing in popularity at Mt. Rushmore, where there are challenging climbs at different levels of difficulty. Novice climbers should be especially cautious, and all climbers should register at park headquarters before starting out. Climbing the memorial is prohibited. Information on particular climbs is available through **Sylvan Rock Climbing School and Guide Service** (tel. 605/574–2425), which is based at Hill City and is open for business from May through September.

Skiing. The most popular cross-country ski areas are Eagle Cliff Ski Area, near O'Neil Pass, and Big Hill Ski Area, near Spearfish—both in the Black Hills National Forest. Passing beneath thick stands of pine and aspen, skiers sometimes see deer, bald eagles, elk, and porcupines. Eagle Cliff is the larger area, and it has consistently better snow. Equipment can be rented for under $10 a day from **Ski Cross Country** (701 3rd St., Spearfish, tel. 605/642–3851). There are two downhill ski resorts in the northern Hills—**Terry Peak Ski Area** (tel. 605/584–2165) and **Deer Mountain Ski Area** (tel. 605/584–3230). Equipment rentals are available at both for $15 a day.

Snowmobiling. More than 300 miles of groomed snowmobile trails link the Black Hills in South Dakota and Wyoming. The most extensive trails with the best snow run through the northern Hills. Snowmobile maps are available free from the South Dakota Department of Tourism (*see* Visitor Information, *above*).

Spelunking. There are numerous caves throughout the limestone rock formations on the edge of the Hills. The biggest and best known are Wind Cave National Park and Jewel Cave National Monument, both in the southern Hills. Caves are always 53°F, so a sweater is recommended. Also wear good walking shoes with nonslip soles to negotiate the uneven, and sometimes wet, walkways.

The third-longest in the country, **Wind Cave** (Hot Springs, tel. 605/745–4600) has 57 miles of mapped routes and is known for its box-work formations. The visitor center is open 8 to 7 in summer and 8 to 5 in winter. There is no fee to enter the park, but you must take a ranger-guided tour to enter the cave. These are given year-round, 8:30 to 6 in summer and varying times in winter. Tours last from 1 to 1³/₄ hours and cost $2 to $5 for adults and $1 to $2.50 for children ages 6–15, although in the dead of winter tours are offered free. In addition, there are two longer tours in summer.

With 84 miles of mapped passages, **Jewel Cave National Monument** (R.R. 1, Box 60AA, Custer, tel. 605/673–2288), west of Custer, is the second-longest cave in the country. It is best known for the calcite crystals in many of its rooms. There is no entrance fee for the park, which is open year-round, but in summer, cave tours cost $4 for adults and $2 for children ages 6–15; in winter they are free. Generally, tours are given from 8:30 to 6 in mid-summer. The limited winter schedule varies.

Swimming. The best beaches in the Black Hills are at Angostura Reservoir, near Hot Springs, which is rimmed with miles of white sand. There are two small, often crowded beaches along Sheridan Lake in the Black Hills National Forest. Both swimming areas have changing rooms, picnic tables, and barbecues, and Angostura also has a snack bar. Neither lake has lifeguards on duty. Center Lake in Custer State Park has good beaches, too.

CHILDREN'S PROGRAMS Children ages 5–12 can take part in the free, two-day **Junior Ranger Program,** in which they learn about nature and Badlands National Park through the use of puzzles and games. The program, which runs from early June to Labor Day, includes several nature hikes led by park rangers, as well as slide shows and demonstrations. Sign up at the desk at Ben Reifel Visitor Center (tel. 605/433–5361).

On Highway 16 leading to Mt. Rushmore, **Reptile Gardens** (tel. 605/342–5873) will delight children with animal shows and hundreds of reptiles and birds on display. It's open daily from 7 AM to 8 PM during the summer, with shorter hours in off-season. Admission is $7.50 for adults, $3.75 for children ages 6–14, and $6.50 for senior citizens.

Bears, elk, mountain lions, wolves, and other animals are displayed in the parklike setting of **Bear Country U.S.A.** (tel. 605/343–2290), which is also on Highway 16. This drive-through park is open daily during summer from 8 to 6:30. It is closed from mid-October to Memorial Day. Admission is $7.50 for adults, $3.50 for children ages 6–15, and $6.50 for senior citizens. The maximum charge is $25 per family vehicle.

Another Highway 16 attraction that your kids will enjoy is the **Marine Life Aquarium** (tel. 605/343–7400), where dolphins and other aquatic creatures can be viewed in tanks and in water shows. Open daily from 8 to 7, the aquarium charges $7.50 for adults, $3.50 for children ages 5–12, and $6.50 for senior citizens.

DINING

Most restaurants are found in the towns surrounding the Badlands National Park and Mt. Rushmore, and visitors should note that many of them close during the winter. Adventurous eaters should try the local specialty: buffalo. The animals are raised on a number of western South Dakota ranches, and the meat is found on the menus of several regional restaurants. It tastes similar to beef but contains less fat and cholesterol. Dress in all the restaurants listed here is casual.

INSIDE THE PARKS **Cedar Pass Lodge Restaurant.** Native American crafts decorate this family restaurant in Badlands National Park, where Native American tacos and quarter-pound buffalo-burgers are featured. Located next to the Ben Reifel Visitor Center, it is the only full-service restaurant in the park. *Cedar Pass, tel. 605/433–5460. Reservations* *not necessary. AE, D, DC, MC, V. Closed Nov. 1–Mar. 31. Inexpensive.*

Mt. Rushmore Dining Room and Snack Bar. Managed by TW Recreational Services, this cafeteria-style eatery is open only from April 10 to September 1. It has a seating capacity of 185, but the tables are set up so that every one of those diners gets a view of the memorial. Breakfast, served from 7 to 11, includes four choices of entrée as well as à la carte items, such as hash browns and freshly made sweet rolls. Lunch is served from 11 to 3; the four hot entrées (beef, pork, fowl, and fish) might include Cajun catfish, New England pot roast, or fried chicken. Desserts are made on the premises. For dinner (served from 5 to 8), the four hot entrées come with salad, potato or vegetable, and a beverage. Dessert and beverages are served from 8:30 to 10. If you prefer a quicker, perhaps lighter, meal, try the adjacent snack bar, which seats 100. Hot dogs, hamburgers, chili, and more are served daily 10 to 9 from June to September 1; a limited menu is offered daily 9 to 5 the rest of the year. *Mt. Rushmore National Memorial, tel. 605/574–2515. Reservations for bus tours appreciated. AE, D, MC, V. Dining room closed Sept.–Apr. 9. Inexpensive.*

NEAR THE PARKS **Casa Del Rey.** The Mexican food at this resaurant, located on the main drag leading to Mt. Rushmore, is mild enough for almost any gringo's taste. Beige plaster walls and greenery create the right atmosphere for corn chips and salsa, chili rellenos, and chimichangas. *1902 Mt. Rushmore Rd., Rapid City, tel. 605/348–5679. Reservations not accepted. AE, MC, V. Moderate.*

Great Wall Chinese Restaurant. Expect up to a 15-minute wait at this popular restaurant, where soft, individual lights shining down on each booth add a romantic touch and fat goldfish swim in an aquarium near the kitchen door. Two popular meals are "Happy Family" (shrimp, scallops, crab, chicken, and vegetables) and "Triple Delight" (chicken, shrimp, and beef, with vegetables). Take-out is available. *315 E. North St., Rapid City, tel. 605/348–1060. Reservations accepted for 5 or more. MC, V. Moderate.*

Saigon Restaurant. This place may look like a hole-in-the-wall, but it has a good reputation for freshly prepared meals that rely heavily on ginger and other spices. Popular dishes include Vietnamese-style shrimp with red sauce and onions, and chicken with broccoli. Order your meal "hot," but watch out. The extremely friendly staff are all family members; service can get a bit hectic during busy periods. Take-out is available. *221 E. North St., Rapid City, tel. 605/348–8523. Reservations accepted. No credit cards. No alcohol served. Closed Sun. and Feb. Moderate.*

Alpine Inn. With a European atmosphere enhanced by opera music, the Alpine Inn serves a Continental lunch, but steak is the only entrée at dinner. Prices for the 6- and 9-ounce steaks are so reasonable that it's no wonder people drive 50 miles and wait half an hour for a table at this restaurant in the rustic logging town of Hill City. The stained-glass windows and rich wood interior offer an unexpected touch of class. *Harney Peak Hotel, Main St., Hill City, tel. 605/574–2749. Reservations accepted for 8 or more. No credit cards. Closed Sun. Inexpensive–Moderate.*

PICNIC SPOTS There are two picnic spots along Highway 240 in Badlands National Park that offer scenic views. **Bigfoot Picnic Area** is near Journey to Wounded Knee Overlook, just a few miles northwest of Cedar Pass, and **Conata Picnic Area** is about 10 miles past that. Picnic supplies can be purchased at grocery stores along I–90 in Wall or Kadoka, or at Badlands Grocery at Interior (*see* General Stores, *above*).

A half-mile from Mt. Rushmore, you'll find the **Grizzly Bear Picnic Ground** turnoff, down Iron Mountain Road. From there a trail goes up Grizzly Creek to a series of small waterfalls, and beyond into the Black Elk Wilderness. Along Iron Mountain Road, not far from the Norbeck Memorial Overlook, lies **Iron Mountain Picnic Ground.** One mile west of Horsethief Lake on Highway 244 is **Elkhorn Picnic Ground,** and 2 miles farther west on Highway 244 is **Willow Creek Horse Camp,** where visitors can pull off the road and spread picnic blankets on the forest floor. All picnic grounds are free. Supplies can be picked up at the Safeway along Mt. Rushmore Road in Rapid City or at Mighty Mart, just east of Hill City (*see* General Stores, *above*.)

LODGING

Hotel rates are highest in summer, but often are reduced by half or more after the peak season. To find the best value for the money, choose a hotel far from I–90, the main tourist route into the Black Hills. Good deals for motels in mountain surroundings can also be found in the smaller Black Hills towns of Hill City, Custer, and Hot Springs, and in the outlying areas. Be sure to make your reservations well in advance, since motels are often booked solid during the summer. No campgrounds or hotels are available at Mt. Rushmore National Memorial, so most visitors to the memorial stay in Rapid City, Hill City, or in motels and campgrounds along the route. Visitors to Badlands National Park can find lodging in the Cedar Pass Lodge Cabins, located inside the park, or in the nearby towns of Interior, Wall, and Kadoka.

INSIDE THE PARKS **Cedar Pass Lodge Cabins.** The jutting peaks of Badlands National Park are visible from the windows of these park cabins, and Ben Reifel Visitor Center is within walking distance. Built in the 1930s, the clean, carpeted cabins were remodeled in 1987, but the knotty-pine walls remain. The cabins are air-conditioned but not equipped with TVs, and there is a restaurant nearby. Reservations are recommended. *Box 5, Interior, SD 57750, tel. 605/433–5460. 24 cabins. AE, D, DC, MC, V. Closed Nov. 1–Apr. 15. Inexpensive.*

NEAR THE PARKS **Hotel Alex Johnson.** This 11-story Rapid City landmark was built in 1928 and is a favorite with business visitors and tour groups. Rooms are small, but guests will enjoy the atmosphere set by the alpine woodwork and Native American artistry. Upper-story rooms have sweeping views of Rapid City, and those on the west side offer glimpses of the Black Hills. The decor in the public spaces is based on a Native American

motif. The fact that five U.S. presidents have stayed here attests to the hotel's good standing. *523 6th St., Rapid City, SD 57701, tel. 605/342–1210 or 800/888–2539. 120 rooms. Facilities: health club, dry sauna, steam showers, room service. AE, D, DC, MC, V. Expensive.*

Edelweiss Mountain Lodging. The 18 houses and many cabins—many of them former homes—sit among pines on a gravel road 3 miles off Highway 385. Each is unique, and the prices range accordingly. Large groups might like the Waite cabin, which has four bedrooms on three carpeted floors and a pool table. *HC33, Box 3128, Rapid City, SD 57702, tel. 605/574–2430. 18 houses and cabins. MC, V. Moderate–Expensive.*

Bel Air Inn. Prices more than double in summer at this motel on the busiest strip in Rapid City. The location is convenient to all the sights, but it can be noisy, particularly in rooms facing the front of the building. Guest rooms have clean bathrooms and firm queen-size beds, but lack the charm of more secluded Black Hills lodgings. *2101 Mt. Rushmore Rd., Rapid City, SD 57701, tel. 605/343–5126 or 800/456–5055. 30 rooms. Facilities: pool, cable TV. AE, D, DC, MC, V. Moderate.*

Castle Inn. This well-kept motel is easy to reach, comfortable, and typical of what is available in Rapid City in the mid-price range. Rooms are spacious enough for families. Again, since it is located in town it can be a bit noisy and lacks the woodsy charm of some other, more rustic, accommodations. *15 E. North St., Rapid City, SD 57701, tel. 605/348–4120 or 800/658–5464. 20 rooms. Facilities: heated pool, cable TV. AE, D, DC, MC, V. Moderate.*

Plains Motel. This remodeled, two-story motel, originally built in the '60s, is just one block from I–90 in downtown Wall, making it an easy base for exploring Badlands National Park. The clean, comfortable rooms are large enough for families, and kids will appreciate the game room with video machines. Ask for one of the newer rooms and be sure to book in advance. *912 Glenn St., Box 393,*

Wall, SD 57790, tel. 605/279–2145 or 800/528–1234. 74 rooms. Facilities: pool, game room, cable TV. AE, D, DC, MC, V. Moderate.

Lewis Park Cabins and Hotel. These cabins on the back streets of Hill City offer small-town living tucked away among mountain ridges and aspen trees. Built in the 1930s, the cabins come with full kitchens and furniture that dates back to the 1950s. There are lawn chairs on the small covered porches, and the buildings are painted a shockingly bright green. The motel-style rooms don't have the old-fashioned character of the cabins. Prices here swing wildly, ranging from $15 in the dead of winter to more than $50 in summer. *110 Park Ave., Box 382, Hill City, SD 57745, tel. 605/574–2565. 5 rooms, 4 cabins. D, MC, V. Inexpensive.*

Spring Creek Inn. This friendly 1950s-era motel earns top honors as one of the best deals in the Black Hills during summer. The white clapboard building doesn't look like much from the outside, but the clean, spacious, knotty-pine rooms fit in well with the mountain setting. Located just 1 mile north of Hill City on Highway 16/385, the place is especially popular with hunters and fishermen. (Don't be surprised to see deer hanging from poles in the front yard during the November hunting season.) In summer, volleyball and croquet games are set up on the grassy lawn, and fishermen angle for trout in nearby Spring Creek. *HCR 87, Box 55, Hill City, SD 57745, tel. 605/574–2591. 14 rooms. D, MC, V. Inexpensive.*

CAMPING

Primitive camping—with no facilities and lots of privacy—is easily found in this part of the United States. You can set up camp in the backcountry of Badlands National Park or off a secluded dirt road in the Black Hills. You can also choose a drive-in campsite at a national forest campground, with the luxury of flush or pit toilets, running water, and fire grates. There is no camping in Mt. Rushmore National Memorial.

The most elaborate camping facilities, with at least water, showers, electricity, and sewage disposal, are in commercial campgrounds scattered across the Black Hills and outlying parts of the Badlands. Most of these have spaces for RVs as well as tents. For a fairly complete listing, check the *South Dakota Campground Guide,* available free from the South Dakota Department of Tourism (*see* Visitor Information, *above*).

INSIDE THE PARKS Within the boundaries of **Badlands National Park** there are two campgrounds, and both assign sites on a first-come, first-served basis. You can also camp in the backcountry of the Badlands, that is if you're willing to hike in.

A short stroll from the Ben Reifel Visitor Center, **Cedar Pass Campground** (tel. 605/433–5361) has 96 sites for tents or RVs with flush and pit toilets, drinking water, disposal station, ranger station, and public phone. The campground is open year-round; sites cost $8 per night in season, but are free in winter, when the water is shut off. Cedar Pass often has space available.

The word to remember at **Sage Creek Primitive Campground** (tel. 605/433–5361) is *primitive*. Located just south of the Sage Creek Rim Road, in the Badlands Sage Creek Wilderness Area, this campground is for those who really like to rough it. There are no set camp sites here: Just park anywhere in the area. There is also no water, and only pit toilets. You pay nothing to stay at Sage Creek, and it's open year-round. Remember, fires are not allowed anywhere in the Badlands.

At campgrounds in the **Black Hills National Forest** (tel. 605/673–2251) you'll find picnic tables, fire grates, flush or vault toilets, and drinking water, but little more. There are usually no showers in national forest campgrounds. The lush forest setting, however, is a big draw, and it helps that sites may be reserved; call **U.S. Forest Reservations** (tel. 800/280–2267) well in advance of your arrival date. It costs $6 per reservation, in addition to the camp fee. Keep in mind that you can usually find an open site without a reservation at most national forest campgrounds

BADLANDS, MT. RUSHMORE, AND THE BLACK HILLS

	Total number of sites	Sites suitable for RVs	Number of hookups	Drive to sites	Hike to sites	Flush toilets	Pit/chemical toilets	Drinking water	Showers	Fire grates	Swimming	Boat access	Playground	Disposal station	Ranger station	Public telephone	Reservation possible	Daily fee per site	Dates open
BADLANDS																			
Cedar Pass	96	96	0	•		•	•	•		•				•	•	•	•*	$8***	year-round
Sage Creek	∞	∞	0	•			•											free	year-round
BLACK HILLS																			
Horsethief Lake	36	36	0	•		•	•	•		•	•					•	•*	$12–$13	Memorial Day–Labor Day
Sheridan Lake Southside	129	129	0	•			•	•	•**	•		•					•*	$9–$11	Memorial Day–Labor Day
Whitetail	17	17	0	•			•	•		•							•*	$7	year-round
Dutchman	45	45	0				•	•		•		•					•*	$7	Memorial Day–Labor Day
Pactola	80	80	0	•		•		•	•	•	•	•				•	•*	$9–$11	Memorial Day–Labor Day
Rod and Gun/Timon	14	14	0				•										•*	$6	year-round
NEAR THE PARKS																			
Berry Patch	130	116	113	•		•		•	•	•	•		•	•		•	•	$15–$19.50	Apr.–early Nov.
Happy Holiday	225	150	150	•		•		•	•	•	•		•	•		•	•	$15–$19.50	year-round
Mt. Rushmore KOA	500	355	355	•		•		•	•	•	•		•	•		•	•	$18.95–$26.95	May–early Oct.
Badlands KOA	130	82	82	•		•		•	•	•	•		•	•		•	•	$16–$19	May–mid-Oct.
Arrow Camp	100	100	72	•		•		•	•	•	•		•	•		•	•	$8.50–$12	May–mid-Oct.

*Reservation fee charged. **Cold water only. ***Free when water is turned off.

in the Black Hills, except for the one at busy Horsethief Lake. The easiest way to find these campgrounds is by buying a Black Hills National Forest recreation map (see Publications, above) and requesting a free list of the campgrounds from the forest service.

Horsethief Lake Campground is the closest forest-service campground to Mt. Rushmore National Memorial, and, as a result, the most crowded. Located 1 mile west of Mt. Rushmore off Highway 244, the 36-site campground is open Memorial Day to Labor Day. It offers easy access to the Black Elk Wilderness, Norbeck Wildlife Preserve, and Centennial Trail. Horsethief Lake has flush chemical toilets. Sites cost $12 to $13 per night.

Also in the national forest, the 129 sites at the **Sheridan Lake Southside Campground** are near a beach, boat ramp, and the Centennial Trail. The best spots are closest to the shoreline. This campground is open from Memorial Day to Labor Day, except for the Rocky Loop, which is open year-round. Sheridan Lake has flush toilets as well as vault toilets. There are cold showers at the lake. Sites cost $9 to $11. (Sheridan Lake North Cove Campground has 58 sites for groups only.)

Whitetail Campground, above Deerfield Reservoir, offers peaceful solitude and good fishing. There are 17 camp sites, which cost $7 per night and are open year-round.

At an elevation of 6,100 feet, **Dutchman Campground** is one of the coolest spots in the Black Hills, allowing campers to escape the summer heat, even in July. The 45 sites are open from Memorial Day to Labor Day and cost $7 per night.

Pactola Campground is large, with 80 sites near Pactola Reservoir, and a boat ramp. In the past few years the water level has been low, exposing mud banks and somewhat marring the normally beautiful lakefront. There are flush toilets and a public phone here; hot showers are at a marina, 1/4 mile away. Sites cost $9 to $11 per night at this national forest campground, which is open from Memorial Day to Labor Day.

Rod and Gun Campground and **Timon Campground** are both small campgrounds that offer secluded camping along Little Spearfish Creek, not far from Roughlock Falls. Open all year, each has seven sites that cost $6 a night.

If you really want to rough it, try camping in the Black Hills backcountry. There are no facilities here, but it's free, it's legal, and campers have complete privacy. The many logging and gravel forest-service roads give access to all parts of the national forest. (You are not allowed to camp in recreation areas, at administrative sites, and in the Black Hills Experimental Forest.) Remember, fires are not allowed in the Black Hills backcountry; if you want to have a campfire you'll have to use the campground fire grates. You can, however, bring a stove.

NEAR MT. RUSHMORE Berry Patch (tel. 605/341–5588), at exit 60 on I–90 in Rapid City, has 14 tent sites and 116 RV sites (113 hookups) on level lots with easy access. There are flush toilets, hot showers, drinking water, fire grates, a playground, swimming, disposal station, and a public phone here. Open from April 1 to November 1, Berry Patch charges $15 to $19.50 per night.

Happy Holiday (tel. 605/342–7365), located across from Reptile Gardens on Mt. Rushmore Road, is conveniently located. It has 150 RV sites with hookups and 75 tent sites, with flush toilets, hot showers, drinking water, fire grates, playground, swimming, disposal station, and public phone. Open year-round, sites cost $15 to $19.50 per night.

Mt. Rushmore KOA (tel. 605/574–2525) is a large commercial campground 5 miles west of Mt. Rushmore on Highway 244, with shuttle service to the Mt. Rushmore Lighting Ceremony, bus tours, restaurant, and car rentals. It has 355 RV sites and 145 tent sites, with flush toilets, hot showers, drinking water, fire grates, playground, swimming, disposal station, and public phone. The KOA is open from May 1 to October 1, and sites cost $18.95 to $26.95 per night.

NEAR BADLANDS The Badlands KOA (tel. 605/433–5337), 4 miles southeast of Interior on Highway 44, has 130 sites (82 hookups), with flush toilets, hot showers, drinking water, fire grates, a playground, a swimming pool, a disposal station, and a public phone. It's open from May 1 to October 15, and sites cost $16 to $19 per night.

The Arrow Camp (tel. 605/279–2112), in Wall, has 100 RV sites (72 hookups) as well as motel units. Here you'll find flush toilets, hot showers, drinking water, fire grates, a playground, a swimming pool, a disposal station, and a public phone. The Arrow Camp is open from May 1 to October 15 and charges $8.50 to $12 per night.

Banff National Park with Yoho and Kootenay National Parks

Alberta and British Columbia

By Peter Oliver

To the unknowing map-scanner with an eye for big mountains, the Canadian Rockies are apt to be a deception. Maps indicate that peak elevations are 2,000 to 3,000 feet lower than elevations in the Colorado Rockies, suggesting that the Canadian Rockies fall short of their southern cousins in alpine grandeur. In truth, however, the tree line (the elevation above which most trees won't grow) in the Canadian Rockies is relatively low—at about 7,000 feet, or more than 3,000 feet lower than the average tree line in the Colorado Rockies. And for that reason more craggy, rugged, high-alpine terrain is exposed. Massive walls of rock, ice, and snow rising high above evergreen forests make the Canadian Rockies appear breathtakingly tall, even if the numbers say it isn't so.

The Canadian Rockies are also still mottled with active glaciers and ice fields, whereas glaciers have all but disappeared from the U.S. Rockies. The pale glacial blue goes hand-somely with the deep-green forests, the gray limestone, and, when the summer blooming season is in session, the multicolored sweep of wildflowers.

The Canadian government first set about the business of creating national parks here in 1885, establishing a small park preserve after the discovery of the Cave and Basin Hot Springs near what is now the town of Banff. Two years later, Canada's Rocky Mountains National Park (later to become Banff National Park) officially came into being. The creation of Yoho and Kootenay national parks would follow, resulting in a parkland totaling 9,360 square kilometers (approximately 3,600 square miles). When Jasper National Park to the north is included, the total contiguous parkland count swells to more than 20,000 square kilometers (about 7,800 square miles). For reasons best understood by students of Canada's provincial politics, a relatively small (386 square kilometers, 149 square miles) but exquisite plot of land southwest of

Banff did not get national-park billing; it was left to British Columbia's government to turn it into Mt. Assiniboine Provincial Park.

Although preservation might have been a major impetus in the creation of the parks, private enterprise had its effect, too. Having completed its route from east to west, the Canadian Pacific Railroad (CPR) was looking to fill train cars, and the tourism business held promise. As CPR general manager W.C. Van Horne said at the time: "If we can't export the scenery, we'll import the tourists!"

They did just that. When the government began setting aside parkland to attract those tourists, CPR basically held a monopolistic stronghold on tourist services in the region. The railroad company built its first hotel, the Banff Springs Hotel, in 1888, and the Lake Louise Chalet, which became the Chateau Lake Louise, followed two years later.

Proprietors other than CPR have since managed to get a foothold in the region, to the point where today the town of Banff overflows with hotels, inns, restaurants, and shops. But development remains concentrated within the Banff and Lake Louise town limits, and the rest of the landscape, except for campgrounds and hiking trails, remains pretty much pristine.

Unlike such U.S. national parks as Yellowstone and Yosemite, the national parks of the Canadian Rockies have few designated tourist attractions and concessions. Beyond the towns, activities are divided between driving the two major highways, Routes 1 and 93, and exploring the mountainous backcountry. The combination of a bustling, full-service community (anathema to national parks in the western United States) and an almost untouched expanse of mountains is apparently hard to resist: More than 3 million visitors annually make Banff the most popular of all national parks in Canada.

A prototypical Banff summer vacation includes a few days in Banff, a few days in Lake Louise, site of the oft-photographed lake and the Victoria Glacier behind it, and a trip along the Icefields Parkway. This is a perfectly pleasant way to experience the parks, whose mountain scenery can overwhelm the senses.

Sticking to the roadways here is, however, like ordering a bottle of fine wine without drinking it. Nearly 2,000 kilometers (1,120 miles) of well-maintained trails in the three parks make this area a mother lode for wanderers of all sorts, from casual walkers to experienced mountaineers.

Banff National Park differs from the western parks of the United States in one other respect: Winter activity is brisk. Skiing is a Banff tradition that predates the park's three lift-serviced ski areas—Mt. Norquay, Lake Louise, and Sunshine Village. Skoki Lodge and Mt. Assiniboine Lodge (in the neighboring provincial park) were built more than 60 years ago with skiing in mind.

ESSENTIAL INFORMATION

VISITOR INFORMATION Principal sources of information are: **Banff National Park Visitor Centre** (Box 900, 224 Banff Ave., Banff, AB T0L 0C0, tel. 403/762–1550), **Yoho National Park Information Centre** (Box 99, Field, BC V0A 1G0, tel. 604/343–6324), the **Canadian Parks Service** (Tourism Services, Box 2989, Station M. Calgary, AB T2P 3H8, tel. 403/292–4401), **Alberta Tourism** (Main Level, City Centre, 10155 102 St., Edmonton, AB T5J 4L6, tel. 800/661–8888), **Tourism British Columbia** (Parliament Bldgs., Victoria, BC V8V 1X4, tel. 604/663–6000). Local information, specifically regarding lodging, dining, and shopping, is available from the **Banff–Lake Louise Chamber of Commerce** (335 Beaver St., Banff, AB T0L 0C0, tel. 403/762–3777). Banff National Park is entirely within Alberta, while Yoho and Kootenay parks are entirely within British Columbia, something to keep in mind when acquiring parks information from either of the provincial agencies. For specific information (e.g., current weather conditions, camping availability) about **Kootenay** (tel. 604/347–9615) and **Lake Louise** (tel. 403/522–3833), contact them directly.

Backcountry campers should ask for a copy of the information pamphlet "Backcountry Visitors' Guide." *The Canadian Rockies Trail Guide* (*see* Publications, *below*) is also a valuable resource for backcountry travelers. Backcountry permits are required for all backcountry campers; these are free and may be obtained from the nearest park visitor center or warden office.

FEES A fee is charged to all vehicles entering the parks (although vehicles in nonstop transit through the parks on Route 1 are not charged). A day pass is $5, a four-day pass is $10, and an annual pass is $30 (all fees are quoted in Canadian currency).

PUBLICATIONS Alberta Tourism, Tourism British Columbia, and the Canadian Parks Service (*see* Visitor Information, *above*) all offer various information packages; those from Alberta Tourism, including the *Alberta Adventure Guide,* tend to be the most thorough. The guide for hikers in all three parks is *The Canadian Rockies Trail Guide*, by Brian Patton and Bart Robinson. Wildflower lovers should look for *Wildflowers of the Canadian Rockies,* by George Scotter and Halle Flygare. Both are available in bookstores and gift shops in Banff.

GEOLOGY AND TERRAIN Formed about 60 to 120 million years ago, the Canadian Rockies are relative youngsters among mountains. Tectonic activity (the shifting of rock layers through faulting, folding, and upthrust), some volcanic activity (long dormant), and erosion have conspired to give the mountains their rugged configurations.

Glaciers have been the main erosive force, gnawing with their infinitely slow appetite at a rock surface composed largely of limestone, sandstone, and shale. Most, though not all, glaciers in the region are receding—getting smaller by shedding their melted ice into the major rivers of western Canada and the northwestern United States. That leaves no shortage of ice, however. The Columbia Icefield alone, at 325 square kilometers (125 square miles), covers about the same surface area as Yellowstone Lake in Yellowstone National Park and is estimated to be more than 1,000 feet thick in places.

Glacial erosion and recession have left a sprawling mountain sculpture catalogued by an arcane alpine terminology. Among the notable land features are cirques (rock amphitheaters), moraines (dikelike deposits of silt and debris), eskers (narrow, glacially deposited ridges of rock and sand), and arêtes (sharp mountain ridges).

Climate, latitude, and glacial activity have contributed to the 7,000-foot tree line. The elevation of the town of Banff, in the Bow River valley, is 4,582 feet, and the highest peaks top off well above 11,000 feet.

FLORA AND FAUNA Coniferous trees—including spruce, fir, and pine—are the predominant growth along mountain slopes, with a few hardwoods, quaking aspens in particular, mixing in at lower elevations. One of the spectacles of fall is the changing color of the larch trees, deciduous members of the pine family, which turn a brilliant gold before shedding their needles.

Above the tree line, what greenery there is consists mostly of meadows and tundra growth. In summer, wildflowers flourish between 6,500 and 9,500 feet. Wildflower varieties are far too numerous to list here, but among the most common are saxifrage and columbine.

Wild animals in general possess an uncanny wisdom in determining zones of safety from their predators (e.g., human hunters). In this region, those zones are defined by national-park boundaries, within which hunting is strictly prohibited.

Guaranteeing anything is begging trouble, but wildlife sightings in Banff, Kootenay, and Yoho are virtually assured. Bighorn sheep (Banff and Kootenay only) and elk tend to graze and wander along highway shoulders, not to mention the highway itself, attracted by roadside grasses and residual road salt. Be alert for animals on the road as well as for cars and humans stopped in unexpected places to photograph them; pull well off onto shoulders, and drive within the speed limit—for your own and the animals' safety.

At higher elevations, marmots and pikas are common, burrowing beneath and between rocks. Much less common are the elusive cougar, bobcat, and mountain goat. (One theory has it that the best way to spot the agile goats is to approach them, if possible, from a higher elevation. According to the theory, the goats reach ridges and ledges inaccessible to other animals and therefore expect no predators above them.) At Kootenay in late spring or early summer, goats are commonly seen along the road at the salt beds at the base of Mt. Wardle.

Vermilion Lakes Drive, just off the west Banff exit from Route 1, can be a gold mine for elk, muskrat, coyote, and the occasional moose. Near the east Banff exit from Route 1 is the buffalo paddock, the place to see buffalo during the summer months.

Bear sightings and encounters are rare, but they do occur. Anyone hiking, biking, or camping in the backcountry should take all the proper precautions: suspending food, cooking and eating away from tent sites, and so on. Bear information is provided upon paying the entry fee to the park and should be read carefully.

WHEN TO GO All three parks are open to visitors year-round, although the relatively few visitor services within Kootenay and Yoho parks are cut back more in winter than those in Banff. The high season runs from July to mid-September, and lodging prices during the period typically jump 50% or more. The Christmas and New Year's period (again, reflected in lodging prices) is the other high season.

People who live in the area invariably say that their favorite time of year is late September into early October. Crowds thin out and prices drop. Better yet, the first lasting snows have usually arrived at higher elevations, providing a backdrop for the radiant fall foliage. Be prepared at this time of year, however, for cooler, though generally pleasant, temperatures and the closing of some services,

such as campgrounds, lodges, and restaurants.

With three major ski areas within Banff National Park and several other ski areas near the park, winter is also an active season. The scenic drives along Route 1 and Route 93 N (the Icefields Parkway) remain open and well-maintained in winter, but snow closes off most backcountry trails to all but hardy skiers experienced in the rigors and hazards of the backcountry winter.

High temperatures in summer typically range from the 60s to the 80s, and midwinter highs range between the teens and the 30s. With every 1,000 feet of elevation gain, temperatures usually drop about 5 degrees. Wild weather swings, however, are common. Snowstorms, especially at higher elevations, and subfreezing temperatures sneak into summer, and warm chinook winds have been known to raise wintertime temperatures, especially along the eastern frontal ranges, into the 70s.

SEASONAL EVENTS Mid-June to mid-August: The Banff Centre (St. Julien Rd., Banff, AB T0L 0C0, tel. 403/762–6100), the cultural epicenter of the parks, hosts the **Festival of the Arts,** which includes classical music, jazz, ballet, opera, and other performing arts. **Mid-February:** At the **Banff Winter Festival** (Box 1976, Banff, AB T0l 0C0, tel. 403/762–3777) lighthearted and die-hard competitions—from tugs-of-war and snow golf to serious cross-country ski races—are mixed with a parade, dances, and wiener roasts.

WHAT TO PACK Casual dress is the rule in this part of the world. Space in your luggage is better used, even for a summer visit, for changes in clothing to match the unpredictable moods of the weather rather than for dresses, jackets, and ties.

Regardless of season, be ready for a wide weather range. Even in summer, pack a warm wool sweater or synthetic-fleece jacket, warm socks, light gloves, and a sturdy windbreaker (preferably of waterproof, breathable material). This is essential gear if you plan to do much hiking, boating, cycling, or other outdoor activity. If you have plans for a half-day hike or longer, or expect to spend much time hiking on cold, glacial ice, bring along a few extra layers, including a layer of polypropylene long underwear, and a warm hat.

GENERAL STORES Regard the town of Banff as a giant, well-stocked general store; pretty much anything you'd ever want or need in the parks, from crampons to crayons, can be found in one of the many stores here. What you won't find are bargains, Banff being not only a resort town (hence resort prices) but also one with a virtual monopoly on park commerce. If you're looking to save money on more costly items (camping gear, for example), shop in Calgary or even Canmore, 26 kilometers (16 miles) east of Banff.

Samson Mall, in Lake Louise, and **Radium Hot Springs,** just outside the Kootenay Park boundary, are other places to stock up on food and equipment. The pickings are slim at grocery and convenience stores in Castle Mountain Village (between Banff and Lake Louise), Field (Yoho National Park), and the Crossing (on the Icefields Parkway).

ARRIVING AND DEPARTING By Plane. Calgary **International Airport** is the most common gateway for travelers arriving by plane. **Air Canada** and **United Airlines** have the most extensive schedules of flights between Calgary and U.S. cities.

By Car and RV. Route 1, the Trans-Canada Highway, is the principal east–west route through the region. Banff is 128 kilometers (80 miles) west of Calgary on Route 1 and 858 kilometers (532 miles) east of Vancouver. The principal routes from the south are: in Alberta, Route 2, which runs directly north to Calgary from the Montana border; and, in British Columbia, Route 93, which runs from Kalispell, Montana, through Radium Hot Springs, British Columbia, and into the southern end of Kootenay National Park.

By Train. Apart from a touring train service that makes a stop at Banff (*see* Guided Tours, *below*), there is no rail service to and from the park. You can, however, take a train to Jasper and the bus from Jasper to Banff.

By Bus. Greyhound Lines (tel. 800/231–2222) provides regular service to Calgary and Vancouver. **Brewster Grayline** (tel. 800/661–1152) offers service between Calgary International Airport and Banff and Lake Louise, in addition to service between Banff and Jasper, a 287-kilometer (178-mile) journey.

EXPLORING

Most people arrive in **Banff** from the east, from Calgary via Route 1. For almost all—casual tourists and avid outdoorspeople alike—the town of Banff is a kind of base camp. The reason is simple: Banff is the only town of size or substance in the three parks. Banff is neither architecturally nor atmospherically an exemplary town; except for the oft-photographed Banff Springs Hotel, its architecture is modern, functional, and undistinguished.

Aside from the hotel, the other major point of reference in Banff is Banff Avenue, the main drag of a town core tightly crammed with shops and restaurants. The shop mix consists of "galleries" selling various art and quasi-art items, clothing stores (with an emphasis on sports and ski wear), and photo stores. If it all seems like shopping overload, remember that, except for a few boutiques at Chateau Lake Louise and Samson Mall, this is about all the shopping there is in the parks. Heading south, Banff Avenue bridges the Bow River, ending at a T in front of the Parks Administration Office.

Lake Louise is 54 kilometers (32 miles) northwest of Banff on Route 1. The actual "town" of Lake Louise is a crossroads barely noticed by most travelers, on their way (another 5 kilometers, or 3 miles) to Chateau Lake Louise. At the edge of the blue-green lake, and with the Victoria Glacier as a backdrop, the château runs head-to-head with the Banff Springs Hotel for the title of most-photographed structure in the Canadian Rockies.

That **Kootenay National Park** is the least-visited of the Canadian Rockies parks is not

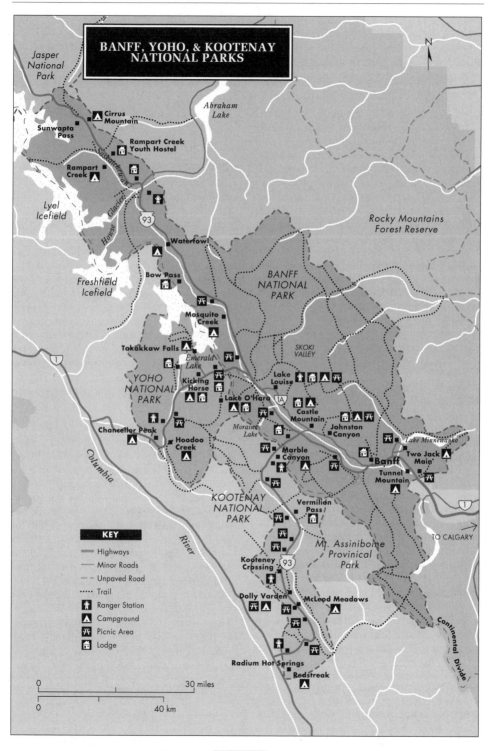

BANFF, YOHO, & KOOTENAY
NATIONAL PARKS

Jasper
National
Park

Abraham
Lake

Cirrus
Mountain

Sunwapta
Pass

Rampart Creek
Youth Hostel

Rampart
Creek

Lyel
Icefield

93

Waterfowl

Freshfield
Icefield

Bow Pass

Rocky Mountains
Forest Reserve

BANFF
NATIONAL
PARK

Mosquito
Creek

Takakkaw Falls

SKOKI
VALLEY

Emerald
Lake

YOHO
NATIONAL
PARK

Kicking
Horse

Lake
Louise

Lake O'Hara

1A

Castle
Mountain

Chancellor Peak

Moraine
Lake

Johnston
Canyon

Lake Minnewanka

Hoodoo
Creek

Columbia

Marble
Canyon

Banff

Two Jack
Main

Tunnel
Mountain

KOOTENAY
NATIONAL
PARK

Vermilion
Pass

Mt. Assiniboine
Provincial
Park

TO CALGARY

1

River

KEY

Kooteney
Crossing

93

Highways

Minor Roads

Unpaved Road

Trail

Ranger Station

Campground

Picnic Area

Lodge

Dolly Varden

McLeod Meadows

Continental
Divide

Radium Hot Springs

Redstreak

0   30 miles

0   40 km

indicative of an intrinsic lack of appeal. Far from it: The deep, narrow valley cut by the Kootenay River, along which the park is contoured, is flanked on the southwest by a steep, extended linkage of peaks, ridges, glaciers, and wall-like cliffs—hence the name "the Rockwall."

What Kootenay is lacking, except at its southern extreme at Radium Hot Springs, is services. There are fewer campgrounds in Kootenay than in any of the other parks, and there is only a single gas station, open only in the summer, at Vermilion Crossing. Most travelers simply use Kootenay as a scenic driving route between Banff and Radium Hot Springs. This is a boon to backpackers, to whom Kootenay offers great opportunities to be away from day hikers and casual walkers.

Yoho is a two-part park: the part north of Route 1, and the part south. It is reached by heading west along Route 1 from its intersection with the Icefields Parkway (Route 93N) just north of Lake Louise. The park name is a Native American (Cree) word that means just what it sounds as though it means: "Wow!" The park indeed is a world of breathtaking scenery—lakes, glaciers, rock walls, ice fields, waterfalls, and more. In short, Yoho has compressed into its relatively small land area a little bit of everything that is the essence of the Canadian Rockies allure.

The Yoho River valley is the main body of the park's northern half, which features some of the finest backpacking and climbing in the parks. **Lake O'Hara** is the physical and spiritual epicenter of the park's southern half. For backcountry enthusiasts, Lake O'Hara is one of the best spots in the Canadian Rockies, the reason that Lake O'Hara Lodge (*see* Lodging, *below*) is usually fully booked many weeks in advance in summer. Other than hiking in, the only way to get to Lake O'Hara is by taking a lodge-run shuttle bus (reservations required and often hard to come by) on an 11-kilometer (7-mile) fire road from Route 1. Contact the Yoho National Park Information Centre (*see* Visitor Information, *above*) for details.

Rock-buttressed mountains and high-alpine lakes—more than two dozen within a few

kilometers of Lake O'Hara itself—are the ingredients of this area's special appeal. It also offers a flavor of the backcountry for people not keen on roughing it, since the lodge is somewhat elegant as backcountry lodges go. Also, with the many climbers, hikers, and lodge guests who congregate here in summer, this is the part of Yoho for people who don't mind sharing the splendor of the backcountry with others.

THE BEST IN ONE DAY Anyone on a short time-budget should plan to spend as few hours as possible in the town of Banff. Weather permitting, perhaps the best program for experiencing the parks and their most renowned attractions is to drive between the town and the Icefield Centre (just north of the Banff/Jasper park boundary), a six-hour round-trip. Leave time for an afternoon hike; a good short-hike area is the Lake Louise/Moraine Lake area, justly famed for its scenery, although hardly undiscovered. If possible, work in time for afternoon tea at Chateau Lake Louise. The town of Banff features the largest concentration of restaurants; the Post Hotel (*see* Dining, *below*) in Lake Louise has perhaps the premier restaurant in the Canadian Rockies.

ORIENTATION PROGRAMS The **Cave and Basin Centennial Centre** (Cave Ave., Banff, tel. 403/762–1557) and **Lake Louise Visitor Centre** (next to the Samson Mall, tel. 403/522–3833) feature a mix of exhibits and multimedia shows that explain the history and geology of the area. The **Banff Park Museum** (93 Banff Ave., tel. 403/762–1558) has wildlife displays, wildlife art, and a library on the natural history of the region. The museum, to which admission is free, is open year-round. The **Whyte Museum** (111 Bear St., tel. 403/762–2291) gives a thorough historical perspective of the region through art, photography, historical artifacts, and rotating exhibits on life in the Canadian Rockies. Admission is $2 for adults and $1 for senior citizens and students (children free); the museum is open 10 to 6 in summer and with somewhat abbreviated hours in winter.

GUIDED TOURS Brewster Transportation and Tours (Box 1140, Banff, AB T0L 0C0, tel. in Banff, 403/762–2241; in Lake Louise, 403/522–3544; in Calgary, 403/221–8242; or 800/661–1152) offers half-day and full-day sightseeing-bus tours of the parks (the most popular being the Icefields Parkway tours). **Tauck Tours** (11 Wilton Rd., Westport, CT 06881, tel. 203/226–6911) arranges multiday bus tours and heli-hiking options in nearby mountain ranges.

Minnewanka Boat Tours (Box 2189, Banff, AB T0L 0C0, tel. 403/762–3473) offers 1¹/₂-hour summer boat cruises on Lake Minnewanka, near Banff ($20 adults, $10 children).

Audiocassette tapes for self-guided auto tours of the parks are produced by **Auto Tape Tours** and **Rocky Mountain Tape Tours**. Tapes can be rented or purchased at newsstands or gift shops in Banff and Lake Louise.

Challenge Enterprises (1300 Railway Ave., Box 2008, Canmore, AB T0L 0M0, tel. 403/678–2628) features one-day and multi-day tour options, including fishing, rafting, and cycling trips.

For hiking, mountaineering, or backcountry ski touring, **Banff Alpine Guides** (Box 1025, Banff, AB T0L 0C0, tel. 403/678–6091) organizes tours according to seasonal conditions.

Rocky Mountaineer Rail Tours (tel. 800/665–7245) takes passengers on a two-day train trip from Vancouver to Calgary, making stops at Kamloops, Jasper, and Banff. Trips run late May to early October and start at $450.

SCENIC DRIVES AND VIEWS Almost obligatory for any vehicle-bound traveler in Banff National Park is **Tunnel Mountain Road,** a 9-kilometer (5¹/₂-mile) loop from the town of Banff. That's not because it's the most scenic drive in the park—though it doesn't lack for scenery—but because it's the most accessible for people staying in Banff.

A good alternative to the busy Route 1 from Banff to Lake Louise is **Route 1A.** The pavement is good (roadwork recently completed) and the views just as rewarding, although the pace is considerably slower. Though hikers can use the Lake Louise trail network to reach **Moraine Lake** in the Valley of the Ten Peaks, less energetic travelers (that is, the vast majority) get to the lake by car or bus, 14 kilometers (8¹/₂ miles) from the Lake Louise crossroads. The lake's mountainous surroundings and its remarkable blue-green color make it a match for any scenic spot anywhere, but it is a tour-bus stop and hence not a hidden alcove for those seeking solitude.

Heading north from Lake Louise on Route 1 and connecting with **Route 93 N** (the Icefields Parkway) leads you to progressively higher, more glaciated country. The road reaches a high point at **Bow Pass,** which at 6,787 feet may be covered with snow as late as May and as early as September. Two lakes, Bow and Peyto, flank the pass; surrounded by rock, snow, and ice, they represent the epitome of Canadian Rockies scenery. This is a premier area for hiking, climbing, and backcountry skiing; the land is high, rugged, and glaciated.

The highway descends gradually from Bow Pass to **Saskatchewan River Crossing**, a utility stop. Almost all travelers on this route stop here for gas, food, or both, but the cafeteria food presents a compelling reason to pack a picnic lunch if you're planning a day trip from Banff.

The road then descends into a valley where three rivers—the Saskatchewan, Howse, and Mistaya—diverge and where glaciers reaching from the giant ice fields ahead can be seen. As the road climbs again toward **Sunwapta Pass** and the juncture of Banff and Jasper parks, keep an eye out on the left for the **Parker Ridge Trail.** The short, moderate walk provides unusually quick access to high-alpine, tundra terrain. Mountain goats are said to enjoy this spot, too, although sightings of the shy goats are rare. From here, the road continues on to the Icefield Centre in Jasper National Park.

Kootenay National Park is reached by heading west/southwest on **Route 93 S** (the Banff/Windermere Highway) which splits from Route 1 about 16 kilometers (10 miles) north of Banff. Of all the major routes through the parks, Route 93S through Kootenay gets the least travel, but the views to the west are consistently stunning. The highway climbs steeply to **Vermilion Pass,** the juncture of Banff and Kootenay parks. This is an eerie but educative spot—a 1968 forest fire has left a charred sweep covering thousands of acres. The forest is regenerating; amid the charred tree skeletons left by the fire, new growth has reached higher than 10 feet.

As the road descends from the pass, look for the **Stanley Glacier trailhead,** the start to an excellent day hike, a moderate 4-kilometer (2½-mile) climb to a large glacial cirque. Continuing south along Route 93S, keep an eye out for the trailhead to **Floe Lake,** one of the park's highlights and a long (20-kilometer, 12-mile, round-trip) day hike. Dark limestone walls that rise 3,300 feet above the lake show off the spectacle of the Rockwall at its most spectacular.

Just before winding through narrow **Sinclair Canyon,** Route 93S reaches the baths of Radium Hot Springs. This is certainly the most populated nook of the park, and the large, hot spring–fed pool on the left side of the road can be packed with people during the summer (*see* Other Activities, *below*). For travelers wanting to make a day of it, lunch and dinner are served at the resort across the road, but given the ho-hum food, taking a picnic lunch on a hike along one of several nearby nature trails, between dips, makes better sense. Dining and lodging options abound in Radium, although they are lacking, for the most part, in distinction.

To reach Yoho National Park, go west from Lake Louise on **Route 1** over Kicking Horse Pass. The first point of interest on the north (left) side of the road is the viewing pull-off for the **Spiral Tunnels.** Built by the Canadian Pacific Railroad as a way of lessening the steepness of the grade for climbing and descending trains, the tunnels are overlapping loops within the mountainside. As a result, if you're passing by when a long train is in transit, it's possible to see the front part of the train emerging from one tunnel-opening at

the same time that the rest of the train is entering a tunnel-opening just below.

To get just a taste of Yoho many travelers make the short excursion to view **Takakkaw Falls,** a slender, 833-foot cascade. The Takakkaw Falls parking lot is also the trailhead for a trail network that leads to Twin Falls and the Little Yoho River valley, both ranked highly among backpacking destinations by people who know. The road to the falls is open mid-June to early October, as snow permits, and is not accessible to trailers or large RVs due to a series of tight switchbacks.

Farther along Route 1, travelers with an interest in geologic history should stop at the **Burgess Shale exhibit,** which contains the fossilized remains of 120 marine species dating back 530 million years. The actual site of the shale is only accessible by taking a difficult guided hike of approximately 20 kilometers (12 miles). Conducted July through mid-September, the hikes can be popular, and reservations, made through the Yoho National Park Information Centre (*see* Visitor Information, *above*), are recommended.

Travelers just looking for an easily accessible nook of relative seclusion should continue on to **Emerald Lake,** a short drive from Route 1. Stroll around the lake (vivid green, as its name suggests), rent a canoe, have a cup of tea at the teahouse, or, if one day isn't enough, spend a night in the fine lodge (*see* Lodging, *below*). Although some tour buses do stop here, Emerald Lake rarely sees crowds comparable to those at stops nearer Banff.

HISTORIC BUILDINGS AND SITES These parks have few historic sites, the presence of settlers in this part of the world being a relatively new phenomenon. The most familiar landmark in the parks is the **Banff Springs Hotel,** worth a visit just to experience the nonstop activity it embraces.

Cave and Basin Centennial Centre, a recently renovated historic building, is on the first site to be given national-park protection (in 1885) after the discovery of hot springs by prospectors in 1883. Of course, long before human beings showed up there were other creatures and the land itself—as evidenced by the **Burgess Shale site** in Yoho National Park, where fossilized remains date back more than 500 million years.

NATURE TRAILS AND SHORT WALKS The twin trails at the **Cave and Basin Centennial Centre** are easy strolls, with signs along the way giving information about regional geology, flora, and fauna. The annotated nature trail encircling **Emerald Lake** is particularly interesting due to the considerably different climate zones and the vegetation on the eastern and western sides of the lake. Twenty-two kilometers (13½ miles) east of Emerald Lake is the **Lake O'Hara** area, accessible only by shuttle bus (*see* Exploring, *above*), and featuring several relatively easy trails in the 3-kilometer (2-mile) range among rock-walled mountains and high-alpine lakes.

The short (3½ kilometers, 2¼ miles) but somewhat steep hike to the **Lake Agnes teahouse,** which seems to hang at the edge of a tiny, mountain-ringed lake, is among the most popular near Lake Louise, as is the somewhat longer (5½ kilometer, 3⅓-mile) hike to the teahouse at the **Plain of the Six Glaciers.** The Lake Agnes hike is a jaunt through the woods; the Six Glaciers hike leads out of the woods onto open glacial moraine. Expect plenty of company on both hikes.

The 2⅖-kilometer (1½-mile) **Parker Ridge trail,** the trailhead just a few kilometers south of the Icefield Centre on Route 93N, offers another opportunity to enjoy high-mountain terrain—with exceptional glacier and icefield views and a minimum amount of effort. The trail is somewhat less traveled than those mentioned around Lake Louise, perhaps because most travelers are rushing on to the Icefield Centre or Jasper.

LONGER HIKES There are over 1,900 kilometers (1,100 miles) of hiking trails in the three parks—maintained hiking trails, that is, since the figure doesn't include the limitless opportunities for scrambling and bushwhacking. The hiking season runs from mid-May into November, the season being shorter on higher trails that may be snow-covered except in summer.

The suggestions here are merely a sampler, one wholly inadequate to do the vast trail system justice. Anyone interested in hiking or backpacking in the parks should get a copy of *The Canadian Rockies Trail Guide*, by Brian Patton and Bart Robinson, widely available in bookshops and gift shops in the area. For hikers sticking to the trails, maps and compasses are optional, since most trails are well maintained and well marked.

For day hikers, the **Lake Louise/Moraine Lake** area offers many exceptional, though well-traveled trails. The trail network connecting the two lakes, with a few fairly steep ups and downs, passes through aptly named Paradise Valley. Day hikers seeking more solitude in Banff National Park are more likely to find it farther north, between **Bow Pass** and the Banff-Jasper boundary. Two worthwhile hikes are the trip to **Nigel Pass,** of moderate difficulty, and the trip to **Sunset Pass,** which is grindingly steep in places. Yoho and Kootenay trails offer better opportunities for escaping the crowds, though some, such as those in the **Yoho River valley,** are quite popular. In Kootenay, the longish round-trip (21 kilometers, 13 miles) to **Floe Lake** from Route 93 is one of the parks' most rewarding.

Backpackers must pick up backcountry-use permits from the nearest visitor center or warden station. Among the best known (hence most populous) backpacking areas are the aforementioned Paradise Valley, the **Skoki Valley** beyond the Lake Louise ski area, and the **Egypt Lake** area beyond Sunshine Village, a lake-dotted high-alpine zone not unlike the Lake O'Hara area. The fact that the Sunshine gondola, which gave less-energetic hikers a quick lift on their way to Egypt Lake, no longer runs in summer might discourage a few backpackers, but don't count on it.

Perhaps the classic, multiday backpacking hike in the area is the rugged **Rockwall Trail** in Kootenay, leading to the Lake O'Hara area in Yoho. The total trip is more than 60 kilometers (40 miles) of considerable ups and downs. Most backpackers do the trail in shorter sections via spurs from Route 93, the choice destinations along the route being Floe Lake, the Rockwall, and tumbling Glacier.

OTHER ACTIVITIES **Back-Road Driving.** Virtually the only way to get off the main highways, Routes 1 and 93, is by foot, horseback, or bike. Nevertheless, if you tire of the big roads and the traffic they attract, there are a few options. Route 1A, running roughly parallel to Route 1, is a slower-paced way to travel between Banff and Lake Louise. Tunnel Mountain Drive offers a quick respite from the bustle of Banff, with various pull-offs for views and photos. In Yoho, many travelers turn off the road at either the Spiral Tunnels viewing point or Takakkaw Falls, but just a bit farther west on Route 1 is the 8-kilometer (5-mile) road to Emerald Lake, a prettier sidetrip.

Biking. The three parks are not especially inspiring for road touring, which is mostly a matter of cycling on the shoulders of the major highways. In recent years, mountain biking has become popular on some hiking trails. Predictably, this has led to disputes among bikers and backpackers. Park officials have been trying to keep the peace by publishing a list of trails (available from the Banff Visitor Centre) on which biking is permitted. Current trail information is posted in the visitor centers at Banff and Lake Louise. Bikes can be rented from **Park and Pedal Bike Shop** (229 Wolf St., tel. 403/762–3191) in Banff.

Several operators offer guided on-road and off-road bike tours. **Rocky Mountain Cycle Tours** (Box 1987, Canmore, AB T0L 0M0, tel. 403/678–6770) features one- to seven-day tours in the Banff area.

Bird-Watching. The 223 species of bird in the park make sightings common; one needn't leave the roadways to spot the many opportunistic scavenger birds, such as jays, magpies, ravens, and crows. Vermilion Lakes are a popular pit stop for migratory fowl, including Canada geese. The parkland is also classic terrain for birds of prey (including hawks, eagles, and owls), many of whom do their preying along open scree (erosion-debris)

slopes, feeding on the rodents that nestle in the rocks.

Boating. Although there are many rivers, lakes, and streams within the parks, few are large enough to support substantial boating activity. The exception is Lake Minnewanka, just 11$^{1}/_{2}$ kilometers (7 miles) from Banff. In addition to tours, **Lake Minnewanka Boat Tours** (Box 2189, Banff, AB T0L 0C0, tel. 403/762–3473) offers boat and canoe rentals. Boats and canoes can also be rented at Emerald Lake in Yoho, and canoes are available at Lake Louise and Moraine Lake in Banff.

Fishing. Various trout species are the principal game fish in the lakes, rivers, and streams of the Canadian Rockies. Their cousins, grayling and salmon, can also be caught. Keep in mind that higher, glacier-fed lakes, rich in glacial silt, usually don't provide very good fishing. The Bow, Kicking Horse, and Kootenay rivers tend to see a lot of action. Information on fishing regulations is available at the visitor center in Banff. A basic, six-day fishing license for non-Canadians is $21; an annual license is $33. Note that separate licenses are required for fishing in Alberta and British Columbia. For more information on licenses, contact the **Ministry of Environment & Parks** (Fish & Wildlife Branch, 780 Blanchard St., Victoria, BC V8V 1X4, tel. 604/387–4573).

Horseback Riding. Trail riding is more restricted in these three parks than it is in Jasper, in nearby Kananaskis Country, and in the mountainous regions surrounding the parks. For that reason, most outfitters operate outside the parks. In its "Adventure Guide," Alberta Tourism lists several reputable outfitters in the area. Other information can be obtained from the **Guide-Outfitters Association** (Box 759, 100 Mile House, BC V0K 2E0, tel. 604/395–2438).

For daily rides and riding instruction, arrangements can be made through the sports desks at Banff Springs Hotel, Chateau Lake Louise, and Emerald Lake Lodge (*see* Lodging, *below*). Arrangements can also be made through **Brewster Stables** (Box 2280, Banff, AB T0L 0C0, tel. 403/762–2832).

Rafting. Trips on the Bow river in Banff, either half-day or full-day, are leisurely, scenic floats, while trips on the Kicking Horse River in Yoho, especially in June when the river is swollen with snowmelt, tend to be more rollicking. For Bow River trips, contact **Rocky Mountain Raft Tours** (Box 1771, Banff, AB T0L 0C0, tel. 403/762–3632); for Kicking Horse River trips, contact **Alpine Rafting Company** (Box 1409, Golden, BC V0A 1H0, tel. 604/344–5016).

Rock Climbing. Great climbs in the park are far too numerous to mention, although the highest peaks—for example, Mt. Temple (11,624 feet)—tend to be considered the classics. Routes can be chosen to include rock climbing, ice climbing, glacier travel, scrambling, or any combination thereof. It is this variety that has lured many Alpine mountaineers to settle in this region.

Many of the Alpine transplants now ply a trade as mountain guides, so there is no shortage of experienced excursion leaders. It's strongly urged that prospective climbers, especially those not familiar with glacier travel, hook up with a guide service. Whether on independent or guided trips, all climbing parties must have permits, available at park warden offices. Climbing is a year-round activity in the Canadian Rockies, although October and November, before icefalls are solid enough to climb, are probably the least desirable months.

The **Canadian School of Mountaineering** (629 10 St., Box 723, Canmore, AB T0L 0M0, tel. 403/678–4134) and **Banff Alpine Guides** (Box 1025, Banff, AB T0L 0C0, tel. 403/762–2791) conduct trips in the parks for climbers of all ability levels. Membership in the **Alpine Club of Canada** (Box 1026, Banff, AB T0L 0C0, tel. 403/678–6091) is also worth considering. The club maintains several backcountry huts in and around the parks and also organizes and leads group climbs.

Skiing. There are three lift-serviced ski areas in Banff National Park: **Lake Louise** (across Rte. 1 from the village of Lake Louise, tel. 403/522–3555), **Mt. Norquay** (on Mt. Norquay Rd., across Rte. 1 from the town of Banff, tel. 403/762–4421), and **Sunshine Village** (on the Sunshine Village Rd., 8 km [5 mi] west of Banff on Rte. 1, tel. 403/762–6500 or 800/661–1363). Lake Louise has the largest variety of terrain; Sunshine features generally moderately pitched, open-bowl skiing; and Mt. Norquay is known for its steepness, although recently installed lifts have helped to expand the intermediate terrain.

Ski Touring. From track skiing to ski mountaineering, the opportunities are limitless. For track skiers, December through March tend to be the best months; after that the snow on the lower-elevation flats starts deteriorating. Backcountry touring tends to be better later in the season (February through April), when temperatures begin warming and snow tends to be (though is not necessarily) more stable with regard to avalanche danger.

Although technically not in the parks, the **Canmore Nordic Centre** (Box 1979, Canmore, AB T0L 0M0, tel. 403/678–2400), 30 kilometers (18 miles) east of Banff, must be noted. Site of the 1988 Olympic cross-country events, the center is among the best anywhere in North America. Approximately 60 kilometers (36 miles) of trails are groomed both for traditional skiing and skating, linking with an extensive ungroomed network. Some trails are lit for night skiing, and, perhaps best of all, there is no trail fee. Groomed tracks (and rental equipment) can also be found near the Banff Springs Hotel and Chateau Lake Louise.

One of the most popular backcountry tours is to Skoki Lodge, 12 kilometers (7¹/₂ miles) from the base of the Lake Louise ski area. The skiing is over generally moderate terrain, with consistently good views. Mt. Assiniboine Lodge, which is in Mt. Assiniboine Provincial Park, and Lake O'Hara Lodge are other popular ski-touring centers (*see* Lodging, *below*). The high country near Bow Pass also has a number of local adherents.

Anyone who ventures into the backcountry should keep in mind that avalanche hazards are considerable. (Avalanche danger information is available at visitor centers and warden offices or by calling 403/762–1460.) One way to lessen backcountry risk is to sign on with a local guide service. The **Canadian School of Mountaineering** and **Banff Alpine Guides** (*see* Rock Climbing, *above*) both lead backcountry tours in the area. The best place in Banff to rent such equipment as cross-country skis, mountaineering skis, and climbing skins is **Mountain Magic** (224 Bear St., tel. 403/762–2591).

Snowmobiling. Snowmobiling, other than for service or emergency purposes, is prohibited in the parks.

Swimming. Cold is the word here. The northerly latitude and the glacial sources of most lakes and rivers make for chilly dipping. The obvious exceptions are the hot-spring–fed pools, though these are obviously intended more for soaking than swimming. The largest of these is the **Radium Hot Springs Pools** in Kootenay (full day: $5.25 adults, $3.25 children 16 and under; half day: $2.75 adults, $1.75 children). The **Upper Hot Springs Pool** (tel. 403/762–1515) is the place to soak in Banff. Suits, towels, and lockers are for rent, and hours vary with the seasons.

CHILDREN'S PROGRAMS With all of the hiking, biking, boating, horseback riding, canoeing, and so on, the three parks could be thought of as a giant camp for children. In addition to the **Banff Park Museum** and **Lake Louise Visitor Centre** (*see* Orientation Programs, *above*), the **Luxton Museum** (1 Birch Ave., Banff, tel. 403/762–2388) is worth a visit with young children. Although the wax-museum format might seem a little hokey, the museum provides some sense of Native American life in the region during the pre-park era.

Outside the national-parks boundaries, **Fort Steele Heritage Park** (16 km [10 mi] northeast of Cranbrook on Rte. 93–95, tel. 604/426–6923) is well worth visiting, especially for travelers arriving from the south. The authentically reconstructed pioneer town is a step back into the 1890s and the glory days of silver and lead mining.

EVENING ACTIVITIES For those most interested in cultural life, **The Banff Centre** (tel. 403/762–6100) is the place in the parks to go for music (classical to pop), dance, and drama.

DINING

BANFF **Le Beaujolais.** In casual Banff, this is the place to find big-city elegance. It can come across as a bit stuffy, but that does nothing to diminish its popularity. Tapestries on the wall give the restaurant a hint of baronial splendor, and the richness of the food is a match for the setting. Traditional French preparations of beef, veal, and duck are featured menu items. *212 Buffalo St. (corner of Banff Ave.), tel. 403/762–2712. Reservations required. Jacket required. AE, MC, V. Dinner only. Very Expensive.*

Giorgio's. This is two restaurants in one: **La Pasta,** a casual spot, is downstairs; the more formal **La Casa** is upstairs. La Pasta is by far the more popular, especially with a young local crowd, who come for the reliably good food, moderate prices, and the warm atmosphere of the dimly lit, tavern-style room. Pasta dishes and small pizzas are the main menu items. La Casa serves more classical Italian fare (veal scallopini, for example) in a romantic, under-the-eaves setting. The main drawback is La Pasta's no-reservations policy; because the restaurant entryway is small, the wait for a table (which can be long during busy periods) can get cramped. *219 Banff Ave., tel. 403/762–5116 (La Casa), 403/762–5114 (La Pasta). Reservations recommended for La Casa. Dress: casual but neat. AE, DC, MC, V. Dinner only. Moderate (La Pasta)–Expensive (La Casa).*

Melissa's Missteak. Behind an ersatz-German-bierhaus facade is an ersatz-log-cabin interior. Any Banff restaurant that serves decent food at fair prices for three meals a day is apt to be popular with families, and so this one is. What's more, an upstairs lounge with video games, TV monitors, and popcorn offers good diversionary fodder for kids. Steaks are the predominant dinner-menu item, although deep-dish pizza is a house specialty. *218 Lynx St., tel. 403/762–5511. Reservations advised for dinner. Dress: casual. AE, MC, V. Moderate.*

Barbary Coast. This sports-theme restaurant with neo-California cuisine has fast become a local favorite. The plant-filled, skylighted dining room is filled with sports paraphernalia—signed race bibs from skiers, hockey skates, old bikes, and more. Pizzas with creative toppings and such oddities as the Einstein Theory Salad (chicken, bananas, and sprouts in a curry dressing) highlight an eclectic menu. Live bands play in the bar (separate from the restaurant) after 9 PM on weekends. *119 Banff Ave., upstairs, tel. 403/762–4616. Reservations for parties of 6 or more only. Dress: casual. AE, MC, V. Inexpensive–Moderate.*

Joe Btfsplk's Diner. It's either fun, camp, or overbearing, depending on your taste. This is a re-created '50s-style diner, with red-vinyl banquettes and chrome-trimmed tables. The menu is right out of the true-American cookbook: eggs and biscuits for breakfast, meat loaf and hash for dinner. Fresh-baked cookies and muffins, available for takeout, are a nice bonus. *221 Banff Ave., tel. 403/762–5529. No reservations. Dress: casual. AE, MC, V. Inexpensive.*

LAKE LOUISE **Post Hotel.** The hotel restaurant is cited in almost every guide and magazine article as one of the true epicurean experiences in the Canadian Rockies. The atmosphere is a mix of farm-home rustic (exposed beams, stone hearth) and citified elegance (tables adorned with fanned, white-linen napkins). Traditional European dishes—with veal and venison the house specialties—are combined with a lighter, California influence. Homemade pastries cap off the meal or can be had earlier (2 PM–5 PM) at tea in the hotel lobby. By Canadian Rockies standards, the service can be overly formal. *Box 69, 200 Pipestone, tel. 403/522–3989. Dress: dressy casual; jacket recommended at dinner. AE, MC, V. Very Expensive.*

Chateau Lake Louise. Five restaurants present an array of options, from light snacking to full-blown, night-on-the-town elegance. Dining in most cases defers to the view of the Lake Louise and Victoria Glacier. The château is perhaps best known—and recommended—

for its meal between meals: afternoon tea in the Lakeside Lounge. Scones, pastries, croissants, and more—along with coffee and tea, of course—are welcome after a day of mountain activities. *Lake Louise Dr., tel. 403/522–3511, ext. 52. Reservations necessary for dinner in summer. Dress: casual at lunch; jacket required at dinner in some areas. AE, DC, MC, V. Moderate–Very Expensive.*

Laggan's Mountain Bakery and Deli. For morning coffee, this small deli-bakery at the Samson Mall is the place where park wardens, mountain guides, and local work crews congregate. Thus, it's a nice place to pick up not only fresh-baked goods (muffins and poppy-seed bread) but a little inside information on what's up in the parks as well. This is a good choice for picnic sandwiches for a hike around Lake Louise or for the drive north along the Icefields Parkway. *Samson Mall, tel. 403/522–2017. Dress: casual. No credit cards. Inexpensive.*

YOHO **Emerald Lake Lodge.** The dining room is a glass-enclosed terrace with views of the lake through tall stands of evergreens. The furnishings are eclectic, some tables with upholstered chairs, some with straight-backs, all evoking a funky-old-lodge atmosphere. Also eclectic is the menu, which mixes familiar Canadian and American fare—steaks, game, fish—with esoteric touches (including ginger-tangerine glaze). More often than not, the odd combos are effective. Salads, quiches, and baked cheeses are served in the dining room and in the lounge area around a giant stone hearth. The lodge also serves an excellent breakfast and lunch. *8 km (5mi) north of Field, tel. 604/343–6321. Reservations recommended, especially for dinner in summer. Dress: dressy casual. AE, MC, V. Moderate–Expensive.*

PICNIC SPOTS A hike of a mile or less gives you a choice of thousands of secluded, scenic picnic spots. If you're not eager to hike, though, picnic sites with tables are numerous along the major roadways. Some of the prettier spots are near Hector Lake, just south of Bow Pass (only on fair-weather days); along the Kicking Horse River beyond Field in

Yoho; and between Vermilion Pass and Vermilion Crossing and at Olive Lake in Kootenay.

LODGING

Finding a place to stay in and around Banff and Lake Louise is not difficult. There are more than 40 hotels, inns, and lodges in and around the park, not including bed-and-breakfasts. Finding reasonably priced lodging can be another story. Travelers on a budget should consider the more moderately priced lodging in Canmore, a 25-minute drive east of Banff. Budget-minded travelers should also avoid the June 15–September 15 peak period, when room rates are typically 25% to 75% higher than during the rest of the year. For basic lodging information, both Alberta Tourism and Tourism British Columbia (*see* Visitor Information, *above*) publish excellent accommodations guides.

Bed-and-breakfast accommodations are plentiful in and around the national parks, but don't expect the quaint-old-home atmosphere you might find elsewhere in North America. Most B&Bs in this part of the world are simply ordinary rooms in ordinary homes, price rather than atmosphere usually being the main attraction. Two agencies that handle bookings in the area are: **Alberta Bed & Breakfast** (Mrs. June Brown, Box 15477, Vancouver, BC V6B 5B2, tel. 604/682–4610) and **Bed and Breakfast Bureau** (Mr. Don Sinclair & Associates, Box 7094, Station "E," Calgary, AB T3C 3L8, tel. 403/242–5555, or Box 369, Banff, AB T0L 0C0, tel. 403/762–5070).

Note also that there are many **guest ranches** near the national parks. Information on guest ranches is included in Alberta Tourism's "Accommodations Guide" and "Adventure Guide." Similarly, publications listing guest ranches are available from Tourism British Columbia. Guest-ranch information can also be obtained from the **Guide-Outfitters Association** (Box 759, 100 Mile House, BC V0K 2E0, tel. 604/395–2438). There is also a hostel network in the parks; for information contact the **Alberta Hosteling Association** (Southern Alberta District, #203, 1414 Kensington Rd. NW, Calgary, AB T2N 3P9, tel. 403/283–5551).

■BANFF■ Banff Springs Hotel. This is the original—the fortresslike hotel, first built in 1888—that established Banff as a tourist destination. The massive, stone-wall hotel is a world of its own, a seemingly endless maze of hallways, stairwells, huge sitting areas, and banquet rooms, with stone, dark wood, and chandeliers abounding. Surprisingly small is the lobby, which can get backed up with guests and luggage at peak check-in times. The layout is both fun and wearying: The orienteering skills of even the most adept adventurer will be challenged; and getting lost, at some point, is a given for all guests. Old-hotel details, such as high ceilings and rattling windows, give the establishment its charm. The hotel is a perpetual, 20-ring circus, anything but a getaway mountain retreat. *Spray Ave., Box 960, Banff, AB T0L 0C0; tel. 403/762–2211 or 800/268–9411. 760 rooms, 69 suites. Facilities: 17 pubs and restaurants, 24-hour room service, meal plans available, cable TV, more than 40 shops and boutiques, health club, tennis courts, riding stables, 27 holes of golf. AE, DC, MC, V. Very Expensive.*

Buffalo Mountain Lodge. The lobby area, with lots of polished pine and exposed, rough-hewn beams, is dominated by a large stone hearth with a buffalo head over the mantel. The layout consists of a main lodge, with lobby and restaurant; a hotel-condo cluster built in 1987; and an older group of chalet buildings. Newer rooms are dressed in pastel shades and have small fireplaces, wicker chairs, and pine cabinetry. Older chalet units are larger, with two bedrooms, and similarly decorated. Although the lodge sits off a high road on the outskirts of Banff, few rooms have views. *Tunnel Mountain Rd., Box 1326, Banff, AB T0L 0C0, tel. 403/762–2400 or 800/661–1367. 85 units, including hotel rooms and 2-bedroom condos. Facilities: cable TV, steam room, hot tub. AE, MC, V. Expensive.*

Storm Mountain Lodge. Built as a backcountry lodge in the 1920s, Storm Mountain is hardly "backcountry" today; Route 93 now passes by the lodge's doorstep on its way through Vermilion Pass. Once you're inside, though, the lodge's roots in tradition are evident in the sitting area, dominated by a large fireplace and the head of a bighorn sheep. The dining area embodies the elegance of simplicity: straight-back wood chairs and white tablecloths on an enclosed porch overlooking the pass. Bedrooms, in separate cabins tucked in the woods, are small but made cozy by fireplaces, old lamps, and down comforters. The lodge is open from late May to early September. *Rte. 93, 4.8 km (3 mi) west of the Rte. 1 interchange, Box 670, Banff, AB T0L 0C0, tel. 403/762–4155. 12 cabins. Facilities: restaurant, immediate access to hiking trails. AE, MC, V. Moderate–Expensive.*

Mt. Assiniboine Lodge. This is another of the original backcountry lodges of the Canadian Rockies. First built in 1928, it is in Mt. Assiniboine Provincial Park, just west of Banff, in a spectacular setting—across Lake Magog from the mountain you may tire of hearing called the Matterhorn of the Canadian Rockies. The log-cabin lodge rooms feature sturdy wood beds covered by down comforters lush enough to disappear in. Opportunities abound for terrific hikes, climbs, and ski tours (unlike Skoki, the lodge does offer a guide service). Guests can hike or ski to the lodge, but there is also helicopter service two days a week. The summer season runs from late June through September; the winter season runs from early February through April. *For reservations: Sepp and Barb Renner, Box 1527, Canmore, AB T0L 0M0, tel. 403/678–2883 or 403/762–5075. Accommodations for 28 in 6 lodge rooms and outlying cabins with propane heat and lights. 3 meals daily and guide service included. Facilities: ski rentals available, sauna, running water in summer, some electricity in summer and winter. No credit cards. Inexpensive–Moderate.*

Red Carpet Inn. This is one of the few moderately priced lodging options in downtown Banff. The inn is basically no-frills: the lobby consists of a desk, an office, and a postcard stand. The motel-style rooms are small, but by Banff standards, so are the prices, slightly below those of the neighboring High Country Inn. Rooms in back, away from Banff Avenue traffic noise, are preferable. *425 Banff Ave., Box 1800, Banff, AB T0L 0C0, tel. 403/762–4184. 46 rooms. Facilities: satellite TV, indoor pool, whirlpool. AE, MC, V. Inexpensive–Moderate.*

Skoki Lodge. You might think a 12-kilometer (7¹/₂-mile) hike (or ski) to a lodge without electricity or running water wouldn't be most people's cup of tea. Yet reservations for this basic lodge must often be made months in advance, especially for weekends. Yet another of the original Canadian Rockies lodges, this one was built of chiseled logs in 1931. There have been additions since, largely in the form of outlying cabins, but the log-cabin motif makes everything seem of the same age. Fill an exposed-log living room with a fireplace, piano, books, and kerosene lamps, and you have just about all that a backcountry lodge is supposed to be. One shortcoming: The lodge offers no hiking or ski-touring guide service. *Reservations through Skiing Louise, Ltd., Box 5, Lake Louise, AB T0L 1E0, tel. 403/522–3555. Reservations must be made in advance. Accommodations for 22 in lodge and cabins with wood-burning stoves; 3 meals a day included. Facilities: sauna. AE, MC, V. Inexpensive–Moderate.*

LAKE LOUISE **Chateau Lake Louise.** Terraces and lawns spread down to the famous aquamarine lake, with the Victoria Glacier as a backdrop. Large, horseshoe-shape windows make the dramatic exterior seem almost a part of the interior, which has been extensively renovated during the past five years. Burgundy and brass and neo-Colonial furnishings lend an appropriately grand-hotel atmosphere, and some guest rooms feature such nice touches as hand-painted floral designs on the doors and cabinetry. In terms of high-quality accommodations, the château is hard to beat in the Canadian Rockies. Unfortunately, it suffers from a circus-in-a-train-station busyness, this being the main Lake Louise stop for tour-bus groups. *Lake Louise Dr., Lake Louise, AB T0L 1E0, tel. 403/522–3511 or 800/268–9411. 515 rooms and suites. Facilities: 5 restaurants, indoor pool, canoe-*

ing, riding stables, whirlpool, steam room, exercise room, more than 20 shops. AE, DC, MC, V. Very Expensive.

Post Hotel. This hotel has the feel of a modern rendition of the country-lodge concept, with a heavy emphasis on gold-color siding and trim in the decor. Rooms come in 15 configurations (and price schemes), from standard doubles to units with sleeping lofts, kitchens, and fireplaces. Bathrooms are large, and most are equipped with whirlpool tubs. Rooms facing away from the highway have good views of Mt. Temple. The restaurant (see Dining, above) is regularly rated as one of the best in the Canadian Rockies. Box 69, Lake Louise, AB T0L 1E0, tel. 403/522–3989 or 800/661–1586. 93 units, some sleeping 6 people. Facilities: cable TV, indoor pool, whirlpool. AE, MC, V. Expensive.

Lake Louise Inn. This five-building complex offers a variety of accommodations, primarily motel rooms and two-bedroom condo units. A three-story building, with 12 one-room suites and 24 motel-style rooms, was completed in 1991 to further expand the array of lodging options. For economy-minded travelers, the Pinery, a separate 56-room building, offers few frills but comfortable accommodations. 210 Village Rd., Box 209, Lake Louise, AB T0L 1E0, tel. 403/522–3791 or 800/661–9237. 222 rooms and condo units. Facilities: restaurant, pub, cable TV, indoor pool, sauna, whirlpool, exercise room. AE, D, DC, MC, V. Moderate.

CANMORE **Rocky Mountain Ski Lodge.** In terms of facilities and price, several motels in Canmore are interchangeable as lower-price alternatives to Banff accommodations. Rocky Mountain Ski Lodge (formerly the Skiland Motel) is a notch above the rest. One reason is that it is comprised of three neighboring lodging establishments under one management. The newer of the two motel properties offers the better accommodations; slanting, exposed wood-beam ceilings give a chaletlike feeling to the otherwise simple motel rooms. Rooms in the older units have kitchenettes. Most recently added to this lodging complex are condo units in what was formerly Rocky

Mountain Chalets. Rte. 1A, Box 696, Canmore, AB T0L 0M0, tel. 403/678–5445. 82 units. Facilities: steam room, exercise room, playground, cable TV. MC, V. Moderate.

KOOTENAY **Kootenay Park Lodge.** In the center of the park, at Vermilion Crossing, this complex of cabins is in a wooded area 45 minutes southwest of Banff, 45 minutes southeast of Lake Louise, and 40 minutes north of Radium Hot Springs. The real log cabins here are surrounded by fir and spruce trees. You can choose one with a queen-size and double bed, a kitchen, and a fireplace, or opt for a simple cabin with double bed only. Unlike other cabin lodgings, the Kootenay Park Lodge has hot water and private showers. All the beds were replaced in 1992. There's a stream nearby for fishing, and lots of hiking trails in the area. Rte. 93 in center of Kootenay, Box 1390, Banff, ALTA T0L 0C0, tel. 403/762–9196. 10 cabins. Facilities: restaurant, library, grocery store, gas station. MC, V. Closed Oct.–early May. Moderate.

YOHO **Emerald Lake Lodge.** A cross between hotel and mountain lodge, this is an enchanted place. Cottages surround the log-cabin main lodge, all set at the edge of a secluded, glacier-fed lake. The 1/4-mile road from the parking lot is restricted to shuttle-van and foot traffic. A sitting area in the main lodge has overstuffed chairs and small tables for light meals around a large, stone hearth. There is also a full bar and an excellent restaurant (see Dining, above) on a glass-enclosed porch. All rooms have fireplaces, and many have balconies with lake views. 8 km (5 mi) north of Field, BC; Box 10, Field BC, V0A 1G0, tel. 604/343–6321 or 800/663–6336. 85 rooms in 24 2- and 4-room cottages. Facilities: restaurant, bar; clubhouse with exercise room, game room, sauna, and outdoor hot tub; teahouse with outdoor deck open in summer; boat rentals, riding stables. AE, MC, V. Expensive.

Lake O'Hara Lodge. This is the lodge for people who like being in a backcountry setting but who aren't keen on things like outhouses and gas lamps. Most of the rooms and cabins have private baths, and the restaurant features à la carte dining (not the one-sitting, family-style dining common to backcountry lodges), with such items on its dinner menu as duck in cherry sauce and chocolate mousse. The lodge, due west from Lake Louise, is in one of the most scenic and popular hiking and climbing areas in the Canadian Rockies, meaning it gets fairly active in the summer. (Reservations for midsummer should be booked several months in advance.) Lodge guests are ferried in by bus along an 11-kilometer (7-mile) fire road between Route 1 and the lodge (other vehicles aren't permitted). In winter, guests must ski to the lodge. *Off Rte. 1 in Yoho National Park, Box 55, Lake Louise, AB T0L 1E0, tel. 604/343–6442 or 403/762–2118 during off-season. 23 units in lodge and cabins. Facilities: restaurant, hiking, climbing, canoeing. MC, V. Closed May, Oct.–Nov. Moderate–Expensive.*

CAMPING

There are more than 20 drive-in campgrounds and 40 designated backcountry campgrounds in the three parks, offering a range of camping options.

In Banff National Park, Tunnel Mountain features three drive-in campgrounds at the edge of the Banff town-site: **Trailer Court**, **Village 1**, and **Village 2**. Convenience is the big asset here; you're just a few minutes from downtown Banff. Similarly, **Lake Louise Campground** offers convenient access to the sites and scenery of Lake Louise, even if the setting itself is not especially scenic.

For more-woodsy privacy, **Johnston Canyon,** on Route 1A between Banff and Lake Louise, is a good place to pull into. There are, however, no hookups.

Two Jack Main, relatively close to the town of Banff, is southwest of Lake Minnewanka. This is a large campground with flush toilets and drinking water but no showers.

Kootenay National Park is a good choice for campers who want to be removed from the settlements of Banff, Lake Louise, and Ra-

dium Hot Springs but who don't want to be far from the action. The **Marble Canyon** campground, closer to Banff, sits alongside the Vermilion River, with mountain ranges rising steeply on either side. The landscape surrounding **McLeod Meadows,** which is closer to Radium Hot Springs, is in the more-open valley of the Kootenay River. Neither campground has hookups. For those, you'll have to stay at **Redstreak**, where there are 242 sites (100 hookups) set in a wooded area near Radium Hot Springs.

More removed from the main park action is **Kicking Horse** campground in Yoho. The campground, alongside the broad, alluvial deposits of the Kicking Horse River, offers good views of the Yoho mountain ranges. Lake Louise is about a half-hour's drive away. If Kicking Horse is full and you don't feel like hiking, Yoho's **Hoodoo Creek** and **Chancellor Peak** campgrounds have drive-in sites. Neither of these has hookups or showers, but Hoodoo Creek does have flush toilets and a disposal station.

Two of the prettiest and most popular spots for backcountry camping in Banff are **Paradise Valley** and **Egypt lakes.** Paradise Valley is just around the corner (as in a few miles around the corner) from Lake Louise; the Upper Meadows campground is a fairly easy 8-kilometer (5-mile) hike from the Paradise Creek parking lot. Egypt Lake is just one of a half-dozen small lakes reached by hiking from the Sunshine Village ski area parking lot. The lake-and-tundra setting is the essence of high-alpine Banff, although if you like your scenery in solitude, avoid the area on summer weekends.

It's hard to imagine a more spectacular campground setting than **Floe Lake,** a small lake lying hard against a 3,000-foot rock wall in Kootenay. Multiday campers can also connect with the equally spectacular, though rugged, Rockwall trail, where there are three other backcountry campgrounds.

Lake O'Hara in Yoho isn't quite the backcountry; there is a lodge here and a daily bus to carry lodgers (and campers, if they wish) along the 11-kilometer (7-mile) fire road con-

BANFF, YOHO, AND KOOTENAY CAMPGROUNDS

Campground	Total number of sites	Sites suitable for RVs	Number of hookups	Drive to sites	Hike to sites	Flush toilets	Pit/chemical toilets	Drinking water	Showers	Fire grates	Swimming	Boat access	Playground	Disposal station	Ranger station	Public telephone	Reservation possible	Daily fee per site*	Dates open
INSIDE BANFF																			
Tunnel Mountain Trailer Court	320	320	320	•		•		•	•					•¹		•		$17.50	mid-May–late Sept.
Tunnel Mountain Village 1	620	620	0	•		•		•	•	•				•		•		$13	mid-May–late Sept.
Tunnel Mountain Village 2	223	188	188	•		•		•	•					•¹		•		$15.50	year-round
Lake Louise	405	189	189	•		•		•	•	•						•		$11.75–$14	year-round
Johnston Canyon	132	132	0	•		•		•		•								$13	mid-May–early Sept.
Two Jack Main	381	381	0	•		•		•		•								$10.50	late June–Labor Day (Fri., Sat., and Sun.)
INSIDE YOHO																			
Hoodoo Creek	106	60	0	•		•		•		•			•	•				$10.50	late June–early Sept.
Chancellor Peak	58	58	0	•			•	•		•								$7.25	early May–mid-Oct.
Kicking Horse	86	50	0	•		•		•	•	•			•	•				$13	mid-May–late Sept.
Lake O'Hara	30	0	0		•		•	•		•					•		•²	$7.25	mid-June–late Sept.
INSIDE KOOTENAY																			
Redstreak	242	242	100	•		•		•	•	•			•	•		•		$13–17.50	mid-May–mid-Sept.
Marble Canyon	60	60	0	•		•		•		•				•				$10.50	mid-June–Labor Day
McLeod Meadows	98	98	0	•		•		•		•		•		•				$10.50	mid-May–mid-Sept.

*Canadian dollars. ¹Tunnel Mountain Trailer Court and Village 2 share a disposal station. ²By reservation only (tel. 403/343–6433).

necting the lake and the Trans-Canada Highway. So camping here might not exactly offer backcountry privacy, but the many short dayhikes in this high-alpine world still make this a great spot to spend a night or three.

On the other side of the Trans-Canada Highway in Yoho are **Twin Falls** and **Little Yoho Valley** campground. A small chalet built in the 1920s near Twin Falls gives that area a slightly more civilized feeling than Little Yoho Valley. The falls are indeed quite a sight, and a day excursion from the campground to the Yoho Glacier is a must. The Little Yoho Valley campground is more secluded, lying on a small meadow near the base of the President Glacier. Even during midsummer, the 10-site campground doesn't usually fill up.

Big Bend National Park
Texas
By Kirby F. Warnock

The Wild West may be no more than a page in history books, but in Big Bend National Park you are reminded that it wasn't so long ago that outlaws and Native Americans roamed the countryside along the Rio Grande. The park remains rugged and remote, preserving a frontier spirit inherited from the Native Americans, cavalrymen, smugglers, cowboys, and Mexican revolutionaries who once called this patch of southwest Texas home.

The Comanches passed through this area each September before swooping across the Rio Grande for their annual raid on Mexican villages and *rancherias*. In the 1800s Big Bend received some more-permanent tenants: A handful of hardy ranching families settled here and proceeded to scrape a living from the unforgiving countryside. Later, during Prohibition, the border along the Rio Grande became a favorite route for bootleggers smuggling mescal and tequila into the

country, and between 1914 and 1917 General John J. "Blackjack" Pershing's attempts to catch the notorious Mexican revolutionary Pancho Villa were centered here. Between 1933 and 1944 Texas acquired the land that was to become Big Bend and donated it to the federal government. Big Bend National Park was established on June 12, 1944.

Named for the bend in the Rio Grande where the park is located, Big Bend spreads over 1,252 rugged square miles. It is more than 230 miles from the nearest airport and more than 100 miles from a town of any considerable size. You cannot fly into the park or arrive by bus or train—the only way to get here is by car, bicycle, or on foot. The terrain in Big Bend is surprisingly diverse: High mountain forests give way abruptly to harsh desert plains and lush river bottomland, all within a day's travel. Visitors can float lazily down a calm stretch of river or hang on for dear life through white-water rapids, ride horseback to the edge of the mountains and down through desert arroyos, and camp in the backcountry. And, like the adventurers who came in the frontier days, visitors can hike along mountain trails deep into a wilderness that is still so remote that one can travel for a day or more without seeing any other people.

Big Bend is the kind of territory that inspired Hollywood's western soundstages: mountains; endless vistas of sky; rugged, mile-high peaks; steep-walled canyons; and broad desert plains punctuated by innumerable species of cactus. And while paved roads will carry you to all the main facilities, there are hundreds of miles of primitive dirt roads that can lead you to desert springs, river crossings, and abandoned mines and ranches. Big Bend is untamed and free, and, in this day and age, it may be the closest you'll get to a true frontier experience.

Another factor that makes Big Bend attractive is its easy access to Mexico, located just across the muddy waters of the Rio Grande. But the Mexico found here is very different from the Mexico of the crowded, overcommercialized border towns of Tijuana and Nuevo Laredo. These Mexican villages—San Carlos, Boquillas, and Santa Elena—are comprised of little more than a few adobe houses, a cantina, and a church. Just as Big Bend offers a no-frills glimpse into America's frontier past, the small villages across the river offer the no-frills simplicity of small-town life in Mexico.

ESSENTIAL INFORMATION

VISITOR INFORMATION The **Panther Junction Visitor Center** (Big Bend National Park, Park Superintendent, Big Bend, TX 79834, tel. 915/477–2251) at the center of the park is the main source for maps, guidebooks, and visitor information. The smaller **Rio Grande Village Visitor Center** (tel. 915/477–2271), located on the Rio Grande along the southeast border of the park, is open only from November through May. **Persimmon Gap** (tel. 915/477–2393) is run by volunteers six days a week and by a ranger one day; it may be

closed on occasion if a volunteer is unable to come in. **Chisos Basin** (tel. 915/477–2264) is open year-round.

A backcountry permit is required if you plan to do any overnight backpacking or primitive camping in the park. These are free at the Panther Junction Visitor Center.

FEES Entrance fees, good for one week, are $5 per vehicle or $3 per person entering on bicycle, motorcycle, or foot. Children under 17 are free, and discounts are available for senior citizens and disabled visitors. If you plan to visit often, you might want to purchase the $15 Big Bend Park Pass, which is valid for one calendar year.

PUBLICATIONS *Big Bend Paisano,* an informative free brochure, which includes a park map, is available at the visitor centers or by writing to the Park Superintendent (Big Bend National Park, Big Bend, TX 79834). Several other excellent publications are available from the **Big Bend Natural History Association** (Box 68, Big Bend National Park, TX 79834, tel. 915/477–2236). For the hiker or backpacker, two essential publications are the *Hiker's Guide* and *Chisos Mountain Trails.* Both of these excellent guides outline a number of hikes and backpacking trips, providing length, degree of difficulty, and tips on what to see along the trail. For canoeing or river rafting on the Rio Grande, choose from three available guidebooks, *River Guides I, II,* and *III,* which detail three different stretches of the river.

Four-wheel-drive enthusiasts will appreciate the *Road Guide to Backcountry Dirt Roads,* while pavement-bound drivers should turn to the popular *Road Guide to Paved Roads.* Both feature maps, photos, and descriptions of the roads in the park. For some colorful folklore of the surrounding countryside, pick up a free copy of *Big Bend Quarterly* at the Panther Junction Visitor Center or at the Chisos Basin.

GEOLOGY AND TERRAIN Covering 800,000 acres, Big Bend National Park is *big*—even by

Texas standards. It is marked by rugged mountains, the tallest of which is Emory Peak (7,835 feet above sea level) in the Chisos Mountain Range. The Chisos Mountains, blanketed in evergreens, are as serene and cool as the surrounding desert is arid and harsh. The cactus-strewn Chihuahuan Desert, stretching from northern Mexico up into Texas, is the second largest in North America. The difference between these two areas is striking: Within an hour's drive from the flatlands near the border up into the Chisos Mountains Basin, a bowl-like canyon at the top of a mountain, the temperature can drop 15 degrees. A third terrain parallels the Rio Grande, where the bottomland is populated with river reeds, salt cedars, and cottonwood trees, and the banks along some stretches of the Rio Grande, worn by centuries of white water, have formed impressive canyons framed by 1,500-foot cliffs.

Nearly 600 million years ago, the Big Bend area was covered by water. As the sea receded, layers of sediment were left behind and eventually hardened to rock. These layers are clearly visible along the Rio Grande in the Santa Elena Canyon. Heavy volcanic activity followed, including lava flows and upthrusts that formed lava domes and mountains. Dinosaurs and crocodiles roamed the Big Bend; in 1975 the remains of the largest flying creature known to man was discovered in the park. Ancient Native American groups lived in caves in the region, leaving pictographs on cave walls. The actual big bend of the Rio Grande was formed over millions of years as the river wore away at the layers of limestone, sandstone, and volcanic rock.

FLORA AND FAUNA Big Bend is a Biosphere Reserve, a unique area of plant and animal life where you will find several species that exist nowhere else on earth. Common in Big Bend but unique to the Chihuahuan Desert is the lechuguilla, a dagger-tipped plant that grows in clusters. The lechuguilla is an important food source for the javelina (pronounced *have-ah-LEEN-ah*), or collared peccary, a curious, piglike animal that can be found throughout the park. Javelinas have poor eyesight but a keen sense of smell.

Also common here is the ocotillo, a 10- to 15-foot plant with slender, thorny stems and a brilliant, red-orange flower. The century plant, a member of the Agave family, has a large stalk growing from the center of its spiny base that produces a bright yellow bloom. Contrary to popular folklore, it does not take the century plant a century to bloom, but it does take many years. And after the plant blooms, it dies.

Aside from the javelina, the park's most common animals include the desert mule deer and a subspecies of white-tailed deer called the Carmen Mountains whitetail. These animals, when seen in the Chisos Basin, have almost completely lost their fear of humans. There are also mountain lions in the Big Bend, although sightings are rare: They are extremely wary of humans and are primarily nocturnal. Among the other animals are jackrabbits, roadrunners, ground squirrels, a family of black bears, and the gray fox and coyote, seen around the Rio Grande Village campgrounds.

Bird species in the area include the golden eagle, turkey vulture, white-winged dove, western bluebird, and endangered peregrine falcon, which nests on the cliffs along the Rio Grande. These birds may be spotted throughout the park, but are most likely to be seen along the Rio Grande and in the Chisos Basin.

Free programs on the park's flora and fauna are given most nights in the amphitheaters at the Chisos Basin and Rio Grande Village (*see* Evening Activities, *below*). For more in-depth looks at the plant and wildlife, you may take part in seminars hosted by the Big Bend Natural History Association (Box 68, Big Bend National Park, TX 79834, tel. 915/477–2236). The seminars are held outdoors, and include hikes and lectures by park rangers and noted area authorities on a variety of related subjects.

WHEN TO GO Big Bend is most popular from March through April, when the desert is in full bloom. If you don't mind fighting the crowds you will be rewarded by the sight of colorful blooming cacti, the giant Big Bend bluebonnets (which stand nearly 2 feet tall), and the cascading blossoms of the yucca plants. The weather is usually very temperate during this season, ranging from the 50s through the 80s, with warm days and cool nights. Since the crowds are biggest during the spring, campsites are usually full and the in-park lodging is booked solid, but you can still get away from the crowds if you don't mind roughing it on the backcountry trails and at the backcountry campsites. It's best to avoid Big Bend altogether during spring break, when high school and college students in Texas descend on the place en masse and even the backcountry campsites are full.

Many visitors opt to visit during the fall, particularly in October, when the crowds are gone and the weather is optimal. Temperatures hover in the high 70s, and the Rio Grande is running at its highest, providing peak white water for rafting or canoeing. Summertime can be unbearably hot along the Rio Grande, where the thermometer regularly rises above 100°F, though it is usually 10 to 20 degrees cooler up in the Chisos Basin. The rainy season falls between late July and October, when sudden cloudbursts can cause flash floods that sometimes impede travel. During the winter, temperatures range between 36°F and 62°F throughout the park, snow is rare, and there are almost no crowds. Bird-watchers will enjoy visiting during the winter, when many migratory birds can be seen on their way south.

SEASONAL EVENTS **February:** The Chihuahuan Desert Mountain Bike Club hosts the **Big Bend Challenge Mountain Bike Festival** (Box 584, Terlingua, TX 79852, tel. 915/424–3366) on President's Day Weekend in Lajitas. Mountain-bike riders from around the nation gather near the Rio Grande to race mountain bikes through the Chihuahuan Desert during this three-day festival. Events include a cross-country race; a circuit race; the Log Pull, in which contestants see how far they can drag a log tied onto their bikes; and the Chainless Race, a downhill race that allows no pedaling (contestants must remove their bike chains before racing). **Big Bend Pioneer Reunion** (tel. 915/477–2236) is also hosted on President's Day weekend in February, with several pioneers and old-timers showing up to exchange tales of life in the Big Bend before it became a national park. The reunion site changes each year; phone ahead for details. **October:** On the third Saturday of the month, Big Bend National Park hosts its **International Good Neighbor Day,** held in cooperation with local Mexican communities. The festival takes place at Rio Grande Village Campground and includes a variety of foods, traditional Mexican dancers, and local arts and crafts that are for sale. Contact the visitor center for more details. **November:** The area's biggest and craziest festival is the **Annual International Championship Chili Cookoff** (tel. 512/629–4275 or 713/523–2362), held the first weekend of the month in Terlingua, a ghost town just 20 miles outside of the park. Chili cooks from around the world descend upon this normally empty town to cook chili, dance, and enjoy the biggest party you can throw in the middle of the desert. Close to 10,000 people come to the area for this weekend, so be sure to reserve lodging in advance if you don't want to camp.

WHAT TO PACK Packing for Big Bend should be adjusted for the season, but there are a few essentials that should be a part of your travel gear no matter what time of year you visit. Good, heavy-duty hiking shoes are a must if you plan to hike any of the trails in the park. A hat or cap is highly recommended, since the sun shines brightly year-round. Sunglasses and sunscreen should also be included, no matter what the season, and moisturizer and lip balm will help fight the effects of the dry desert air. Whether you will be driving or hiking, a pair of binoculars can prove useful in this vast wilderness.

Dress in Big Bend is ultracasual: This is rough country, so wear clothes that you don't mind roughing up a bit. Always pack a light jacket or sweater—the nights are cool, even in the summertime. Nighttime temperatures can drop into the 50s in the middle of July. During the winter bring plenty of warm clothing, including a hat and gloves. Also, a tough windbreaker is essential for those fierce west Texas winds.

Hikers should bring a canteen for water and water-purification tablets: Even if you do come across a spring or water hole along the trail, there is no guarantee that it's safe to drink from. Be sure that you have a good spare tire and jack in your car, and carry spare water in case your car or you overheat.

GENERAL STORES The nearest full-service grocery stores are in Alpine and Fort Stockton, approximately 100 and 140 miles from the park, respectively. **Furr's Supermarket** (104 N. 2nd, tel. 915/837–3295) and **Alpine IGA** (101 E. Sul Ross Ave., tel. 915/837–7307) are in Alpine. Furr's is open daily 8 AM to 9 PM but closes on Thanksgiving and Christmas. The Alpine IGA is open Monday through Saturday 8 AM to midnight and Sunday 8 AM to 10 PM. It is also closed on Thanksgiving and Christmas. In Fort Stockton, **Furr's Grocery** (1300 W. Dickinson St., tel. 915/336–3341) is open daily 7 AM to 10 PM; it's closed Christmas Day and closes early Easter and Thanksgiving. You can also buy food at **Lowe's** (108 W. 10th St., tel. 915/336–3919), open Monday to Saturday from 8 AM to 10 PM and Sunday from 8 AM to 9 PM, closed Christmas Day. The town's **Wal-Mart** (1700 W. Dickinson St., tel. 915/336–3389) is a good place to stock up on any other supplies you might need. It's open 7 AM to 9 PM Monday through Saturday, and 9 AM to 7 PM Sunday, closed Thanksgiving and Christmas Day. Note: The drive-through window at Fort Stockton's **First National Bank** (1000 W. Dickinson St.) has the only ATM in the entire region.

Smaller general stores selling gas, ice, beer, and some staples are located inside the park at the **Rio Grande Village Campground** (tel. 915/477–2293) and the **Chisos Basin** (tel. 915/477–2291). Outside the park you can find a few basic items at the **Lajitas Trading Post** (tel. 915/424–3234) in Lajitas (40 miles west on Hwy. 170), at the **Study Butte Store** (tel. 915/371–2231) in Study Butte (26 miles west on Hwy. 118), and at the **Stillwell Store** (tel. 915/376–2244), located just north of the park on Route 2627, 6 miles off Highway 385.

The Lajitas Trading Post is open daily 8 to 7 (closed Christmas); the Study Butte Store is open daily 8 to 8 (closed Christmas and New Year's Day morning); and the Stillwell Store is open daily 7 AM to 8 PM, 365 days a year.

ARRIVING AND DEPARTING Big Bend is not a park that is usually visited on a tour of national parks. It is located in a remote corner of Texas, hours away from any sizable city. The park is vast, and although public transportation can deliver you to some of the nearby towns, there is no way to travel through the park itself except in a car. Remember, too, that gas stations are few and far between, so always fill your tank whenever you have a chance.

By Plane. The nearest airport—really just an airstrip—is **Alpine Airport** (tel. 915/837–3009), 100 miles away. It's served by Lone Star Airlines (tel. 800/877–3932). Larger but farther are **Midland International Airport** (tel. 915/563–1460), 238 miles away, and **El Paso International Airport** (tel. 915/772–4271), 325 miles away. Private planes can land on dirt airstrips at Lajitas and Terlingua Ranch, at Alpine Airport, and on a paved landing strip in Marfa.

By Car and RV. I–10 is the major artery that cuts across this part of Texas, nearly 140 miles north of the park. You can reach I–10 from several directions, including I–20 from Dallas/Fort Worth. At Fort Stockton leave I–10 and pick up Highway 385 south to Panther Junction in the park. If you are coming from El Paso in the west, you may follow I–10 to Van Horn, pick up Highway 90 south to Alpine, then take Highway 118 to Study Butte at the park's western border. Be prepared to drive distances of 70 miles or more between gas stations, phones, and food.

By Train. Amtrak (tel. 800/872–7245) has stations in Sanderson and Alpine and makes regular stops at both depots. There are no car-rental agencies in Sanderson, but in Alpine you can rent a car at the **Siesta Country Inn** (1200 E. Holland, tel. 915/837–2503) and at **Aerflite Auto Rental** (Alpine Airport, tel. 915/837–2744).

By Bus. Greyhound Lines (tel. 800/231–2222) and Kerrville Bus Company (tel. 915/336–5151) can bring you into Alpine, where you can rent a car (*see* By Train, *above*).

EXPLORING

While hikes and bicycle trips are useful for experiencing small sections of the park up close, Big Bend's vast acreage can be thoroughly explored only by car. A drive/hike combination, which you can tailor to suit your needs, is the best formula. It is possible to see all the major sites from your car in a day; if you'd like to stop to take a closer look at the sites, allow yourself three days. But if you want to take in all the sites, do some hiking, go river rafting, explore by horseback, and enjoy the evening programs held in the amphitheaters, give yourself at least five days. Big Bend is huge, and you would be shortchanging yourself if you rushed through it. You could spend three days exploring the Chisos Basin alone and another three days just paddling on a raft trip down the Rio Grande. Pick the activities that are most important to you, and take it from there.

THE BEST IN ONE DAY Stow a picnic lunch in the car and drive up to the Chisos Lodge Restaurant at daybreak for breakfast and some beautiful views of the Chisos Basin, the bowl-shape canyon at the top of the mountain. Early morning is the best time to spot wildlife, and along this drive you are likely to spot javelinas and deer; if you are very lucky, you might even see a black bear. Enjoy breakfast as you watch the sun rise over the mountains, then don your hiking gear and head over to the Window hiking trail. This moderate, 5¹/₄-mile round-trip hike leads down through a dry creek bed and along a narrow canyon, ending at a scenic overlook that becomes a waterfall whenever it rains. You can look out through a "window" formed by the canyon walls at the desert below.

Return to your car and then head down the Basin drive toward Panther Junction. Go past the park headquarters and continue southeast toward Rio Grande Village Campground. Watch closely for the Dugout Wells cutoff, a well-maintained dirt road on the left. Make this left, and after ¹/₄ mile you will reach a group of huge cottonwood trees, which have been growing over a seep here for decades. There are some picnic tables under the trees, always ensuring a shady place for a picnic lunch. After lunch follow the short nature trail, reading the display boards that tell the history of this water hole.

Drive back to the main road and continue to follow it toward Boquillas. You will be driving toward Rio Grande Village, but you should turn off at the Boquillas Village cutoff (not the Boquillas Canyon Overlook). Park your car in the gravel lot and follow the pathway down to the river's edge, where a boatman will row you across the Rio Grande for about $2. On the other side you can rent a burro for about $4 to ride up the hill to the village of Boquillas or make your way on foot. Boquillas is not much of a town—just a few adobe houses, a bar, a restaurant, and a church—but you'll feel like you've gone back in time and entered the world of one of Clint Eastwood's spaghetti Westerns. Have a seat on the patio of the restaurant, order up some soft tacos and a cold beer or soft drink, and sit back and take it easy for a while. When you are ready to leave, go back to the river and the waiting boatman. Once back in your car, retrace your steps to the main road to return to your camp or lodge.

ORIENTATION PROGRAMS There are a number of daily activities held throughout the park that are designed as informative introductions to area attractions. At least one nature walk is organized most days, and there is a variety of workshops and lectures. At the Persimmon Gap, Basin, and Rio Grande visitor centers you will find a Big Bend orientation video, which can be viewed on request. Check with any of the visitor centers for a schedule of events occurring during your visit.

GUIDED TOURS The Big Bend Natural History Association (Box 68, Big Bend National Park, TX 79834, tel. 915/477–2236) offers seminars covering a range of topics, including birds, nature photography, and wildflow-

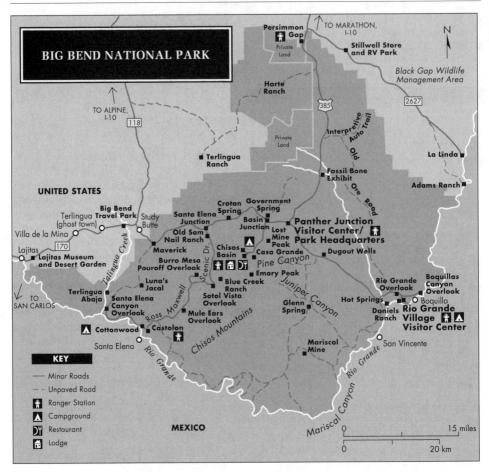

KEY

— Minor Roads

- - Unpaved Road

🛉 Ranger Station

⛺ Campground

🍴 Restaurant

🏠 Lodge

ers. The seminars are led either by park rangers, professors from nearby Sul Ross State University, or other knowledgeable professionals, and cost between $40 and $300.

A variety of guided horseback and river rafting tours are conducted daily by private, local outfitters (*see* Other Activities, *below*).

SCENIC DRIVES AND VIEWS The **Ross Maxwell Scenic Drive,** named after Big Bend's first park superintendent, makes a great tour of the scenery inside the park. Winding between the Chisos Mountains and Burro Mesa, the 30-mile road climbs up along the western edge of the Chisos to the Sotol Vista Overlook and then heads southward past Mule Ears Peaks into Castolon and Cottonwood campgrounds, ending at the mouth of Santa Elena

Canyon. Paved side roads lead to the Sotol Vista Overlook, Burro Mesa Pouroff, and Mule Ears Viewpoint, all worthy detours. Parts of this road are very steep and winding, and the park service suggests that trailers over 20 feet and RVs over 24 feet do not attempt the drive.

The drive to the **Chisos Basin** is a steep uphill climb through canyon country. Although it is only 7 miles long, the sharp curves and steep grade make it a challenging drive, to be taken slowly; it is not recommended for trailers over 20 feet and RVs over 24 feet. Once you reach the Basin you'll find several hiking trails, including the Window Trail, the Lost Mine Trail, and the challenging 14-mile South Rim hike.

HISTORIC BUILDINGS AND SITES There are many structures of historic interest in Big Bend, including ranches, cavalry outposts, and vestiges of farming and mining communities, all listed on the National Register of Historic Places. One special site is the **Hot Springs Hotel and Post Office.** The geothermal mineral spring at this site was used for medicinal purposes by Native Americans, and around the turn of the century J. O. Langford built a resort here. The stone buildings may be abandoned and crumbling, but the springs are still flowing. Bring your swimsuit and soak in these hot mineral springs alongside the Rio Grande, a sure tonic after a long day of driving and hiking.

Although the park service tore down many of the buildings on the area's various ranches in the park's early days, some do remain. One is located off Ross Maxwell Scenic Drive, between Santa Elena Junction and the Sotol Vista Overlook. It was part of the **Blue Creek Ranch,** which was owned by Homer Wilson, a successful rancher in the Big Bend area. The structure was the ranch-foreman's house.

On the Old Maverick Road, south of Chimneys West primitive campsite, is a structure known as **Luna's Jacal,** an old earthen, wood, and thatch structure built by Gilberto Luna, who farmed the floodplains of Alamo Creek from the mid-1800s until the National Park Service bought his land in the 1940s. With a succession of wives, Luna raised dozens of children in the barren desert and lived to the age of 108. If you follow the dirt road south toward Santa Elena you will find the ruins of the farming community called **Terlingua Abaja,** just west of the Terlingua Abaja primitive campsite.

The largest historic structure in the park is the **Mariscal Mine,** an abandoned mercury mine that was in operation until about 1944. It is located off the four-wheel-drive dirt road that runs by Mariscal Mountain. The retorts are still standing, as are several shacks that once housed the Mexican miners who crossed the river to work here. The old, open retorts, where mercury ore was extracted, are still partially intact: These contraptions are considered by some to have contributed to the deaths of dozens of Mexican laborers who breathed the mercury fumes during the smelting process.

There are literally hundreds of ruins in the abandoned mining village of Terlingua, located about 12 miles outside the park's border on Highway 170 to Lajitas. Old mine shafts and miners' houses stand as testimony to what was once a bustling village—there is even an abandoned opera house and an old cemetery.

NATURE TRAILS AND SHORT WALKS The **Rio Grande Village Nature Trail** is a 1¼-mile loop that runs along the Rio Grande and has several markers noting area plant and animal life.

At Dugout Wells is the **Chihuahuan Desert Nature Trail,** an easy ½-mile round-trip that serves as an excellent introduction to the vast shrub-desert habitat.

The **Fossil Bone Exhibit,** 9 miles north of park headquarters, displays re-created fossilized bones of 50-million-year-old mammals. Part of the exhibit compares the vista from the area in prehistoric times to the current view.

The **Santa Elena Canyon Trail** is a 1¾-mile round-trip walk right down the canyon walls to the Rio Grande. Concrete steps and handrails have been added, making this hike more accessible to frailer visitors and children.

Boquillas Canyon, another of the spectacular sights in Big Bend, is accessible via a 1½-mile round-trip hike, which starts at the end of the Boquillas Canyon Road, near Rio Grande Village.

LONGER HIKES Longer hikes out here can mean anything from a 14-mile all-day stroll to a multiday backpacking excursion into lands that are accessible only by foot. The most popular and scenic of the longer hikes goes to the **South Rim** by way of a network of trails called the High Chisos trails. This 14-mile round-trip trek up from the Chisos Basin runs through the mountains to an overlook at the south rim of the Chisos Mountain Range. The view from this point over the mountains and the desert below is breathtaking. Many people take two days or more to make this trip, camping overnight at one of the back-country campsites along the way (you'll need a permit). Bring water and ready-to-eat meals; wood fires are not allowed. This trip is for the physically fit only.

The **Lost Mine Trail** is another of the more popular hikes in the Chisos Mountains. Nearly 5 miles round-trip, the trail passes Casa Grande, rounds the head of Juniper Canyon, and ends overlooking Pine Canyon, going from an elevation of 5,600 feet to 6,850 feet. The hike is not too strenuous but can be tough if you are out of shape.

To reach **Boot Canyon** you can start out on the Pinnacles Trail from the Chisos Basin Trail-head. You'll pass the cowboy boot–shape landmark that gives the canyon its name on this 9-mile round-trip hike. Boot Springs, located just off the trail, is a popular (although unreliable) freshwater spring used by high-country hikers. Any water used for drinking that comes from this spring should be treated or filtered first.

The truly adventurous will want a crack at the **Strawhouse–Telephone Canyon Trail.** The 24-mile one-way path weaves through a labyrinth of dense brush and mesquite and takes at least two days to complete. There is no water available along the entire route, and summer temperatures can top 100°F, so be sure to carry plenty of water and have lots of protection against the sun.

For a complete, descriptive list of trails, get a copy of the *Hiker's Guide* (*see* Publications, *above*).

OTHER ACTIVITIES **Back-Road Driving.** No off-road driving is permitted inside the park, but there are several primitive roads where you will need a four-wheel-drive vehicle, or at least one with a high clearance, spare tire, jack, and plenty of water. If you should break down, stay with your car. Do not attempt to walk for help. A disabled vehicle is much easier to spot from the air than a solitary figure walking across the desert. It is very important that you carry at least a gallon of water per person per day on any back-road trip, no matter how short it may be. Check with a ranger before you head out.

Biking. Cycling is permitted on all designated roads but not on any hiking paths or off-road. Rental bicycles are available from **Desert Sports** (Box 584, Terlingua, TX 79852, tel. 915/424–3366) in Lajitas, about 17 miles west of the park's western entrance on Highway 170.

Bird-Watching. Bird-watching is excellent throughout the park. Varieties and species vary with the seasons and the migration patterns. The best spots to watch are the Chisos Basin and the Rio Grande. The rare peregrine falcon nests and breeds on many peaks in the Chisos Mountains and along the Rio Grande's sheer cliffs from February through August. Other species include the golden eagle, turkey vulture, scaled quail, and the western bluebird. Check with the rangers to find out which species are in the area during your visit. Bird-watching tours are offered by Jim Hines of **Big Bend Birding Expeditions** (tel. 915/424–3313).

Fishing. Fishing is permitted in the Rio Grande, and the catch is primarily catfish. No fishing license is necessary. Trot lines may not extend across the river, and jug fishing is not allowed.

Horseback Riding. The **Chisos Remuda** (Chisos Basin, Big Bend, TX 79834, tel. 915/477–2374), located in the Chisos Basin, offers daily guided horseback trips to the South Rim and the Window Trail. Advance reservations are a must. The Window Trail is a half-day ride, but the South Rim ride is an all-day trip, and you must pack your own lunch.

Outside the park, try **Lajitas Stables** (Star Rte. 70, Box 380, Terlingua, TX 79852, tel. 915/424–3238), in nearby Lajitas. The staff will take riders on guided trips on private land and property not located inside Big Bend National Park. Rides range from one-hour tours to multiday trips and can be combined with river-rafting trips. Reservations are suggested.

Rafting. Rafting is permitted on the Rio Grande with a free float permit obtained at Panther Junction. Because of the fickle nature of the river—switching quickly from slow and lazy to roaring white water—it is recommended that you go with one of the outfitters in the region. Should you go on the river without a guide, be sure to ask the park rangers to recommend the best stretch of river to suit your abilities. You should also consult one of the books in the *River Guide* series (*see* Publications, *above*).

Rafts are available for rent from **Rio Grande River Outfitters** (tel. 915/371–2424), based in the old Lajitas Trading Post in Lajitas. Some of the more popular trips include those through the Mariscal Canyon and Colorado Canyon, but the best one-day raft trip, strictly for experienced rafters, is the Santa Elena Canyon tour, which passes through a stretch of canyon known as the Rock Slide. Huge rocks, some as large as houses, have fallen off the canyon walls over the centuries, creating an obstacle course of narrow channels through the rocks.

The river-running outfitters in the area all offer one-day trips, which cost from $70 to $100. They will handle all the work and will even supply a buffet lunch. Some of the local river guides and outfitters are **Far Flung Adventures** (Box 377, Terlingua, TX 79852, tel. 915/371–2489 or 800/359–4138), **Outback Expeditions** (General Delivery, Study Butte, TX 79852, tel. 915/371–2490), and **Big Bend River Tours** (Box 317, Lajitas, TX 79852, tel. 915/424–3219 or 800/545–4240).

Travel into Mexico. The only barrier between the United States and Mexico is the Rio Grande, so if you raft or canoe you can easily leave the country just by beaching your craft on the opposite shore. Passports are not needed and there is no customs office along the river: People come and go as they wish here, as they have for centuries. The only place that you may be stopped and asked to produce proof of citizenship will be at a border-patrol roadblock on Highway 118 or Highway 385, 50 to 75 miles north of the park.

No exchange of currency is necessary, despite what some natives will tell you.

The villages along the Rio Grande do not offer much in the way of tourist attractions, but they do provide a glimpse at the lives many of the Mexicans lead. **Boquillas,** a town near Rio Grande Village Campground, has an open-air café, a bar, a school, two stores, and a church. You can catch a ride across the river from a boatman who charges about $2 round-trip. Once on the other side, you can rent a burro for about $4 to ride up to the village, or walk the 3/4 mile into town.

Santa Elena is across the river from Cottonwood Campground. It has two small restaurants where women cook and serve traditional Mexican food in their homes. Passage across the river is by a boatman. The largest village is **San Carlos,** which is nearly 20 miles across the river from Lajitas up a bumpy dirt road. **Kikko Garcias** (tel. 915/424–3221), who can usually be found at the Lajitas Trading Post, offers San Carlos tours. Gray Line he isn't, but his day-long trips in a Suburban over the dirt roads are fun for the adventurous, offering spectacular scenery—including mountain waterfalls and hot springs. Rates of $50 per person per day include lunch; there's a three-person minimum. Some brave souls have walked or ridden mountain bikes to San Carlos, but it's not encouraged.

Rock Climbing. Climbing is discouraged because the rock in the Big Bend is very unstable and fragmented. Some rappelling is done in the Chisos Basin, but check with the rangers beforehand; some peaks are off limits during certain wildlife-breeding seasons.

Swimming. Swimming in the Rio Grande is allowed, but because of currents, drop-offs, and submerged hazards it is not encouraged. However, one spot where people do swim regularly is at the hot springs just upriver from the Rio Grande Village Visitor Center. Bathers can alternate between the warm, soothing waters of the springs and the cold Rio Grande running alongside. You can also come down to the hot springs at night and soak while you watch the stars above you.

Bring a lantern: There is no lighting along the narrow footpath leading to the springs. Overnight use of the hot-springs area is not allowed.

CHILDREN'S PROGRAMS Educational workshops geared specifically to children are conducted on a variety of related topics. Past programs have covered such topics as Native American life in Big Bend, predator/prey relationships, reptiles and amphibians, and dinosaurs. Programs are usually held at the Panther Junction Auditorium. Although these programs are held year-round, they do occur more frequently during school holidays. Call 915/477–2251 for a detailed schedule of events.

EVENING ACTIVITIES Free informational sessions are held on most nights in the amphitheaters located at the Rio Grande Village and the Chisos Basin campgrounds. The programs rotate, and a different topic is addressed each night, covering everything from bats to Columbus and the Comanches. Schedules are available at the ranger stations. The hour-long, ranger-led shows, accompanied by slides, usually begin shortly after dark. Bring a flashlight and a jacket, and arrive early for the best seats.

DINING

The rough-and-ready frontier atmosphere of Big Bend is reflected in the area's informal restaurants, which vary from rustic adobe huts to classic southwestern ranch buildings, complete with antique furniture and candles. You won't find any low-cal dishes or nouvelle cuisine, but what you will find is simple, inexpensive, hearty fare, enjoyed by cowboys and oil tycoons alike and consisting mainly of Tex-Mex, steaks and burgers, and barbecue, all in healthy portions that are meant to stick to your ribs.

INSIDE THE PARK Chisos Mountain Lodge. The main attraction at this, the only restaurant located within Big Bend National Park, is the phenomenal view. Large picture windows on three sides of the restaurant allow diners to soak in the beauty of the Chisos Basin. Juniper and piñon trees and steep, red-rock cliffs encircle the restaurant, which is run by the National Park Concessions. Such basic dishes as chicken-fried steak, chicken, and burgers are served. The quality of the food can be inconsistent; the best time to come here is early morning, when you can sip a cup of coffee and watch the sun rise over the mountainside. *Chisos Basin, tel. 915/ 477–2291. Reservations not accepted. AE, DC, MC, V. Moderate.*

NEAR THE PARK McFarland's. This restaurant may be a considerable hike north of the park, but it's as close as you'll come to upscale dining in the Big Bend area. McFarland's is located in downtown Alpine's old Holland Hotel; white tablecloths and a pleasant decor set the mood. The menu, which changes daily, often includes good seafood such as oysters on the half-shell, fresh shrimp, and Gulf snapper. Try the steak McFarland, a rib eye stuffed with ham and Monterey Jack cheese and topped with sautéed mushrooms. *207 W. Holland, Alpine, tel. 915/837–3455. Reservations suggested. Dress: casual. AE, D, MC, V. Closed Sun.; closed Mon., Memorial Day–Labor Day. Moderate.*

Starlight Theatre. This restaurant in Terlingua was built in 1937 by Howard E. Perry as a movie house for his workers in the Terlingua Mining Company. The old adobe building has been completely remodeled and now has a southwestern decor, with pink-adobe walls, green door frames, mesquite-wood chairs, and dark-green tablecloths. The handmade mesquite bar is a showpiece. Local musicians frequently perform here before a largely local audience. Order a large T-bone or New York strip steak, or try one of the authentic Mexican dishes, which include home-style tamales. *Off Hwy. 170, Terlingua, tel. 915/371–2326. Reservations not necessary. Dress: casual. MC, V. Moderate.*

Big Bend Motor Inn Café. This small café, located next to the Big Bend Motor Inn at the intersection of Highways 170 and 118, offers basic truck-stop fare: burgers, chicken-fried steak, and sandwiches. The atmosphere is unpretentious and down-home. *Hwy. 170 and Hwy. 118, Terlingua, tel. 915/371–2218. AE, D, DC, MC, V. Inexpensive.*

Desert Deli and Diner. For a casual lunch with a good view of the Chisos Mountains, this funky little adobe diner, 8 miles outside the park in Terlingua, is the place to come. The chili and burgers are popular with locals and with Rio Grande rafters. Try the breakfast burrito to go in the morning, and the BLT and turkey sandwich for lunch. *Hwy. 118, Terlingua, tel. 915/371–2305. No credit cards. Closed Mon. Inexpensive.*

Gage Hotel Restaurant. Located 70 miles north of Big Bend National Park in the small town of Marathon, the Gage Hotel's full-service restaurant is the last place where you can get a full-course meal before driving down into the park. Located in a historical landmark building, the Gage offers entrées ranging from Tex-Mex to steaks, chicken, and fish. The decor is authentic southwestern, with stuffed animal heads, Native American artifacts, saddles, and wood tables and chairs. At breakfast don't miss the homemade oatmeal with plump raisins and cinnamon. This is a popular spot for local ranchers, who stop by for their morning coffee when they come into town. *Hwy. 90W, Marathon, tel. 915/386–4205. D, MC, V. Inexpensive.*

La Kiva. This restaurant/bar is decorated like a desert oasis, with an entryway modeled after a Navajo kiva, or underground ceremonial chamber. A cavelike passageway leads to a lower-level bar, and there is a large patio out back. The menu emphasizes barbecue—beef, ribs, and chicken—but also includes filet mignon. *Hwy. 170W, Terlingua Creek, tel. 915/371–2250. AE, MC, V. Closed lunch. Inexpensive.*

Sarah's Café. The last word in authentic Tex-Mex for Big Bend, Sarah's has been operated by the Castello family for more than 60 years. The lunch crowd that packs this place includes local politicians, oil men, and ranchers, while dinner sees more families. The tangy dishes are all prepared from scratch with ingredients that are made fresh daily. Try the enchiladas, the chile relleno, or Sarah's Special, a huge sampler platter with a little of everything. This place is quite a drive from the park, but if you're passing through Fort Stockton, don't miss it. *106 S. Nelson, Fort Stockton, tel. 915/336–7124. MC, V. Closed Sun. Inexpensive.*

PICNIC SPOTS If you'd like to picnic in the shade, head to the **Dugout Wells** picnic tables, located in the middle of the desert off the main road from Panther Junction to Rio Grande Village. Tables are tucked inside the long and leafy branches of some giant cottonwood trees growing in the moist ground over a nearby seep. For a close-up view of the Rio Grande, try the picnic table located underneath a desert palm tree just down the path from the old **Hot Springs Post Office.** You'll have a good view of the river rafters and the bathers hiking to the hot springs a few hundred yards downriver. A premium place for the picnicking crowd is the **Chisos Basin,** although it can be a bit chilly to eat outside here in the winter months.

LODGING

Most of the accommodations in and around Big Bend National Park are very basic, moderately priced motels in rustic settings. But what the accommodations may lack in luxury, they more than make up for in friendly service. Most of the motels in the region do not have telephones or televisions in every room, and some of them require that you share a bathroom, but you'll find that the staff will usually go out of their way to try to make you comfortable.

The park's one motel is very popular, and during the peak spring season you are unlikely to find a room available unless you book as much as a year in advance or stumble across a cancellation. The park is so large, however, that visitors who stay in surrounding towns often drive no farther than those staying inside the park to visit certain sights.

INSIDE THE PARK **Chisos Mountain Lodge.** Centrally located in Chisos Basin and adjacent to the more popular hiking trails as well as horseback-riding facilities, this establishment is well liked by senior citizens and families. The lodge features basic motel decor—nothing fancy, but clean—but there are no phones or televisions in any of the rooms. The newest addition is the Casa Grande Lodge, with private balconies and a second story, but the most sought-after accommodations are the six stone cottages. Book your reservations well in advance of your trip. *Big Bend National Park, Big Bend, TX 79834, 915/477–2291, fax 915/477–2352. 72 rooms, 6 cabins. Facilities: restaurant, souvenir shop, store. AE, DC, MC, V. Moderate.*

NEAR THE PARK **Badlands Hotel/Cavalry Post Motel.** The Badlands and the Cavalry offer two types of accommodations in a resort complex in Lajitas that incorporates numerous shops, tour outfitters, restaurants, stables, and even a museum. Although the complex is not even 20 years old, it was carefully constructed to look like an old western town, complete with wood sidewalks and a saloon. The resort is located 45 miles from the Panther Junction Ranger Station and is right next to the Rio Grande and the 240,000-acre Big Bend Ranch State Natural Area. The two-story Badlands Hotel is in the center of town, and the Cavalry, about 200 yards away, was built on the foundations of the original cavalry headquarters that stood here at the turn of the century. Both offer simple lodging in rooms decorated in generic motel style. The hotel and motel are popular with river rafters, golfers, and people planning day trips into the nearby Mexican village of San Carlos. *Rte. 170, Terlingua, TX 79852, tel. 915/424–3471 or 800/527–4078, fax 915/424–3277. 82 rooms, 27 condominium units. Facilities: restaurant, bar, lounge, pool, 2 tennis courts, 9-hole golf course, horseback riding, shops. AE, DC, MC, V. Moderate–Expensive.*

Big Bend Motor Inn. This small motel is located just 3 miles from the park's western border at the intersection of Highways 118 and 170. The "we aim to please" attitude of the friendly employees, and the convenient location, make up for the basic, somewhat spartan, motel rooms. There is a large RV park located behind the motel. *Box 336, Terlingua, TX 79852, tel. 915/371–2218 or 800/848–2363. 82 rooms, 10 with kitchenettes. Facilities: restaurant, pool. AE, D, DC, MC, V. Moderate.*

Gage Hotel. Without a doubt, this is the best place to stay in Big Bend; its romantic ambience can't be beat. Built in 1928 by wealthy rancher Alfred Gage as a place to lodge his numerous friends and business contacts, the restored building is a registered Texas Historical Landmark. Each room is unique, furnished with handmade, antique ranch furniture in wood and leather. Walls are covered with southwestern artifacts and paintings, and the lobby is filled with stuffed animal heads, saddles, and cowboy gear. There are no phones or televisions, and, while some rooms come with a private bath, most guests must share a community bathroom. The hotel has a great front porch with oversize rocking chairs for sitting and contemplating. The new Los Portales addition across the road has 20 rooms, all with private baths (but no TVs or phones) and all decorated in Old West–style, including viga-beam ceilings and cowboy paraphernalia on the walls. Couples, river rafters, cowboys, and senior citizens frequent this establishment. *Box 46, Marathon, TX 79842, tel. 915/386–4205, fax 915/386–4510. 40 rooms, 27 with private bath. Facilities: restaurant, activities desk, pool. D, MC, V. Moderate.*

Mission Lodge. This recently constructed motel is owned and operated by the same folks who own the Big Bend Motor Inn across the road. The sparsely decorated rooms all have queen-size beds. *Box 169, Terlingua, TX 79852, tel. 915/371–2555. 24 rooms. AE, D, DC, MC, V. Moderate.*

Chisos Mining Company/Easter Egg Valley. These no-frills motel rooms and cabins in Study Butte all have kitchenettes, but no rooms have phones, and only some have televisions. *Box 229, Terlingua, TX 79852, tel. 915/371–2254. 28 rooms, 8 cabins with kitch-*

enettes. *Facilities: shop, RV park. AE, D, MC, V. Inexpensive.*

Terlingua Lodge. If you're looking for a remote getaway, this is it: The Terlingua Lodge can be reached only by driving 18 miles down a dirt road off Highway 118. The lodge is situated on the private Terlingua Ranch at the base of the Christmas Mountains, almost 60 miles from Panther Junction. This is a very quiet spot, with big skies, mountainous landscapes, and starry nights. There are no phones and no televisions in the rooms. *HC 675, Box 220, Alpine, TX 79830, tel. 915/371–2416. 32 rooms. Facilities: restaurant, pool, gift shop, private airstrip. MC, V. Inexpensive.*

CAMPING

Camping is extremely popular in Big Bend, where you can choose from isolated primitive sites and three major campgrounds with toilets and grills. Only one campground has RV hookups. Sites at the park's campgrounds are assigned on a first-come, first-served basis, and a single stay is limited to 14 days. Nightly fees vary according to the campsite: $5 at Rio Grande Village Campsites and Chisos Basin campground, and $3 at Cottonwood Campground; primitive backcountry camping is free. All campgrounds are open year-round.

All major campgrounds are usually filled to capacity during Easter, spring break, Thanksgiving, and Labor Day, particularly the popular Chisos Basin Campground. Primitive backcountry campsites are usually available, except at spring break, but some of these are accessible only with a high-clearance vehicle.

INSIDE THE PARK The **Chisos Basin** (63 sites) remains the most popular campground because of its scenery, wildlife, and easy access to several hiking trails. It is also near a store and a restaurant, and rest rooms are close by. The campsites are fairly close to each other, and many hikers pass through the campground on their way to the trails; nevertheless, it is surprisingly quiet.

You can get more isolation down at **Cottonwood Campground** (35 sites), located next to the Rio Grande, where the only people you will see are other campers and the occasional river rafter. Campsites are beneath the shade of a grove of large cottonwood trees. There are pit toilets, grills, picnic tables, and water.

The campgrounds with the most amenities are located at **Rio Grande Village.** The park-service campground here has 100 sites, with picnic tables, grills, and nearby rest rooms. A park concessionaire runs 25 RV sites with full hookups near the fairly well-stocked general store. There are also laundry facilities, showers, and a service station at the store. Rio Grande Village is also close to the hot springs, where you can go for a relaxing natural Jacuzzi, and the village of Boquillas, should you want to make a quick trip across the border into Mexico.

If you really want to get away from it all, try a primitive, backcountry roadside campsite. There are 43 of them along the dirt roads in the park, some of which can only be reached by four-wheel-drive vehicle or on foot. There are no facilities at these spots. One of the most remote and peaceful is the **Fresno primitive campsite,** a short walk from the abandoned Mariscal Mine. It is too hot to camp here during the summer, but in fall and winter the solitude is inspirational.

NEAR THE PARK Since there is only one campground with full RV hookups located in the park, many RVers go to sites outside the park, including those at nearby RV parks in Study Butte, Lajitas, Terlingua, and at the Stillwell Store.

The **Big Bend Motor Inn** (Box 336, Terlingua, TX 79852, tel. 915/371–2218), located at the intersection of Highways 170 and 118 in Study Butte, has a swimming pool and a restaurant, as well as picnic tables, grills, water, electric, and fuel. The 75 RV sites here cost $12.50 each per night; tent sites cost $10.

Big Bend Travel Park (Box 146, Terlingua, TX 79852, tel. 915/371–2250) is located next to the La Kiva restaurant, on Highway 170 in Study Butte. The 45 RV sites cost $10 each per night, including full hookup. Facilities

BIG BEND CAMPGROUNDS

	Chisos Basin	Cottonwood	Rio Grande Village	Primitive campsites	Big Bend Motor Inn	Big Bend Travel Park	Lajitas RV Park	Terlingua Ranch	Stillwell RV Park
	INSIDE THE PARK				**NEAR THE PARK**				
Total number of sites	63	35	125	43	80	95	94	24	8
Sites suitable for RVs	0	0	125	0	75	45	77	22	80
Number of hookups	0	0	25	0	75	45	77	22	80
Drive to sites	•	•	•		•	•	•	•	•
Hike to sites				•					
Flush toilets	•		•		•	•	•		•
Pit/chemical toilets	•	•							•
Drinking water	•	•	•		•	•	•	•	•
Showers			•		•	•	•	•	•
Fire grates	•	•	•		•	•	•		•
Swimming					•		•	•	
Boat access			•						
Playground								•	
Disposal station					•	•	•	•	•
Ranger station	•	•	•						
Public telephone	•	•	•		•	•	•	•	•
Reservation possible					•	•	•	•	•
Daily fee per site	$5	$3	$5–$11	free	$10–$12.50	$10	$8–$12	$4.50–$6.50	$10.60–$11.75
Dates open	year-round	year-round	year-round	year-round	year-round	year-round	year-round	year-round	year-round

include a restaurant, showers, and a laundry facility. Tent sites are also available.

Found next to the Lajitas Resort on Highway 170, the **Lajitas RV Park** (HC70, Box 400, Terlingua, TX 79852, tel. 915/424–3471 or 800/527–4078) has 77 full hookup sites, 58 of which have cable television, for $12 each per night or $72 per week. There is also a nine-hole golf course, two tennis courts, and a pool. The 17 tent sites cost $8 per night.

The 24 sites at **Terlingua Ranch** (Box 220, HC65, Alpine, TX 79830, tel. 915/371–2416) are located 26 miles north of the park off Highway 118. Facilities here include water, sewer, electricity, and gravel pads; costs range from $4.50 to $6.50 per night.

A gem of a campground, **Stillwell RV Park** (Box 430, Alpine, TX 79830, tel. 915/376–2244) is located off FM 2627, 30 miles north of the park, on a large west Texas ranch owned and operated by Hallie Stillwell. Ms. Stillwell is a true Big Bend pioneer and is the Annual Queen of the Chili Cookoff in Terlingua. The campground boasts 80 RV sites and unlimited tent sites, a well-stocked general store, and a museum. Four-wheel-drive tours to view ancient Native American campsite pictographs are available, and films about the region are run nightly. There is also a laundry facility and showers; water, gravel pads, and electricity are available. Sites cost between $10.60 and $11.75 per night.

Bryce Canyon National Park
Utah

By Tom Wharton

The first view of Bryce Canyon's iridescent colors defies belief. It is almost impossible to imagine such brilliant hues of red, buff, and tan existing in nature. And then there are the shapes—fantastic shapes resembling spires, cathedrals, goblins, and the tops of fairy castles. For years people have tried with little success to describe this brightly colored land.

One of the most heartfelt descriptions allegedly came from Ebenezer Bryce, the Mormon settler who came here in 1875 and gave his name to the park. Folklore has it that Bryce exclaimed that this was "a hell of a place to lose a cow!" Others gave the trails and major formations such names as Fairyland Point, the Queen's Garden, Peekaboo Loop, the Silent City, and the Chinese Wall. Nearly 50 years after Ebenezer Bryce built his homestead in the canyon, Congress established the area as Utah National Park. In 1928, several thousand acres were added and its name was changed officially to Bryce Canyon National Park.

You may be surprised to find out that Bryce Canyon is really not a canyon; it's a natural amphitheater carved from the encircling cliffs by rain, snow, and ice. To walk through it in the early morning or late afternoon is to see its deepest colors, colors that change with the season, time of day, and weather—colors that almost seem to glow.

Except during the height of the summer travel season, when the lodge is full and finding a motel room near the park can be difficult, Bryce is a relatively quiet place, easily seen from the 18 miles of main road and four major spur roads that lead to the park's 13 overlooks. For many, simply sitting on a bench at the edge of Sunrise or Sunset points and contemplating the vista is enough; those who want a more complete experience will need to hike down into the amphitheater or explore the park by horse.

ESSENTIAL INFORMATION

VISITOR INFORMATION Write to **Bryce Canyon National Park**, Bryce Canyon, Utah 84717; or call 801/834–5322. A free permit available from the visitor center is required for overnight backcountry trips, which are allowed only on the Under-the-Rim Trail south of Bryce Point.

FEES The entrance fee is $5 per vehicle for a seven-day pass or $3 per person arriving by bus. An annual park pass, good from January 1 through December 31, costs $15.

PUBLICATIONS Useful maps and publications can be purchased from the **Bryce Canyon Natural History Association** (Bryce Canyon, UT 84717, tel. 801/834–5322). *Bryce Canyon National Park,* by Fred Hirschmann, is the best of the color photo books. Tully Stoud's 44-page *Bryce Canyon Auto and Hiking Guide* includes information on the geology and history of the area. The "Bryce Canyon Hiking Guide," with an amphitheater hiking map and aerial photo, supplements the free map given to park visitors at the entrance. The "Kid's Guide to Bryce Canyon" introduces the region to children 5–10 years old.

GEOLOGY AND TERRAIN Fifty million years of geologic history can be studied through the oddly shaped and colored limestone and sandstone rock formations in Bryce Canyon National Park. The park comprises 35,835 acres. Its main formation is the Pink Cliffs, which sit atop a larger geological formation, the Grand Staircase. This begins at the bottom of the Grand Canyon and gradually ascends, both in elevation and in geological time, to a height of 9,100 feet at Bryce. Thus the park stands at a higher elevation than the other national parks in Utah—Arches, Canyonlands, Capitol Reef, and Zion—and instead of finding those parks' desert ecologies, visitors to Bryce will enjoy cooler temperatures and an alpine environment. Stands of piñon-juniper in the lower parts of Bryce give way to communities of huge, majestic ponderosa pines and then, near Rainbow Point, to forests of spruce, aspen, and fir.

Unlike many of the parks in the Colorado Plateau region, where sandstone is the dominant rock, Bryce is filled with brightly colored, almost glowing, limestone, and the forces of flowing water, rain, snow, and ice have eroded the limestone into exotic shapes.

Like other parks in this area, Bryce was once covered by vast lakes, and the red rocks were under water. About 15 million years ago, the pressures associated with continental drift that created the coastal mountains also raised much of the western half of North America as high as 2 miles above sea level, causing these enormous lakes to disappear. This increase in altitude contributed to a change in the weather patterns of the area, bringing more precipitation, which carved out the mostly bare rock of Bryce.

FLORA AND FAUNA Spotted on rare occasions browsing in the meadows in the early morning or late evening, the elk is the largest mammal you're likely to see in Bryce. Porcupines, mule deer, skunks, gray foxes, coyotes, and a number of small rodents, such as chipmunks, marmots, pine squirrels, and prairie dogs, also inhabit the park.

Birders have identified 172 species of bird in the park, including the common nighthawk, three kinds of hummingbirds, the northern flicker, Steller's jay, pygmy nuthatch, meadowlark, bluebird, robin, swift, and swallow. A checklist is available at the visitor center.

Bryce's often long and snowy winters are a prelude to spectacular displays of wildflowers in the spring and early summer, with sego lilies, pentstemons, asters, clematis, evening primrose, skyrocket gilias, Indian paintbrush, and wild iris common from May through June. Rabbitbrush and goldenrod bloom later.

WHEN TO GO At a higher elevation than other Utah parks and with cooler summer temperatures (daytime highs in the low 80s, evenings in the mid-40s), Bryce would be an ideal summer vacation area if only no one else knew about it. Some 75% of Bryce's visitors come in the summer months—June, July, and August—and the crowds can pack trails, local motels, and campgrounds to capacity. Although thunderstorms may dampen a summer trip, the resulting rainbows and the play of the thunderclouds and sunlight on the red rocks more than make up for the inconvenience. The lodge is open from mid-April through October, during which time horseback riding and many interpretative activities are available.

By contrast, when the snow begins to fall and cover the formations, Bryce is nearly deserted. Although the major road into the park is almost always open and local motels offer winter specials and discounted rates, only a few lucky visitors have discovered the benefits of a winter trip to this area. Conditions are usually good for snowshoeing and cross-country skiing from late December into March, and the park offers free use of snowshoes. Taking a lonely snowshoe trip down into the Bryce amphitheater on a clear, blue January morning ranks among the most pleasurable experiences to be had in any Utah park. Skiing along the rim of the amphitheater and out to several of the major overlooks allows a visitor to see a face of the park enjoyed by few. Temperatures, however, can be low; Bryce Canyon regularly records some of the coldest readings in all of Utah. In January, for example, the average high is 39°F and the average low 9°F, although temperatures as low as -30°F have been recorded.

Fall may be the best season to see Bryce. The weather is usually quite clear; temperatures rise into the 70s during the day and dip into the 30s at night; the aspens begin to turn gold and, seen against the park's evergreens, create a spectacular sight. What's more, the summer crowds have subsided, and the park is quiet and serene.

The weather is a bit more unpredictable in the spring, often bringing rain and snow. Trails, though passable, can be muddy, and average lows remain below freezing well into May. But on a clear spring day when the leaves just begin to peek out and the first warm sun hits the amphitheater, such inconveniences are soon forgotten.

SEASONAL EVENTS Except for the town celebrations honoring Mormon pioneers, the following events are hosted by Ruby's Inn (tel. 801/834–5341).

President's Day Weekend: The **Winter Festival** features a 10-kilometer cross-country ski race, a dance, Nordic tours, and ski clinics. **Memorial Day to Labor Day:** Step into the Wild West six nights a week at the **Bryce Canyon Rodeo,** held in an arena near the park entrance. **First weekend in June:** Take rides in the area surrounding Bryce Canyon during the **Mountain Bike Festival,** and learn what your bike and you can do. **Saturday closest to July 24:** Towns near Bryce Canyon, including Tropic, Panguitch, Cannonville, and Hatch, hold local celebrations to honor the day the **Mormon pioneers** first came to the Salt Lake Valley.

WHAT TO PACK You won't need any special equipment in Bryce. In spring, when the hiking trails tend to be muddy, an extra pair of shoes can come in handy, and since nights can be cool, even in the middle of the summer, bring a warm jacket or light parka. Because the sun is usually out, in both summer and winter, a good sunscreen, long sleeves, and a hat are recommended. And don't forget to bring an adequate supply of water bottles—especially if you plan to be out on the trails in June, July, or August.

GENERAL STORES The **General Store at Bryce Canyon** (tel. 801/834–5361) is the only store in the park (except for the gift shop at the lodge). Located near Sunrise Point, the shop sells film, souvenirs, and groceries from the end of April through October. It is open daily 7 AM to 9 PM.

Ruby's Inn (tel. 801/834–5341), located north of the park boundary on Highway 63, is a larger facility with a good selection of groceries, souvenirs, and camping equipment. Ruby's is open daily year-round 7 AM to 10:30 PM.

Four miles northwest of the park, **Fosters** (tel. 801/834–5327) has a general store, with a bakery, which is open daily in spring, summer, and fall, 7 AM to 8 PM. Fosters's 24-hour towing and car-repair service provides good, honest service year-round.

Doug's (tel. 801/679–8633), a small general grocery store in Tropic, is usually open daily in summer 7 AM to 11 PM. Winter hours vary according to the owner's discretion.

ARRIVING AND DEPARTING As is the case for many national parks, the easiest way to get to Bryce Canyon is by car, driving from Las Vegas (237 miles) or Salt Lake City (256 miles). The nearest small city from which you can rent a car or board a tour bus is Cedar City, 78 miles west of the park, but you can also rent a car in St. George, 126 miles southwest of Bryce.

By Plane. Bryce Canyon airport is located 4 miles from the entrance to the park. It is larger than other southern Utah airports because it is used for emergency landings. **Bryce Air Service** (tel. 801/834–5208) has rental cars ($30 half day, $45 full day) and rental vans ($55 half day, $80 full day, for up to 15 passengers); it also shuttles visitors from the airport to Bryce Lodge or Ruby's Inn for $6 one-way.

Air Nevada Airlines (tel. 800/634–6377) flies daily year-round from Las Vegas to Bryce as long as there are at least four people flying. It costs about $258 to fly round-trip.

If you fly into Las Vegas, Salt Lake City, Cedar City, or St. George, you can rent a car or limousine from these airports and drive to the park. It generally costs just under $40 per day to rent a compact car, but better prices may be arranged when calling in advance for a reservation.

Cedar City car rentals include: **Avis** (Municipal Airport, tel. 801/586–3033), **Hertz** (943 S. Main St., tel. 801/586–6096), **National Car Rental** (Municipal Airport, tel. 801/586–7059), and **Speedy Rental** (650 N. Main St., tel. 801/586–7368).

You can rent a car in St. George from: **A–1 Car Rental** (590 E. St. George Blvd., tel. 801/673–8811), **Avis** (St. George Municipal Airport, tel. 801/673–3686), **Budget** (1275 N. Highland Dr., tel. 801/673–6825), **Dollar Rent-A-**

Car (1175 S. 150 E., tel. 801/628–6549), and **National** (St. George Municipal Airport, tel. 801/673–5098).

To rent a car in Salt Lake City or Las Vegas, call **Avis** (tel. 800/331–1212), **Hertz** (tel. 800/654–3131), **Thrifty** (tel. 800/367–2277), or **Budget** (tel. 800/527–0700).

By Car and RV. It is about a six-hour drive from either Salt Lake City or Las Vegas to Bryce Canyon. Many people combine a trip to Bryce with visits to Zion National Park (an 84-mile, two-hour drive) and, during summer, the North Rim of the Grand Canyon (a 152-mile, three-hour drive).

There are three ways to approach Bryce. The entrance is in the northwest of the park and can be approached from the south on U.S. 89 via Kanab and Hatch or from the north on U.S. 89 via Panguitch. You will have to turn east onto Route 12 and then south onto Highway 63, which leads directly to the park entrance. From U.S. 89 it is about 17 miles to the Bryce entrance. An alternate route, making a loop toward Capitol Reef National Park, will take you along what is perhaps the most scenic road in the state. From Salt Lake City, take I–15 to the Scipio exit. Pick up U.S. 50 to I–70 and then at the Sigurd exit take Route 24 to Route 12. You will drive near Capitol Reef, through the Dixie National Forest, and past the Anasazi Indian Village and Escalante Petrified Forest state parks to enter Bryce after passing through the town of Tropic. The section of road between the towns of Grover and Boulder on Route 12 is particularly beautiful. When you reach the juncture of Highways 12 and 63, turn left onto Highway 63 and drive 3¹/₂ miles to the park entrance.

Trailers cannot be taken beyond the Sunset campground near the park's entrance, because the road running south into the park is narrow and twisting. They can be left at the visitor-center parking area. RVs longer than 25 feet are not allowed on the Bryce/Paria Point Road.

By Train. The **Amtrak** station (tel. 800/872–7245) closest to Bryce is in the tiny hamlet of Milford, about 52 miles north of Cedar City, but there are no buses or rental cars in Milford. Amtrak serves Salt Lake City and Las Vegas, where you can rent a car (*see* By Plane, *above*) or sign up for a commercial bus tour (*see* Guided Tours, *below*).

By Bus. Greyhound Lines (tel. 801/355–4684) serves St. George and Cedar City. From either city you can rent a car, take a taxi, or take a tour bus to the park (*see* Guided Tours, *below*).

EXPLORING

Bryce Canyon is a relatively easy park to visit, largely because so much of it can be viewed from the 13 major overlooks, which are connected by an 18-mile paved rim road. In a day, it's possible to drive the rim, go for a short hike, take a horseback ride into the canyon, and come away with a decent sense of what the park has to offer.

Visitors with extra time should consider either taking an all-day hike into the amphitheater or driving to nearby Kodachrome Basin State Park, Anasazi Indian Village, Escalante Petrified Forest State Park, or Dixie National Forest (tel. 801/865–3700) to enjoy the area's varied and unusual scenery. (For information about any Utah state park, call 801/538–7221.)

Regardless of how much time you have, be sure to explore the park in the very early morning or in the late afternoon, when the sun sets the rocks ablaze with color. You should also set aside 30 minutes or more to descend, if only briefly, into the amphitheater.

THE BEST IN ONE DAY Visitors with only one day to spare in Bryce should get up before sunrise and grab a quick breakfast at either Ruby's Inn or the Lodge (*see* Dining, *below*) before heading to Sunrise Point. The Point is a photographer's heaven in early morning, and those who watch the sun come up will experience the park when it's most peaceful.

Consider hiking into the Queen's Garden (*see* Nature Trails and Short Walks, *below*) and, depending on how much energy you have,

perhaps tackling the 1¹/₂-mile Navajo Loop Trail (*see* Longer Hikes, *below*). It takes about three hours to hike both trails, and you'll end up back on the rim at Sunset Point, a ¹/₂-mile walk from Sunrise Point. It should be time for that leisurely picnic lunch you packed.

After lunch, you have several options: You could wander back to the visitor center to browse through books and watch the slide show; tag along on an interpretative hike with a ranger; saddle up a horse for a half-day trot; or head for the helipad at Ruby's Inn, where you'll be airlifted over the canyon.

If you don't mind sitting in your car, it is possible to gaze out over all 13 overlooks in one afternoon, but their beauty begins to pall after you've seen five or six. A better idea is to stop at the ones that you *feel* like stopping at and take brief walks along the rim trail. If it isn't too hot, a good choice of hikes is the 1¹/₂-mile round-trip Bristlecone Loop trail from Rainbow Point, which takes you through a forest of bristlecone pine.

Make sure you end the day at sunset, and make sure you're standing at Sunset Point, camera in hand.

ORIENTATION PROGRAMS The 10-minute introductory slide show at the visitor center is worth viewing. It runs every 30 minutes during peak season; on request off-season. The rangers also offer a number of interpretative programs and guided hikes during the summer months. Check at the visitor center for times and topics.

GUIDED TOURS Several operators offer tours of Bryce Canyon, often combined with trips to the North Rim of the Grand Canyon and Zion National Park. Perhaps the best known and most reliable is **Scenic West Tours** (Box 369, Draper, UT 84020, tel. 800/723–6429), which offers specialized package tours from Salt Lake City to Bryce, Zion, and Grand Canyon national parks from May through October. A three-day, two-night trip costs $350. Operators with more personalized service and flexible tours include **On the Town Tours** (Box 510541, Salt Lake City, UT 84151–0541, tel. 801/575–6040), **Toraco Enterprises** (747

E. St. George Blvd., St. George, UT 84770, tel. 801/628–8687), and **Western Leisure** (1172 Brickyard Rd., Suite 200, Salt Lake City, UT 84106, tel. 800/532–2113).

Take a step back in time and see the park through the windows of a **White Touring Limo** (tel. 801/834–5361), restored from the days when Union Pacific Railroad operated the Bryce Canyon Lodge. The car, with guide, leaves the lodge at 9, 11:30, 1:30, and 3:30 daily and stops at three points in the course of 1½ hours. The touring car remains in operation from late April through mid-October. Prices are $7 for adults and $3.50 for children under 12. Reservations are required.

You can spend from 10 minutes to 3 hours in the skies above Bryce Canyon with **Bryce Canyon Helicopters** (Box 41, Ruby's Inn, Bryce Canyon, UT 84764, tel. 801/834–5341). Prices run from $63 to $90 per person.

Air Nevada Airlines (tel. 800/634–6377) offers a $179 one-day package that is a good deal for those with limited time: Sightseers are picked up at any hotel in Las Vegas and driven to the airport, where they board a Cesna seven- to nine-seater plane, on which they are guaranteed a window seat. The plane flies over the Valley of Fire outside Las Vegas, Zion National Park, and Bryce Canyon National Park. At Bryce Canyon airport a buffet lunch is served, and visitors are then given a bus tour of Bryce, before flying back to Las Vegas.

For information about bicycle and horseback riding tours, *see* Other Activities, *below*.

SCENIC DRIVES AND VIEWS Only two roads pass through Bryce Canyon National Park: a section of **Highway 12** in the northern end of the park and **Highway 63,** which leads south to the main entrance and becomes the **Park Road**. It then dead-ends 18 miles from the park entrance at **Rainbow Point,** where there is a superb 270-degree view of the surrounding canyon country. The park's most famous formations are best viewed just after sunrise or just before sunset from Fairyland, Sunrise, Sunset, Inspiration, and Bryce points, as well as from Paria View.

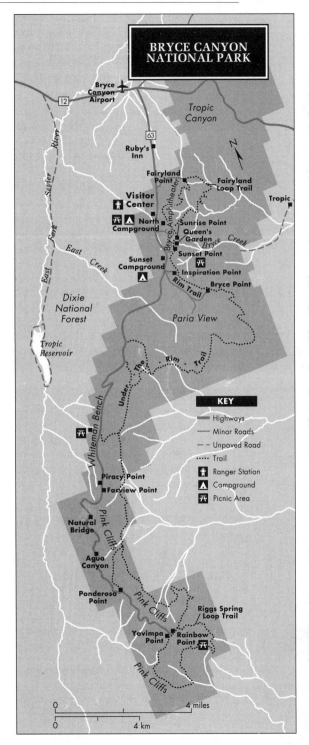

BRYCE CANYON NATIONAL PARK

KEY
- Highways
- Minor Roads
- Unpaved Road
- Trail
- Ranger Station
- Campground
- Picnic Area

RVs are allowed on the Park Road, but trailers are not permitted beyond the Sunset Campground (leave them in the visitor center parking lot). The road is open year-round, but after a heavy snowfall it may be closed for a few hours while crews clear the way.

Both walkers and wheelchair-bound visitors enjoy the trail that runs along the rim of the Bryce Amphitheater. Paved for the 1/2 mile from Sunset Point to Sunrise Point, the trail parallels the road and is 11 miles long. Major overlooks are rarely more than a one-minute walk from the parking areas.

HISTORIC BUILDINGS AND SITES Designed by Stanley Gilbert Underwood for the Union Pacific Railroad and built in the mid-1920s, the **Bryce Canyon Lodge** is one of the few park lodges that hasn't been the victim of a fire. (The Union Pacific also constructed lodges at Zion and at the North Rim of the Grand Canyon, but both of these later burned.) A National Historic Landmark, it has been faithfully restored, right down to the reproduced hickory furniture, which was built by the same company that produced the originals.

Outside the park's main entrance stands **Ruby's Inn,** an area landmark that has been operated by the Syrett family since 1919. Unfortunately, the building has been the victim of several fires, and although parts of the inn retain a rustic look, the facility is relatively new.

NATURE TRAILS AND SHORT WALKS Those who prefer their exercise in short, slow doses will find any stretch of the 11-mile **Rim Trail** suitable for strolling, especially the paved area between Sunrise and Sunset points. If it's a long stroll you want, but one that's not too strenuous, consider trading keys with another driver so that you can walk along the entire rim of the Bryce Amphitheater and have a car on the other end to take you back.

There are few short easy walks into the canyon, largely because the sloping nature of the amphitheater forces hikers to descend quickly. If you are willing to put a little work into your walk try the moderately strenuous

1 1/2-mile round-trip trek to the **Queen's Garden.** This is the easiest hike into the canyon itself, with a descent—and subsequent ascent—of 320 feet. Another short hike is the **Bristlecone Loop,** a 1 1/2-mile round-trip jaunt beside a bristlecone forest.

LONGER HIKES You can get down into the Bryce Amphitheater, but be warned: All of the trails that bring you closer to the forces that shape the canyon involve some steep descents and ascents. These trails are demanding, especially in the hot summer months. Be prepared with hat, sunscreen, and plenty of water.

One of the longest trails in the park, and the only one along which overnight stays are allowed, is the **Under-the-Rim Trail,** which begins at Bryce Point on the north side of the park and runs for just over 22 1/2 miles to Rainbow Point on the far southern end. From there, it's another 4 miles to Riggs Springs. You can choose to start at a different point to shorten the trip, but if you want to go the entire distance, give yourself two to three days and prepare for a 1,500-foot change in elevation.

Perhaps the best and most popular half-day hike is one that combines **Queen's Garden** and the **Navajo Loop Trail.** This hike covers 3 miles round-trip, with a 521-foot ascent, and leads through the most dramatic parts of the amphitheater. The trail is open year-round, unless ice makes it impassable. The least strenuous way to hike this route is to begin at Sunset Point, descending the switchbacks of the Navajo Loop first. The section of the trail near the Queen's Garden is not as steep, so it will be less work to ascend there. You will end up at Sunrise Point; the walk along the rim back to Sunset Point adds 1/2 mile.

The 5 1/2- to 7 1/2-mile round-trip trek on the **Peekaboo Loop** will take you three to four hours, and you'll have to work a little harder than on the Navajo Trail. You can start at Sunrise, Sunset, or Bryce points, and depending on which you choose, you will have to climb 500 to 800 feet. Along the way you'll happen upon some terrific formations: the

Cathedral, the Three Wisemen, and the Wall of Windows. This trail is intended for those on horseback; if you cover it on foot, be sure to give way to horses.

OTHER ACTIVITIES Biking. The 18-mile main road that passes through Bryce can provide an enjoyable half-day to day-long bicycle trip, but it can also be dangerous. The road has only two lanes, and there is no shoulder, so cyclists must always be on the lookout for cars, especially during the summer. Ruby's Inn (tel. 801/834–5341), near the park's northwest entrance, rents bicycles for $4 an hour, $12 for 4 hours, and $20 for 24 hours. Bike racks are few in the park, so if you want to leave your bike unattended, you may have trouble finding somewhere to lock it up.

Bikes are not allowed on any of the trails inside the park, so mountain bikers should head for **Dixie National Forest** (tel. 801/865–3700), where backcountry roads and mountain biking trails abound.

Backcountry Bicycle Tours (Box 4029, Bozeman, MT 59772, tel. 406/586–3556) offers relatively easy, fully supported, and catered six-day bike trips to Bryce and Zion, and **Backroads Bicycle Touring, Inc.** (1516 5th St., Suite Q333, Berkeley, CA 94710–1740, tel. 510/527–1555 or 800/245–3874; fax 510/527–1444) has a nine-day trip to Bryce and Zion.

Bird-Watching. More than 170 bird species have been spotted at Bryce. The best time to see them is from May through July, during the migration season in the high alpine area. A checklist is available at the visitor center.

Boating and Fishing. There's no boating or fishing inside the park, but you can do both at nearby Otter Creek Reservoir in **Otter Creek State Park** (tel. 801/538–7221), at the **Escalante Petrified Forest State Park** (tel. 801/538–7221), and at **Tropic Resevoir, Pine Lake,** and **Panguitch Lake** in Dixie National Forest (tel. 801/865–3700).

Horseback Riding. Bryce–Zion–Grand Canyon Trail Rides (Box 128, Tropic, UT 84736, tel. 801/679–8665 or 801/834–5219) offers two-hour ($20) and half-day ($30) rides into Bryce Canyon on the Peekaboo Loop trail, from early April through early October. Advance reservations are suggested.

Ski Touring. Unlike Utah's four other national parks, Bryce Canyon usually receives plenty of snow, making it an ideal and increasingly popular cross-country ski area. You can rent skis from **Ruby's Inn** (tel. 801/834–5341), which grooms a 10-kilometer trail outside the park that connects with the Fairyland Trail in Bryce Canyon. The park service does not plow the roads to Fairyland and Paria points. The 2½-mile Fairyland Trail is marked by blue diamonds, and the 5-mile Paria Loop, which runs through ponderosa forests into long, open meadows, is marked with orange. Skiing into the canyon itself is allowed but not recommended because drop-offs are steep and trails are narrow.

Snowshoeing. The National Park Service offers free use of snowshoes at the Bryce Visitor Center. Just leave your driver's license or a major credit card with a ranger for as many pairs of snowshoes as your group needs. Snowshoeing the Queen's Garden or Navajo Loop trails when the snow is several feet deep can be exhilarating, and there are days when snowshoers have the entire amphitheater area to themselves. Because some of the trails and drop-offs are so steep, snowshoes or even good winter boots may be preferable to cross-country skis as a means of getting into the canyon.

Swimming. There is no place to swim in the park, but **Escalante Petrified Forest State Park** (tel. 801/538–7221), about 40 miles east of Bryce, has an attractive swimming beach at Wide Hollow Reservoir, which is next to a campground.

CHILDREN'S PROGRAMS The Junior Ranger program runs from Memorial Day to Labor Day; children ages 6–12 can sign up at the park visitor center. In addition, some interpretative programs and hikes are geared especially for kids. To prepare your children for the trip, consider ordering the 32-page "Kid's

Guide to Bryce Canyon," for children 5–10 (see Publications, above).

EVENING ACTIVITIES Bryce Canyon and the surrounding area have little in the way of formal nightlife. In summer the National Park Service offers campfire programs nightly near the campgrounds. Check at the visitor center for details. A popular nighttime activity is the Bryce Canyon Rodeo, which runs every night but Sunday from Memorial Day to Labor Day. Tickets cost $5 for adults and $3 for children under 12; they may be purchased the day of the show at Old Bryce Town, across the street from Ruby's Inn (tel. 801/834-5341), which hosts the event.

DINING

Restaurants in the area surrounding Bryce lack pretension: They serve filling, Western-style foods in simple but pleasant settings. Steak is the food of choice, so vegetarians will have to make do with salad bars. Prices in this part of Utah are low; the most expensive entrée on the dinner menu at the relatively posh Bryce Canyon Lodge is $16.95. Most restaurants are clustered outside the main park entrance, and none of these requires reservations.

INSIDE THE PARK Bryce Canyon Lodge. Nestled among towering pines, this rustic old stone and wood lodge is the only place to dine within the park. Meals here are probably the best the area has to offer, although the lunch menu is rather standard. Among the most interesting choices are a Navajo taco (fry-bread covered with chili, tomatoes, and cheese) and the buffalo-burgers. For dinner, try the roast pork, fried chicken, or ground buffalo. *Bryce Canyon, UT, tel. 801/834–5361. Reservations required. AE, DC, MC, V. Closed late Oct.–late Apr. Moderate.*

NEAR THE PARK Bryce Canyon Pines Restaurant. If you have hungry kids, head for this small restaurant, where the children's menu runs from $2 for a hot dog to $4.75 for fish and chips. For adults there are consistently good six-course dinners, including hamburger steak and tenderloin. Other specialties are homemade soup, chili, and banana-blueberry pie. *Hwy. 12 (7 mi from park entrance), tel. 801/834–5441. D, DC, MC, V. Closed Dec.–Feb. Moderate.*

Doug's Place. Located in the tiny hamlet of Tropic, east of Bryce, Doug's Place specializes in steak. The variety of steak dishes includes breaded *Milanesa* (with tomato sauce), and a *Milanesa ala Neopolitonia* (with ham and Swiss cheese). Also on the menu are inexpensive taco salads, hamburgers, soft flour tacos, and homemade pies and sweet rolls. On Friday and Saturday nights Doug's serves a great prime-rib dinner. The restaurant is licensed to sell beer only. *141 N. Main St., Tropic, UT, tel. 801/679–8633. AE, D, DC, MC, V. Moderate.*

Fosters Family Steakhouse. With its stone fireplace and picture windows, Fosters is a clean, relatively quiet, modern steakhouse, and one of the most pleasant restaurants in the area. The menu features prime rib, steaks, and basic chicken and seafood dishes. Only wine and beer are served. It is located 4 miles from the entrance to the park on Highway 12, just west of the juncture of Highways 12 and 63. *Hwy. 12, tel. 801/834–5227. AE, D, MC, V. Closed Jan. Moderate.*

Hungry Coyote. Decorated with antiques and pictures from the area, this five-table restaurant in the Bryce Valley Inn specializes in Mexican food. Don't miss the Number One Burrito—seasoned chicken or beef on a 12-inch tortilla covered with salsa and cheese. *Bryce Valley Inn, 200 N. Main St., Tropic, UT, tel. 801/679–8811. AE, MC, V. Moderate.*

Ruby's Inn. This historic motel, store, and dining complex has been owned by the Syrett family since 1919. The victim of several fires, Ruby's has been remodeled many times over the years, but it continues to attract hordes of Bryce visitors. So many people pass through the doors every day that the food, while solid, is a bit lackluster. Best bets for dinner are the country-fried steaks or the fillet steak wrapped in bacon. There's a sandwich bar, children's menu, and a good soup-and-salad bar, as well as an all-you-can-eat buffet for lunch and dinner. *Hwy. 63 (1 mi north of park* *entrance), tel. 801/834–5341. AE, D, DC, MC, V. Moderate.*

Harold's Place. Located on Highway 12, at the entrance to Red Canyon and about 15 miles west of Bryce, Harold's specializes in Philly burgers (¹/₃-pound burger with green peppers, onions, mushrooms, and melted Swiss cheese), Italian meatball sandwiches, fajitas, and Mexican-style pizza. At lunch, mostly Mexican dishes are served, and at dinner, you'll find mainly Chinese dishes and steaks. Harold's has a beer license only. *3066 Hwy. 12, tel. 801/676–2350. No credit cards. Closed Oct.–Mar. Inexpensive–Moderate.*

PICNIC SPOTS There are three picnic areas inside the park. The one near **Rainbow Point,** at the southern end of the park, and the one near the **North Campground** are the most developed. The Rainbow Point picnic area is the more scenic of the two. Another, smaller facility is located half-way between the entrance and Rainbow Point, just north of a place locals call Piracy Point (unmarked). Picnic supplies are available inside the park from a small general store near Sunrise Point (open daylight hours).

LODGING

Lodging choices in the Bryce Canyon area are few. The nearest town of any significance, Panguitch, is 24 miles from the park entrance. With the exception of the Bryce Canyon Lodge, inside the park, don't expect anything more than a roadside motel. The facilities listed below are clustered around the main entrance, in the northwest corner of the park. Advance reservations are a must in summer. At the very least arrive early in the day.

INSIDE THE PARK **Bryce Canyon Lodge.** In an attempt to preserve the past, many of the materials from the original Bryce Canyon Lodge were used in the stone and timber building's 1989 reconstruction. The lodge and its western-style cabins therefore retain the rustic feel of an authentic 1930s retreat. Weary hikers rest on replica bark-covered hickory chairs while warming their hands before the lobby's grand limestone fireplace.

The main lobby of this National Historic Landmark is lighted by a log and wrought-iron chandelier. There are four recently refurbished suites on the second floor, and 40 lodgepole-pine units are scattered across the property. These sleep up to four people, and most feature 12-foot cathedral ceilings and gas fireplaces. There are also two motel-style buildings with 70 additional rooms that have either groundfloor porches or upstairs balconies. Reservations are hard to come by: Call several months ahead, or, if you're feeling lucky, call the day before your arrival—cancellations occasionally make last-minute bookings possible. *Bryce Canyon, Box 400, Cedar City, UT, 84721, tel. 801/586–7686, fax 801/586–3157. 114 rooms with bath. Facilities: restaurant, gift shop. AE, DC, MC, V. Closed Nov.–late-Apr. Moderate–Expensive.*

NEAR THE PARK **Bryce Canyon Pines Motel and Restaurant.** This quiet, relatively modern motel complex is nestled in the woods 6 miles from the park entrance. Most of the rooms offer excellent mountain views. Two housekeeping cottages and three cabin-suites are available. *Hwy. 12, Box 43, Bryce, UT 84764, tel. 801/834–5441. 51 rooms with bath. Facilities: restaurant, campground park, RV park, indoor pool. D, DC, MC, V. Moderate–Expensive.*

Bryce Valley Inn. Located in the tiny community of Tropic at the base of the national park, this new facility, more like a motel than an inn, is decorated inside and out with wood. It provides shuttle service for hikers and bicyclists to the park. A gift shop sells Native American crafts. *200 N. Main St., Box A, Tropic, UT 84776, tel. 801/679–8811. 63 rooms. Facilities: restaurant, gift shop, laundromat. AE, MC, V. Moderate.*

Ruby's Inn. A member of the Best Western chain, Ruby's is the largest and longest-operating facility in the area. It is also the most complete—with restaurant, gas station, store, shopping complex, nightly rodeo in summer, helicopters, RV park, horseback riding, ski and bicycle rentals, and even a U.S. post office. The rooms are relatively new or recently refurbished and typical of Best

Westerns. Reserve far in advance. *Hwy. 63 (1 mi north of park entrance), Box 1, Bryce, UT 84764, tel. 801/834–5341 or 800/528–1234, fax 801/ 834–5265. 216 rooms with bath. Facilities: restaurant, RV park, pool, shops. AE, D, DC, MC, V. Moderate.*

CAMPING

INSIDE THE PARK There are two large public campgrounds, the **North Campground** and **Sunset Campground,** in Bryce Canyon National Park, with a total of 218 sites for both tents and RVs. No reservations are accepted, and the campgrounds generally fill every night from mid-May through mid-September. It is best to arrive by 2 PM. To find out in advance if sites are available, call the visitor center (tel. 801/834–5322). Before planning a winter camping trip, check with park headquarters; budget cuts have caused the campground to close during recent winters. The camping fee is $7 per night in both campgrounds.

There are some designated RV sites at these campgrounds, and tenters may have an RV in the site next to them. Hookups are not available at either campground, and the maximum RV length is 30 feet. A sewage dump station is located near the North Campground, but it's shut down during the winter months.

Set amid pine trees, all the sites in these campgrounds are similar; each has a fire grate and picnic table. Restrooms scattered throughout the areas have flush toilets and cold running water. During the summer, campers can enjoy evening programs at both facilities.

A store, pay showers ($1.50 for seven to nine minutes), and laundry facilities ($1.25 to wash and dry one load) are located near Sunrise Point, just a short distance from either campground. These are open from early May through mid-October.

Hikers who choose to overnight on the Under-the-Rim Trail must camp at designated backcountry sites and must have a free backcountry permit. There are 11 of these sites along the trail—at Yellow Creek (3), Sheep Creek, Swamp Canyon (2), Natural Bridge, Corral Hollow, Yovimpa Pass, and Riggs Spring (2). They are nothing more than cleared areas for tents. Only six people may camp in each site with one permit; if your party consists of 7 to 10 people you must obtain a special permit for one of the group sites at Yellow Creek or Riggs Spring. Open campfires are not allowed, so if you plan to cook, bring a portable stove.

NEAR THE PARK There are two relatively primitive but spectacular U.S. Forest Service camping areas in the Dixie National Forest near Bryce Canyon. Appropriately named **Red Canyon** (tel. 801/676–8815 or, for reservations only, 800/280–2267), on Highway 12 about 8 miles from the entrance to Bryce, has 39 sites for tent or RV. It is surrounded by pine trees in a brilliant red rock canyon not unlike the Bryce amphitheater. On Highway 143, 2 1/2 miles from Panguitch and about 30 miles from Bryce, **White Bridge** (tel. 801/865–3200) has 29 sites, for tent or RV, set in another quiet red rock canyon. Both areas have fire grates and drinking water and flush toilets until the weather turns cold. They are open from mid-May to mid-September. Sites cost $7 per night.

Tenters will enjoy staying at the alpine setting of **King's Creek campground** (tel. 801/676–8815), also in Dixie National Forest. It is about 11 miles from Bryce, just west of the park boundary and near Tropic Reservoir; to get there, you will have to turn off Highway 12 west of the juncture with Highway 63 and drive south for 7 miles down a dirt road. King's Creek has 34 individual sites for tents or RVs and one group site. The campground is open from mid-May to mid-September. Sites cost $6 per night.

Two of the best public campgrounds east of the park are found at **Kodachrome Basin State Park** and at **Escalante Petrified Forest State Park.** Kodachrome Basin is 9 miles southeast of the town of Cannonville and about 23 miles east of Bryce. Its unusual monolithic rock formations make it an attraction in its own right, and the 24-site campground there ranks among the best in Utah.

BRYCE CANYON CAMPGROUNDS

	INSIDE THE PARK		NEAR THE PARK									
	North	Sunset	Red Canyon (National Forest)	White Bridge (National Forest)	King's Creek (National Forest)	Kodachrome Basin State Park	Escalante Petrified Forest State Park	Ruby's Inn	Bryce Canyon Pines	Bryce/Zion KOA	Red Canyon RV Park	Riverside
Total number of sites	107	111	39	29	34	24	22	200	50	80	35	124
Sites suitable for RVs	75	83	28	29	25	24	22	100	25	60	30	124
Number of hookups	0	0	0	0	0	0	0	100	25	50	30	58
Drive to sites	•	•	•	•	•	•	•	•	•	•	•	•
Hike to sites												
Flush toilets	•	•	•	•		•	•	•	•	•	•	•
Pit/chemical toilets			•		•							
Drinking water	•	•	•	•	•	•	•	•	•	•	•	•
Showers		•			•	•	•	•	•	•	•	•
Fire grates	•	•	•	•	•	•	•	•	•	•	•	•
Swimming							•	•	•	•		•
Boat access												
Playground								•	•	•	•	
Disposal station					•	•		•	•	•	•	•
Ranger station	•	•										
Public telephone	•	•			•			•	•	•	•	•
Reservation possible			•*			•*	•*	•	•	•	•	•
Daily fee per site	$7	$7	$7	$7	$6	$9–$10	$9–$10	$12–$19	$10–$14	$15–$18.50	$8–$17	$11–$13
Dates open	early May–mid-Oct.	year-round	mid-May–mid-Sept.	late May–mid-Sept.	mid-May–mid-Sept.	mid-Mar.–late Oct.	mid-Apr.–late Oct.	Apr.–Nov.	early May–mid-Oct.	mid-Apr.–mid-Oct.	mid-Mar.–Nov.	year-round

*Reservation fee charged.

Escalante Petrified Forest is about 45 miles east of the park on Highway 12 and has 22 sites for tents and RVs (no hookups). Both campgrounds have showers, flush toilets, drinking water, fire grates, and a disposal station. Both charge $9 a night Sun.–Thurs. and $10 on Fri. and Sat. Campground sites at any Utah state park can be reserved for $5 by calling 800/322–3770; call 801/538–7221 for general information.

Several private campgrounds are located near the park. One of the closest is **Ruby's Inn** (tel. 801/834–5301), which has 200 RV and tent sites with 100 hookups, most set in shaded areas. Ruby's has everything a camper could ask for—flush toilets, showers, drinking water, fire grates, disposal station, public phone, laundry room, heated pool, and game room—but staying here is not exactly a peaceful outdoors experience. It's open from April to November; sites cost $12 to $19.

Shady, quiet sites in a wooded setting can be found at **Bryce Canyon Pines** (tel. 801/834–5441), 6 miles from the park entrance on Highway 12. This smaller campground has 50 sites for tents and RVs (25 hookups), with flush toilets, hot showers, drinking water, fire grates, playground, disposal station, and public phones. Campers can enjoy horseback riding, a game room, and a swimming pool. There is also a convenience store, laundromat, and gas station. Sites cost $10 to $14 per day. The campground is open from mid-April to late October.

If you are heading to Zion, you could break up your trip by staying at the **Bryce/Zion KOA,** on Highway 89, about 50 miles from both Bryce and Zion and 90 minutes from the Grand Canyon. This secluded campground is set amid juniper and oak trees at the base of majestic pink cliffs. It has 60 RV (30 water/electric and 20 full hookups) and 20 tent sites as well as two large group sites that can accommodate up to 40 people. There are flush toilets, hot showers, drinking water, fire grates, a disposal station, and a public phone here. Laundry facilities and a general store are convenient additions, and the playground, swimming pool, hiking trails, and guided horse tours will keep campers busy. The KOA is open from May 1 to October 15. Sites cost $15 to $18.50 and should be reserved in advance. Contact Glendale KOA, Box 186, Glendale, UT 84729, tel. 801/648–2490.

The **Red Canyon RV Park** (tel. 801/676–2690) is 16 miles from Bryce; it's near a red canyon on Highway 12, 1 mile east of U.S. 89. The 30 RV sites all have full hookups, and visitors can choose to stay in either a tepee that sleeps up to five or one of four log cabins. A desert campground where sage brush and mountain views are plentiful, Red Canyon has a recently constructed shower and rest room facility, as well as fire grates, a playground, and a public phone. Tenters can use the sites for $8 per site per night; RVers pay $11 per site, and kids under 10 stay free. Cabins start at $17. This campground is open from mid-March into November.

The **Riverside Campground** (tel. 801/735–4223 or 800/824–5651) is located ¹/₂ mile north of Hatch on U.S. 89. Its 124 sites (58 with full hookups) are nestled together well off the road. Open year-round, Riverside has flush toilets, drinking water, showers, fire grates, river swimming, a playground, a disposal station, and a public phone, as well as eight motel units. Campsites cost $11 to $13.

Canyon de Chelly National Monument

Arizona

By Ron Butler
Updated by Edie Jarolim

In Canyon de Chelly, nature paints the landscape using very broad strokes. Walls of rock rise hundreds of feet above the canyon floor, like sentinels guarding the desert's history. Tall monoliths point accusing fingers of red rock toward the heavens, and massive red sandstone buttes and mesas dot the landscape. Gracious cottonwoods and tilled fields on the canyon floor, however, reveal a softer, more hospitable side of this imposing land.

Located in the northeast corner of Arizona, Canyon de Chelly (pronounced *deh-SHAY*) occupies 131 square miles of Navajoland, the largest Native American reservation in North America. It was officially declared a reservation in 1868, but the Navajo, now numbering about 200,000, have occupied this land for almost 400 years. Their 25,000-square-mile reservation, spreading across Arizona, New Mexico, and Utah, is near such famous American landmarks as Monument Valley, the Petrified Forest, the Painted Desert, and

Glen Canyon. But the most impressive and dramatic of the area's sights is certainly Canyon de Chelly National Monument, which encompasses three of the most magnificent canyons in the Southwest: Canyon de Chelly, Canyon del Muerto, and Monument Canyon.

Beautiful though it may be, Canyon de Chelly National Monument offers visitors much more than just another pretty rock face: The landscape here serves as the backdrop for a wealth of Native American history. The Anasazi, "the ancient ones," were the early ancestors of the Pueblo people, and ruins in the form of more than 100 village sites dating back as far as the 4th century are located here. All types of Anasazi architecture are found, from simple pit houses to multistory pueblos, history's first apartment houses. Canyon del Muerto's famous Mummy Cave, with its three-story tower, is where two mummies were found preserved by the desert's dryness. Other prize archaeological finds include Antelope House, named for the Navajo antelope drawings found on its walls, and White House, the upper section of which is white-washed.

The Navajo who farm Canyon de Chelly's bottomland today moved in some 300 years after the original Anasazi tenants had migrated late in the 13th century. It was from here in 1864 that Kit Carson and his troops forced the Navajo to make the infamous 300-mile Long March to the Bosque Redondo in eastern New Mexico. Of the 9,000 Navajos taken captive, 3,000 to 4,000 died, many stricken by smallpox once they arrived in New Mexico. The Navajo resettled Canyon de Chelly in 1868, and today they continue to farm and raise sheep here in the tradition of their forefathers. The area became a national monument in 1931.

Visitors to this area should remember to respect the privacy and customs of the Navajo people. Approach homes only when invited, and do not wander across residential areas or disturb property. Also, obtain permission before taking photographs of Navajo people; a small gratuity may be expected.

ESSENTIAL INFORMATION

VISITOR INFORMATION For specific information about Canyon de Chelly contact the Superintendent's office at **Canyon de Chelly National Monument** (Box 588, Chinle, AZ 86503, tel. 602/674–5500 or 602/674–5501). The **Arizona Office of Tourism** (1100 W. Washington St., Phoenix, AZ 85007, tel. 602/542–TOUR or 800/842–8257) provides a variety of informative printed material. For information and help with hotel reservations, contact the **Native American Tourist Center** (4130 N. Goldwater Blvd., Scottsdale, AZ 85251, tel. 602/945–0771), and for additional information regarding Navajo country, contact the **Navajoland Tourism Department** (Box 663, Window Rock, AZ 86515, tel. 602/871–6659 or 602/871–7371).

The visitor center opens at 8 AM year-round and closes at 7 PM from Memorial Day to Labor Day and at 5 PM the rest of the year.

Note: Although the Navajo nation in Arizona observes Daylight Savings Time from April 7 through October 27, the rest of Arizona and the Hopi Reservation (located virtually in the center of the Navajo Reservation) remain on Mountain Standard Time. Plan accordingly.

FEES Admission to Canyon de Chelly and its visitor center is free; this includes the North and South rim drives and the self-guided tour to the White House Ruin. In addition, there are free canyon hikes led by a ranger that depart from the visitor center at 9 AM daily from Memorial Day through Labor Day. The number of people allowed on these tours is limited, so arrive early.

All other tours of Canyon de Chelly and its tributaries, made either on foot, horse, or in four-wheel-drive vehicles, must be made in the company of authorized Navajo guides, who are available for hire at the visitor center. The beautiful rock formations seen here are not without their hazards. Loose rocks, quicksand, and flash floods are common in these canyons: Guides are necessary to ensure the safety of visitors. The cost for a guide in a four-wheel-drive vehicle provided by the visitor (one guide required per five vehicles) is $10 per hour; four-hour Navajo-led hikes cost $10 per person (maximum 15 people) or $10 per hour for a smaller, more personalized tour. Guided tours on horseback are offered by a concessionaire (*see* Guided Tours, *below*). You must have a permit, available free at the visitor center, to participate in any tour.

PUBLICATIONS The Canyon de Chelly Visitor Center offers a good selection of books and publications about both the canyon and Native American country. Some that will prove particularly enlightening are *Canyon de Chelly: Its People and Rock Art,* by Campbell Grant; *Women in Navajo Society,* by Ruth Roessel, and the inexpensive *Canyon de Chelly Handbook,* offering practical tips for exploring and enjoying the spectacular canyon.

Other books worth reading include *A Celebration of Being,* by Susanne Page (with a forward by Robert Redford), which chronicles the activities that make up the circles of

Navajo and Hopi lives; *The Book of the Navajo,* by Raymond Friday Locke, perhaps the most comprehensive survey of the history and legends of the Navajo people; *The Main Stalk: A Synthesis of Navajo Philosophy,* by John R Farella; *Sa'anii Dahataat: The Women are Singing,* by Luci Tapahonso; *Navajo Rugs: How to Find, Evaluate, Buy and Care for Them,* by Don Dedera; *Dine' Behane': The Navajo Creation Story,* by Paul G. Zolbrod; *Indian Rock Art of the Southwest,* by Polly Schaafsma; and *Pueblos: Prehistoric Indian Cultures of the Southwest,* by Sylvio Acatos.

Free brochures such as "Canyon Overlook," "Navajoland Visitors Guide," and "Ya' a' Teeh from the Navajo Nation" are available at most area hotels, shops, and restaurants.

Because of Navajoland's sheer expanse, you'll find a good road map indispensable. An excellent map containing lists of area attractions is available free from the Navajoland Tourism Department (Box 663, Window Rock, AZ 86515, tel. 602/871–6659 or 602/871–7371).

GEOLOGY AND TERRAIN Sheer sandstone cliffs, though heavily eroded over time, still rise as high as 1,000 feet within the Canyon de Chelly. Their evolution began about 50 to 60 million years ago, when a group of rock formations nearly 50 miles wide and 100 miles long began to uplift along what is now the northern border of Arizona and New Mexico. Over the millennia this piece of land, known geologically as the Defiance Uplift, underwent upheaval that wrenched and twisted the layers of colored rock. Meanwhile, raging rivers from the nearby Chuska Mountains cut deeply at the foundations, forming the canyons. Over the years, a persistent wind, still experienced by those who visit today, has carved swirling striations into the sheer cliff walls, and manganese deposits from rain and river runoff painted a black wash on the red rocks—a striking phenomenon known as desert varnish.

Today, area streams are usually dry, although they do run fast in the spring, when filled with runoff from the mountain snows, and during the summer rainy season. The main canyons, Canyon de Chelly and Canyon de Muerto, both about 26 miles long, continue to stand over yesterday's ruins and today's fields, pastures, and traditional Navajo hogans (dwellings made of logs and mud), despite the harsh treatment of centuries of wind and water.

FLORA AND FAUNA The 24,347 square miles that make up the Navajo reservation are mostly arid or semiarid, with coniferous vegetation at the higher levels. While various forms of cactus, such as the prickly pear, and other desert plants can be found on the Canyon de Chelly plateau, it is the common reed and the sacred datura that are most often associated with the area. Douglas and Canadian fir trees grow along the upper reaches where snow lingers longest. Piñon pines, whose small edible nuts are prized, and juniper trees can be found along the canyon rim. At the lower altitudes are cottonwood trees, coyote willow, tamarisk, and Russian olive, the latter brought from western Asia in the 1800s to help stop water erosion in the area. Wildflowers such as beeplant and paintbrush cover the canyon floor in profusion during the spring and summer.

Animal life consists primarily of desert rodents: squirrels, chipmunks, skunks, and raccoons, all especially pesky from August through September, during the corn harvesting season. Hawks and eagles soar gracefully overhead, and canyon wrens, ravens, swallows, and piñon jays are also at home here.

WHEN TO GO Canyon de Chelly is open to visitors year-round, but during the cold winter months most travelers steer clear of the area's snow and hazardous road and trail conditions. The more sensible time to visit is between May and September, when the weather is more hospitable and all of the ranger-led activities, canyon hikes, and other programs are in full swing. October is also a very pleasant month in which to visit. Daytime temperatures from April through November range from 60°F to 98°F, but it can cool down considerably after sunset. Winter daytime temperatures fall between 30°F and 65°F but can quickly drop to below zero; also, the wind at the canyon's higher altitudes can be fierce. KTNN radio (AM 660), broadcasting from Window Rock, offers periodic weather updates in English and Navajo.

SEASONAL EVENTS July 1 to 4: The Navajo nation hosts more Native American rodeos than any other Native American reserve in the United States or Canada, and the **Fourth of July Rodeo**, held 65 miles south of Canyon de Chelly in Window Rock, capital of the Navajo nation, is by far the most spectacular. The simultaneous **Navajo Nation Powwow** is the world's largest Native American fair. For information call 602/871–6478, 602/871–6702, or the Navajoland Tourism Department at 602/871–6659 or 602/871–7371. **Late August/Early September:** Two similar events, both involving lots of food, dances, and arts and crafts, take place in late summer on the reservation—first the smaller **Central Navajo Fair** held in Chinle, then the **Annual Navajo Nation Fair** in Window Rock. For information, contact the Navajoland Tourism Department (*see above*).

WHAT TO PACK If you're planning to hike into the canyons, you'll need good walking shoes, binoculars, sunglasses, sunscreen, insect repellent, a canteen full of water (and an extra for emergencies), snacks, a broad-brim hat, camera equipment, tissues, and a small towel (be prepared to walk through water). Dress casually, and if you're going to be out after sunset be sure to bring a sweater or jacket; the temperature can drop dramatically. Winter temperatures can hover around 0°F, so if you're planning an off-season visit, be sure to dress warmly.

GENERAL STORES The tiny town of Chinle is roughly 3 miles west of Canyon de Chelly. You can find most of what you need at the **Tseyi Shopping Center** on Highway 191. It has a large **Bashas'** supermarket (tel. 602/674–3464 or 602/674–3465), open daily year-round, 8 AM to 10 PM Monday through Saturday and 8 to 8 Sunday. Also in the shopping center, **West World** (tel. 602/674–3610) is a western outfitter that can supply saddles, boots, blankets, and other western gear. It is open year-round, 9 to 8 Monday

through Saturday and 10 to 6 Sundays and holidays. In addition, there are some small grocery stores, gas stations, laundromats, and a few fast-food outlets in Chinle. There are no banks or ATMs in Chinle: The nearest bank is in Window Rock, some 65 miles to the south. While you're in town you might want to scout about the local shops for an early masterpiece by the famed Navajo artist R.C. Gorman, who grew up in Canyon de Chelly.

Driving south on U.S. 191 for about 45 minutes, you'll come to the famous **Hubbell Trading Post** (Rte. 264, 1 mile west of Ganado, tel. 602/755–3475), a museum and general trading post that is listed on the National Register of Historic Sites and operates much as it did over a century ago (*see* Historic Buildings and Sites, *below*). It is open daily 8 to 6 from June to September, and 8 to 5 from October to May; it's closed Thanksgiving, December 25, and January 1.

ARRIVING AND DEPARTING Although public transportation serves several towns on the outskirts of the reservation, there is no major air, train, or bus service to Navajoland itself, making it best to travel here by car.

By Plane. The closest commuter air connections are in Gallup, NM, (airport tel. 505/722–4896) located on Old Hwy 66 in western New Mexico, about 100 miles from the park. Other options are the airport in Flagstaff, located on I–40, 216 miles from the park, just outside the southwestern corner of the Navajo reservation, or in Page, on U.S. 89 near Lake Powell and Arizona's northern border, 180 miles from the park. Arizona's major air hub for these areas is **Sky Harbor International Airport** (tel. 602/273–3300) in Phoenix, served by nearly all major U.S. airlines. **America West** (tel. 800/235–9292) has daily flights from Phoenix to Gallup. Flights from Phoenix to Flagstaff are offered by Delta via **Sky West** commuter service (tel. 800/453–9417) and by America West. The town of Page is also served by Delta's Sky West commuter service.

At the airport in Gallup, **Avis** (tel. 505/863–9309) and **National** (tel. 505/863–6578) rent cars. Car rentals available at Flagstaff Municipal Airport include **Avis** (tel. 800/331–1212),

Budget (tel. 800/527–0700), and **Hertz** (tel. 800/654–3131). At Page Airport, try **Budget** (tel. 602/645–3977), but note that it's considerably less expensive to rent a car in Flagstaff than it is to rent one in Page.

By Car and RV. To reach Canyon de Chelly National Monument from Flagstaff, take I–40 east to Chambers, then U.S. 191 north to Ganado, where the road jogs west for 6 miles, and continue on U.S. 191 for another 47 miles north to Chinle. If you're driving from Page, take Route 98 southeast to Highway 160, which you must take north to Highway 59. Follow Highway 59 southeast to Many Farms, then pick up U.S. 191 south to Chinle. The monument is located approximately 2 miles east of Chinle on Indian Route 7.

Drivers need to remain alert for animals on the roads, especially after dark. The Navajo reservation has an open range policy; livestock are not fenced in and frequently wander onto roadways.

By Train. Amtrak (tel. 800/872–7245) provides daily service into Arizona from east and west, making scheduled stops in Gallup and Flagstaff from both directions. The Gallup station is at 201 East Highway 66, and car rentals are available at the airport, 2¹/₂ miles away. The station in Flagstaff is located downtown, within walking distance of **Budget** (100 N. Humphreys St., Flagstaff, AZ, tel. 602/774–2763) and **Admiral's** (602 W. Highway 66, Flagstaff, AZ, tel. 602/774–7394) car-rental offices.

By Bus. Greyhound Lines (tel. 800/231–2222) offers bus service to numerous Arizona destinations, including Page and Flagstaff, where car rentals are available. You can also take a Greyhound bus to Gallup, New Mexico (bus depot, tel. 505/863–3761), and make a connection with a Navajo Nation Transit bus, which will take you to Fort Defiance and on to Chinle. The Navajo Transit buses run Monday through Friday only, and you must catch the 2:25 bus out of Gallup in order to make the connecting bus in Fort Defiance that travels to Chinle. You must purchase two tickets, which together will cost less than $10. Call

Navajo Nation Transit (tel. 602/729–5449) to check the schedule.

EXPLORING

For excellent views of the canyon and ruins, there are two spectacular rim drives: the South Rim Drive, covering 36 miles round-trip and leading to eight dramatic overlooks, and the North Rim Drive, which is 34 miles round-trip and leads to four overlooks (*see* Scenic Drives, *below*). The White House Ruins trail, beginning at White House Trail Overlook, about 6 miles south of the visitor center, can be hiked independently; arrangements for the Navajo guides required for the many other spectacular hikes into the canyon can be made at the visitor center. You will need a permit (ask at the visitor center) and a guide to take a four-wheel-drive or horseback tour into the canyon (*see* Guided Tours, *below*). Be aware that canyon roads and trails are often impassable in winter and during and after heavy rains. Visitors are not allowed to enter any of the ruins.

THE BEST IN ONE DAY The visitor center opens at 8 AM, and this is the best place and time to begin your visit. Throughout the summer, special programs, hikes, and performances are scheduled on short notice and this is the place to find out about them. This is also a good time to browse through the center's bookstore and museum and pick up literature and maps. In the busy summer season, ranger talks are given daily, but the schedule varies, so check for times.

During the summer at 9 AM, the daily ranger-led tour into the canyon begins, a fascinating three-hour hike that explores the canyon's geology, plants, animals, ancient pictographs, and spellbinding ruins (*see* Guided Tours, *below*). The free hike is limited to 25 people, and participants must sign up in person at the visitor center no earlier than 48 hours in advance. If you can't secure a space on the gratis tour, you'll find that authorized guides lead other groups into the canyon throughout the day, at a cost of $10 per person (*see* Guided Tours, *below*). The hikes are rather strenuous, so all who join these in-

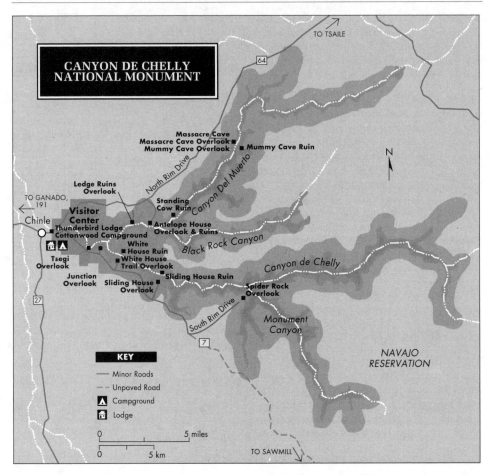

trepid bands of adventurers should be in relatively good physical condition.

If you take the 9 AM hike you'll be back in time for a well-earned lunch before joining the 2:15 PM ranger talk and demonstration held daily at the visitor center. At the afternoon lecture rangers discuss aspects of the Navajo culture and demonstrate such skills as basket weaving and flint knapping. If you've missed the morning hike, you can catch the two-hour archeology walk that leaves daily at 3:45 PM from Junction Overlook; check at the visitor center for information. Or, at any time of year, you can take the short unguided White Horse Trail hike (see Nature Trails and Short Walks, below). Later in the afternoon you might drive along the North and South rims for an overall

view of everything you've just seen up close (see Scenic Drives and Views, below).

ORIENTATION PROGRAMS The helpful ranger staff at Canyon de Chelly National Monument gives a variety of afternoon and evening demonstrations and talks. Topics include the history of the park and the Navajo people, Native American crafts, and Navajo mythology. For a full schedule of programs offered at the park, consult the visitor center (tel. 602/674–5500). The visitor-center museum has a wealth of displays providing background on the Anasazi cliff dwellers who lived in Canyon de Chelly from about AD 300 to 1300 and on the Navajo people who followed.

GUIDED TOURS Visitors are free to explore the rim of the canyon or hike the well-marked trail to the White House Ruin unescorted, but no one may explore the bottom of the canyon without a permit and a guide. You can almost always book a guided hike, even during off-season, but in summer, there are free ranger-led tours. Since the number of people allowed on these walks is limited, you must sign up no more than 48 hours in advance at the visitor center. The three-hour tour leaves from the visitor center at 9 AM daily, Memorial Day through Labor Day.

In order to hire one of the canyon's knowledgeable, authorized guides, almost always resident Navajo, stop by or phone the visitor center (tel. 602/674–5500 or 602/674–5501). These guides are available for four-hour tours for walking parties of up to 15 people; the cost is $10 per person (minimum $50 for four persons or less). As many as three hikes are offered each day during the busy season (April through October or November): generally, a morning hike, from 8:30 AM to 12:30 PM; an afternoon hike from 1 to 5; and a shorter, less expensive ($5 per person) trek from 4 to 6. The hikes, which go into either the Canyon de Chelly or the Canyon del Muerto, are approximately 4 miles round-trip. Note: Although a descent into the canyon is an extremely rewarding experience, some of the guided hikes are rather strenuous; trails are not graded and routes may involve steep ascents. Those who have a health problem or a fear of heights should question the guide carefully about the difficulty of the hike they're considering. Guides for smaller groups or individuals may also be hired for $10 per hour.

Visitors who plan on driving their own four-wheel-drive, high-clearance trucks through the canyon can hire one guide for groups of as many as five vehicles for $10 per hour. Free permits are required for anyone hiking or driving into the canyon; they can be obtained at the visitor-center information desk.

The **Thunderbird Lodge** (tel. 602/674–5841) offers tours into the canyon via heavy-duty four- and six-wheel-drive vehicles, appropriate for the rugged desert terrain. Daylong tours, offered from late spring through early fall, depart from the lodge at 9 and return at 5:30. This comprehensive tour costs $51.45 per person, including lunch. Two daily half-day tours from Thunderbird Lodge are offered year-round, one from 9 to 12:30, and the other from 2 to 5:30. The half-day tours take canyon goers halfway up Canyon del Muerto and Canyon de Chelly. The cost is $31.50 per person; $22.50 for children 12 and under.

Two authorized operators offer guided tours on horseback: **Justin's Horse Rental** (Box 881, Chinle, AZ 86503, tel. 602/674–5678), which is located beside the park entrance on South Rim Drive, and **Twin Trail Tours** (Box 1706, Window Rock, AZ 86515, tel. 602/674–8425, summer only), which is on North Rim Drive, just past Antelope House turnoff. Rates at Justin's are $8 per hour for each horse and $8 per hour for the requisite guide. Extended and overnight trips by horseback are also available.

A package photo tour of Canyon de Chelly National Monument and the Annual Navajo Nation Fair at Chinle is frequently offered to photography buffs by the **Friends of Arizona Highways** (tel. 602/271–5904) in the autumn. The package tour includes instruction by professional photographers, transportation from Phoenix, Navajo guides, four nights' lodging at the Thunderbird Lodge, snacks, background lectures on Navajo culture, slide shows, and photo tips. The cost is $925 per person, double occupancy.

SCENIC DRIVES AND VIEWS The **South Rim Drive** covers 36 miles round-trip and includes eight important overlooks, so it can take about two hours to make the trip. The first stop is **Tsegi Overlook**, from which you'll get a breath-stopping glimpse down the sheer canyon face to tranquil Navajo farming fields below. The hogan (many-sided Navajo home) that you can see on the farm is occupied during the warm weather. At the next stop, **Junction Overlook**, canyon walls come together, forming a tall, circular peninsula where Canyon del Muerto meets Canyon de Chelly. Two Anasazi cliff dwellings can be glimpsed from this vantage point. **White House Overlook** offers access, via a 2½-mile round-trip trail, to the best-known Anasazi cliff dwelling, White House, named after a long wall in the upper part of the ruin that's covered with white plaster (*see* Historic Buildings and Sites, *below*). Farther down South Rim Drive (another 3 miles) is **Sliding House Overlook**, from which you will see an ancient ruin perched so precariously along a narrow ledge that it appears about to topple into the canyon far below. **Wild Cherry Overlook** provides more stunning canyon vistas, while **Face Rock Overlook** offers a bird's-eye view of ancient canyon dwellings high in an opposite wall. **Spider Rock Overlook**, at the end of the route, is best saved for last. Here the walls drop more than 1,000 feet, and the slender, 800-foot-high Spider Rock monolith rises majestically from the canyon floor. Spider Rock was named by the Navajos as the legendary home of Spider Woman, the person who brought weaving to the tribe.

The **North Rim Drive**, along Canyon del Muerto, covers 34 miles round-trip and leads to four important overlooks; it, too, can be a two-hour ride. **Ledge Ruin Overlook** is the first stop. From here you'll see some of the Anasazi ruins and get sweeping views up and down the canyon. Four miles up the road are the two overlooks at **Antelope House**, located at the point where Canyon del Muerto and Black Rock Canyon join (*see* Historic Buildings and Sites, *below*). Skillful paintings of antelopes, attributed to a Navajo artist who lived here in the 1830s, are drawn on the canyon wall to the left of the ruin. The towering Navajo Fortress, once an important refuge from enemy raiders, can be seen across the canyon. The next turnoff, 8 miles up the highway on the right, brings you to two overlooks in Canyon del Muerto. **Mummy Cave Overlook** is a remarkably unspoiled pueblo dwelling so named because two mummies were found inside, preserved by the dryness of the cave. From nearby **Massacre Cave Overlook,** you can glimpse the ledge where more than 100 men, women, and children were slaughtered by the Spanish. The North Rim Drive turns into Highway 64, which runs

northwest into Tsaile, home of the Navajo Community College.

HISTORIC BUILDINGS AND SITES White House, Antelope House, and the other well-preserved ruins at Canyon de Chelly are among the best examples of multistory Anasazi pueblos to be found anywhere in the Southwest. People are not allowed to enter any of the ruins.

A 2½-mile round-trip trail leads to **White House**, the best-known Anasazi cliff dwelling. In the upper part of the ruin, there is a long wall that's covered with white plaster, which gives the ruin its name. It is believed that the construction of the White House, set into the cliffs "between heaven and earth," was begun around 1060. The two-level structure may have originally contained as many as 80 rooms, but today there are only 60 of them, along with four kivas (ceremonial structures), some of which could be reached only by ladders. Historians believe that once safely inside, the occupants withdrew the ladders so that intruders could not enter. White House, which could accommodate 50 or 60 people, was inhabited from the 11th to the 13th centuries. Near this pueblo are some of the unique, foot-size steps that Anasazi throughout the Southwest chipped into steep canyon walls to facilitate the climb to their dwellings high in the cliffs. The trail to White House is the only area in Canyon de Chelly that may be visited without a guide. Archaeological digs take place here from May through August.

Antelope House, an ancient Anasazi dwelling, is named for its colorful antelope drawings, made by a Navajo artist more than 150 years ago. A pit house under this impressive ruin dates to AD 693, and the site was probably occupied from then until the middle of the 13th century. The circular pits found here held kivas, and 91 rooms—some used for storage, some for living quarters—are still intact. From the overlook here, visitors can see the juncture of Canyon del Muerto and Black Rock Canyon.

The **Hubbell Trading Post** (*see* General Stores, *above*), a museum and historic shop, is listed on the National Register of Historic Sites. Navajo men and women give frequent demonstrations of jewelry-making and other traditional crafts. The trading post, now operated by the National Park Service, was founded in 1878 by John Lorenzo Hubbell, who was not only a merchant, but a friend, teacher, and frequently a doctor to the Navajo people; during the smallpox epidemic Hubbell's home was transformed into a hospital where he cared for the sick and dying. Hubbell, who died in 1930, is buried not far from the trading post.

The **Thunderbird Lodge** (*see* Lodging, *below*) in Chinle also began as a trading post, built in 1902 by trader Sam Day. Like other trading posts on the reservation, it served not only as a store but also as a bank, post office, community meeting place, and courtroom (with Day serving as sheriff, judge, and jury). On occasion, the lodge was even used as a makeshift hotel and hospital. The original trading-post building, which has changed owners many times over the years, is now part of a much larger facility incorporating a hotel and cafeteria.

Although not a historic building, the free **Ned Hatathli Museum** (tel. 602/724–3311), at the Navajo Community College in Tsaile, has an extensive collection of historic Navajo and other Native American arts, crafts, and artifacts. Many of the artworks and handicraft items are for sale. There's also a cafeteria, open to the public. The museum is usually open weekdays from 8 to 5, but call ahead to check the times.

NATURE TRAILS AND SHORT WALKS The only trail at Canyon de Chelly that visitors may explore without a guide is the well-maintained, 2½-mile round-trip **White House Trail** from the White House Overlook to the White House Ruin. The moderately difficult trail descends to the canyon floor 600 feet below. Hikers should be prepared to wade across Chinle Wash. Rangers and Navajo guides are emphatic about protecting the canyons: Visitors are cautioned not to pick up or remove any objects and not to sit on the walls of canyons or ruins. Be sure to carry water.

There is a ½-mile round-trip walk along the rim at **Spider Rock**, at the end of the South Rim Drive, with a number of scenic vantage points. This hike takes about 10 minutes. Brochures are available at the visitor center.

LONGER HIKES Hikers interested in making longer treks into Canyon de Chelly's backcountry must do so with a hired guide (*see* Guided Tours, *above*). There are no consistently marked trails in the park—only undesignated treks through the stark yet stunning, high-desert canyon country.

CHILDREN'S PROGRAMS All activities and programs at Canyon de Chelly are family oriented. Check the bulletin board at the visitor center (tel. 602/674–5500 or 602/674–5501) for specially scheduled children's activities. A Junior Ranger activity sheet is available for children, who can check off the plants, animals, and overlooks they see during the day, then turn in the completed sheet at the visitor center to get a certificate confirming their accomplishment.

EVENING ACTIVITIES The nightly 9 PM campfire program at the Campground Amphitheater is devoted to a different subject each night; topics include Navajo history, rock painting, and Anasazi culture. Check at the visitor center, the Thunderbird Lodge, or on the campground bulletin board for schedules.

DINING

There is very little of what might be considered fine dining in Canyon de Chelly country. The best restaurant in the region is also the newest: The cheerful lobby dining room in the Holiday Inn Canyon de Chelly (*see* Lodging, *below*), is low-key by big-city standards, but serves well-prepared versions of Native American dishes and good fish, pasta, and meat entrées. It also has the only salad bar around, although it's rather sickly. The other two motels in town (*see* Lodging, *below*) offer hearty, basic American-style cuisine and some Native American specialties such as fry bread and Navajo stew. Otherwise, only fast-food establishments are available. These include **Taco Bell** (tel. 602/674–5376) and **Burger King** (tel. 602/674–3700). All are located in Chinle. **Bashas'** supermarket in Chinle (Hwy. 191, tel. 602/674–3464 or 602/674–3465) has a deli section; sandwiches, salads, fried chicken, and other dishes may be carried to a small upstairs lounge with booths and tables.

LODGING

There is only one lodging inside the park, and if you are hoping to find a long strip of pulsating neon motel signs you will have to look elsewhere: There are only two other motels, and one smaller, traditional Navajo lodging, in the area.

INSIDE THE PARK **Thunderbird Lodge**. Ideally located at the mouth of Canyon de Chelly, in a grove of cottonwood trees $1/2$ mile southwest of the visitor center, this National Park Service–authorized hotel and restaurant traces its history to the turn of the century; its stone and adobe units match the architecture of the site's original trading-post building, now part of the Thunderbird's cafeteria. The large air-conditioned guest rooms have ceilings of exposed, hand-hewn beams; rustic wood furniture; and Native American decor throughout. Southwestern and Native American motifs are found in the cafeteria as well, where inexpensive American cuisine, ranging from soups and salads to complete chicken and steak meals, is offered. *Box 548, Chinle, AZ 86503, tel. 602/674–5841. 72 rooms. Facilities: cafeteria, gift shop, tour service. AE, DC, MC, V. Expensive.*

NEAR THE PARK **Canyon de Chelly Motel**. This low-slung Spanish-tile roof motel nearly doubled its capacity when it added an upper tier of rooms in 1993. Old and new accommodations are equally attractive, decorated in shades of turquoise and terra-cotta, with solid oak furnishings and Navajo art prints and patterns on drapes and bedspreads. All have air-conditioning, color cable TV, clocks, and coffee makers; the new rooms also have refrigerators. Such dishes as roast beef, chicken, and fish are typical of the restaurant's basic American fare. *Hwy. 64, $1/4$ mi east of U.S. 191, Box 295, Chinle, AZ 86503,*

tel. 602/674–5875. or 800/327–0354. 102 rooms. Facilities: restaurant, indoor pool, gift shop. AE, D, DC, MC, V. Expensive.

Coyote Pass Hospitality. This unusual lodging, a roving bed-and-breakfast run by the Coyote Pass clan of the Navajo Nation, isn't for everyone: Guests sleep on a mattress on the dirt floor of a hogan (the location depends on the season, but most are near the Canyon de Chelly), use an outhouse, and eat a traditional Navajo breakfast prepared on a wood-burning stove. But for those who don't mind roughing it a bit, this is a rare opportunity to be immersed in a Native American culture in beautiful surroundings. Guided hikes, nature programs, and other meals are optional. Rates for lodging are $75 for the first person, $10 for each additional person (maximum group size 15). *Contact Will Tsosie Jr., Box 91, Tsaile, AZ 86556, tel. 602/724–3383 or 602/674–9655. No credit cards. Expensive.*

Holiday Inn Canyon de Chelly. Opened in late 1992, the newest lodging near Canyon de Chelly is less generic than one might expect: This territorial-style, Navajo-staffed complex is built on the site of a former trading post and incorporates part of the historic structure. Rooms, on the other hand, are predictably pastel-toned and contemporary. Service is a bit erratic in the attractive lobby restaurant, but the food more than compensates. *BIA Rte. 7, Box 1889, Chinle, AZ 86503, tel. 602/674–5000 or 800/23–HOTEL, fax 602/674–8264. 108 rooms. Restaurant, pool, evening Native American dance and music performances in season, gift shop. AE, D, DC, MC, V. Expensive.*

CAMPING

There is only one camping facility in Canyon de Chelly National Park, which, remember, is part of the Navajo Reservation. Because of the rough, rugged terrain and the fact that visitors are not permitted to wander without a seasoned guide, camping in the backcountry is both illegal and foolhardy.

Near the visitor center is **Cottonwood Campground** (tel. 602/674–5500), which offers free camping at 52 RV sites (maximum length 35 feet) and 95 tent sites. The campground is open year-round, but running water and flush toilets are available only from April through October; visitors must use portable chemical toilets from November through March. Each site has a fire grate and picnic table, and there is a disposal station that's open from April through October. Campground hosts are on duty in summer only.

Campsites at Cottonwood are available on a first-come, first-served basis, and during the busy summer months you should try to arrive by 3 PM to be assured of a space, particularly if you have an RV. There is a five-day maximum stay for campers. Group sites, in which RVs are not allowed, can be reserved 90 days in advance for a maximum of three days. Campers are advised to bring their own fuel. Fires are permitted only in the available grills; no open-ground fires are permitted in the campground. Be aware that the possession and consumption of alcoholic beverages is illegal at Canyon de Chelly and everywhere else on the reservation.

Carlsbad Caverns National Park
New Mexico

By Ron Butler
Updated by Edie Jarolim

The huge, subterranean chambers, fantastic rock formations, and delicate mineral sculptures of Carlsbad Caverns National Park draw about three-quarters of a million people each year to a remote corner of southeast New Mexico. Although the park is in the Chihuahuan desert foothills, near the rugged canyons and peaks of the Guadalupe mountain range and the piñon and ponderosa pines of Lincoln National Forest, the most spectacular sights here are all below the earth's surface, with such evocative names as the Green Lake Room, the King's Palace, the Devil's Den, the Monarch Room, the China Wall, and Iceberg Rock. Delicate aragonite crystals, massive stalactites and stalagmites—the deeper you go, the more your mind soars.

This cave system, millions of years in the making, is one of the world's largest and most impressive, but it was rediscovered only in the last century. Pictographs near the cave entrance tell us that Native Americans took shelter in Carlsbad Caverns more than 1,000 years ago, but archaeologists doubt they ventured in very far: Access to the depths was limited, and the tribe may have believed that the dwellings of the dead lay below.

It wasn't until the 1880s that nearby settlers, curious about the huge numbers of bats they saw in the area, rediscovered the caves. In the early 20th century, the caves were mined for bat guano (dung), which was used as fertilizer. It was one of the guano miners, Jim White, who explored the caves and began telling people about this amazing underground universe.

White brought a photographer, Ray Davis, to bear witness to his extravagant claims for the place. Displayed in the nearby town of Carlsbad in 1915, Davis's black-and-white pictures astounded people and heightened interest in the caverns. White turned tour operator, taking people down 170 feet in a bat-guano bucket, lighting their way with kerosene lamps.

In the early 1920s, the folks in Washington became convinced that this natural wonder should be checked out, and in 1923 inspector Robert Holley was dispatched by the U.S. Department of the Interior to investigate. His report was instrumental in getting Carlsbad Caverns declared a national monument later that year by President Calvin Coolidge. The area was designated a national park in 1930.

Carlsbad Caverns National Park was much in the news early in 1991 when Emily Davis Mobley, an expert caver, broke her left leg some 1,000 feet underground while mapping one of the park's rugged backcountry caves. It took rescuers four days to carry, lift, and pull her over gaping pits and narrow passageways to safety, while the world held its breath. Of course, unless you're an expert, you won't be allowed to explore the same route or even anything like it. Of the 80 caves in the park, only two, Carlsbad Cavern and Slaughter Canyon Cave (formerly called New Cave), are open to the public.

ESSENTIAL INFORMATION

VISITOR INFORMATION Contact the **Carlsbad Caverns National Park**, 3225 National Parks Highway, Carlsbad, NM 88220, tel. 505/785–2232 (24-hour information line). Other sources of information on the area surrounding Carlsbad are: **Guadalupe Mountains National Park** (HC 60, Box 400, Salt Flat, TX 79847, tel. 915/828–3251), **Lincoln National Forest** (Guadalupe Ranger District, Federal Building, Room 159, Carlsbad, NM 88220, tel. 505/885–4181), **Living Desert State Park** (Box 100, Carlsbad, NM 88220, tel. 505/887–5516), **Brantley Lake State Park** (Box 2288, Carlsbad, NM 88220, tel. 505/457–2384), and **Carlsbad Chamber of Commerce** (302 S. Canal St., Carlsbad, NM 88220, tel. 505/887–6516).

All hikers are advised to stop at the visitor-center information desk to get current information about trails; those planning overnight hikes must get a free backcountry permit.

Trails are poorly defined but can be followed by using a topographic map.

FEES There is no fee to enter the above-ground portion of the park, but to descend into Carlsbad Cavern adults pay $5 and children ages 6 to 15 pay $3, and to enter lantern-lit Slaughter Canyon Cave, adults pay $6 and children $3. The fee for periodic, special guided trips into other undeveloped caves is $10 a person. Golden Age and Golden Access Passport holders receive a 50% discount.

PUBLICATIONS The **Carlsbad Caverns-Guadalupe Mountains Association** (Box 1417, Carlsbad, NM 88221–1417, tel. 505/785–2318), a nonprofit, educational organization, sells a number of books, maps, posters, and booklets. The association is open to public membership ($25 annual dues); members receive a 15% discount on all purchases, special discounts on seminars, and a quarterly newsletter.

Visitors planning a trip to Carlsbad Caverns should find the following books of particular interest: *Bats of Carlsbad Caverns* (30 pages, with color photos), by noted bat researchers Dr. Scott Altenbach and Dr. Ken Geluso, along with cave expert Ronal Kerbo, examines the bat phenomenon of the area, shedding light in dark places; *Carlsbad Caverns: Silent Chambers of Timeless Beauty* (32 pages, with color photos), by former park naturalist John Barnett, covers the history, geology, and surface features, as well as the underground features, of Carlsbad Caverns National Park; *Stories from Stone* (42 pages, with color photos), by geologist David Jaganow and writer Rebecca Jaganow, tells about the geography of the Guadalupe Mountains and Carlsbad Caverns; *Caves Beyond* (238 pages, with black-and-white photos), by Joe Lawrence, Jr., and Roger W. Brucker, takes a look at famous caves throughout the United States; *Speleology* (150 pages, with black-and-white photos), by George W. Moore and G. Nicholas Sullivan, is a general guide to cave exploring. If bats hold your interest and you want a simple introductory souvenir of your visit to Carlsbad Caverns, the first two books listed should fill the bill. Readers seeking a more detailed examination of caves and cave-exploring will find the latter books compelling.

The association also publishes *Capitan Reef,* a 12-page quarterly covering Carlsbad Caverns as well as other nearby recreational areas. For a free copy, write to the address above.

GEOLOGY AND TERRAIN The vast cave system that comprises Carlsbad Caverns National Park owes its existence as much to slow drips and accretions as to cataclysmic events. Its origins go back some 250 million years, when 400-mile-long Capitan Reef formed around the edge of the warm, shallow sea that once covered this region. After its connection to the ocean to the southwest was cut off, the sea evaporated and the reef was buried until a few million years ago, when it was slowly pushed above the surface to form a part of the Guadalupe Mountains. Over the millennia, huge cavities formed when surface water, passing through soil and rock, became acidic and slowly dissolved the soft limestone and dolomite of which the reef was made. The dissolved limestone, in turn, was deposited on the ceilings of these vast rooms as carbon dioxide in the mineral-laden drops of water escaped into the cave air. These limestone deposits grew into great hanging stalactites, and, over time, massive stalagmites and other more delicate formations—cave pearls, draperies, popcorn, and lily pads—also formed.

FLORA AND FAUNA Occasionally raccoons or ringtail cats may wander into the caverns, but, below ground, Mexican free-tail bats rule the roost. They share their spacious home with other species but not ones that most visitors would want to contemplate—generally, arthropods and crawling insects. (The bats, who dine out every evening, prefer the flying kind.) Human misconceptions about bats, along with the use of pesticides, have helped cause some species—there are more than 900—to become endangered, but the fact is, few of these flying mammals are rabid and none are attracted to human hair; their unique echolocation system enables them to avoid people. Scientists have not yet figured

out how a bat hanging upside down in a dark cave knows when the sun has set outside.

Some algae grows around the entrance to the caves and around the electric lights, but most plants need more light and moisture than caves provide. It is the inanimate, intricately shaped, and often beautifully colored mineral formations that are the natural attractions in this subterranean world.

On the surface, the park's terrain varies with its many elevation levels, so vegetation is diverse. Texas black walnut, oak, desert willow, and hackberry proliferate along the canyon bottoms. The ridges and walls of the canyons contain a variety of desert plants—yucca, agave, sotol, sticklike branches of ocotillo, and clusters of sparse desert grass. Plants—even clumps of grass—stand far apart on the desert so that their roots will not compete for water. Higher up, piñon pine, juniper, ponderosa pine, and Douglas fir dominate.

Animals that scamper about or roam the area at a more leisurely pace include raccoon, skunk, rabbit, fox, gopher, mice, porcupine, mule deer, coyote, and the ever-elusive badger, bobcat, and mountain lion. There are plenty of snakes in the region, including western diamondback rattlers and banded rock rattlers, but since they are both nocturnal and shy, visitors rarely see them. Snakes generally appear in summer; if you see one, give it a wide berth. More than 270 species of bird come and go at Carlsbad, including the magnificent golden eagle.

WHEN TO GO For most people, weather is not a major factor in deciding when to visit the park. The caves are a constant temperature year-round: 56°F in Carlsbad Cavern and 62°F in Slaughter Canyon Cave. Above ground, the climate of the park is semiarid, with hot summers and mild winters. The sun shines 74% of the daylight hours, and humidity is generally low.

If you're interested in hiking the backcountry, summer days may be too hot, with high temperatures from mid-May through mid-September almost always exceeding 90°F and frequently climbing over 100°F. Even during the hottest periods, however, nights are comfortably cool.

Winters are dry and sunny, with January, the coldest month, averaging daylight shade temperatures of 58°F.

You'll avoid the crowds if you come between late September and early May, except during the Christmas, New Year, and Easter holiday periods. Hiking will be the most comfortable during those months, but you may miss the bats, which winter in Mexico. Their nightly (around sunset) forays and dawn returns en masse begin in May and usually continue through October. The nightly ranger program at the cave entrance is one of the highlights of a visit to Carlsbad Caverns.

SEASONAL EVENTS **August:** It's not exactly the swallows returning to Capistrano, but usually on the second Thursday of August each year, early risers—would you believe 5 AM?—gather for a **Bat Flight Breakfast** at the entrance to Carlsbad Cavern. More than 400 bat fanciers may show up to watch tens of thousands of bats return from a night out feeding on insects and fly back into a black hole descending steeply into the ground. Park rangers are on hand for a talk and to answer questions. The bats' homecoming may be viewed each morning (although there is no formal program) from mid-May through October, but the breakfast is a once-a-year affair. For additional information, contact Superintendent, Carlsbad Caverns National Park *(see* Visitor Information, *above).*

WHAT TO PACK The temperature inside Carlsbad Cavern remains at a constant 56°F, but it's damp, so a sweater or flannel shirt and slacks rather than shorts are recommended. Comfortable, nonskid shoes are essential. Because of the moisture, the underground walkways are slippery. Slaughter Canyon Cave is a bit warmer (a constant 62°F) but even more rugged: If you're planning to do some serious spelunking, take strong-grip hiking shoes. In addition, anyone wishing to visit Slaughter Canyon Cave must bring along a flashlight and water.

Once you've explored the caverns, you'll likely be spending lots of time outdoors. Carlsbad's weather is generally delightful year-round (*see* When to Go, *above*). The air is dry, so bring along moisturizers as well as sunscreen and sunglasses. New Mexico's state symbol is a sunburst for good reason.

Southwest informality prevails throughout all of New Mexico, and even more so in Carlsbad. You won't need anything dressy, no matter where you plan to go in the evening.

GENERAL STORES In 1927, Charlie L. White established White's Cavern Camp 7 miles from the entrance to Carlsbad Cavern as a convenience to the ever-growing number of tourists who were coming to the area to see the spectacular cave. It has since grown to White's City, providing lodging, food, and shopping facilities. The small **White's City Grocery and Drug Store** (tel. 505/785–2291) sells camping supplies as well as groceries and sundries and is open daily year-round, 7 to 7.

You'll have a better selection, however, if you head 20 miles north to the city of Carlsbad, which hosts a large variety of supermarkets and general stores. Among them are **Albertson's** (808 N. Canal St., tel 505/885–2161), which is open daily 6 AM to 11 PM; **Thriftway** (1301 S. Canal St., tel. 505/887–5514), open 7 AM to 9 PM, and **IGA Foodliner** (609 S. Canal St., tel. 505/887–3074), open Monday through Saturday 8 to 8 and Sunday 9 to 6.

ARRIVING AND DEPARTING Carlsbad Caverns National Park is 27 miles southwest of Carlsbad, New Mexico, on U.S. 62–180, in the southeastern part of the state. The park is 35 miles north of Guadalupe Mountains National Park, about 250 miles from Big Bend National Park, and 210 miles from Pecos National Historical Park.

By Plane. The newly expanded and remodeled **Albuquerque International Airport,** 380 miles north of Carlsbad, is the gateway to New Mexico and is served by most major airlines. Air shuttle service via **Mesa Airlines** (tel. 505/885–0245 or 800/637–2247) connects to Cavern City Air Terminal in

Carlsbad. There are four flights daily Monday through Friday, two flights on Saturday, and three on Sunday. Flying time aboard the 19-passenger Beechcraft 1900s is about 60 minutes. The highest fares are $104 one-way, $139 round-trip, but discount fares are available on advance ticket purchases.

Carlsbad car-rental agencies include **Hertz** (tel. 505/887–1500) at Cavern City Air Terminal and **Independent** (tel. 505/887–1469) at Park Inn International. Taxi transfers from the Carlsbad airport are also available via **Cavern City Cab Company** (tel. 505/887–0994).

By Car and RV. From Albuquerque drive south on I–25 for about 77 miles, exit onto U.S. 380 East, and continue for 165 miles to Roswell. There switch to U.S. 285 and go south directly to the town of Carlsbad, about 75 miles from Roswell (a total of 320 miles from Albuquerque). The last part of the drive is monotonous, with miles of uninterrupted flat, scrubby brush as far as the eye can see, but the U.S. 380 leg through the Valley of Fire lava flows and the hilly Lincoln National Forest offers some dramatic scenery. You can stop in the historic towns of Capitan (home of Smoky Bear State Park) and Lincoln, where the Lincoln County War was centered.

A little quicker but less scenic route is to take I–40 east of Albuquerque to Clines Corners, then U.S. 285 south to Carlsbad. Watch for pronghorn antelope grazing near the highway. From El Paso, Texas, going east on U.S. 180, the distance to Carlsbad Caverns is 147 miles. Eighty-four miles northwest of Pecos, Texas, Carlsbad can be reached via U.S. 285.

By Train. The closest city to Carlsbad served by **Amtrak** (tel. 800/872–7245) is El Paso, Texas, 147 miles away. Car rentals are available at the airport, which is roughly 20 minutes from the train station. Try **Alamo** (tel. 800/327–9633), **Hertz** (tel. 800/654–3131), or **Budget** (tel. 800/527–0700).

By Bus and Van. TNM&O Greyhound (tel. 505/887–1108 or 800/231–2222) provides transcontinental bus service to Carlsbad. **Sun-Country Tours** (tel. 505/785–2291) offers van service between Carlsbad Caverns

National Park and White's City; buses leave from the gift shop at White's City (where you can purchase tickets) and from the park's visitor center. The round-trip fare is $15 for up to three people, $5 per additional person.

EXPLORING

If you don't have a car you're limited in what you can do in the park. Tour buses go to Carlsbad Cavern, but that's their only stop. Hikers have lots of scenic—if rugged—backcountry trails to choose from, but those who'd like to get to Slaughter Canyon Cave from Carlsbad Cavern without a car or bicycle are out of luck: It's a 25-mile trek across flat, unshaded terrain.

You can easily see what most people come to see, Carlsbad Cavern, in one day, but it would be a pity not to explore other sites in this unique area. Plan to spend a couple of days hiking the park trails or visiting one of the nearby natural attractions: Guadalupe Mountains National Park, Lincoln National Forest, Living Desert State Park, or Brantley Lake State Park (*see* Visitor Information, *above*).

THE BEST IN ONE DAY Your schedule for the park will be determined largely by the amount of time you want to spend below ground: Caving enthusiasts will be interested in exploring the Slaughter Canyon Cave as well as Carlsbad Cavern, while those who prefer fresh air have a number of outdoor options.

The trip through **Carlsbad Cavern** is an experience like none other. Whether you take the long route or the elevator shortcut, the trek is long, and you may find yourself getting a bit disoriented. The sheer vastness of the interior is overwhelming, and the proportions seem to change as one goes along. In places where pools of water have formed beside the walkway, reflections and reality merge; you may have to pause for a moment to gain your equilibrium.

Although you may be tempted to touch the cave's walls and jutting rock formations, heed the ranger's warning against doing so. Oil from the human hand forms a type of waterproofing that inhibits the natural water seepage. One or two people pawing at the rocks wouldn't make much of a difference, but thousands tour the cavern daily, and, over time, the formations are discolored by touching. Also, some of the formations are easily broken. Visitors are also warned not to leave the guided pathways. They're not always told, however, that if they wander astray, alarms may quickly summon park rangers. The interior of Carlsbad Cavern is well lighted, but many people seem more concerned about where they're stepping than what's ahead and make much of the trip looking down at their feet. Walk cautiously, but take time to stop and look up as well as around you.

There are two self-guided tours through parts of Carlsbad Cavern and one guided tour. Each covers about 1 mile. On the self-guided Natural Entrance Tour you walk from the cave entrance along the paved walkway that winds down the Main Corridor of the cavern. You pass through a series of underground rooms, including Devil's Den and the Boneyard, and past 200,000-ton Iceberg Rock. The trail can be slick in parts, and the grades are fairly steep as you descend to a depth of about 780 feet. The Main Corridor is distinguished by its size: It's more than $1^1/_4$ miles long, and parts of its ceiling are 200 feet high. It does not, however, contain many cave formations. To see those, you will have to continue to another tour. The Natural Entrance Tour ends at the base of the high-speed elevator, which is where the self-guided Big Room Tour and the guided King's Palace Tour begin (you can take the elevator down from the visitor center to start here).

On the Big Room Tour, you walk around the T-shape Big Room, which has a floor area equal to that of 14 Houston Astrodomes. The ceiling is as high as 255 feet; the White House could fit in one corner. The room has many cave formations—stalagmites, stalactites, columns, draperies, and flowstone—and such natural phenomena as Mirror Lake and the Bottomless Pit. This is a circular tour.

Also leaving from (and returning to) the elevator area is the King's Palace Tour, a guided walk that lasts about one hour. You are escorted through four rooms with beautiful formations: the Green Lake Room, the King's Palace, the Queen's Chamber, and the Papoose Room. These tours generally leave daily at 9, 11, 1, and 3, but there are sometimes as many as eight tours per day during the busy summer season. You must join a guided tour in order to see these four rooms.

No matter which tour or tours you choose, you should be able to stop at the gift shop and exhibit displays by late morning. In the afternoon, take a picnic lunch to **Rattlesnake Springs** (don't let the name scare you—rattlesnakes are rarely seen there). To get there take Highway 62–180 from White's City 5 miles south and turn onto Route 418, traveling 3 miles west. It's about 25 minutes by car from the visitor center. Rattlesnake Springs has a pleasant picnic area with shade trees, grass, tables, water, and grills. Close to the Black River, it was a source of water for Native Americans hundreds of years ago. Army troops exploring the area used it as well, and it was also the site of a Civilian Conservation Corps camp. Today it's the main water source for all of the park facilities. It is also a favorite spot for bird-watchers.

If you have an appetite for more underground adventure, head for **Slaughter Canyon Cave** after lunch (you must make a reservation several weeks in advance). It's 25 miles from Carlsbad Cavern and much less accessible: You'll have to provide your own transportation to get there; the last few miles of the roadway that leads to the cave are gravel, and the mouth of the cave is a $^1/_2$-mile climb up a 500-foot rise. It takes about 30 to 45 minutes to walk to the entrance from the parking area. Reservations are required for the two-hour ranger-led tour (tel. 505/785–2232); children under 6 are not permitted. You'll need to bring along your own flashlight, hiking boots or good walking shoes with rubber soles (sneakers are not recommended), and drinking water. Tours are offered daily in summer but only on weekends during the winter season.

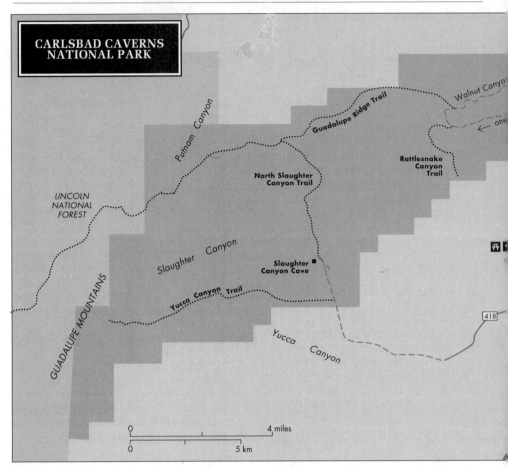

Slaughter Canyon Cave, located in remote Slaughter Canyon, was not discovered until 1937, when Tom Tucker, a local goatherd, came across it. Because it was discovered later than Carlsbad Cavern, it was for many years called New Cave at Slaughter Canyon. The name was eventually shortened to New Cave, but in 1992 the park service began calling it Slaughter Canyon Cave in order to avoid confusion with such other "new"—that is, unexplored—caves as Lechuguilla Cave.

Slaughter Canyon Cave consists primarily of a single corridor, 1,140 feet long, with numerous side passages. The lowest point is 250 feet below the surface. Outstanding formations are Christmas Tree, the Monarch Room, Klansman, Tear Drop, and the China Wall.

Photographs are permitted, but no tripod setups are allowed since the group moves along at a relatively brisk pace, and you *really* wouldn't want to be left behind (the cave is so dark that the flick of a cigarette lighter has been known to cause temporary blindness). Unless you're in good physical shape, with a long attention span, Slaughter Canyon Cave may be more cave-peeping than you bargained for.

If you'd like to stay above ground, you can get a bit of exercise after lunch by taking the self-guided **Desert Nature Walk** (*see* Nature Trails and Short Walks, *below*). Afterward, if you don't want to venture too far afield, take the 9½-mile **Walnut Canyon Desert Drive** (*see* Scenic Drives and Views, *below*), which

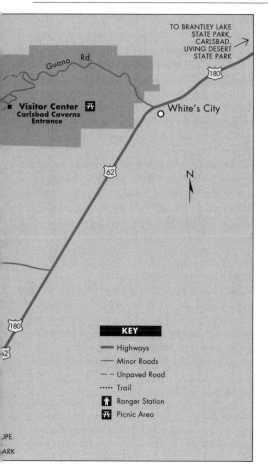

Whatever you do during the daylight hours, if you visit the park from late May through mid-October, be sure to come back to Carlsbad Cavern to view the **nightly bat flight.** Each evening at about sunset, bats by the tens of thousands go out from the natural entrance of the cave and scout about the countryside for flying insects. They consume them in flight, collectively more than three tons of yummy bugs per night. Because bats, albeit less lovable than furry kittens, are among the most maligned and misunderstood of creatures, park rangers give informative talks about them each evening prior to the mass exodus, sometime around sunset. The time of the bat flights varies over the course of the season, so ranger lectures are flexible as well; the time is usually posted, but if not, check at the visitor center. Lectures are suspended during the winter months, when the bats leave for Mexico.

ORIENTATION PROGRAMS An exhibit area at the visitor center (tel. 505/785–2232) features a model of Carlsbad Cavern as well as displays detailing the archaeology, geology, and history of the area. Photos from the guano mining days are fascinating. You can also see a 10-minute slide program outlining the attractions at Carlsbad Caverns National Park and the other parks in the area. In addition, a movie on bat flight is shown on request. This is especially worthwhile if you visit in the winter, when the bats are away, or if you don't plan to be around in the evening to see them for yourself.

Before you embark on your underground adventure, a park ranger gives an orientation talk. And from late May to mid-October, the rangers give nightly lectures on bats (*see* The Best in One Day, *above*).

GUIDED TOURS The King's Palace Tour (*see* The Best in One Day, *above*) is the only guided tour through Carlsbad Cavern. It covers four of the cavern's decorated rooms in one hour. In addition, rangers lead a two-hour guided tour of Slaughter Canyon Cave (*see* The Best in One Day, *above*).

For self-guided tours of Carlsbad Cavern, you can rent small radio receivers detailing attrac-

starts near the visitor center. Another good option for the afternoon is the nearby **Living Desert State Park** (*see* Visitor Information, *above*), atop Ocotillo Hills, about 1¹/₂ miles northwest of the town of Carlsbad (off U.S. 285; look for the signs). It contains an impressive outdoor collection of plants and animals native to the Chihuahuan Desert living in natural surroundings. The park is home to mountain lions, deer, elk, wolves, buffalo, rattlesnakes, and other indigenous species. The park's Desert Arboretum has hundreds of exotic cacti and succulents from around the world. Admission is $3 for adults; children 6 and under are free. It's open daily 8 to 8 May 15 to Labor Day, 9 to 5 the rest of the year (closed Christmas Day).

tions along the cave route, in Spanish or English, for 50¢ each; you'll receive a total of 43 messages as you walk through the cave's various listening zones.

Monthly interpretative explorations of the Chihuahuan Desert offered by the nearby **Living Desert State Park** (tel. 505/887–5516) sometimes venture into the Guadalupe Mountains. Near the time you're thinking of visiting, call to find out what special tours are being run. If you're not a Friend of the Park, you'll have to pay your own expenses for the excursion.

The **Carlsbad Caverns-Guadalupe Mountains Association** (*see* Publications, *above*) sponsors a year-round seminar program featuring 1- to 5-day, in-depth programs on caving, geology, nature photography, bird-watching, and history. Write or call for a free catalog.

SCENIC DRIVES AND VIEWS **Walnut Canyon Desert Drive,** a 9½-mile loop that begins ½ mile from the visitor center, travels along the top of the Guadalupe Ridge to the edge of Rattlesnake Canyon and back down through upper Walnut Canyon to the main entrance road. The trip, along a twisty one-way gravel road, takes about an hour to an hour and a half for a leisurely drive. It's perfect for late afternoon or early morning, when you can enjoy the full spectrum of the desert's changing light and dancing colors. A pamphlet describing this drive is available at the visitor center bookstore.

NATURE TRAILS AND SHORT WALKS Try taking the ½-mile self-guided **Desert Nature Walk** that begins off the cavern entrance trail, 200 yards east of the visitor center, while waiting for the nightly bat flight program to begin. The tagged and identified flowers and plants make this a good place to get acquainted with much of the local desert flora. Take the short (¼-mile) **Rattlesnake Canyon Overlook Trail,** off Walnut Canyon Desert Drive, to get superlative views of Rattlesnake Canyon.

LONGER HIKES Backcountry hiking in Carlsbad Caverns National Park can be exhilarating—the desert terrain is stark and awesome—but few trails are as clearly marked as those in other national parks and there is no water, so you'll need to bring plenty. It is recommended that you carry from two quarts to one gallon per person for each day hike. Topographic maps, available at the visitor center, are essential on all but the most well-marked trails. Permits aren't required, except for overnight backpacking trips, but all hikers are requested to register at the information desk at the visitor center. If you don't register and you get lost, it's likely that you won't be found for a long time in this little-trafficked area. No pets or guns are permitted. Following is a sampling of some of the most interesting and most easily accessible trails.

Guadalupe Ridge Trail starts at the west end of the Walnut Canyon Desert Drive loop and covers 13½ miles one way, mostly along ridge tops, to Putnam Cabin in Guadalupe Mountains National Park. The 2,050-foot ascent is a gradual climb to the highest point in the park. Count on spending the night in the backcountry here to make this 27-mile round-trip hike.

Guano Road, a little more than 3½ miles one-way, was originally the truck and wagon route that miners used to transport bat dung (a fertilizer) from Carlsbad Cavern to Carlsbad. The first visitors to Carlsbad Cavern also took this route, which follows the escarpment ridge south of the entrance road. Starting out from the Bat Flight Amphitheater, the trail affords good views of the eastern escarpment of the Guadalupe Mountains. The terrain is mostly flat but drops sharply down to the White's City campground at the end. Because the trail follows a more direct route, it covers about half the distance of the highway to White's City. Give yourself two to three hours to complete the walk.

The 6-mile round-trip **Rattlesnake Canyon Trail** descends from 4,570 to 3,900 feet as it winds down into the canyon. This trail, which is defined and marked with rock cairns, starts at marker number 9 on Walnut Canyon Desert Drive. It will take three to four hours to trek down into the canyon and make the somewhat strenuous climb out.

Yucca Canyon Trail, about 6 miles long one-way, begins at the mouth of Yucca Canyon, which is reached by taking the Slaughter Canyon Cave road to the park boundary, then turning west along the boundary fence line to the trailhead. This trail climbs up to the top of the escarpment, then follows the ridge top westward to the junction of Double Canyon Trail (the elevation ranges from 4,300 to 6,150 feet); at the top of the ridge, a level, well-marked route offers sweeping views of the Guadalupe escarpment and El Capitan. Along much of the trail you'll see oak, piñon, and juniper, with a sprinkling of ponderosa pine. This somewhat strenuous hike takes from six to eight hours round-trip.

OTHER ACTIVITIES For the most part, unless you bring along your own horse, boat, fishing gear, or bicycle, you're somewhat restricted in the ways you can enjoy nature in the area.

Back-Road Driving. The 9¹/₂-mile Walnut Canyon Desert Drive (*see* Scenic Drives and Views, *above*) is the only unpaved road recommended by the rangers; a number of people who have taken the Guadalupe Ridge Trail, which heads west along the north edge of the designated wilderness area, have found themselves stranded.

Biking. The park is not a favorite with bicyclists. The entrance road is too narrow and congested for bicycles, and the unpaved Walnut Canyon Desert Drive and Slaughter Canyon Cave roads are narrow and dusty and not conducive to safe and enjoyable riding. Mountain bikers will do no better here: Bikes are not allowed on park trails, and cross-country travel is prohibited.

Bird-Watching. From turkey vultures to golden eagles, some 273 bird species have been identified in Carlsbad Caverns National Park. The best place to go birding in the park, if not the entire state, is Rattlesnake Springs, a desert oasis located on Route 418, 3 miles off Highway 180–62 and 5 miles south of White's City. Ask for a checklist at the visitor center, and then start checking: red-tailed hawk, red-winged blackbird, white-throated swift, northern flicker, pygmy nuthatches, yellow-billed cuckoo, roadrunner, mallard, American coot, green- and blue-winged teals, among others. Another good bird-watching spot is at Oak Springs, west of the visitor center. Also ask about the occasional ranger-led bird-watching walks.

Boating. There's very little water in Carlsbad Caverns National Park, but the Pecos River, which runs through Carlsbad, has been dammed up to form a long, narrow lake in the middle of the town. The upper lake attracts jetskiers, waterskiers, and boaters, but you have to bring your own equipment.

If you're hauling a boat trailer, you can set your vessel afloat at the upper lake or 12 miles north in **Brantley Lake State Park** (tel. 505/457–2384), where the views are especially dreamy. In late afternoon in summer, dark storm clouds form in the distance over Brantley Lake, and shafts of golden sunlight streak through vivid green trees. The state park has a well-developed campground, boat ramps, a day-use area with a playground, and good fishing most of the year.

Caving. Only two of Carlsbad's 80 caves are open to the public, but 10 backcountry caves may be explored by serious cavers under the park's Cave Management Plan and permit system. Those who have training from one of the chapters (called Grottos) of the National Speleological Society, headquartered in Huntsville, Alabama, should contact the **Cave Resources Office** (tel. 505/785–2232) for more information. Nonaffiliated amateur cavers may catch the occasional ranger-guided trip to Spider Cave or to an undeveloped area of Carlsbad Cavern; however, these trips are unscheduled, so you'll need to call ahead for information or check at the visitor center when you arrive.

Fishing. There is no fishing in the park, but Carlsbad's lower municipal lake is popular with anglers, who know that it is stocked with trout in winter. Bass and catfish nibble the lines at **Carlsbad Municipal Beach Park** (tel. 505/887–6516), which covers the shores of the river from where it is crossed by the

Hobbs Highway Bridge in the south up through the North Canal Street Bridge. Cast off from the fishing dock at **Brantley Lake State Park** (*see above*) for black bass, white bass, walleye, channel catfish, and bluegill. Anyone over 12 must have a New Mexico fishing license, which can be obtained from a local sporting goods store, or any store that carries fishing or hunting equipment. A one-day license costs $8.50, and a five-day license costs $15. For more information, call the **New Mexico Department of Game and Fish** (tel. 505/841–8881).

Horseback Riding. It's too hot much of the year to make renting horses a worthwhile proposition for area residents. Horseback riding is permitted in Carlsbad Caverns National Park, but there are only limited corral facilities to accommodate those traveling with horse trailers, and the trails are not particularly good for riding. A better place to bring a horse is **Guadalupe Mountains National Park** (*see* Visitor Information, *above*), 30 miles from Carlsbad, which has two visitor corrals, one at Pine Springs, the other at Dog Canyon (reservations are required). Horseback riding is permitted on approximately 80% of the park's 80 miles of mountain trails, most of which are moderately difficult. For a view of the high country conifer forest, the Tejas Trail is particularly recommended. The El Capitan–Williams Ranch Trail also provides for an excellent ride, with sweeping views of the salt flats and Patterson Hills from the base of El Capitan's sheer cliff face.

Swimming. From early May to Labor Day, lifeguards are on duty at the **Carlsbad Municipal Beach Park** (*see above*). Across the river, at **President's Park** (tel. 505/887–0512), there's lifeguarded swimming at the lake from Memorial Day to Labor Day. If you don't mind taking an unsupervised plunge, the water at **Brantley Lake State Park** (*see above*) is fine.

CHILDREN'S PROGRAMS Although there are no regularly scheduled children's programs per se, the interpretative headsets that may be rented for 50¢ (*see* Guided Tours, *above*) come in a children's version (English only). Call the visitor center (tel. 505/785–2232) for information about occasional special tours for kids.

The long trek through the cavern is a bit much for little children, and baby strollers are not permitted on the narrow cave trails because of safety considerations. The park no longer has a nursery, but there are baby-sitting services in Carlsbad. Ask your hotel for recommendations.

EVENING ACTIVITIES Aside from the bat flight program at the entrance of Carlsbad Caverns at sunset (*see* The Best in One Day, *above*), there are no regularly scheduled evening activities offered in the park. Interpretive programs are given only when a special event, such as a meteor shower or lunar eclipse, occurs.

At **Guadalupe Mountains National Park** (tel. 915/828–3251), ranger programs addressing both the natural and the cultural histories of the Guadalupe Mountains are offered nightly from late May through early September, and on Friday and Saturday nights in the fall and spring.

DINING

At press time, box lunches could still be bought at the underground lunchroom, but the facility may be closed by the time this book is printed. The park has a full-service restaurant above ground with an extensive menu, including Mexican dishes, fish, chicken, steak, soups, hot dogs, and burgers, at moderate prices. Nearby White's City and Carlsbad have a good number of eateries, but don't expect haute cuisine; in this part of the country, your best bet is always Mexican.

NEAR THE PARK **Old City Hall Restaurant.** For many years, this late-19th-century building housed the town's marriage license bureau, fire department, police department, and any other city service you can think of. Now some of the most innovative food in town is served in this two-level restaurant lined with photos of Carlsbad in the old days. Along with such standards as prime rib and broiled lobster, the menu lists pork teriyaki, coconut fried shrimp, blackened trout, and Caribbean-style catfish. There's also an Italian menu Thursday through Saturday. The beautiful old bar upstairs was brought over from a drugstore in Corona, New Mexico. *222 W. Fox St., tel. 505/887–0934. Reservations not required. Dress: casual but neat. AE, D, MC, V. Moderate–Expensive.*

Lucy's. This popular, family-owned (Lucy and Justo Yanez) Mexican restaurant doesn't have much in the way of atmosphere. A large-screen TV blares accompaniment to meals, which are served in the restaurant and, when it gets crowded, the adjoining lounge. But the food is fresh, the service is friendly, and this is one of the few places in town that has a liquor license. All the New Mexican standards are available, including Chapa chicken tacos (named for Chapa, a former waitress who ate the chicken tacos all the time) and Tucson-style *chimichangas* (flour tortillas stuffed with beans, meat, or chicken, deep-fried, and topped with sour cream). *701 S. Canal St., Carlsbad, tel. 505/887–7714. Reservations not required. Dress: casual. AE, D, MC, V. Moderate.*

Velvet Garter Restaurant and Saloon/Fast Jack's. You can take your pick at these two adjoining White's City restaurants in a pueblo-style building: At the slightly more upscale Velvet Garter, you'll find steak, chicken, catfish, shrimp, and Mexican food in a whoopee Wild West atmosphere with bawdy paintings on the wall, the Carlsbad Cavern in stained glass, and honky-tonk background music. At Fast Jack's next door, you can eat good burgers, 32 flavors of homemade ice cream, and fresh baked pies at either a counter or a booth. Jack White, whose grandfather founded White's City and who owns almost everything in this tiny tourist town, is a Stanford graduate with an electrical engineering degree. He makes sure his restaurant's bank of video games and souvenir slot machines are all in working order. *26 Carlsbad Caverns Hwy., White's City, tel. 505/785–2291. Reservations not required. Dress: casual. D, DC, MC, V. Inexpensive–Moderate.*

Cortez. This charming family-owned Mexican restaurant, with an all-brick interior and

photo murals of Old Mexico, has been in business for more than half a century. Nothing on the menu costs more than $7.50. Try the combination plate, fajitas (tortillas stuffed with chunks of beef or pork), or sour-cream enchiladas. *506 S. Canal St., Carlsbad, tel. 505/885–4747. Reservations accepted. Dress: casual. No credit cards. Inexpensive.*

LODGING

Since tourism is a major industry in Carlsbad, the area offers a wide choice of motels and other services, although few provide much in the way of charm or individuality. Most of them are strung out along the highway going to the caverns, appropriately called National Parks Highway. At the turnoff from the highway to the caverns, White's City is a honky-tonk tourist complex, with three motels, a tent and RV campground, restaurants, a post office, souvenir shops, a small amusement park and museum, a miniature golf course, and a saloon.

NEAR THE PARK **Holiday Inn Carlsbad.** This Spanish Colonial–style link in the Holiday Inn chain, with a tan stucco exterior, red-tile roofs, and portale-style balconies, opened in June 1993. Rooms are attractively decorated in deep tones from the Southwest, with misty blue-and-maroon pattern bedspreads and curtains, light oak furniture, and Native American prints. Those seeking amenities not widely available in the area—in-room safes, key-card security, nonsmoking and fully accessible rooms, fitness center and spa—might find it worth paying slightly higher rates to stay here. *601 S. Canal St., Carlsbad, NM 88220, tel. 505/885–8500, 800/742–9586, or, for reservations, 800/HOLIDAY. 100 rooms. Facilities: 2 restaurants, children's playground, pool, conference facilities. AE, D, DC, MC, V. Expensive.*

Best Western Cavern Inn. A two-story motor inn with southwestern-style rooms, this Best Western offers the nearest accommodations to Carlsbad Caverns, and is an immediate neighbor of the popular Velvet Garter Restaurant (*see* Dining, *above*). It's a pleasant, friendly place, determined to help you have a good time. Tour groups frequent the Best Western, as do families; nonsmoking rooms are available. *17 Carlsbad Caverns Hwy., White's City, NM 88266, tel. 505/785–2291 or, for reservations, 800/528–1234. 63 rooms. Facilities: café, restaurant, lounge, pool, tennis, spa, in-room whirlpools, playground. AE, DC, MC, V. Moderate.*

Best Western Motel Stevens. An old favorite, both locally and with tour groups, this is a reliable, well-operated place. Guest rooms feature bright desert colors, mirrored vanities, and modern furnishings. Some have kitchenettes, some have private patios, and some have both. Buildings are scattered over a landscaped area covering more than a city block. The motel's Flume Room, an elegant local favorite dining spot, features steaks and prime ribs. There's also a coffee shop offering regional and Mexican specialties, and the Silver Spur Bar and Lounge, where country western music plays long and loud. The hotel is owned by Carlsbad's mayor, Bob Forrest, but even knowing him won't get you a table in the Silver Spur on a Saturday night when the Chaparrals are playing. *1829 S. Canal St., Box 580, Carlsbad, NM 88220, tel. 505/887–2851 or, for reservations, 800/528–1234. 202 rooms. Facilities: restaurant, café, lounge, pool, guest laundry, playground. AE, D, DC, MC, V. Moderate.*

Carlsbad Travelodge South. One mile from the airport, and one block from the Convention Center in Carlsbad, this three-story motel has rooms decorated in bright desert colors, although the furnishings are generic. Breakfast is free for up to two adults sharing a room and for children under 6, and it costs $2 each for additional people in the room. There is no restaurant on the premises, but Jerry's restaurant, in the immediate vicinity, serves standard coffee-shop fare 24 hours a day. *3817 National Parks Hwy., Carlsbad, NM 88220, tel. 505/887–8888 or, for reservations, 800/578–7878. 60 rooms. Facilities: pool, Jacuzzi, free airport transfers. AE, D, DC, MC, V. Moderate.*

Park Inn International. This two-story, stone-facade property encloses a landscaped patio with a pool and sun deck about as large as an aircraft hangar. Rooms are comfortable, with undistinguished modern furnishings and king-size or two double beds with bright Native American–design bedspreads. The Café in the Park serves breakfast and lunch, and the Chaparral Grill Room, a more formal dining room, is open for dinner. Scott's Archery Range is next door. *3706 National Parks Hwy., Carlsbad, NM 88220, tel. 505/887–2861, 800/321–2861, or, for reservations, 800/437–7275. 124 rooms. Facilities: 2 restaurants, bar, hot tub, pool, game room, laundry, gift shop, free airport/bus-terminal transfers. AE, D, DC, MC, V. Moderate.*

Stagecoach Inn. Close to many of the major Carlsbad attractions, this family-style motor inn offers generically furnished rooms at affordable rates. It has a shaded playground and picnic area. *1819 S. Canal St., Carlsbad, NM 88220, tel. 505/887–1148. 56 rooms. Facilities: restaurant, pool, wading pool, Jacuzzi, laundry, truck parking. AE, D, DC, MC, V. Moderate.*

Continental Inn. South of Carlsbad on National Parks Highway, 30 minutes from Carlsbad Caverns, Continental Inn has simple rooms with matching curtains and bedspreads in colorful southwestern patterns. All rooms have coffeemakers and cable TV with free HBO. The small grounds are beautifully landscaped and well kept. Rates are about as low as they come in town. *3820 National Parks Hwy., Carlsbad, NM 88220, tel. 505/887–0341. 60 rooms. Facilities: heated pool in season, airport pickups, truck parking. AE, D, DC, MC, V. Inexpensive.*

CAMPING

You will have to hike into the backcountry to set up a campsite within the confines of Carlsbad Caverns National Park, and your site must be far enough from established roadways so as not to be seen or heard.

If you want an RV hookup or a drive-in campsite, you will have to camp outside the park. Public campgrounds include those in nearby Guadalupe Mountains National Park;

Brantley Lake State Park, the newest state park in New Mexico; and Lincoln National Forest. In addition, a number of commercial sites are available at White's City.

INSIDE THE PARK You will need a free backcountry permit to camp in Carlsbad Caverns National Park, which has no designated campsites. Permits can be obtained at the visitor center, where you can also pick up a map of areas closed to camping. Campfires are illegal in Carlsbad, but you may use a camp stove. There is no water in the backcountry, so be sure to bring an adequate supply (at least one gallon per person per day).

Use of the backcountry here is presently very light, so you need not worry about crowds. The rugged beauty of Slaughter Canyon, the ridge above Yucca Canyon, and the far western part of the park near Putman Patrol Cabin are attractive destinations for those who are strong and determined enough to reach them.

NEAR THE PARK Twelve miles north of Carlsbad via Highway 285, and another 4½ miles east via Capitan Reef Road, **Brantley Lake State Park** campground (Box 2288, Carlsbad NM 88221, tel. 505/457–2384) has 51 sites, including 48 water and electric hookups. It also has a primitive camping area, where there are no designated sites (just pull off the dirt road wherever you please). The established campground has flush toilets, drinking water, fire grates, showers, a disposal station, a ranger station, and a public phone. The primitive camping area has only chemical toilets. You can swim in the lake at your own risk. Boating is allowed, but rentals are not available. The campground is open year-round; sites cost $11 per night with hookups, $7 per night in developed campground, $6 per night in primitive area. Reservations are not accepted.

You can camp anywhere you like in the **Lincoln National Forest** (tel. 505/437–6030), which abuts the southwest corner of Carlsbad Caverns National Monument. The lovely Sitting Bull Falls picnic area has tables, grills, toilets, and water, but it's for day use only; the camping areas have no facilities, so bring water and proper clothing for backcountry

camping. Watch your campfire very carefully and make sure it is out before you leave.

In the heart of White's City, the popular **AAA White's City RV Park** (31 Carlsbad Caverns Hwy., Box 128, White's City, NM 88268, tel. 505/785–2291 or, for reservations, 800/228–3767) has 50 full hookups and 22 water and electric hookups, as well as an open area that can accommodate 40 to 50 tents. There are flush toilets, hot showers, drinking water, barbecue grills, and shaded picnic tables. Guests can use two pools and two Jacuzzis at nearby motels. Sites cost $16 per night. Make reservations at least two weeks in advance during the summer season.

The shaded, full-service **Carlsbad Kampgrounds** (4301 National Parks Hwy., Star Rte. 1, Box 34, Carlsbad, NM 88220, tel. 505/885–6333) has 114 level gravel sites of which 46 have full hookups and 68 have water and electric hookups. For tents there are 40 additional grass sites. The campground has canopied picnic tables, an indoor swimming pool, laundry, public phone and phone hookups, hot showers, flush toilets, a grocery store, grills, and sewage disposal. A professional RV service station is located next door. Open year-round, this campground charges $9.50 to $11.50 for two persons; electric hookups are $1.50 extra. Reservations are recommended Memorial Day through Labor Day.

Windmill RV Park (3624 National Parks Hwy., Carlsbad, NM 88220, tel. 505/885–9761) has 61 RV sites, all of which have hookups. There are laundry facilities, hot showers, and flush toilets here. In summer, guests use the outdoor pool. Open year-round, Windmill charges $11 per site per night, $1.50 extra for cable TV hookup.

Run by the town of Carlsbad, the **Lake Carlsbad Campground** (Greene St., Box 1569, Carlsbad, NM 88220, tel. 505/885–4435) is located right on the Pecos River, about a mile from downtown Carlsbad. There are no designated sites here, but half of the camping area is gravel and half is grass. The campground has flush toilets, hot showers, drinking water, picnic tables, and grills. Each car or camper is charged $4.45 per night.

Crater Lake National Park
Oregon
By Jeff Kuechle

If old Mt. Mazama had held its powder 7,700 years ago, this area in Oregon's southern Cascades might never have rated a national park. Geologists say it was a big mountain, perhaps the highest in the state, but otherwise unremarkable.

As it happens, though, the mountain blew its top in an eruption that would have made the 1980 eruption of its northern cousin Mt. St. Helens look like a cherry bomb. But Mazama spewed out so much debris that, when it was all over, the mountain collapsed. And the result is a unique body of crystal-clear water encased in a goblet of a mountain. The park, at 183,224 acres among the smallest in the West, is sometimes derided as having little to it other than the lake, beautiful as it may be. But if Crater Lake lacks the three-ring circus lineup of Yellowstone and Yosemite, it also lacks anything resembling the crowds. About 500,000 visitors annually drink in the sights

at Crater Lake, compared to the millions that throng the other parks.

Crater Lake remains an undiscovered gem among national parks, in part because the region is so remote—the nearest major metropolitan area, Portland, is 250 miles away—and in part because the high mountain environment is so unforgiving that little development has taken place. Only on the caldera's south rim is there any development of consequence. But even there, at 7,100 feet, 50-foot snowdrifts have taken their toll. The Crater Lake Lodge, built from 1909 to 1915, has been closed for several years now, the victim of weak construction and more than 70 winters. The lodge is undergoing an extensive rehabilitation, but the work won't be finished until 1995.

The main attraction here is the lake, mesmerizing with its pure blue color and dizzying setting. The first look at its placid, clear waters will take your breath away. The lake is about 6 miles across and 1,000 or more feet below the rim, which ranges from 6,600 to 8,000 feet in elevation. This makes a little shortness of breath only natural. The winds on the rim can be bracing, if not brisk, and the vertiginous heights and sheer cliffs make everyone feel exposed. If you have trouble with heights, you may have second thoughts about coming here.

Once you descend to the surface of the lake, however, the mood changes. The protective cliffs cradle the lake, and in calm weather its mirrorlike surface is sometimes hauntingly still. At 1,932 feet it's the deepest lake in the United States.

At times this huge body of water seems to be an illusion, a giant mirage. The reflective visitor might think about the first European Americans to see the lake in 1853. Out of food at the headwaters of the Rogue River, near what is now the northwestern corner of the park, a party of prospectors set off in search of game. Two of them came up a long slope that simply broke off into space. Beneath them hung this huge, incredibly blue lake. The men continued their search for food, encountering some Native Americans nearby who vehemently denied the existence of any such lake. To them, the lake was sacred, and they believed that anyone with the temerity to gaze into its depths would be struck dead.

Crater Lake lay undisturbed by European Americans for another decade. In fact, the shore of the lake was not reached until 1865. The lake wasn't photographed until 1874, when pioneer photographer Peter Britt's images of the still-unexplored splendors of the West captivated the nation. A 16-year-old Kansas schoolboy named William Gladstone Steel saw an article about Crater Lake in a local newspaper and decided he would journey there and row out to the strange cinder cone now called Wizard Island. In 1885 he did just that, and then he dedicated himself to making Crater Lake a national park.

The battle went on for 16 years. Bills to preserve Crater Lake were introduced in each Congress and routinely dismissed after lobbying by ranchers, land speculators, and tim-

ber tycoons. But Steel persevered, and in 1902 he found a friendly ear in conservation-minded President Theodore Roosevelt. Crater Lake became the nation's sixth national park.

ESSENTIAL INFORMATION

VISITOR INFORMATION Write to **Crater Lake National Park,** Box 7, Crater Lake, Oregon 97604; or call 503/594–2211. Free backcountry permits are required for overnight stays in the backcountry. These are available at any information center within the park.

FEES The entrance fee is $5, June to September; there is no fee for off-season entrance. *Note:* Oregon Highway 62 passes through the southwest corner of the park, and no fee is charged unless the visitor turns north at the Annie Spring Entrance Station toward the lake.

PUBLICATIONS A handy mail order catalog of books and maps about the park is available from the **Crater Lake Natural History Association** (Box 157, Crater Lake, OR, 97604), as are the following books:

Ron Warfield's *A Guide to Crater Lake National Park—the Mountain that Used to Be* provides a useful and lushly illustrated overview of Crater Lake's history and physical features. The National Park Service uses Stephen Harris's *Fire Mountains of the West* in its ranger training; the detailed handbook covers Cascade range geology. *Field Guide to the Olympics and Cascades,* by Steven Whitney, is an easy-to-use guide to the flora and fauna of the Northwest's mountainous areas. For information on the park's natural history, geology, plants, and wildlife, use Jeffrey P. Schaffer's *Crater Lake National Park and Vicinity,* a readable guide with excellent topographic trail maps, or KC Publication's *Crater Lake, the Story Behind the Scenery.*

GEOLOGY AND TERRAIN Crater Lake National Park encompasses about 400 square miles of high alpine meadows, the lunar-looking Pumice Desert, deep canyons, snowy peaks, and, of course, the natural wonder for which the park is named.

The park straddles the southern Cascade range and is part of a network of high mountain wilderness areas that stretch from North Cascades National Park in northern Washington to California's Sequoia National Park. The northern third of Crater Lake National Park contains a small, broad plain of volcanic dust called the Pumice Desert. Located at about 5,000 feet, this very dry and fragile area supports only small ground-hugging vegetation.

Toward the northwest end of the park, on the moister Pacific side of the Cascades, the dry pumice gradually gives way to lush alpine meadows and forests. Here the famous Rogue River begins its 150-mile journey to the sea in a series of springs embedded in a high cliff. Streams such as Crater Creek, Bybee Creek, and Castle Creek in the western section of the park carve deep canyons through pumice and layer upon layer of lava flows. The most dramatic is Castle Creek Canyon, which is filled with mammoth pumice spires 100 feet high. Highway 62 enters the park from the west and follows Castle Creek on its way toward the rim. On the western edge of the park, south of Castle Creek and Highway 62, Union Creek erupts from a hillside at Thousand Springs.

Union Peak, a 7,709-foot hunk of stone that is actually a volcanic plug, holds sway over the southern part of the park, giving way to a smaller volcanic area known as Pumice Flat and the canyon of Annie Creek, which heads southeast toward upper Klamath Lake. Farther east are the high, wild slopes of Crater Peak and the park's other notable geologic oddity: the Pinnacles.

Basically, the Pinnacles are the fused remnants of ancient ash flows. Mt. Mazama's catastrophic collapse filled the canyons of Annie Creek, Sun Creek, Wheeler Creek, and Sand Creek with hundreds of feet of ash. As hot gases bubbled to the surface, fumaroles (holes from which gases can escape) were formed, and the material around the holes fused into hardened "pipes" as the superheated gas escaped. Over time, streams caused the erosion of the softer ash material, leaving pillars of heat-tempered ash behind.

Now the pillars dot the canyons of the park's southeastern section.

The relatively narrow eastern part of the park is high, wild, and completely undeveloped. Mt. Scott, at 8,926 feet the highest point in the park, is the main landmark in this 45-square-mile section of meadows and pine forests.

In the middle of the park is the lake itself, surrounded by cliffs that range from 500 feet to almost 2,000 feet above the water's surface. South of the rim, you'll see U-shape valleys carved by glaciers that once existed on the ancestral Mt. Mazama.

Other geologic features of note are within the lake itself. Near the western shore is Wizard Island, a 700-foot-high cinder cone that is the product of eruptions that occurred after Mazama's cataclysmic collapse. In the southeast portion of the lake is the Phantom Ship, a tattered, eerie island of basalt that, in certain lights, resembles the Flying Dutchman of maritime legend.

FLORA AND FAUNA Crater Lake National Park offers an excellent cross section of Cascade range vegetation and wildlife. In the west, the dominant trees are Douglas fir, interspersed with sugar pine and mountain hemlock. To the east are white fir, ponderosa pine, and lodgepole pine, found everywhere but the austere precincts of the Pumice Desert. Around the rim, where harsh winterlike conditions can occur any time of the year, white-bark pines, the mainstay of the High Sierras, are found.

In the high country, growing seasons are very short, but the park fosters a wide variety of wildflowers. Glacier lilies are the first to appear, breaking through the snowbanks in spring. Western pasqueflowers, which evolve into the white-bearded "old men of the mountain" also flourish by the vanishing snowbanks. Newberry knotweed, lupines, pentstemon, phlox, pussy paws, monkey paws, Jacob's ladders, forget-me-nots, and bleeding hearts are all found in fissures, bogs, and meadows of the park.

Crater Lake's larger wildlife are a shy lot. Roosevelt elk roam in the southern portion of the park and near Union Peak, and black bears inhabit much of the park. Neither species is often seen by visitors, because the animals tend to stay away from roads and buildings. The Sky Lakes Wilderness, due south of the park, stretches some 40 miles before hitting a road. The Union Creek and Red Blanket Creek canyons are also remote and provide a good haven for the animals. Deer, both mule and black-tailed, are common, as are red foxes, yellow-bellied marmots, and the rabbitlike pika.

The park is also home to a wide range of bird life. Clark's nutcracker is most common, but ravens are also plentiful, gliding above the rim. Great horned owls, water ouzels, hairy woodpeckers, red-breasted nuthatches, mountain chickadees, golden-crowned kinglets, red crossbills, and dark-eyed juncos are regularly sighted. Hawks—red-tailed, marsh, and goshawks—are found near Mt. Scott, where rare sightings of bald eagles also occur.

Fish were introduced to Crater Lake in 1888 by William Steel. Stocking continued until 1941. Only two species, rainbow trout and kokanee salmon, remain.

WHEN TO GO Summer here—above 7,000 feet in the Cascades—is a relative thing. Midsummer snowstorms on the rim of Crater Lake are not uncommon. Nor, of course, is the bright, clear December day in the 50°F range.

High season for the park is July and August. Although temperatures in the surrounding lower valleys often reach 110°F during the summer, in the higher elevation of the park it is usually a breezy 75°F to 80°F, even during the hottest months. Warm, clear days are the rule for July and August, but because of the elevation, at night the temperature can fall below freezing, even after a day when it has been in the 70s.

The average yearly precipitation at park headquarters is 69 inches. Most of the rain comes in winter, spring, and fall and quickly turns to snow. And it is the snow that is the park's main source of moisture. Outside of Mt. Rainier, no other national park receives as much annual snowfall as Crater Lake. In the steeply sloped area, drifts of up to 50 feet are common. A year without at least 10 feet (120 inches) of snow at Rim Village is considered abnormal.

During winter, temperatures range from 20°F to 40°F and rarely fall below zero. The lake seldom freezes. The last hard freeze of Crater Lake occurred in 1949.

WHAT TO PACK As in other high mountain areas, it is best to wear layered clothing at Crater Lake, and because most of the trails are steep and rocky, sturdy hiking boots are a good bet. For sightseeing above or on the lake, binoculars are a must.

GENERAL STORES Inside the park, there is only one store, **Camper's Service Store** (tel. 503/594–2511), located at Mazama Village, near Highway 62. The store is small, but carries food supplies and such camping necessities as stove fuel and lantern mantels. It is open daily, weather permitting, from early May through late October. The hours are 7 AM to 10 PM from June through September and 10 to 6 in May and October.

There are no other stores within 20 miles of the park. **Diamond Lake Resort** (tel. 503/793–3333 or 800/733–7593), 25 miles north on Highway 138, has basic food supplies and fishing tackle. Daily summer hours are 7 AM to 10 PM, and winter hours are 8 to 6. Some 25 miles southwest of the park on Highway 62 is **Union Creek Resort** (tel. 503/560–3565), which also stocks staples and fishing gear. The store is open daily year-round. Summer hours are 8 to 8; winter hours vary month to month.

ARRIVING AND DEPARTING There are three entrances to Crater Lake—the North entrance on Highway 138 and the west and south entrances on Highway 62. Which you choose depends on the season in which you're traveling and where you're coming from. The most popular route is Highway 62, which visitors take northeast from Medford or northwest from Klamath Falls. This is also the only road to the park kept open during the winter.

By Plane. The closest airport of any size is in Medford, 75 miles southwest of the park. Medford has daily service on United and Horizon airlines from Portland, the Bay Area, and points beyond. There is no public transportation to Crater Lake. Car rentals are available from **Avis** (tel. 503/773–3003), **Budget** (tel. 503/773–7023), **Hertz** (tel. 503/773–4293), and **National** (tel. 503/779–4863).

By Car and RV. The drive from Medford, Oregon (population 55,000), to the park runs on Highway 62 northeast along the Rogue River, gradually gaining elevation through thick forests. The trip is about 80 miles and takes about two hours. This route provides the quickest access to Rim Village.

To get to the park from Klamath Falls (population 17,000), travel north on U.S. 97 for 30 miles and then pick up Highway 62 traveling northwest for another 25 miles to the park entrance.

The park is about a two-hour drive from Bend, Oregon (population 20,000), south along U.S. 97 and west on Highway 138. Visitors arriving from Willamette Valley to the west or central Oregon to the east can also enter the park via Highway 138. From Roseburg (population 15,000) to the west, this road twists up the canyon of the North Umpqua River skirting the northern edge of the park. A hundred miles (2¹/₂ hours) from Roseburg it reaches the North entrance and then continues east to U.S. 97.

From Portland—about 250 miles away—the park is a six-hour drive by one of several routes, most involving one or two mountain passes. The fastest, with the least amount of climbing, is I–5 to Eugene, about 100 miles south of Portland, then east on Highway 58, south on U.S. 97, and west on Highway 138. Crater Lake is about 400 miles, via Portland, from Mt. Rainier National Park. Lassen Volcanic Park is about 300 miles to the southeast, traveling along Highway 62 to Medford and then taking I–5 to Redding, California, and Route 44 east.

By Train. The nearest **Amtrak** station (tel. 800/872–7245) is in the town of Chemult (population 250) about 40 minutes away by car. Chemult has no car rentals, however, and no public transportation to the park. Klamath Falls has an Amtrak station and car rentals (call Avis, tel. 503/882–7232) but no public transportation to the park.

By Bus. There are **Greyhound** bus depots in Roseburg, Chemult, Bend, Klamath Falls, Medford, and Grants Pass, but there is no public transportation to the park from any of those locations. Car rentals are available in Roseburg from **Chrysler Rental Service** (tel. 503/672–6555), in Bend from **Hertz** (tel. 503/388–1535), in Klamath Falls from **Avis** (tel. 503/882–7232), and in Medford from **Hertz** (tel. 503/773–4293) or **National** (tel. 503/779–4863).

EXPLORING

A car and a pair of reliable hiking shoes can get you around Crater Lake quite nicely. The 33-mile Rim Drive encircles the lake, providing access to better than a dozen viewpoints, some of which are right on the road and others that are less than a mile from the road.

A thorough job of rounding the lake can take up an entire day, although most visitors find a half day more than adequate. Biking the Rim Drive provides more time to observe, but only able bicyclists should make the journey. The road is on average at an elevation of 7,000 feet, and some portions are steep and narrow. The Pacific Crest Trail (which leads from Canada to Mexico) runs through the western section of the park, but it is never within sight of the lake. The lake itself can be reached only on foot, and it can be explored only aboard one of the park's motor launches. Touring the lake properly is also a full day's job, although many do it in half that time.

THE BEST IN ONE DAY About 95% of the people who visit Crater Lake never actually stick a finger in the lake itself. Why? The main reason is that the lake is only accessible by one very steep, 2-mile round-trip trail: Getting down isn't so difficult, but the climb back

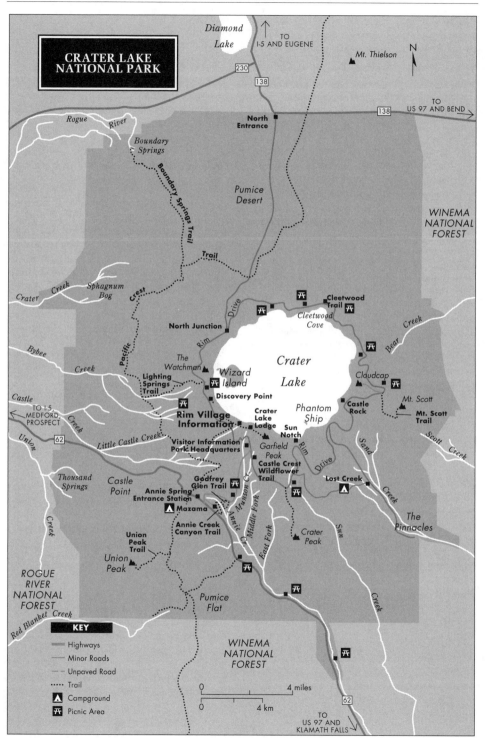

CRATER LAKE
NATIONAL PARK

Diamond
Lake

TO
I-5 AND EUGENE

Mt. Thielson

N

230

138

138

TO
US 97 AND BEND

North
Entrance

Rogue   River

Boundary
Springs

Pumice
Desert

WINEMA
NATIONAL
FOREST

Crater   Creek

Sphagnum
Bog

Trail

Cleetwood
Trail

Cleetwood
Cove

Bear   Creek

North Junction

Crater

Bybee   Creek

The
Watchman

Lighting
Springs
Trail

Wizard
Island

Discovery Point

Crater
Lake

Cloudcap

Mt. Scott

Castle   Creek

TO I-5,
MEDFORD,
PROSPECT

Rim Village
Information

Crater
Lake
Lodge

Phantom
Ship

Castle
Rock

Mt. Scott
Trail

62

Little Castle Creek

Union   Creek

Visitor Information
Park Headquarters

Sun
Notch

Garfield
Peak

Castle Crest
Wildflower
Trail

Lost Creek

Scott   Creek

Thousand
Springs

Castle
Point

Godfrey
Glen Trail

Annie Spring
Entrance Station

Mazama

Annie Creek
Canyon Trail

The
Pinnacles

Union
Peak
Trail

Union
Peak

Crater
Peak

ROGUE
RIVER
NATIONAL
FOREST

Red Blanket Creek

Pumice
Flat

WINEMA
NATIONAL
FOREST

62

TO
US 97 AND
KLAMATH FALLS

KEY

Highways
Minor Roads
Unpaved Road
Trail
Campground
Picnic Area

0   4 miles

0   4 km

up is a deterrent. If you really want to understand the power and scope of the lake, however, take the trouble to get down to the water.

To reach the boats, head north from Rim Village along Rim Drive. The road has excellent views of the lake for several miles, with numerous turnouts for picture taking. If you get up really early you should be able to get in one good hike before you reach the boat launch, and that hike should be the almost 3/4-mile uphill trek to the Watchman, an 8,035-foot precipice complete with lookout tower. Park in the large parking area at the Watchman overlook and look for signs to the Watchman trail. From here you can look down 2,000 feet into the lagoon of Wizard Island, where the boat will soon be taking you.

After the hike, continue along Rim Drive, which pulls away from the lake for a few miles affording views of spirelike Mt. Thielsen, lying just north of the park. The road returns to hug the rim just east of Llao Rock, one of the park's most distinctive features. Picnic areas along here are good for brief stops.

It's an 11-mile, 30-minute drive from Rim Village to Cleetwood Trail, which you must descend to reach the boats. It takes about 25 minutes to walk down the 1-mile trail. Give yourself enough time, and try to catch the first boat, which usually leaves at 10 AM (tour times vary due to weather and anticipated number of visitors). The boat ride takes about an hour and 45 minutes, including a five-minute stopover at Wizard Island. The adventuresome get off at the island and spend most of the day hiking, climbing, fishing, and picnicking; the truly intrepid even swim in the incredibly clear, cold, 45°F to 55°F water. If you have the time, it's worthwhile to spend at least some time on the island, but remember the last launch leaves at about 4:30 PM. Boat hours are posted, and a ranger roams the island warning any tardy sojourners.

When you return to the mainland, give yourself at least an hour for the hike out—unless you're in extremely good shape. If you chose not to stay on Wizard Island, it will be early afternoon when you disembark, and you'll have the rest of the day to make it around Rim Drive. From Cleetwood Trail, continue clockwise around the lake.

The next stop is Cloudcap, a lookout that you can reach via a mile-long spur road at the far eastern end of the lake. From here, Wizard Island and all the postcard views of the lake are several miles away. If you're interested in observing the park from a different perspective and have the time, the view from Cloudcap is well worth the trek.

Circling back west, the visitor will reach the 7-mile spur road that leads to the Pinnacles, a spooky area of volcanic spires. The weary sightseer may be discouraged by the fact that the road dead-ends, which makes it necessary to drive the same stretch twice. But hang in there. The Pinnacles and the canyons leading up to them are spectacular, and although many a traveler pass them by, you should not. Unfortunately, there are no trails out here.

After viewing the Pinnacles, you'll have to backtrack to Rim Drive and continue west. The road veers away from the lake, climbing around Garfield Peak just east of Rim Village, at the lake's southern edge. If you have any energy left, trek the 1 3/4 miles one way from the old lodge to the top of Garfield Peak, where you'll be rewarded with good views of the entire lake.

ORIENTATION PROGRAMS Ranger-led talks (10 to 15 minutes) on the origins of Crater Lake are presented every half-hour at the Sinnott Memorial Overlook in Rim Village. A scale model of the lake helps visitors understand the forces at work even today at Crater Lake. Rangers are well prepared to answer questions.

At park headquarters, an 18-minute video shown every half-hour introduces visitors to the park. There's some decent footage, but the small screen does little to capture the grandeur of the setting, and you may want to avoid it, unless you're unlucky enough to arrive on one of the park's snowy or foggy days.

GUIDED TOURS The only guided tours in Crater Lake are aboard the lake boats. Run by the park's concessionaire, the launches carry 60 passengers on a one-hour, 45-minute tour accompanied by a ranger. No private boats are allowed on the water, so this is your only opportunity to get a close-up look at the lake.

Depending upon the weather and on how well the boats survived the winter, boat tours usually begin by July 1 and end in mid-September. The first of nine hourly tours leaves the dock at 10 AM; the last departs at 4:30 PM. The fee is $10 for adults and $5.50 for children 11 and under. Children under two can sit on laps and ride free.

SCENIC DRIVES AND VIEWS The 33-mile **Rim Drive** is the main scenic route, affording views of the lake and its cliffs from every conceivable angle. The drive alone takes over an hour. Frequent stops at viewpoints and short hikes stretch this to half a day.

All along Rim Drive are scenic turnouts and picnic areas. Two of the best spots to stop are on the north side of the lake, between Llao Rock and Cleetwood Cove, where the cliffs are nearly vertical (watch for signs).

If you want to walk for your views, and be rewarded for your walks, the best short hike is to the Watchman. While the hike is less than a mile each way, the trail climbs more than 400 feet—not counting the steps up to the actual lookout.

The only other scenic drive is the 7-mile trip to the **Pinnacles,** to the southeast, off Rim Drive. The road scoots along the Sand Creek Canyon with its weird volcanic landscape and ends up at the Pinnacles, a canyon full of strange-looking spires composed of hardened ash deposits.

NATURE TRAILS AND SHORT WALKS The three best nature hikes are in the Munson Valley, where Mazama Village and park headquarters are located. The ³/₄-mile loop of **Castle Crest Wildflower Trail** runs along the upper reaches of Munson Creek. Park your car at park headquarters' Steel Center, cross the street, and look for the sign pointing the way

to the trailhead. The creekside walk is easy going, and in July the wildflowers are in full fragrant force. Drive 2 miles farther down the Munson Valley, and you will reach the parking area for **Godfrey Glen Trail.** This 2-mile loop takes you through an excellent example of what geologists term a hanging valley—the place where one valley hangs over a lower valley, with a cliff and a waterfall between them. Deer are frequently seen here, and the flowers are plentiful. The **Annie Creek Canyon Trail,** which sets off from Mazama Campground, is more strenuous but still easy compared to some of the steep rim hikes, such as that of the Watchman Trail. The 2-mile loop threads through the Annie Creek Canyon, giving views of the narrow cleft, scarred by volcanism and carpeted with lichen.

LONGER HIKES The 2³/₄-mile **Mt. Scott Trail** takes you to the park's highest point, the top of Mt. Scott, at 8,926 feet. It will take the average hiker 60 to 90 minutes to make the steep uphill trek and about 45 minutes to get down. The trail starts at an elevation of about 7,800 feet, so the climb is not extreme but does get steep in spots. The elevation, however, will make the unfit quickly short of breath. The view of the lake is wonderful. Views to the east and south of the broad Klamath Basin are equally spectacular. Mt. Scott is an older volcano than Mt. Mazama.

The **Pacific Crest Trail** extends from Mexico to Canada and winds for more than 30 miles through the park, entering it about a mile east of the North entrance road and shadowing the road across the Pumice Desert for about 6 miles. While the trail offers the prime backcountry experience of the park, it offers no views of the lake. The trail keeps to the west side of the rim at about 6,000 feet, although it dips in and out of frequent canyons. After crossing Highway 62 near Mazama Village, the trail enters the wildest area of the park. It gets steeper as it passes by Union Peak and skirts the wide expanse of Pumice Flat before leaving the park and entering the 40-mile-long Sky Lakes Wilderness Area.

Hikers of the Pacific Crest wishing to see Crater Lake often detour along the 4-mile one-way **Lightning Springs Trail,** which approximates the trek of the old prospectors. The trail connects the Pacific Crest Trail with Rim Drive about 1 mile south of the Watchman, climbing from about 5,700 feet to 7,172 feet in elevation. Many hikers will walk down Lightning Springs from Rim Drive and continue all the way to Mazama Campground—a 10-mile, mostly downhill hike that takes several hours.

For the intrepid hiker, a trip to Boundary Springs may be in order. The 8-mile one-way **Boundary Springs Trail** splits from the Pacific Crest Trail 3¹/₄ miles after the Pacific Crest crosses the North entrance road. There is parking on the road, but you must watch closely for the signs. From here, the trail eases down the gradually sloping northwestern shoulders of the old Mt. Mazama. To the east you'll see the barren Desert Cone and the Pumice Desert. To the west the thick forests begin. The trail angles toward them, ending up at Boundary Springs, one of the sources of the Rogue River. To avoid a long walk back, many hikers arrange to be picked up at Lake West, a small campground outside the park, easily accessible via Highway 230 from the Diamond Lake area.

Beginning at the Pacific Crest Trail about 4 miles south of Highway 62, the poorly maintained **Union Peak Trail** scales 7,709-foot-high Union Peak in the far southeast corner of the park. Elk herds roam the area, and bear sightings are frequent here. There is no view of the lake from the top, but the vistas west and south to the Union Creek, Red Blanket Creek, and Rogue canyons are excellent.

OTHER ACTIVITIES There are several activities you cannot do in this park. There is no off-road driving or bicycling because of the fragile alpine and volcanic soils. No private craft are allowed on the lake, no boat rentals are available, and rock climbing is not permitted within the caldera.

Biking. The 33-mile Rim Drive is popular with bicyclists, although no designated bike route exists. The road is steep and narrow in places, and the shoulder is dangerously small, so use extreme caution. No bike rentals are available in the park.

Bird-Watching. Clark's nutcracker is found throughout the park, and ravens strut and croak near virtually all rim viewpoints. Hawks and bald eagles are sighted only in the Mt. Scott area.

Fishing. Fishing is allowed but impractical in the lake. A state fishing license is not required. Those who do fish try the area near the boat launch or take poles on the boat tour and fish off Wizard Island. Rainbow trout and kokanee salmon lurk in Crater Lake's aquamarine depths, some growing to monster lunker size. The problem is finding them—or, rather, getting them to find you.

Horseback Riding. Few people ride in the park. There are no stables in the park, and only three trails are open to horses, mules, and llamas: the Pacific Crest Trail, the Lightning Springs Trail, and the Bald Crater Loop. Only pelletized feed is allowed; riders must carry enough for their entire stay. A free brochure on park regulations is available at visitor centers.

Ski Touring. Equipment rentals are available at Rim Village (tel. 503/594–2511) for $12 per day. There are no maintained trails. Most cross-country skiers follow a portion of Rim Drive as best they can. The road is plowed to Rim Village, but it may be closed temporarily by severe storms.

Snowmobiling. Snowmobiling is allowed only on the North entrance road up to its junction with Rim Drive. Tours are offered by Diamond Lake Resort (tel. 503/793–3333), 25 miles northwest, for $66–$125 per person. Some adventurous cross-country skiers snowmobile to the remote north rim area to ski that area or the large flat area of the Pumice Desert.

Snowshoeing. Rentals are available at Rim Village (tel. 503/594–2511) for $8 a day or $4 for a half-day and at Diamond Lake Resort (*see above*) for $3 a day. Snowshoeing can be difficult in the deep, drifting snow around the rim, but this is still the most popular area in the park for the sport.

Swimming. Swimming is allowed in the lake, but not usually advised. Made up entirely of snowmelt, Crater Lake is very cold—about 45°F to 55°F during summer. What swimming does take place is in a lagoon on Wizard Island, but even then it's only appealing when the air temperature rises above 80°F.

CHILDREN'S PROGRAMS From late June to Labor Day, Crater Lake offers a junior ranger program. Contact the visitors center for details.

EVENING ACTIVITIES During the summer, the park service offers slide shows at an outdoor amphitheater near Mazama Campground. The shows focus on natural and cultural history and are well attended by overnight visitors.

DINING

If you can't survive without espresso and duck à l'orange, Crater Lake is not the place for you. In the park itself, fast food is the only alternative to the picnic basket. The old lodge used to serve up very nice trout, salmon, and steak, but it has been closed since 1988. And the park is so isolated that few other dining options exist nearby.

INSIDE THE PARK **The Watchman.** More sophisticated than the other dining options within the park (at least until the dining room at the newly renovated Crater Lake Lodge opens in 1995), this full-service dining room offers an array of steak and seafood choices. Try the Lake Majesty (vegetarian patty with sprouts and avocados) or the Mount Lazama Burger (with cheese and mushrooms) for lunch, or the broiled salmon or shrimp stir-fry for dinner. *Rim Village, tel. 503/594–2211. MC, V. Closed Sept.–May. Moderate.*

Lao Rock Cafeteria. This barnlike cafeteria, where diners eat family-style at long tables, features hamburgers, simple sandwiches, and drinks. *Rim Village, tel. 503/594–2211. MC , V. Inexpensive.*

Wizard Pizza. This park institution is known for its fresh-baked pizza and fried chicken. As an added bonus, they'll deliver to the nearby campgrounds. *Rim Village, tel. 503/594–2211. MC, V. Closed Sept.–May. Inexpensive.*

NEAR THE PARK **Diamond Lake Resort.** The resort has three restaurants, ranging from a snack bar to sit-down formal. The small, informal ground floor café is best suited for hearty breakfasts and lunches. On the far side of the lake is a standard pizza parlor. Upstairs at the lodge is the rustic Dinner House, where specialties include prime rib and surprisingly good veal cordon bleu. *25 mi from Crater Lake on Hwy. 138, Diamond Lake, OR, tel. 503/793–3333. MC, V. Inexpensive–Moderate.*

Beckies Café. Beckies is a local institution, serving up home-cooked meals to hungry hunters, fishermen, loggers, and park rangers for more than 60 years. The trout is excellent, and the tiny café is famous for its succulent huckleberry pie. *25 mi south of park on Hwy. 62, Union Creek Resort, Prospect, OR, tel. 503/560–3563. MC, V. Inexpensive.*

Prospect Hotel Restaurant. The dining room of this beautiful old hotel secluded on a mountain serves up hearty food in suprisingly civilized surroundings. Dinners are four courses, with such entrées as rack of lamb and fresh seafood. There's also a champagne brunch, from 8 to 2 on weekends, where you can design your own omelet. *391 Millcreek, Prospect, tel. 503/560–3664. MC, V. Inexpensive.*

NOT SO NEAR THE PARK The Medford–Ashland area, about 60 miles south of the park on Highway 62, has southern Oregon's broadest array of dining options, centered around Ashland's Tony Award–winning Oregon Shakespeare Festival. Standouts include: **Chata** (1212 S. Pacific Hwy., Talent, OR, tel. 503/535–2575), a friendly, family-oriented place serving such hearty Eastern European peasant food as *mamaliga de aur* (cheesy cornmeal cakes in a rich sauce of cream, wine, and mushrooms); **Chateaulin** (50 E. Main St., Ashland, OR, tel. 503/482–2264), a classic French restaurant with an elegant, romantic, ivy-walled ambience; **Gen Kai** (1763 E. McAndrew Rd., Medford, OR, tel. 503/779–7933), the best in Japanese dining; **Thai Pepper** (84 N. Main St., Ashland, OR, tel. 503/482–8058), offering fiery and satisfying (if not scrupulously authentic) Thai food in a soothing creekside setting; and **Winchester Country Inn** (35 S. 2nd St., Ashland, OR, tel. 503/488–1113), another classic French restaurant that competes with Chateaulin as Ashland's best, and usually scores higher for imaginative dishes.

PICNIC SPOTS Rim Drive has perhaps a dozen picnic-area turnouts. While all offer good views, they can get very windy. If something a little less spectacular and more peaceful appeals, try some of the spots off the rim proper. The Vidae Falls picnic area on the upper reaches of Sun Creek has an alpine setting, as does a small picnic area between Mazama Village and park headquarters, near the Godfrey Glen trailhead.

LODGING

Accommodations are limited in or near the park. There are fewer than 150 units of any kind within a 25-mile radius of Crater Lake. The good news is that prices are low, especially during the winter.

INSIDE THE PARK **Mazama Village.** The only lodging within the park, this 80-unit motel complex is located near Highway 62. Built in low-slung four-plexes meant to weather the winter, the accommodations are basic with few frills. *Box 128, Crater Lake, OR 97604, tel. 503/594–2511. 80 rooms. MC, V. Closed Nov.–Apr. Moderate–Expensive.*

NEAR THE PARK **Diamond Lake Resort.** Located on a mountain lake 25 miles northwest of Crater Lake, this large resort has 50 motel rooms and 40 cabins. The cabins are simple and rustic while the motel rooms are modern and plain. *Diamond Lake, OR 97731–9708, tel. 503/793–3333. 50 rooms and 40 cabins. Facilities: 3 restaurants, lounge, fishing, boat rentals. MC, V. Moderate.*

Prospect Historical Hotel & Motel. This lovely old roadhouse hotel, built in 1889, was brought back from the dead in 1990. Looking like a set from a John Ford movie, it lies 34 miles from the park entrance. There are 8 smallish (but nice) rooms in the main hotel, where the tariff includes breakfast. The 15 new motel rooms out back are larger and better for families. *391 Millcreek, Prospect, OR 97536, tel. 503/560–3664, fax 503/560–3825. 23 rooms. Facilities: restaurant, lounge, cable TV. MC, V. Moderate.*

Union Creek Resort. This resort is 3,000 feet lower than Rim Village, and although it gets plenty of snow, the climate is much warmer. The lodge and adjacent cabins were built by the Civilian Conservation Corps during the 1930s, and the entire settlement is listed on the National Register of Historic Places. The bulk of the accommodations are in 13 individual cabins strung out behind the lodge. These vary from very small sleeping cabins to creekside A-frames with decks. The nine heavy-timbered lodge rooms are more colorful, but cramped and sometimes noisy. *Prospect, OR 97965, tel. 503/560–3565. 9 rooms and 13 cabins. MC, V. Inexpensive–Moderate.*

CAMPING

Crater Lake has two camping areas: the large, 198-site **Mazama Campground** (flush toilets, hot water, drinking water, laundry facilities, fire grates, disposal station, public phone) and the smaller, more remote, 16-site **Lost Creek Campground** (chemical flush toilets, drinking water, fire grates). Mazama is open from mid-June through mid-October, and sites cost $11 per night. You can camp at Lost Creek from mid-July through mid-September for $6 per night. Reservations are not accepted, but sites are usually available on a daily basis. During July and August arrive early to ensure getting a spot. Call the main park office (tel. 503/594–2211) to check on space availability.

RVs must stay at Mazama; Lost Creek is for tent campers only. The road is too steep. About half the spaces at Mazama are pull-throughs meant for RVs, but no hookups are available. The best tent spots are on some of the outer loops above Annie Creek Canyon.

Death Valley National Monument
California

By Matt Peters
Updated by Mimi Kmet

 here is a general misconception that Death Valley National Monument consists of mile upon endless mile of flat desert sands, scattered cacti, and an occasional cow skull. Many people don't realize that across the valley floor from Badwater, the lowest point in the Western Hemisphere, towers 11,049-foot Telescope Peak. In fact, Death Valley is surrounded by rugged, seemingly impassable mountain ranges. At the park's western entrance, motorists drive from sea level to nearly 5,000 feet in a space of 20 miles.

Botanists say there are 900 species of plants here, but at times that's hard to believe. Many plants lie dormant for all but a few days of the year, when spring rains trigger a bloom. The rest are congregated around limited sources of water. Part of the attraction of Death Valley, however, is observing how plants, animals, and humans survive in this extremely harsh environment, one that can quickly become life-threatening.

The air-conditioned auto may have eliminated many of the rigors of a trip through the area, but Death Valley National Monument is still a desolate place in an isolated location, and, outside of Furnace Creek, there are very limited facilities. This is a unique land: the hottest, driest climate in North America, where nights are marked by star-filled skies and howling coyotes.

But in the middle of this desert is the oasis at Furnace Creek, a popular resort where people come to golf, play tennis, swim, and dine. The atmosphere here is low-key, with many visitors content to stroll among the palms, relax poolside after a day of exploring, or browse in the souvenir shop at the general store. Warm, dry winters attract a large contingent of senior citizens, who drive their motor homes or pull their fifth-wheelers to Furnace Creek for a stay of up to a month.

Long before the creation of RVs, Furnace Creek was home to generations of Shoshone tribespeople. In 1849, emigrants looking for the California gold fields accidentally stumbled into the valley, and eventually prospectors came looking for gold and silver, which went largely unfound. In 1881, borax, the so-called white gold of the desert, was discovered near Furnace Creek, and its harvesting and mining soon followed. Twenty-mule teams operated from 1883 to 1889, carrying the borax out of Death Valley, over passes in the Panamint Mountains and through the desert to the railroad station at Mojave.

In 1882, Bellerin Tex Bennett founded the Greenland Ranch, and in 1888 he sold the property to the Pacific Coast Borax Company, which called it the Furnace Creek Ranch. In 1927, in response to growing interest in the area, the company opened the Furnace Creek Inn to provide more luxurious accommodations to travelers. The Fred Harvey Company assumed operation of the inn in 1956 and purchased the property in 1969.

It was officials of the Pacific Coast Borax Company who brought the beauty of Death Valley to the attention of the National Park Service. President Hoover signed a bill creating Death Valley National Monument on February 11, 1933. At press time, the Desert Protection Act, which would add 1.2 million acres to Death Valley and change its status from a national monument to a national park, was pending in the U.S. Congress.

ESSENTIAL INFORMATION

VISITOR INFORMATION Contact the Superintendent, **Death Valley National Monument**, Death Valley, CA, 92328, tel. 619/786–2331; 619/786–2471 for the hearing impaired (8 AM–5 PM).

A backcountry permit is not required, but those planning to visit the backcountry are encouraged to complete a backcountry registration form at the visitor center. Backcountry camping is allowed in areas that are at least 1 mile from the main paved or unpaved roads and 1/4 mile from water sources. Most abandoned mining areas are restricted to day use. Visitors should check the "Dirt Road Travel

and Backcountry Camping" guide available at the visitor center.

FEES The entrance fee is $5 per vehicle and $3 for those entering on foot, bus, bike, or motorcycle; it covers seven days. Annual park passes, which are valid only at Death Valley, are $15.

PUBLICATIONS The **Death Valley Natural History Association** (Box 188, Death Valley, CA 92328, tel. 619/786–2331, ext. 286) publishes a number of pamphlets enabling visitors to take self-guided tours to many of the monument's attractions. These pamphlets cost only 50¢ to $1 and are generally available at the visitor center or at the beginning of the walk or trail. The association also sells an illustrated waterproof, tear-proof trail map of the park with a backcountry and hiking guide for $7.95.

One of the most comprehensive guides to the park, including its natural and cultural history, is Richard Lingenfelter's *Death Valley and the Amargosa—A Land of Illusion.* The 600-page book covers the valley's evolution from precivilization to the present and includes old maps and pictures of the area. Bob and Barbara Dedecker's *Road Guide to Death Valley* lists the best vehicle-access areas for sightseeing and picture taking. The 80-page *Exploring Death Valley,* by longtime resident Ruth Kirk, includes an introduction to the area's geology, accounts of the prospectors' arrival in 1849, and the life of the Shoshone; it also gives information on where to go and what to see. Chuck Gebhardt, who has spent a lot of time in Death Valley, has drawn on his experience to write *Inside Death Valley,* a comprehensive guide to back-road driving and hiking destinations, with information on the area's geology and history; his *Backpacking in Death Valley* gives ideas for day hikes and overnight hikes in the valley, with trail descriptions. The latter discusses necessary precautions for surviving in the desert. Those interested in the area's natural history should check out Michael Collier's *An Introduction to the Geology of Death Valley,* which provides a detailed account of the area's natural evolution to date in a style that is easily understood.

GEOLOGY AND TERRAIN Part of the Mojave Desert, Death Valley National Monument, which covers just over 2 million acres, ranges from 6 to 15 miles wide and measures 125 miles north to south. The elevation varies from 282 feet below sea level near Badwater, the lowest point in the Western Hemisphere, to 11,049 feet at Telescope Peak. The highest point reached by auto is at the Charcoal Kilns, an elevation of approximately 7,000 feet. The Panamint Range parallels Death Valley to the west, the Amargosa Range to the east. Minerals and ores in the rugged, barren mountains turn them a variety of shades, from green to yellow to brown to white to black. Scores of alluvial fans spread across the valley floor, which is comprised of alkali flats and sand dunes. Relief from the desert environment can be found around the oasis at Furnace Creek, where warm-water springs support a variety of vegetation, including cottonwoods and palms.

Death Valley is located in a vast area geologists call the basin-and-range province. Block faulting and tectonic forces caused part of the land to uplift to form mountain ranges, while adjacent areas dropped to form valley floors. Lava and cinder cones are evidence of occasional volcanic activity. The major forces of erosion here are wind and rain, which carve away the soft spots in rocks, creating strange formations.

FLORA AND FAUNA A majority of the plant and animal life in Death Valley is found near the limited sources of water. One seldom-seen mammal here is the bighorn sheep, which spends most of its time in the secluded upper reaches of the park's rugged mountain ranges, finding toeholds and perches on rock faces where there seemingly are none. Other four-footed park inhabitants include bobcats, coyotes, and rodents. The coyotes can often be seen lazing in the shade next to the golf course and have been known to run onto the fairways to steal a golf ball.

The only type of fish found in the park is the pupfish, which grows to slightly more than 1

inch in length. During winter, when the water is cold, the fish lie dormant in the bottom mud. They become active again in the spring. The Salt Creek Nature Trail pamphlet points out the best places to spot the Salt Creek pupfish. Because they are wary of large moving shapes, you must stand quietly over a pool at Salt Creek in order to see them. Pickleweed and salt grass are found in the Salt Creek marsh, and ravens, killdeer, and great blue herons may be sighted.

Between 60 and 100 feral burros, descendants of the miners' stock, still wander the park. But because these burros were overgrazing on the bighorn sheep's habitat, more than 6,000 burros were removed in recent years. One might also see a kit fox or a desert banded gecko here. The gecko is 3 to 4 inches long and is colored bright yellow and pink with white banding. There are more than 250 species of bird in Death Valley, including yellow warblers, kingfishers, hawks, peregrine falcons, Canada geese, and an occasional golden eagle. The best areas to bird-watch are Scotty's Castle and Salt Creek.

Because the park receives an average of less than 2 inches of rainfall per year, most of the low-elevation vegetation is concentrated around the oases at Furnace Creek and Scotty's Castle, where magnolias, palms, and cottonwoods grow. At the higher elevations, visitors will find piñon, juniper, and bristlecone pines. A majority of the monument's wildflowers are seen for a few days each spring, with rainfall and temperature largely determining when they bloom. There are several publications that can help visitors locate various plants and animals within the park. These are available at the visitor center or from the Death Valley Natural History Association (*see* Publications, *above*).

WHEN TO GO Amazingly, an increasing number of visitors come to the park each year during the summer. Death Valley is the hottest place in North America, and they want to see the place at its fiery best.

Some are disappointed if they don't arrive on the hottest day of the year. In 1913, the temperature hit 134°F, for many years a world record. From May through September, daytime highs are 99.5°F to 116°F. It is not unusual for summertime temperatures, including the overnight low, to remain above 100°F for a week. In December, January, and February, daytime highs are 65°F to 73°F, while overnight lows are 40°F to 50°F.

The majority of the park's 900,000 annual visitors still come between late fall and early spring, taking advantage of moderate temperatures and the lack of rainfall. Although during these cooler months you will need to book a room in advance, the park never feels crowded.

During the winter, the tops of the mountain ranges surrounding the park are often dusted with snow. Although precipitation in the park averages less than 2 inches annually, rainfall here can be a dramatic occurrence. Because there is little vegetation and the ground is too hard to soak up the rain, flash floods are common; sections of roadway can be flooded or washed away. The wettest month of the year is February, when the park receives an average of .33 inch of rain.

Generally, the air in the park is dry year-round, except during an infrequent storm. The dry air can wick moisture from the body without causing a sweat, so visitors should remember to drink plenty of water. In several places within the park it is possible to drive to an elevation higher than 5,000 feet, where the air temperature is generally 15 to 20 degrees cooler than on the valley floor. Winds are not uncommon, especially at higher elevations at sunrise and sunset. Most facilities remain open year-round, although the historic Furnace Creek Inn closes from mid-May through mid-October.

SEASONAL EVENTS **Early November:** The **Death Valley Encampment,** which sprang from a centennial celebration held in 1949 honoring the area's first European emigrants, annually draws thousands of visitors from around the world. The week-long celebration includes art shows, organized seminars and walks, demonstrations, and dances. For information, call the park at 619/786–2331.

WHAT TO PACK The weather here can be extreme—extremely hot and dry. Bring a wide-brim hat, sunglasses, sunscreen, and skin lotion. Whether hiking or driving, you should always have an ample supply of water—for you and your car. Comfortable walking shoes are necessary. Motorists should take note of signs giving the distance to the next service area. Make sure you have enough cash: There are no banks in Death Valley. Most purchases can be made with major credit cards, but the soda machines won't take your plastic. In winter months, a sweater or sweatshirt and long pants are often necessary. And although it seldom rains, when the skies open up here, you'll be glad you brought a waterproof jacket.

GENERAL STORES There are two general stores in Death Valley: The one in **Furnace Creek** (tel. 619/786–2345, ext. 210) is open year-round, 7 AM to 10 PM, and the one in **Stovepipe Wells Village** (tel. 619/786–2387) is open year-round, 8 AM to 8 PM. Both carry food, sundry items, souvenirs, camping supplies, film, and many necessities. Prices in these stores are 20% to 50% higher than those in grocery stores in most urban areas.

ARRIVING AND DEPARTING Visitors to Death Valley don't have a lot of options when it comes to selecting a mode of transportation. No trains or public bus routes service the area, although motorized tours are available once you reach the park. There are public airstrips where you could land a small plane near Furnace Creek and Stovepipe Wells Village, but, basically, the only way to get to Death Valley is to drive. Because the park's sights are so distant from each other, having a car will enhance your visit. Motorists should bear in mind that gas is available only in Stovepipe Wells, Furnace Creek, and Scotty's Castle: Fill up whenever possible. Diesel fuel is available in the park at Furnace Creek; you can also get it in Beatty, Amargosa, Baker, Lone Pine, Olancha, Trona, and Pahrump. Entering the monument from the north allows visitors to see Scotty's Castle and Ubehebe Crater, the two major draws at the park's northern end, more than 50 miles from Furnace Creek.

By Plane. The nearest major airport is **McCarron International Airport** (tel. 702/739–5743) in Las Vegas, 140 miles away. About 30 car-rental agencies serve the airport. Within Death Valley, there are public airstrips near Furnace Creek and Stovepipe Wells.

By Car and RV. Death Valley is not easily reached by car. When choosing a route, keep in mind that the drive to the park can be part of the Death Valley and Mojave Desert experience. Be aware of possible winter closures or driving restrictions due to snow. Call the California State Department of Transportation hotline (tel. 800/427–ROAD) for updates on road conditions.

It is 140 to 155 miles from Las Vegas to Death Valley, about a three-hour drive; 260 to 315 miles from Los Angeles, a 6½-hour haul; and about 645 miles from San Francisco, which will take you 9½ to 12 hours to travel by car. The nearest national parks are Sequoia and Kings Canyon, from which you can reach Death Valley in about eight or nine hours traveling about 430 miles, and Yosemite, which is about 530 miles away and will take up to 10½ hours to drive.

There are two major routes to Death Valley out of **Las Vegas.** The first is on U.S. 95 north for 86 miles to Amargosa Valley and the town of Lathrop Wells, where you can turn south on Nevada Highway 373 (which turns into Highway 127) to Death Valley Junction. From Death Valley Junction, take California Highway 190 west for 29 miles to Furnace Creek.

You could also take U.S. 95 all the way to Beatty (an additional 28½ miles from Lathrop Wells), where there are several casinos and motels, then turn onto Nevada Highway 374 (which turns into California Highway 190) west for the approximately 25½-mile trip into the monument. This road passes the ghost town of Rhyolite.

The most scenic route out of Las Vegas is on Nevada Highway 160 west. Drive for 42 miles, then take the Old Spanish Trail, which will be on your left and runs for 35 miles to Tecopa, California, and the public mineral baths in Hot Springs, California (adjacent to Tecopa). Tecopa has an RV park, restaurant, stores, and a post office. Hot Springs has several RV parks. From Tecopa, continue west on the Old Spanish Trail for 4 miles to California Highway 127, which you must take north for 8 miles to Shoshone, which is a dusty wide spot in the road with a motel and service station. From Shoshone you will enter the park by traveling 69 miles on Highway 178 west to Furnace Creek, or by going north on Highway 127 for 28 miles to Death Valley Junction and taking Highway 190 into the park.

You also have the option of taking Highway 160 all the way to Pahrump, Nevada (50 miles), where there is casino gambling, golf, and bowling. From Pahrump, travel on Nevada Highway 372 west to the California–Nevada state line, and then on California Highway 178 for a total of 29 miles to Shoshone, from which you can follow the directions above.

From **Los Angeles,** there are two main routes, each with two options. You can take I–5 to San Fernando, then travel east on Highway 14 for 129 miles to U.S. 395, or you can take I–15 to reach U.S. 395, which leads to Red Mountain, where you must pick up Highway 178 to Ridgecrest and Trona. You could also continue on U.S. 395 to Lone Pine and pick up Highway 190 east into the park. Either way, you will be entering the park over Towne Pass, then passing Stovepipe Wells and the sand dunes.

The southeastern route passing through the eastern Mojave Desert from Los Angeles is the most scenic. Take I–15 through Barstow and Baker, then go north on Highway 127 at Baker to Shoshone. At Shoshone, you have the option of turning west on Highway 178 and driving through the park to Furnace Creek (gas up: there are no services for 69 miles from Shoshone to Furnace Creek), or continuing north on Highway 127 to Death Valley Junction, where you must take Highway 190 into the park.

From **San Francisco** take I–80 over the Oakland Bridge to I–580 east, which will bring you to I–5. Travel south on I–5 for 204 miles toward Bakersfield. At Highway 58, go east 126 miles to Highway 14 (watch for the cutoff sign as you approach Mojave) and follow the directions for routes out of Los Angeles, above.

EXPLORING

The distances between the major attractions in Death Valley make it necessary to travel by car or bus to cover all of the park's cultural and natural-history offerings. Much of the park can be toured on a variety of regularly scheduled bus tours, but these often don't allow time for hikes to sites not seen from the road, such as Salt Creek, Golden Canyon, and Natural Bridge. It is best to drive to a number of the sites, get out of the car, and walk.

You will get a feeling for the park after spending two full days driving and hiking here, but if you have five or six days you won't run out of short hikes and things to see and do.

THE BEST IN ONE DAY What you can see and do in one day at Death Valley depends a lot on where you plan to enter and exit the park. If you have only one day, it is best for that day to be during the spring or fall, when the days are still long and the temperatures are more moderate.

If you begin the day in Furnace Creek, you can see a lot of different sights without doing a lot of driving. Get up early and drive the 21 miles on Highway 178 (*see* Scenic Drives and Views, *below*) to Badwater, which looks out to the lowest point in the Western Hemisphere and which is a fine place to watch the sunrise. Returning north, stop at Natural Bridge, a medium-size limestone rock formation that has been hollowed at its base to form a span across two rocks, and then at the Devil's Golf Course, so named because of the large balls of salt present here. These balls, which are about a foot in diameter, formed when an ancient lake that covered the area evaporated. Detour to the right onto Artists Drive, a 7-mile route that passes Artists Palette. The reds, yellows, oranges, and greens here are evidence of the minerals in the rocks and the earth. Four miles north of Artists

Drive you will come to the Golden Canyon Interpretive Trail, a 2-mile round-trip that winds through a canyon with colorful rock walls. Just before Furnace Creek, take a short side trip on Highway 190 east 3 miles to Zabriskie Point (another good place to watch the sunrise) and the Twenty Mule Team Canyon. By this time you will be ready to return to Furnace Creek, where you can have lunch either before or after visiting the Death Valley Museum. The museum features photographs and artifacts, some with accompanying push-button audio presentations, that outline the natural and cultural history of the valley. There are slide presentations and movies in the museum's theater, and a three-dimensional model illustrates the topography of the area.

Heading north from Furnace Creek, pull off the highway and take a gander at the Harmony Borax Works (*see* Nature Trails and Short Walks, *below*). Twenty miles up the road are the sand dunes, a good place to be at sunset.

A major consideration for those who have but one day is whether to make the one-hour drive to the park's north end for a tour of Scotty's Castle, with its unique construction and living-history program (*see* Historic Buildings and Sites, *below*), and the nearby Ubehebe Crater—a volcanic crater well worth a visit. The in-season wait at Scotty's can be from one to two hours (reservations are offered to organized tours), but you could time it so that you take your lunch break while you wait. If you get up and catch the sunrise at Badwater, you can hit all these sights and visit Scotty's Castle, with enough time left to be back at the dunes to watch the sunset.

ORIENTATION PROGRAMS Year-round, the **Death Valley Museum** (tel. 619/786–2331) offers orientation programs every half hour. Special programs are offered each evening in the fall, winter, and spring (check visitor center for times). Subjects include birds of the park, characters of Death Valley during the 1900s, desert sheep, the differences between America's deserts, the area's geology, and the mining of borax. These high-quality, informa-

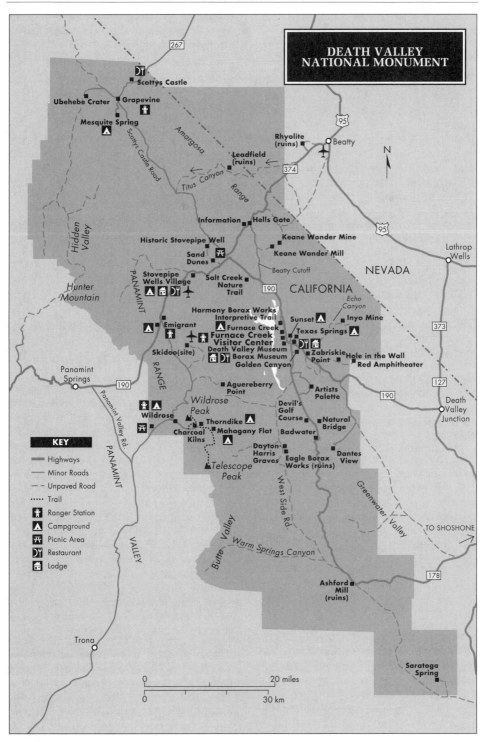

DEATH VALLEY NATIONAL MONUMENT

267

Scottys Castle

Ubehebe Crater ■ ■ Grapevine

Mesquite Spring

Amargosa

95

Rhyolite (ruins) ■ ○ Beatty

Leadfield (ruins) ■

374

Scottys Castle Road

Titus Canyon

Range

Hidden Valley

Information ■ Hells Gate

Keane Wonder Mine ■

Historic Stovepipe Well ■

Sand Dunes

Keane Wonder Mill ■

95

Lathrop Wells ○

Beatty Cutoff

NEVADA

Hunter Mountain

Stovepipe Wells Village ■

PANAMINT

Salt Creek Nature Trail

190

CALIFORNIA

Echo Canyon

Inyo Mine ■

373

Harmony Borax Works Interpretive Trail

Sunset ■

Emigrant ■

Furnace Creek

Texas Springs ■

Furnace Creek Visitor Center

Death Valley Museum

Skidoo (site) ■

Borax Museum

Zabriskie Point ■

Hole in the Wall Red Amphitheater ■

Panamint Springs ○

RANGE

Golden Canyon

190

127

Death Valley Junction ○

Aguereberry Point ■

Artists Palette

190

Wildrose Peak

Devil's Golf Course

Wildrose ■

Thorndike ▲

Natural Bridge ■

Charcoal Kilns

Mahogany Flat ▲

Badwater

Dantes View

PANAMINT

Dayton-Harris Graves ■

Eagle Borax Works (ruins) ■

Telescope Peak

West Side Rd.

Greenwater Valley

TO SHOSHONE →

VALLEY

Butte Valley

Warm Springs Canyon

178

KEY
━━━ Highways
─── Minor Roads
- - - Unpaved Road
······ Trail
🚹 Ranger Station
▲ Campground
⛉ Picnic Area
🍴 Restaurant
🏠 Lodge

Panamint Valley Rd.

Trona ○

Ashford Mill (ruins) ■

0 _____ 20 miles

0 _____ 30 km

N

Saratoga Spring ■

145

tive presentations are led by park rangers and are free.

GUIDED TOURS Guided tours in passenger vans are operated October through May by the **Fred Harvey Company** (tel. 619/786–2345, ext. 222), which holds the concession rights in Furnace Creek and Stovepipe Wells. These tours all leave from Furnace Creek, cost from $20 to $30 for adults (less for children and seniors), and have a four-adult minimum. Among the offerings are a half-day trip to **Scotty's Castle,** including a ranger-led tour of the mansion and stops at nearby Ubehebe Crater, the original Stovepipe Well (an early water source for prospectors), and the sand dunes; a **Lower Valley Tour,** with stops at such natural wonders as Mushroom Rock, the Devil's Golf Course, Badwater, and Mustard Canyon, as well as at the Harmony Borax Works; a drive to **Dante's View,** at 5,475 feet the highest point reachable by car on the east side of the valley, with a look at the U.S. Borax–owned town of Ryan (closed in the 1930s), and the American Borate Company–owned Billie Mine (which reopened recently), and the Twenty Mule Team Canyon; and an evening at Death Valley Junction's **Amargosa Opera,** where the renowned Marta Beckett performs dance-mime interpretations.

Fred Harvey also offers special tours that must be arranged 24 hours in advance and have a four-person minimum: the **Charcoal Kilns and Aguereberry Point,** the **Titus Canyon** backcountry excursion, and **casino/gaming** trips to Beatty or Pahrump, Nevada. Call for prices and times.

The National Park Service runs 50-minute walking tours of Scotty's Castle led by park rangers. These tours are offered from October through April, hourly from 9 to 5. During the summer season, tours are held periodically throughout the day. Call the visitor center (tel. 619/786–2331) or Scotty's Castle (tel. 619/786–2392) for tour times. Tickets are sold the day of the tour on a first-come, first-served basis and cost $6 for adults, $3 for those over 62, and $3 for children ages 6 to 11. Children under age 6 are free. Tours are limited to 19

people, and during holiday periods they are sometimes shortened to 30 minutes and fees are reduced to half-price.

SCENIC DRIVES AND VIEWS Titus Canyon, named for a young mining engineer who perished there, is a box canyon where limestone walls tower several hundred feet above the floor. From Furnace Creek, you can reach the beginning of the one-way road that passes through the canyon by taking Highway 190 west to the Beatty cutoff, then following that north and picking up Highway 374 east. The entrance to the canyon will be on your left, about 17 miles from the point where you enter Highway 374. It is about 42 miles from Furnace Creek. A steep, occasionally rough gravel road makes the 26-mile descent through the canyon. The lighting is best at midday, when the sunshine is able to filter between the steep canyon walls. You will exit the canyon onto Scotty's Castle Road, which you can take southeast for 36 miles back to Furnace Creek. Allow six hours for the trip. *Note:* Titus Canyon is normally only open October through April.

Another pleasurable drive from Furnace Creek is over 24 miles to **Dante's View,** a trip that will take about 40 minutes. Drive east on Highway 190 for 11 miles, stopping at Zabriskie Point (try to be here at sunrise) and detouring on the **Twenty Mule Team Canyon drive,** a graded dirt road that passes through mudstone hills formed in an ancient lake that has since evaporated. Turn right onto the Dante's Point spur; it's 13 miles to the end. From this 5,475-foot vantage point, it is nearly a sheer drop to Badwater, at 282 feet below sea level. You can see much of Death Valley and, across the valley, the Panamint Range and 11,049-foot Telescope Peak. No buses or trailers are allowed on the Twenty Mule Team Canyon drive or on the last few miles of the road to Dante's View.

The lowest point in the Western Hemisphere can be seen from **Badwater,** located 20 miles south of Furnace Creek on **Highway 178** east. Make this a predawn drive and watch the sunrise here. As you drive back to Furnace Creek, there are several sights worth stopping for, but you will have to hike a short distance to them. Just 4 miles north of Badwater is a right-hand turnoff for **Natural Bridge,** which spans a colorful canyon. The road to the trailhead is a rough 1/2 mile, but it's an easy 1/4-mile walk to the arch. Returning to Highway 178, it is just 1 1/2 miles to the left-hand turnoff to the **Devil's Golf Course,** the name given to the huge beds of rugged salt crystals that pioneers crossed in covered wagons in 1849. A bumpy 1/2-mile dirt road puts tourists at the edge of the area. The one-way **Artists Drive** is 5 miles farther up Highway 178. The 7-mile drive winds through country that is popular among painters because of its colorful rocks. Yet another spur road brings you to the trailhead for the moderate 2-mile trek to **Golden Canyon,** where the rocks range from deep purple to gold. Look for Mushroom Rock along the side of Highway 178.

HISTORIC BUILDINGS AND SITES Located in the northern end of Death Valley, **Scotty's Castle** is a Mediterranean-style hacienda that was built as a winter retreat by Albert Johnson and his wife, Bessie. The castle is named for Walter Scott, also known as Death Valley Scotty, who was financed by the Johnsons, visited them often during their stays at the castle, and lived the final six years of his life on the castle grounds after Walter Scott died in 1948. Death Valley Scotty, who claimed to be a prospector but was seldom known to work, became notorious in the valley for his long-winded, creative tales of the adventures of himself and others. Scotty's Castle has elaborate Spanish tiling, a 56-foot clock tower, and sits amid an oasis created by springs bubbling from the mountainside. Rooms are decorated with the original furniture and bedding and rugs from Majorca. Employees dressed in costumes of the era lead living-history tours, in which they recount the stories of Scotty, the Johnsons, and the valley.

The **Furnace Creek Inn** is situated on the spring-fed oasis at Furnace Creek. It was built in 1927 by the Pacific Coast Borax Company in answer to what company officials recognized as a growing tourist interest in Death Valley. The inn is similar in architecture to Scotty's Castle (*see* Lodging, *below*).

If you want to see a genuine ghost town, travel 35 miles from Death Valley toward Beatty, Nevada, to **Rhyolite,** which was once the largest town in the Death Valley area. In the gold boom of the early 1900s, Rhyolite supported from 2,000 to 10,000 people and was called the Queen City of Death Valley. Today visitors can see the old train depot, as well as the Bottle House, the jailhouse, and the remains of a few three-story stone buildings.

NATURE TRAILS AND SHORT WALKS To explore the **sand dunes,** begin from either Highway 190, 2 miles east of Stovepipe Wells, or the sand-dunes picnic area, 19 miles from the Furnace Creek Visitor Center. There are no trails here; hikers are free to roam where they please. Watch for animal tracks and interesting sand formations. Remember where you parked your car: It is easy to become slightly disoriented in this ocean of sand. If you lose your bearings, simply climb to the top of a dune and spot the parking lot.

Take a close look at Salt Creek—its vegetation, birds, and desert pupfish—on the 1/2-mile **Salt Creek Nature Trail,** a circuit of dirt and boardwalk that loops through a spring-fed wash. The small nearby hills are brown and gray, but the floor of the creek's wash is alive with aquatic plants such as pickleweed and salt grass. Look closely and you may find the tracks of nocturnal visitors such as lizards, bobcats, coyotes, ravens, and snakes. The tiny pupfish is the only surviving fish in Death Valley. Stand still and you may see one of these inch-long fish moving in the shadows of overhanging vegetation. The trailhead is located 1 mile down a gravel road off Highway 190, 23 miles north of the visitor center.

To understand more of the history of Death Valley stroll down the 1/4-mile **Harmony Borax Works Interpretive Trail,** located 2 miles north of the visitor center. The hard-surface trail leads to adobe ruins, borax-mining equipment, and a 20-mule-team wagon from the 1880s.

It is best to hike the 2-mile round-trip **Golden Canyon Interpretive Trail** in late afternoon, when diffused sunlight accentuates the rock colors. This gradual uphill trail meanders through rock canyons, and you can continue from here to Zabriskie Point (*see* Longer Hikes, *below*) or Red Amphitheater. The trailhead is located on Badwater Road, 5 miles south of the visitor center.

Natural Bridge Canyon, a ¹/₂-mile round-trip, begins 3 miles off Badwater Road, 15 miles south of the visitor center. Although the access road can be rough, the uphill walk is gradual, with interesting geological features beyond the natural bridge.

Seven miles east of Wildrose Canyon off Highway 178, you will come to the **Charcoal Kilns.** Charcoal produced in these beehive-shape kilns was transported to ore smelters in the Argus Range.

There are several short walks at **Scotty's Castle.** A ¹/₂-mile loop explores the grounds at the castle and signs explain the construction of the building. The ³/₄-mile **Windy Point Trail** climbs 160 feet to a view of Scotty's grave and an overview of the Death Valley Ranch, on which Scotty's Castle sits. The **Tie Canyon Trail** is an easy ³/₄-mile walk through a canyon once used to store building materials for the castle.

LONGER HIKES A moderately strenuous, unmaintained trail from **Golden Canyon** to **Zabriskie Point** climbs over ridges in Golden Canyon. Rock formations tinted red, green, yellow, orange, and purple rise on both sides of the trail; at Zabriskie Point you get a view of Death Valley. Return to your starting place along the major drainage to Highway 190, then hike north along the trail to Golden Canyon parking lot. The trailhead is 3 miles south of Furnace Creek, off Highway 190, and the route is 5 miles round-trip. This trail can be a little tricky to follow; be sure to obtain a free trail map at the visitor center.

You can reach the western entrance of the **Titus Canyon Narrows** via a 2-mile dirt road off Scottys Castle Road, 37 miles north of the visitor center. The narrow canyon bottom is hard-packed gravel and dirt, and it serves as a one-way road as well as a trail (*see* Scenic Drives and Views, *above*). Watch for cars, which will be traveling in the opposite direction. For hikers, this is a constant, moderate uphill walk. Klare Spring and some petroglyphs are located 5¹/₂ miles from the mouth of the canyon, but you can get a feeling for the area on a shorter walk. The views here are vertical: canyon walls rising 40 to 60 feet and the rugged, rocky ridges above them. The sheltered, shadowy trail is almost eerie.

Allow two hours for the 2-mile round-trip trail that follows a historic aerial tramway to the **Keane Wonder Mine.** The way is very steep, but the views of the valley make it worth the extra effort. Do not enter the tunnels or hike beyond the top of the tramway—it's dangerous. The trailhead is located 3 miles off the Beatty Cutoff road, 16 miles northeast of the visitor center. The road to the trailhead is unpaved and bumpy.

A gradual uphill trail winds 2 miles through the smoothly polished walls of narrow **Mosaic Canyon.** There are dry falls to climb at the upper end of the canyon. The trailhead is 3 miles off Highway 190, just west of Stovepipe Wells Village, via a dirt road that can be rough but is accessible to most vehicles.

The 8¹/₄-mile round-trip **Wildrose Peak Trail** starts at the Charcoal Kilns and moves through piñon- and juniper-pine country. Moderately steep, it offers sweeping views of the valley; it is best hiked in the afternoon, when the sinking sun adds color and dimension to the Funeral Range, across the valley to the east.

The 14-mile round-trip **Telescope Peak Trail** begins at Mahogany Flat Campground (or start at the Charcoal Kilns and add 4 miles), 9 miles east of Wildrose Campground. A steep trail winds through piñon, juniper, and bristlecone pines, with excellent views of Death Valley and Panamint Valley. Ice axes and crampons may be necessary in the winter—check at the visitor center. It will take a minimum of eight hours to hike in and out.

OTHER ACTIVITIES **Back-Road Driving.** With almost 1 1/2 million acres of backcountry and 150 miles of back roads open to camping and day use, Death Valley is a popular destination among four-wheel-drive enthusiasts. Numerous suggested four-wheel-drive routes and a map of where to find them are found in a pamphlet entitled "Dirt Road Travel and Backcountry Camping," available free at the visitor center. Driving off established roads is strictly prohibited. Overnight camping is permitted, but you must be at least 5 miles from a maintained campground, 1 mile from major roads, and 1/4 mile from any backcountry water source. Topographic maps for all areas within the monument are available for $4 to $6 at the visitor center or by writing the Death Valley Natural History Association (*see* Publications, *above*).

The more popular back-road destinations include Butte Valley, Hunter Mountain, and Echo Canyon. Butte Valley is a 21-mile trail (via Warm Spring Canyon) that climbs from 200 feet below sea level to an elevation of 4,000 feet. The geological formations along this drive reveal the development of Death Valley. Hunter Mountain (from Teakettle Junction to Monument Boundary) is 20 miles long and climbs from 4,100 feet to 7,200 feet in elevation. It winds through a piñon-and-juniper forest. This route may be closed or muddy in winter and spring. Echo Canyon (from Highway 190 to Highway 29) is 30 miles long, climbing 4,400 feet and topping out at 4,800 feet in elevation. There is no camping along the first 4 miles of this trail.

Biking. There are no bike rentals in the park, but mountain biking is permitted on any of the back roads open to the public. These roads receive very little traffic. A flier on suggested bike routes is available free at the visitor center. Easy routes include Mustard Canyon (2 miles), Desolation Canyon (1 mile), and Twenty Mule Team Canyon (6 miles). Among the moderate routes are Hole-in-the-Wall (6 miles) and Skidoo (6 miles). Racetrack (28 miles), Hidden Valley (30–35 miles), Cottonwood Canyon (20 miles), Greenwater Valley (30 miles), West Side Road (40 miles), and Artists Drive (8 miles, paved) are more difficult to negotiate.

On-road bicycling is becoming increasingly popular along the paved roads of Death Valley, particularly in the cooler months from late fall through early spring. But be aware that there are no shoulders on these roads and that drivers are often distracted by the surrounding scenery.

Bird-Watching. Approximately 250 species of bird have been identified in Death Valley. The best place to bird-watch is along the Salt Creek Nature Trail, where you might see ravens, common snipes, spotted sandpipers, killdeer, and great blue herons. At the golf course at Furnace Creek (stay off the greens) look for kingfishers, peregrine falcons, hawks, Canada geese, yellow warblers, and an occasional golden eagle.

Golf. The 6,037-yard, par-70 course at the **Furnace Creek Golf Club** (tel. 619/786–2301, ext. 270) is open year-round. Greens fees are $28 for 18 holes, $14 for nine holes. Cart rentals are $16 for 18 holes and $8 for nine holes. Club-rental is $5 for nine holes and $10 for 18 holes. Special rates for 2 to 20 weeks of play are available. Foursomes should make reservations for winter mornings.

Horseback Riding. Guided horseback and carriage rides are available at **Furnace Creek Ranch** (tel. 619/786–2345) October through May. Horseback rides cost $15 per person for one hour, $25 for two hours. Moonlight rides are $20. Hour-long, morning wagon-rides depart from the general store and cost $3. Evening carriage-rides take passengers around the golf course and Furnace Creek Ranch. Cost is $3 per person. Special cocktail rides, with champagne, margaritas, hot spiced wine, and peppermint patties, are available for $6 per person; reservations are required.

Swimming. There are pools at the Furnace Creek Inn, Furnace Creek Ranch, and Stovepipe Wells Village. The pools at Furnace Creek Ranch and Stovepipe Wells are open to the public (nonguests pay $2). Both pools at Furnace Creek are spring-fed, with no filters, and remain just over 80°F. They are closed during summer, but the Stovepipe Wells pool is open year-round.

Tennis. There are four lighted tennis courts at Furnace Creek Inn (guests only, tel. 619/786–2361) and two lighted courts at Furnace Creek Ranch (public welcome, tel. 619/786–2345). There is no fee to play tennis at the ranch.

CHILDREN'S PROGRAMS A junior-ranger program is in its early phases—children can go on special hikes and earn badges. Call the Furnace Creek Visitor Center (tel. 619/786–2331) to find out if any junior-ranger activities will happen during your visit.

EVENING ACTIVITIES During the fall, winter, and spring months, evening programs are held nightly at the visitor center, beginning at 7:30 PM. Subjects include birds of Death Valley, characters from the early 1900s, borax mining, desert sheep, types of deserts, and Death Valley's geology. For more information, contact the visitor center (tel. 619/786–2331).

DINING

There aren't a lot of dining options in Death Valley, and it's 40 miles to the nearest town. Fortunately for the monument's visitors, the restaurants that are here have good food and a wide price range.

INSIDE THE PARK **Inn Dining Room.** Located in the Furnace Creek Inn, which was built in 1927, this restaurant provides silver service in a grand-hotel setting, with lace table linens, crystal, and candlelight. The building's adobe walls contrast with its redwood ceiling beams. There are two fireplaces and views of the valley. Guests at the Furnace Creek Inn enjoy breakfast and dinner here under a modified American plan, in which these meals are included with lodging. Nonguests are welcome. A large selection of California premium wines ranges from $12 to $70. Popular entrées include lobster del mar and orange roughy prepared in a lemon herb sauce. *Furnace Creek Inn, CA, tel. 619/786–2361. Reservations required. Dress: casual in daytime; jackets required at dinner. AE, D,*

DC, MC, V. Closed Mother's Day–2nd Thurs. in Oct. Moderate–Expensive.

L'Ottimo's. Gourmet southern Italian cuisine is served in this Furnace Creek Inn restaurant, an alternative to the inn's dining room. Decorated in greens and creams, L'Ottimo's has glass-top tables set with Palermo china. Veal and pasta entrées are complemented by Caesar salads made table-side. The most acclaimed dishes are the veal picatta and the chicken *imbattiti* (stuffed with spinach and covered with green peppercorn sauce). *Furnace Creek Inn, CA, tel. 619/786–2361. Reservations required. Dress: casual. AE, D, DC, MC, V. Closed Mother's Day–mid-Oct. Moderate.*

Toll Road Restaurant. There are wagon wheels in the yard and Old West artifacts on the interior walls at this restaurant in Stovepipe Wells Village. A stone fireplace heats the dining room. A full menu, with steaks, chicken, fish, and pasta, is served October through mid-May; breakfast and dinner buffets are offered during summer. *Stovepipe Wells Village, CA, tel. 619/786–2387, fax 619/786–2389. Dress: casual. MC, V. Moderate.*

Furnace Creek Ranch. Several family-style restaurants are housed in one complex at the ranch. Options include a steak house, coffee shop, pizza parlor, Western buffet, and Mexican restaurant. Breakfast is available only in the coffee shop. Each of these restaurants serves good food in a simple setting. The steak house is slightly more formal than the others, and patrons pay slightly higher prices for more attentive service. Reservations are recommended for the steak house during peak hours. *Furnace Creek Ranch, CA, tel. 619/786–2345. Dress: casual. AE, D, DC, MC, V. Inexpensive–Moderate.*

19th Hole. This open-air lunch spot located at the Furnace Creek Golf Club is designed with the active golfer in mind. The menu includes hot dogs, chicken sandwiches, and the special Mulligan Burger, which has twice the beef, twice the cheese, and twice the bun of a regular burger and is topped with green chilies and a Secret Duffer Sauce. It comes with potato chips and iced tea. *Furnace Creek, CA, tel. 619/786–2345. Dress: casual. AE, D, DC, MC, V. Inexpensive.*

NEAR THE PARK The closest restaurants outside the park are located in Beatty, Nevada, 40 miles from Furnace Creek. Beatty sees many travelers on the Reno–Las Vegas run and many heading to or from Death Valley, so the restaurants are filled with an eclectic bunch. There is also a popular café in Shoshone, which is 89 miles from Furnace Creek.

Burro Inn. This restaurant is part of a casino/inn complex in Beatty, Nevada, but the seven booths, six tables, and 11 counter seats here fill up with visitors of all types, including families. Breakfast, lunch, and dinner are served around the clock—such American basics as eggs, pancakes, hamburgers, and hot and cold sandwiches. There are daily dinner specials after 5; the prime rib, on Friday and Saturday, includes hors d'oeuvres, salad or soup, and a potato (baked, mashed, or french fried). *Hwy. 95 and 3rd St., Beatty, NV, tel. 702/553–2225. Reservations not required. Dress: casual. AE, MC, V. Inexpensive.*

Exchange Club Motel. Also part of a casino/motel complex in Beatty and also open 24 hours a day, the Exchange Club seats 133 people at booths, tables, and a small counter. Many a traveler stops here while passing through, but the atmosphere is relatively quiet and the kids can choose from their own menu. Breakfasts include eggs, pancakes, or waffles; lunch is cold or hot sandwiches or burgers. One of the most popular specials is the Friday catfish dinner, which features catfish panfried to order, hush puppies, and homemade baked beans. Prime rib is served Friday and Saturday; it usually sells out. For vegetarians, there's a chef's salad. Try the lemon meringue or blueberry pie—they're homemade. *702 Main St., Beatty, NV, tel. 702/553–2368. Reservations not required. Dress: casual. AE, MC, V. Inexpensive.*

Red Buggy Café. This café has shared the same wood building with an adjacent saloon for 60 years. Located in the old mining town of Shoshone, the Red Buggy has a half-dozen wood tables with red-and-white tablecloths, red curtains, and a counter that seats 11 people. Photographs of the town's mining heyday hang on the walls. The menu comes in the form of a newspaper (yes, you can keep it), with Mexican and American selections that fill two pages. The only thing the Red Buggy doesn't have is hot dogs. All the food is homemade, from the potato salad to the spaghetti sauce to the bread pudding. The most popular specials are Saturday's meatloaf and Friday's grilled cod. *Hwy. 127, Shoshone, CA, tel. 619/852–9908. Reservations not required. Dress: casual. AE, MC, V. Closed Christmas Day. Inexpensive.*

Stagecoach Hotel. Remodeled in 1991, the brick-walled Stagecoach has light-color booths surrounding a center fountain. It seats 100 and has a no-smoking section in the back. Breakfasts include such standards as eggs, pancakes, and waffles; sandwiches and burgers are served for lunch. Pizza, meat loaf, and chicken-fried steak are among the dinner specials; those watching the calories can order a dieter's plate or a chef's salad. *U.S. 95 N, Beatty, NV, tel. 702/553–2419. Reservations not required. Dress: casual. AE, D, MC, V. Inexpensive.*

PICNIC SPOTS If you're looking for a shady spot to lay down a blanket, your choices are limited to the oasis at **Furnace Creek** and **Scotty's Castle,** where many visitors opt to eat lunch while waiting the hour or two for a tour. A luncheon stand there sells hot dogs and hamburgers. The soft sand of the dunes also makes a good picnic spot, providing a comfortable seat and mattress. It's possible to find shade under a mesquite tree or shelter from the wind behind one of the dunes. There are picnic tables at the **Salt Creek** trailhead but no shade. The area is located at the end of a 1-mile bumpy road and gets less traffic than other areas; the self-guided tour around the creek's marsh provides an easy after-meal stroll. There are also several picnic tables by the date grove in the Furnace Creek area. Supplies can be purchased at the general stores at Furnace Creek or Stovepipe Wells Village.

LODGING

In addition to campgrounds, there are three places to lay your head within the confines of Death Valley National Monument: Furnace Creek Inn, Furnace Creek Ranch, and Stovepipe Wells Village Motel. Furnace Creek resembles a small resort. Accommodations there are centrally located, close to the visitor center, museum, and many of the monument's natural attractions. A golf course is shared by guests of the two Furnace Creek hotels and is open to the public. Campers may use the tennis courts at the Furnace Creek Ranch. During the park's busy season, from November through March, reservations should be made one month in advance.

There are a number of moderately priced motels (with casinos) in Beatty, Nevada, located 40 miles from Furnace Creek. Many visitors stop in Shoshone, 89 miles from the park, but there is only one hotel there.

INSIDE THE PARK **Furnace Creek Inn.** This stone-and-adobe Spanish-villa inn was built in 1927 and is designated a U.S. Historical Landmark. It sits next to natural springs on a hill above Furnace Creek, and most rooms have a view of the valley. The others face a spring-fed garden, where a stone walkway meanders through lush grasses, magnolias, and 50-foot palm trees. The rooms have Spanish-tile floors, antique ceiling fans, brass beds, and pedestal sinks; some have balconies and Jacuzzis. Amenities include refrigerators, hair dryers, alarm clocks, and irons. Room rates include breakfast and dinner at the Inn Dining Room or L'Ottimo's. Reservations for spring weekends should be made one to two months in advance. Some guests have been coming here for 40 years. The inn is operated by the Fred Harvey Company. *Box 1, Death Valley, CA 92328, tel. 619/786–2361 or 800/528–6367, fax 619/786–2514. 68 rooms. Facilities: 2 restaurants, lounge, exercise area, masseuse, pool, Jacuzzi, 4 lighted tennis courts, golf course, concierge, salon, gift shop, library, observatory. AE, D, DC, MC, V. Closed day after Mother's Day–2nd Thurs. in Oct. Expensive.*

Furnace Creek Ranch. Also operated by the Fred Harvey Company, the ranch offers less than the Furnace Creek Inn, but it is also less expensive. A clean, quiet motel, with one- and two-story buildings, it has a pool and tennis courts on the grounds and is within walking distance of the golf course, visitor center and museum, post office, general store, and a half-dozen restaurants. Many of the rooms overlook the golf course or a large lawn area near the pool. Each room has two double beds and air-conditioning, but not all of them have TVs. *Box 1, Death Valley, CA 92328, tel. 619/786–2345 or 800/528–6367, fax 619/786–2514. 224 rooms. Facilities: 6 restaurants, saloon, pool, 2 lighted tennis courts, golf course. AE, D, DC, MC, V. Moderate–Expensive.*

Stovepipe Wells Village Motel. This roadside motel is a scaled-down version of the Furnace Creek Ranch and is also operated by the Fred Harvey Company. It is primarily for visitors who use their room only to shower and sleep. There are no phones or TVs in the rooms. *Stovepipe Wells Village, Death Valley, CA 92328, tel. 619/786–2387. 83 rooms. Facilities: restaurant, swimming pool, general store, 14 RV hookups. MC, V. Moderate.*

NEAR THE PARK **Amargosa Hotel.** The Pacific Coast Borax Company built the Amargosa in 1923 to serve railroad passengers stopping in Death Valley Junction, then a borax-mining town. Neighbor to the Amargosa Opera House, the adobe building was renovated and reopened in 1991. Its rooms have one or two double beds but no phones and no TVs. A free breakfast of cold cereal, rolls, toast, juice, and coffee is served in the dining room October through mid-May. Reservations should be made at least one to two months in advance. *Box 614, Death Valley Junction, CA 92328, tel. 619/852–4441. 15 rooms. MC, V. Moderate.*

Burro Inn. This two-story wood structure is 10 years old. Each room has queen-size beds and a private bath. The guests include senior citizens, families, and Europeans heading to Death Valley. *U.S. 95 and 3rd St., Box 7, Beatty, NV 89003, tel. 702/553–2225. 62* *rooms. Facilities: restaurant, casino. AE, MC, V. Inexpensive–Moderate.*

Exchange Club Motel. Many guests at this three-year-old hotel would give it three stars. It's clean and quiet, and each carpeted room has a refrigerator and a cable TV with remote control. Two rooms are disabled-accessible. *604 Main St., Box 97, Beatty, NV 89003, tel. 702/553–2333. 44 rooms. Facilities: restaurant, casino, laundry. AE, MC, V. Inexpensive–Moderate.*

Shoshone Inn. The dusty town of Shoshone is only a wide spot in the highway, and the rustic Shoshone Inn is the only hotel in town. It features a hodgepodge of architectural styles. The accommodations here are adequate, and each room has a private bath. Advance reservations are advisable year-round. *Hwy. 127, Box 67, Shoshone, CA 92384, tel. 619/852–4335. 16 rooms. Facilities: pool. AE, MC, V. Inexpensive–Moderate.*

Stagecoach Hotel. In 1991 the 32 rooms in this eight-year-old hotel were remodeled, and 16 new rooms were constructed. The remodeling included adding tile in the bathrooms. Each room also got new curtains, a refrigerator, and cable TV with remote control. *U.S. 95 N, Box 836, Beatty, NV 89003, tel. 702/553–2419 or 800/424–4496. 48 rooms. Facilities: restaurant, casino, pool, Jacuzzi. AE, D, MC, V. Inexpensive–Moderate.*

CAMPING

There are more than 1,500 campsites at nine campgrounds in Death Valley National Monument, although not all of them are open year-round. Furnace Creek, Mesquite Spring, and Wildrose campgrounds are open throughout the year; Texas Spring, Sunset, and Stovepipe Wells are open November to April; Emigrant is open April to October; Thorndike and Mahogany Flat are open March to November. Reservations for individuals are available only at Furnace Creek; make them through Mistix (tel. 800/365–2267). Holidays that fall from October through March are busy times in Death Valley, but the only time it may be difficult to

find a site is during the 49er Encampment Days, which are held the first through second weekends in November.

There are two group campsites for 40 people each at Texas Spring campground. They cost $40 per night, per group, and may also be reserved through Mistix (*see above*).

Although there are electric, water, and sewer hookups at small commercial campgrounds in Furnace Creek and Stovepipe Wells Village, it is next to impossible to get a site there; they are usually taken by annual visitors and seasonal residents.

Fires are allowed in fire grates, but wood-gathering is prohibited. Firewood is available at general stores in Furnace Creek and Stovepipe Wells, but campers should bring their own.

The **Sunset** campground (flush and pit toilets, drinking water, playground, disposal station, ranger station, public phone), located 1 mile north of the Furnace Creek Visitor Center, is a gravel-and-asphalt RV mecca with 1,000 sites. It also serves as an overflow site for tents. Hookups are not available, but campers can walk across the street for pay showers, laundry facilities, and a swimming pool at the Furnace Creek Ranch. Many of the campers here are senior citizens who migrate to Death Valley each winter to play golf and tennis or just enjoy the mild, dry climate. Sites cost $4 per night per vehicle. Pull-throughs are available here and at Stovepipe Wells.

With more than 200 sites, **Stovepipe Wells** (drinking water, public phone) is the second-largest campground in the park. Like Sunset, this area is little more than a giant parking lot, but it has flush toilets and a dump station. Pay showers and laundry facilities are available at the Stovepipe Wells motel. Sites cost $4 per vehicle per night.

The most popular low-elevation campgrounds are **Furnace Creek** (135 sites, flush and pit toilets, hot water, showers, drinking water, fire grates, playground, swimming, disposal station, ranger station, public phone), **Texas Springs** (93 sites, flush and pit toilets, showers, drinking water, fire grates, playground, swimming, disposal station), and **Mesquite Spring** (50 sites, flush toilets, drinking water, disposal station), primarily because each of these areas has vegetation. In terms of natural ambience, there is little difference between the three: In each of them the campsites sit among dry, dusty, rock-strewn terrain. Furnace Creek and Texas Springs, however, are near the hub of valley civilization, and so they draw a wide variety of campers, from senior citizens to foreigners to families. Mesquite Spring, on the other hand, is more removed, the only campground in the north end of the park, and so it is frequented by a younger group intent on getting away from the crowds. Sites cost $5 per vehicle per night at Mesquite Spring and Texas Springs, but $8 per vehicle for a night at Furnace Creek.

During the summer months, some campers prefer the higher-elevation campsites of **Wildrose** (4,100 feet), **Thorndike** (7,500 feet), and **Mahogany Flat** (8,200 feet), where the temperature is generally 15 to 20 degrees cooler than it is on the valley floor. The road into Thorndike and Mahogany Flat is not suitable for trailers, campers, and motor homes, and at times it is necessary to have a high-clearance or four-wheel-drive vehicle to get through. Mahogany Flat (10 sites, pit toilets, fire grates) is the most scenic campground, set among piñon pines and junipers, with a view of the valley. Thorndike has 8 sites, pit toilets, and fire grates. Since it is at a lower elevation, Wildrose (30 sites, pit toilets, fire grates) is less likely to be closed because of snow in the winter. The view here is not as spectacular as that from Thorndike or Mahogany Flat, but it does offer a panorama of the northern end of the valley. It should be mentioned that although there is much more vegetation at these three campgrounds than at any of those in the valley, you still won't be camping under the shade of a large tree; the harsh climate here tends to result in dwarfed vegetation. There is no fee charged at these campgrounds.

The 10-site campground at **Emigrant** (flush toilets, drinking water), located near the western entrance to the park, is one of the least scenic campgrounds. The surrounding rock formations here are less dramatic than those at other campgrounds in the valley. Still, Emigrant has potable water and no fee is charged to camp here, making it an acceptable spot when no others are available.

Backcountry camping is allowed in most areas 1 mile back from main paved or unpaved roads and 1/4 mile from water sources. For restrictions, check the "Dirt Road Travel and Backcountry Camping" guide, available at the visitor center. For your own safety, fill out a voluntary backcountry registration form so the rangers know where to find you.

Denali National Park and Preserve
Alaska

By Barbara Hodgin
Updated by M.T. Schwartzman

 vast wilderness of taiga and tundra, with blue glacial pools and seamless snowfields, Denali National Park and Preserve is, and has always been, best known as the home of 20,320-foot Mt. McKinley, the highest mountain in North America. In fact, the park is named for the mountain, which Native Americans called *Denali* (The High One).

Climbers from all over the world come to scale the rugged Alaska Range, and dramatic Mt. McKinley offers the greatest challenge. The first successful ascent occurred in 1913, but is was not until 1967 that a team of climbers actually reached the apex in the middle of winter. Today, climbing parties assemble at the village of Talkeetna, just south of the park near mile 99 on the George Parks Highway. On any spring day, you will find them at the airstrip preparing for their ascent.

But these mountains were not always so accessible. The area was first established as Mount McKinley National Park in 1917 (the name was changed in 1980); it was set up as a game refuge to protect moose, sheep, and caribou from exploitation by market hunters from Fairbanks and the Alaska Railroad construction camps. But when the railroad was completed, in 1923, the first commercial tours of the area began to trickle in.

You need not climb Mt. McKinley to appreciate Denali; the park is both a hiker's paradise and a wildlife-watcher's playground. The one 88-mile road into the heart of the park is unpaved after the first 14.8 miles, and summer visitors now travel it on free shuttle buses, from which they watch for grizzly bears, wolves, caribou, and moose. The bulk of the parkland, however, is only accessible on foot in summer or by dog team or cross-country skis in winter. Don't let that discourage you: Most of the park lies above the tree line, and in summer there are 16 to 20 hours of daylight here. That means you have a lot of time to enjoy the expansive views of unspoiled landscape and to catch a few glimpses of Alaskan wildlife in the open spaces. Make sure you bring binoculars and a camera—Denali is one of the country's premier outdoor photography locations. Just outside the park, there's also horseback riding on wilderness trails, boating and whitewater rafting on the Nenana River, and helicopter or fixed-wing flightseeing in the skies above Mt. McKinley.

ESSENTIAL INFORMATION

VISITOR INFORMATION Visitors can obtain information about the park by writing to: Superintendent, **Denali National Park and Preserve,** Box 9, Denali National Park, AK 99755, in winter, tel. 907/683–2294, in summer, 907/683–1266 or 907/683–2686 for recorded updates. Information is also available at the **Alaska Public Lands Information Center,** 605 W. 4th Ave., Anchorage, AK 99501, tel. 907/271–2737; and 250 Cushman St., Fairbanks, AK 99701, tel. 907/451–7352.

Backcountry permits are required for all overnight trips in the park and can be obtained at the Visitor Access Center located at the park entrance. Since there are no maintained trails in the backcountry, hikers should be skilled in reading topographic maps, which are available at the park visitor centers. Most private cars are banned from the 88-mile park road beyond the Savage River Bridge (mile 14.8).

FEES Admission to the park is $3 per person or $5 per family for seven days. You may opt for an annual pass costing $15, which entitles visitors to unlimited entry for the calendar year. Visitors pay $12 per night for campgrounds, and $3 at the Morino backpacker campground, which has limited facilities (*see* Camping, *below*).

PUBLICATIONS Read the park's annual newspaper, the *Denali Alpenglow,* as well as the park brochure, which are both available at the Visitor Access Center. While you're there, pick up a guide describing the broad array of local birds and mammals. You can also purchase the *Denali Road Guide,* which gives a

mile-by-mile description of the geological history, terrain, and wildlife visible from the park road.

The **Alaska Natural History Association** (Box 230, Denali National Park, AK 99755, tel. 907/683–1258, fax 907/683–1408) will send you their latest mail-order brochure. It is an extensive listing of helpful books on natural history, wildlife, and mountaineering in Alaska. *Denali,* published by the **Alaska Geographic Society** (Box 93370, Anchorage, AK 99509, tel. 907/562–0164, fax 907/562–0479), describes the history, geology, flora, and fauna of the park, utilizing numerous color plates of the mountain and the surrounding preserve. **Trails Illustrated** (tel. 800/962–1643), based in Evergreen, Colorado, sells detailed maps of the area.

GEOLOGY AND TERRAIN Denali National Park and Preserve spans 6 million acres of taiga, tundra, and high mountain peaks—it's actually larger than the state of Massachusetts. The park entrance is in the taiga (Russian for "land of little sticks"), a coniferous forest lying in the lower river valleys, where there is more moisture and the micro-climate is a little warmer. Taiga within the park reaches elevations up to 2,700 feet.

The tundra begins at tree line. Covering more of the slopes and sitting at higher elevations, this ecosystem of small shrubs and miniature wildflowers knows a short, cool three-month growing season. Tundra may be moist, with swampy fields of tussocks, or it may be dry and brittle, on high, rocky ground.

The most prominent geological feature of the park are the high peaks of the Alaska Range, a 600-mile-long crescent of summits that separates southcentral Alaska from its vast interior. These peaks are all immense, but the truly towering ones are Mt. Hunter (14,573 feet), Mt. Foraker (17,400 feet), and Mt. McKinley (20,320 feet). These mountains are the result of tectonic plate activity along the Denali Fault, North America's largest crustal break, and earthquakes are still common in the park. In fact, a major quake hit in the spring of 1992, terrifying climbers and resulting in the avalanches that pummeled the Ruth Amphitheater.

Mt. McKinley rises from 2,000-foot lowlands at Wonder Lake, and when measured from base to peak it is nearly the tallest mountain in the world, second only to Nanga Parbat in the Himalayas. Because it reaches so far above every other feature around it, this mountain makes its own weather. Climbers often fail to reach McKinley's peak because of its powerful storms, which obscure the mountain and drive temperatures down. During the first successful winter ascent in 1967, climbers calculated that the temperature, adjusted for wind-chill, was -168°F.

Mt. McKinley's granite heart is covered with glacial ice, which is hundreds of feet thick in places. Glaciers, in fact, are abundant along the entire Alaska Range, and a few are visible from the Park Road. Muldrow Glacier is only $1/2$ mile from the Park Road, near mile 67.

Glaciers in turn are largely responsible for forming and feeding the rivers of the park. The Savage River valley seen from the Park Road was created by their advance and retreat, and with time, the river flowing from the mouth of a glacier cut a V-shape valley out of its U-shape floor. You can clearly observe this pattern at mile 14. Note that most glacial rivers, are murky: This is caused by the glacier, which grinds rocks and dirt in its path into a fine silt that does not clear in the water. This is why a glacial river can be especially dangerous to cross on foot: The bottom is not visible, and its water level can rise and fall dramatically during the day as the sun warms and melts the glacier that feeds it.

FLORA AND FAUNA The taiga is typified by small spruce, interspersed with aspens, birch, and balsam poplar. Ground cover in the taiga forest includes such shrubs as dwarf birch, blueberry, and willows. Alders occur along riverbanks. From the road the taiga looks open, with wide views and very few trees, but the dense bushes make it difficult for the inexperienced to hike here.

Tundra is a fascinating miniature forest. Get down at eye level to examine the variety of miniature plants; you may have seen their full-size counterparts elsewhere in the park. Fireweed, the ubiquitous pinkish-purple stalk of flowers that bloom along Alaska roads in late summer, has a tundra version—a tiny beauty less than 6 inches high. Berries are a common tundra food source; low bush cranberries, blueberries, and crowberries are all prized by Alaskans. In the wide pass south of the park near Cantwell, late August finds families picking blueberries on the tundra. Berry-picking season has begun in full force, while the tundra flora generates brilliant color: Bearberry leaves turn bright red, boasting their shiny dark-blue berries; the mountain slopes turn deep gold and orange; and the fragrant bouquet of wine permeates the tundra as fruit ferments on the bush.

Although Denali's unique landscape and sensational wildflower displays deserve high accolades, it is the animals that are the best reason to visit. You might see grizzly bears, caribou, moose, and Dall sheep, as well as smaller mammals and a variety of birds.

Grizzlies appear routinely in the park, but black bears are seldom sighted (although they do appear along the wooded rivers to the north and east). Don't expect to identify a bear by its color; grizzlies can range from very light gold to chocolate to black. What distinguishes a grizzly from a black bear is the large hump across its shoulders and its broad, dish-shape face. With a heavier-set stature than a black bear, a male grizzly typically weighs 450 pounds, a female 260.

The bears of Denali Park generally don't fear humans, and they can be dangerous, especially if surprised. Although most charges are bluffs, bears should always be considered unpredictable; it's wise to heed the park administration's guidelines on how to avoid problems. Leave dogs in the camper or car and keep food smells off yourself and your clothes. If you see a bear, make noise, alter your route, and back off. If a bear approaches, speak calmly, hold up your arms, and back away. If the bear runs at you, do not run away. If contact is imminent experts advise falling to the ground, tucking into a fetal position to better take the blow, and playing dead. You can't outdistance a grizzly, which can run 40 miles per hour.

The Denali caribou herd has diminished over the years from between 15,000 and 20,000 during the 1940s to some 2,200 animals today. Frequently spotted from the Park Road, male caribou in particular have large antlers and big, round hooves that provide good support in snow and on the tundra. They forage for green sprouts, lichens, willow, and sedge grasses. Flies and mosquitoes are a special nuisance to the caribou; flies lay eggs on their coats and the larvae penetrate the body. A caribou can commonly be seen holding its nose close to the wet ground for relief from the nostril flies that enter it. Hot, calm days encourage the flies; the herd will look for high breezy ground to forage.

Moose don't travel in herds; they are commonly seen in small groups or wandering alone in Denali. Bulls may weigh as much as 1,500 pounds and sport 70-inch antlers. Both sexes should be considered potentially dangerous, especially when it comes to protecting their calves. Equipped with strong legs, they manage a powerful kick. Being herbivores, moose look for tender tips of willow and birch in winter, and in summer they eat grasses from lake bottoms—emerging from the water with grass trailing out of their mouths and water pouring off their antlers. Look for evidence of winter browsing along roads and trails; moose like the easy access to bushes. Willows are often eaten back to the thicker branches.

Dall sheep roam the higher elevations of the park during the summer season and are commonly seen on slopes above the first 70 miles of the Park Road. These bright white animals travel in bands of about 60. Males have big, curling horns; females flaunt little spikes. Eager shuttle-bus passengers scan the rocky hillsides for this Denali Park favorite. Look for them grazing on grasses and at natural salt licks.

Denali Park wolves are extremely wary and seldom seen. They are occasionally sighted in packs during winter months and, from time to time, wandering on their own.

Smaller mammals commonly spotted in the park are arctic ground squirrels (whose quick whistle and prairie dog–like stance are easily recognized on tundra slopes), hoary marmots, red foxes, lynx, wolverines, martens, mink, and weasels. Beavers inhabit the park's lakes and rivers. A total of 37 species of mammal reside in the preserve.

There are also 159 species of bird in the park. Often seen are ravens—big, bossy black birds that would happily frequent hotel dumpsters and garbage cans were the containers not bear- and raven-proof. Look for the incredibly dull-witted willow ptarmigan, Alaska's state bird, a type of grouse with feathered feet. These birds are brown and white speckled in summer and will freeze when approached.

WHEN TO GO Summer is the most popular season to visit the park. Most campgrounds open Memorial Day weekend and close in mid-September. From June through August you can expect high temperatures to be about 65°F and lows around 40°F. In early summer, trails may be muddy and all the trees won't be fully leafed out, but young animals may be more readily visible. High run-off in early summer may limit rafting activities on the Nenana River. Late in summer, the tundra colors and fragrances brighten up; berry picking, a traditional Alaska activity for both bears and people, is allowed in Denali. Rain is common throughout summer.

During this time, waiting periods for a shuttle-bus pass can be as long as two or three days and for campsites even longer. At press time, shuttle-bus reservations (tel. 800/622–7275) were being offered on a trial basis for $4 per person for summer 1994.

Fall comes and goes quickly. Autumn colors peak the third week in August and disappear by September. Snow automatically closes western portions of the Park Road any time after mid-September, and they are not open again before the first week in June. If you're fortunate enough to be in the park during an early snowfall—before the tourism season is over and the hotels have closed—you'll experience a taste of the Denali winter. Those braving the winter climate find good cross-country skiing, dogsled touring, and solitude but limited guest facilities. Although Riley Creek campground is open all year, winter snow and cold discourage any but the hardiest. The January low temperature averages -7°F but can drop as low as -50°F.

SEASONAL EVENTS June 21: Alaskans celebrate the **summer solstice** with all-night softball games, barbecues, and footraces at midnight. Though this does not occur inside the park, you can check with park visitor centers, concessionaires, and local restaurants and hotels for locations.

WHAT TO PACK Wildlife viewing is the park's main attraction for most visitors, so binoculars and specialized camera equipment are important (*see* Photography, *below*).

Mosquitoes can be a problem, especially in swampy parts of the park. Alaskans carry insect repellent everywhere. If you're hiking overnight into the backcountry, you might even want to bring a head net.

Rain gear, a hat with a brim, a warm sweater, and sturdy footwear will ensure that the weather won't inhibit your plans. Light walking shoes are not suitable for hiking in the backcountry; bring waterproof or quick-drying hiking boots. Sneakers will suffice for the trails near the Riley Creek campground and the Visitor Access Center.

Some people have trouble sleeping in the long daylight of Alaska summers, so a great many hotels have black-out drapes. In campgrounds eyeshades would help.

There is no food available west of the Denali National Park Hotel; shuttle-bus riders should pack a lunch or have their hotel supply one. A thermos for hot coffee can make a long, wet day on the bus more pleasant. The only stop for water is at the Eielson Visitor Center (mile 66).

GENERAL STORES **McKinley Mercantile** (tel. 907/683–2215) is located at mile 1.4 on the Park Road and carries gas, groceries, and pro-

pane. There are showers ($2) in back of the building. It's open daily 7 AM to 10 PM during peak summer season, 8 AM to 9 PM in spring and fall. The **Lynx Creek Campground general store** (tel. 907/683–2548) is at mile 238.6 on the George Parks Highway, 1¹/₂-miles north of the park entrance on the river side of the road. A good selection of staples, prepared foods, liquor, gas, and ice are on sale here. It's open daily 24 hours June through August, dawn to dusk in May and September.

ARRIVING AND DEPARTING Denali Park is accessible by road and railroad from Anchorage and Fairbanks. This trip is recommended because the scenery between the cities and the park is nearly as lovely as the park itself. The railroad generally stays close to the road, but occasionally it detours into more remote country.

By Plane. There is no scheduled service to the park, but you can charter a flight from Anchorage or Fairbanks, the nearest major airports.

By Car and RV. The park is 237 miles north of Anchorage and 121 miles south of Fairbanks on the George Parks Highway (Hwy. 3). Roadhouses, which sell food and gas, appear every 50 miles or so along the highway. In winter, the roads are often snow-packed and you should always travel with emergency supplies, including a warm sleeping bag and a change of clothing, in the car. Studded tires help. Also note that from September through May there may be a span of 200 miles without an open gas station, especially at night. Gas up whenever you can.

Count on a five-hour drive to the park from Anchorage and a three-hour drive from Fairbanks. The country is mostly wilderness with broad views to the mountains. Streams along the way offer fine fishing opportunities. Byers Lake, 147 miles north of Anchorage, has picnic tables and is a good spot for a picnic lunch en route. It's also frequented by black bears.

RV rentals are available for travelers wishing to drive to the park and camp. Typically, a four-person motor home rents for between

$125 and $150 per day. Try **Murphy's RV** (Box 202063, Anchorage, AK 99520–2063, tel. 907/276–0688), **ABC Motorhome Rentals** (2360 Commercial Dr., Anchorage, AK 99501, tel. 907/279–2000), or **Clippership Motorhome Rentals** (5401 Old Seward Hwy., Anchorage, AK 99518, tel. 907/562–7051).

By Train. The **Alaska Railroad** (Box 107500, Anchorage, AK 99510–7500, tel. 907/265–2494 in Anchorage, 907/456–4155 in Fairbanks, or 800/544–0552) runs daily trains from Anchorage and Fairbanks to the park. It's a good option since private cars are severely limited inside the park, and shuttle and wildlife-tour buses are the main transport. Hotels outside the park entrance offer transportation to and from the train depot, which is right across the street from the Denali National Park Hotel, inside the park entrance. The northbound train leaves Anchorage at 8:30 AM, arriving at the park at 3:45 PM. The southbound train leaves Fairbanks at 8:30 AM, arriving at 12:30 PM. The round-trip fare from Anchorage is $170 and from Fairbanks $90. The Alaska Railroad has a vista dome car on each train, and passengers can sit up top. Locals bring a picnic lunch, but in summer there's a restaurant on board.

Private tour companies hook up plush touring cars to the train. **Princess Tours'** *Midnight Sun Express* (519 W. 4th Ave., Anchorage, AK 99501, tel. 907/276–7711 or 3045 Davis Rd., Fairbanks, AK 99709, tel. 907/479–9660) and **Gray Line of Alaska's** *McKinley Explorer* (745 W. 4th Ave, Anchorage, AK 99501, tel. 907/277–5581 or 1980 S. Cushman Ave., Fairbanks, AK 99701, tel. 907/456–7742) charge $228 round-trip from Anchorage and $112 round-trip from Fairbanks.

By Bus. Gray Line of Alaska (*see* By Train, *above*) offers round-trip bus transportation from Anchorage for $130 and from Fairbanks for $80.

EXPLORING

Most visitors to Denali Park ride the park service shuttle buses, some of which are accessible to people with disabilities. The park hotel also runs narrated bus tours (*see* Guided Tours, *below*).

Bicycles are currently allowed on the Park Road. The Alaska Railroad transports bikes on the baggage car if space is available. The road is suitable only for mountain bikes. The only cars allowed on the Park Road beyond mile 14.8 are those that belong to campers who are staying in the Teklanika River campground.

The real wilderness experience in Denali is reserved for those who get off the buses and walk. There are excellent day hikes near the entrance, and overnight options are unlimited, since there are no formal trails. Many hikers follow river beds or ridges. Of course, the real wilderness experience includes the possibility of encounters with potentially dangerous wildlife. Follow the advice of park rangers about routes and safe behavior.

THE BEST IN ONE DAY Because half a million visitors come to Denali each year, shuttle bus coupons can be as rare and valuable as a gold nugget in the Kantishna Hills; you may need to wait a day or two to secure a coupon. Day-trippers unable to wait this long can explore the area near the park entrance. Here they will find hiking trails—the only marked paths in the park—and dogsled demonstrations at the kennels near park headquarters.

At the Denali National Park Hotel, try catching some of the afternoon films and interpretative activities planned in the hotel auditorium. Most of these programs run during the mid-afternoon. The half-hour "Denali Wilderness" is particularly good.

Assuming you're here during the summer months, you still have plenty of sunlight left, so those of you in need of a little action should experience firsthand the rapids of the Nenana River. A two-hour trip costs $35 per person (*see* Guided Tours, *below*). Then, after choosing one of the area's eateries for dinner (*see* Dining, *below*), stretch your legs with a 1-mile hike down to Horseshoe Lake, a little jewel surrounded by birch forest.

ORIENTATION PROGRAMS The **Visitor Access Center** (tel. 907/683–1266) at the entrance offers a 15-minute orientation to the park throughout the day. Ranger-naturalist–led activities are provided near the park entrance daily. Sled dog demonstrations at the dog kennels on the park road are scheduled three times daily. Bus transportation from the Visitor Access Center and the park hotel is provided. At 8 PM nightly in the park hotel auditorium, rangers show slides or films about the park.

GUIDED TOURS Rangers offer free daily walks at Eielson Visitor Center, at mile 66 on the Park Road. Staff members also lead daily off-road discovery hikes exploring ridges, tundra, and river valleys in the park. Registration for these off-road hikes is required at the Visitor Access Center.

Guided bus tours depart from the Denali National Park Hotel (Box 87, Denali Park, AK 99755, tel. 907/276–7234 or 907/683–2215) daily at 6 AM and 3 PM. These buses are more comfortable than the park service's school buses, and they provide lunch. The tour is six or seven hours and costs $45 per adult, $22 for children ages 11 and under. Shorter (three- to four-hour) natural history tours cost $25 per adult and $14 for children. The advantage is that you can book these private tours well in advance of your arrival.

Denali Air (Box 82, Denali National Park, AK 99755, tel. 907/683–2261) gives 70-minute small-plane tours of the park, departing from the park landing strip. **K2 Aviation** (Box 545, Talkeetna, AK 99676, tel. 907/733–2291) and **Doug Geeting Aviation** (Box 42, Talkeetna, AK 99676, tel. 907/733–2366) are air taxi services that fly out of a village on a spur road off mile 99 on the George Parks Highway; both offer flightseeing tours of the mountain. Prices range from $70 to $150 per person, depending on the operator, number of persons, length of the flight, and if a glacier landing is included. **ERA Helicopters** (6160 Airpark Dr., Anchorage, AK 99502, tel. 907/683–2574 or 800/843–1947) operates 50-minute tours for $165 per person from its helipad ½ mile north of the park entrance.

Raft trips down the icy, class-four white-water Nenana River attract visitors and locals alike. Operators provide waterproof gear, and some tours include a shore lunch with a campfire. The river is run in two stretches. The part south of the park entrance is not as scary, and is more suitable for children. The rapids are found in the northern section. **Denali Raft Adventures** (Denali National Park, AK 99755, tel. 907/683–2234) offers four different river excursions ranging from an all-day outing ($125 per person) to two-hour canyon rapids or scenic float trips (both $36 per person). These latter two-hour trips may be combined. **McKinley Raft Tours** (Box 138, Denali National Park, AK 99755, tel. 907/683–2392) offers a two-hour white-water canyon run or a two-hour scenic tour for $35, or a combination of both for $48.

Kantishna Wilderness Trails (Box 130, Denali National Park, AK 99755, tel. 907/479–2436 or 800/942–7420, fax 907/479–2611) provides private bus transportation to Kantishna Roadhouse, at the end of the park Road. Have lunch at the new log lodge, then spend the day hiking and panning for gold.

SCENIC DRIVES AND VIEWS Visitors can disembark at any shuttle-bus stop in the park for hiking and sightseeing, then catch the next bus in either direction to continue the trip. Buses generally run every half hour. **Polychrome Pass** is a popular place to disembark, walk around, and look at the wide views of the streams below.

Wonder Lake, at the end of the road, is a good spot to picnic, hike, and enjoy the tundra before the long ride back to the park entrance at Riley Creek. There are good views here of the north face of Mt. McKinley.

HISTORIC BUILDINGS AND SITES In the early days of the park, horse-drawn carriages brought visitors to the **Savage Road Camp** just south of the present Savage River campground. Campers stayed overnight on cots in canvas tents. The stage route fell out of use in the early 1940s. A few yards south of the campground, indentations from the old camp can still be seen in the fragile tundra.

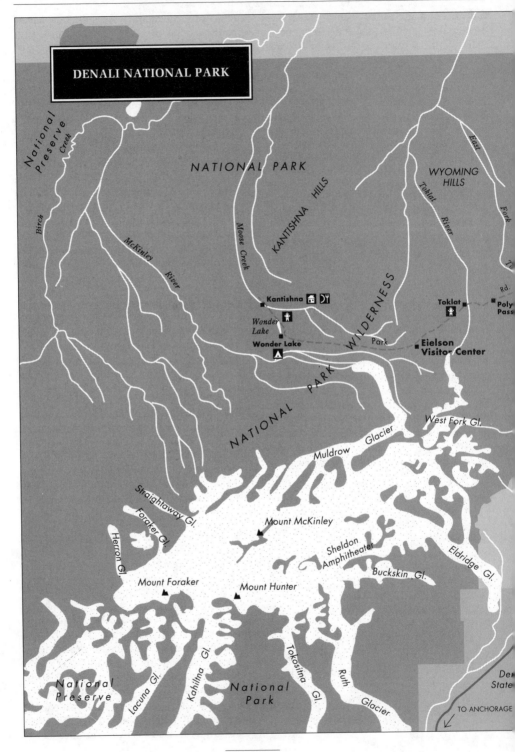

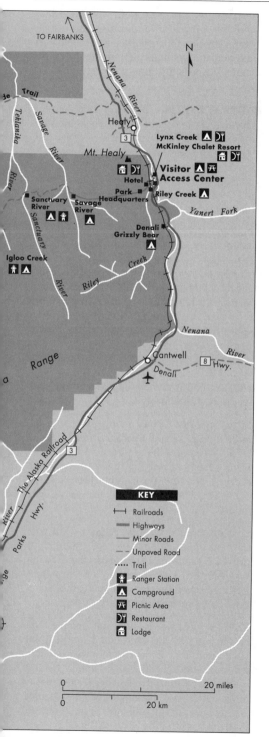

TO FAIRBANKS

N

Healy

Lynx Creek
McKinley Chalet Resort

Mt. Healy

Visitor
Access Center
Hotel

Park
Headquarters

Riley Creek

Sanctuary
River

Savage
River

Yanert Fork

Denali
Grizzly Bear

Igloo Creek

Riley

Creek

Nenana

Range

Cantwell

River

Denali

8 Hwy.

The Alaska Railroad

Parks Hwy.

KEY

⊢⊣	Railroads
▬▬	Highways
—	Minor Roads
– –	Unpaved Road
·····	Trail
🧍	Ranger Station
▲	Campground
🏕	Picnic Area
🍴	Restaurant
🏠	Lodge

0   20 miles

0   20 km

The old **Kantishna Roadhouse** at the end of the Park Road, beyond Wonder Lake, was part of the old townsite of Kantishna. The gold rush in the Kantishna Hills at the turn of the century attracted more than 2,500 people to the area. The roadhouse is now one of four private wilderness lodges located in the old gold mining district (*see* Lodging, *below*).

NATURE TRAILS AND SHORT WALKS All developed trails are near the park entrance at Riley Creek. The **Taiga Trail Loop** is a 1^1/₃-mile easy walk through dense spruce forest near the campground and has enticing views of the rushing creek. It starts and ends at the Denali National Park Hotel and will take no more than an hour to complete. The **Horseshoe Lake Trail** is a 1-mile hike, also beginning near the park hotel, to small Horseshoe Lake at the bottom of a canyon. Look for arctic ground squirrels along the way.

LONGER HIKES The **Mt. Healy Overlook Trail** gains 1,700 feet in 2^1/₂ miles and takes about four hours round-trip, with outstanding views of the Nenana River below and the Alaska Range above. Carry water.

This hike is the only relatively long, marked trial for hiking in the park. What remains is a tremendous opportunity for overnight backcountry hiking. Know ahead of time that, though backcountry hiking is somewhat unrestricted throughout the park, wise and careful planning is necessary to undertake any overnight or even daylong trek through Denali's rugged and often unpredictable wilderness. At the very least, you should consult with park rangers at the Visitor Access Center well before departing. You cannot make advance reservations to hike and camp in a particular region of the park; however, you can ask the rangers for practical advice on where best to take advantage of Denali's vast resources — and where bears have been sighted recently. If time allows, you might even consult the Alaska Public Lands Information Centers in either Anchorage (tel. 907/271–2737) or Fairbanks (tel. 907/451–7352).

The day of your hike, you will have to stop in at the Visitor Access Center (open summer 7 to 6) to pick up your free backcountry permit if you plan to camp overnight. On the map, Denali is divided into three sections: Denali National Park Wilderness (through which the Park Road passes), Denali National Park, and Denali National Preserve. Different regulations apply to the three regions: Campfires, firearms, and pets are prohibited in the Wilderness backcountry. Fishing is allowed with a license in the Park and Perserve; and without a license in the Wilderness backcountry. Sport hunting with a license is allowed in the Perserve only (*see* Other Activities, *below*).

Learn to use a topographic map; some of the areas in the park are extremely dense with brush, and in these regions it's very easy to become lost. It's safest to hike along ridge tops and alongside gravel riverbeds, away from the brush. The park is replete with glacial rivers, many of them dangerous to cross. Ask rangers about techniques for crossing these rivers. Never attempt to cross a river barefoot, and always choose a route that allows you the option of returning to the shoreline. If in a group, walk side by side, thereby minimizing the tendency to imprint your own trail on the delicate tundra. Because of Denali's fierce subarctic climate, the earth beneath you is easily damaged and repairs itself slowly. It is important to realize that the number of visitors to the park—which has risen dramatically in recent years—poses a great threat to both the precious wildlife and the fragile terrain. A study done 10 years ago showed that the increase in numbers had begun to disturb the park's ecosystem and reduce the number of wildlife sightings. It is your responsibility to leave the park exactly as you found it.

Remember also that private dwellings are scattered throughout Denali National Park and Preserve. No camping is allowed within sight of lodges or private property, or within 1/2 mile of the Park Road, and you must not hike through private property. Hiking in the backcountry is carefully trafficked by the Visitor Access Center, and, depending on the crowds, you may not be permitted to hike in certain regions of the park. Again, the key to successful and enjoyable hiking is re-searching your trip prudently and checking with the appropriate authorities. The unique character and climate of Denali National Park may make a spontaneous odyssey over the tundra impossible, but persevere: The rewards are well worth it.

OTHER ACTIVITIES All-terrain vehicles and bicycles are not permitted to leave the park road. In winter, you can travel wherever you wish on a dogsled, snowshoes, or cross-country skis; however, as with hiking, you should plan ahead and consult rangers before setting off. Commonly used trails make travel easier than breaking new trail.

Biking. Bicycling in Denali has caught on in recent years. Given the restricted use of the Park Road, however, cyclists should pick up a copy of the park brochure "*Rules of the Road*" before departing. A travel permit is not required, but bicycles are not allowed off the roadways. Also, if you're planning an overnight trip, you must register with the Visitor Access Center, just as if you were planning an overnight hike (*see* Longer Hikes, *above*). The **Denali Princess Lodge** (tel. 907/683–2283 or 800/426–0500) outside the park entrance has mountain bikes for rent.

Bird-Watching. Denali is an excellent park for watching several species of bird. The ubiquitous song of the tundra, a falling "Three Blind Mice," is sung by the white-crowned sparrow, common throughout Alaska. There are also golden eagles, falcons, ducks, and loons.

Boating. Denali Wildlife Safaris (Box 181, Cantwell, AK 99729, tel. 907/768–2660) provides narrated trips down the Nenana River aboard covered, heated tour boats that lead to an operating prospector's camp. Tours last 3¹/₂ hours and cost $75.

Fishing. Interior Alaska is not home to the best fishing in the state, but it's still quite good. A number of local rivers and lakes offer grayling and pike fishing. Though fishing licenses are required in the more remote areas of Denali (Denali National Park and Denali National Preserve), a license is not required for fishing within the limits of Denali Wilderness; check with the Visitor Access Center to learn Wilderness boundaries. A three-day, nonresident license costs $15 and is available at most general stores and gas stations.

Flight Seeing. The vastness of the park takes on new dimensions when you view it from the air. Helicopter and small-plane rides are available (*see* Guided Tours, *above*).

Horseback Riding. You can't ride a horse inside the park unless you're a guest at Kantishna Roadhouse (*see* Guided Tours, *above*, and Lodging, *below*). **Denali Wilderness Lodge** (907/683–1287 or 800/541–9779), 30 miles east of the park, offers horseback riding, with daily fly-in packages to its grounds; the property is a former bush camp, homestead, and hunting lodge, first settled after the turn of the century. **Wolf Point Ranch** (tel. 907/768–2620) offers guided horseback riding just south of the park in Cantwell.

Photography. Denali is renowned among outdoor photographers. Big skies, big mammals, and the biggest mountain in North America provide plenty of subject matter. The shot of a moose wading in Wonder Lake, water cascading from its antlers, is a classic. Necessary equipment includes a telephoto lens (to get visually close to potentially dangerous animals), a polarizing filter (to cut through haze) or 81-series amber warming filter (to balance cool light of overcast skies), and a tripod. Bring plenty of film—long summer days allow for plenty of photo opportunities.

Rafting. Rafters should not attempt the portion of the Nenana River north of the park entrance unless they have scouted the rapids by running it with a commercial operator (*see* Guided Tours, *above*) and have skills to navigate class four or higher white water. Several people have died on this river.

Ski Touring. Opportunities for wintertime cross-country skiing are unlimited in the backcountry. Cross-country skis and camping gear can be rented in Anchorage at **REI** (1200 W. Northern Lights Blvd., Anchorage, AK 99503, tel. 907/272–4565).

CHILDREN'S PROGRAMS The park rangers offer limited junior ranger programs during summer. Check at the Visitor Access Center.

EVENING ACTIVITIES The Alaska Cabin Nite dinner theater at the McKinley Chalet Resort (tel. 907/683–2215) has seatings twice nightly during spring and fall, three times nightly during summer, at $29 for adults and $17 for children under 12. Waiters and waitresses perform musical skits recalling the gold rush days in Alaska. Reservations are recommended.

Riley Creek, Savage, Teklanika, and Wonder Lake campgrounds have evening programs led by ranger-naturalists. Check the bulletin boards for times and topics.

Ranger's talks, movies, and slide shows take place at 8 PM in the Denali National Park Hotel auditorium. The topics presented vary from year to year.

DINING

One drawback of a road trip in Alaska or the Yukon is the dearth of good food you'll encounter along the way. Denali National Park and Preserve is unfortunately no exception. Alaska hotels and roadhouses generally serve good hamburgers and seafood. In Denali, basic is usually better. Dress is extremely casual, so don't feel obligated to don your sharpest duds.

Alaska Cabin Nite at McKinley Chalet Resort. This family-style establishment offers surprisingly good barbecued ribs, salmon, and halibut at its dinner and show. Nearly two hours of gold rush–era skits and a barbecue feast for $29 per person make this a good value. *George Parks Hwy., 1¹/₂ mi north of park entrance, tel. 907/683–2215. Reservations recommended. AE, D, MC, V. Closed winter. Expensive.*

Summit Restaurant. In the Denali Princess Lodge, the Summit Restaurant offers a sophisticated interpretation of a predictable menu consisting of steak, salmon, and pasta. Since local salmon become mushy after their long journey up the interior rivers, the fish here come from southcentral ports; ask for them grilled. A wood-paneled dining room overlooks the Nenana River, so be sure to request a window table. *George Parks Hwy., 1 mi north of park entrance, Denali, tel. 907/683–2283. Reservations recommended. AE, MC, V. Closed winter. Expensive.*

Lynx Creek Campground Pizza & Pub. This modest, low-frame building beside the gas station is unattractive outside and in, but it's popular with young park and hotel workers. The jukebox is usually blaring rock 'n' roll, and friendly folks can be found mingling at the common tables. You might avoid the Mexican food; this eatery is a bit too far from the border. Ask for reindeer-sausage pizza, and wash it down with locally brewed Alaskan beer. *George Parks Hwy., 1¹/₂ mi north of park entrance, tel. 907/683–2548. No reservations. No credit cards. Closed winter. Inexpensive.*

PICNIC SPOTS You can picnic anywhere along the park road. Tundra is soft and smells like medicinal potpourri, and napping here is pleasant after lunch on a sunny day. Ask the shuttle-bus driver where bears have been spotted that day and avoid those areas. Horseshoe Lake is an easy short walk (*see* Nature Trails and Short Walks, *above*) for lunch near the park hotel.

LODGING

There is only one hotel inside the park entrance. Lodges in the Kantishna gold-mining district offer a true wilderness experience without sacrificing the modern comforts of hot showers and queen-size beds. These properties are very expensive, averaging almost $250 per person, per night, and some require a minimum two- or three-night stay. There are several large hotels and cabin compounds near the park.

INSIDE THE PARK **Denali National Park Hotel.** Built in 1973, this hotel consists of modular buildings. The construction is purely practical inside and out. The hotel's only advantage over others in the area is its convenience to the railroad station and shut-

tle buses. Ranger talks are given nightly in the hotel's 300-seat auditorium. *ARA Denali Park Hotels, Box 87, Denali Park, AK 99755, tel. 907/276–7234 or 907/683–2215. 100 rooms. Facilities: cafeteria, snack shop, auditorium. AE, D, MC, V. Closed winter. Expensive.*

Kantishna Roadhouse. This roadhouse, which is at the end of the Park Road, takes as long as five to six hours to reach by bus from the park entrance. Surrounding the historic roadhouse are 27 log cabins with private bath, and a new, hand-hewn log lodge. Available activities include gold panning, mountain bike riding, horseback riding, and sightseeing by plane. Meals are included in the rather pricey rates; the chef will accommodate dietary restrictions. Pre-payment, in full, by check or money order is required 45 days prior to your stay. *Box 130, Denali Park, Kantishna, AK 99755, tel. 907/479–2436 or 800/942–7420, fax 907/479–2611. Facilities: dining room, saloon, sauna, library. Closed Sept.–May. Expensive.*

The Kantishna district's other wilderness lodges are **Camp Denali** (Box 67, Denali Park, AK 99755, tel. or fax 907/683–2290, Expensive); **Denali Backcountry Lodge** (Box 189, Denali Park, AK 99755, tel. 907/683–2594 or 800/841–0692, fax 907/683–1341, Expensive); and **North Face Lodge** (Box 67, Denali Park, AK 99755, tel. or fax 907/683–2290, Expensive).

NEAR THE PARK **Denali Princess Lodge.** This grand, wood-sided hotel prides itself on being the most luxurious in the Denali area. Since its opening in 1987, the property has been expanded twice and now houses 280 rooms. Big wood decks off the back of the hotel overlook the Nenana River. The interior has a log-cabin feel to it, but it is sophisticated, with fine carpets and fabrics in jewel tones. A free shuttle takes guests to the park. *George Parks Hwy., 1 mi north of park entrance, Box 110, Denali Park, AK 99755, tel. 907/683–2283 Reservations: 2815 Second Ave., Suite 400, Seattle, WA 98121–1299, tel. 800/426–0500. Facilities: 2 restaurants, outdoor hot tubs, Jacuzzis in suites, meeting rooms. AE, MC, V. Closed winter. Expensive.*

McKinley Chalet Resort. This is a sprawling complex of chalet-style cedar lodges on the George Parks Highway. Grouped on a bluff overlooking the Nenana River, the log buildings house a number of river-view rooms. All 288 mini-suites have a sitting area that can serve as a second bedroom. The dinner theater is home to Alaska Cabin Nite (*see* Dining, *above*). You can arrange for the kitchen to pack you a shuttle-bus lunch. *George Parks Hwy., 1½ mi north of park entrance. ARA Denali Park Hotels, Box 87, Denali Park, AK 99755, tel. 907/276–7234 or 907/683–2215. Facilities: restaurant, dinner theater, pool, hot tub, exercise room. AE, D, MC, V. Closed winter. Expensive.*

Other lodge-type options near the park are the **Denali Crow's Nest Log Cabins** (Box 70, Denali Park, AK 99755, tel. 907/683–2723, Expensive), **Denali Cabins** (Box 229, Denali Park, AK 99755, tel. 907/683–2643, Expensive), and **Denali Grizzly Bear Cabins and Campground** (Box 7, Denali Park, AK 99755, tel. 907/683–2696, Moderate–Expensive). The **Denali Hostel** (Box 801, Denali Park, AK 99755, tel. 907/683–1295, Inexpensive) is located 10 miles north of the park entrance, near Healy, and offers bus service back and forth to the park. All of these lodgings are open in summer only; the actual dates vary depending on the weather. Always call or write ahead.

CAMPING

INSIDE THE PARK There are seven campgrounds in the park. The dates of opening and closing depend on snow conditions, but most years the campgrounds are closed from late September to late May. Riley Creek is at least partially open year-round, but there is no water in winter.

Patience and planning are the keys to obtaining one of Denali's 228 sites (including 60 spaces for backpackers at Morino). Each site is assigned at the Visitor Access Center. You might consider devising the following strategy: First, call the **Alaska Public Lands Information Center** in Anchorage (tel. 907/271–2737) or Fairbanks (tel. 907/451–7352)

to find out whether the park service is allowing any reservations of campsites in advance. The park's policy changes from time to time as it tries valiantly to accommodate the increasing number of campers to Denali each year. Usually you will find that campgrounds are full and that your best bet is to come to Denali, register at the Visitor Access Center (registration is not permitted more than a day or two in advance), and spend your one- or two-day wait at a nearby private campground. A number of these private establishments, in addition to the two described below, are listed on the Visitor Access Center bulletin board. Be aware that stays in the park are limited to 14 days during the summer (30 during winter), and nonrefundable payment is due upon registration. There are no RV hookups. At press time, the campgrounds at Sanctuary River and Igloo Creek offered no water supplies. No fee was being charged at these sites.

Riley Creek is ¼ mile west of the George Parks Highway, on the Park Road. It has 102 RV and tent sites, with flush toilets, piped water except during winter, and a pay phone. Sites cost $12 per night. **Morino Backpacker Campground** is on mile 1.9 and has room for 60 backpackers. There is piped water here, as well as chemical toilets and a pay phone. Sites cost $3 per night. **Savage River,** with 34 RV and tent sites and 3 group sites that accommodate between 9 and 20 persons each, is on mile 13. It has piped water and flush toilets. Sites cost $12 per night and $20 per group site. **Sanctuary River,** on mile 23, has 7 tent sites, with chemical toilets. **Teklanika River** is on mile 29. It has 50 RV and tent sites, piped water, and chemical toilets. Sites cost $12 per night. **Igloo Creek,** on mile 34, has 7 tent sites, and pit toilets. **Wonder Lake** is on mile 85. It has 28 tent sites, piped water, and flush toilets. Sites cost $12 per night. Note that Wonder Lake is closed, due to snow, for a longer period of the year than the others; check the Visitor Access Center for exact dates and a number of additional rules and regulations that apply to each campground. Fire is never allowed outside of established grates, and pets must be on a leash at all times.

Bears are a potential problem at all of Denali's campgrounds. Always keep food, fragrant toiletries, and food-soiled clothing out of your tent. Clean up after meals and store food in your car or in the food storage locker. Backcountry camping is allowed by permit anywhere in the park, unless restricted for safety or wildlife-preservation reasons. These sections change from time to time, so check with the ranger before setting out. Apply for a permit at the Visitor Access Center (*see* Longer Hikes, *above*).

NEAR THE PARK Outside the park, several campgrounds offer full-service campsites for tents and RVs. The best are:

Denali Grizzly Bear Cabins and Campground. An Alaskan family has owned and operated this campground since 1958. A number of authentically restored trapper's cabins, dating back to 1904, may be found on the grounds. Campsites cost $15 per night plus $5 for an electrical hookup and $1 for a water hookup. The walled tents are the bargain of the area: only $23 a night for three if you bring your own linens. The campground is located 6 miles south of the park entrance. Reservations are recommended. *Box 7, Denali Park, AK 99755, tel. 907/683–2696. 59 campsites, 17 cabins. V.*

Lynx Creek Campground. Located next to the Nenana River, 1½ miles north of the park entrance, this campground has 25 sites, 12 with electrical hookups ($20 per night) and 13 without electricity ($15 per night). A bar, pizzeria, dump station, and showers are available. No reservations are accepted. *Box 118, Denali Park, AK 99755, tel. 907/683–2548. D, MC, V.*

Grand Canyon National Park
Arizona

By William E. Hafford
Updated by Deke Castleman

he Grand Canyon is often called the Temple of the World because of the reverence it instills in virtually all who view it for the first time. Naturalist John Muir, more than a century ago, said of the canyon, "It will seem as novel to you, as unearthly in the color and grandeur and quantity of its architecture, as if you had found it after death, on some other star."

Creation of the canyon began more than 80 million years ago when a great upheaval of the earth's crust began forming what is now the huge domelike Colorado Plateau in northern Arizona. Nearly 6 million years ago the force of the Colorado River began carving an erratic path through the uplifted region, sculpting a gorge that is, today, 277 miles long, as much as 17 miles wide, and nearly 6,000 feet deep in some places.

Although the great buttes and erosion-blasted gorges of the canyon have been in place for millions of years, the canyon provides an ever-changing drama for those who visit. Clouds, shadows, and the moving sun constantly repaint what the viewer sees. The sharply defined colors of the rock merge and soften as sunlight shifts. Clouds float by and purple shadows creep into the depths. During the gentle fall of rain, a haze tints and softens the landscape. As the sun flames in the west, some of the canyon walls turn almost blood red. Then, as night falls, the depths become obscured, and the purples get deeper and deeper, until finally all is cloaked in darkness. Next day, the show begins anew.

There are clearly plenty of reasons why the Grand Canyon is such a thrilling destination for those who like to bathe their eyes with visual adventure. And the regions immediately surrounding the canyon offer similarly stunning views: North and west of the canyon's North Rim are the wonders of Zion and Bryce Canyon national parks, both in southwestern Utah. The magnificent emerald waters of Lake Powell and thousands of square miles of the Glen Canyon National Recreation Area lie north and east of the Grand Canyon. Directly to the east is the sprawling 25,000-square-mile Navajo Indian Reservation, a land of red dunes and soaring buttes where the silent cliff dwellings of Betatakin and Canyon de Chelly reveal evidence of Pueblo cultures that existed long before Europeans arrived in the Southwest. It's no wonder that more than 4 million visitors come to Grand Canyon country each year.

There are certain differences between the North and South rims of the Grand Canyon: The South Rim is more accessible, more developed, and more likely to be crowded. (From Flagstaff it's 81 miles to the South Rim and 210 miles to the North Rim.) There are more services, attractions, and amenities at the South Rim, but the North Rim is set in a lush forest where you can find sylvan solitude only a few yards from motel and campground areas. The long drive to the North Rim is through lonely but impressively scenic country.

ESSENTIAL INFORMATION

VISITOR INFORMATION For detailed information about the park, write to: **Grand Canyon National Park,** Box 129, Grand Canyon, AZ 86023, or call 602/638–7888. The **Arizona Office of Tourism** (1100 W. Washington, Phoenix, AZ 85007, tel. 602/542–8687) is also a great source of information on the park and other tourist attractions in the state. If you have questions about lodging, touring, and recreation, contact **Grand Canyon Park Lodges** (Box 699, Grand Canyon, AZ 86023, tel. 602/638–2401) on the South Rim and **TW Recreational Services** (Box 400, Cedar City, UT 84720, tel. 801/586–7686) on the North Rim.

Hikers descending into the canyon (via any of the numerous trails) for an overnight stay need a free backcountry permit, which must be obtained in person or by writing: **Backcountry Reservation Office,** Box 129, Grand Canyon, AZ 86023, tel. 602/638–7888. Permits are limited, so make your reservation at least several months in advance. Day hikes into the canyon or anywhere else in the national park do not require a permit; overnight stays at Phantom Ranch require reservations but no permits. Before attempting a descent to the bottom of the canyon, discuss your plans with a park ranger, and acquaint yourself with all the required safety precautions. Unless you have a backcountry permit, overnight camping in the national park is restricted to designated campgrounds.

FEES The National Park Service charges visitors $10 to enter Grand Canyon National Park by car, regardless of the number of passengers. Individuals arriving by public conveyance (bus, taxi, or train) pay $4. The entrance gates are open 24 hours a day but are generally attended from about 7 to 6. If you arrive when a gate is unpatrolled, you may enter legally without paying the fee.

PUBLICATIONS Visitors at either rim are given *The Guide,* a free newspaper, as they enter the park. It contains a detailed area map, a complete schedule of the free programs offered, and other useful information. It's also available at the visitor centers and lodges. Maps are available at the visitor centers and at many of the lodges and stores. Grand Canyon National Park (*see* Visitor Information, *above*) sends out the *Trip Planner,* a newsletter for those planning a visit to the park, on request. Many other publications are on sale in the visitor centers, various gift shops, and museums at both rims.

The **Grand Canyon Natural History Association** (Box 399, Grand Canyon, AZ 86023, tel. 602/638–2481) has a listing of informative publications on Northern Arizona. Some of the better books available through this organization are *Along the Rim,* by Nancy Loving, a short but helpful guide to the flora and fauna you'll encounter on both rims; *Introduction to Grand Canyon Geology,* by Michael Collier, which offers a concise and easy-to-follow overview of the park's geology; and *In the House of Stone and Light,* by J. Donald Hughes, a careful and revealing history of the canyon. These books and many others can be ordered by mail or over the phone.

GEOLOGY AND TERRAIN Grand Canyon National Park consists of more than 1,900 square miles, and both rims are surrounded by the vast Kaibab National Forest. The inner canyon—that immense and imposing area below the rims—reflects a geologic profile of the earth's history. At the very bottom of the canyon is a layer of rock called Vishnu Schist, which is more than 2 billion years old.

The terrain at the North Rim of the canyon is a part of the Kaibab Plateau, a heavily forested region as high as 9,000 feet. The South Rim, part of the Coconino Plateau, lies in an area that is essentially flat, at an elevation of about 7,000 feet, where highland trees are abundant.

FLORA AND FAUNA The South Rim of the canyon is forested primarily by stands of ponderosa pine, piñon pine, and Utah juniper. Shrubs include cliffrose, mountain mahogany, and fernbush. The Kaibab Plateau on the North Rim is thickly forested with ponderosa pine, spruce, fir, and quaking aspen.

Animal life abounds in the park on both rims. Seventy-five different species of mammal, 24 types of lizard, 24 kinds of snake, and 300 species of bird inhabit the park. Two species are unique to the Grand Canyon: The rare Kaibab squirrel with its white tail and tufted ears is found only on the North Rim, and the pink rattlesnake stays at lower elevations in the canyon, the only place it is found. Mule deer are often seen in the park—frequently crossing the roads—so drive carefully. Coyotes are seldom seen but often heard as they howl and yip at night. Hawks and ravens are regularly observed riding on the updrafts over the canyon. It is illegal and unsafe to feed the animals: Their health can be maintained only on a natural diet, and visitors have been bitten while feeding.

WHEN TO GO The high and low seasons at Grand Canyon are not sharply defined. Changes in activities, prices, and the availability of services are often based on demand, funding, and weather. For example, the number of months that the free shuttles run at Grand Canyon Village (South Rim) may depend in part on the availability of National Park Service funding. When the number of visitors remains high, retail stores continue their longer summer hours well into the fall. Although crowds start arriving around Easter and stay until November, and warm weather can last from May to September, for practical purposes, consider the term "summer season" to mean roughly the months of June, July, and August. The term "colder months" means roughly all the others.

Because it stands at only 7,000 feet, you can visit the South Rim any time of year. Most summers offer shirt-sleeve days and crisp evenings with short, but somewhat frequent, afternoon thundershowers. Spring and fall are moderate: temperatures generally stay above 32°F and often climb into the 70s. In winter, days typically range from about 20°F to 50°F, although subzero temperatures are not uncommon in midwinter. Snowfall is common during winter months, but it enhances the beauty of the canyon, and the roads are kept open. The North Rim, situated in country often higher than 8,000 feet, can be hit with extremely heavy snowfall: It is generally open from mid-May through late October, but unexpected snow can change these dates. As at the South Rim, afternoon rains are common here.

Summer crowds at the South Rim can be a major irritation. More than 4 million people come to the canyon each year, and 90% of them arrive at the popular and much more accessible South Rim. If you choose to visit in spring, fall, or winter, there are fewer crowds. However, since spring and fall are far better for inner-canyon hiking than summer, backcountry permits can be just as hard to get, and aside from occasional winter specials, prices are not lower. Lodging prices outside the national park and in such northwestern Arizona communities as Flagstaff and Williams generally do drop during colder months.

WHAT TO PACK Dress at the Grand Canyon is informal. Even at the elegant El Tovar Hotel restaurant, ties are not required. Jeans, shorts, and casual slacks are seen everywhere. In summer, bring lightweight upper-body wear for warm sunny days and heavier clothes for chilly evenings, including light jackets and sweaters. There are myriad walking and hiking opportunities, so pack appropriate footwear. Most hikers wear hiking boots, but some prefer running shoes. If you plan on hiking more than a mile round-trip anywhere in the park, be sure to pack the proper equipment, including at least one water bottle or canteen. A light slicker or water-repellent windbreaker should be carried when clouds threaten. Suntan lotion is also advised. In colder months, wear heavy jackets, scarves, warm headgear, and mittens.

GENERAL STORES Both rims of the Grand Canyon offer convenient locations for buying groceries and other necessities. On the South Rim a convenient stop for all types of necessities is **Babbitt's General Store,** which has locations in Grand Canyon Village (tel. 602/638–2262), Tusayan (5 mi south of Grand Canyon Village on U.S. 180, tel. 602/638–2854), and Desert View (near the east entrance to the South Rim on Rte. 64, tel. 602/638–2393). All three locations are well stocked for the traveler, but the main store in Grand Canyon Village has the widest range of goods: groceries, deli food, clothing, camping and hiking equipment, and RV supplies. Hours vary from store to store but are generally 8 to 8 during summer and 9 to 6 during winter; all Babbitt's stores are open daily year-round. The nearby village of Tusayan also has several other convenience stops and service stations.

On the North Rim, groceries, traveler's supplies, and some clothing can be found at the **North Rim General Store** (2 mi north of Grand Canyon Lodge off Rte. 67, tel. 602/638–2611, ext. 370).

Automotive service on the South Rim is available year-round, daily 8 to 5, at the **Fred Harvey Garage** (tel. 602/638–2225) in Grand Canyon Village. There are other South Rim service stations in the nearby village of Tusayan. On the North Rim, the **Chevron Service Station** (tel. 602/638–2611, ext. 290) repairs cars year-round, daily 8 to 7; it is located inside the park on the access road leading to the North Rim Campground.

There is a gift shop, general store, trading post, and service station at **Desert View** (tel. 602/638–2736). The general store is open daily year-round (except holidays), 9 to 5.

ARRIVING AND DEPARTING Without a doubt, the best way to visit the Grand Canyon is by car. There is so much to see, in addition to the Grand Canyon, and distances between points are often so great, that a car is a tremendous asset. The South Rim is more accessible than the North Rim, since it is less than 100 miles from Flagstaff, while the North Rim is 235 miles from the South Rim and not terribly convenient to any major towns or cities. The South Rim is roughly 250 miles from Phoenix and 260 miles from Las Vegas. It's also within a 300-mile radius of Bryce, Canyon de Chelly, Mesa Verde, and Zion national parks. Once you arrive at Grand Canyon Village on the South Rim, you can either walk or catch a shuttle (summer only), commercial shuttle, or taxi to get around.

By Plane. Sky Harbor International Airport (tel. 602/273–3300), in Phoenix, and **McCarran International Airport** (tel. 702/261–5743), in Las Vegas, both served by all major airlines, are the most accessible airports. From Las Vegas you can catch a connecting flight to the South Rim's **Grand Canyon Airport** (tel. 602/638–2446), located about 6 miles from Grand Canyon Village. There is no commercial airline service to the North Rim of the Grand Canyon, but air travelers can take the **Trans Canyon shuttle** (tel. 602/638–2820) 235 miles from the Bright Angel Lodge in Grand Canyon Village to the North Rim. The shuttle, the only public transportation to the North Rim, leaves daily May 15 to October 21 at 1:30 PM, takes 4½ hours, and costs $60 one-way, or $100 round-trip. Reservations should be made two weeks in advance. You can also rent a car at Grand Canyon Airport from either **Budget** (tel. 800/527–0700) or **Dollar** (tel. 602/638–2625).

Most visitors who arrive at the South Rim's Grand Canyon Airport have lodging reservations in either the village of Tusayan, 6 miles south of Grand Canyon National Park, or in Grand Canyon Village on the South Rim. Transportation to either location is offered by the **Tusayan/Grand Canyon Shuttle** (tel. 602/638–2475) for all arriving flights. Fare one-way is $5 for adults, $4 for children under 12. The 24-hour, **Grand Canyon Village taxi service** (tel. 602/638–2822) will take you from the airport to Tusayan, Grand Canyon Village, and other points in the area.

By Car and RV. If you're traveling from the east or south, your best access to the Grand Canyon's South Rim is from Flagstaff or Williams, both on I–40. You have two routes out of Flagstaff: One, U.S. 180, heads 81 miles northwest to Grand Canyon Village; the other runs north on U.S. 89 and then turns west on Route 64—a total of 107 miles to Grand Canyon Village. The former route is generally considered the more scenic but can be dangerous or impassable during the winter.

If you're crossing Arizona on I–40 from the west, the most direct route to the South Rim is on Route 64 from Williams to Grand Canyon Village, a distance of 58 miles.

To reach the North Rim from Flagstaff, proceed north on U.S. 89 to Bitter Springs, then take U.S. 89A to Route 67, and head south to the North Rim, a total distance of 210 miles.

By Train. Amtrak (tel. 800/872–7245) provides daily service into Arizona from both east and west. The stop for the Grand Canyon is Flagstaff. From here bus connections can be made to Grand Canyon Village through **Nava-Hopi Tours** (tel. 602/774–5003). To continue on to the North Rim, take the **Trans Canyon shuttle** (*see above*).

The famous steam-engine service resumed several years ago between Williams (63 miles away) and the South Rim's Santa Fe Railway Station. The handsome 1923 passenger cars, which chug along behind near-turn-of-the-century engines, transport visitors year-round (limited schedule between early October and early April). Reservations and schedule information are available by contacting the **Grand Canyon Railway** (tel.

800/843–8724). The cost of this 4$^{1}/_{4}$-hour round-trip (same-day) treat is $47.50 for adults, $23.50 for teenagers, and $14.50 for children 12 and under.

By Bus. Greyhound Lines (tel. 800/231–2222) provides bus service from all over the United States to either Flagstaff or Williams. From either town, continue to the South Rim with **Nava-Hopi Tours** and on to the North Rim on the **Trans-Canyon shuttle** (*see above*, for both).

EXPLORING

Though having a car makes sightseeing a little easier, most scenic views, museums, hotels, and restaurants are within easy walking distance of both Grand Canyon Village, on the South Rim, and Grand Canyon Lodge, on the North Rim. Those sights that require more than a short walk are usually accessible by shuttle or taxi, and you can always opt to take a bus tour of either rim.

Having a car, on the other hand, allows you to take advantage of the myriad opportunities for scenic drives in and around the national park. Visitors will generally find from October through May that traveling by car or RV increases flexibility and convenience. If you're going to the South Rim during summer months an RV may be more trouble than it's worth; RV parking is extremely limited. Roads in Grand Canyon Village can also be very congested during high season, as can those on the North Rim.

THE BEST IN ONE DAY Although Grand Canyon National Park covers more than 1,900 square miles, you can see all the primary sights at either rim in one full day, but you will most likely enjoy the experience more if you plan two days. If you did not arrive the night before, a one-day visit to the North Rim is difficult, since it takes several hours just to get there. At the South Rim, you can drive all of the suggested roads (*see* Scenic Drives and Views, *below*) if you start early and move briskly, or get out of your car and take the Rim Trail (*see* Nature Trails and Short Walks, *below*). It covers a small area and short dis-

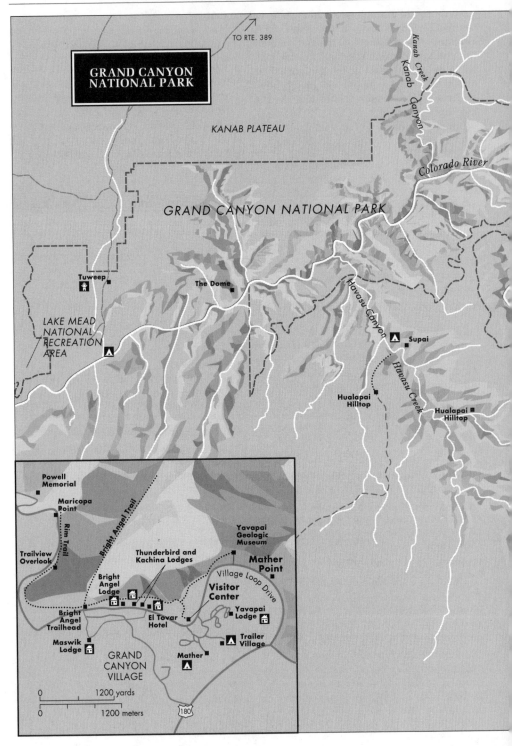

TO RTE. 389

GRAND CANYON NATIONAL PARK

KANAB PLATEAU

Kanab Creek

Kanab Canyon

Colorado River

GRAND CANYON NATIONAL PARK

Tuweep

The Dome

Havasu Canyon

LAKE MEAD NATIONAL RECREATION AREA

Supai

Havasu Creek

Hualapai Hilltop

Hualapai Hilltop

Powell Memorial

Maricopa Point

Bright Angel Trail

Rim Trail

Trailview Overlook

Thunderbird and Kachina Lodges

Bright Angel Lodge

Bright Angel Trailhead

El Tovar Hotel

Maswik Lodge

GRAND CANYON VILLAGE

Mather

Yavapai Geologic Museum

Mather Point

Village Loop Drive

Visitor Center

Yavapai Lodge

Trailer Village

0   1200 yards

0   1200 meters

180

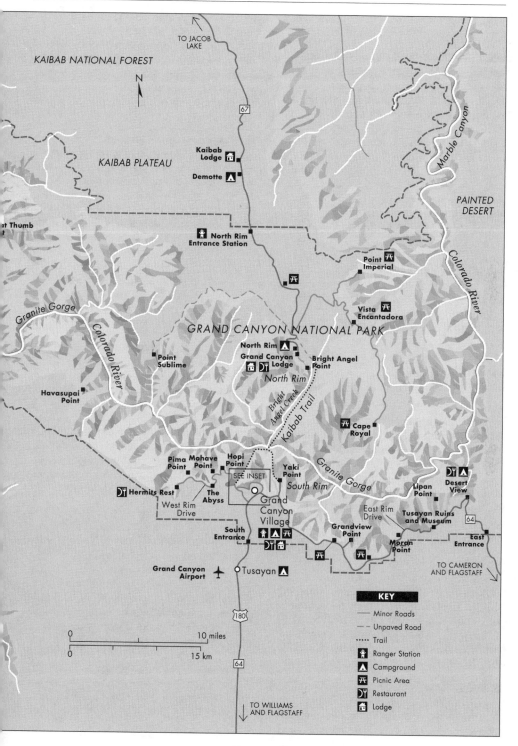

KAIBAB NATIONAL FOREST

N

KAIBAB PLATEAU

Kaibab Lodge 🏨

Demotte 🏕️

67

TO JACOB LAKE

Marble Canyon

PAINTED DESERT

🚶 North Rim Entrance Station

Point Imperial 🏕️

Colorado River

Granite Gorge

Colorado River

t Thumb

GRAND CANYON NATIONAL PARK

Vista Encantadora 🏕️

Point Sublime

North Rim 🏕️
Grand Canyon 🏨🍴 Lodge

Bright Angel Point

North Rim

Havasupai Point

Bright Angel Creek

Kaibab Trail

🏕️ Cape Royal

Pima Mohave Point
Point

Hopi Point

Yaki Point

🍴 Hermits Rest

SEE INSET

South Rim

Granite Gorge

The Abyss
West Rim Drive

Grand Canyon Village

Lipan Point

🍴🏕️ Desert View

East Rim Drive

Tusayan Ruins and Museum

South Entrance
🚶🏕️🏕️
🍴🏨

Grandview Point

Moran Point

🏕️

🏕️

64

East Entrance

Grand Canyon Airport ✈️ ⭕ Tusayan 🏕️

TO CAMERON AND FLAGSTAFF

180

64

TO WILLIAMS AND FLAGSTAFF

KEY	
——	Minor Roads
- - -	Unpaved Road
·····	Trail
🚶	Ranger Station
🏕️	Campground
🏕️	Picnic Area
🍴	Restaurant
🏨	Lodge

0 ——————— 10 miles

0 ——————— 15 km

tances, but it does allow visitors to gain a sense of what the canyon has to offer.

ORIENTATION PROGRAMS There are quite a few orientation activities offered on a daily basis by the National Park Service at both the North and South rims. These include lectures on nearly every aspect of the canyon—from geology, plants, and wildlife to history and ancient inhabitants. Guided tours and hikes are also available. The *Grand Canyon Guide,* which is free to all visitors, contains a daily schedule of such activities. Programs are presented throughout the day and into the evening. For a truly dazzling introduction to the Grand Canyon, head to the **IMAX Theatre** (tel. 602/638–2203) in nearby Tusayan. It shows *Grand Canyon, Hidden Secrets* via the world's largest motion-picture system, a huge specially designed screen that draws the viewer right into the picture. The script is highly informative, and some of the aerial shots and those of boats running rapids are absolutely dizzying. Tickets are $7 for adults and $4 for children under 17. The theater is open daily 8:30 to 8:30 with shows starting on the half-hour.

A quick tour of the South Rim Visitor Center will probably enhance your stay in the park. The center provides comprehensive orientation on many facets of the Grand Canyon, and it's also an excellent source of trip information on lodging, dining, transportation, and recreation within the park. The visitor center's numerous exhibits present an intriguing profile of the canyon's natural history and a chronicle of pre-Columbian human life in the region. Short movies and slide programs are shown, and a bookstore offers a variety of publications, videotapes, and slides. Park rangers are on duty to answer questions and aid you in planning your excursions. Contact the **South Rim Visitor Center** (tel. 602/638–7888) or the **North Rim Visitor Center** (tel. 602/638–7864) for a complete list of orientation programs.

GUIDED TOURS There are four types of tours given at Grand Canyon National Park: air, bus, mule, and raft. Raft trips demand good health, reservations six months or more in

advance, and a high fee. Mule trips to the bottom of the canyon also require that you be in excellent shape, and these too should be reserved as far in advance as possible. If you are at the South Rim during the summer months, you can put together your own tour by hopping from one free shuttle bus to another.

Those wishing to see the canyon by air can opt to take a plane or helicopter ride over it. A number of Tusayan-based companies offer these tours, including **Air Grand Canyon** (tel. 602/638–2618) and **Kenai Helicopters** (tel. 602/638–2764). Helicopters usually hold up to six passengers; planes between 5 and 20. Flights typically last 30 to 90 minutes and cost $50 to $150 per person, depending on the aircraft and the length of the trip. A 50-minute flight allows excellent coverage of both rims as well as the inner canyon. Most of these companies accept major credit cards. No flights are available from the North Rim.

The **Fred Harvey Transportation Company** (Grand Canyon Village, South Rim, tel. 602/638–2401) offers a variety of motorcoach sightseeing trips along the South Rim and as far away as Monument Valley on the Navajo Reservation. The tour guides are experienced and the commentary is thorough. Prices range from $11 for short excursions to $65 for all-day tours. Children under 16 pay half-price for trips within the park; children under 12 pay half-price for longer trips.

From either rim, there are plenty of options for mule rides into the canyon. Note, however, that you must be over 4' 7" tall and under 200 pounds. You should also check for other regulations, as visitors need to be in fairly good physical condition to ride a mule. A typical two-hour ride costs about $25. All-day trips, which include lunch, cost $70, and overnights to Phantom Ranch at the bottom of the canyon are $260 per person or $463 per couple. The overnight price includes lodging and meals. Make reservations as far in advance as possible by writing to the **Reservations Department** (Box 699, Grand Canyon, AZ 86023, tel. 602/638–2401). All major credit cards are accepted.

White-water trips down the Colorado River and through the Grand Canyon are said by most rafting aficionados to be the adventure of a lifetime. These trips can also be quite expensive, and reservations need to be made sometimes as much as one year in advance, though it is possible to book some shorter and less spectacular trips, particularly during the off-season, as few as three or four days in advance. Some trips cover more than 200 miles; those that terminate at Phantom Ranch, at the bottom of the canyon, are about 100 miles. More than 25 companies offer raft trips on the Colorado. Among them you might try: **Canyoneers, Inc.** (tel. 602/526–0924), **Diamond River Adventures** (tel. 602/645–8866), and **Expeditions Inc.** (tel. 602/774–8176). Smooth-water, one-day trips in the stretch from Glen Canyon Dam to Lees Ferry (where the canyon officially begins) are given by the **Fred Harvey Transportation Company** (*see above*) and start at $75. White-water trips the length of the canyon (14 days or more) can cost well over $1,000.

SCENIC DRIVES AND VIEWS Perhaps the highlight of any trip to the Grand Canyon is a visitor's first look into the awesome gorge. Mather Point, which is an ideal spot for this moving experience, is about 24 miles from the east entrance and 4 miles from the south entrance. At the junction of Route 64 and U.S. 180, drive about 3/4 mile toward Grand Canyon Village on **Village Loop Drive**, and park in the lot. From this lookout, you'll have an extraordinary view of the Inner Gorge and numerous buttes that rise out of the chasm.

The **East Rim Drive** is 25 miles one-way and takes visitors to several of the Grand Canyon's most spectacular turnouts. There are four well-marked picnic areas along the route, and rest rooms are available at Tusayan Museum and Desert View. From the South Rim Visitor Center, drive a couple of miles east on East Rim Drive, turning left on a short, well-marked road leading to Yaki Point. Here, you'll be treated to an impressive view of Wotan's Throne, a massive flat-top butte about 6 miles to the northeast. This is also the point where the popular but challenging South Kaibab Trail starts its canyon descent

(*see* Longer Hikes, *below*). Next, travel about 7 miles east to Grandview Point, one of the higher spots along this drive, which reveals a group of dominant buttes, including Krishna Shrine and Vishnu Temple, as well as a short stretch of the Colorado River below. Here you'll find large stands of piñon and ponderosa pine, juniper, and Gambel oak. Other stops along the route include Moran Point; Tusayan Ruin and Museum, where you can see evidence of pre-Columbian inhabitants and learn about the Anasazi people who inhabited the region roughly 800 years ago; and Lipan Point. Desert View and Watchtower, the final stops on the tour, are at the highest elevation on the South Rim (7,500 feet). The view is enhanced by a climb to the top of the stone-and-mortar Watchtower, which replicates early Native American architecture. From here you can see the muted pastels of the Painted Desert to the east, the 1,000-foot Vermilion Cliffs to the north, and an impressive stretch of the Colorado River in the canyon gorge below. It costs 25¢ to climb the Watchtower. If you're without a car, the **Fred Harvey Transportation Company** (*see* Guided Tours, *above*) gives a daily, four-hour bus tour of the area. The price is $17 for adults and $8.50 for children under 16.

You cannot use your own car for the 8-mile **West Rim Drive** during the summer—the roads are closed to private automobiles. However, it's still worth making this rewarding trip via the park's free shuttle service. If you are traveling between late September and Memorial Day and have a car, start a little more than a mile west of the South Rim Visitor Center. Then head west on West Rim Drive, where you'll encounter 10 scenic turnouts. First you'll come to Trailview Overlook, from which you can see the San Francisco Peaks, Red Butte, and Bill Williams Mountain all to the southeast. There's also a good canyon view of where Bright Angel Trail (*see* Longer Hikes, *below*) loops its way down to the Inner Gorge. Subsequent stops along this road are: The Powell Memorial, a large granite monument dedicated to the early canyon explorer John Wesley Powell; Hopi Point, where you can see down to the Colorado River at one of its widest points (350 feet); Mojave Point,

GRAND CANYON NATIONAL PARK

which reveals three sets of white-water rapids in the river below; The Abyss, where there is a sheer canyon drop of 3,000 feet to the Tonto Platform; and Pima Point, which offers a clear view of the Tonto Trail as it winds its way for more than 70 miles through the canyon. The last stop on this tour is Hermits Rest, named for a reclusive 19th-century prospector, Louis Boucher, who lived in the canyon. The stone building at this vista point sells refreshments and is the site of the only rest rooms on the West Rim.

The **South Rim–North Rim Drive** is one very long journey: 235 miles to be exact. From Grand Canyon Village, take Route 64 east out of the park for 55 miles, turn left onto U.S. 89, and head north another mile to the old Cameron Trading Post (tel. 602/679–2231). Founded in 1916, this historic establishment has a truly extensive stock of authentic Native American jewelry, rugs, baskets, and pottery. There's also a restaurant and motel. After filling your trunk with curios, continue north on U.S. 89. On the right, the road is bordered by the Painted Desert, which consists of thousands of square miles of mesas and windswept plains painted by nature in muted pastel colors. Forty miles north of the trading post, drive beside the Echo Cliffs, which rise to more than 1,000 feet in many places. At Bitter Springs, bear left onto U.S. 89A. Driving west 14 miles, cross over the canyon on the still-sturdy, 1929 bridge that hangs 500 feet over the Colorado River. There is a parking area on the north side of the bridge, a favorite spot for photographers. As you proceed west a few miles through the sparsely populated land of the Arizona Strip, you will soon encounter three small way stations—Marble Canyon, Vermilion Cliffs, and Cliff Dwellers—that have gas, food, and motel rooms. Here you'll also be treated to views of the Vermilion Cliffs. These rock formations, which are among the most spectacular in the world, rise more than 1,000 feet from the plateau floor. As you continue west, 18 miles from Marble Canyon, you will pass the San Bartolome Historic Site. Pull into the parking area and read the plaques that tell the tale of the Escalante and Dominguez expedition—one of the earliest undertaken by white men

in this harsh and forbidding wilderness—which traversed the river near this point in 1776. At Jacob Lake, 55 miles past Marble Canyon, turn left and drive south on Route 67; the remaining 45 miles to the North Rim of the Grand Canyon lie ahead. Along this road, you'll drive over the summit of the 9,000-foot Kaibab Plateau.

On the North Rim, one final scenic drive to a pair of the area's best-loved canyon vistas awaits you. Starting at Grand Canyon Lodge, drive north on the **Cape Royal Road** for a couple miles, and bear left at the fork. Continue north 11 miles to Point Imperial—at 8,803 feet, it's the highest vista on either rim. Point Imperial affords visitors an excellent view of the canyon, not to mention thousands of square miles of the surrounding countryside in all directions. After stopping here, backtrack the 11 miles to the fork and head southeast on the road to Cape Royal: It's about a 15-mile drive on paved road. This is the site of Angel's Window, a giant, erosion-formed hole through which you can see South Rim across the canyon; it's just beyond the trailhead for Cliff Springs Trail (*see* Nature Trails and Short Walks, *below*). The drive back to Grand Canyon Lodge is 23 miles.

HISTORIC BUILDINGS AND SITES Nearly everyone who comes to the South Rim visits the lobby and public areas of the magnificent **El Tovar Hotel** (*see* Lodging, *below*). Built in 1904 by the Fred Harvey Company, this historic hotel is named in honor of the Spanish explorer Pedro de Tovar. Constructed to resemble a European hunting lodge, it was designed by architect Charles Whittlesey and incorporates native stone and Oregon pine. Feel free to wander in and browse the rustic lobby, warm your hands in front of the huge fireplace, and people-watch. The hotel is located on Village Loop Drive, a short walk from the visitor center, in the heart of the South Rim's historic district. You'll find a number of buildings in this area, most of which are open to the public, that date back to the Grand Canyon's early days. All of these are within short walking distance of each other. Sights include the **Kolb Studio**, built in 1904, where the Kolb brothers showed films

178

and held dances throughout the early half of the century; the 1914 **Lookout Studio** (a competitor of the Kolb brothers' establishment), which was built with rough-cut limestone and now houses a gift shop, museum, and lookout loft; the **Buckey O'Neill Cabin,** which is the oldest surviving structure on the rim; **Hopi House**, built in 1905 as an outlet for Native American crafts and now one of the best-stocked gift shops in the area; the **Santa Fe Railway Station,** which received train passengers to the park for nearly 70 years until ending service in 1968 (it resumed service in 1989); and the **First National Park Service Administration Building,** erected in 1921 and indicative of the park service's attempt to design buildings that fit in with their natural environments. Finally, a restful place to finish your tour of the district is the **Bright Angel Lodge** (*see* Dining *and* Lodging, *below*), another of the canyon's historic hotels. The hotel has a dining room and a soda fountain and is a good spot to relax after your invigorating jaunt.

Rugged and spacious, created of massive stone walls and timber ceilings, the **Grand Canyon Lodge** sits at the very edge of the North Rim. Built by a subsidiary of the Union Pacific Railroad and opened in 1936, the complex originally consisted of a main building and 125 cabins scattered in the deep forest. Its architect, Gilbert Stanley Underwood, also designed the national-park hotels in Yosemite Valley and Bryce Canyon. The lodge is listed in the National Register of Historic Places.

NATURE TRAILS AND SHORT WALKS In Grand Canyon National Park the opportunities to walk and explore on foot are many. The most popular walking path at the South Rim is the 10-mile one-way **Rim Trail,** which runs along the edge of the canyon from Yavapai Museum in Grand Canyon Village west to Hermits Rest. This walk, which is paved to Maricopa Point, allows visits to several of the South Rim's historic landmarks (*see* Historic Buildings and Sites, *above*). Start at the **Yavapai Museum** (on the east side of Grand Canyon Village, tel. 602/638–7888), where exhibits trace the long geological history of the can-

yon, and polarized picture windows provide excellent views into the depths of the gorge. Purchase natural-history and geology booklets (25¢ apiece for your self-guided tour along the rim) at the museum. From here, take the paved, level Rim Trail west for easy access to many views of the canyon. You'll pass Bright Angel Trailhead (*see* Longer Hikes, *below*), a well-maintained avenue to the bottom of the canyon for mules and foot traffic. Beyond this you'll walk roughly a mile paralleling West Rim Drive (*see* Scenic Drives and Views, *above*) to reach Maricopa Point. You can continue beyond this point to Hermits Rest, but be warned that this stretch of the Rim Trail is unpaved and runs close to the edge in places. Those uncomfortable with heights should stop at Maricopa Point.

Popular walks at the North Rim are the 1½-mile **Transept Trail**, which starts near the Grand Canyon Lodge, and **Cliff Springs Trail** near Cape Royal. This easy 1-mile round-trip walk leads you through a ravine to another impressive view of the canyon.

LONGER HIKES The treks into the canyon are rewarding for their views, but be prepared for their considerable difficulty. Bright Angel, Hermit, and South Kaibab trails are the most popular from the South Rim; North Kaibab Trail is the best from the North Rim. When hiking down the South Kaibab Trail, be sure to move to the inside when mule trains pass.

Caution: A hike down into the Grand Canyon may be relatively easy, but, beware: Coming back up can be painfully exhausting. For every hour you hike downhill, allow two hours for the uphill return. Wear hiking or running shoes, and dress appropriately for the season (*see* What to Pack, *above*). Always carry water, and consult park rangers before you set off. Summer temperatures in the canyon frequently exceed 100°F, and hikers run the risk of heat exhaustion. Journeys to the bottom of the canyon are recommended only for people in excellent health and with backcountry hiking experience. The park service specifically advises against attempting to hike from the rim to the river and back in one day.

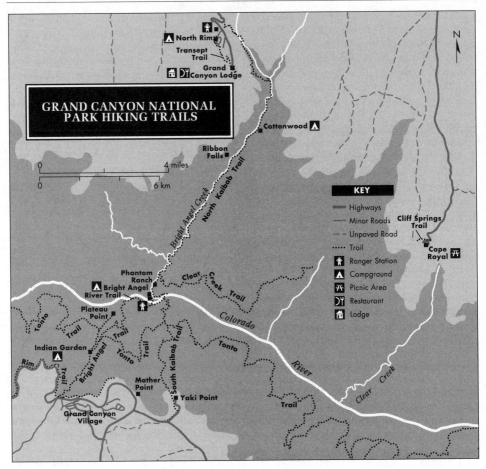

From a trailhead on the South Rim near Grand Canyon Village, **Bright Angel Trail** descends 4,460 feet to the Colorado River and is 6 miles one-way. Phantom Ranch awaits hikers at the bottom of the canyon. This historic route was used by Native Americans for centuries before the arrival of Europeans. Drinking water is available 1¹/₂ miles into the canyon. There you will find tables, water, and shade trees.

The 6-mile round-trip **Hermit Trail,** which you begin on the South Rim beyond Hermits Rest, drops 4,300 feet to Dripping Springs and takes almost a full day. Hermit Creek, which flows year-round, is partially responsible for the lush growth and abundant bird- and animal-life in the campsite area. You're quite likely to see desert bighorn sheep on this strenuous hike, which should be attempted by serious hikers only.

The **South Kaibab Trail** starts at Yaki Point, 4 miles east of Grand Canyon Village. This is a steep trail, so many hikers return via the less-demanding Bright Angel Trail. During this 6¹/₄-mile trek to the Colorado River, you're likely to encounter mule trains and riders. At the river, the trail crosses a suspension bridge and runs on to Phantom Ranch.

On the North Rim, the trailhead to the **North Kaibab Trail** is about 2 miles north of the Grand Canyon Lodge and is open only from May through October. This is a long, steep hike that drops 5,840 feet over a distance of 14¹/₄ miles and is recommended for strong, experienced hikers only. After about 7 miles, you might stop at the Cottonwood Campground, which is equipped with drinking water, rest rooms, shade trees, and a ranger. Additional campground and lodging facilities are located at Phantom Ranch (*see* Lodging, *below*), at the bottom of the canyon.

OTHER ACTIVITIES Back-Road Driving. Automobiles and RVs are permitted to drive on primary paved roads, secondary dirt roads, and fire roads within Grand Canyon National Park. Driving off-road is strictly prohibited and violators will be cited and fined.

Biking. Cyclists will find miles of scenic roads to ride on, including paved roads for all types of bicycles and dirt roads for mountain bikes. However, most dirt roads open to mountain bikers are in the national forest lands that border the park to the north and south. Roads are generally level at the South Rim and gently rolling with some steeper hills on the North Rim. Be aware that bicycles are not permitted on any of the walking trails in the national park. Bring your own bike; there are no rentals in or near the Grand Canyon.

Fishing. The high plateau country of northwestern Arizona is a land of limited rain and quick runoffs. Fishing opportunities are few. However, Lake Powell, on U.S. 89, 140 miles north of the South Rim, is known for its largemouth, smallmouth, and striped bass; northern and walleye pike; catfish; and crappie. The Colorado River, below Lake Powell's Glen Canyon Dam and as far south as Lees Ferry, yields trophy-size trout. Before wetting your line, be sure to obtain an Arizona fishing permit, available at marinas and sporting-goods stores in the vicinity of Page and at Marble Canyon Lodge (*see* Lodging, *below*).

Flight-Seeing. There's nothing quite like the view of the canyon from the air. Helicopter and small-plane rides are available (*see* Guided Tours, *above*).

Horseback and Mule Riding. On the South Rim, gentle horses can be rented from **Apache Stables** (tel. 602/638–2891) at Moqui Lodge in Tusayan. Rentals cost about $20 per hour,

$34 for two hours. The stable is open daily from April through November. At the North Rim, short mule rides are offered by the **Grand Canyon Lodge** (tel. 602/638–2292). These trips are extremely popular so reserve far in advance. A trusty mule rents for about $10 per hour. Rides are available daily May through October. Full-day and overnight (South Rim only) mule rides are also available at the park (*see* Guided Tours, *above*).

Rafting. You can bring your own rafts to the canyon, but the waiting list for private permits is six to eight years long. White- and smooth-water guided trips through the canyon are offered (*see* Guided Tours, *above*).

Ski Touring. The North Rim of the canyon is part of the Kaibab Plateau, which reaches up to 9,200 feet in elevation. Snow is plentiful here, and cross-country skiing is a great way to get around. If you want to overnight in the area, try the backcountry **Kaibab Lodge** (Box 2997, Flagstaff, AZ 86003, tel. 602/526–0924 or 800/525–0924, fax 602/527–9398), which is accessible only by enclosed tracked Snowvan. It is home to the North Rim Nordic Center, which has 54 kilometers of groomed trails, as well as 20 kilometers of forested backcountry trails, which are marked but ungroomed. Guided tours are available.

CHILDREN'S PROGRAMS The Grand Canyon is full of family-oriented activities and programs, and children can take part in nearly everything available to their parents. On the South Rim, kids can try horseback riding, and, on the North Rim, mules are similarly appropriate (*see* Other Activities, *above*). On both rims, the National Park Service offers an extensive menu of free daily programs, which change seasonally and are listed in *The Guide* (*see* Publications, *above*). Typical programs and activities are nature walks, geology talks, and natural-history discussions. Also, children as well as adults will enjoy the film *Grand Canyon, Hidden Secrets*, shown outside the park at the IMAX Theater in Tusayan (*see* Orientation Programs, *above*).

EVENING ACTIVITIES Entertainment and nightlife in this part of the world often consists of watching a full moon hover above the soaring buttes of the Grand Canyon, roasting marshmallows over a crackling fire, and crawling into your sleeping bag beside a lonely canyon trail. However, there are a few cocktail lounges in Grand Canyon hotels and motels. The **El Tovar Hotel** has a piano bar, **Bright Angel Restaurant** and **the Moqui Lounge** both have occasional live entertainment, **Maswik Lodge** is home of the region's sports bar, and there is dancing at the **Yavapai Lodge. Grand Canyon Lodge** on the North Rim also has a lounge. The phone number for each of these lounges is 602/638–2401.

Additionally, the National Park Service at both rims presents informative evening programs on subjects related to the Grand Canyon. For a complete daily schedule of these activities, consult a copy of the free newspaper, *The Guide.*

DINING

Throughout Grand Canyon country, restaurants cater to tourists on the move. Therefore, most places offer standard American fare, prepared quickly and at a reasonable price. If you want a more elaborate dining experience try the El Tovar Hotel dining room, but be prepared to pay as much as $30 for a complete dinner. If you are primarily seeking sustenance at a good price, eat at the cafeterias. Dress is always casual.

NORTH RIM Grand Canyon Lodge Dining Room. The historic lodge, built of native stone and logs, houses a huge, high-ceiling dining room that serves well-prepared entrées, including steak, shrimp tempura, rainbow trout, and vegetable lasagna in marinara sauce. *Grand Canyon Lodge, Bright Angel Point, tel. 801/586–7686 or 602/638–2611. Reservations advised. AE, D, DC, MC, V. Closed winter. Moderate.*

Grand Canyon Lodge Cafeteria. Dining choices are very limited on the North Rim, so this is your best bet for a meal tailored to a budget. There are plenty of good selections. *Grand Canyon Lodge, Bright Angel Point, tel. 801/586–7686 or 602/638–2611. Reserva-*

tions not accepted. AE, D, DC, MC, V. Closed winter. Inexpensive.

NEAR NORTH RIM Vermilion Cliffs Restaurant. If you make the long drive up U.S. 89 to the North Rim, you'll need at least one food stop, and this may be the best along the route. It has rock walls, a rustic interior, and surprisingly good American fare. *Lees Ferry Lodge, U.S. 89A near Marble Canyon Bridge, tel. 602/355–2231. Reservations not accepted. MC, V. Closed winter. Inexpensive.*

SOUTH RIM El Tovar Dining Room. This world-class restaurant in the historic old El Tovar Hotel is known for its Continental cuisine (including veal Française with lemon butter) and such American dishes as prime rib and fresh fish. Breakfast and lunch are great, too. *El Tovar Hotel, Grand Canyon Village, tel. 602/638–2401. Reservations advised. AE, D, DC, MC, V. Expensive.*

Bright Angel Restaurant. This is a memorable but informal place for breakfast, lunch, or dinner, serving good breast of chicken almondine, barbecued ribs, and prime rib. *Grand Canyon Village, tel. 602/638–2401. Reservations advised. AE, D, DC, MC, V. Moderate.*

Fred Harvey Cafeterias. There are three cafeterias at the South Rim, all offering wide selections and all run by the Fred Harvey Company. Two are in Grand Canyon Village at **Maswik Lodge** and **Yavapai Lodge** (tel. 602/638–2401 for both); the third is at **Desert View Trading Post** (tel. 602/638–2360), 23 miles east of Grand Canyon Village on Rte. 64. *AE, D, DC, MC, V. Yavapai Lodge cafeteria closed winter. Inexpensive.*

NEAR SOUTH RIM The Steak House. This is the place for a warm Western atmosphere, right down to checkered tablecloths and steaks and chicken prepared over an open wood grill. *Tusayan, 6 mi south of the park entrance on U.S. 180, tel. 602/638–2780. Reservations not accepted. AE, MC, V. Closed winter. Inexpensive.*

PICNIC SPOTS There are a number of designated picnic areas within the national park at both rims. The free newspaper *The Guide* points out their locations. On the South Rim, try the picnic area near **Grandview Point** on the East Rim Drive. At the North Rim, a truly scenic spot is near the parking area at **Cape Royal,** where pit toilets are also provided.

LODGING

For summer lodging reservations, call as far in advance as possible. Often, Grand Canyon hotels and motels are booked for the summer season six months to a year in advance. If you can't get rooms near the canyon, you might find vacancies in Flagstaff or Williams or on the Navajo Reservation at the Cameron Trading Post (tel. 602/679–2231) on U.S. 89. Also consider Tuba City Motel (tel. 602/283–4545) on U.S. 160. Prices at motels and hotels inside the national park generally remain the same year-round. Motels outside the park frequently lower prices about 10% during the colder months.

NORTH RIM **Grand Canyon Lodge.** Located a few yards from the canyon rim, the main building has massive limestone walls and timber ceilings. There are also rustic cabins and traditional motel units scattered among the pines. *Bright Angel Point, tel. 801/586–7686. 201 rooms. Facilities: restaurant, cafeteria, lounge, gift shop. AE, D, DC, MC, V. Moderate.*

NEAR NORTH RIM If you are unable to obtain rooms at the North Rim, there are plenty of clean alternatives on the North Rim approach on U.S. 89A. These are no-frills, roadside motels that range from Native American–style rock-and-mortar units to frame cabins. **Marble Canyon Lodge** (tel. 602/355–2225), **Lees Ferry Lodge** (tel. 602/355–2231), and **Cliff Dwellers Lodge** (tel. 602/355–2228) are all 70 to 80 miles from the North Rim. All accept MC and V. **Jacob Lake Inn** (tel. 602/643–7232; AE, MC, V) is 45 miles from the North Rim. All four motels are Inexpensive to Moderate.

SOUTH RIM **El Tovar Hotel.** Built in 1904 of native stone and heavy pine logs, the El Tovar reflects the style of old European hunting lodges and is regarded as one of the finest national park hotels. *Grand Canyon Village, tel. 602/638–2401. 65 rooms and suites. Facilities: restaurant, lounge, gift shop. AE, D, DC, MC, V. Expensive.*

Bright Angel Lodge. This rustic Fred Harvey hostelry, built in 1935, sits within a few yards of the canyon rim. It has rooms in the main lodge and in quaint cabins. *Grand Canyon Village, tel. 602/638–2401. 90 rooms. Facilities: restaurant, lounge, fountain, gift shop. AE, D, DC, MC, V. Moderate–Expensive.*

Fred Harvey Motels. In addition to the Bright Angel Lodge and El Tovar Hotel, the Fred Harvey Company operates five other clean, comfortable, and nicely appointed lodges at the South Rim: **Maswik Lodge, Yavapai Lodge, Moqui Lodge, Kachina Lodge,** and **Thunderbird Lodge.** *In or near Grand Canyon Village, tel. 602/638–2401. AE, D, DC, MC, V. Moderate–Expensive.*

Phantom Ranch. Located at the bottom of the Grand Canyon and accessible only to hikers and mule riders, the ranch offers a dormitory for hikers with backcountry permits; cabins are exclusively for mule riders (*see* Guided Tours, *above*). *Tel. 602/638–2401. AE, D, DC, MC, V. Dormitory rate $21 per person.*

NEAR SOUTH RIM **Best Western Grand Canyon Squire.** Rooms are standard American-roadside design and decor, lacking some of the charm of the older lodges in Grand Canyon Village but with a nice list of amenities. *6 mi south of rim on U.S. 180, Tusayan, tel. 602/638–2681 or 800/528–1234. 150 units. Facilities: restaurant, coffee shop, heated pool, tennis courts, indoor whirlpool. AE, D, DC, MC, V. Moderate–Expensive.*

Quality Inn. Here you'll find typical chain-motel architecture and decor, but it's clean and comfortable. *6 mi south of rim on U.S. 180, Tusayan, tel. 602/638–2673. 185 units. Facilities: restaurant, coffee shop, gift shop, heated pool. AE, D, DC, MC, V. Inexpensive–Moderate.*

CAMPING

All campgrounds in and around the park are located in gorgeous country, most of it pine forest. If you can't get a site in the park, you can camp in the surrounding Kaibab National Forest.

Three backcountry campgrounds in the park—**Indian Garden** (15 sites), **Bright Angel** (33 sites), and **Cottonwood** (12 sites)—are free and open year-round, but only Bright Angel has flush toilets. All have drinking water. Fires are forbidden.

NORTH RIM **North Rim Campground.** Situated in a grove of pines near a general store, the 82 RV and tent sites are convenient to flush toilets, fire grates, showers, drinking water, a disposal station, and a ranger station but have no hookups. *3 mi north of rim. Reservations through Mistix, tel. 800/365–2267. Closed mid-Oct.–Apr. Cost: $10 per day.*

NEAR NORTH RIM **Demotte Campground.** Operated by the U.S. Forest Service, this attractive site is surrounded by tall pines. The 22 RV and tent sites have use of pit toilets, picnic tables, fire grates, and drinking water, but there are no hookups. *20 mi north of rim on Rte. 67, tel. 602/643–7395. No reservations. Closed Nov.–Apr. Cost: $8 per day.*

Jacob Lake Campground. This forest-service campground offers 53 tent and RV sites in the secluded pine country of the Kaibab Plateau. It has pit toilets, fire grates, drinking water, and a visitor-information station but no hookups. Demotte and Jacob Lake are run by the Southwest Natural and Cultural Heritage Association, which sponsors evening programs at both campgrounds. *Junction U.S. 89A and Rte. 67, about 45 mi north of rim, tel. 602/643–7395. No reservations. Closed Nov.–Apr. Cost: $10 per day.*

Jacob Lake RV Park. In a wooded area near a store, gas station, and restaurant, this is the closest campground to the North Rim with full hookups. Eighty RV sites and 60 tent sites have pit toilets, fire grates, drinking water, and a disposal station. *Junction U.S. 89A and Rte. 67, about 45 mi north of rim, tel. 602/643–7804 or 801/628–8851 in winter. Reservations advised. Open most of year, depending on weather. Cost: $18 for full hookup, $10 for no hookup or for tent site.*

SOUTH RIM **Desert View Campground.** A grocery store, service station, and trading post make Desert View extremely popular—and then there's the spectacular view of the canyon from nearby Watchtower Lookout. There are 50 tent and RV sites with flush toilets, drinking water, fire grates, and a ranger station, but there are no hookups. *On Rte. 64, 23 mi east of Grand Canyon Village, tel. 602/638–7888. No reservations. Closed Nov.–Apr. Cost: $10 per day.*

Mather Campground. In the heart of Grand Canyon Village, this campground's 319 tent and RV sites are popular and heavily booked in summer. Make reservations as early as the campground will accept them. Mather is equipped with flush toilets, showers, drinking water, fire grates, a disposal station, and a ranger station but has no hookups. *Near South Rim Visitor Center, tel. 602/638–7888. Reservations through Mistix, tel. 800/365–2267. Open all year. Cost: $10 per day.*

Trailer Village. Near the visitor center, Mather Campground, and a five-minute walk from the general store, this RV area has 78 50-foot sites with full hookups. Every site has fire grates, and the facility has potable water, a dump station, flush toilets, and phones. There are hot showers at Mather. *Near South Rim Visitor Center. Reservations advised (Grand Canyon South Rim Reservations, tel. 602/638–2401). Cost: $17 per day.*

NEAR SOUTH RIM **Grand Canyon Camper Village.** This commercially operated campground is generally rated among the best in the South Rim area. You'll find 200 RV sites (with full hookups) and 60 tent sites, flush toilets, showers, drinking water, fire grates, and a disposal station. *1 mi south of park entrance on U.S. 180, tel. 602/638–2887. Reservations advised. Open all year. Cost: $20 for full hookup, $18 for water and electricity, $13 for tent site.*

GRAND CANYON CAMPGROUNDS

	NORTH RIM	NEAR NORTH RIM			SOUTH RIM			NEAR SOUTH RIM	INNER CANYON			
	North Rim	Demotte (National Forest)	Jacob Lake (National Forest)	Jacob Lake RV Park	Desert View	Mather	Trailer Village	Grand Canyon Camper Village	Indian Garden	Bright Angel	Cottonwood
Total number of sites	82	22	53	140	50	319	78	260	15	33	12
Sites suitable for RVs	82	22	53	80	50	319	78	200	0	0	0
Number of hookups	0	0	0	80	0	0	78	200	0	0	0
Drive to sites	•	•	•	•	•	•	•	•			
Hike to sites									•	•	•
Flush toilets	•				•	•	•	•		•	
Pit/chemical toilets		•	•	•					•		•
Drinking water	•	•	•	•	•	•	•	•	•	•	•
Showers	•					•		•			
Fire grates	•	•	•	•	•	•	•	•			
Swimming											
Boat access											
Playground											
Disposal station	•			•		•	•	•			
Ranger station	•				•	•					
Public telephone	•	•	•	•	•	•	•	•			
Reservation possible	•			•		•	•	•	•	•	•
Daily fee per site	$10	$8	$10	$10–$18	$10	$10	$17	$13–$20	free	free	free
Dates open	May–mid-Oct.	May–Nov.	May–Nov.	year-round	May–mid-Nov.	year-round	year-round	year-round	year-round	year-round	year-round

Grand Teton National Park

Wyoming

By Andrew Giarelli
Updated by Candy Moulton

Many travelers treat Grand Teton National Park simply as a strip of Rocky Mountain scenery crossed on the way to Yellowstone National Park's roadside wonders. Its intimidating profile makes Grand Teton seem less accessible than its neighbor to the north: The jagged vertical peaks of the Teton Range rise precipitously, as high as 7,000 feet above the Snake River plain (or 13,000 feet above sea level), north of Jackson, Wyoming. You can't just drive into those steep peaks the way you can cruise over Yellowstone's mountain passes.

But those who venture even a few hundred yards off the Jackson Hole Highway, which crosses the east side of the park's 310,000 rugged acres, are quickly rewarded. Mountain glaciers creep imperceptibly down 12,605-foot Mt. Moran, multicolored wildflowers coat the Jackson Hole valley floor, and Wyoming's great abundance of wildlife scampers about the meadows and mountains.

On a drive along Teton Park Road you get close-ups of magnificent peaks, and, as you pull off Jenny Lake Road at Cathedral Group Turnout, Mts. Grand, Owen, and Teewinot dominate the massif that rises abruptly from the valley floor. Short trails lead through sagebrush near the Snake River and through willow flats near Jackson Lake, and concession-operated boats skim the waters of Jackson and Jenny lakes, depositing you on the wild western shore of the latter. There are also guided float trips down a calm stretch of the tortuous Snake River, and if you take to the backcountry—with 200 miles of trails, from the novice's Cascade Canyon to the expert's Teton Crest—you will discover the majesty of what the Gros Ventre and Shoshoni tribes called Teewinot (Many Pinnacles).

French trappers, who entered the region about 1820, named the range Les Trois Tetons (The Three Breasts). Today, as you drive through the park, the three most prominent peaks—Grand, Owen, and Teewinot—come into view around Moose Junction, on the west side of the road. Beneath these 12,000- to 13,700-foot peaks stretches a 40-mile-long valley, which the American trappers who arrived after the French dubbed Jackson's Hole (after David E. Jackson, a trapper who reportedly spent the winter of 1829 along Jackson Lake). And through this valley the Snake River winds in braided channels for more than 40 miles. Between the Snake and the Tetons lies a string of sparkling lakes: Phelps, Taggart, Jenny, Leigh, and Jackson, to name only a few.

Jackson Hole was first settled during the 1880s, and it quickly became a splendid hunting ground, with locals leading wealthy outsiders into the Tetons. But early conservationists recognized the environmental significance of the area and first proposed that it be added to Yellowstone National Park. As early as 1897, environmentalists successfully lobbied Congress and President Grover Cleveland to establish the Teton Forest Reserve, which covered much of the valley floor. The reserve became Teton National Forest in 1908. In 1929 Congress set aside 96,000 acres—covering the main part of the Teton Range itself and most glacial lakes at the base of the mountains—as Grand Teton National Park.

Meanwhile, John D. Rockefeller, Jr., started buying land in Jackson Hole, intending to preserve the wild and scenic character of the mountains, as well as their valley foreground. In 1943 President Franklin D. Roosevelt established Jackson Hole National Monument, whose 221,000 acres included some of the national forest and federal land in Jackson Hole. The Rockefellers donated nearly 33,000 acres to the monument in 1949, and in 1950 Congress merged the park and the monument into today's Grand Teton National Park.

The opportunities at Grand Teton for rigorous hiking, climbing, and rafting are many, but you can forego an exhilarating day of rappelling for a gentle meander around Jenny Lake or for an evening drink looking out over the Tetons from the veranda of the Jackson Lake Lodge. And if that's just too much relaxation, you can always spend the night whooping it up in Jackson Hole at the Million Dollar Cowboy Bar.

ESSENTIAL INFORMATION

VISITOR INFORMATION For detailed information about the park, write to the Superintendent, **Grand Teton National Park,** Drawer 170, Moose, WY 83012; or call 307/739–3300. **Colter Bay Visitor Center** (tel. 307/739–3591) has information on activities at Jackson Lake. The park's largest lodging, dining, and tour concessionaire is **Grand Teton Lodge Company** (Box 240, Moran, WY 83013, tel. 307/543–2811, 307/733–2811, or 800/628–9988).

For information on Jackson and its environs contact **Jackson Hole Chamber of Commerce** (Box E, Jackson, WY 83001, tel. 307/733–3316), **Jackson Hole Visitors Council** (Box 982, Dept. 41, Jackson Hole, WY 83001, tel. 307/733–7606 or 800/782–0011, fax 307/733–5585), or **Wyoming Division of Tourism** (I–25 at College Dr., Cheyenne, WY 82002, tel. 307/777–7777 or 800/225–5996, fax 307/777–6904).

Backcountry permits, which must be obtained in person at the Moose or Colter Bay visitor centers or the Jenny Lake Ranger Station, are free and required for all overnight stays outside designated campgrounds. Unlike Yellowstone, Grand Teton allows off-trail hiking; register at the Jenny Lake Ranger Station. Pets, which must be leashed at all times, are not permitted on trails. Campfires are prohibited in the backcountry except at designated lakeshore campsites.

FEES Park entrance fees are $10 per vehicle and $4 per individual on foot, bicycle, or motorcycle and are payable at the Moose and Moran entrances. Passes are good for seven days in both Grand Teton and Yellowstone parks. Boat permits, available at Moose visitor center year-round and at Colter Bay, Signal Mountain, and Buffalo ranger stations during summer, cost $10 for motorized craft and $5 for nonmotorized craft.

PUBLICATIONS The *Grand Teton Official Map and Guide* and the seasonal park newspaper, *Teewinot,* are distributed free at park entrances. **Trails Illustrated** (Box 3610, Evergreen, CO 80439, tel. 800/962–1643) sells an excellent waterproof, tear-proof topographic map of the park. That map and all 13 park USGS quadrangle topographical maps are available from the **Grand Teton Natural History Association** (Box 170, Moose, WY 83012, tel. 307/739–3606). This nonprofit organization, which operates bookstores at both park visitor centers, also has a wide range of adult and children's books and videos on the park and its environs. Among the best are: *Guide to Exploring Grand Teton National Park,* by park naturalists Linda Olson and Tim Bywater, which contains natural history, scenic drives, and tips for exploring; *Creation of the Teton Landscape,* by J.D. Love and J.C. Reed, a classic short geologic history with color illustrations and maps; *Birds of Grand Teton and the Surrounding Area,* by Bert Raynes; *Plants of Yellowstone and Grand Teton,* by Dr. J. Richard Shaw, with black-and-white illustrations; *Wildlife of Yellowstone and Grand Teton,* by F. Douglas and Suvi Scott; and *Origins: Place Names of Grand Teton,* by Cynthia Nielsen and Elizabeth Weid Hayden.

GEOLOGY AND TERRAIN As recently as 9 million years ago, the dramatic sawtooth Teton skyline lay under a flat layer of sandstone that today lies more than 4½ miles beneath the earth's surface. You can still see sections of this sandstone on top of Mt. Moran.

To get an idea of why the valley of Jackson Hole sits beside the immense Teton Range without even the slightest foothill between them, picture the preformed mountains as a flat, rectangular block of granite and gneiss. Tension in the earth's crust caused several vertical breaks in the overlying layer of sandstone. The Teton Fault, the most intense of these breaks, appeared as a vertical fissure broken top to bottom through the block's midsection. The land east of the fault sank, while the block to the west of the fault rose sharply above the landscape.

Several conditions account for the jagged, unpredictable appearance of today's Teton Range. Essentially, the park is set on two blocks of stone: The range, thrust upward and west of the fault, is the higher block, while Jackson Hole dropped downward to the east. During three ice ages that followed the great rift, and the warming spells that followed the ice ages, glaciers (some as thick as 3,000 feet) cut uneven gorges out of the uplifted fault block creating vast canyons, such as Cascade and Leigh. These same glaciers carried layer upon layer of sedimentary rock east of the fault. As the glaciers melted, the numerous lakes that now occupy Jackson Hole formed, as a result of natural damming, in the shadow of the mountains.

Glaciers are responsible for the Teton Range's sheer walls, rugged ridges, and sharp peaks, and a dozen re-established glaciers now slowly flow from the sharp, angular amphitheaters (also called cirques) cut out of the mountainsides by their ice-age ancestors. Schoolroom Glacier, visible up close from the South Fork of Cascade Canyon Trail, has an easily recognizable cirque and outflow. Another good spot for seeing glaciers is Mt. Moran Turnout, also on Teton Park Road, where you have a good view of Mt. Moran, home to Skillet Glacier on its east face and Falling Ice Glacier on its southeast face.

Originating near Yellowstone's South Entrance, the Snake River flows into Jackson Lake; it exits through Jackson Lake Dam, rushing eastward through an Ice-Age glacial trough. The Snake turns suddenly southwest at Moran Junction, following the widened bed of the ancestral Snake, carved 20,000 years ago by the last Ice-Age advance down from Yellowstone Plateau. Visible from Jackson Hole Highway, the sagebrush flats along the Snake's twisting southern path were created when torrential glacial meltwaters washed away moisture-holding clay.

FLORA AND FAUNA Close to 900 wildflower varieties bloom in the park's three-phase explosion of summer color. Following the receding snow on the valley floor are sagebrush buttercups, then spring beauties and yellow-bells. In late June the valley is covered by blue lupine, yellow balsamroot, scarlet gilia, and purple larkspur. In July and August, wild-flowers flourish in meadows along canyon trails at 7,000 to 10,000 feet. In August, at alpine elevations of over 9,000 feet, a low, brilliant cushion of color includes the official park flower, the alpine forget-me-not. Visitor centers distribute a free wildflower check-list, and the Grand Teton Natural History Association (*see* Publications, *above*) sells more-extensive wildflower guides.

The Snake's ongoing pattern of floods and channel-changing (a fine example of the latter is visible at Oxbow Bend Turnout) keep spruce trees from dominating the land close to the river. Thanks to nature's upheavals, tall cottonwoods and low willows compete with spruce in the valley, thereby creating a perfect moose-and-beaver habitat. As you move up into the mountains you'll find the mix of trees turning to spruce, fir, aspen, and lodgepole pine.

Elk are the region's most common large mammals. The best place to view the herd during the winter is south of the park on the National Elk Refuge, where some 7,500 of them spend the colder months. In summer, elk and mule deer haunt forest edges along Teton Park Road at sunrise and sunset. Oxbow Bend and Willow Flats are good places to look for moose, beaver, and otter. Pronghorn antelope and, occasionally, bison appear in summer along Jackson Hole Highway and Antelope Flats Road (especially at dawn and dusk), and black bear inhabit the backcountry, although sightings are not common. Birds include bald eagles and ospreys, which can be spotted along the Snake, as well as a colony of great blue herons that lives near Oxbow Bend. In addition, there are killdeer in marshy areas and trumpeter swans, mallards, and Canada geese around ponds.

WHEN TO GO July and August are the park's most crowded months. In winter, when park lodgings close, the crowds are genuinely sparse, and, although most of Teton Park Road is also closed, Jackson Hole Highway remains open, providing access to cross-country ski trails and frozen Jackson Lake. Moose Visitor Center stays open all winter except on Christmas Day. Winter dining and lodging rates at Teton Village are often higher than in summer because of the popularity of nearby downhill skiing. In Jackson, rates are generally higher during the summer; the low-est rates, and smallest crowds, can be found during spring and fall. In April most of Teton Park Road is open to bicyclists and hikers only, an off-season treat for observers of young wildlife.

The average high temperature in Grand Teton in July is 81°F, the average low, 41°F. Locals say there are three seasons here: July, August, and winter. Although that is an exaggeration, snow is possible year-round. A spring of mild days and cold nights extends into June, when the average high is 71°F and the average low is 37°F. Snow begins falling in October, with temperatures averaging a high of 57°F and a low of 24°F. In January the thermometer can drop as low as -46°F and rise as high as 50°F but usually falls between 2°F and 25°F. The park averages 49 inches of snow in January and 160 inches each year. July and August are generally the driest months, and May is the rainiest, with an average of 3 inches of rain.

SEASONAL EVENTS Unless stated otherwise, more information on the following events can be obtained from the Jackson Hole Chamber of Commerce and the park visitor centers (*see* Visitor Information, *above*).

Early April: The **Pole-Pedal-Paddle** is a ski-cycle-canoe relay race starting at Jackson Hole Ski Resort and finishing down the Snake River. **Mid-May:** At the **Elk Antler Auction** in Jackson you'll find roughly three tons of ant-lers shed by the herd that winters at the National Elk Refuge. **Late May: Old West Days** in Jackson features a rodeo, Native American dancers, a Western swing contest, cowboy poetry, and a mountain-man rendez-vous. **May to August: Teton County Histori-cal Society** (tel. 307/733–9605) sponsors monthly field trips to regional sites. **Early June to late September: Teton Science School** (tel. 307/733–4765) offers one- to six-day natural-science seminars at its park campus.

Topics include flora and fauna field-study, wilderness skills and ethics, and geology. Enrollment costs $50 to $300 (*see* Children's Programs, *below*). **June to September: Jackson Hole Summer Rodeo** (tel. 307/733–2805) runs Wednesday and Saturday near downtown Jackson. **Early July to late August:** The **Grand Teton Music Festival** schedules nightly classical and modern orchestral concerts performed at Teton Village by more than 115 musicians from orchestras worldwide. **Mid-September to early October: Jackson Hole Fall Arts Festival** (tel. 307/733–3316) offers gallery shows, artist's workshops, concerts, dance, and theater. **Early October: Quilting in the Tetons** features workshops and exhibits in Jackson. **Early December to early April: Ski races** for qualifying amateurs and the general public are sponsored by Jackson Hole Ski Club (tel. 307/733–6433), Grand Targhee Resort (tel. 307/353–2300), and Snow King Resort (tel. 307/733–5200). **December to March: Winter Speaker Series** sponsored by Teton Science School (tel. 307/733–4765) features twice-monthly natural-science speakers. **Year-round:** The **speaker series** offered by Teton County Historical Center (tel. 307/733–9605) features monthly programs on regional history.

WHAT TO PACK Remember the wind-chill factor even in July, and pack extra warm clothing and rain gear. Wearing several layers is the best safeguard against Grand Teton's fickle weather. In summer, shorts and a light cotton shirt should suffice, but have a wool sweater or thick sweatshirt handy, as well as a hooded nylon windbreaker and long pants. Walking shoes—and hiking boots if you plan on hitting the trail—are essential. Wool socks and extra warm clothing are recommended if you're taking a Snake River float trip (*see* Guided Tours, *below*). Insect repellent, sunscreen, sunglasses, and a hat are also worth carrying.

In winter, consider donning polypropylene underwear and socks; these wick away skin moisture while retaining body heat. Over the polypropylene, wear fleece and/or wool, along with warm headgear and gloves or mittens. Insulated boots are also necessary during the winter. Sunscreen and sunglasses will protect you from snow-reflected glare.

GENERAL STORES Colter Bay Grocery and General Store, along with **Colter Bay Tackle and Gift Shop** (both tel. 307/543–2811), is open daily 7:30 AM to 10 PM from mid-May through late September. **Flagg Ranch Grocery Store** (tel. 307/543–2868), 4 miles north of the park, is open daily 7 AM to 10 PM in summer and 9 to 5 the rest of the year. **Dornans' Grocery** (tel. 307/733–2415), west of Moose Junction, is open daily 8 to 8 from May to October and 9 to 6 at other times. **Jenny Lake Store** (tel. 307/733–3708), on Jenny Lake Road, is open daily 8 to 7 from June to mid-September. **Moose Village Store** (tel. 307/733–3471), in Moose, is open daily 8 to 6 from mid-May to mid-September. **Signal Mountain Lodge Convenience Store** (tel. 307/543–2831), on Teton Park Road, is open daily 7 AM to 9 PM mid-May to mid-October. These stores sell canned, frozen, and some fresh food, as well as most outdoors essentials (from ponchos to camping knives), but don't plan to stock your entire camping trip at any of them. Instead, rely on supermarkets in Jackson.

Nearby **Jackson** is a shopper's mecca of Western wear, gear, crafts, and souvenirs, with several minimalls off its old-fashion downtown boardwalks. Some of the more popular stores include **The Hole Works** (tel. 307/733–7000); **Warbonnet Indian Arts** (tel. 307/733–6158), which has a fine selection of Navajo rugs woven on the premises; and **Valley Bookstore** (tel. 307/733–4533), with numerous books on regional history, mountaineering, guides, and travel.

ARRIVING AND DEPARTING The park is just over 7 miles from Yellowstone's south entrance on the John D. Rockefeller, Jr., Memorial Parkway, which is often crowded in July and August. Less crowded is the eastern entrance on U.S. 26–287 from Dubois, Wyoming, through Moran Junction. The most popular route is through bustling Jackson, 12 miles south of the park on the Jackson Hole Highway. This is also the most scenic route, offering panoramic views of Jackson Hole, the

Gros Ventre Range to the east, and the Teton Range to the west.

The cities nearest Grand Teton are: Rock Springs, Wyoming, 177 miles southeast of Jackson on U.S. 191; Pocatello, Idaho, 150 miles from Jackson on U.S. 89 and Route 30; and Salt Lake City, Utah, 269 miles from Jackson on U.S. 89 and I–15.

By Plane. Jackson Hole Airport (tel. 307/733–7682), 8 miles north of town, off Jackson Hole Highway, receives daily flights connecting from Denver and Salt Lake City, home of the closest international airport. **Grand Teton Lodge Company** (*see* Visitor Information, *above*) offers a shuttle between the airport and Jackson Lake Lodge several times daily for $10 per person one-way, and some Jackson lodgings provide free airport shuttle service for guests. One-way taxi fare from the airport to Jackson is about $12; taxi companies include **All Star Transportation** (tel. 307/733–2888), **Buckboard Cab** (tel. 307/733–1112), and **Jackson Hole Transportation Company** (tel. 307/733–3135). Car rentals at the Jackson Airport are available through **Avis** (tel. 307/733–3422 or 800/331–1212), **Dollar** (tel. 307/733–0935 or 800/800–4000), **Eagle** (tel. 307/739–9999 or 800/582–2128), **Hertz** (tel. 307/733–2272 or 800/654–3131), **Jackson Hole Car Rental** (tel. 307/733–6868 or 800/722–2002), **National** (tel. 307/733–0735 or 800/CAR–RENT), and **Rent-a-Wreck** (tel. 307/733–5014 or 800/289–3538).

By Car and RV. Jackson Hole Highway (U.S. 26–89–191) runs the entire length of the park, from Jackson to Yellowstone's South entrance. This road is open all year from Jackson to Moran Junction and north to Flagg Ranch, 2 miles south of Yellowstone. (The road into Yellowstone, however, is closed in winter.) The section of the highway that runs east from Moran Junction over Togwotee Pass (U.S. 26–287) is also open year-round.

Depending on traffic, the southern Moose Entrance to Grand Teton is about 20 minutes from downtown Jackson. West Yellowstone, Montana, the western gateway to Yellowstone park, is 58 miles, or two hours, from

Teton park via Yellowstone's often crowded Lower Loop Road.

Two back-road entrances are for the adventurous and properly equipped. The Moose–Wilson Road passes Teton Village resort 12 miles from Jackson off Route 22 before continuing another 3 unpaved miles to the Moose Entrance; it is closed to trucks, trailers, and RVs. Even rougher is the 60-mile Grassy Lake Road, which heads east from Ashton, Idaho, through Targhee National Forest to the John D. Rockefeller, Jr., Memorial Parkway (a park, not a road). Grassy Lake Road (dirt and gravel) is off Route 32 just a mile south of Ashton. Much of it is one lane, so it's closed to trailers and large RVs. Both roads are closed by snow and are heavily rutted through June.

By Bus. Jackson Hole has no interstate bus service. **Grand Teton Lodge Company** (*see* Visitor Information, *above*) runs daily buses from Jackson's Town Square to Jackson Lake Lodge for $10 one-way or $15 round-trip; it also shuttles passengers between Jackson Lake Lodge and Colter Bay Visitor Center hourly from 7 to 5, early June to mid-September. Jackson's **START Bus** runs regularly from Town Square to Teton Village, from late May to mid-September and from early December to early April, 6 AM to 11 PM. Fares are 50¢ in town and $1 between end points. **Gray Line of Jackson Hole** (330 N. Glenwood, tel. 307/733–4325) makes regular day trips during the summer from Jackson to Grand Teton National Park for $3 per person, round trip.

EXPLORING

Unlike Yellowstone's Grand Loop, Grand Teton's road system doesn't allow for easy tour-bus access to all major sights. A car will get you close to Jenny Lake, into the remote eastern hills, and to the top of Signal Mountain. Easy interpretative trails make some sights accessible to most visitors. If your time and ability allow it, bicycling is easier here than in Yellowstone: Teton Park Road and Jackson Hole Highway are either flat or feature long, gradual inclines. And they have well-marked shoulders and less traffic than the roads at Yellowstone. While you can breeze through

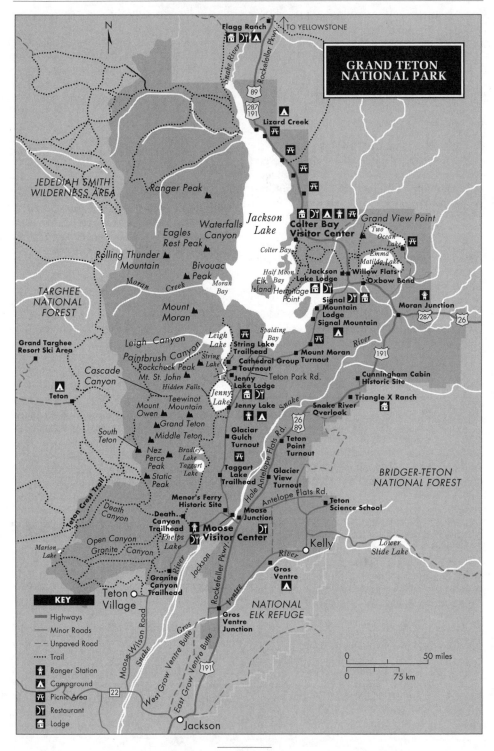

GRAND TETON NATIONAL PARK

TO YELLOWSTONE

Flagg Ranch

Snake River

Rockefeller Pkwy.

89

287
191

Lizard Creek

JEDEDIAH SMITH
WILDERNESS AREA

Ranger Peak

Jackson
Lake

Colter Bay
Visitor Center

Grand View Point

Two
Ocean
Lake

Eagles
Rest Peak

Waterfalls
Canyon

Colter Bay

Emma
Matilda Lake

Rolling Thunder
Mountain

Bivouac
Peak

Half Moon
Bay

Jackson
Lake Lodge

Willow Flats
Oxbow Bend

TARGHEE
NATIONAL
FOREST

Moran   Creek

Moran
Bay

Elk
Bay

Island
Hermitage
Point

Moran Junction

287   26

Mount
Moran

Signal
Mountain
Lodge

Signal Mountain

River

Grand Targhee
Resort Ski Area

Leigh Canyon

Leigh
Lake

String
Lake
Trailhead

Spalding
Bay

Mount Moran
Turnout

191

Paintbrush Canyon

String
Lake

Cathedral Group
Tournout

Cunningham Cabin
Historic Site

Cascade
Canyon

Rockchuck Peak
Mt. St. John

Hidden Falls

Jenny
Lake Lodge

Teton Park Rd.

Triangle X Ranch

Teton

Teewinot
Mountain

Jenny
Lake

Jenny Lake

Snake

Snake River
Overlook

Mount
Owen

Grand Teton

26
89

South
Teton

Middle Teton

Glaciar
Gulch
Turnout

Teton
Point
Turnout

BRIDGER-TETON
NATIONAL FOREST

Nez
Perce
Peak

Bradley
Lake
Taggart
Lake

Static
Peak

Taggart
Lake
Trailhead

Glacier
View
Turnout

Menor's Ferry
Historic Site

Hole Antelope Flats Rd.

Teton
Science School

Death
Canyon

Death
Canyon
Trailhead

Phelps
Lake

Moose
Junction

Antelope Flats Rd.

Open Canyon

Granite   Canyon

Moose
Visitor Center

Kelly

Lower
Slide Lake

Marion
Lake

River

Jackson

River

Gros
Ventre

Granite
Canyon
Trailhead

Teton
Village

NATIONAL
ELK REFUGE

Rockefeller Pkwy.

Gros Ventre

Gros
Ventre
Junction

Moose-Wilson Road

Snake

West Gros Ventre Butte

East Gros Ventre Butte

22

191

Jackson

KEY
— Highways
— Minor Roads
--- Unpaved Road
···· Trail
Ranger Station
Campground
Picnic Area
Restaurant
Lodge

0   50 miles
0   75 km

the park by car in two to three hours, you should spend at least two days in Grand Teton. Dedicated hikers and outdoor enthusiasts could easily find two weeks worth of adventurous camping.

THE BEST IN ONE DAY Get to Moose Visitor Center in time for a 9 AM, two-hour, guided Snake River float trip (you'll have to make reservations in advance with one of the dozen or so outfitters that offer the trip). Although mild white water is the roughest stuff you'll experience, this is an exhilarating ride, and you might see moose and bison along the way. When you're back on dry ground, drive north on Teton Park Road, stopping at scenic turnouts—don't miss Teton Glacier—until you reach Jenny Lake Road. Because traffic on this road runs in only one direction, you will have to drive to the far end of the road, turning left onto it at North Jenny Lake Junction. After a brief stop at Cathedral Group Turnout, from which you'll see Grand, Owen, and Teewinot peaks up close, park at the South Jenny Lake Ranger Station and take the 20-minute boat ride to Cascade Canyon Trailhead. An easy 1/2-mile walk up Cascade Canyon Trail takes you to Hidden Falls, a shaded, pine-scented picnic site. Return to your car by early afternoon, drive back to Teton Park Road, and head north to Signal Mountain Road, a spur road that leads to a top-of-the-park view of the Tetons. In late afternoon descend the mountain and continue north on Teton Park Road. At Jackson Lake Junction, you can go east to Oxbow Bend or north to Willow Flats, both excellent spots for wildlife-viewing. An early dinner in Jackson Lake Lodge looking out at the Tetons will rejuvenate you just enough for the trip north to Colter Bay Marina, from which you can take a 1½-hour sunset cruise across Jackson Lake to Waterfalls Canyon (*see* Guided Tours, *below*). The nearest Yellowstone lodgings are slightly more than an hour away from Colter Bay, but consider staying in cabins here or back at Jackson Lake Lodge. Do not go on to Yellowstone expecting a room without a reservation.

You can reverse this route if you're heading south from Yellowstone: Start the day with a 7:30 breakfast cruise from Colter Bay, and end it with a sunset float down the Snake.

ORIENTATION PROGRAMS Colter Bay Visitor Center auditorium hosts several free daily programs. A 30-minute ranger lecture, *Teton Highlights,* offers tips on park activities daily at 11 and 3. Several times daily, Colter Bay shows *The Nature of Grand Teton,* a 15-minute slide show on park geological history, and *Bald Eagles,* a 10-minute slide show. Two 25-minute movies—*Song Dog,* about coyotes, and *Elk of the Northern Herd*—are each shown once daily. Every other day, Colter Bay shows the 25-minute Native American film *In Quest Of a Vision.*

Moose Visitor Center plays video versions of *The Nature of Grand Teton* and *Teton Highlights. Song Dog* and *Elk of the Northern Herd* are among the videos shown on rainy days.

GUIDED TOURS **Grand Teton Lodge Company** (Box 240, Moran, WY 83013, tel. 307/543–2811 or 307/733–2811) offers 1½-hour Jackson Lake cruises from Colter Bay Marina throughout the day, from mid-May to mid-September. With excellent captain's narration on geology and wildlife, these cruises cost $9.25 for adults and $5.75 for children under 12. Sunset cruises to the base of Waterfalls Canyon are offered mid-June to mid-August for the same price. Daily breakfast cruises ($17.50 adults, $10.50 children under 12) depart from the marina from late May to late September. Run on Wednesday and Saturday evenings, early June to mid-September, steak-fry cruises cost $29.75 for adults and $20.50 for children under 12.

Access Tours (Box 2985, Jackson, WY 83001, tel. 307/733–6664) caters to people with physical disabilities, offering educational, multiday park tours from motels, ideal for those who want to move at a slower pace. **Grayline Tours** (Box 411, Jackson, WY 83001, tel. 307/733–4325 or 800/443–6133, fax 307/733–2689) departs from Dirty Jack's Theatre (140 N. Cache St., Jackson, WY) for a daily 9 to 3:30, $36 guided park tour.

There are many guided float trips through calm-water sections of the Snake River; these pick up clients at the Float Trip parking area near Moose Visitor Center for a 10- to 20-minute drive to upriver launch sites. Ten-mile floats last two to three hours and 5-mile floats last one to two hours. All concessionaires provide ponchos and life preservers. You should wear soft-sole shoes and carry a jacket or sweater for early morning and evening floats (best bets for wildlife-sighting). Oarspeople provide a narrative. Float season runs mid-May to mid-September. **Barker-Ewing Scenic Tours** (Box 100, Moose, WY 83012, tel. 307/733–1800 or 800/365–1800) specializes in 10-mile floats. They cost $30 for adults and $20 for children 4–12. Dinner trips cost $10 more per person. **Grand Teton Lodge Company** (*see above*) gathers floaters from Colter Bay and Jackson Lake Lodge for 10-mile trips ($22.50 adults, $12.50 children 6–16) and lunch and supper floats ($30 adults, $19.50 children 6–16). **National Park** (tel. 307/733–6445), **Osprey** (tel. 307/733–5500), and **Triangle X Float Trips** (tel. 307/733–5500) are all part of Triangle X Ranch (Moose, WY 83012), which is located between Moose and Moran junctions off Jackson Hole Highway; pickups are in downtown Jackson, Moose parking lot, and Triangle X Ranch, depending on the float. Ten-mile trips are $29 for adults and $18 for children under 16; 5-mile trips cost $19 for adults and $14 for children under 12; supper floats are $39 for adults, $26 for children under 12. **Signal Mountain Lodge** (*see* Lodging, *below*) takes floaters from the lodge for 10-mile trips ($25 adults, $15 children under 16). **Solitude Float Trips** (Box 112, Moose, WY 83012, tel. 307/733–2871) depart six times daily, charging $18 for adults and $15 for children under 13 on 5-mile trips, $28 for adults and $18 for children under 13 on 10-mile trips.

Rangers lead free walks, from a one-hour lakeside stroll at Colter Bay to an all-day, 10-mile mountain hike from Moose (early June to early September). Some of these require reservations; call the park (*see* Visitor Information, *above*) in advance. **National Elk Refuge Horse-Drawn Sleigh Rides** (Box C, Jackson, WY 83001, tel. 307/733–8084 or 307/733–9212) depart continuously from 9 to 4, late December to late March, from the ref-uge visitor center; fares are $6 for adults, $3 for children ages 6 to 12. **Teton Village Aerial Tram** (Teton Village, WY 83025, tel. 307/733–2292) departs every half hour, late May to late September, for a 20-minute ride with an informal conductor's narrative up 10,450-foot Rendezvous Mountain, which has a viewing platform, snack bar, and trailhead. Tickets must be purchased in person: $14 adults, $11 senior citizens, $7 children 13–17, $5 children 6–12 without an adult, free for children under 12 with an adult. **Wild West Jeep Tours** (Box 7506, Jackson, WY 83001, tel. 307/733–9036) departs three times daily, early June to early September, from the Wildlife Museum of Jackson Hole on West Broadway for rides through the Teton backcountry. Fare is $30 adults, $18 for children under 12. **Jackson Hole Museum** (Box 1005, corner Deloney and Glenwood Sts., Jackson, WY 83001, tel. 307/733–2414) tours historic Jackson on foot from the museum daily at 11 except Sunday, early June to late September ($2 adults and children, $1 senior citizens).

SCENIC DRIVES AND VIEWS Starting at Moose, you can combine several park roads for a 60-mile, three- to five-hour loop past major sights. Displays at Teton Park Road and Jackson Hole Highway turnouts identify mountains and explain geology. Watch carefully for oncoming traffic at turnouts north of Jackson Lake Lodge; the road is narrow and the curves are sharp.

Your first stop on **Teton Park Road** is just a few hundred yards past Moose Entrance, where a short road leads to the Chapel of the Transfiguration. The chapel was built in 1925, and its altar window frames the Grand Teton. Past Teton Park Road's Windy Point and Teton Glacier turnouts, one-way **Jenny Lake Scenic Drive** offers the park's best roadside Teton close-ups. The road winds south past groves of lodgepole pine and open meadows from North Jenny Lake Junction, 12 miles north of Moose. Roughly 2 miles down Jenny Lake Road, the Cathedral Group Turnout faces 13,770-foot Grand Teton (the range's highest peak), which is flanked by 12,928-foot Mt. Owen and 12,325-foot Mt. Teewinot. Just before you rejoin Teton Park Road at

South Jenny Lake Junction, you'll see Jenny Lake, named after a mountain man's Native American wife, and today a favorite hiking area. Beware: Steep, unguarded drop-offs border the right side of the road.

Back on Teton Park Road, Mt. Moran Turnout affords you your first view of the northern Tetons that surround 12,605-foot Mt. Moran. Detouring on **Signal Mountain Road,** you climb 800 feet on a 5-mile stretch of switchbacks with this peak dominating the view. The trip ends with a sweeping view of Jackson Hole and the entire 40-mile Teton Range. Sunrise and sunset are the best times to make the climb up Signal Mountain, so you may want to return later. Back on Teton Park Road, continue north to the log Chapel of the Sacred Heart, which has a picnic area overlooking southern Jackson Lake. A mile north of Jackson Lake Junction, Willow Flats Turnout surveys Mt. Moran, 10,825-foot Bivouac Peak, 10,908-foot Rolling Thunder Mountain, 11,258-foot Eagles Rest Peak, and 11,355-foot Ranger Peak. The willow thickets here are an excellent wildlife habitat and are especially lively in the morning. Scan the flats with binoculars to find moose feeding.

Colter Bay Visitor Center, at the north end of this driving tour, has an airy, three-level Native American Arts Museum with displays of hide paintings, beadwork, headdresses, weapons, and tools. When you're through browsing in the museum, backtrack on Teton Park Road to Jackson Lake Junction and turn left onto **Jackson Hole Highway** toward Moran Junction. One mile down this road, Oxbow Bend Turnout overlooks a quiet backwater left by the Snake River when it cut a new southern channel. White pelicans stop here on their spring migration—many staying on through summer—trumpeter swans visit frequently, and a colony of great blue herons nests amid the cottonwoods along the river. Use binoculars to search for these waterfowl as well as for bald eagles, ospreys, moose, beaver, and otter. The Oxbow is also known for the reflection of Mt. Moran that marks its calm waters in early morning.

At Moran Junction bear right, continuing south on the Jackson Hole Highway. Nine miles south, at Snake River Overlook, you may recognize the view of this river bend—it is immortalized in an Ansel Adams photograph. Five miles farther south, stop at Glacier View Turnout for a look at Teton Glacier. About 2 miles before you reach Moose Junction, turn left onto **Antelope Flats Road,** which wanders eastward through ranches and over rolling plains and river flats that are home to antelope, as well as bison and moose during the spring and fall. Turning right off this road at the four-way intersection, you can loop around past Kelly and the Gros Ventre campground and back to the highway at Gros Ventre Junction.

HISTORIC BUILDINGS AND SITES To reach the **Menor's Ferry Historic Site,** take the ¹/₂-mile Menor's Ferry Interpretive Trail at the Chapel of the Transfiguration parking lot, just past Moose Entrance. The easy ¹/₂-hour riverside walk passes a small free history museum, 19th-century homesteader Bill Menor's log cabin, the old site of the Snake River Ferry, and an indoor historic-photo exhibit. These exhibits are open year-round, and a pamphlet on the area is available for 25¢ at the trailhead.

Six miles south of Moran, a gravel spur road leads to the **Cunningham Cabin Historic Site.** An easy ³/₄-mile trail runs through sagebrush around Pierce Cunningham's 1890 log-cabin homestead. Cunningham, an early Jackson Hole homesteader and civic leader, built his cabin in Appalachian dogtrot style, joining two halves with a roofed veranda. Watch for badgers, coyotes, and Uinta ground squirrels in the area. The site is open year-round, and a 25¢ pamphlet is available at the trailhead.

NATURE TRAILS AND SHORT WALKS Beginning at the Death Canyon Trailhead, the **Phelps Lake Overlook Trail** is an easy 1-mile, two-hour round-trip walk up conifer- and aspen-lined glacial moraine to views of this valley lake, accessible only by trail. Expect abundant birdlife: Western tanagers, northern flickers, and ruby-crowned kinglets thrive in the bordering woods, and hummingbirds feed on scarlet gilia beneath the overlook. To reach the trailhead from Teton Park Road, turn left onto Moose–Wilson Road just before the Moose Entrance, go 4¹/₂ miles, and turn right. The trailhead and parking area is near the White Grass Ranger Station, just 1¹/₂ miles ahead (*see* Longer Hikes, *below*).

Off Jenny Lake Road, before it reaches Jenny Lake, you'll come to the String Lake parking area and trailhead, from which two easy hikes begin. The flat 2-mile, one-hour round-trip **Leigh Lake Trail** follows String Lake's northeastern shore to Leigh Lake's south shore. This hike can be extended into a still-easy 7¹/₂-mile, four-hour round-trip by following the forested east shore of Leigh Lake to Bearpaw Lake. Along the way you'll have views of Mt. Moran across the lake, and you may be lucky enough to spot a moose. Also starting from this parking area is the 3¹/₂-mile, three-hour **String Lake Trail** loop, which sits in the shadows of 11,144-foot Rockchuck Peak and 11,430-foot Mt. Saint John. This trail starts out running with the Leigh Lake Trail, but it splits off at the north end of String Lake.

Lunchtree Hill Trail, one of the park's easiest, leaves Jackson Lake Lodge for a ¹/₂-mile, ¹/₂-hour round-trip walk to the top of a hill above Willow Flats. This area's willow thickets, beaver ponds, and wet, grassy meadows make it a birder's paradise. Look for sandhill cranes, hummingbirds, and many types of songbirds described in the free bird guide available at visitor centers. Another very easy two-hour walk is the **Colter Bay Nature Trail Loop,** a 1³/₄-mile round-trip excursion with views of Jackson Lake and the Tetons. Start at the Colter Bay Visitor Center and walk about ¹/₃ mile to the trailhead, where you can pick up a trail leaflet. The level trail follows the forest's edge. You may see lakeside moose and bald eagles. Also starting from this trailhead, the 3-mile, two-hour, mostly level **Heron Pond–Swan Lake Trail** passes through areas with willows and aspens and traverses a marshy, stream-crossed terrain favored by beaver and waterfowl.

You can take the 20-minute boat ride from the Jenny Lake dock to the **Cascade Canyon Trailhead,** from which it is a gentle, ¹/₂-mile climb one-way to 200-foot Hidden Falls, the park's most popular and crowded trail destination. Listen here for the distinctive bleating of the rabbitlike pika among the glacial boulders and pines. Or skip the boat ride and walk to Hidden Falls from the Jenny Lake Ranger Station by following the mostly level **Jenny Lake Trail** around the south shore of the lake and joining the Cascade Canyon Trail to the falls. The Jenny Lake Trail continues around the lake for 6¹/₂ miles, an easy hike that should take about four hours and offers views of the Tetons from the eastern shore.

LONGER HIKES From the Death Canyon Trailhead, you can hike out to the Phelps Lake Overlook (*see* Nature Trails and Short Walks, *above*), then continue down to the lake via the **Death Canyon Trail.** This 4-mile, three-hour hike entails a steep return hike.

You can also take the **Death Canyon Trail** from Phelps Lake Overlook up into Death Canyon. The trail passes wildflower meadows and follows the north side of Death Canyon Creek for a 7¹/₂-mile, six-hour round-trip from the Death Canyon Trailhead to the Static Peak Trail Junction and back. As you ascend the canyon, listen for the whistle of marmots and the bleating of pika, two small mammals that are common in the park, and keep an eye out for moose, mule deer, and the occasional black bear. From the junction, the **Static Peak Divide Trail** switchbacks through a white-bark-pine forest, then climbs a steep slope to the foot of Static Peak. This is one of the roughest trails in the park, and in order to traverse it early in the season you must have an ice axe and know how to use it (check conditions at the Jenny Lake Ranger Station). Static Peak Divide, at 10,800 feet in altitude, is the highest point on a maintained trail in the park. Your reward on this 15¹/₂-mile, 10-hour round-trip hike from Death Canyon Trailhead will be sweeping views of the Tetons and Jackson Hole.

A somewhat less strenuous southern-Tetons day hike is the 17¹/₂-mile round-trip **Marion Lake Trail,** which climbs nearly 3,000 feet from Granite Canyon Trailhead, off the

Moose-Wilson Road (the trailhead is about 2 miles south of the turnoff for the Death Canyon Trailhead). About 1¹/₂ miles in from the trailhead you climb through a talus field and then follow Granite Creek for about 4 miles, sometimes winding through willows close to the creek, where chances of moose sightings are excellent. The trail traces Granite Canyon up to subalpine meadows near Marion Lake that in August are brilliantly painted with wildflowers. Just above tree line you turn right for a brief stretch on the Teton Crest Trail until you reach tiny Marion Lake. It will take about 12 hours to hike to Marion Lake and back. You can shorten this spectacular hike— and make it even more spectacular—by returning south from Marion Lake along the **Teton Crest Trail,** past the turnoff for the Granite Canyon Trail, and looping eastward to the top of the tram that runs from Teton Village. The tram will take you down to the village, where you should have parked a car. To get from Granite Canyon Trailhead to Teton Village via the Marion Lake Trail and the tram, you must cover 12¹/₂ miles, a seven-hour journey.

Two more-moderate hikes in the southern Tetons are the **Bradley Lake** and **Taggart Lake–Beaver Creek** trails, which begin as one trail at the Taggart Lake Trailhead, some 3 miles north of the Moose Visitor Center on Teton Park Road. Each of these trails is 4 miles round-trip and takes about three hours to hike. You will pass through a major portion of land burned during a 1985 fire. The Bradley Lake Trail branches north (right) 1 mile from the trailhead, and the Taggart Lake Trail continues west (left) ¹/₂ mile to Taggart Lake's south end, climbing glacial moraines surrounding the lake. When you reach Taggart Lake you may continue along its east shore to the north end, climbing the moraine between Taggart and Bradley lakes to join the Bradley Lake Trail. This adds about a mile to the hike and makes it a little more difficult, but it also increases your chances of spotting wildlife.

At Jenny Lake the **Cascade Canyon Trail** past Hidden falls (*see* Nature Trails and Short Walks, *above*) gets strenuous as it climbs an-

other ¹/₂ mile to Inspiration Point, from which there are sweeping views of Jenny Lake and Jackson Hole below and Cascade Canyon's wall of mountains above. The Cascade Canyon Trail up to Inspiration Point is the park's most crowded, but beyond that point the crowds thin. The trail continues up the canyon and has great views of Mt. Teewinot, Mt. Owen, and Grand Teton (in that order, on your left). At times the trail crosses talus slopes where, in August, wild raspberries and thimbleberries grow. Along the way there are a couple of stream crossings that make good lunch spots. To get from the trailhead to the point where the trail forks (it follows the two forks of Cascade Creek) and back, you'll hike 13 miles in about seven hours.

The **Grand View Point Trail** offers a good introduction to the backcountry in the northeastern section of the park. The trailhead is at the end of a 1-mile dirt road that turns right off U.S. 89–191–287 about 2¹/₂ miles north of Jackson Lake Junction. Watch for moose in the marshy area at the base of the trail, which switchbacks up moderately through old-growth Douglas firs that support woodpeckers, many kinds of songbirds, and grouse. From the 7,327-foot summit, you'll see long, sparkling Two Ocean Lake below to the northeast and Emma Matilda Lake to the southeast. Red-tailed hawks, pelicans, and eagles may be sighted above the waters. The hike to the summit and back is just over 2 miles and will take about two hours. If you want to go farther, continue down through stands of pine and aspen to the northwest shore of Two Ocean Lake, circle around the lake's north shore, and then trace the north shore of Emma Matilda Lake, returning to the Grand View Point Trailhead. On this route you'll hear many more songbirds, and you will likely see trumpeter swans near the lakes. The loop around the lakes, however, covers approximately 10 miles from the trailhead and takes about five hours.

From the Colter Bay Trailhead (*see* Nature Trails and Short Walks, *above*), the **Hermitage Point Trail** traverses gentle terrain with pine forests and willow thickets that are prime moose and beaver habitat. Watch for ducks at Swan Lake and Heron Pond along the way. The trail covers a 9-mile loop to Heritage Point on Jackson Lake and takes about four hours to hike.

OTHER ACTIVITIES **Back-Road Driving.** Except for short dirt roads to trailheads and the two back-road entrances (*see* Arriving and Departing, *above*), no back-road driving is allowed inside the park. Four-wheeling is, however, possible in national forests outside Grand Teton.

Biking. Jackson Hole's long, flat profile and mountain scenery attracts even novice 10-speed and mountain bikers. The River Road, 4 miles north of Moose, is an easy four-hour mountain-bike ride along the Snake River. A bike lane allows for northbound bike traffic along the one-way Jenny Lake Loop Road, a one-hour ride. A four-hour, moderate ride on paved road goes from Gros Ventre Junction to Lower Slide Lake. The three-hour Shadow Mountain Road loop off Antelope Flats Road gives experienced mountain bikers an aerobic workout and spectacular Snake River views. For a true bike odyssey, try all or part of the 60-mile Ashton–Flagg Ranch Road (*see* Arriving and Departing, *above*). Bicycles are not allowed on trails or in the backcountry.

The closest bike-rental and repair shop is **Mountain Bike Outfitters** (Box 303, Moose, WY 83012, tel. 307/733–3314), which offers excellent advice on cycling. The shop is located at Dornan's Corners, just before Moose Visitor Center. Mountain bike rentals cost $6 per hour, $16 per half-day, and $24 for a full day; sport bikes are $7 per hour, $20 per half-day, and $28 for a full day, including water bottle, cage, helmet, and lock. **Teton Cyclery** (175 N. Glenwood St., Jackson, WY 83001, tel. 307/733–4386) offers in-town rentals and repairs.

Bird-Watching. Among Teton-country birds are great blue herons and osprey, who nest at Oxbow Bend from spring through fall. White pelicans also stop at the Oxbow on their southward journey in spring, and bald eagles remain all year to fish in the shallow water. Nearby Willow Flats is host to similar birdlife. Trumpeter swans, rare in Yellowstone, are more common in Grand Teton; look for them at Oxbow Bend and Two Ocean Lake. Look for songbirds, such as pine grosbeaks and Cassin's finches, in surrounding open pine and aspen forests. Similar songbirds inhabit Grandview Point, as do blue and ruffed grouse. Keep binoculars handy while traveling along Antelope Flats Road: You may spot red-tailed hawks and prairie falcons. At Taggart Lake you'll see woodpeckers, bluebirds, and hummingbirds.

Boating. Motorboats are allowed on Jenny (7½-horsepower maximum), Jackson, and Phelps lakes. Grand Teton Lodge Company (tel. 307/543–2811 or 307/733-2811) rents 9.9 HP motorboats at Colter Bay Marina for $13 per hour and $90 per eight-hour day, with a $50 deposit. A two-hour minimum is required. Rowboats and canoes are $7 per hour. Reservations are not accepted. **Signal Mountain Lodge Marina** (tel. 307/543–2831 or 307/733–5470) rents pontoon boats ($110 half-day, $165 full-day), ski boats ($140 half-day, $190 full-day), motorboats ($60 half-day, $90 full-day), and rowboats and canoes ($7.50 per hour, $50 full-day). The **Teton Boating Company** (tel. 307/733–2703) operates a shuttle that will run you across Jenny Lake to Hidden Falls. It costs $3.50 round-trip for adults and $1.75 for children under 18.

Fishing. Native cutthroat, rainbow, brook, and lake trout are caught in Grand Teton National Park waters. The Snake's 120 miles of river and tributary are world famous. Unlike Yellowstone, the park requires a Wyoming fishing license, which costs $12.50 for residents and $40 for nonresidents for the entire fishing season. Nonresident licenses for one, five, and 10 days may be purchased for $5, $15, and $25, respectively. Fishing licenses are available at the Wyoming Game and Fish Department (Box 67, 360 N. Cache St., Jackson, WY 83001, tel. 307/733–2321), Colter Bay Marina, and most of the area's sporting-goods stores. Jenny and Leigh lakes are open for fishing year-round, Jackson Lake is closed to anglers during October, and the Snake River is closed November 1 to March 31. Only in the park's northern half, including Jackson Lake, are you allowed to use live bait. **Grand Teton Lodge Company** (*see* Guided Tours, *above*) offers guided Jackson Lake fishing trips with boat, guide, and tackle costing $43 per hour for up to three people and $8 per hour for each additional person. **Signal Mountain Lodge** (*see above*) offers similar trips at $30 per hour for up to two people and $5 per hour for each additional person.

Horseback Riding. Grand Teton Lodge Company (*see above*) runs one-hour to half-day trail rides from the Jackson Lake Lodge and Colter Bay Village corrals, ranging in price from $16 to $34 per person. One-hour rides offer an overview of the Jackson Lake Lodge area; two-hour rides depart from the lodge corral to Emma Matilda Lake, Oxbow Bend, and Christian Pond, or from Colter Bay to a variety of destinations. Half-day trips, for advanced riders only, depart from Jackson Lake Lodge Corral to Two Ocean Lake and from Colter Bay Village Corral to Hermitage Point.

Rafting. If you're floating the Snake River on your own, check at visitor centers or the Buffalo Ranger Station near Moran Junction for current conditions. Permits, which are required, cost $5 per raft and are valid for the entire season. There are a variety of guided trips as well (*see* Guided Tours, *above*).

Rock Climbing. The Teton Range offers the nation's most diverse general mountaineering. Excellent rock, snow, and ice routes abound for the inexperienced as well as the advanced climber. Among the peaks that can be ascended in a day are Cube Point, a moderate climb approached via Hanging Canyon west of Jenny Lake, and nearby Symmetry Spire, which features long, moderately difficult pitches. Grand Teton itself is one of the world's classic two-day climbs: Moderately difficult Exum Ridge is the most popular ascent, but the original Owen-Spalding Route is easier. Mt. Moran offers the range's most commanding views, with two-day ascents via the standard route or Skillet Glacier, the range's most popular snow climb. Mt. Owen's two-day Koven Route and the more difficult East Ridge both combine rock with steep

snow up to the Tetons' most difficult summit. Between June and mid-September all climbers can sign in and out at Jenny Lake Ranger Station and from mid-September to May at Moose Visitor Center. **Exum Mountain Guides** (Box 56, Moose, WY 83012, tel. 307/733–2297) runs one-day basic ($50), intermediate ($70), and advanced ($90) schools from June through September, as well as a winter Snow School. **Jackson Hole Mountain Guides** (Box 7477, Jackson, WY 83001, tel. 307/733–4979) has similar courses.

Ski Touring. Grand Teton has some of North America's finest and most varied cross-country skiing. Ski the gentle 3-mile Swan Lake–Heron Pond Loop near Colter Bay Visitor Center, the mostly level 9-mile Jenny Lake Trail, or the moderate 4-mile Taggart Lake–Beaver Creek Loop and 5-mile Phelps Lake Overlook, which have some steep descents. Advanced skiers should head for the Teton Crest Trail. During the winter all backcountry travelers must register at park headquarters in Moose to obtain a free permit.

Rossignol Nordic Ski Center (Box 290, Teton Village, WY 83025, tel. 307/739–2629), at Teton Village, rents skis and offers about 10 miles of groomed trails. **Jack Dennis Outdoor Shop** (Chet's Way on the Town Square, Jackson, tel. 307/733–3270; Teton Village, tel. 307/733–6838), **Wildernest Sports** (Teton Village, tel. 307/733–4297), and **Teton Village Sports** (Teton Village, tel. 307/733–2181) also rent equipment.

Snowmobiling. Designated unplowed sections of Teton Park Road are open to snowmobiles, and you can also snowmobile on Jackson Lake. Annual $5 permits must be purchased at Moose Visitor Center or Colter Bay Ranger Station. The speed limit is 45 miles per hour. **Flagg Ranch Village** (Box 187, John D. Rockefeller, Jr., Memorial Parkway, Moran, WY, tel. 307/543–2861) and **Togwotee Mountain Lodge** (Box 91-J, U.S. 26–287, Moran, WY, tel. 307/543–2847) rent snowmobiles.

CHILDREN'S PROGRAMS The Teton Science School (tel. 307/733–4765) offers weekday Young Naturalists programs for children in grades 3 and 4 from late July through early August. Children may be enrolled in the program for up to 10 days and will pay $11 to $14 per day, depending on length of enrollment. The Junior Science School program, for children in grades 5 through 7, runs from June through August and costs $95 to $115 per week, depending on the number of weeks the child is enrolled (there's a nine-week limit). These outdoor programs are led by experienced environmental educators. In previous years, program topics have included "Making Your Own Nature Journal," "Weird Science," and "Wild Animals Need Wild Lands."

EVENING ACTIVITIES Ranger-led activities include campfire programs at the Colter Bay, Gros Ventre, and Signal Mountain amphitheaters with slides shown nightly from June through September. The **Flagg Ranch Campfire Program** is held several times a week. The **Moose Visitor Center** holds a free monthly Full Moon Walk on the night of the full moon from June through August, and the **Jackson Lake Lodge Wapiti Room** hosts a slide-illustrated ranger talk several evenings each week from July through mid-August, where you'll learn about park wildlife, geology, flora, and more.

DINING

While the park itself has some excellent restaurants, don't miss dining in Jackson, the hub of Rocky Mountain cuisine. Several innovative restaurants combine native game, fowl, and fish with Old World preparations and new-age health consciousness. Steaks are usually cut from sage-fed Wyoming beef. Poultry and pasta dishes are still heavily influenced by Alpine tradition, but new styles of preparation are quickly becoming popular. Whole-grain breakfasts and homemade soups are crowding out eggs and burgers, too. Casual, neat dress is accepted everywhere.

INSIDE THE PARK Jackson Lake Lodge **Mural Room.** The ultimate park dining experience is found right off the lodge's Blue Heron Lounge. Raised, rose-color banquette tables face tall windows that look out at Mt. Moran and the neighboring northern Tetons.

The room gets its name from a mural painted by western artist Carl Roters on 11 eight-foot-tall rosewood-and-walnut panels covering 700 square feet. The mural details an 1837 Wyoming mountain-man rendezvous and covers two walls of the dining room. The larger East Mural Room toward the back of the restaurant offers views of Gravelly Peak, especially at sunset or sunrise. Try sautéed Snake River trout topped with hazelnuts and grapes, or smoked and roasted Wyoming buffalo sirloin in a three-peppercorn sauce. Recommended appetizers include the cured salmon in sweet mustard and sage, and the onion au gratin and mushroom soups. *Jackson Lake Lodge, Moran, tel. 307/543–2811. Reservations advised. AE, DC, MC, V. Closed early Oct.–late May. Moderate–Expensive.*

The Aspens. Part of Signal Mountain Lodge, this modern lavender room has exposed ceiling beams and big square windows overlooking southern Jackson Lake and the Tetons. The emphasis here is on fish: Rocky Mountain trout is marinated, lightly floured, and grilled, or simply grilled and topped with lemon-parsley butter. Also good are the brace of quail, broiled and basted in a tangy vinaigrette. *Signal Mountain Lodge, Teton Park Rd., Moran, tel. 307/543–2831, fax 307/543–2569. Reservations advised. D, MC, V. Closed mid-Oct.–mid-May. Moderate.*

Jackson Lake Lodge Pioneer Grill. With an old-fashion soda fountain, friendly service, and seats along a winding counter, this eatery recalls the pre-yuppified Middle American luncheonette. It's favored by families and senior citizens: Tour groups crowd the counter at lunch, often ordering the daily specials, such as hot-dog-and-potato casserole or chicken and dumplings. The buffalo-and-barley soup is excellent. Dinner specials include grilled pork chops with home fries and applesauce, and local trout in egg batter with home fries. The walls are decorated with antique ranch tools. *Jackson Lake Lodge, Moran, tel. 307/543–2811, ext. 1911. Reservations not accepted. AE, DC, MC, V. Closed early Oct.–late May. Inexpensive–Moderate.*

John Colter Grill and **Chuckwagon Restaurant.** The grill and restaurant are connected in a sprawling, pine-shaded building across from Colter Bay Marina. The grill and marina draw families staying at Colter Bay's lodgings as well as sightseers from Jackson Lake's boat tours. Fare and decor are bland compared to the equally budget-friendly Pioneer Grill (*see above*). The all-you-can-eat cowboy beef stew is plain but hearty; Jackson Lake fisherfolk often come here to eat trout they've caught themselves, which must be cleaned and presented to the chef by 4 and can be served any time between 5:30 and 9, when the restaurant is open for dinner. *Jackson Lake Lodge, Colter Bay Village, Moran, tel. 307/543–2811. Reservations not accepted. AE, DC, MC, V. Closed late Sept.–late May. Inexpensive–Moderate.*

NEAR THE PARK **The Granary.** Located on a butte just south of town, this restaurant, which is part of Spring Creek Resort, is best known for its consistently fine nouvelle Western cuisine served amid stunning views of the Teton Range. The downstairs, open-beam lodgepole-pine interior is decorated with Northern Plains Native American art and Teton photos. In summer, the deck is open. Outstanding entrées include sautéed elk medallions in morel-port sauce with spaetzle; poached salmon in cucumber-dill sauce; and a mixed grill of quail, lamb, and elk with roasted garlic. For starters, try pheasant-and-duck pâté with cranberry-bourbon relish. *1800 Spirit Dance Rd., Jackson, tel. 307/733–8833 or 800/443–6139. Reservations advised. AE, D, DC, MC, V. Expensive.*

Louie's Steak and Seafood. One block north of Town Square, in a 1930s log house with red window-frames and a giant wood butterfly on the siding near the door, Louie's combines Continental with American cuisine. Three intimate, lavender-wallpapered rooms are furnished with simple pine tables and decorated with the region's omnipresent Teton wildlife photos. Try the swordfish steak over lime *beurre blanc;* or Wyoming Wellington, a beef fillet with mushroom pâté baked in a pastry shell, with bordelaise sauce. Sautéed breaded shrimp dipped in artichoke hearts and mustard is a popular appetizer. *175 N. Center St., Jackson, tel. 307/733–6803. Reservations required. AE, MC, V. No lunch. Expensive.*

Sweetwater Restaurant. A three-room, historic downtown log cabin enhanced by stained-glass windows, a chandelier, and a deck, Sweetwater is crowded with locals drawn by its Greek and American fare. Especially good are the mesquite-grilled Atlantic salmon with raspberry-cream sauce and the moussaka. *Kolokythopita* (feta and Parmesan cheeses with zucchini, baked in phyllo) is an outstanding appetizer. *Corner King and Pearl Sts., Jackson, tel. 307/733–3553. Reservations advised. AE, MC, V. Expensive.*

Cadillac Grille and **Billy's Burger Bar.** The Cadillac is as slick as Jackson's eateries get: art-deco decor, glass tabletops, classic-car photos, low ceiling fans, and a marble floor. Unfortunately, the nouvelle Western menu doesn't always live up to the restaurant's pretensions. Among entrées that do are buffalo in zinfandel-blackberry sauce with polenta, venison medallions with chanterelle mushrooms and ancho chile sauce, and blackened orange roughy in pineapple butter. Exotic renditions of antelope, wild boar, caribou, and pheasant are sometimes available. Across the front lobby of the Cadillac Grille is Billy's, with a tiled diner floor and reliable food. Jackson's biggest burgers are cooked at the counter right before your eyes. *Cache St. on Town Square, Jackson, tel. 307/733–3279. Reservations required for Cadillac; not accepted at Billy's. AE, DC, MC, V. Cadillac, Moderate–Expensive; Billy's, Inexpensive.*

Anthony's. Inconspicuously set on a downtown Jackson side street, this homey local favorite, run by a New York émigré, befits New York's Jackson Heights more than Wyoming's Jackson Hole. Past a lounge with an antique barber chair and '60s kitsch tables rescued from a local bar (the owner is also an antiques dealer), you'll find southern Italian abundance. Anthony's minestrone comes with a thick, spicy broth; his chicken Marsala is smothered in mushrooms and prosciutto. Lasagna and a spicy Cajun fettuccine with chicken, shrimp, and sausage are also popular. *62 S. Glenwood St., Jackson, tel. 307/733–3717. Reservations advised. MC, V. No lunch. Moderate.*

Bar J Chuckwagon Suppers. Jackson Hole's Western lifestyle is the theme at this "best buy" in the valley. Besides an all-you-can-eat meal of barbecued beef, potatoes, beans, biscuits, cake, and coffee or lemonade, you get a first-class Western show featuring the Bar J Wranglers. Recalling the days of cattle drives and the old West, the show provides a full hour of entertainment in the form of cowboy yodeling, cowboy poetry, and Western stories. *Teton Village Rd., Wilson, tel. 307/733–3370. Reservations advised. AE, MC, V. Inexpensive.*

Bubba's Bar-B-Que. Not your average beef 'n' beans joint, this traditional favorite has wood booths, antique signs, and paintings of Western gunmen, as well as groaning beef, pork, turkey, and chicken barbecue platters. Chili, chocolate-buttermilk pie, and the tremendous salad bar are also popular with locals and families. *515 W. Broadway, Jackson, tel. 307/733–2288. No reservations. D, MC, V. Inexpensive.*

The Bunnery. This lively pine-panel wholegrain restaurant and bakery is hidden in a bustling nook called the Hole-in-the-Wall Mall. A favorite hearty breakfast, the Mother Earth, includes mushrooms, tomatoes, and broccoli piled upon a bed of home fries covered with melted cheddar. Many meals are served on or with the Bunnery's multigrain bread. Lunches and suppers feature hot sandwiches, burgers, and Mexican fare. There are daily baked specials, and beer and espresso are served. *130 N. Cache St., Jackson, tel. 307/733–5474. Reservations not accepted. MC, V. No dinner early Sept.–early June. Inexpensive.*

Jedediah's House of Sourdough. Mountainman memorabilia decorates this laid-back, somewhat noisy, log cabin breakfast-and-lunch spot, which serves sourdough and whole-grain pancakes, waffles, and biscuits—not to mention buffalo burgers. *1 block east of Town Square on E. Broadway, Jackson,* *tel. 307/733–5671. Reservations not accepted. AE, MC, V. No dinner. Inexpensive.*

PICNIC SPOTS The park has 11 designated picnic areas, each with tables, grills, pit toilets, and water pumps or faucets. Those at **Signal Mountain Lodge** and **Colter Bay Visitor Center** are also close to flush toilets and stores. Colter Bay's big picnic area is spectacularly located right on the beach at Jackson Lake (continue north past the visitor center to reach it), and it gets crowded in July and August. The Signal Mountain Lodge picnic area is a slightly less crowded alternative; it, too, can accommodate a big group and is also lakeside. A more intimate lakeside picnic area is near the **Chapel of the Sacred Heart,** on Jackson Lake, about a mile north of Signal Mountain Lodge. From this area you will enjoy great views across southern Jackson Lake to Mt. Moran.

Another scenic although, again, often crowded picnic area is at the **String Lake Trailhead.** To reach it, turn right onto the spur road off Jenny Lake Road, just north of Jenny Lake. Jenny Lake itself has no designated areas, but you can improvise along the Jenny Lake Trail or at popular Hidden Falls (buy supplies at the Jenny Lake Store). Farther south, just north of the **Taggart Lake Trailhead,** on the east side of Teton Park Road, a picnic area offers views of the Snake River Valley to the east and the southern Tetons to the west.

One of the park's most isolated and uncrowded picnic sites is in the **Two Ocean Lake** area. Drive about 1 mile north of Moran Junction on the Jackson Hole Highway, then turn right onto the Pacific Creek Road, following signs to the lake for about 4 miles. North of Colter Bay, four scenic roadside picnic areas dot the east shore of Jackson Lake. The northernmost, near **Lizard Creek Campground,** is closer to the Flagg Ranch Village stores than it is to Colter Bay's facilities.

LODGING

The park itself doesn't have Yellowstone's quantity or variety of accommodations. A much better range is available in Jackson and Teton Village, which have everything from bare-bones hostels to expensive time-share condominiums. Jackson has several excellent bed-and-breakfasts, too. Make reservations for July and August park lodgings two months ahead. Outside the park, ski season raises winter rates $10 to $40 per night. Many lodgings offer April to May shoulder-season bargains. You can reserve some rooms outside the park through **Jackson Hole Central Reservations** (Box 510, Teton Village, WY 83025, tel. 307/733–4005 or 800/443–6931), which handles hotels as well as B&Bs.

INSIDE THE PARK Jackson Lake Lodge. Built in 1955, John D. Rockefeller, Jr.'s, contribution to park architecture is a massive brown stone edifice perched on a bluff overlooking the Willow Flats. With walls bordered with Native American designs, the freshly renovated lobby leads to the main guest lounge and is worth a visit even if you're not staying here. Buttressed with giant concrete beams stained to resemble wood and Idaho stone columns, the lounge has two walk-in fireplaces and a 60-foot-high window overlooking Willow Flats. Teton travelers can relax on the thick old leather chairs and sofas. A 1989 addition to the main lounge, the Blue Heron cocktail lounge, also has big windows. In comparison to the lounges' sumptuous furnishings, the 37 rooms within the lodge proper are a letdown: They lack adequate ventilation, and they're the smallest and least desirable rooms in the complex. On the other hand, the 343 motor-lodge rooms on either side of the main building are a pleasant surprise. Each room has log partitions, oak furniture, Native American quilts, ceiling fans, and 19th-century prints of the Tetons. Half of them were renovated in 1990, and renovations on the rest were completed by 1993. An outdoor heated pool has a tepee-shape cabana. *Grand Teton Lodge Company, Box 240, Moran, WY 83013, tel. 307/543–2855 or 800/628–9988, fax 307/543–2869. 385 rooms. Facilities: 2 restaurants, lounge, business center, 5 shops. AE, DC, MC, V. Closed early Oct.–late May. Expensive.*

Jenny Lake Lodge. This is the most expensive—some say overpriced—lodging in the entire national park system. Nestled well off Jenny Lake Road (only the main building is visible from the road), the lodge borders a wildflower meadow, and its guest cabins are adequately spaced in lodgepole-pine groves. The main guest lounge is of open-beam construction and has a tidy raised stone fireplace and pine furniture. Cabin interiors, with their sturdy pine beds and handmade quilts and electric blankets, live up to the elegant rustic theme. Cabin suites have fireplaces. Lodging is on the Modified American Plan, with breakfast and dinner in the excellent lodge restaurant included. *Grand Teton Lodge Company, Box 240, Moran, WY 83013, tel. 307/543–2855 or 800/628–9988, fax 307/543–2869. 37 cabins, 6 suites. Facilities: restaurant, cocktail lounge. AE, DC, MC, V. Closed mid-Sept.–late May. Expensive.*

Signal Mountain Lodge. The only park lodging not run by Grand Teton Lodge Company, Signal Mountain Lodge offers a refreshing change of pace from Colter Bay's commotion and Jackson and Jenny Lake lodges' toniness. The main building's volcanic travertine and pine-shingle exterior gives way to a cramped lobby and cozy lounge with Adirondack stick furniture, a fireplace, a piano, and a television (a rarity within the park). Out back is a grand, open pine deck. The rooms here are not in the lodge; instead, there are clusters of four cabinlike units with modern upholstered furniture, sleek kitchens, and pine tables. The larger units sleep up to six people. Numbers 151 to 178 overlook Jackson Lake. Smaller shaded log cabins have carpeting and rustic pine furniture; eight have fireplaces. *Teton Park Rd., Box 50, Moran, WY 83013, tel. 307/543–2831 or 307/733–5470, fax 307/543–2569. 79 units. Facilities: restaurant, bar, business center, store, 3 shops, marina. AE, D, MC, V. Closed mid-Oct.–early May. Moderate–Expensive.*

Colter Bay Cabins. These log structures, some of which are remodeled settlers' cabins, line a terraced drive overlooking Jackson Lake. Furniture is sturdy, simple pine. Odd-numbered cabins 1001 to 1011 and even numbers 468 to 492 offer the best views. *Colter Bay Village, Grand Teton Lodge Company, Box 240, Moran, WY 83013, tel. 307/543–2855, 800/628–9988, 307/543–2811 for same-day reservations; fax 307/543–2869. 209 cabins, most with bath. Facilities: 3 restaurants, bar, 3 shops, laundromat. AE, DC, MC, V. Closed late Sept.–mid-May. Moderate.*

Colter Bay Tent Cabins. The walls of these cabins are canvas on log frames, and there are minimal furnishings and shared baths, but the price and central location are unbeatable. Each cabin has an outdoor grill, a wood-burning stove, and two double-decker bunks. The cabins are all set around a circular drive, with rest rooms and showers in the middle. *Colter Bay Village, Grand Teton Lodge Company, Box 240, Moran, WY 83013, tel. 307/543–2855, 800/628–9988, 307/543–2811 for same-day reservations; fax 307/543–2869. 72 cabins. Facilities: see Colter Bay Cabins, above. AE, DC, MC, V. Closed early Sept.–early June. Inexpensive.*

NEAR THE PARK **Best Western Inn at Jackson Hole.** Far superior in quality to most of the area's chain motels, the Best Western, set slightly back from the rest of Teton Village's commotion, is actually a distinctive, first-rate hotel. Stone floors, a fireplace, and tree-trunk tables in the lobby are matched by the airy, natural decor of a broad range of rooms renovated during the past few years. Deluxe rooms with lofts feature four-poster lodgepole or bamboo beds, fireplaces, oak or cherry-wood furniture, and a beige color scheme. Even standard and economy rooms have this fine furniture, but the latter are without mountain views. A popular cocktail lounge named Beaver Dick's and two restaurants are located in a modern atrium. The inn also has the best outdoor poolside view of the Tetons. *Box 328, Teton Village, WY 83025, tel. 307/733–2311 or 800/842–7666, fax 307/733–0844. 83 rooms. Facilities: 2 restaurants, bar, sauna, 3 Jacuzzis, laundromat, gift shop, heated outdoor pool. AE, D, DC, MC, V. Expensive.*

Flagg Ranch Village. A sprawling year-round resort 4 miles north of the park, the Flagg Ranch is at least convenient. Recently renovated two-story motel units on the Snake River are still bland, except for the view they give of the northern Tetons; cabins have more attractive pine furnishings but lack views. With its snack bar, float trips that leave from the premises, games, and patio movies, Flagg Ranch is particularly popular with families. *Box 187, John D. Rockefeller, Jr., Memorial Parkway, Moran, WY 83013, tel. 307/543–2861 or 800/443–2311, fax 307/543–2356. 54 rooms, 6 cabins. Facilities: 2 restaurants, bar, 2 Jacuzzis, 3 shops, laundry. MC, V. Closed mid-Oct.–mid-Dec. and mid-Mar.–mid-May. Expensive.*

Jackson Hole Lodge. Like the Wort Hotel (*see below*), Jackson Hole Lodge dates from the early '40s, but despite renovations a few years ago, this in-town lodge has not aged quite as gracefully. Hand-hewn lodgepole pine and a stone fireplace accent the lobby, and stuffed '40s furniture adds character to a comfortable upstairs sitting room. Antique Oregon white pine, originally in the lobby, has been reused in the lodge rooms, which get too much street noise. The condominiums and some motel rooms are quieter. A game room and a big indoor pool keep the children happy. *420 W. Broadway, Box 1805–B, Jackson, WY 83001, tel. 307/733–2992, fax 307/739–2144. 26 rooms, 33 condominiums. Facilities: health club, indoor pool, sauna, 2 Jacuzzis. AE, D, DC, MC, V. Expensive.*

Spring Creek Resort. Fifteen minutes from downtown Jackson, yet isolated atop 7,000-foot East Gros Ventre Butte, this elegant group of log buildings occupies 1,000 acres of sagebrush and wildflower meadows adjacent to a mule-deer refuge. Most buildings are of open-beam lodgepole construction, and the main building's intimate lobby is decorated with homey plaid-upholstered chairs. There are four single-bedroom units in some buildings and blocks of four to six two-bedroom condominiums. All include floor-to-ceiling stone fireplaces, pine beds and furniture, Native American hangings and prints, and porches with views of the Tetons. Guided horseback rides are available at Spring Creek, and there are stables where you can board your own horse. The resort also has a Nordic ski center and offers dogsled trips. Shoulder-season specials for couples make this romantic setting especially affordable from April to May and mid-October to November. *1800 Spirit Dance Rd., Jackson, WY 83001, tel. 307/733–8833 or 800/443–6139, fax 307/733–1524. 117 units. Facilities: restaurant, cocktail lounge, outdoor pool, Jacuzzi, concierge, business center. AE, D, DC, MC, V. Expensive.*

Wort Hotel. Built by a rodeo cowboy in 1942, during Jackson's earlier incarnation as a winter hideaway for wealthy Hollywood and East Coast residents, this dandy old downtown-Jackson hotel was rebuilt after a 1980 fire and redecorated in 1993. Beyond its stone facade and big front staircase, a pine-panel lounge features Southwest-style furniture and a stone fireplace topped by a massive moose head. Halls are lined with photos of the many Hollywood cowboys who worked and played here, among them Alan Ladd, who's renowned for his fight scene in the movie *Shane.* A vintage slot machine in the hall is the lone remnant of the Wort's past as an illegal but tolerated gambling house. Look for the old photo of the row of slots that was once hidden under a stairway. Down one hall is JJ's Silver Dollar Bar, inlaid with 2,032 uncirculated 1921 silver dollars. Rooms have modern oak furniture and flowered quilts, and some even have Murphy beds. Second-floor rooms are quieter, and some feature lodgepole furniture. *Corner Broadway and Glenwood Sts., Box 69, Jackson, WY 83001, tel. 307/733–2190 or 800/322–2727, fax 307/733–2067. 60 rooms. Facilities: restaurant, bar, health club, 2 Jacuzzis, business center. AE, D, DC, MC, V. Expensive.*

Cowboy Village Resort. Log cabins with porches, barbecue grills, and picnic tables make this quasi-rural establishment, on a quiet side street south of downtown Jackson, a desirable home base for families. *Flat Creek Rd., Box 1747, Jackson, WY 83001, tel. 307/733–3121 or 800/962–4988, fax 307/739–1955. 57 cabins. Facilities: Jacuzzi. AE, D, MC, V. Moderate.*

Grand Targhee Resort. On the west side of the Tetons, this popular ski center is also a summer resort with hiking trails, horseback riding, and other outdoor activities. The motel-style rooms are undistinguished. *12 mi east of Driggs, ID, off U.S. 33 on Grand Targhee Rd., Box SKI, Alta, WY 83422, tel. 307/353–2300 or 800/827–4433, fax 307/353–8148. 63 rooms. Facilities: restaurant, bar, pool, Jacuzzi, laundromat. AE, MC, V. Moderate.*

Split Creek Ranch. Modest, carpeted rooms with electric heat in a log lodge are set 1½ miles west of Gros Ventre Junction south of the park. These are quiet country accommodations without phones or TVs. *Zenith Dr., Box 3463, Jackson, WY 83001, tel. 307/733–7522. 8 rooms. Facilities: Jacuzzi, laundry. MC, V. Moderate.*

Togwotee Mountain Lodge. Seventeen miles from the Moran entrance, this big, family-oriented log lodge has a central fireside room and a game room. The lodge also offers horseback riding and snowmobile rentals. *U.S. 26–287, Box 91–J, Moran, WY 83013, tel. 307/543–2847 or 800/543–2847. 35 rooms. Facilities: restaurant, bar, sauna, Jacuzzi, laundry. AE, D, V. Moderate.*

The Hostel. Favored in summer and winter by young, budget-conscious outdoorspeople, this modest Teton Village lodging has four beds (a bunk bed and two twins) per room. The downstairs lounge has a huge stone fireplace; skiing and mountaineering movies are shown here. The rooms have no phones or TVs. *Box 546, Teton Village, WY 83025, tel. 307/733–3415, fax 307/739–1142. 60 rooms. Facilities: laundry, game room. MC, V. Inexpensive.*

On the Teton Village Road (Highway 390), about 8 miles from Jackson and 3 miles from Teton Village, visitors will find two of the area's best B&Bs, the Painted Porch Bed and Breakfast and the Wildflower Inn, as well as the largest condominium-rental complex. The **Painted Porch Bed and Breakfast** (Teton Village Rd., Box 7453, Jackson, WY 83001, tel. 307/733–1981) is a modern house with five guest rooms, each with a private bath. It also has two Japanese soaking tubs and a restaurant. Right next door is the **Wildflower Inn** (Teton Village Rd., Box 3724, Jackson, WY 83001, tel. 307/733–4710), a sprawling log home on 3 acres, with five sunny rooms with private baths, a restaurant, Jacuzzi, and game room. Right next to these two B&Bs is the vast **Jackson Hole Racquet Club Resort** (Teton Village Rd., Box 3647, Jackson, WY 83001, tel. 307/733–3990), which has 120 condos ranging from studios to three-bedroom units. The complex has a restaurant, bar, sauna/Jacuzzi, laundry, in-room fireplaces, convention facilities, and a fitness center. All of the above accommodations are rated Expensive, although there is a large gap in price between a single room and a three-bedroom condo.

In Jackson there are a number of nondescript but adequate lodgings, most of which are franchises of large, national hotel chains. These include: The **Best Western Executive Inn** (325 W. Pearl St., Box 1101, Jackson, WY 83001, tel. 307/733–4340 or 800/528–1234; Expensive), the **Days Inn** (1280 W. Broadway, Jackson, WY 83001, tel. 307/739–9010 or 800/325–2525; Expensive), the **Forty-Niner Motel** (330 W. Pearl Ave., Box 575, Jackson, WY 83001, tel. 307/733–7550 or 800/451–2980; Moderate–Expensive), the **Virginian Lodge** (Box 1052, 750 W. Broadway, Jackson, WY 83001, tel. 307/733–2792 or 800/262–4999; Moderate–Expensive), the **Antler Motel** (43 W. Pearl Ave., Box 575, Jackson, WY 83001, tel. 307/733–2535; Moderate), the **Super 8 Motel** (Box 1382, 1520 S. U.S. 89, Jackson, WY 83001, tel. 307/733–6833 or 800/800–8000; Moderate), the **Trapper Motel** (Box 1712, 235 N. Cache St., Jackson, WY 83001, tel. 307/733–2648 or 800/341–8000; Moderate), the **Wagon Wheel Motel** (Box 525, 435 N. Cache St., Jackson, WY 83001, tel. 307/733–2357 or 800/323-9279; Moderate), the **Hoback River Resort** (Star Rte., Box 23, U.S. 89, Jackson, WY 83001, tel. 307/733–5129; Inexpensive–Moderate), and the **Motel 6** (1370 W. Broadway, Jackson, WY 83001, tel. 307/733–1620; Inexpensive).

CAMPING

Camping possibilities are abundant and varied both inside and outside the park. Inside the park, facilities range from a concessionaire-operated RV site with full hookups to isolated primitive sites in the backcountry. Outside the park there are commercial RV-and-tent campgrounds, as well as roadside campgrounds and backcountry sites on national-forest lands surrounding the park. Always remember that Grand Teton is high, wild country; even if you camp in Colter Bay Village, down the road from a snack bar and laundry, take precautions against bears, and be prepared for temperatures that can dip below freezing even on a night in July.

INSIDE THE PARK Within Grand Teton National Park, the National Park Service operates five campgrounds: Colter Bay, Gros Ventre, Lizard Creek, Signal Mountain, and Jenny Lake. The campground at Jenny Lake allows tenters and small camping vehicles, but no trailers. The others accommodate tents, trailers, and RVs. There are no hookups available in these campgrounds, but all of them have fire grates, drinking water, and modern restrooms with cold water. Only Colter Bay has hot showers. Fees are $8 per vehicle per night at every National Park Service campground.

A maximum stay of seven days is allowed at Jenny Lake and 14 days at the others. You might consider checking in as early as possible—sites are assigned on a first-come, first-served basis; no reservations are accepted. In July and August most campgrounds are filled by day's end; however, you can usually find a campsite in one of several commercial Jackson Hole campgrounds or in nearby Bridger-Teton and Targhee national forests.

You also have the option of camping in the park's backcountry, which can be done year-round if you're able to gain access to it. Remember that snow remains in the high country through much of the summer. Between June 1 and September 15, backcountry campers in the park are limited to stays of fewer than 11 days.

GRAND TETON CAMPGROUNDS

*Number of campgrounds. **Reservation fee charged.

	INSIDE THE PARK						NEAR THE PARK		
	Colter Bay	Gros Ventre	Jenny Lake	Lizard Creek	Signal Mountain	Colter Bay Trailer Village	Flagg Ranch Village	Bridger-Teton National Forest	Targhee National Forest
Total number of sites	310	360	49	60	86	112	175	39*	30*
Sites suitable for RVs	310	360	0	NA	80	112	100		
Number of hookups	0	0	0	0	0	112	100	0	0
Drive to sites	•	•	•	•	•	•	•	•	•
Hike to sites									
Flush toilets	•	•	•	•	•	•	•		
Pit/chemical toilets								•	•
Drinking water	•	•	•	•	•	•	•	•	•
Showers	•				•	•	•		
Fire grates	•	•	•	•	•		•	•	•
Swimming									
Boat access	•		•	•	•				
Playground									
Disposal station	•	•			•	•	•		
Ranger station	•	•	•		•	•	•		
Public telephone	•	•	•		•	•	•		
Reservation possible						•	•	•**	•**
Daily fee per site	$8	$8	$8	$8	$8	$17–$21	$16–$21	$4–$6	$3–$9
Dates open	mid-May–late Sept.	early May–mid-Oct.	late May–late Sept.	mid-June–early Sept.	early May–mid-Oct.	mid-May–Oct.	mid-May–mid-Oct.	mid-May–mid-Sept.	Memorial Day–Labor Day

For visitors with RVs, two concessionaire-operated campgrounds, Colter Bay Trailer Village and Flagg Ranch Village (which is outside the park), provide hookups.

Busy, noisy, and filled by noon, the **Colter Bay** campground has one great advantage: It's centrally located. There are 310 tent and RV sites, hot showers, a ranger station, a disposal station, and public phones, as well as boat access. Try to get a site as far from the nearby cabin road as possible. Don't confuse this campground with the roadside Colter Bay Trailer Village, operated by Grand Teton Lodge Company, which charges $21 per site with full hookup. Colter Bay is open from mid-May to late September, depending on weather conditions.

Gros Ventre is the park's biggest campground, but it is as isolated as Colter Bay is centrally located. It has 360 tent and RV sites set in an open, grassy area on the bank of the Gros Ventre River, away from the mountains. Here you might see moose and antelope. Try to get a site close to the river. The campground usually doesn't fill until nightfall, if at all, but it's closed from mid-October to early May. It is on Gros Ventre Road, 2 miles southwest of Kelly, which has a general store.

The campground at **Jenny Lake** has 49 wooded sites and lovely views across the water that make it the most desirable campground in the park. It is small and quiet and allows tents and small camping vehicles, but no trailers. Close to the Jenny Lake trailhead, this campground is extremely popular and usually fills by 8 AM in July and August. Jenny Lake has phones, boat access, and a ranger station; it is open from the end of May to late September.

With 60 sites, **Lizard Creek** probably has the park's best combination of views and relative isolation, although like Gros Ventre it is not near stores or other facilities. For that you'll have to drive 8 miles north to Flagg Ranch or 8 miles south to Colter Bay. The campground is set on a wooded point of land close to northern Jackson Lake and across the water from Webb Canyon, the park's most primitive hiking area. There is no shuttle-boat service

across the lake from here, but many backcountry hikers use their own boats. Lizard Creek usually fills by 2 PM in summer and is closed from early September through mid-June. RVs longer than 25 feet are not allowed.

Providing much better Teton views than Colter Bay campground, **Signal Mountain** campground has boat access on southern Jackson Lake. Its 86 sites set on the lakeshore are close to nearby stores and services and, in July and August, are filled by 9 AM. Signal Mountain has public phones, a disposal station, and a ranger station. It's open from early May to mid-October.

Colter Bay Trailer Village, near Colter Bay Marina, is ideal for RVers toting boats. This large, often crowded 112-site RV park is also close to horseback riding, stores, and the Colter Bay Visitor Center. It is an open, flat area that is not very attractive. Sites are paved or gravel, all with full hookups, and cost $17 from May to early June; $21 late June to early September; and $17 September 6 to October 3. Colter Bay Trailer Village has rest rooms with hot showers, boat access, a disposal station, a ranger station, and public phones. LP gas is available at village stores. The trailer park is run by the Grand Teton Lodge Company (Box 240, Moran, WY 83013, tel. 307/733–2811). Reservations are strongly advised in July and August; the campground is open from mid-May to October.

NEAR THE PARK The **Flagg Ranch Village Campground** (Box 187, Moran, WY 83013, tel. 307/543–2861 or 800/443–2311, fax 307/543–2356) is reached from a turnoff just north of the bustling main Flagg Ranch Village turnoff (*see* Lodging, *above*), 4 miles north of the park on U.S. 89–287. It is on the John D. Rockefeller, Jr., Memorial Parkway, which is also administered by the National Park Service. Set in a wooded area near the north bank of the Snake River, the campground has 100 RV sites, with full hookups, that vary in width and length. Tenters can be accommodated in 75 additional sites. The campground has a ranger station, a disposal station, hot showers, and fire grates. LP gas is sold. Reservations are advised. Sites cost $21 for a full hookup and $16 for a tent site. The campground is open mid-May to mid-October.

There are 39 campgrounds scattered across **Bridger-Teton National Forest,** a huge expanse of land that stretches south and east of Grand Teton and Yellowstone national parks. These campgrounds are best suited to tent camping (only a few can accommodate RVs) and typically have drinking water, pit toilets, and fire grates, although facilities do vary from place to place. Most Bridger-Teton National Forest campgrounds charge $4 to $6 per night, but in some places you can camp for free. The majority of these campgrounds are open from mid-May to mid-September. Reservations are accepted at 15 of the campgrounds—some through L&L, Inc. (tel. 800/342–2267), others through U.S. Forest Reservations (tel. 800/280–2267)—and sites are assigned on a first-come, first-served basis at the rest. You can also camp free in the backcountry here, but be sure to find out about restricted areas and fire dangers before heading out. It's a good idea to stop at the National Forest Service Visitor Center (340 N. Cache) in Jackson. For more information, call 307/733–2752.

Of the 30 or so campgrounds in **Targhee National Forest,** on the west side of the park, 22 are close to Grand Teton. These also typically have drinking water, pit toilets, and fire grates. RVs can be accommodated, but there are no hookups. Most Targhee National Forest campgrounds accept reservations, which must be made through U.S. Forest Reservations (*see above*); sites at others are available only on a first-come, first-served basis. These campgrounds are officially open Memorial Day to Labor Day, but you may camp in many of them (unless there is a barricade) until access is blocked by snow. Most sites cost $3 to $9; some are free. Backcountry camping is allowed in most areas, but be sure to call the forest service to find out about restrictions. For more information, call 208/624–3151.

Jasper National Park
Alberta
By Peter Oliver

hould you doubt that Jasper is the largest of the Canadian Rockies national parks, talk to an experienced Jasper backpacker. With 10,878 square kilometers (4,200 square miles), Jasper has plenty of room to roam; extended trips of more than 160 kilometers (100 miles) without crossing any paved roads are possible. Because of its expansive back-country, Jasper tends to draw a higher percentage of willing-to-rough-it types than does Banff National Park to the south.

This should not suggest, however, that the park comes up short in easily accessible attractions. The Icefield area, near the park's southern border with Banff, is among the most visited sites in all of the parks, getting its share of day trippers from the towns of Banff and Lake Louise. Other Jasper sites of note are Maligne Lake and Maligne Canyon, Pyramid Lake, and the Whistlers, the mountain near the town of Jasper serviced by an aerial tram.

It took the Canadian government somewhat longer to create a national park around Jasper than it did to create one around Banff, essentially because of slower railroad development. The priority of the Canadian Pacific Railroad in the late 1800s was to complete an east–west route that passed south of Jasper. This development led to fears of heavy land speculation, which in turn inspired government officials to establish Jasper National Park in 1907. The Grand Trunk Pacific Railway route through Jasper's Yellowhead Pass (through which Route 16 now passes) was finally completed in 1911.

The park's boundaries did not, however, incorporate what is perhaps the most remarkable—certainly the highest—mountain in all of the Canadian Rockies. Mt. Robson, at 12,931 feet, is a stark, often cloud-shrouded colossus of tumbling glaciers and rock walls more than 2 kilometers (1¼ miles) high and prone to violent weather and avalanches. It's no matter that the mountain is part of Mt.

Robson Provincial Park rather than Jasper National Park. The two parks are contiguous, and Route 16 and hiking trails (to a much lesser extent) make travel between the two easy.

Jasper National Park is really two parks in one, a southern half and a northern half. The southern half, with most of the park's featured attractions, is by far the more heavily visited. The landscape here consists largely of what the Canadian Rockies are known for: rugged peaks and glaciers. When visitors combine Banff and Jasper national parks in their travels—a popular vacation program—most stay in the town of Jasper and stick to the park's southern half.

The northern half, by contrast, has minimal trails and even fewer roads. Although mountains are many, the high, glaciated peaks common in the south are rare in the north. This is getaway land, choice country for wilderness backpackers, packhorse adventurers, and anglers.

Many of the people who prefer to center their Canadian Rockies travels in Jasper do so to escape the crowds and commercial bustle of Banff. The pace of Jasper is more easygoing, although Jasper is similar to Banff in one respect: It is no quaint mountain village. Its architecture is plain, clean, and functional. Jasper is no more than it needs to be: a base of operations for exploring the park's considerable natural riches.

ESSENTIAL INFORMATION

VISITOR INFORMATION The major sources of information are: Superintendent, **Jasper National Park** (Box 10, Jasper, AB T0E 1E0, tel. 403/852–6161), **Alberta Tourism** (Main Level, City Centre, 10155 102 St., Edmonton, AB T5J 4L6, tel. 800/661–8888), **The Canadian Parks Service** (Information Services, Box 2989, Station M, Calgary, AB T2P 3H8, tel. 403/292–4401), and **Jasper Tourism and Commerce** (Box 98, Jasper, AB T0E 1E0, tel. 403/852–3858). There is also a Parks Service information office in Banff (224 Banff Ave., Banff, AB T0L 0C0, tel. 403/762–4256). All of

Jasper is within Alberta; travelers planning to venture into neighboring British Columbia should contact **Tourism British Columbia** (Parliament Bldgs., Victoria, BC V8V 1X4, tel. 604/663–6000).

FEES All vehicles entering the park are assessed a visitors' fee. A day pass is $4.25, a four-day pass is $9.50, and an annual pass is $26.75 (all fees are quoted in Canadian currency). You may leave and re-enter the park for the duration of the pass without additional charge. Any pass is good for visiting any of the nearby national parks.

PUBLICATIONS Alberta Tourism and the Canadian Parks Service (*see* Visitor Information, *above*) have extensive lists of maps, booklets, and brochures. Among the best are Alberta Tourism's *Alberta Touring Guide* and *Alberta Adventure Guide.* Indispensable for hikers in the park is *The Canadian Rockies Trail Guide,* by Brian Patton and Bart Robinson.

GEOLOGY AND TERRAIN *See* the Banff National Park chapter.

FLORA AND FAUNA *See* the Banff National Park chapter.

WHEN TO GO The park is open year-round, with the high season from late June to mid-September. Not surprisingly, lodging prices are highest in summer; room rates before September 15 (or thereabouts) are typically 50% or more above what they are later in the fall. With the snowcapped mountains, changing foliage, and generally warm days and cool nights, late September is a prime time to visit the park. However, Jasper slows down in fall and winter more than Banff does, and a few services, hotels, and outlying lodges shut down by mid-October.

Jasper is still quite popular in winter, when visitors enjoy downhill skiing and ski touring. And don't be misled into thinking Jasper's northerly latitude assures a cold winter climate. Because the town of Jasper is about 1,000 feet lower in elevation than Banff, and because it receives a greater share of the

Pacific Ocean's maritime effects, its average temperatures are surprisingly moderate.

High temperatures in summer typically range from the upper 60s to the lower 80s, with midwinter highs ranging between the teens and the 30s. With every 1,000 feet of elevation gain, temperatures usually drop about 5 degrees. Yet July snowstorms, especially at higher elevations, are not unheard of, and warm chinook winds have been known to raise winter temperatures into the 70s.

SEASONAL EVENTS January is considered winter-festival time in Jasper, but "festival" is a loosely used term. The main push of the winter-festival concept is to attract visitors to the park—that is, to fill hotel rooms—during normally slow months. Hence, room rates are widely discounted, and special events, tending heavily toward ski-related promotions, are widely scattered.

Every **August** in even-number years, the **Jasper Folk Festival** attracts musicians, both the famous and the obscure, from the United States and Canada for a series of concerts and informal performances. The other notable summer event is the **Jasper Indoor Rodeo,** testament to the cowboy-and-ranching culture that remains a vital part of the Canadian west.

WHAT TO PACK Casual dress is the way of the world here, unless you plan to spend time at Jasper Park Lodge, a last outpost of an old-fashion, more formal dress code (although, even at the lodge, you can get away with neat sportswear). The first rule in packing for the Canadian Rockies is to be ready for almost any weather. Even in summer, pack a warm wool sweater or synthetic-fleece jacket, warm socks, light gloves, and a windbreaker, especially if you have such outdoor activities as hiking, biking, or boating in mind. If you are planning hikes of a half-day or longer or expect to spend much time above the tree line, bring extra layers, especially a layer of polypropylene long underwear, and a warm hat.

GENERAL STORES Basically, the only place in the park for supplies is in the town of Jasper itself. There is a small convenience store near Pocahontas, at the Miette Hotsprings turnoff, but it's hardly a place for stocking up. Hinton, just east of the park gate on Route 16, is a good place for last-minute shopping before entering the park.

ARRIVING AND DEPARTING **By Plane.** The nearest international airport is **Edmonton International Airport,** served by several major U.S. and Canadian airlines. Travelers making a combined trip to Banff and Jasper national parks might prefer flying into **Calgary International Airport,** which is much nearer to Banff.

By Car and RV. The main east–west route through the park is Route 16. The town of Jasper is 360 kilometers (224 miles) west of Edmonton on Route 16, an easy four-hour drive. Many park visitors, however, come into the park from the south—from Banff and Calgary—via Route 93. The town of Jasper, at the juncture of Routes 16 and 93, is 287 kilometers (178 miles) from the town of Banff; the Jasper park border, near the Icefield Centre, is 180 kilometers (110 miles) from the town of Banff.

By Train. VIA Rail Canada (tel. 800/361–3677) provides connecting service between Jasper and Toronto, Edmonton, and Vancouver. Call for schedules and fares.

By Bus. Greyhound Lines (in Edmonton, tel. 800/231–2222) provides regular ser-vice between Edmonton and Vancouver, with a stop at Jasper. **Brewster Transportation** (tel. 403/852–3332 or 800/661–1152) in Jasper has regular service between Banff and Jasper.

EXPLORING

For anyone traveling between Jasper and Banff, the **Icefield Centre** is a hard place not to stop. An approximate halfway point along the Icefields Parkway—125 kilometers (75 miles) from Lake Louise and 105 kilometers (62 miles) from the town of Jasper—it's a logical service stop for gas, food, and even lodging. Its primary purpose, however, is as a starting point for people viewing or venturing onto the Athabasca Glacier.

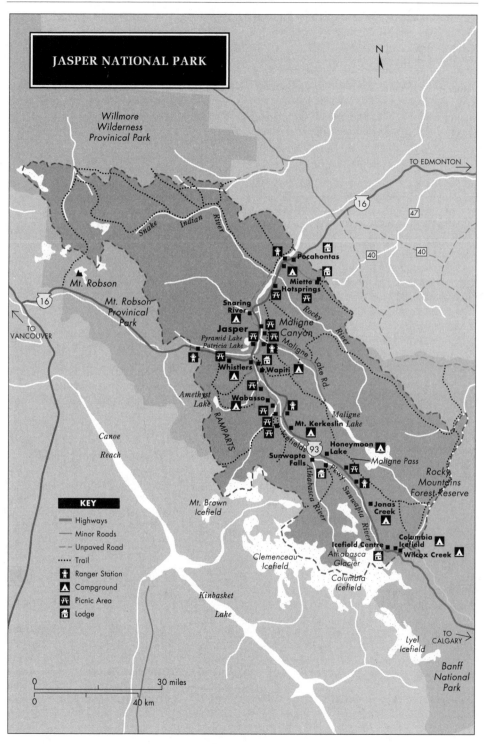

JASPER NATIONAL PARK

Willmore
Wilderness
Provinical Park

TO EDMONTON

Mt. Robson

Mt. Robson
Provinical
Park

TO VANCOUVER

Pocahontas

Miette
Hotsprings

Snaring
River

Jasper

Pyramid Lake
Patricia Lake

Maligne
Canyon

Maligne Lake Rd

Whistlers

Wapiti

Amethyst
Lake

Wabasso

Maligne
Lake

RAMPARTS

Mt. Kerkeslin

Canoe
Reach

Honeymoon
Lake

Maligne Pass

Sunwapta
Falls

Rocky
Mountains
Forest Reserve

Mt. Brown
Icefield

Jonas
Creek

Clemenceau
Icefield

Icefield Centre

Athabasca
Glacier

Columbia
Icefield

Wilcox Creek

Columbia
Icefield

Kinbasket
Lake

TO CALGARY

Lyel
Icefield

Banff
National
Park

KEY

Highways
Minor Roads
Unpaved Road
Trail
Ranger Station
Campground
Picnic Area
Lodge

0   30 miles
0   40 km

The **Columbia Icefield,** covering approximately 325 square kilometers (125 square miles), is the largest single mass of ice in subarctic North America. It's just one of a number of ice fields in the area that are the collective source of numerous rivers in western Canada and the United States. From the Icefield Centre, the Athabasca Glacier, just across the highway, is the most immediate indication of the great store of ice that lies beyond.

Interpretive exhibits and an audiovisual presentation at the center explain the dynamics of this frigid geology. But unless the weather is uncooperative, it's imperative to get a closer, firsthand look at the ice. There are two ways of going about it: by snow coaches (special buses for driving on ice) or by foot, with guided hikes conducted in June through August (*see* Guided Tours, *below*). One point worth noting: The midday (11–3) rush—the prime tour-bus time slot—is so intense that even ice field promotional materials suggest you choose another time of day to come.

Two attractions very close to town are the **Jasper Tramway** and **Pyramid and Patricia lakes.** The side-by-side lakes, at the foot of Pyramid Mountain, are a pretty and popular place for a variety of activities, including hiking, horseback riding, swimming, and boating. The tramway, 7 kilometers (4¹/₃ miles) south of town on the Whistlers Road (off Route 93) rises 3,000 feet up the steep flank of **Whistlers.** The view from the top is two-fold—to the east are the Athabasca and Miette river valleys, and to the west is mighty Mt. Robson, highest of the Canadian Rockies. (For tramway information, call 403/852–3093.) The tramway is open late March through mid-October; perhaps the best time to ride is on a fair-weather evening (the tram runs until 10:30 in summer), to take in the sunset. It's a good idea to bring an evening picnic, although the tram-top restaurant serves adequate food.

Although the Columbia Icefield and the attractions around Jasper are well worth visiting, Jasper is a park that can be fully appreciated only by venturing into its considerable backcountry. Many long, well-maintained hiking trails—some open to horse-pack trips—establish Jasper's preeminence among parks in the North American west in making accessible large expanses of wilderness (*see* Longer Hikes *and* Other Activities, *below*).

THE BEST IN ONE DAY Because Jasper is such a large park and its best-known sites (the Columbia Icefield, Maligne Lake, Miette Hotsprings) are so widely scattered, the one-day visitor is forced to be selective.

Assuming that the town of Jasper is your starting point, the drive to the Icefield Centre and back (about a 200-kilometer, or 120-mile, round-trip) is a worthwhile, if time-consuming, venture. Unless you get a bright and early start, don't expect to be back in Jasper before early afternoon after the drive and the ice-field tour. Also, although the Jasper ice-fields drive is scenic, it's not nearly as spectacular as the drive to the ice-field area from Banff.

Perhaps a better one-day program is to drive to Maligne Lake, stopping at Maligne Canyon along the way. Rent a boat, take a boat tour, take a hike, and have a picnic lunch at the docks or around the lake. A day at Maligne will give you a good sense of what there is to see and do in Jasper.

After Maligne Lake, an afternoon soak in Miette Hotsprings (about a 1¹/₂-hour drive from the lake) is a good option. Dinner at the top of the Jasper tram is an enjoyable way to finish the day, the sunset view being the main attraction.

If all of that sounds like a lot of driving, a good (though expensive) one-day alternative is simply to hang out at Jasper Park Lodge. All of the activities at your doorstep make the lodge seem like the most extravagant summer camp you've ever been to.

ORIENTATION PROGRAMS The **Jasper Information Centre** (500 Connaught Dr., Jasper, AB T0E 1E0, tel. 403/852–6176) is administered by the Canadian Parks Service. Call or visit for a schedule of programs on the history, geology, and wildlife of the park. Other exhibits on the history of the area are displayed at the **Jasper–Yellowhead Museum** (400 Pyramid Lake Rd., tel. 403/852–3013, closed Thurs.) and occasionally in the **Jasper Activity Centre** (303 Pyramid Ave., tel. 403/852–3381).

GUIDED TOURS **Brewster Transportation and Tours** (Box 1140, Banff, AB T0L 0C0, tel. 800/661–1152 or 403/852–3332 in Jasper) offers full- and half-day bus tours of the park, some of which combine with Maligne Lake boat tours, rafting trips, or tram rides.

Maligne Lake is Jasper's boat-tour center. **Maligne Tours** (Box 280, 626 Connaught Dr., Jasper, AB T0E 1E0, tel. 403/852–3370) conducts 1¹/₂-hour tours of the lake early June through September; they also sponsor winter tours of Maligne Canyon. Lake-tour arrangements can also be made through **Brewster Transportation and Tours** (*see above*).

Audiocassette tapes for self-guided auto tours of Jasper and the neighboring parks are produced by **Audio Tape Tours** and **Rocky Mountain Tape Tours.** Tapes can be rented or purchased at newsstands or gift shops in Jasper.

Snow coaches, buses adapted for travel on glacial ice, carry sightseers onto the Athabasca Glacier. The 1¹/₂-hour tours are conducted from the end of May to mid-October. Tickets are available through the ice-field information center or **Brewster Transportation and Tours** (*see above*). Three- and five-hour ice-field walking tours are also conducted June through August (tel. 403/852–4242).

Jasper Climbing School and Mountaineering Service (Box 452, Jasper, AB T0E 1E0, tel. 403/852–3964) leads hiking and mountaineering tours in summer and ski tours in winter, with private guides available. The **Jasper Park Riding Academy** (tel. 403/852–3363) at Jasper Park Lodge offers summer-evening hayrides and winter sleigh rides.

SCENIC DRIVES AND VIEWS The scenic roadways of Jasper can be divided into four basic drives: the drive on the Icefields Parkway, the drive to Maligne Lake, the drive to Miette Hotsprings, and the drive to Mt. Robson. Each is distinctly different, a testament to Jasper's diverse landscape. On a poor-weather day, the best option is probably the drive to Miette. Not only does the possibility of better weather improve by heading east, but also the broad Athabasca River can be appreciated in sun or gloom.

The drive on the **Icefields Parkway** north from the ice field is a gradual descent toward Jasper, the elevation of the Icefield Centre being about 2,500 feet higher than that of the town. This is not to say the drive lacks mountain scenery. Most prominent to the west are the rock-and-ice massifs of Mt. Fryatt and Mt. Edith Cavell along the string of peaks demarcating the Continental Divide.

Among several turnoffs along the way you'll see Sunwapta Falls and Athabasca Falls. Both falls are hydrodynamic reminders of what happens to glacial ice when it's no longer ice: It turns to water. Since viewing the falls in either case requires very little hiking, visitors are usually plentiful. An alternative for solitude seekers is to take the 5-kilometer (3-mile) gravel road from Route 93A, just past Athabasca Falls, that leads to the Geraldine Lakes trail. The 4-kilometer (2¹/₂-mile) trail to Geraldine Falls requires some climbing, and it's the physical exertion that leaves the crowds behind.

Route 93A, an alternate route to Jasper that reunites with Route 93 just before the Route 16 juncture, leads to the access road for Tonquin Valley, one of the most popular backpacking and horse-packing areas of the park.

When Route 93 intersects with Route 16, going straight leads into the town of Jasper. Jasper is more functional than scenic; people come and stay here to avail themselves of the natural attractions nearby, not for the town itself.

The drive to **Maligne Lake,** 50 kilometers (30 miles) southeast of Jasper (take Maligne Lake Road from Route 16 east), is almost obligatory for visitors. In the middle of a summer day there are likely to be sizable crowds of people and vehicles here. That's the bad news; the good news is that boat rentals and several hiking trails make escaping the masses relatively easy. The more popular activity at Maligne Lake is to take a 1½-hour scenic cruise (*see* Guided Tours, *below*) on the lake, the cruise highlight being Spirit Island, a small, often mist-shrouded outcropping.

On the way to or from Maligne Lake, a short walking excursion to Maligne Canyon, where the Maligne River pushes through a narrow limestone gorge, is well worthwhile. Another point of note is Medicine Lake, just north of Maligne Lake. An unusual underground drainage system completely empties the lake at times, leaving only puddles, rivulets, and glacial silt.

Another excursion is the drive east from Jasper to **Miette Hotsprings,** 50 kilometers (30 miles) from Jasper. Following the flood basin of the Athabasca River, the scenery changes, trees begin to thin out, the valley opens up, and glaciers and residual snow patches disappear. All are indications that you're passing through the eastern Frontal Ranges (Rocky Mountains) and toward the more arid climate of the prairie. The naturally heated waters of the springs are actually too hot; when fed into the bathing pools, they must be diluted with colder water to make them tolerable to human skin.

The fourth drive in Jasper leads out of the park, 80 kilometers (50 miles) westward on Route 16 to **Mt. Robson,** a mountain technically within the British Columbia provincial park that bears its name. Pick a clear day to go, since Mt. Robson is notorious for attracting foul weather. So substantial is the challenge imposed upon climbers by the cliffs, glaciers, and weather moods of Mt. Robson that it is ranked among the world's classic climbs by alpinists. You needn't climb it to appreciate it; the 5-kilometer (3-mile) hike to Kinney Lake (for day trippers) and the 18-kilometer (11-mile) hike to Berg Lake (for backpackers) offer good views of the mountain. Berg Lake, incidentally, is so called because of the large chunks of ice that are often released into the lake from Robson's glaciers.

HISTORIC BUILDINGS AND SITES Jasper's relatively recent development is responsible for its preservation today as a wild, scenic area. Prospectors, fur traders, and surveyors did not arrive until the latter half of the 19th century, while the town of Jasper itself was not established until the early 20th century. Most traces of the pathfinding days have vanished, although exhibits and archives at the **Jasper–Yellowhead Museum** (400 Pyramid Lake Rd., tel. 403/852–3013) give some sense of life in the previous century.

Although not especially old, **Jasper Park Lodge** is of some historical significance in being the first resort lodge built in the park—Jasper's equivalent to the much older Banff Springs Hotel in Banff. It's the lodge, to adulterize a phrase, that launched 1,000 trainloads of tourists.

NATURE TRAILS AND SHORT WALKS Perhaps one of the most popular trails in Jasper is along **Maligne Canyon,** which can be approached either from above (from the Maligne Lake Road) or below (from Route 16, where the Maligne River empties into the Athabasca River). The shorter loop takes 20 minutes, and the longer 1¼-mile route takes 45 minutes. Despite plenty of company along the trail, the sight of the river rushing through the limestone canyon makes the trip well worthwhile, especially when the water is high in late spring.

A network of mostly gentle, mostly wooded trails just west of town winds through a cluster of small lakes (Pyramid and Patricia lakes being the best known). Anyone looking for an easy, half-day jaunt should consider the 9-kilometer (5½-mile) loop to tiny **Mina and Riley lakes.**

There is a short trail—less than 1½ kilometers (1 mile)—to **Sunwapta Falls** (50 kilometers, or 30 miles, north of the Icefield Centre). Many people take this route, but they're still a small percentage of the travelers along the Icefields Parkway. The view of the falls and of distant, glaciated peaks makes the trip enjoyable despite the considerable company, and the leg stretch is a good way to break up the hours of car travel along the parkway.

LONGER HIKES Here lies the essence of Jasper. Think this way: There are long hikes, longer hikes, and Jasper hikes. In Jasper, it's literally possible to hike for weeks without crossing a paved road.

The two longest hikes, the **North Boundary** and **South Boundary trails,** both exceed 160 kilometers (100 miles). Although neither presents consistently spectacular scenery, they do offer considerable opportunity for wildlife encounters—caribou, elk, goats, bear—while leading hikers into the most remote sections of the park.

With many fine options, choosing a single route is a real backpackers' dilemma in Jasper. The most popular choices are **Tonquin Valley** and the **Skyline Trail.** It's easy to understand why: The valley's scenery is highlighted by the twin Amethyst Lakes, lying before the backdrop of a 3,300-foot palisades called the Ramparts. Before setting out, be aware that a 21-kilometer (13-mile) one-way hike makes the valley mainly an overnight, not a day-trip, destination. The Skyline Trail leads 45 kilometers (28 miles) in a northerly direction from Maligne Lake and is marked by long stretches of alpine meadows strewn with wildflowers if the season is right. Heading south from Maligne Lake toward Maligne Pass can be equally rewarding though more rugged, with the trail leading over a series of high passes. Depending on how far you want to go, this southerly route continues for more than 90 kilometers (56 miles) to connect with the trail system of Banff National Park.

Backpackers must obtain permits, and the park does try to keep a limit on backcountry trail-and-campground use. The quota can be reached quickly in midsummer in popular areas, such as Tonquin Valley. Reservations can be made three weeks in advance by writing or calling the Superintendent, Jasper National Park, Box 10, Jasper, AB T0E 1E0, tel. 403/852–6177.

Longer backpacking trips are Jasper's strong suit; good day-hikes are somewhat fewer. The Maligne Lake trail system, offering several options, is probably the best day-hiking area. On a good-weather day, the 4-kilometer (2½-mile) hike to **Wilcox Pass** just north of the Banff-Jasper park boundary leads to alpine tundra that opens up to a wide, glacial panorama.

OTHER ACTIVITIES Back-Road Driving. Roads (much less back roads) are few in Jasper. Indeed, the way to experience Jasper in its glory is to get off the road, on foot or on horseback; anyone who doesn't is short-changing herself. Other than the two main highways (Routes 16 and 93) the park has only two smaller roads of note: **Maligne Lake Road** and **Route 93A,** which connects with Marmot Basin Road and Edith Cavell Road. Put simply, enthusiasts of touring along winding old country roads should look elsewhere. Four-wheel-drive vehicles are not permitted on the park's fire roads.

Biking. Given the shortage of back roads in Jasper, road cycling is somewhat limited. A good short ride (about a 12-kilometer, or 7-mile, round-trip) is from Jasper to Pyramid Lake and back, the climb on the way giving the legs and lungs a good, quick burn. Two longer rides from Jasper are to Maligne Lake or eastward along Route 16; the first ride has plenty of ups and downs, the second is for the most part flat, with several turnoff spots along the Athabasca River. The drawback in both cases is the considerable traffic, at least in summer.

With the increasing popularity of mountain biking in recent years, the Canadian Parks Service has been grappling with the issue of backcountry bike use. Hikers have complained not only of the intrusion but of the hazard of allowing bikers on hiking trails, and the parks people are trying to satisfy both sides in working out a compromise. Suffice it to say that mountain bikers are permitted on some trails but not on others. Before hitting the trail, check with the information centers for a list of those open to cyclists.

Mountain bikes can be rented from **Freewheel Cycle** (611 Patricia St., tel. 403/852–5380) and **Beyond Bikes** (4 Cedar Ave., tel. 403/852–5922). Bikes can also be rented at **Sandy's** (tel. 403/852–3301, ext. 6190) at the marina at Jasper Park Lodge. **Rocky Moun-**

tain Cycle Tours (Box 1987, Canmore, AB T0L 0M0, tel. 403/678–6770) conducts tours through Jasper as well as through Banff National Park and the surrounding area.

Bird-Watching. Although such scavenger birds as ravens, jays, and magpies are the most ubiquitous of the more than 200 species in the park, this is the kind of country made for birds of prey. Eagles, hawks, owls, and others can regularly be seen circling on the intense thermal updrafts that build around the mountain flanks rising along the Athabasca River east of Jasper. Sighting chances also increase near scree (erosion-debris) slopes at higher elevations, as hawks and eagles prey upon such rodents as pikas that scurry among the rocks.

Boating. Those looking to go boating in Jasper should head to Maligne Lake, Pyramid Lake, or Lac Beauvert. Maligne Lake, being by far the largest, offers considerably more exploratory possibilities. However, because of the types of rental boats available at all of the lakes—canoes; rowboats; small, lightly powered electric motorboats; sailboards; pedal boats—the distances covered and the pace of travel are limited. Rentals at Maligne Lake are available at the lake boat-house through **Maligne Tours** (*see* Guided Tours, *above*). Pyramid Lake is the only lake that allows gas-powered motor boats; rentals are available at the lake through **Pyramid Lake Resort** (*see* Lodging, *below,* tel. 403/852–3536). Lac Beauvert rentals are available through **Sandy's** (tel. 403/852–3301, ext. 6190) at the marina at Jasper Park Lodge.

Fishing. Perhaps the best fishing in all of the Jasper-Banff area is in the northern half of Jasper. Because the large tract of land (more than 3,000 square kilometers, or 1,150 square miles) is accessible only by foot or by horseback—though off-road vehicles may show up from time to time from neighboring Willmore Wilderness Park—the many rivers, lakes, and streams here see relatively few fishermen. Good fishing can also be had at Maligne Lake (where the Alberta-record rainbow trout, weighing over 20 pounds, was caught) and Amethyst Lakes in the Tonquin Valley.

The principal game fish are trout, grayling, and their various cousins. Information on fishing regulations is available at the **Jasper National Park Office** (*see* Visitor Information, *above*). A basic, six-day fishing license for non-Canadians is $15; an annual license is $27. Note that separate licenses are required for fishing in Alberta and British Columbia. For more information on licenses, contact the **Ministry of Environment & Parks** (Fish & Wildlife Branch, 780 Blanchard St., Victoria, BC V8V 1X4, tel. 604/387– 4573).

Several fishing guides operate within the park; for a recommended guide service (depending on the part of the park and the type of fishing you are interested in) contact **Jasper Tourism and Commerce** (*see* Visitor Information, *above*) or the activities desk at Jasper Park Lodge. **Currie's Guiding & Tackle** (416 Connaught Dr., Box 202, Jasper, AB T0E 1E0, tel. 403/852–5650) offers half- to multi-day fishing packages, accommodations included.

Horseback Riding. Depending on trail conditions, the riding season in Jasper runs approximately from May through October. Horse-pack trips are a highlight of any visit to Jasper and the surrounding area; with the large expanses of roadless wilderness, it's easy to understand why. Shorter trips (two- to four-day rides) tend toward Tonquin Valley, but the understandable popularity of this stunning spot make this option less than a wilderness getaway. For that, horse-pack vacationers head to the park's northern half for one- and two-week trips.

Several horse-pack operators guide trips in and around the park, with rates generally ranging between $80 and $100 per person per day. For a listing of outfitters, see Alberta Tourism's "Adventure Guide." For shorter rides (and instruction), there are two stables in Jasper: **Jasper Park Riding Academy** (tel. 403/852–3301, ext. 6052) at Jasper Park Lodge and **Pyramid Riding Stables** (Pyramid Lake Rd., Box 787, tel. 403/852–3562).

Rafting. If you're looking for white water, the Maligne River in late June is the place you want to be; if a scenic float is your preference, opt instead for a ride along the Athabasca River. Regardless of your choice, your trip will be relatively short, three hours being the usual time frame.

The rafting season generally runs from late May into September, with early-season waters, swollen by snowmelt, usually swifter and more rollicking. **Jasper Raft Tours** (Box 398, Jasper, AB T0E 1E0, tel. 403/852–3613) runs one- to three-hour trips on the Athabasca River and also offers canoe rentals; **Maligne River Adventures** (626 Connaught Dr., Jasper, AB T0E 1E0, tel. 403/852–3370) runs half-day trips on the Maligne River.

Rock Climbing. In general, Jasper is better for ice climbing and glacier travel than it is for rock climbing; the sedimentary underpinnings of many of the mountains here are loose, crumbly rock. This isn't to say that there is a dearth of rock climbing in Jasper; in a park of this size, with this many mountains, there's something for every type of climber and scrambler. It's just that the best Jasper has to offer—around the ice fields at the southern extreme of the park—tends to be ice oriented.

Climbers differ in their opinions of which mountain in this area offers the best climbing, but all will agree that any one of the peaks here is unsurpassed in the variety and challenge of terrain and in the summit views of the vast ice fields below. The highest peak is Mt. Columbia, at 12,294 feet, but more accessible climbs are Mt. Athabasca (11,452 feet) and Snow Dome (11,340 feet).

All of these climbs are almost entirely on ice. For those seeking a combination of rock and ice, Mt. Edith Cavell, the 11,033-foot peak south of the town of Jasper, is a good choice. And for those seeking the ultimate challenge, there is Mt. Robson, just west of the park boundary.

This is big country, and all but the most experienced climbers are urged to sign on with a local guide service. **Jasper Climbing School and Mountaineering Service** (Box 452, Jasper, AB T0E 1E0, tel. 403/852–3964) and **Peter Amann** (Box 1495, Jasper, AB T0E 1E0, tel. 403/852–3237) lead climbs and offer

instruction for climbers of all abilities. Prospective climbers might also want to consider membership in the **Alpine Club of Canada** (Box 2040, 278 St. Barbara's Terr., Canmore, AB T0L 0M0, tel. 403/678–3200), which leads climbs and maintains several backcountry huts in and around the park.

Skiing. The one lift-serviced ski area in the park is **Marmot Basin** (Box 1300, Jasper, AB T0E 1E0, tel. 403/852–3816), 19 kilometers (12 miles) south of Jasper. Overshadowed by Banff's ski areas, Marmot Basin tends to be the forgotten ski area of the Canadian Rockies. With 2,300 feet of vertical rise; a good variety of open-bowl and trail skiing; a new, high-speed quad; and relatively few visitors, Marmot holds up well against its competitors to the south. The 2,300 feet, incidentally, is just the lift-serviced vertical rise.

Ski Touring. Track skiers who like flatter terrain should head for the Jasper Park Lodge's 25-kilometer (15-mile) groomed-trail network, which loops around Lac Beauvert and the lodge golf course. Those looking for more rolling terrain should head up to the trail network around Patricia and Pyramid lakes. And for those who can't get track skiing out of their system, the 5-kilometer (3-mile) groomed trail at Whistlers Campground is lit at night.

For touring/backcountry skiing, a logical place to start in Jasper is around Maligne Lake. There's a good mix of terrain here; relatively flat skiing along the lake is possible, but those who like moderate climbing and gentle slopes for telemark turning should head for the Bald Hills, overlooking the lake.

For true touring enthusiasts, however, Maligne Lake skiing is merely a small taste of the skiing possible in a park with a hiking-trail network of nearly 1,000 kilometers (612 miles). An excellent and popular backcountry tour is the 22-kilometer (14-mile) ski into Tonquin Valley. Small, rustic cabins can be reserved through **Tonquin Valley Ski Tours** (Box 550, Jasper, AB T0E 1E0, tel. 403/852–3909). The sensible plan is to reserve a cabin for at least two nights, to allow time for skiing and exploring around Amethyst Lakes.

All but the most experienced ski tourers and mountaineers are strongly advised to enlist a guide service for longer trips; try **Caribou Outings** (4 Cedar Ave., tel. 403/852–5922) and **Spirit of Skiing** (Jasper Park Lodge, tel. 403/852–3433). Backcountry enthusiasts might also want to contact the **Alpine Club of Canada** (*see above*). The club maintains a hut system within the national parks and organizes outings and expeditions. Full membership isn't necessary to reserve huts or participate in outings, but nonmembers are charged considerably higher rates.

Snowmobiling. Snowmobiling, other than for service or emergency reasons, is prohibited in the park.

Swimming. This is cold-water country, and the antidote is the pool of **Miette Hotsprings** (tel. 403/866–3750), a three-spring combo said to produce the hottest water in the Canadian Rockies. The pool is open from mid-May to early September, 8:30 AM to 10:30 PM; admission is $2.50 adults, $1.50 children. **Jasper Aquatic Centre** (tel. 403/852–3356) is open to the public year-round (rates and hours vary). Suits, towels, and lockers can be rented at both places. There is also good free swimming at **Lake Annette**, **Lake Edith**, and **Pyramid Lake**. These lakes have unsupervised beaches, and all are near the town of Jasper.

CHILDREN'S PROGRAMS The question in Jasper is more, What *can't* you see and do with children? Hiking, rafting, horseback riding, boating, swimming—all activities that appeal to adults are likely to delight the kids, too. **Pyramid Lake,** on the outskirts of the town of Jasper, and **Jasper Park Lodge** are the two best places to find a variety of activities in one location; the rates for boat and horse rentals are more modest at Pyramid Lake. There isn't much in Jasper for children on a bad-weather day; the **Jasper-Yellowhead Museum** is worth a visit, but it will hardly be a daylong affair.

DINING

Charlton's Chateau Jasper. When locals go out for a special meal, this is often the place they go. The Chateau Jasper, with upholstered chairs, blue tablecloths, and crimson walls with wood trim, has elegant touches. Meat's the main thing on the menu, good choices being lamb in pesto sauce and an elk-beef-pork mélange. The giant Sunday-brunch buffet has epic-feast potential for active outdoorspeople. *96 Giekie St., in Charlton's Chateau Jasper hotel, tel. 403/852–5644, ext. 179. Dinner reservations advised in summer. Dress: casual; jacket advised for dinner. AE, MC, V. Expensive.*

Edith Cavell Room and **Moose's Nook.** For big-hotel–style dining, this is the place around Jasper. Table-side service, a harpist, and the view of Lac Beauvert lend atmosphere to an otherwise cool, stone-pillared dining room and a straightforward, Continental menu. Moose Nook is more intimate and its menu more imaginative, leaning heavily on food-of-the-hunt dishes: pheasant, reindeer, buffalo, and so on. *Jasper Park Lodge, Rte. 16, tel. 403/852–3301. Reservations required for dinner. Jacket advised for dinner. AE, MC, V. Expensive.*

Palisades Restaurant. A surprisingly rich Greek streak runs through Jasper, and this restaurant is just the place to get a feel for it. It's not just in the decor, which, with its bright white walls, greenhouse ceiling, and numerous plants, evokes a Mediterranean mood, but in the food as well. Moussaka and souvlaki, along with baklava for desert, are among the characteristic Greek items. Pizzas are available, too. *Cedar Ave. near Connaught Dr., tel. 403/852–5222. Dinner reservations accepted. Dress: casual. AE, MC, V. Inexpensive–Moderate.*

Mountain Foods Café. The café is a combination health-food store and deli/luncheonette. That means that while you're picking up a picnic sandwich or salad—the best in town—you can read about how healthy your lunch is by browsing through the book rack. Healthier foods, such as tabbouleh salad, are emphasized, though you can still get a three-meat grinder if that's more your thing. *606 Connaught Dr., tel. 403/852–4050. No reservations. Dress: casual. No credit cards. Inexpensive.*

PICNIC SPOTS Good picnic spots in the park are limitless for anyone willing to walk a mile or two. A good choice, for scenery if not necessarily solitude, is **Cavell Meadows.** For nonwalkers, picnic areas with tables are scattered around the park. Among the prettiest (and most populated) are at **Lake Annette, Maligne Lake, Pyramid Lake,** and **Athabasca Falls.** The **Medicine Lake** picnic area, just off the Maligne Lake road, is somewhat more private, but it's also quite small and not especially scenic.

LODGING

Park lodging, for the most part, begins and ends in and around the town of Jasper. Options boil down to cabins or motel-style accommodations, unless there is room in your budget for the high-end Jasper Park Lodge. Following is a selection of some of the better lodging choices in Jasper. **Jasper Experience** (Box 1570, Jasper, AB T0E 1E0, tel. 403/852–4242) books rooms in private homes for an $11 fee; **Jasper Travel Agency** (Box 320, Jasper, AB T0E 1E0, tel. 403/852–4400) reserves rooms in hotels as well as private homes for a $9 fee.

As for bed-and-breakfast accommodations, don't expect anything fancy; in Jasper, as in Banff, B&Bs tend to be ordinary rooms in ordinary homes. Two agencies that handle bookings in and around Jasper are: **Alberta Bed & Breakfast,** c/o Mrs. June Brown, Box 15477, Vancouver, BC V6B 5B2, tel. 604/682–4610; and **Bed and Breakfast Bureau,** c/o Mr. Don Sinclair & Associates, Box 7094, Station E, Calgary, AB T3C 3L8, tel. 403/242–5555.

Guest ranches are a popular lodging choice on the eastern (Alberta) periphery of the park. Guest-ranch information is included in Tourism Alberta's *Accommodations Guide* and *Adventure Guide.* There are also five hostels in Jasper; for hostel information contact **Al-**

berta Hosteling Association, Northern Alberta District, 10926 88 Ave., Edmonton, AB T6E OZ1, tel. 403/433–5513.

Charlton's Chateau Jasper. Big wood beams cantilevered over the front door suggest a Scandinavian interior. Not so. Rooms are in an American motel style, the beds adorned with Colonial-style headboards. Kitchen areas are spare but functional and may be little used, since the hotel's restaurant (*see* Dining, *above*) is excellent. *96 Giekie St., Box 1418, Jasper, AB T0E 1E0, tel. 403/852–5644. 121 rooms. Facilities: satellite TV, heated indoor parking, indoor swimming pool and whirlpool, rooftop sun deck, kitchens in some rooms. AE, MC, V. Expensive.*

Jasper Park Lodge. This is Jasper's original resort, a lakeside compound northeast of town that hums with on-site activities, such as golf, tennis, boating, bicycling, horseback riding, and fishing. The main lodge, overlooking Lac Beauvert and the mountains, features polished-stone floors, totem-pole pillars, and high ceilings. Outlying bungalows feature log-cabin walls, bright down comforters, and, in some cases, sitting areas overlooking the lake. Breakfast and dinner are included in most room rates (the priciest in Jasper). *4 km (2 mi) northeast of Jasper on Rte. 16, Box 40, Jasper, AB T0E 1E0, tel. 403/852–3301. 437 rooms. Facilities: 6 restaurants and lounges, satellite TV, many rooms with fireplaces and sitting rooms, golf, tennis, horseback riding, boating, and bicycling on site. AE, DC, MC, V. Expensive.*

Jasper Inn. A variety of lodging is offered here, from motel-style rooms to two-bedroom condos featuring modern, functional design and architecture. The rates are surprisingly reasonable given the inn's convenient location and amenities. Condo accommodations are especially suitable for families. The full-service restaurant serves a range of dishes, from pasta to seafood to meat entrées. *Geike St. and Bonhomme Ave., Box 879, T0E 1E0, tel. 403/852–4461 or 800/661–1933. 138 units. Facilities: satellite TV, 2 restaurants, indoor pool, sauna, whirlpool, steam bath. AE, MC, V. Moderate–Expensive.*

Alpine Village. A cluster of pine-log cabins 1 kilometer (²/₃ mile) south of town, this family-run operation is one of Jasper's bargains. The exposed-log interior of many cabins makes for an old-lodge atmosphere. Furnishings are garage-sale eclectic. The 12 newer cabins are preferable to the older, smaller ones. The view of Mt. Edith Cavell and the sound of the Athabasca River, just across a small road, create a quiet, country atmosphere. *1 km (²/₃ mi) south of Jasper on Rte. 93A, Box 610, Jasper AB, T0E 1E0, tel. 403/852–3285. 41 units, from 1-room sleeping cabins to 2-bedroom cabins with full kitchens. MC, V. Closed mid-Oct.–Apr. Moderate.*

Pyramid Lake Resort. Located on the shore of popular Pyramid Lake, this place is for those who enjoy hiking, boating, horseback riding, and sunrises. Thirty-two modern units in four log-cabin lodges are preferable to the older bungalows, which are closer to the lake but more timeworn. The restaurant is adequate, but all units have kitchenettes, and Jasper, just a few kilometers down the road, has a good selection of restaurants. *Pyramid Lake Rd., 4.6 km (3 mi) from Jasper, Box 388, Jasper, AB T0E 1E0, tel. 403/852–4900, fax 403/852–7007. 10 bungalows, 4 lodges. Facilities: satellite TV; dock with boat, canoe, paddleboat and sailboard rentals; kitchenettes; whirlpool baths in some rooms. MC, V. Moderate.*

CAMPING

Camping information can be obtained at the **Jasper Information Centre** (500 Connaught Dr., Jasper, AB T0E 1E0, tel. 403/852–6176) or from **Jasper National Park** (Box 10, Jasper, AB T0E 1E0, tel. 403/852–6161). Drive-in campgrounds are generally open from mid-May to early fall. Camping in the park costs between $7 and $17.50 per site, depending on whether you require a hookup.

INSIDE THE PARK Because of the park's size, campground selection depends largely on which parts of the park you're most interested in exploring. The drive-in campgrounds listed below are all on or near Route 16. All

of them have drinking water and public phones.

Pocahontas (130 sites and 10 walk-in tent sites, flush toilets, fire grates, $9.25), which sits in the Athabasca River valley and is nearest Miette Hotsprings, is 44 kilometers (27 miles) north of the town of Jasper. It tends to be very crowded on weekends.

Snaring River (56 sites and 10 walk-in sites, pit toilets, $7.25), **Whistlers** (781 sites, of which 113 have RV hookups; flush toilets; fire grates; showers; disposal station; playground; $12 to $16.50), **Wapiti** (366 sites, of which 40 have RV hookups; fire grates; showers; disposal station; flush toilets; $12 to $14), and **Wabasso** (232 sites and 6 walk-in tent sites, fire grates, disposal station, flush toilets, $9.25) are all within 17 kilometers (10 miles) of the center of Jasper. Whistlers is probably the best-serviced and most conveniently located in the park, but you must be willing to put up with the high volume of campers.

Thirty-five kilometers (21 miles) south of town is **Mt. Kerkeslin** (42 sites, pit toilets, $7.25), which is a little quieter but more primitive than many of the others. Other smaller grounds between Mt. Kerkeslin and the Columbia Icefield are **Honeymoon Lake** (35 sites, pit toilets, fire grates, $7.25) and **Jonas Creek** (13 sites and 12 walk-in tent sites, pit toilets, $7.25).

In the Columbia Icefield region, you have a choice of two good campgrounds. Climbers tend to prefer the somewhat exposed-to-the-elements **Columbia Icefield** campground (22 tent sites and 11 walk-in sites, pit toilets, fire grates, $7.25) because it is a closer starting point for exploring the Athabasca Glacier. **Wilcox Creek** (46 sites, disposal station, pit toilets, $7.25) is considered more comfortable and is still near all there is to do in the ice-field area of the park.

Off the beaten track there are a number of backcountry campgrounds scattered throughout the park. These grounds are free and require free overnight permits that can be obtained at any of the information centers;

JASPER CAMPGROUNDS

*Canadian dollars

	Pocahontas	Snaring River	Whistlers	Wapiti	Wabasso	Mt. Kerkeslin	Honeymoon Lake	Jonas Creek	Columbia Icefield	Wilcox Creek
Total number of sites	140	66	781	366	238	42	35	25	33	46
Sites suitable for RVs	130	56	360	70	200	42	35	13	22	46
Number of hookups	0	0	113	40	0	0	0	0	0	0
Drive to sites	•	•	•	•	•	•	•	•	•	•
Hike to sites	•	•			•			•	•	
Flush toilets	•	•	•	•						
Pit/chemical toilets	•					•	•	•	•	•
Drinking water	•	•	•	•	•	•		•	•	•
Showers			•	•						
Fire grates	•		•	•		•	•		•	
Swimming										
Boat access										
Playground			•							
Disposal station	•		•	•						•
Ranger station										
Public telephone	•	•	•	•	•	•	•	•	•	•
Reservation possible										
Daily fee per site*	$9.25	$7.25	$12–$16.50	$12–$14	$9.25	$7.25	$7.25	$7.25	$7.25	$7.25
Dates open	mid-May–Sept.	mid-May–Oct.	mid-May–Oct.	June–Sept.	late June–Sept.	mid-May–Sept.	June–mid-Oct.	late May–Oct.	mid-May–mid-Oct.	June–Sept.

they are open year-round, but winter camping in this part of the world can be rugged. For backcountry campers, *The Canadian Rockies Trail Guide,* by Brian Patton and Bart Robinson, is a valuable resource. Below is a sampling of what Jasper's backcountry has to offer.

The beauty of **Tonquin Valley** is an allure for many Jasper backpackers, although backcountry campers who aren't fond of sharing their world with horse packers should go elsewhere. There are four campgrounds in the valley as well as small cabins that can be reserved through **Tonquin Valley Ski Tours** (Box 550, Jasper, AB T0E 1E0, tel. 403/852–3909).

For a relatively long but relatively flat hike to a pretty backcountry lake, the trip to the **Jacques Lake** campground is tough to beat. For those who prefer camping on high-country meadows, the **Watchtower Basin** campground, a 10-kilometer (6-mile) hike from the Maligne Lake Road, is the place to go, although the hike in is anything but flat.

Perhaps *the* classic backpacking trip in Jasper is the Skyline Trail, which begins at Maligne Lake. A stopover at the **Little Shovel Pass** campground, about 8 kilometers (5 miles) from Maligne Lake, provides a brief introduction to the sprawling meadows and mountain views that lie ahead on a trail that continues for another 37 kilometers (23 miles). Because of the fragile, alpine-meadow vegetation along the trail, campground use may be limited by a quota system.

Another classic hike that isn't in the national park (it's in adjoining Mt. Robson Provincial Park) is the trip to the **Berg Lake** campground. It's a fairly long poke for one day—19 kilometers (12 miles)—although there are other campgrounds along the way. The incredible rock-and-glacier mass of Mt. Robson rising above the lake inspires awe—if it's visible. Campers heading for Berg Lake should be prepared for Mt. Robson's often foul weather.

Joshua Tree National Monument
California

By Matt Peters
Updated by Mimi Kmet

ormon pioneers in the 19th century likened the Joshua trees to a Biblical prophet who, in different versions, was either beseeching the heavens with upraised arms or pointing travelers toward a promised land. There are thousands of Joshua trees in the national monument bearing their name. No two alike, their multiple and varied arms end in fists of elongated, needlelike leaves. But many of the one million annual visitors to the Southern California park don't come for the Joshua trees. They come for the rocks.

The abundant outcroppings of weathered igneous boulders draw rock climbers from around the world, and on any day of the week, climbers of various abilities can be seen clambering up and around them. Sightseers, also, are drawn to the rocks. Boulder gardens filled with fascinating natural sculptures are the result of the way in which the rocks were formed and have since been eroding.

There are few facilities within the park, but there are towns within a few minutes' drive of any of the three entrances. In addition, Palm Springs is 25 to 40 miles away (depending on which entrance you choose), and Los Angeles, 140 miles. The park does get crowded, especially on weekends from fall through spring, but there are plenty of trails on which visitors can find solitude only a short walk from their car. Since the number of tours available is limited and there is no public transportation within the monument, it is difficult to see Joshua Tree without a car. But whether you remain here for one day or one week, you should make it a point to hike away from the roads and the crowds, to let the desert's beauty and solitude seep into your soul.

The monument owes its existence to the efforts of Minerva Hamilton Hoyt, a Pasadena resident who, during the 1920s, became concerned with the removal and destruction of Joshua trees and cacti from the area. Vandals were uprooting cacti and palms to transport them to suburban gardens, and Joshua trees were being burned to mark a nightime path across the desert.

Hoyt launched a grass-roots campaign to protect the region, lobbying for the creation of an enormous federal desert park. It took several years of battling the bureaucracy and swaying public opinion, but, finally, on August 10, 1936, an 825,000-acre Joshua Tree National Monument was established by President Franklin D. Roosevelt. For more than 15 years, however, prospectors fought for the right to continue searching for new mineral and iron-ore deposits in the monument. Fearing the eventual repeal of Roosevelt's original proclamation, conservation groups decided to compromise with the miners and agreed to return over a quarter of a million acres to the public domain. Today, Joshua Tree National Monument comprises 558,000 acres. At the time this edition was printed, however, the Desert Protection Act was pending in the U.S. Congress. If passed, it would change the status of Joshua Tree from a national monument to a national park and add about 230,000 acres to the area.

ESSENTIAL INFORMATION

VISITOR INFORMATION Contact the Superintendent, **Joshua Tree National Monument,** 74485 National Monument Dr., Twentynine Palms, CA 92277, tel. 619/367–7511.

If you plan to enter the monument's backcountry you must self-register at one of 12 designated backcountry boards located throughout the park. Unregistered vehicles and registered vehicles left overnight anywhere other than a backcountry road are subject to citation and/or towing. Camping is prohibited within 1 mile of any road, 500 feet of any trail, in washes, and in areas designated for day use only. The latter restriction allows the park's animals to make use of watering holes at night. Pets are prohibited in the backcountry. Maps locating backcountry registration boards and day-use areas are available at any of the park's three visitor

centers or by writing to the superintendent (*see above*).

FEES The entry fee is $5 per vehicle and is good for seven days. Bus passengers, cyclists, and travelers on foot pay $3 each. An annual pass for Joshua Tree National Monument (good for the calendar year) is $15.

PUBLICATIONS Several publications, in addition to the park's free newspaper, *Joshua Tree Journal*, provide background information and suggestions on what to do and where to go within the monument. You can order them through the **Joshua Tree Natural History Association** (74485 National Monument Dr., Twentynine Palms, CA 92277, tel. 619/367–1488), or look for them at the park's three visitor centers.

Joshua Tree National Monument, a Visitor's Guide, by Bob Cates, provides most of the basic information necessary for exploring the park. It consists of about 100 pages, including maps, discussions of natural and cultural history, and overviews of different areas within the monument. Steve Trimble's *Joshua Tree: Desert Reflections* is filled with four-color photos of the monument, with running text that describes park features and history. Hikers will want to have a copy of *Hikes and Walks, 25 Trails in Joshua Tree,* by Patty Knapp, a pocket-size book that covers the most popular of Joshua Tree's trails. This book will tell you how long and how difficult each trail is. Also useful is a topographic map published by Trails Illustrated and *The Desert Survival Handbook,* which teaches ways to survive in the desert.

GEOLOGY AND TERRAIN Joshua Tree National Monument sits on the eastern edge of the Transverse Ranges in southern California. Its 558,000 acres straddle the area where two deserts, the Colorado and the Mojave, meet. The eastern side of the monument is part of the lower-lying Colorado Desert, where the elevation is generally below 3,000 feet. This area is characterized by creosote bushes and ocotillo and jumping cholla cactus, the latter named for its propensity to seemingly leap onto the pant legs of those passing through. The western half of the monument, most of which sits at elevations exceeding 3,000 feet, is primarily part of the Mojave Desert. Temperatures are cooler here, and the relatively higher precipitation results in more abundant vegetation. It is in these upper elevations that the namesake Joshua tree is found in the greatest numbers.

The area's geological instability is responsible for the monument's striking landscape, which is characterized by a handful of mountain ranges that rise sharply from the desert floor. A number of major and hundreds of minor faults cut through the monument, and over the millennia they have caused huge masses of rock to rise above the desert areas. In fact, the land comprising Joshua Tree has sunk below sea level at least 10 times in the past 800 million years, only to resurface through the radical uplifting of surface rock. Particularly dramatic examples of this uprising are the Pinto Mountains, which form the northern border of the park, and the Little San Bernardino Mountains on the southwestern edge. Other ranges in Joshua Tree are the Hexie Mountains in the monument's center, the Cottonwood Mountains to the south, and the Eagle and Coxcomb mountains to the east.

Fault zones also have played an important role in the creation of Joshua Tree's five fan-palm oases. The famous San Andreas Fault skims the monument's southwestern border. The movement of earth around this and other faults causes the underground rock to splinter, and the resulting bits of rock form dams that stop the flow of groundwater. The groundwater is then forced to rise through the cracks to the surface, where it gives life to limited numbers of plants and animals.

Another prominent geological feature in the monument is the monzogranite intrusions-boulder gardens filled with multiton building blocks stacked in intriguing formations. Their form is the result of spheroidal and cavernous weathering, complicated processes that involve the expansion of fissures (called joints) in the rocks; the chemical and mechanical weathering of the rocks; and the accumulation of minerals, water, and lichen on the rocks, resulting in their decomposi-

tion. The Wonderland of Rocks, Ryan Campground, and Split Rock areas are good examples of spheroidal weathering; cavernous weathering was responsible for the formation of Skull Rock, in the Jumbo Rocks area.

FLORA AND FAUNA The desert is a land of precarious existence; plants and animals have adapted to the harsh temperatures and dry climate. To an untrained eye, the desert appears to be relatively void of life, but on closer inspection, it becomes apparent that this land is very much alive.

Seventeen species of cactus are found within Joshua Tree National Monument. The self-guiding nature trail at the Cholla Cactus Garden takes you through an area concentrated with bigelow cactus, a cholla cactus that is also known as the teddy bear cholla and usually grows waist high. Nearby is the Ocotillo Patch, where the long skinny spines of the ocotillo can be seen stretching up to 12 feet into the air. During periods of relatively heavy moisture the ocotillo even produces leaves.

Joshua trees can be seen throughout the western portion of the park, generally in elevations above 3,000 feet. They are especially abundant in Queen Valley and Lost Horse Valley. A member of the agave family, the Joshua tree, or *Yucca brevifolia,* is sometimes called the tree yucca. It is difficult to determine the age of a Joshua tree, because, unlike most trees, it has no annual growth ring; its trunk is composed of countless tiny fibers. The Joshua tree is also known for its seldom-seen white blossoms, which can appear anytime from February through April but only when the temperature and precipitation in a given year have been just right. You may have to return to the monument for many years before you catch a bloom.

Rising spring temperatures will trigger an outburst of wildflowers that paints the desert carpet myriad colors. Among the fields of flowers, you may see the desert five-spot, which draws its name from the dark spot located toward the center of each of its five pinkish petals. The pinkish-white desert primrose grows in wide circles of ground cover. Also look for purple lupine, sandmat, and locoweed. These spring blooms vary greatly from one year to the next, depending on rainfall during fall and winter and temperatures in spring. Many of the desert annuals need a good soaking to germinate, usually from September through mid-December, and the timing of the fall rains will determine what happens in the spring. The lower elevations begin blooming around February, and the upper elevations start in March and April. Some areas above 5,000 feet see blooms as late as June. Spectacular desert blooms typically occur only once every 20 years; the last such spectacle was in 1988.

When the sun has set and the air has cooled, the desert's creatures emerge from their hiding places to hunt and forage. The wildlife in Joshua Tree National Monument includes coyotes, burrowing owls, kangaroo rats, yucca night lizards, bobcats, sidewinders, roadrunners, golden eagles, bighorn sheep, and tarantulas. The desert tortoise, a protected species, makes its home in the north end of the monument, although it is not commonly seen.

WHEN TO GO It is best to visit Joshua Tree National Monument from October through May, when the weather is most comfortable and the number of activities being held in the park and nearby communities is greatest. Of course, that is when most of the 1 million visitors choose to visit, so the park's roads and campgrounds can become crowded, especially on weekends.

You are most likely to see cacti and wildflowers blooming in March, April, and May. Rainfall is not really a factor at any time of the year, although the wettest month is August, when an average of less then 3/4 inches of rain falls each year. July is the hottest month, with daytime highs averaging 104.7°F. During the summer months, nights usually cool down to 65°F to 70°F. Average high temperatures are 85°F in October, 62°F in January, and 90°F in May. From November through March, overnight lows get down into the high 30s and low 40s. The park has an average of 81 days per year above 100°F, with 100-degree temperatures recorded as early as April 18 and as late as October 19. Temperatures are 5°F to 10°F cooler in the higher elevations, where the campgrounds are located. With the exception of two campgrounds that may be closed during the summer, the park's facilities are open year-round.

SEASONAL EVENTS **May:** In Yucca Valley, the **Grubb Steak Days** (tel. 619/365–6323) are held annually on Memorial Day weekend, with dancing, a parade, and a rodeo. **October:** Grab a seat and watch five-person teams of enthusiastic potty-pushers racing their handmade outhouses-on-wheels at the Twentynine Palms **Outhouse Races.** In the later part of the month, the town hosts **Pioneer Days,** its version of the Grubb Steak Days, with a rodeo and assorted festivities. Contact the Chamber of Commerce (tel. 619/367–3445).

Throughout the year, the **Andromeda Astronomical Society** (tel. 619/228–1977) conducts occasional stargazing programs.

WHAT TO PACK No matter what time of year you visit Joshua Tree, bring a wide-brimmed hat, sunglasses, and sunscreen to combat the heat and glare, but also pack a jacket for the relatively cool nights. A long-sleeved shirt and long pants will help minimize water loss due to perspiration. Carry at least one gallon of water per person for each day you plan to be in the park—whether you are hiking *or* driving—and bring additional water for your vehicle. Sturdy hiking boots are best for extended walks, and an extra pair of socks is worth its weight in gold. Hikers should also carry maps and a compass. Campers must bring their own firewood: Wood gathering is illegal.

GENERAL STORES There are no stores in the park, but there are many in the Morongo Basin, through which Highway 62 travels. In Yucca Valley, **Von's** (57590 Twentynine Palms Hwy., tel. 619/365–8998), open 7 AM to 11 PM, sells groceries. Camping supplies can be purchased at **K-Mart** (57725 Twentynine Palms Hwy., tel. 619/365–0628), which is open 9 to 9. In Twentynine Palms, groceries can be purchased at **Stater Bros.** (71727

Twentynine Palms Hwy., tel. 619/367–6535), open daily 7 AM to 10 PM. These stores are open year-round.

ARRIVING AND DEPARTING Joshua Tree National Monument is 140 miles northeast of Los Angeles, 40 miles east of Palm Springs. There is no public transportation through the monument, so the best way to visit Joshua Tree is by car. Because the entire monument can be seen in one day of driving, it really doesn't matter which of the park's three entrances you choose. The West (Joshua Tree) and North (Twentynine Palms) entrances, off Highway 62, are closer to the main loop of the road along which most of the scenic attractions are located. But most visitors wind up heading for the Ocotillo Patch and Cholla Cactus Garden at some point during their stay, and these are closer to the South (Cottonwood Springs) entrance, which is reached off I–10, east of Indio. There are visitor centers at the Twentynine Palms and Cottonwood Springs entrances and an entrance station at the Joshua Tree entrance.

By Plane. Many major airlines serve **Palm Springs Regional Airport** (tel. 619/323–8161), which is 2 miles east of the downtown area. Most hotels provide transportation to and from the terminal, but visitors staying in towns closer to the park should rent a car. Try **Avis** (tel. 800/331–1212), **Budget** (tel. 800/527–0700), **Dollar** (tel. 800/800–4000), **Hertz** (tel. 800/654–3131), or **National** (tel. 800/328–4567).

By Car and RV. To reach the park from Los Angeles, take I–10 east to the Cottonwood entrance (a lefthand turn just before Chiriaco Summit), or take I–10 east and turn onto Highway 62 (Twentynine Palms Highway) going east. Both the West entrance and the North entrance can be reached from Highway 62; four short spur roads also stem off Highway 62 and dead-end just inside the park boundary. From Palm Springs, take Indian Avenue north 3 miles to I–10 and turn left (west) to reach Highway 62 in 3 miles (it's 29 miles east to the West entrance) or turn right (east) on I–10 to reach the Cottonwood entrance in 48 miles.

Those headed to Death Valley have the option of traveling from Joshua Tree through the Eastern Mojave Desert, not the shortest route, but certainly the most scenic. From the town of Twentynine Palms, take Amboy Road north to Amboy (ask someone for directions to Amboy Road), then take the Kelbaker Road to Baker, where you can pick up Highway 127 north to Shoshone. From Shoshone, there are numerous options for entering Death Valley (*see* the Death Valley National Monument chapter). The scenery along this route—sand dunes and rugged mountains painted by various ores and minerals—makes this a trip to remember. But the way is long and isolated. Approximately 260 miles are covered, and there is a 35-mile stretch of gravel road and a 65-mile stretch between services.

A more populated route from Twentynine Palms starts out on Highway 62 west, then moves north on Highway 247 to Barstow, where you must take I–15 east to Baker. At Baker, Highway 127 runs north to Shoshone.

By Train. Amtrak (tel. 800/872–7245) passenger trains service Indio, located 25 miles west of the park's South entrance and 20 miles east of Palm Springs. For $3.75 one-way, Greyhound Lines takes passengers from Indio to Palm Springs, where there are buses to Twentynine Palms (*see below*). The bus station is just five blocks from the train station, and taxis are on hand to meet incoming trains.

By Bus. Greyhound Lines bus service is available from most major cities to the Greyhound–Trailways Terminal in Palm Springs (311 N. Indian Ave., tel. 619/325–2053). From there, **Desert Stage Lines** (tel. 619/367–3581) serves the towns of Yucca Valley, Joshua Tree, and Twentynine Palms. A one-way bus ticket from Palm Springs to Twentynine Palms costs about $9; it's about a 90-minute ride.

EXPLORING

It's easy to motor your way through Joshua Tree in one day. A number of companies offer organized tours of the monument for those who would rather leave the driving to some-

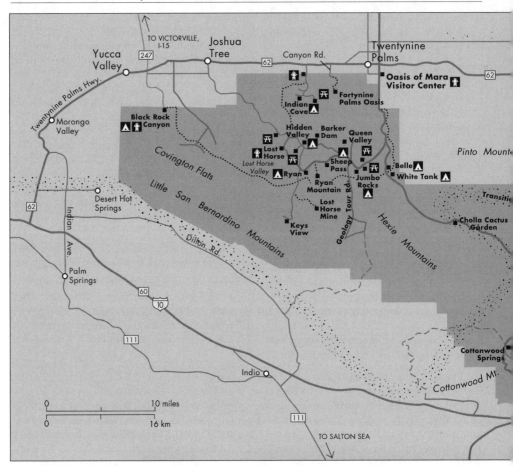

one else, but Joshua Tree is the kind of place where you'll want to pull off the road to further explore something that catches your eye. A few of the park's dirt roads are unpassable by passenger vehicles, so a mountain bike may come in handy. Bikes are permitted on all of the park's roads (they are not permitted off-road), but with motorists constantly craning their necks to look at rock formations and other sites, most of these narrow two-lane roadways aren't where a cyclist wants to be.

Water is not available in the park, so hikers must carry it—a lot of it—making backpacking trips only for the hardiest of visitors. There are, however, a multitude of short hikes, and it is easy to take a few of these and still see the park in one day. On the other

hand, the air is clean, the stars shine bright at night, and the desert calms even the most frazzled nerves. You might want to kick back for a couple of days, maybe more, and wait to hear the coyotes calling.

THE BEST IN ONE DAY Start out from the Twentynine Palms entrance and drive the 11 miles to the Jumbo Rocks area, a plateau rimmed by huge and splendid boulder formations, formed by the work of 800 million years of tectonic and erosive forces. Head out early enough to catch the sunrise; it paints these giant boulders pink and yellow. By 8 AM the Oasis Visitor Center will open, and it's worth your while to backtrack so as to stop there. You'll learn about the park's natural and cultural history and become acquainted with the

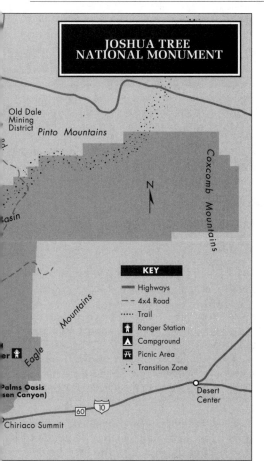

JOSHUA TREE NATIONAL MONUMENT

Old Dale Mining District

Pinto Mountains

Coxcomb Mountains

N

...asin

KEY

— Highways
– – 4x4 Road
····· Trail
🚹 Ranger Station
⛺ Campground
🪧 Picnic Area
∴ Transition Zone

Mountains

Eagle

Palms Oasis (...sen Canyon)

Desert Center

60 10

Chiriaco Summit

differences between the two deserts present within the park boundaries. Displays also tell how the plants and animals eke out an existence here. Take the ¹/₂-mile nature walk through the nearby Oasis of Mara, which was used by miners, early settlers, and Native Americans. The area features cottonwood trees, palm trees, arrowweed, and mesquite shrubs.

From the Oasis Visitor Center, drive up the hill leading back into the park. At about the 5-mile mark, take the fork to the left and continue another 9 miles to the Ocotillo Patch, where the sun fills the cactus needles with light. As the road descends toward the Ocotillo Patch, note the transition from high desert to low desert. Get out of the car and

wander around the patch, then drive back 2¹/₂ miles west to the Cholla Cactus Garden, where there is a short self-guiding nature trail (pamphlets at the site). Now drive back up the hill to the fork in the road; this time turn left toward the Jumbo Rocks (clearly marked with a road sign). After 2 miles, there's a short, well-marked paved road on the right that leads to the Split Rock picnic area.

Continue west on the main road for 1 mile, stopping to view Skull Rock alongside the road (see Nature Trails and Short Walks, below). As you drive west, you will approach the higher desert and the Jumbo Rocks area, where you may have watched the sun rise. Start keeping an eye out for rock climbers. Binoculars will help you to see their spider-like feats. By now it should be lunchtime, and the huge boulders in Hidden Valley provide a multitude of private places to spread a picnic blanket (the number of picnic tables is limited). Before or after lunch, take an hour to walk the easy 1-mile Hidden Valley Trail, which winds its way through boulders into an area where cattle rustlers once allegedly kept their liberated livestock. From the Hidden Valley area, backtrack to the 6-mile drive out to Keys View (see Scenic Drives and Views, below). On a clear day, you'll be able to see the Coachella Valley, the Salton Sea, and into Mexico. From late fall through early spring it can be chilly at the lookout, so bring a sweater or sweatshirt. Backtrack on the Keys View spur road to the main park road and return to Hidden Valley.

At the Hidden Valley campground, look for the signs leading to the Barker Dam Trail (see Nature Trails and Short Hikes, below). At this point, you have two options: Continue through the park to Highway 62 and Joshua Tree, or return to Keys View to watch the sun set.

ORIENTATION PROGRAMS On Friday, Saturday, and Sunday, from mid-October through mid-December and mid-January through mid-May, rangers lead a variety of programs, many of which repeat over the course of the day or weekend. Meeting times and places are listed in the free newspaper *Joshua Tree Jour-*

nal, available at any of the visitor or information centers.

Campfire Coffee programs at Black Rock Canyon and Cottonwood campgrounds run from 45 minutes to one hour; coffee, tea, and hot chocolate (bring your own mug) are served while a park ranger or camp host answers your questions. On the **Keys Ranch Tour** you will explore the homestead (also known as Desert Queen Ranch) of one of the few ranchers to successfully endure in this harsh land. The 90-minute tour covers 1 mile and is free. Admission is limited to 20 people on a first-come, first-served basis (*see* Historic Buildings and Sights, *below*).

A number of free ranger-guided hikes are also offered, although they vary from year to year. Among them: the **Fortynine Palms Oasis Hike** covers 3 miles in 3 hours; the 3-mile **Mastodon Peak Hike** explores the Cottonwood area and the Mastodon Gold Mine in 2¹/₂ hours; the 3-mile, 3-hour **Ryan Mountain Hike** heads to a summit offering some of the best views in the park; on the 1-mile, one-hour **Barker Dam Walk** you will learn about some of the historical uses of Barker Dam, as well as the area's natural history; covering 2¹/₂ miles in two hours, the **Wall Street Mill Hike** tells the tales of many of the rugged people who mined for gold in the desert; a ranger leads the short (¹/₄-mile) 45-minute **Cholla Walk** through the Cholla Cactus Garden, explaining how the cholla and the pack rat interact; on the ¹/₂-mile **Geology Walk** you'll stroll for 1¹/₂ hours among some of the rock formations that make Joshua Tree famous and learn about their origin.

GUIDED TOURS Technical rock-climbing classes, ranging from two-day courses for beginners to one-day private sessions, are taught by skilled climbers from the **Wilderness Connection** (Box 29, Joshua Tree, CA 92252, tel. 619/366–4745), a school that has been in operation since 1989 and is accredited by the American Guides Association. Wilderness Connection provides all equipment for the classes, which are offered from October through May. A two-day basic course is $150 per person; private guides cost $160

per day for one person, with diminishing rates for additional climbers.

The oldest climbing school in the area is **Vertical Adventures** (Box 7548, Newport Beach, CA 92658, tel. 714/854–6250), which has more than 10 years of experience and instructs about 1,000 climbers each year. The school's most popular class is a two-day, $130 beginner's seminar. A two-day intermediate course is $145. Classes run from November through May; it's best to sign up at least two weeks in advance.

SCENIC DRIVES AND VIEWS A 6-mile spur road heads south from the park's main road just west of the Ryan campground and leads to 5,185-foot **Keys View,** from which you can see the Salton Sea, the Coachella Valley, the mountains of the San Bernardino National Forest, and on a rare clear day, a mountain peak in Mexico. About halfway to the point there is a 4-mile round-trip trail that leads to the Lost Horse Mine, a reminder of the monument's gold prospecting and mining history. As you head back north on the road, you'll have an excellent view of the Lost Horse Valley. Keys View is a good place to watch the sunset.

Some of the monument's most fascinating landscapes can be observed from the 18-mile **Geology Tour Road,** a dirt road that should be negotiated only with a four-wheel-drive vehicle. Not only is this road rough and ill-maintained, it also has several sandy stretches that can snag two-wheel-drive vehicles (think about the towing bill). It will take four to six hours to make the round-trip journey. Along the way, you'll see a volcanic hill, a 100-year-old stone dam called Squaw Tank, old mines, archaeological sites, and a large plain with an abundance of Joshua trees.

HISTORIC BUILDINGS AND SITES The 150-acre **Keys Ranch** (also known as Desert Queen Ranch) was one of the most successful attempts at homesteading in the area, lasting for more than 50 years. Located in an open area surrounded by huge boulders, the ranch now consists of the main dwelling and several outbuildings (which you can not enter), gardens, and some wells. It was started by Bill

Keys, who dug the wells by hand, built a concrete dam and an earthen levee, and installed an irrigation system to water his vegetable gardens, fruit orchards, and wheat and alfalfa fields. The only way to see the Keys Ranch is to take a guided tour led by the Joshua Tree Natural History Association guides (tel. 619/367–1488). These free tours are held on Saturday and Sunday at 9 AM and 11 AM from October through May and are limited to the first 20 people to arrive at the ranch.

NATURE TRAILS AND SHORT WALKS Starting at the White Tank campground, a 1/3-mile loop leads to **Arch Rock.** Signs along the trail give information on the geology of the area and the formation of this natural arch. A 1-mile loop beginning 2 miles northeast of the Hidden Valley campground passes **Barker Dam,** built by early cattle ranchers to provide water for their stock. After the dam, this trail proceeds past a group of Native American petroglyphs, which, unfortunately, were once painted over by a film crew attempting to make them more visible. The geology and plant life of the Mojave Desert are explained along a 1/2-mile loop trail that begins at the **Cap Rock** parking area. This trail moves through fascinating rock formations; it is one of the park's top geology trails and is paved for handicapped access. Twenty miles north of the Cottonwood Visitor Center is the **Cholla Cactus Garden,** where visitors can walk the 1/4-mile loop through a dense concentration of bigelow cholla. A brochure available at the start of the trail helps identify the well-camouflaged homes of pack rats in the garden. Head to the **Cottonwood Springs Oasis** via the 1-mile round-trip trail that begins at sites 13A and 13B of the Cottonwood campground. Signs tell about the plants and animals of the Colorado Desert. The **High View Nature Trail** is a 1 1/3-mile loop that climbs nearly to the top of Summit Peak (elevation 4,500 feet). The view makes the moderately steep, 300-foot elevation gain worth the effort. Start 1/2 mile west of the Black Rock Canyon campground. Look for desert tortoises along the 1/2-mile loop of **Indian Cove Trail,** but if you see one, observe it from a distance—it's protected by state law.

This trail begins at the west end of Indian Cove campground and follows a desert wash. The 1 3/4-mile loop of the **Skull Rock Trail** begins near the loop E entrance at Jumbo Rocks campground and guides hikers through boulder piles, desert washes, and a rocky alley. Don't miss the 1/2-mile paved **Oasis of Mara** trail or the 1-mile **Hidden Valley** loop (*see* The Best in One Day, *above*).

LONGER HIKES The **Fortynine Palms Oasis Trail** is a 3-mile round-trip that begins at the end of Canyon Road, which is located off Highway 62, 4 miles west of the town of Twentynine Palms. Hikers should allow three hours for this moderately strenuous walk. The trail makes a steep climb into the hills, from which there is a good view of the lush oasis, then drops down into the canyon where the oasis is found. Sights within the oasis include fan palms, pools of water, and evidence of fires built by Native Americans for cooking and, occasionally, warmth. Petroglyphs can be found in some of the canyons above the oasis.

The 4-mile round-trip **Lost Horse Mine Trail** makes for a fairly strenuous hike along a former mining road to the site of a well-preserved stamp mill. The mill was used during the late 1890s to crush rock mined from the nearby mountain in a search for gold. The operation was one of the most successful in the area, and the mine's cyanide settling tanks and stone buildings are the area's best-preserved. You'll notice the relative absence of Joshua trees, which were used for fuel and have yet to regenerate. The hike begins at the parking area 1 1/4 miles east of Keys View Road. From the mine area, a short but steep 10-minute side trip takes visitors to the top of a 5,278-foot summit. Allow three to four hours for the entire walk.

Allow four to six hours for the moderately strenuous, 7 1/2-mile round-trip **Lost Palms Oasis Trail,** which leads from Cottonwood Springs campground to the largest palm oasis in the monument, with more than 100 palm trees set at the base of rugged canyon walls. The spring here bubbles from boulders, but disappears into the sandy, boulder-strewn canyon. This area, located in the park's southeast corner, is one of the places where you might be lucky enough to spot a bighorn sheep. From this trail, there are more strenuous side trips into Munsen Canyon that involve boulder scrambling.

The **Mastodon Peak Trail** is a 3-mile loop that starts at the Cottonwood Spring Oasis and climbs 420 feet in elevation. Gold was mined along this trail from 1919 to 1932; hikers should be careful not to walk too close to the mouths of open mines. Southeast of the mining area, the trail heads for the peak. It involves an easy-to-moderate boulder scramble to reach the top, but from the 3,371-foot summit, there are views of the Hexie Mountains, the Pinto Basin, and the Salton Sea. The peak draws its name from a large rock formation that miners during the late 1890s believed looked like the head of a prehistoric behemoth. It takes about two hours to hike to the top and back.

One of the best panoramic views in the park is your reward for hiking to the top of 5,461-foot **Ryan Mountain.** It's a 3-mile round-trip journey that will take two to three hours to complete. The elevation gain is 981 feet. From the top, hikers can see Mount San Jacinto, Mount San Gregornio, Monument Valley, the Pinto Basin, and Queen and Pleasant valleys.

The 16-mile round-trip **Boy Scout Trail** runs through the westernmost edge of the Wonderland of Rocks. The northern trailhead is up the road from Indian Cove Campground; the southern trailhead is about 4 miles west of Hidden Valley Campground along the main park road. On this moderately difficult trail you will see some of the park's most fascinating rock outcroppings.

The **California Riding and Hiking Trail** stretches for 35 miles between Black Rock Canyon Campground, in the west, and the North entrance, in the east. It is accessible to hikers and horseback riders. You can reach sections of the trail at its junction with Covington Flats, Keys View, and Geology Tour (near Squaw Tank) roads and at Ryan Campground, which means you don't have to cover the entire 35 miles, a trek that takes two to three days. The trail will give you a feeling for the higher elevations of Joshua Tree.

OTHER ACTIVITIES **Back-Road Driving.** Vehicles are not allowed off-road in Joshua Tree National Monument, but there are a limited number of roads where four-wheel-drive is recommended. Before venturing out on any of these roads check first with park officials. (For road description, *see* Bicycling, *below.*)

Biking. Cyclists should restrict the amount of time they spend on the park's fairly narrow main roads, where two-way traffic can be heavy. Mountain bikes are welcome in Joshua Tree, although they must remain on established roads. This is critical in this fragile environment, where off-road tracks can last for many years. Some suggested routes for mountain biking follow.

Beginning at the Cottonwood Visitor Center, the challenging 20-mile **Pinkham Canyon Road** travels along Smoke Tree Wash, then cuts down Pinkham Canyon. The road crosses soft sand and rocky flood plains and ends at a service road near I–10. The **Black Eagle Mountain Road** is a dead end that begins 6½ miles north of the Cottonwood Visitor Center. This road runs along the edge of Pinto Basin, then crosses a number of dry washes before navigating several of Eagle Mountain's canyons. The first 6 miles are within the monument. Beyond is Bureau of Land Management land and a number of side roads. Stay away from the old mines you may see along the way. Beginning at the same place as the Black Eagle Road is the 23-mile **Old Dale Road.** The first 11 miles of this route run across Pinto Basin, which is a flat, sandy, and dry lake bed. The road then ascends a steep hill, crossing the national monument boundary. At this point several side roads head off toward old mines and private residences. If you stay on the main road, you will come out on Highway 62, 15 miles east of Twentynine Palms.

A network of roads, totaling 13½ miles, winds through **Queen Valley** and a huge grove of Joshua trees. You can begin at the Hidden Valley campground or at the dirt road across from the Geology Tour Road. Bike racks in the area allow riders to lock up their bikes and go hiking. The **Geology Tour Road** turns south from the main paved road 2 miles west of Jumbo Rocks. The first 5^1/$_2$-mile sandy and bumpy downhill leads to Squaw Tank, where a 6-mile circular route can be taken through Pleasant Valley. A guide to Geology Tour Road is available at the beginning of the road and at visitor centers.

Several roads in the **Covington Flats** area offer access to some of the monument's largest Joshua trees, in addition to piñon pines, junipers, and areas of lush desert vegetation. One suggested ride runs from the Covington Flats picnic area to Eureka Peak, 3^3/$_4$ miles one way. The dirt road is steep toward the end, but at the top riders are rewarded with views of Palm Springs, the surrounding mountains, and the Morongo Basin. Add 6^1/$_2$ miles to the trip by riding to the backcountry board, where you have the option of taking one of several excellent hikes.

Rock Climbing. It is difficult to spend much time in Joshua Tree without seeing rock climbers. The monument is one of the most popular climbing areas in the world, boasting more than 4,000 climbs. Signs mark the primary routes from parking areas to popular climbing spots. Information on specific climbing routes may be obtained by contacting any of the visitor centers. At least two companies offer schools for climbers of varying abilities (*see* Guided Tours, *above*). The "Joshua Tree Climbers' Brochure," written by climbers and park staff members, offers suggestions for reducing the impact of climbing on natural resources. Read it before you start out for the day.

CHILDREN'S PROGRAMS Programs designed to help children explore the desert environment are offered from time to time, depending largely on the park's budget and staff during the given year. Call the superintendent's office (*see* Visitor Information, *above*) for current details. The park also offers programs for school groups on a limited basis; prior arrangements are necessary.

EVENING ACTIVITIES Park rangers or volunteers present one-hour traditional campfire or slide programs every Saturday night from October through April. Topics covered include history, wildlife, and park management. The programs begin at 7 PM from October through the beginning of daylight saving time (sometime in April), then move to 8 PM through the end of April. They may be held at the Black Rock Canyon information center, the Cottonwood campground campfire circle, the Indian Cove campground campfire circle, and the Jumbo Rocks campground amphitheater. Check visitor centers for a current schedule.

DINING

There are no restaurants within Joshua Tree National Monument, but there is a wide selection in the Morongo Basin, which borders the monument's northern boundary. The area's eateries range from moderately priced to inexpensive and include plenty of fast-food franchises. Dress is casual at all of these establishments.

Stefano's. The best Italian restaurant in the basin, this small brasserie has only 16 tables set in two bright, airy dining rooms, with lots of plants. The Venetian-style cuisine includes such specialties as chicken in marsala sauce with mushrooms and veal à la limon. Also popular are the daily fish combinations. If you're lucky the restaurant will be serving the sea bass and scampi, steamed, with tarantino sauce and champagne. The red snapper and salmon combo is delicious, too. Stefano's is located on Highway 62, 2 miles west of the turnoff to the park's Black Rock entrance. *55509 Twentynine Palms Hwy., Yucca Valley, tel. 619/228–3118. Reservations recommended. D, MC, V. No lunch Sun. Moderate.*

Twentynine Palms Inn Restaurant. In its own building on the grounds of the historic Twentynine Palms Inn, this informal restaurant feels much like a resort. A dozen interior tables share a room with a cocktail bar, and outside, diners at the half-dozen tables encircling the pool are warmed with portable heaters. The service is friendly and efficient.

Local residents mix with first-time and re-turning guests. The menu is primarily steak and seafood but includes chicken and vege-tarian dishes. The breads are homemade, and the herbs, in season, come from the inn's garden. The restaurant hosts Sunday brunches. *73950 Inn Ave., Twentynine Palms, tel. 619/367–3505. Reservations recom-mended on weekends. AE, MC, V. Moderate.*

Yucca Inn Restaurant. Light pours through the many windows of this large, airy restau-rant in the Yucca Inn. Frequented by locals, it serves seafood, chicken, steak, pasta, ribs, baked ham, and burgers—the works. Stand-ard American breakfasts and lunches, from the Denver omelet to the BLT, are also served. *7500 Camino Del Cielo, Yucca Valley, tel. 619/365–0043. Reservations recommended on weekends. D, MC, V. Moderate.*

Edchada's. This Yucca Valley Mexican res-taurant is where all the rock climbers congre-gate on weekends. It's large, crowded, and noisy—but everyone has a good time. The servings are big, too. *56805 Twentynine Palms Hwy., Yucca Valley, tel. 619/365–7655. AE, MC, V. Inexpensive.*

Ramona's. Located on the main drag at the west end of Twentynine Palms, Ramona's has a basic interior with Formica tables and ami-able service. But it's what comes out of the kitchen that counts here. Try the burrito ranchero, an all-beef burrito with guacamole, sour cream, green chiles, onions, and a spe-cial ranchero sauce; or the large combo, which includes two tacos, a chicken enchi-lada, a chile relleno, rice, and beans. *72115 Twentynine Palms Hwy., Twentynine Palms, tel. 619/367–1929. Reservations recom-mended on weekends. MC, V. Closed Sun. Inexpensive.*

Rocky's Pizzeria. Residents of Twentynine Palms come here when it's pizza they're look-ing for. You order your food at the counter, but it is served to you at your table or booth. The oft-crowded restaurant can hold 185 peo-ple, and there is a party room that seats 45. There are no tablecloths on the Formica ta-bles, and the plates are plastic; Rocky's is simple but neat. The large selection of pizzas

is supplemented by lasagna, spaghetti, and sandwiches—including meatball, pastrami, and a super-sub served hot or cold. *73737 Twentynine Palms Hwy., Twentynine Palms, tel. 619/367–9525. No credit cards. Inexpen-sive.*

PICNIC SPOTS Since there are no stores or restaurants inside the monument, you will have to pack a picnic lunch. Several stores in the Morongo Basin sell groceries and sand-wiches to go, and the restaurant at the Twen-tynine Palms Inn, located off the park's North entrance, sells tasty box lunches for $7 each morning.

Among the many good places where one can find shelter and solitude amid the giant boul-ders, a few stand out from the lot. The desig-nated picnic spot at **Hidden Valley** has a limited number of tables but lots of shade. A 1-mile self-guided tour of the area provides an easy after-lunch walk. Vandals set fire to the picnic tables at **Split Rock,** but nearby is **Live Oak,** which has tables, rock formations, and Joshua trees. Across the main road from the entrance to the Hidden Valley picnic area is a dirt road leading to **Barker Dam,** a re-freshing spot for a picnic. There are numer-ous picnic tables in the Jumbo Rocks area, but it can get crowded. Still, it's a good choice if you want to find shade beneath a boulder.

LODGING

Although there are no accommodations within the monument's boundaries, a variety of lodgings are located in the Morongo Basin, and these are open year-round. Among the pickings are bed-and-breakfasts with only two guest rooms, standard motor lodges, and resorts that are more than 60 years old. If you are looking for a luxury hotel, however, you'll have to travel the 40 miles to Palm Springs. Lodgings in Twentynine Palms and Yucca Valley are within a few minutes' drive of the monument's two northern entrances. The more desirable locations usually require re-servations 30 days in advance for in-season weekends and the month of April.

Best Western Gardens. This two-story motel is located on the Twentynine Palms Highway, close to the Twentynine Palms entrance to the park. It is in a business district and has no view and no trees, but does provide Best Western–standard rooms. Suites with kitchenettes are located next to the pool. *71487 Twentynine Palms Hwy., Twentynine Palms, CA 92277, tel. 619/367-9141. 64 rooms, 8 suites with kitchenettes. Facilities: pool, Jacuzzi. AE, DC, MC, V. Moderate–Expensive.*

Twentynine Palms Inn. This inn in the Oasis of Mara has been in the family of owner Jane Grunt since it was built in the 1920s, before Joshua Tree became a national monument. The grounds comprise 30 acres with fan palms, a garden, and a 1-acre pond with ducks and a houseboat. The 17 separate cabins accommodate from two to five guests; 10 of them are constructed from adobe and 10 have a fireplace. All of the cabins have porches. The inn gets a lot of repeat customers who cherish its intimacy and don't mind its offbeat nature. *73950 Inn Ave., Twentynine Palms, CA 92277, tel. 619/367-3505. 17 units. Facilities: restaurant, cocktail lounge, pool, Jacuzzi. AE, MC, V. Moderate–Expensive.*

Circle C. Don't let the cinderblock construction of this Twentynine Palms motel fool you. Owners Dick and Edna Miller have worked to make guests feel at home. Of the 11 units, 10 have kitchens stocked with a stove, refrigerator, microwave, coffeepot, dishes, and utensils. Rooms here average 450 square feet and have a TV and VCR. The two wings enclose a large, private garden area with pool, Jacuzzi, barbecue pits (necessities provided), and picnic tables. Each morning the staff sets out a Continental breakfast in the motel reception room. *6340 El Ray Ave., Twentynine Palms, CA 92277, tel. 619/367-7615. 11 units. Facilities: pool, Jacuzzi. AE, DC, MC, V. Moderate.*

Tower Homestead. Located at the corner of Amboy and Mojave roads in Twentynine Palms, this bed-and-breakfast is owned by Dona Schutz. Built in 1932, the house sits on 160 acres at the edge of town. The two high-ceiling guest suites are filled with functional antiques; each has its own living room and fireplace. Dona cooks breakfast every day. *Box C-141, Twentynine Palms, CA 92277, tel. 619/367-7936. 2 rooms. Moderate.*

Yucca Inn Motor Hotel. This motel is nondescript, but it is conveniently located within a couple of miles of the park's Black Rock entrance and very near a golf course. *7500 Camino Del Cielo, Yucca Valley, CA 92284, tel. 619/365-3311. 74 rooms. Facilities: restaurant, workout room, pool, sauna, Jacuzzi. AE, D, DC, MC, V. Inexpensive.*

CAMPING

INSIDE THE PARK Joshua Tree National Monument has nine campgrounds with a total of 494 individual campsites and 22 group sites. On many weekends in fall and spring, all of these campgrounds will fill up, so plan on arriving by Friday morning at the latest if you expect to find a site (especially from mid-March through mid-May). If you arrive later, try Cottonwood, Indian Cove, or Black Rock campgrounds first; these are usually the last to fill up. Reservations for group sites and for sites at Black Rock Canyon may be made eight weeks in advance through Mistix (tel. 800/365-2267). At all other campgrounds, sites are assigned on a first-come, first-served basis.

Although RVs are permitted at all campgrounds, no hookups are available. RVs should probably stay away from Belle and White Tank campgrounds, because these have small sites with very little space for a large vehicle to maneuver. Dump stations are located at the Black Rock Canyon and Cottonwood campgrounds.

Camping within the monument leans toward the primitive. Only Cottonwood and Black Rock Canyon have flush toilets and drinking water. All other campgrounds have chemical toilets and no water; be sure to bring a gallon of water per person per day. Showers do not exist anywhere in the monument. Each individual site can accommodate two cars, two tents, and six people, and each has a fire grate and picnic table. Campfires are allowed only in fire grates, and all wood must be brought in. It is illegal to collect and burn any vegetation in the monument. Night temperatures at Joshua Tree can be cool any time of the year— bring a sweater or light jacket. The area is noted for its clean air, which provides good stargazing.

At the south end of the park, located at an elevation of 3,000 feet, the **Cottonwood Campground** is usually the last to fill up. There are 62 individual sites here and 3 group sites that hold 10 to 70 people. The individual sites cost $8 per night per campsite, and the group sites are $15 per night for the entire site. All stays are limited to 14 days. The campground has flush toilets, drinking water, a disposal station, and a ranger station. It is open year-round.

Moving toward the interior of the park, **Belle** and **White Tank** campgrounds are next to each other at an elevation of 3,800 feet. These small, quiet campgrounds are very similar to each other: Belle has 17 campsites, White Tank has 15, and they both tend to draw a lot of families. Both have pit toilets, but no water; the nearest water is found at the Cottonwood Visitor Center, roughly 18 miles away. There are a few big boulders to scramble on in this area, and a trail from White Tank leads to a natural arch. Belle is usually open from September through May, and White Tank is usually open year-round. (Both will close if the number of visitors to the park drops greatly, so it's best to call ahead.) There is no fee to camp at either place.

There are four campgrounds in the center of the park, located on the perimeter of Queen Valley: Jumbo Rocks, Ryan, Hidden Valley, and Sheep Pass. They are located at elevations of 4,200 to 4,500 feet, with cool nights from fall through spring. All four of these areas are very popular with climbers and tend to fill first.

Jumbo Rocks, with 125 sites, is located in the heart of the park, near Geology Tour Road. There are pit toilets and no water. The campground is open year-round, with no fee for camping. **Ryan Campground,** which closes

during summer, sits at the base of Ryan Mountain and has 29 sites. This is one of two areas in the park where horses are permitted overnight, although the only corral is located at Black Rock Canyon Campground (*see below*). It is also one of the more vegetated areas. Of these four campgrounds **Hidden Valley** is the most popular among rock climbers, who make this a semipermanent home when Yosemite Valley becomes too cold for climbing. The 39-site campground tends to be crowded until about June, when the rocks get too hot for climbers. It is situated among large boulders and relatively abundant vegetation, just off a dirt road that leads to Barker Dam. The **Sheep Pass Campground** is much like the Hidden Valley site, but it is reserved for groups only. There are six sites that accommodate 10 to 70 people each. The fee is $10 per night for the entire site, with a 14-day maximum stay. At 4,500 feet, Sheep Pass is the highest campground in the monument. It is an isolated area, set among large boulders and relatively dense vegetation. The nearest water is found at the Oasis Visitor Center, 18 miles away.

The 107-site **Indian Cove Campground** is also very popular with the climbing community, primarily because it sits at the base of the Wonderland of Rocks. The wonderland, which separates this campground from the balance of the park, is so named for the more than 50 square miles of rugged mountains and boulder formations. The campground, at an elevation of 3,200 feet, can only be reached via a spur road off Highway 62, between Joshua Tree and Twentynine Palms. The campground has pit toilets but no water. Indian Cove is open year-round and camping is free, on a first-come, first-served basis. There is a ranger station nearby. Indian Cove also has 13 group sites. Sites 1 and 2 cost $30 per night and each can accommodate up to 70 people; sites 3 to 13 cost $15 per night and each holds up to 50.

Finally, there is the **Black Rock Canyon Campground,** which is reached via a 5-mile drive off Highway 62, just east of Yucca Valley. The 100 campsites sit among piñon pines, junipers, and Joshua trees. It is open from September through May. There are flush toilets and drinking water, and a ranger station is nearby. Horses are permitted here. The fee is $10 per vehicle per night.

NEAR THE PARK In Twentynine Palms, the **Twentynine Palms RV Resort** (4949 Desert Knoll Ave., Twentynine Palms, CA 92277, tel. 619/367–3320) has 197 full hookups, tennis courts, a playground, Jacuzzi, sauna, exercise room, and a pool. It is situated in a barren, desert setting, but is adjacent to a golf course. Rates are $19 per night, $96 per week.

Also in Twentynine Palms is the county-operated **Knott's Sky RV Park** (6897 El Sol Ave., Twentynine Palms, CA, 92277, tel. 619/367–9669), which has 40 sites, with water and electric hookups, a dump station, and rest rooms with showers. This RV park is also in a desert setting, but it has a grass playground, a few trees, and picnic tables. Tent camping is allowed. The area tends to draw senior citizens and foreigners. There is a security patrol. Rates are $10.70 per night for any site.

Mount Rainier National Park
Washington
By Jeff Kuechle

he awestruck local Native Americans called it Tahoma, "the mountain that was God," and dared not ascend its eternally ice-bound summit. In 1792 the first white man to visit the region, the British explorer George Vancouver, gazed in amazement at its majestic dome and named it after his friend Rear Admiral Peter Rainier.

Two centuries later, Mt. Rainier, visible from a distance of 200 miles, still fills visitors and natives with wonder. Like a mysterious white-clad virgin, often veiled in cloud even when the surrounding forests and fields are bathed in sunlight, the 14,410-foot mountain is the centerpiece of Mt. Rainier National Park in northwest Washington. Surrounded by some of the finest old-growth forests left on earth, gnawed at by the most extensive system of glaciers in the contiguous United States, supporting a rich array of plant and animal life, Mt. Rainier rewards daytrippers and experienced mountaineers alike.

At one time an unbroken wilderness stretched for hundreds of miles in every direction around this summit, but today Mt. Rainier National Park is an oasis of wilderness in a sea of clearcuts. Its 235,404 acres were preserved by President McKinley in 1899, and in its cathedral-like groves—some more than 1,000 years old—the visitor can experience the grandeur of America's now nearly vanished old-growth forests (all but 1% have been clearcut). Water and lush greenery are everywhere in the park, and dozens of waterfalls, accessible from the road or by a short hike, fill the air with thundering mist.

Higher, above the timberline, are flower-filled meadows thronged with life during Rainier's brief 11-week summer. Higher still, the mountain's glaciated ridges are studies in the elemental forces of geology. Nearly 3 miles high, Rainier's summit is one of the Cascade Range's most challenging mountaineering adventures; serious climbers use Rainier's walls and crevassed ice fields to prepare for such Himalayan peaks as Everest. Every year 8,000 climbers take on the Rainier challenge.

Most visitors to Mt. Rainier, however, aren't prepared for or inclined to participate in dangerous climbs. A well-designed road system at the park allows casual summer visitors to get a sense of the mountain's greatness without leaving their cars. Most head first to gorgeous Paradise Valley, high on the mountain's south flank, half an hour's drive from the Nisqually entrance. From there they might choose to hike a few of the 305 miles of well-maintained trails. The adventurous circle the mountain on the spectacular 93-mile loop of the Wonderland Trail.

Close to the densely populated area of Puget Sound, the park is accessible to anyone who cares to explore it: More than 2 million visitors arrive every year. But mountain wilderness lovers will still find Rainier just the way it has always been: majestic, beautiful, and remarkably unspoiled.

ESSENTIAL INFORMATION

VISITOR INFORMATION Contact the Superintendent, **Mt. Rainier National Park,** Tahoma Woods, Star Route, Ashford, WA 98304, tel. 206/569–2211.

Free wilderness use permits are available from the visitor information centers at Longmire, Paradise, Ohanapecosh, and Sunrise; at the hiker information centers at Longmire and White River; and at any of the park's 21 ranger stations. These permits are required for all overnight stays in the park's wilderness areas.

FEES Single-visit passes at Mt. Rainier, valid for seven days, cost $5 per vehicle. Bicyclists, bus passengers, and travelers on foot pay $3 each. Annual passes are available for $15. Class A sites at Rainier's five auto campgrounds cost $6 per night (except at Ohanapecosh, where the charge is $8 per night); Class B sites, with fewer amenities, cost $5 per night.

PUBLICATIONS The park service has free fliers, brochures, and maps covering various aspects of Mt. Rainier ecology, geology, history, trails, camping, and climbing opportunities. To get copies of these write or call the Superintendent (*see* Visitor Information, *above*). The Superintendent's office also distributes a useful, free four-page guide for those planning overnight trips in the backcountry, "Backcountry Trip Planner: A Hiker's Guide to the Wilderness of Mt. Rainier National Park."

The best general guide to the park, *A Traveler's Companion to Mt. Rainier National Park,* is available through the Northwest Interpretative Association, Longmire, WA 98397 for $5, as is a list of books and park publications, the "Catalogue of Books and Maps—Mt. Rainier National Park." You can also purchase books at bookstores in the Jackson Visitor Center at Paradise and the Longmire Museum.

One publication worth considering is *Cascade and Olympic Natural History,* by Daniel Matthews, a fine regional overview and trailside companion for those interested in the flora, fauna, and geology of the park. *Mt. Rainier: The Story Behind the Scenery*, by Ray Snow, is a colorful, touristy backgrounder on the park, and *Wilderness Above the Sound*, by Arthur Martinson, supplies an illustrated history.

For a concise and useful map and guide to Rainier's trail system, buy *50 Hikes in Mt. Rainier National Park*, by Ira Spring and Harvey Manning. If you are curious about glaciers, Carolyn Driedger's pamphlet "Visitor's Guide to Mt. Rainier's Glaciers" will give you an easy-to-understand explanation of the forces that continue to shape the mountain.

GEOLOGY AND TERRAIN Mt. Rainier rises abruptly from its surrounding terrain in northwest Washington, towering above a series of jagged, heavily forested ridges in the Cascade Range. From an airplane the land surrounding the mountain's base looks like a crumpled sheet of green paper; roads and trails within the 235,404-acre park are steep and winding.

Rainier is a young mountain, less than a million years old. And the area that now comprises Mt. Rainier National Park was not always part of a mountain range. Fifty million years ago, the Cascades did not exist. This area was lowland, with rivers, lakes, and even saltwater bays. Volcanic eruptions in these lowlands spread layer upon layer of debris in the form of ash and lava flows that hardened into rock, which later broke and folded and was eventually uplifted into mountains. The mountains wore away, and the Cascade Range began to form across the low hills that remained. Rivers cut rugged paths through the range, but before the birth of Rainier the highest point in the Cascades was only 6,000 feet.

Rainier was formed between half a million and a million years ago, when a weak spot in the earth's crust allowed deeply buried molten rock to ooze to the surface. Lava flowed from Rainier's central vent as far as 15 miles through the Cascades' deep valleys. The high cone of the mountain was formed later, by lava flows that were smaller and thinner and thus did not travel as far from the vent. When the Mt. Rainier volcano calmed, it immediately began to undergo erosion. There are now three "summits" to Mt. Rainier: Liberty Cap and Point Success, the sides of the old cinder cone, and Columbia Crest, the top of a more recently formed cone and the highest point, at 14,410 feet.

Deep valleys; serrated, sheer-sided ridges; and lesser mountains 6,000 to 10,000 feet high radiate outward from Rainier's domed summit. Those smaller peaks on the westward, or windward, side of Rainier are covered with the dripping green of rain forests at their lower elevations, and, at higher elevations, an average of 620 inches of snow falls during the long winters. To the east, Rainier's vast bulk casts a considerable "rain shadow," and the vegetation in this shadow, though still impressive, is sparser. The twisting 14-mile road from the park's eastern entrance, at White River, to the 6,400-foot Sunrise Visitor Center passes through stately lowland, silver fir, and subalpine forests, emerging from the timberline at about 5,500 feet in a zone of verdant alpine meadows. The exposed visitor center provides what many consider to be the park's most breathtaking views of the mountain and its Cascade neighbors, Mt. Adams, Mt. St. Helens, and Mt. Hood.

This is a peak shaped by fire and ice. An active volcano, it is capable of the same suicidal violence that decapitated nearby Mt. St. Helens in May 1980. In fact, Rainier used to be 2,000 feet taller. About 5,000 years ago the mountain's volcanic grumblings triggered a vast mudslide. When it was over, the unstable summit had vanished, and debris covered nearly 200 square miles around the mountain's base. The volcano's last major eruption occurred about 2,500 years ago, but scientists expect another outburst some time in the next 500 years.

Further change is wrought by Rainier's 26 named glaciers and 50 smaller ice patches, which combined contain more than a cubic mile of ice and are fueled by as much as 90 feet of fresh snow every year. The glaciers continually eat away at the mountain's sturdy flanks; some creep downhill more than a foot a day. Carbon Glacier, on the mountain's north face, is the longest in the continental United States; Emmons Glacier, on the northeast side, is 1 mile wide by $4^{1}/_{3}$ miles long, the largest U.S. glacier outside Alaska.

At Kautz Creek, just east of the park's Nisqually entrance, rank upon rank of dead weather-silvered snags march toward the mountain's slopes, silent witnesses to the destructive power of Rainier's glacier-spawned mudslides, or *jökulhlaups* (pronounced *YO-kul-loips*). In 1947 torrential rains weakened the front edge of the Kautz Glacier, and a roaring wall of mud and debris swept down, carrying along boulders up to 13 feet in diameter, snapping ancient firs like pencils, and burying the landscape in an estimated 50 million cubic yards of cementlike mud. Scientists believe that at Mt. Rainier jökulhlaups like this one occur when glacial cavities that are filled with water from snow, ice melt, and rain are "opened" by increased water pressure, and the stored water is released in violent flows.

Because it is the highest peak in the Cascades, Mt. Rainier has a profound effect on local weather, which in turn affects the geology of this young mountain. Moisture-laden storms off the Pacific rise to pass over Rainier's summit; as the moisture rises, it cools and condenses into snow, which begets glaciers. Over the course of millions of years these glaciers will reduce Mt. Rainier and the Cascades to the stature of the East Coast's Blue Ridge and Catskill mountains.

FLORA AND FAUNA The undisturbed forest and alpine biosphere of Mt. Rainier supports dozens of mammal species, 150 species of bird, more than 100 different flowering plants, and hundreds of trees, shrubs, and other plants. These interact with a temperate lowland climate and plentiful rainfall to weave a complex and interdependent tapestry of life. Scientists are only now beginning to unravel its secrets. Trees and plants provide food and shelter for the animals, who in turn fertilize the plant life and, by scattering seeds, help them to reproduce. The visitor centers and naturalist activities at Longmire, Sunrise, Ohanapecosh, and Paradise each address different facets of park ecology.

The park's flora runs the gamut from the tiny to the tremendous. Immense old-growth Douglas firs shade minuscule ferns and epiphytes, or "air plants." Roosevelt elk inhabit the park in summer; their mating bugles resound through the high ridges on the east side of the park in September. The best place to see them is the Shriner Peak area, reached by trail from Ohanapecosh. Their smaller cousins, the shy black-tailed deer, are often seen from the park roads in early morning and at twilight; spotted, wobbly legged fawns appear in May and June.

White-wooled mountain goats bound from crag to crag near the snowline on their strong legs and soft black hooves. They are most common at Van Trump Park, west of Paradise; at Emerald Ridge, in the southwest corner of the park; in the Colonnades, just east of Sunset Park; and at Cowlitz Chimneys, on the east side of the park.

Black bears are present but rarely seen. More common are Rainier's chubby raccoons and porcupines, which prowl the lowland forests nibbling the tender inner bark of young trees. Pikas, timid ground-dwelling rodents with soft gray fur, rounded ears, and no discernible tail, inhabit the talus slopes and rock piles of the highlands, gathering forage for winter. Watch for their tiny piles of "hay" drying in the sun on rocks, and listen for their shrill "eek!"s of alarm.

Rainier is particularly rich in avian life. In the winter, pigeon-size ptarmigan turn snow-white and travel on feathery "snowshoes." Flycatchers, hawks, owls, pileated woodpeckers, and the occasional golden eagle roost in snags in the lowland forest. The cheerful, bubbling calls and sprightly antics of the gray-and-black water ouzel charm hikers along forest streams.

These and dozens of other species depend on the dense woodland to survive. The Douglas fir, monarch of the Northwest forest, towers hundreds of feet in the air. Crinkle-barked spruce and hemlock and thick-boled cedar can grow almost as large. The trees in the Grove of the Patriarchs, in the park's southeast corner, protected from fire by nearby rivers, are thought to be more than 1,000 years old. In their shadows grow slimy 6-inch banana slugs, mushrooms, mosses, ferns, and a particularly nasty lowland species called devil's club, whose extravagant spines and serrated barbs make it the punk rocker of local plant life. Fortunately—or, perhaps, unfortunately—devil's club grows only in the Pacific Northwest.

Rainier's extensive alpine meadows, accessible by car at the Paradise and Sunrise visitor centers, are one of the park's special attractions. From late June to early September flowers follow the retreating snows and bloom in profusion, sometimes thrusting their blossoms through several inches of snow in their haste to reproduce. Avalanche lilies, pentstemon, monkey-flower, partridge-foot, cinquefoil, and dozens of other species bring color to the meadows, then wither away before the arctic blasts of winter.

WHEN TO GO The ideal time to visit Mt. Rainier is late September through the first week of October. Although most of the wildflowers have vanished by then, the weather is still fine, the huckleberries and vine maples turn brilliant fall colors, all the park's roads and facilities are still open, and most important of all, the summer crowds have melted away. Half of Rainier's 2 million annual visitors arrive in July and August, a human flood that continues well into September.

From December to April deep winter grips the park, burying the lodge at Paradise up to its high-gabled roof in snow and closing access to most of the park. Only the road from Nisqually to Paradise is kept plowed; the north and east sides of the park are completely inaccessible by vehicle. The cross-country skiing and snowshoeing, however, are exquisite, and the crowds thin (only about 100,000 people visit the park in winter). At the same time, the mountain, covered with a deep blanket of fresh snow, is at its most beautiful.

When it can be seen, that is. In winter, the mountain is frequently socked in for weeks on end, and many visitors depart without ever seeing it. Of course, even in summer, fog and clouds rising from Rainier's extensive glaciers can hide it from view.

SEASONAL EVENTS **May to early June:** The **birth of fawns** to the park's black-tailed deer herds occurs. **December to April: Ski season** (*see* Other Activities, *below*). **Last week of June to first week of September:** Enjoy the colors of the **wildflower season** in subalpine meadows. **September to early October:** During **elk-mating season** the bulls bugle and fight for harems of females.

From early June through September, **Pacific Northwest Field Seminars** (83 S. King St., Suite 212, Seattle, WA 98104, tel. 206/553–2636) leads educational classes and seminars on various aspects of the park's natural treasures: "Ancient Forests of Mt. Rainier," "Photographing Nature at Mt. Rainier," "Backpacking for Women," to name a few. There are also classes available for children.

Classes last from one to four days and cost an average of $35 per day per person.

WHAT TO PACK Over the years, visitors to this inclement mountain have bestowed on it the sardonic nickname Rainiest. Campers and hikers in particular should be sure to bring adequate rain gear. Those planning extended stays in the backcountry will need to bring some means of purifying drinking water: vessels for boiling or lightweight, hand-pumped filters. Even the pure and plentiful mountain streams of Mt. Rainier may contain organisms that cause giardiasis, a particularly distressing intestinal disease. Although many old-timers scoff that they've drunk untreated water for years without ill effects, it's better to be safe than sorry.

GENERAL STORES Inside the park, **Longmire Service Station** (tel. 206/569–2411) sells gas and oil and rents tire chains. The **General Store at Longmire's National Park Inn** (tel. 206/569–2411) stocks food, gifts, camping supplies, and other basic necessities. From mid-June to mid-October, the store is open 8 to 8, the gas station 9 to 7. The rest of the year, the store is open 10 to 5 and the gas station 9 to 5. Groceries are also available at **Sunrise Lodge** (tel. 206/569–2211, Ext. 2357), which is open from early June to early September, 10 to 6.

Outside the park, the nearest gas and groceries are found at **Ashford,** near the park's Nisqually entrance; at **Packwood,** near the Ohanapecosh Visitor Center; and at **Fairfax,** near the Carbon River entrance. The nearest large grocery stores are the **Ashford Valley Grocery** (tel. 206/569–2560) in Ashford, and the **Eatonville Market** (tel. 206/832–4551) in Eatonville.

ARRIVING AND DEPARTING The vast majority of visitors to Mt. Rainier National Park arrive via Highway 706 and the Nisqually entrance, at the park's southwest corner. Highways 410 and 123 enter the park from the east and southeast, respectively; both routes are usually closed in winter. Highway 165 leads to Ipsut Creek Campground through the Carbon River entrance and to Mowich Lake, in the park's northwest corner. The Nisqually entrance is preferred because of its proximity to I–5, and because the road from it links the popular Paradise area with Ohanapecosh and Sunrise. In winter, this route dead-ends at Paradise, but the other roads within the park are not plowed at all.

By Plane. The nearest airport is Seattle–Tacoma International, 70 miles and two hours northeast of the park. No public ground transportation is currently available from the airport, but all major car rental agencies service Seattle and Tacoma. Try **Budget** (tel. 800/345–6655 or, in Washington, 800/435–1880) or **Avis** (tel. 206/433–5231).

By Car and RV. Seattle is 80 miles from the park, and Tacoma is 55 miles. It takes about 2¹/₂ hours by car to get to the Nisqually entrance from Seattle and two hours from Tacoma. From both cities, take I–5 south to Highway 7 east, which will bring you to Route 706 and Mt. Rainier.

A scenic alternate route (impassable in winter) starts in Renton, 10 miles southeast of downtown Seattle. Follow Highway 169 east from Renton and pick up Highway 410 at Enumclaw. This road follows the eastern edge of the park to Chinook Pass, where you pick up Highway 123 south to its junction with Stevens Canyon Road. Take Stevens Canyon Road west to its junction with the Paradise–Nisqually Entrance road, which runs west through Longmire and exits the park at Nisqually. This route covers about 100 miles and will take you three to four hours to drive with minimal stops.

If you are coming from the east through Yakima, take Highway 12 northwest. Just past Naches the road will split: You can either continue on Highway 12 and pick up 123 north to Ohanapecosh, or take Highway 410 west to Chinook and Cayuse passes and enter the park via the White River entrance.

From Portland, take I–5 north toward Olympia, then take Highway 12 east to Route 7 at Morton and then Highway 706 to Mt. Rainier.

By Train. There is no commercial rail service to the park; the nearest **Amtrak** (800/USA-RAIL) station is in Tacoma. **Budget** (tel. 800/345–6655 or, in Washington, 800/435–1880) and **Hertz** (tel. 206/922–6688) provide free shuttle service from the station to their offices. From May to October, the **Mount Rainier Scenic Railroad** (tel. 206/569–2588) offers 90-minute round-trip excursions from Elbe to Mineral Lake.

By Bus. There is no public bus transportation to the park. For guided bus tours, *see* Guided Tours, *below*.

EXPLORING

A single, narrow, winding paved road links the main attractions at Rainier, and during the peak months of July and August, traffic can be torturously slow and heavy. Despite this, a combination of driving and hiking is your best bet for exploring the park. The ideal trip would include 10 to 14 days to hike the Wonderland Trail (*see* Longer Hikes, *below*), the magnificent 93-mile circuit of Mt. Rainier, but time and rugged terrain make this option impractical for most visitors.

The main park road from Nisqually climbs through towering forests toward Paradise, then loops around the east side of the mountain and exits at the park's northeast corner, a total of about 50 miles. The unpaved Westside Road, which is now closed because of flood damage, runs northward for 3 miles into the mountains from the Nisqually entrance. Two short gravel roads in the northwest corner of the park dead-end at Mowich Lake Campground and Ipsut Creek Campground. The rest of the park interior is roadless, and feet, horses, cross-country skis, and snowshoes are the only means of exploration.

It is possible to sample Rainier's main attractions—Longmire, Paradise, the Grove of Patriarchs, and Sunrise—in a single day by car, but you should plan on spending at least two days or, better, three, hiking the park's multitude of forest, meadow, and high mountain trails.

Every year, more than 8,000 people take the most adventurous exploring option of all—a

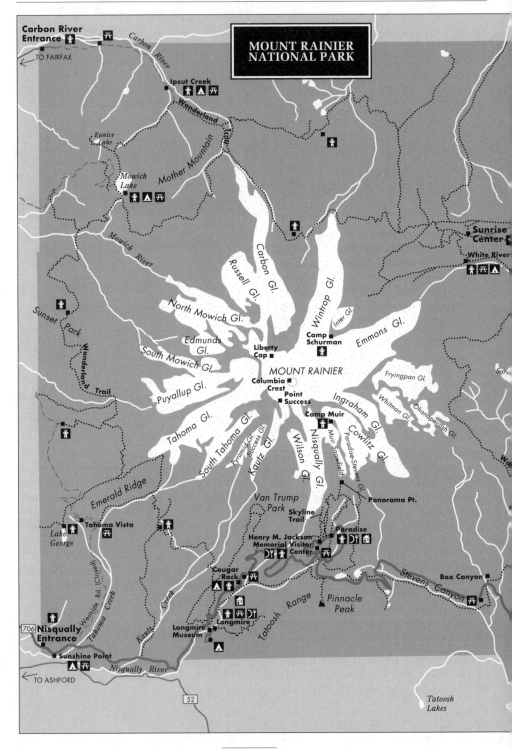

MOUNT RAINIER NATIONAL PARK

Carbon River Entrance

TO FAIRFAX

Ipsut Creek

Eunice Lake

Mowich Lake

Mother Mountain

Wonderland Trail

Carbon River

Carbon Gl.

Russell Gl.

Wintrop Gl.

Sunrise Center

White River

Mowich River

North Mowich Gl.

Edmunds Gl.

South Mowich Gl.

Sunset Park

Wonderland Trail

Puyallup Gl.

Camp Schurman

Liberty Cap

Inter Gl.

Emmons Gl.

MOUNT RAINIER

Columbia Crest

Point Success

Fryingpan Gl.

Sarv

Ingraham Gl.

Whitman Gl.

Ohanapecosh Gl.

Tahoma Gl.

South Tahoma Gl.

Pyramid Gl.

Success Gl.

Kautz Gl.

Camp Muir

Cowlitz Gl.

Wilson Gl.

Nisqually Gl.

Muir Snowfield

Paradise-Stevens Gl.

Panorama Pt.

Emerald Ridge

Van Trump Park

Skyline Trail

Tahoma Vista

Lake George

Westside Rd. (Closed)

Tahoma Creek

Kautz Creek

Henry M. Jackson Memorial Visitor Center

Paradise

Box Canyon

Stevens Canyon

Cougar Rock

Pinnacle Peak

Tatoosh Range

Longmire

Longmire Museum

706 Nisqually Entrance

Sunshine Point

Nisqually River

TO ASHFORD

52

Tatoosh Lakes

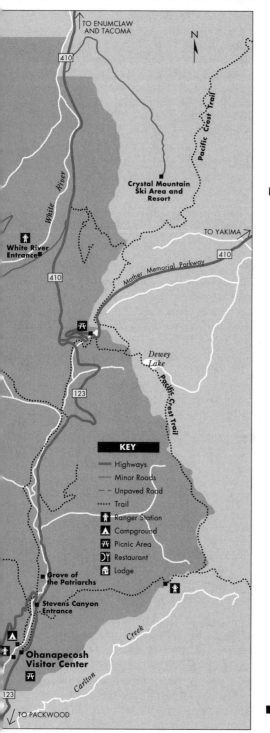

climb to Rainier's 14,410-foot summit. Novice climbers complete a one-day snow and ice-climbing school taught by park concessionaire Rainier Mountaineering Inc. (*see* Other Activities, *below*), then make the two-day climb to the top. This transcendent mountain adventure, open even to those with no previous climbing experience if they are up for the rigorous physical demands of a summit attempt, is one of the things that distinguishes Mt. Rainier from other places in the National Park system.

THE BEST IN ONE DAY The best way to get a complete overview of Mt. Rainier's charms in a day or less is to enter via Nisqually, and begin your tour by browsing in the Longmire Museum. The ¹/₂-mile Trail of Shadows nature loop will acquaint you with the environment in and around Longmire Meadow, as well as with the overgrown ruins of the Longmire Springs Hotel.

From Longmire, the road climbs northeast into the mountains toward Paradise. Take a moment to explore gorgeous Christine Falls, just north of the road 1¹/₂ miles past Cougar Rock Campground, and Narada Falls, 3 miles farther on; both are spanned by graceful stone footbridges. Fantastic mountain views, alpine meadows crosshatched with nature trails, a welcoming lodge and restaurant, and the excellent Henry M. Jackson Memorial Visitor Center combine to make lofty Paradise the primary goal of most park visitors. One outstanding—but grueling—way to explore the high country is to hike the 5-mile Skyline Trail to Panorama Point, which has stunning 360-degree views (*see* Longer Hikes, *below*).

Continue eastward for 21 miles and leave your car for an hour to explore the incomparable, thousand-year-old Grove of the Patriarchs, a small, protected island where a 1¹/₃-mile nature trail leads through towering Douglas fir, cedar, and hemlock. Afterward, turn your car north toward White River and the Sunrise Visitor Center, from which you can watch the alpenglow fade from Mt. Rainier's domed summit.

ORIENTATION PROGRAMS From Fourth of July weekend through Labor Day, park rangers and naturalists lead daily nature walks and illustrated campfire talks at Paradise, Longmire, Sunrise, Ohanapecosh, and Ipsut Creek. See bulletin boards at campgrounds, ranger stations, and visitor centers for dates, times, and subjects; or call the main park phone number (tel. 206/569–2211).

The park's four visitor centers each focus on a different aspect of park ecology, and all are a worthwhile first stop on your explorations. The **Longmire Museum**'s simple glass cases contain hundreds of preserved plants and animals from the park, including a large, friendly-looking stuffed cougar. Other exhibits give an overview of park history. Longmire is open daily all year 9 to 4:30.

At disk-shape **Jackson Memorial Visitor Center** at Paradise, high on the mountain's southern flank, the exhibits focus on geology, mountaineering, glaciology, winter storms, and alpine ecology. Two worthwhile 20-minute multimedia programs repeat at half-hour intervals. The center is open daily 9 to 6 from early May to mid-October and 10 to 5 weekends and holidays only from mid-October to early May.

At **Ohanapecosh Visitor Center** you will learn about the region's dense old-growth forests from late May to October, daily 9 to 6.

The **Sunrise Visitor Center,** open daily 9 to 6 from early July to Labor Day, features exhibits on that region's sparser alpine and subalpine ecology.

GUIDED TOURS **Gray Line of Seattle** (tel. 206/624–5813) offers daily bus tours to Mt. Rainier, with stops at Paradise and Longmire, from May 1 through mid-October. The tours leave at 8 AM from the Seattle Sheraton, downtown at 6th and Pike, and cost $34 per person. Lunch is not included in the price of this 10-hour trip. Reservations are required. **Cascade** (tel. 800/824–8897) bus service also runs tours to Mt. Rainier.

SCENIC DRIVES AND VIEWS There are four paved roads that form one continuous route through the park, with a spur road from the White River entrance to the Sunrise Visitor Center. The main road starts at the Nisqually entrance and traces the southern boundary of the park, turning north in the southeast corner, and traveling along the east side of the mountain until it exits the park in the northeast corner (*see* The Best in One Day, *above*). Every foot of this 50-mile route is scenic. Along the 7 miles of road between the Nisqually entrance and Longmire, deer stalk the shadows, and the narrow thoroughfare, wrapping around gigantic old trees, gives the right-of-way to nature. This is one of the most beautiful stretches of forest road in the world.

The kinks and twistings of the 15-mile spur road from the White River entrance to Sunrise give the best views of the mountain.

Two unnamed roads that start at the Carbon River entrance provide access to some of the park's steepest, wildest, and most densely wooded sections. These roads are not plowed in winter and are often closed by mudslides, but in dry summer months you can cover them even without a four-wheel-drive vehicle. Be careful—the roads are narrow and winding. The two northern roads connect with Ipsut Creek campground and Mowich Lake campground.

HISTORIC BUILDINGS AND SITES The **Paradise Inn,** in continuous operation since 1917, has sheltered the likes of Shirley Temple, Cecil B. DeMille, John D. Rockefeller, and Tyrone Power. Its high, gable roof, massive beams, and parquet floors were constructed from Alaska cedars salvaged during the building of the road to this high mountain meadow. Through the inn's tall, many-paned windows you will be treated to unequaled views of the mountain. The property is on the National Register of Historic Places.

A smaller sister establishment, the **National Park Inn at Longmire,** is also a national historic landmark, and like many of the park service buildings at Longmire, it is worth a look for its massive stone-and-timber construction and hand-forged wrought iron. Its rooms lost much of their historic character in a 1990 renovation.

NATURE TRAILS AND SHORT WALKS The ½-mile **Trail of Shadows** begins just across the road from the National Park Inn at Longmire. It's notable for its insights into meadowland ecology, its colorful soda springs, James Longmire's old homestead cabin, and the foundation of the old Longmire Springs Hotel, which was destroyed around the turn of the century.

A 1⅓-mile loop takes hikers through one of the park's most stunning features, the **Grove of the Patriarchs,** a lush old-growth forest in Rainier's southeastern corner. The trail begins just west of the Stevens Canyon entrance and leads over a bridge to an island covered with thousand-year-old trees, among the oldest in the Northwest; they have been protected from forest fires and other disasters by the rushing waters to either side.

The mile-long loop of the **Sourdough Ridge Self-Guiding Trail** moves through the delicate sub-alpine meadows near the Sunrise Visitor Center. The trail begins at the north side of the parking area; a gradual climb to the ridge top yields magnificent views of Mt. Rainier and neighboring peaks Baker, Adams, and Glacier.

Equally popular in summer and winter, the 1¼-mile round-trip **Nisqually Vista Trail** heads out from the Jackson Visitor Center at Paradise, through subalpine meadows, to an overlook point for Nisqually Glacier. In winter, the snow-covered, gradually sloping trail is a favorite venue for cross-country skiers. In summer, listen for the shrill alarm-calls of the area's marmots.

LONGER HIKES All other Mt. Rainier hikes pale in comparison to the stunning 93-mile **Wonderland Trail,** which completely encircles the mountain. The Wonderland passes through all the major life-zones of the park, from the old-growth forests of the lowlands to the wildflowers and goat-haunted glaciers of the highlands. It's a rugged trail; elevation gains and losses totaling 3,500 feet are common in a day's hike, which averages 8 miles. Most hikers start out from either Longmire or Sunrise and take 10 to 14 days to cover the 93-mile route, but why hurry? Snow lingers

on the high passes well into June, and you can count on rain any time of year. Campsites are primitive trailside areas with pit toilets and water that must be purified before drinking. Only the hardy and well-equipped should attempt this trip, but few who complete the journey are ever quite the same again.

Those who lack the time or the conditioning to complete the entire Wonderland loop can sample an 18-mile section of the trail that leaves Stevens Canyon Road at Box Canyon, runs northward along the mountain's east flank, and connects with the road to Sunrise near the White River entrance to the park. In three or four days of hiking, you can cover a microcosm of Rainier's scenic glories.

The 5-mile loop of the **Skyline Trail,** one of the highest in the park, beckons day-trippers with an exhilarating *Sound of Music* vista of alpine ridges and, in summer, meadows filled with brilliant flowers and birds. At 6,800-foot Panorama Point, the spine of the Cascade Range spreads away to the east, and Nisqually Glacier grumbles its way downslope. The trail begins and ends in the Paradise parking lot, just west of the inn.

OTHER ACTIVITIES **Back-Road Driving.** All vehicles are required to stay on constructed roads; off-road vehicles are not allowed in the park.

Biking. This is not a prime activity in the park. Bikes are allowed, but only on constructed roads; off-road mountain biking is prohibited. Park roads are narrow, winding, and, in summer, extremely crowded with cars. Bike rentals are not available within the park.

Bird-Watching. Watch for kestrels, red-tailed hawks, and, occasionally, golden eagles on snags in the lowland forests. Rarely seen, but also present at Rainier, are great horned owls, spotted owls, and screech owls. Iridescent hummingbirds flit from blossom to blossom in the drowsy summer lowlands, and there are sprightly water ouzels in the many forest creeks. Raucous Steller's jays and gray jays scold passersby from trees, often darting boldly down to steal morsels from unguarded picnic tables. At higher elevations, look for the pure white plumage of the white-tailed ptarmigan as it hunts for seeds and insects in winter. Waxwings, vireos, nuthatches, sapsuckers, warblers, flycatchers, larks, thrushes, siskins, tanagers, and finches are common throughout the park in every season but winter.

Boating. There are no boat rentals inside the park. Nonmotorized boating is permitted on all lakes inside the park except Frozen Lake, Ghost Lake, Reflection Lakes, and Tipsoo Lake.

Fishing. Fishing in Rainier's unstocked lakes and rivers is apt to be an unproductive experience; the park isn't known for its fishing, but you're welcome to try. Small trout are the main quarry, and park rangers encourage "fishing for fun," with barbless hooks. No license is required, but seasonal regulations are enforced. The Ohanapecosh River and its tributaries are open to fly-fishing only.

Horseback Riding. Nearly 100 of the park's 300 miles of trails are open to horseback riding, and parties with horses may use four backcountry camps—Deer Creek, Mowich River, North Puyallup River, and Three Lakes. There are no horse rentals within the park, but they are available at **Bar B Ranch** (tel. 206/569–2989) in Ashford.

Mountain Climbing. The highly regarded concessionaire **Rainier Mountaineering Inc.,** cofounded by Himalayan adventurer Lou Whittaker, makes climbing the Queen of the Cascades an adventure open to anyone in good health and physical condition. The company teaches the fundamentals of mountaineering at one-day classes held during the climbing season, late May through early September. Participants in these classes are evaluated for their fitness for the climb; they must be able to withstand a 16-mile round-trip with a 9,000-foot gain in elevation. Those who meet the fitness requirement choose between guided two- and four-day summit climbs, the latter via more-demanding Emmons Glacier. Experienced climbers can fill out a climbing card at the Paradise, White River, or Carbon River ranger stations and

lead their own groups of two or more. Contact Rainier Mountaineering Inc. (535 Dock St., Suite 209, Tacoma, WA 98402, tel. in winter 206/627–6242, in summer 206/569–2227).

Ski Touring. Mt. Rainier is a major Nordic ski center. Equipment rentals are available at the **Longmire Ski Touring Center** (tel. 206/569–2411), adjacent to the National Park Inn at Longmire, for $10.50 per day. Trails are not groomed. Those around Paradise are extremely popular; if you want to ski with fewer people try the trails in and around the Ohanapecosh/Stevens Canyon area, which are just as beautiful. Visitors should never ski on the plowed main roads, especially in the Paradise area—the snowplow operator can't see you.

Snowmobiling. Snowmobiling is allowed on the east side of the park, on sections of Highway 123 and Stevens Canyon Road—between the ranger station at Ohanapecosh Visitor Center and Box Canyon—and on Highway 410, which is accessible from the north entrance and unplowed after its junction with the road to the Crystal Mountain Ski Area. A $10 State of Washington Sno-Park permit, available at stores and gas stations throughout the area, is required to park in the area near the north park entrance arch.

Snowshoeing. Deep snows make Mt. Rainier a snowshoeing capital. Rentals are available at the **Longmire Ski Touring Center** (tel. 206/569–2411), adjacent to the National Park Inn, for $7.25 per day. From December through April, park rangers lead free twice-daily snowshoe walks that start at Jackson Memorial Visitor Center at Paradise and cover $1^{1}/_{4}$ miles in about two hours. The network of trails in the Paradise area makes it most popular for snowshoers, but the park's eastside roads, Highways 123 and 410, are unplowed and provide another good snowshoeing venue.

Swimming. There are 62 lakes and countless streams and rivers within the park, but all are fed by glacial snowmelt. Unless your tolerance for bone-chilling cold exceeds that of a walrus, it is best to avoid Rainier's waters.

CHILDREN'S PROGRAMS Every Saturday at 10 AM a park naturalist escorts visitors on a two-hour, ½-mile walk through the old-growth forest around Ohanapecosh Campground. They can also meet a park naturalist at the Cougar Rock Campground Amphitheater at 2 on Tuesday and Saturday for a two-hour, ½-mile walk that includes nature activities. Both outings are geared to children as well as adults.

EVENING ACTIVITIES Rangers and naturalists lead campfire talks and slide shows at park campgrounds from June to mid-September. Consult bulletin boards at the campgrounds, visitor centers, and ranger stations for dates, times, locations, and subjects.

DINING

Dining options inside Mt. Rainier National Park are somewhat better than average because of the capable chefs at the National Park Inn at Longmire and (in summer) lofty Paradise Inn. Outside park boundaries, dining options are somewhat austere given Rainier's proximity to the cosmopolitan Puget Sound area. A 7½% Washington sales tax is added to the bill.

INSIDE THE PARK **Paradise Inn.** Where else can you get a decent Sunday brunch in a historic heavy-timbered lodge halfway up a mountain? Tall many-paned windows offer terrific views of Rainier, and the warm glow of native wood permeates the large dining room. The menu is simple and healthy: vegetable stir-fry, fettuccine Paradise with chicken and mushrooms in a creamy Parmesan sauce, fresh salmon poached with lemon butter, and a decadent warm blackberry pie. *Paradise, tel. 206/569-2413. Reservations not accepted. Dress: casual. MC, V. Closed Oct.–late May. Moderate.*

National Park Inn. This historic inn at Longmire was completely remodeled in 1990, a process that robbed it of some of its old-fashioned rustic charm but left it looking decidedly more cheerful. Photos of Mt. Rainier taken by some of the Northwest's top photographers adorn the walls of the inn's

bright, clean dining room—a bonus on the many days the mountain refuses to show itself. The small menu changes seasonally and emphasizes such simple healthy fare as pan-fried snapper with lemon butter and wine, chicken and vegetable skewers marinated and charbroiled, hearty broiled steaks, and spicy pasta with fennel sausage. For breakfast, don't miss the home-baked cinnamon rolls with cream-cheese frosting. The prices are reasonable, a real boon for families with hungry children. *Longmire, tel. 206/569-2275. Reservations not accepted. Dress: casual. MC, V. Inexpensive–Moderate.*

The **Paradise** and **Sunset visitor complexes** also have modestly priced snack bars serving burgers, sandwiches, and salads.

NEAR THE PARK **Alexander's Country Inn.** Yet another historic inn, Alexander's offers the closest thing to gourmet within a 50-mile radius of the park. This comfortable, eccentrically turreted 1912-vintage inn sets a mean dinner table. Meals start with roasted garlic, olive oil, and Parmesan-cheese dip and fresh-baked bread, and there are always three or four special entrées from which to choose. Fresh seafood figures heavily in the permanent menu: chinook salmon baked with cider butter sauce; halibut with sweet red bell-pepper sauce; pork chops duxelles with raspberry glaze; thick pan-fried steaks; and Greek chicken fettuccine. Don't forget the fresh blackberry pie for dessert. *37515 Hwy. 706 E, 4 mi east of Ashford, tel. 206/569-2300. Reservations suggested in summer. Dress: casual. MC, V. Closed weekdays (except holidays) Nov.–mid-May. Moderate–Expensive.*

Baumgartner's. Picnickers alert: Located at the junction of Route 169 and Highway 410, this is the best place in the park's vicinity to stock up on fresh baked goods, imported meats and cheeses, deli sandwiches, beer and wine, and heavenly desserts. You can eat in, in the small and casual dining area, for lunch and early dinner. *1008 E. Roosevelt, Enumclaw, tel. 206/825-1067. Reservations not necessary. Dress: casual. MC, V. Inexpensive.*

Wild Berry Restaurant. This funky, organic eatery just down the road from Alexander's is the place where the mountain's laid-back ski-and-hot-tub crowd stokes up for a long day in the woods. Hefty salads, pizzas, crepes, sandwiches, and home-baked desserts are served in relaxed (though far from luxurious) surroundings. *37720 Hwy. 706 E, 4 mi east of Ashford, tel. 206/569–2628. Dress: casual. MC, V. Inexpensive.*

PICNIC SPOTS The picnic areas at **Sunrise** and **Paradise** are justly famous, especially in summer, when wildflowers fill the meadows and friendly yellow pine chipmunks dart hopefully about in search of handouts. (Never stray from the paths when traversing the meadows. The vegetation is extremely fragile; some plants grow only fractions of an inch every few years.) After picnicking at Paradise, you can take an easy hike to one of the numerous waterfalls in the area—Sluiskin, Myrtle, or Narada, to name a few.

Although many maps of Mt. Rainier show the Tahoma Vista picnic area, 6 miles up the unpaved Westside Road, you won't be able to spread out a picnic feast there. The area was washed out several years ago, and because of continuous outburst floods there are no plans to replace it.

LODGING

The Mt. Rainier area is singularly bereft of quality lodging, a fact that may be a result of its proximity to Seattle. The two National Park lodges, at Longmire and Paradise, are attractive and well maintained, and ooze history and charm, but unless you've made your summer reservations a year in advance, you probably won't get a room in either one. There are dozens of motels and cabin complexes near the park entrances, but the vast majority are disappointingly plain, overpriced, or downright dilapidated. With just a few exceptions, you're better off camping. The room tax in Washington is 9¹/₂%.

INSIDE THE PARK **National Park Inn.** This smaller, more modern, and more intimate version of the Paradise Inn (*see below*) lost a little of its old rustic flair but gained a lot of comfort in an extensive 1990 renovation. The old stone fireplaces are still here, but the public areas are freshly painted and carpeted. The small rooms mix budget-motel functionality (though without TVs and telephones) with such wistful backwoods touches as antique bentwood headboards and graceful wrought-iron lamps. There's a good restaurant on the ground floor. Located down the hill at heavily wooded Longmire, the inn is the only year-round lodging in the park, and it makes a great base camp for day explorers. Again, reservations well in advance are a must. *Box 108, Ashford, WA 98304, tel. 206/569–2275. 25 rooms, 18 with bath. Facilities: restaurant, gift shop, general store. MC, V. Moderate.*

Paradise Inn. With its hand-carved cedar logs, burnished parquet floors, stone fireplaces, Indian rugs, and glorious mountain views, this 75-year-old inn is loaded with high-mountain atmosphere. Its smallish, sparsely furnished rooms, however, are not equipped with TVs or telephones and have thin walls and showers that tend to run cold during periods of peak use. The attraction here is the 5,400-foot alpine setting, so lovely you expect Julie Andrews to stroll by at any moment. There's a small, crowded bar and a competent dining room as well. *Box 108, Ashford, WA 98304, tel. 206/569–2275. 127 rooms, 96 with bath. Facilities: restaurant, snack bar, lounge, gift shop. MC, V. Closed early Oct.–late May. Moderate.*

NEAR THE PARK **Alexander's Country Inn.** This freshly renovated 1912-vintage inn towers over its Rainier-area competition like a grand old Douglas fir over seedlings. From the big hot tub overlooking the trout pond out back to the hand-quilted antique warmth of its 14 rooms, Alexander's understands hospitality. Presidents Theodore Roosevelt and William Taft stayed here during visits to the mountain. The big second-floor sitting room, with its fireplace, deep couches, stained glass, and complimentary evening wine, has changed for the better since their day. The guest rooms sparkle with fresh paint, carpeting, antiques, and marble-top pine bedside tables. One word of warning: The walls are rather thin, so it's possible to catch phrases from conversations three rooms away. All in all, though, the popular inn is the place to stay near Mt. Rainier. A delicious farm breakfast, served in the downstairs restaurant, is included in the price of the room; lunch and dinner are extra. *37515 Hwy. 706 E (4 mi east of Ashford), Ashford, WA 98304, tel. 206/569–2300 or 800/654–7615. 14 rooms, 10 with bath plus a 3-bedroom, 2-bath house that accommodates 8. Facilities: restaurant, hot tub, trout pond. MC, V. Moderate.*

Nisqually Lodge. Built in 1989, this brand-new motor lodge has an intimate Swiss-chalet feel, with a big stone fireplace, exposed beams, and lots of knotty pine in the lobby. The 24 earth-tone rooms are spacious; furnishings are department-store-modern. Even though the motel is located on busy Highway 706, the rooms' double insulation keeps them quiet. A Continental breakfast is included in the room price. *31609 Hwy. 706 E (2 mi east of Ashford), Ashford, WA 98304, tel. 206/569–8804. 21 rooms. AE, DC, MC, V. Moderate.*

The Lodge Near Mt. Rainier. Scattered over 16 wooded acres are four cabins and three lodges of varying size and quality. The large, modern Chalet and charming, wood-paneled Large Lodge (the latter built in 1917) both feature a huge restaurant-style kitchen. They sleep 12 to 25 people in relative comfort. The smaller Cedar Log Cabin is perfect for a single family. The other units—notably the run-down, noisy Small Lodge—should be avoided. *38608 S.R. 706 E (5 mi east of Ashford), Ashford, WA 98304, tel. 206/569–2312. 9 units. MC, V. Inexpensive–Moderate.*

Between the park's Nisqually entrance and the town of Ashford, 11 miles east, Highway 706 is crowded with privately owned bed-and-breakfasts, motels, and cabin complexes. Most are rather small and primitive, but they fill up quickly in summer. These include the **Gateway Inn** (tel. 206/569–2506), the **Growly Bear Bed & Breakfast** (tel. 206/569–2339), **Mountain Meadows Inn** (tel. 206/569–

2788), **Mounthaven** (tel. 206/569–2594), and **Rainier Country Cabins** (tel. 206/569–2355).

CAMPING

INSIDE THE PARK There are five drive-in campgrounds in the park—Cougar Rock, Ipsut Creek, Ohanapecosh, Sunshine Point, and White River—with almost 700 campsites for tents and RVs. These campgrounds are categorized Class A, B, or C, and all have parking spaces, drinking water, garbage cans, fire grates, and picnic tables with benches. There is a ranger station at each campground, as well as a public phone at Class A sites. Class A sites have flush toilets and a concrete parking pad and cost $6 to $8 per night. Class B sites have pit toilets and cost $5 per night. Group sites are Class C and cost $2 per person. There is no hot water in the park campgrounds, and RV hookups are not available. (Showers are available only at Jackson Memorial Visitor Center.)

Just past the Nisqually entrance is **Sunshine Point,** which has 18 Class B sites that are the only drive-in sites open all year. It's a pleasant, wooded riverside campground, the most crowded in the park. Farther up the road, 2½ miles north of Longmire, is **Cougar Rock,** a secluded, heavily wooded campground that is very popular. It has a mix of 200 Class A and Class B sites, 60 of which are pull-throughs. There are also five group sites here. Open from late May to mid-October, this campground has an amphitheater and a trailer dump station. In the southeast corner of the park is lush green **Ohanapecosh,** with 205 Class A sites including 10 walk-ins. Open from May to late October, Ohanapecosh has a visitor center, amphitheater, dumping station, and self-guided trail. The **White River** campground, in the northeastern section of the park, has 117 Class A sites that are available from late June to late September. At an elevation of 4,400 feet, it's the highest and least wooded campground in the park; it has partial views of Mt. Rainier's summit. Here you can enjoy campfire programs and self-guided trails. With only 31 Class B sites and 2 group sites, **Isput Creek** is the quietest park campground, but also the most difficult to reach. In the remote northwest corner of the park, it is open from May through October and has weekend campfire programs and self-guided trails. Set in the middle of a wet, green, and rugged wilderness, this is a popular starting point for those venturing out on the Wonderland trail and well worth the effort it takes to find it.

Reservations are not accepted at any of the campgrounds; it's strictly first-come, first-served. Sunshine Point, Cougar Rock, and Ohanapecosh tend to fill up first; White River, the highest and last to open in spring, is also busy but harder to get to. Cougar Rock, Ohanapecosh, and Sunshine Point have the best RV access. The road to White River is paved. Ipsut Creek is accessible only by a 5-mile convoluted gravel road.

Camping is also allowed throughout the back-country, but you must have a free wilderness permit—ask at the visitor centers (*see* Visitor Information, *above*). Primitive sites are spaced at 7- or 8-mile intervals along the Wonderland Trail. A copy of "Backcountry Trip Planner: A Hiker's Guide to the Wilderness of Mt. Rainier National Park," available from any of the park's four visitor centers or through the superintendent's office (*see* Visitor Information, *above*), is an invaluable guide for those planning overnight backcountry stays.

Olympic National Park
Washington
By Jeff Kuechle

ust off the Washington coast, where the farthest northwestern horn of the continental United States gores the Pacific, is Destruction Island, a barnacle-crusted monolith crowned by a mournful lighthouse. To the north, the rock-fanged coast of the Olympic Peninsula curves gracefully outward toward Japan, a wild, lush coastline without roads, souvenir shops, golf courses, or crowded resorts. Marked only by the tracks of black bear, Roosevelt elk, bobcat, and other wildlife, these are the last wilderness beaches left in the contiguous United States, and just one area of Olympic National Park.

Traveling east from the coastline, visitors will reach the gateway to the park's most remarkable zone: a rare temperate rain forest. This type of rain forest exists only here on the northwest coast and in a few other isolated areas of the world.

The jagged Olympic Mountains gash the passing Pacific storm fronts, causing the forests and highlands to soak up as much as 200 inches of rain and snow each year, as much as 11 inches in one day. Olympic National Park contains the largest, wildest ancient forest in the lower 48, with vast old Douglas fir, Western hemlock, Sitka spruce, and Western red cedar whose shallow roots spread over the mountains that feed them. The heavily forested park is divided into five biological zones: lush, mossy temperate rain forest in the coastal valleys; richly diverse lowland forests found at elevations up to 3,000 feet; the snowier but still biologically dense montane forest, from 3,000 to 4,500 feet; the austere subalpine forest from about 4,500 to 6,500 feet; and alpine meadows on the highest slopes.

A range of sharp, snow-frosted peaks rules the interior of the peninsula. In the regal shadow of 7,965-foot Mt. Olympus are alpine meadows bursting with frantic life during the all-too-brief summer, glacial lakes of sapphire blue, lonely hiking trails to fill the soul with wonder, and living glaciers that can advance or retreat a few feet each year.

Olympic is one of the least-sullied of our national parks, partly because it is one of the least accessible. Although 15 roads enter the park from different directions, none traverse it, and none penetrate more than a few miles. In most of the park's interior, horses and hiking boots are the only means of transportation.

The secrets of the Olympic Peninsula have always been guarded well. Two of the first seaborne expeditions to alight here—Bodega y Quadra's in 1775 and Captain Charles Barclay's in 1787—suffered massacres at the hands of the local Native Americans. It wasn't until 1889 that the first organized exploration of what is now Olympic National Park took place. The expedition, sponsored by the *Seattle Press,* took almost six months to hack its way from Port Angeles to Lake Quinault, about 50 miles south.

These virgin forests were preserved for posterity by federal mandate in 1897 and further protected by Theodore Roosevelt, who proclaimed the area a national monument in 1909. Official national park status was conferred in 1938.

ESSENTIAL INFORMATION

VISITOR INFORMATION For more information about the park, write to **Olympic National Park,** 600 E. Park Ave., Port Angeles, WA 98362; or call 206/452–0330.

Olympic's wilderness is a fragile web of life, and park regulations are designed to keep it as healthy and unsullied as possible. A copy of "Olympic National Park: Backcountry Use Guidelines," available from any of the park's five visitor centers or through the address above, is an invaluable guide for those planning overnight stays in the park.

Free backcountry permits, available from self-registration stations at most of the major trailheads, are required for all overnight stays

in the park's wilderness areas. The permits are also available at all of the visitor centers and 24 ranger stations.

FEES Visitors to Hurricane Ridge, Hoh, Staircase, Elwha, and Sol Duc are charged $4 per vehicle during peak season, mid-May to September 30; at other entrances there is currently no fee.

PUBLICATIONS The park service publishes a variety of free fliers on specific aspects of the park, including "Suggested Day Hikes," "Facilities and Services," and "Climate and Seasons." These are available at the visitor centers, or by writing the park (*see* Visitor Information, *above*).

A handy mail-order catalogue of books and maps of the park is available from the **Northwest Interpretive Association** (3002 Mt. Angeles Rd., Port Angeles, WA 98362, tel. 206/452–4501, ext. 239), as are the following books:

Robert L. Wood's *Olympic Mountains Trail Guide* is a bible for both day hikers and those planning longer excursions. Stephen Whitney's *Field Guide to the Cascades and Olympics* is an excellent trailside reference covering more than 500 plant and animal species found in the park. Rowland W. Tabor's *Geology of Olympic National Park* provides a detailed history of the forces that shape the Olympic Peninsula and guides geophiles to geologic points of interest within the park. Robert Steelquist's *Olympic National Park and the Olympic Peninsula* offers travelers a lavishly illustrated overview of the park, complete with detailed maps.

GEOLOGY AND TERRAIN The rocky 57-mile coastal strip of Olympic National Park has claimed hundreds of ships over the years, and their weedy bones protruding from the surf at low tide lend poignancy to the gorgeous vistas of wave-tortured stone. Hikers who explore the long, driftwood-choked gray-sand beaches linked by slick, steep forest trails find teeming tide pools, vast galleries of rock sculptures, and brooding, forested headlands. The incoming tides are strong and fast, and the surf often carries logs that can weigh several tons and have killed some unwary waders and swimmers over the years.

The coastal portion of the park is separated from its mountainous interior by a broad band of privately owned land, most of which was logged off early this century. Passing through this belt of savage clear-cuts—a zone of stumps and erosion-gashed hillsides—the visitor enters the dense, protected virgin forests along the Olympic Mountains' western slopes in the lush valleys of the Hoh, Queets, Quinault, and Bogachiel rivers. These valleys were scoured out of the sandstone mountains by glaciers and water, a process that continues to this day.

Towering above, the Olympic Mountains are an austere rampart of glacier-carved stone a mile and a half high, with waterfalls, meadows, and clear glacial lakes. These are young mountains. Less than 30 million years ago the Olympic peninsula was under water. Then the tremendous tectonic forces of the Pacific's "Ring of Fire" crumpled the floor of the sea and thrust it skyward. As the mountains rose, they intercepted moisture from the Pacific. Streams and glaciers formed, and the intricate carving of the Olympics began. Today the park contains some 60 glaciers, vast sheets of ice in constant restless motion. The Blue, White, and Hoh glaciers of Mount Olympus are the most impressive.

FLORA AND FAUNA A mild climate, torrential rainfall, warm sunlight, and a wealth of plant and animal species have combined to produce the complex ecological system of Olympic's temperate rain forest. Gigantic, elephant-bark Douglas fir, shaggy cedar, and lordly Sitka spruce thrust hundreds of feet heavenward. One Douglas fir, on the South Fork of the Hoh River, stands 298 feet high; another, near the Queets River, is 44 feet in circumference. A thick carpet of moss cushions the forest floor, and dense fern glades provide cover for a myriad of small animals. Epiphytes, or "air plants," pluck moisture from the musky air.

As the elevation increases, the junglelike lowland and montane forests give way to a sparser subalpine zone of stunted, widely spaced clumps of subalpine fir, Western hemlock, and yellow cedar. Above the timberline, where the snow can last into August, magnificent alpine meadows bloom with wildflowers during the brief summers (mid-July to mid-September). There is a profusion of lupines, wallflowers, orchids, paintbrushes, phlox, and monkeyflowers, as well as some species that are found only in the Olympics, such as the delicate, six-petaled Pipers bellflower.

Herds of Roosevelt elk, some weighing 1,000 pounds, wander the park, their bellows of challenge echoing through the forest during the September mating season. Black bears, coyotes, and cougars haunt the highlands (Olympic is believed to contain the largest cougar population of any national park). Black-tailed deer are also plentiful—and unafraid of human visitors.

Among the park's most unique and charming inhabitants is the chubby and gregarious Olympic marmot. These cat-size rodents, related to the eastern woodchuck, inhabit the high meadows and talus slopes of the park. This species of marmot is found nowhere else in the world. Their shrill whistles of alarm greet hikers throughout the high country; their friendly antics are an inexhaustible source of entertainment. Squirrels, chipmunks, weasels, river otters, and hundreds of other mammals also inhabit the park.

A colony of sea otters, re-introduced after the original population was hunted to extinction, can be seen floating in the offshore kelp beds by coastal hikers. Seals are plentiful, and in late March and early April pods of Pacific gray whales pass on their way south. In early fall they return, heading north toward Alaska.

Aloft, avian life thrives from the coastal estuaries to the high mountain crags. Bald eagles and red-tailed hawks ride the winds in search of prey. Great blue herons, with their 6-foot wingspans, stalk the estuaries. Glossy, long-billed black oystercatchers patrol the shoreline, while brilliant hummingbirds dip nectar from the flowers. The water ouzel, found in forest streams from the high slopes to the sea, dives and walks along the river bottom to find its meals. The raven-size pileated woodpecker, with its red head and haunting call, is another star performer.

There are those who believe Olympic National Park's vast wilderness houses another rare and timid species: Bigfoot, or Sasquatch, whose tracks local residents occasionally claim to find. When asked about the legendary creature, park rangers usually wink and smile.

WHEN TO GO Because of the park's vastly varied terrain, it's difficult to generalize about weather at Olympic. Even at the height of summer (late July to early September) the temperature rarely exceeds 80°F anywhere on the peninsula, and it is usually 45°F to 75°F. Autumn is usually cool and wet, with temperatures in the 35°F to 60°F range. In winter, the park's windward mountains receive as much as 100 feet of snow, though the lowlands seldom receive more than a few inches at a time. Springs are wet, mild, and windy throughout the park. Three-quarters of Olympic's considerable precipitation falls between October 1 and March 31.

The coastal lowlands and forested areas of the park are accessible year-round, and they are always teeming with plant and animal life. The highlands tend to be snowed in well into summer; the best time to observe the flora and wildlife is during August and September. Like most national parks, Olympic is most crowded in July, August, and September, when the weather is drier and plant and animal life are at their peak.

Starting in July, park rangers offer free nature walks, lectures, and in the evenings, campfire programs on various aspects of park ecology. Overall, the weeks from mid-September to early October offer the best balance between plant and animal activity, good weather, and diminished crowds.

The dense snowpack in the mountains begins to accumulate in October, and from December to late March the area around Hurricane Ridge offers good Nordic skiing.

SEASONAL EVENTS **July to early September:** Park rangers offer nature walks, lectures, and fireside programs. See the bulletin boards at the visitor centers and campgrounds for dates, times, and subjects. **Late March to early November:** The **Olympic Park Institute** (HC 62, Box 9T, Port Angeles, WA 98362, tel. 206/928–3720 or 800/775–3720) runs one- to five-day seminars on various aspects of park ecology, history, native culture, and such arts as writing, painting, and photography. Whale- and bird-watching in the spring and guided backpacking, kayaking, and day trips in the summer and fall give visitors an opportunity for more in-depth study of given aspects of the park. Classes are led by wildlife experts, local artists, and park rangers and cost $12 to $242 per person. **Late March to mid-April:** Coastal hikers can watch the stately passage of Pacific gray whales on their 12,000-mile annual migration from the Bering Sea to the Sea of Cortez. In October they pass in the opposite direction.

WHAT TO PACK Visitors to the peninsula, particularly campers and hikers, should be sure to bring adequate rain gear. Hikers should always carry a first-aid kit, flashlight, pocketknife, map and compass, matches and fire-starter, food and water (allow for two extra days), extra clothing, sun protection, and a tent. Those planning extended stays in the backcountry will need to bring some means of purifying drinking water: vessels for boiling or lightweight, hand-pumped filters, available from outdoor supply stores. Even the clear and plentiful mountain streams of the Olympics may contain organisms that cause giardiasis, a particularly distressing intestinal disease. Although many old-timers scoff that they've drunk untreated water for years without ill effects, it's better to be safe than sorry.

GENERAL STORES The main shopping area for the park is **Port Angeles,** the Olympic Peninsula's largest community, located at the northern (Hurricane Ridge) entrance to the park. Visitors can choose from a variety of modern supermarkets and convenience and specialty stores.

Elsewhere, stores are fewer and farther between. Continuing counterclockwise around the park, there is a small general store at **Fairholm** (tel. 206/928–3020), a tiny community on Highway 101 at the west end of Lake Crescent. Food, gas, camping supplies, fishing tackle, and boat rentals are available there. The store is open daily from May 1 to September 30, 9 to 6; in June, July, and August it stays open from 8 to 7.

Gas, food, and other supplies are available from several stores in the town of **Sappho** and its larger neighbor, **Forks.**

A small store at **Sol Duc Hot Springs Resort** (tel. 206/327–3583), in the northwestern corner of the park, stocks food, fishing tackle, and camping supplies; it's open 8 AM to 9 PM, mid-May through late September.

Another general store is located at **Kalaloch Lodge** (pronounced *Clay-lock*) (tel. 206/962–2271), on Highway 101, at the southern end of the park's coastal strip. It sells gas, food, fishing tackle, and camping supplies, and is open daily 8 AM to 9 PM year-round.

ARRIVING AND DEPARTING The best way to reach Olympic National Park is by car. Though no roads traverse the park, and much of the coastline is roadless, Highway 101 circles the park, and spur roads offer access to it at various points. Visitor information is available at the Olympic Park Visitor Center, in Port Angeles, and the Hoh Rain Forest Visitor Center, in the western section of the park, as well as at the Storm King Information Station, on Lake Crescent, and the Kalaloch Information Station, on the southern coast. The long stretch of highway from Kalaloch to Port Angeles, along the west and northwest edges of the park, has the best views of ocean, forest, and mountains.

By Plane. Visitors can fly into either Seattle-Tacoma International Airport, located 10 miles south of downtown Seattle and a three-hour drive from the park, or Fairchild International Airport, at Port Angeles, the park's northern gateway. Both airports are served by **Horizon Air** (tel. 800/547–9308). Dozens of car-rental firms service Seattle's airport, the

regions's busiest; call Sea-Tac information (tel. 206/433–5217) for specific agencies. At Fairchild, try **Budget Rent-A-Car** (tel. 206/457–4246).

By Car and RV. The eastern boundary of the park is less than 50 miles from downtown Seattle as the crow flies; unfortunately, Puget Sound lies in between, and the drive from Seattle to Kalaloch takes four to five hours. From Seattle or parts north, drivers can either cross the spectacular Tacoma Narrows Bridge or take a cheap, quick ferry ride, a relaxing way to see the island-dotted expanse of Puget Sound and get rewarding glimpses of the Olympics. Seattle–Winslow, Seattle–Bremerton, and Edmonds–Kingston are the most popular ferry routes to the peninsula. Call 206/464–6400 for scheduling information. The cost is $6.65 one-way for a car and driver, plus $3.30 for each passenger. Foot passengers pay $3.30 westbound only. The Winslow and Bremerton ferries depart downtown Seattle from Pier 52. The Edmonds–Kingston ferry departs from Edmonds, 15 miles north of Seattle: From I–5, take the Edmonds exit and follow the signs to the ferry terminal. Once you are in Bremerton, drive north on Route 3, turn left onto Route 104, and then turn right onto Highway 101, which leads directly to Olympic's main entrance, in Port Angeles. From Winslow, you'll take 305 north to Route 3 and follow the directions above, and from Kingston you'll drive west on 104, also following the directions above. The drive from each of these three towns is between 70 and 75 miles and takes roughly 1¹/₂ hours. Those arriving from the south via I–5 should turn westward on Highway 101 at Olympia.

By Train. There is no passenger train service on the Olympic Peninsula. Seattle, Tacoma, and Olympia are served by **Amtrak** (tel. 800/872–7245). Rental cars are available in all three cities.

By Bus. Port Angeles, the park's northern gateway, is served by **Greyhound Lines** (tel. 206/452–8311 or 800/231–2222). One bus connects daily with Seattle and costs $16 one-way. **Clallam Transit** (tel. 206/452–4511 or 800/858–3747) runs winter weekend trips from downtown Port Angeles to spectacular Hurricane Ridge (about $8 round-trip) high in the Olympics and offers commuter bus service to Sequim, Lake Crescent, Forks, and La Push (50¢–75¢ one-way).

EXPLORING

It is possible to acquire an overview of Olympic's wonders by driving up the coast from Kalaloch, visiting the Hoh Rain Forest, then continuing on to Hurricane Ridge, but only those willing to hike a few miles off the main roads will discover the park's hidden grandeur. Visitors should plan to spend at least a day—but preferably several days—in each of the park's three wilderness environments: coastal, forest, and mountain. Try camping in several of the 17 campgrounds, or break up your visit with a stay at Kalaloch Lodge or one of the bed-and-breakfasts in Port Townsend.

THE BEST IN ONE DAY Those who have just one day to see Olympic National Park and want to cover all three zones must have a car. It's best to start in the mountains and work your way toward the sea. Begin your tour at Hurricane Ridge, 17 miles south of Port Angeles. There are soul-stirring mountain views from this point, 5,200 feet up in the Olympics, and in summer, the green alpine meadows are grazed by shy black-tailed deer. A warm, modern lodgelike visitor center with food service and observation platforms serves as a base for visitors. Hikes, short and long, radiate from the ridge in all directions. To get a good introduction to the mountains take the 1½-mile-long paved Hurricane Hill Lookout Trail, which leaves the parking lot and climbs through meadows and stands of fir to the site of a former fire lookout.

Returning to Highway 101, drive west to limpid, mountain-girded Lake Crescent, and take the trail to Marymere Falls. This short, 1-mile trail ascends through dense forest to the base of the falls, a 90-foot cascade falling into a moss-hung grotto.

Continue along Highway 101, stopping for lunch in the town of Forks. Staying on the same road—the only road—travel south and follow the signs toward the Hoh Rain Forest, 14 miles from the Highway 101 turnoff up the Hoh River. A somewhat rudimentary visitor center will acquaint you with the basic ecology of the ancient forests that blanket this portion of the park. Behind the building is the beginning of the Hall of Mosses nature trail, an easy ¾-mile loop over chuckling creeks and through stately, somber forests that have never known an ax. Signs explain many facets of the rich and complex forest biosphere.

You'll have to backtrack to Highway 101 and continue west to end the day's tour at Ruby Beach, where the road enters the park's coastal zone. The restless Pacific has slashed away at the rocky coast, creating a series of much-photographed natural pillars, monoliths, and sea stacks. The beach is accessible by a short, steep trail from the parking area; look for shells and green-glass fishermen's floats from Japan along the shore. Watching a melancholy sunset through the rocks is a fitting end to any tour.

ORIENTATION PROGRAMS The best place to get a quick overview of the park is the **Olympic Park Visitor Center** (3002 Mt. Angeles Rd., Port Angeles, tel. 206/452–0330), which is open year-round, daily 9 to 4 (8:30 to 6 in July and August). A wealth of written materials is available at the center, and there are displays on park geology, history, and wildlife. Well worth your while is a 13-minute slide show, shown on request, which provides an excellent survey of the history and main features of the park.

The park's other information centers are located at Hoh Rain Forest, Hurricane Ridge, Kalaloch, and the ranger stations at Dosewallips, Elwha, Mora, Ozette, Queets, Lake Quinault, Sol Duc, and Staircase. These tend to be more limited in scope, providing information more specific to the area in which they are located. All are open daily 9 to 5 year-round, except Dosewallips and Kalaloch, which are closed from October to May, and Sol Duc and Hurricane Ridge, which close if it snows.

From July 1 through Labor Day, park naturalists lead nature walks that last from one to several hours through Olympic's kaleido-scopic array of forests, meadows, and tidal areas. These highly informative walks give visitors a hands-on experience and are an excellent way to get to know different aspects of park ecology. Weekly schedules are posted on the bulletin boards at visitor centers and campgrounds. During the summer, a newslet-ter lists naturalist activities.

GUIDED TOURS An area native with a genu-ine love for the park heads up **Olympic Van Tours** (Box 273, Port Angeles, WA 98362, tel. 206/452–3858) and personally leads trips in air-conditioned 10-passenger vans to Hurri-cane Ridge. The three-hour tour departs from downtown Port Angeles two times a day from mid-June to Labor Day and costs $12 per person, and an all-day trip is also available. Tours to the Hoh Rain Forest, Lake Crescent, Marymere Falls, and other destinations can be arranged upon request. Full-day trips cost $25 to $30 per person.

Those whose backcountry skills are a little rusty can choose from four operators that lead guided backpacking trips through Olympic National Park: **America's Adventure Inc.** (2245 Stonecrop Way, Golden, CO 80401, tel. 303/526–0806), **Mountain Madness Inc.** (4218 S.W. Alaska, Suite 206, Seattle, WA 98116, tel. 206/937–8389, fax 206/937–1772), **Trailmark Outdoor Adventures Inc.** (16 Schuyler Rd., Nyack, NY 10960, tel. 914/358–0262), and **Wilderness Ventures Inc.** (Box 2768, Jackson Hole, WY 83001, tel. 307/733–2122).

Olympic's rugged wilderness also lends itself well to travel with llamas, who carry the equipment while you walk. Two firms offer llama pack trips: **Kit's Llamas** (Box 116, Olalla, WA 98359, tel. 206/857–5274) and **Watts-A-Llama Leisure Treks** (735 Peters St., Raymond, WA 98577, tel. 206/942–5239).

SCENIC DRIVES AND VIEWS **Highway 101** cir-cles the park, and those who take the time to explore its length will find much to enthrall them. The 91-mile drive from Kalaloch to Port Angeles offers an ever-changing series of shoreline, forest, lake, and mountain views. Clear-cuts mar the road from the Hoh River to

Sappho; take a good long moment to contem-plate the destruction. Stop and stretch your legs at La Poel Picnic Area, on the south shore of the deep blue-green Lake Crescent. The snow-capped ramparts of the Olympics are beyond.

To get a look at the forest in restoration—that is, a heavy second-growth forest—as well as an old-growth forest, backtrack 2 miles and turn left down **Sol Duc River Road.** This paved spur road runs for about 10 miles and ends at the trailhead to lovely Sol Duc Falls, about a mile's hike one-way.

The 17 serpentine miles of **Hurricane Ridge Road** run from Port Angeles into the moun-tains, providing unequaled glimpses of the peninsula's glacier-sculpted interior. At the 9-mile point, the wayside at Lookout Rock overlooks the Strait of Juan de Fuca, Dunge-ness Spit, and Vancouver Island. Following a paved path at Lookout Rock, visitors are re-warded with views of the crags of the Olym-pics.

NATURE TRAILS AND SHORT WALKS Olympic National Park abounds in short exploratory walks showcasing various aspects of park ecology. Probably the best known of these is the **Hall of Mosses Trail,** which begins at the Hoh Rain Forest Visitor Center. This gentle 3/4-mile loop takes hikers through the forest and into a fanciful grove of maple and alder dripping with green-gold moss.

At **Second Beach,** 14 miles west of Highway 101 on the La Push Road, a 1/2-mile trail leads to a broad, tide pool–filled beach with excel-lent views of the offshore sea stacks.

The **Quinault Rain Forest Nature Trail,** also known as the Big Tree Grove Nature Trail, leads through one of the finest groves of old-growth Douglas fir left in the world. These magnificent, near-primeval evergreens are re-markable for their uniform age and size—500 years old and 250 to 275 feet tall. The 1/2-mile (one-way) trail meanders through the somber forest, and benches are placed along the way for quiet contemplation. The trailhead is lo-cated at the parking area west of Willaby

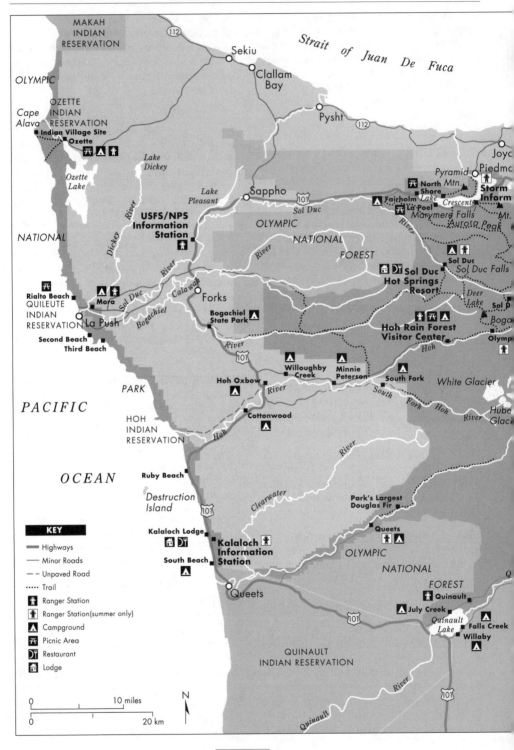

MAKAH
INDIAN
RESERVATION

112

Sekiu

Clallam
Bay

Strait of Juan De Fuca

OLYMPIC

Pysht

112

Joyc

OZETTE
INDIAN
RESERVATION

Cape
Alava

Indian Village Site
Ozette

Ozette
Lake

Lake
Dickey

Lake
Pleasant

Sappho

101

Sol Duc

River

Piedmo

Pyramid
Mtn.
North
Shore

Storm
Inform

Fairholm

La Poel

Crescent Lake

Mt.

Marymere Falls
Aurora Peak

NATIONAL

Dickey

River

USFS/NPS
Information
Station

OLYMPIC

NATIONAL

FOREST

River

Sol Duc

Sol Duc Falls

Deer
Lake

Sol p

Sol Duc
Hot Springs
Resort

Rialto Beach
QUILEUTE
INDIAN
RESERVATION

Mora

La Push

Sol Duc

Bogachiel

River

Calawah

Forks

Bogachiel
State Park

Hoh Rain Forest
Visitor Center

Boga

Olymp

Second Beach
Third Beach

River

101

Hoh

Willoughby
Creek

Minnie
Peterson

South Fork

White Glacier

PARK

Hoh Oxbow

River

South

Fork

Hoh

River

Hube
Glac

PACIFIC

HOH
INDIAN
RESERVATION

Cottonwood

Hoh

OCEAN

Ruby Beach

Destruction
Island

101

Clearwater

River

Park's Largest
Douglas Fir

Kalaloch Lodge

South Beach

Kalaloch
Information
Station

Queets

OLYMPIC

NATIONAL

KEY

Highways
Minor Roads
Unpaved Road
Trail
Ranger Station
Ranger Station(summer only)
Campground
Picnic Area
Restaurant
Lodge

Queets

FOREST

Q

Quinault

July Creek

Quinault
Lake

Falls Creek

Willaby

0   10 miles

0   20 km

N

QUINAULT
INDIAN
RESERVATION

River

101

Quinault

262

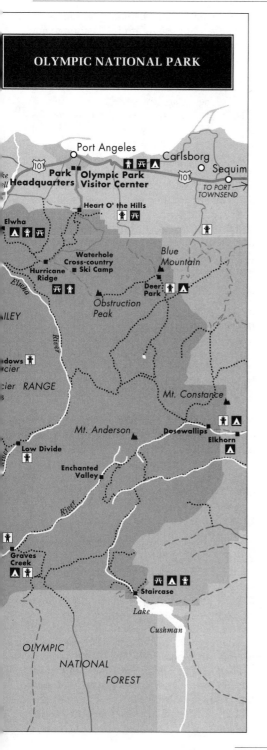

OLYMPIC NATIONAL PARK

Creek, 1 1/2 miles northeast of Highway 101 on Lake Quinault's South Shore Road.

LONGER HIKES Olympic's 600 miles of trails require 23,000 man-hours of maintenance work annually, and many of the park's most precious treasures are accessible only on foot.

Wilderness beaches provide the park's most unusual hiking experience: an opportunity to explore a green Pacific coastline essentially unaltered by humans. Raccoons waddle from the forest to pluck dinner from the tide pools; bald eagles stoop over fantastic tangles of bleached drift-logs, the bones of ancient forests. The three-day hike from **Rialto Beach to Cape Alava** is especially rewarding. Hikers—equipped with backcountry permit, current tide table, a durable tent, and rain gear—generally camp on the beach. To reach Rialto Beach take Highway 101 to the point just north of Forks where signs point the way west to the shore. Park at the picnic area.

One note of caution: Beach hikers should beware of the peninsula's strong incoming tides and beach logs, some of which weigh several tons. Logs roll unpredictably in the surf and have killed unwary waders and swimmers over the years. You should also use extreme caution when hiking around the park's many protruding headlands—incoming tides may trap you, rendering it impossible to advance or retreat. When hiking the coastal strip, always carry a current tide table, available at all visitor centers and many stores; many headlands can only be crossed at low tide.

For a long hike combining the best of Olympic's forest and mountain areas, take Sol Duc River Road to the end and park at the trailhead. The 8 1/2-mile **Sol Duc Trail** first passes lovely Sol Duc Falls, then follows the river through colonnades of huge Douglas fir, hemlock, and cedar. The trail climbs steeply after the falls, toiling toward its junction with the spectacular **High Divide Trail** at Sol Duc Park, a perfect base camp for an exploration of the alpine meadows and peaks nearby. Turning west along the High Divide Trail, you'll enjoy incredible mountain vistas in every direction, particularly of Mt. Olympus and the Bailey Range. The trail tightropes along the spine of the mountains for a little over 2 miles; at Bogachiel Peak, turn north on the **Bogachiel Trail** toward Deer Lake, reentering the forest. After about 4 miles you'll reach the lake and the juncture of the **Canyon Creek Trail,** which leads you back to Sol Duc Falls. The loop totals about 17¹/₂ miles and runs through steep and mountainous terrain; plan on taking your time and spending two or, better, three nights along the trail.

For all their splendor, the trails in the Sol Duc region are probably the most-trampled trails in the park. Rangers, fearing the long-term environmental effects of heavy wear on the trails, have instituted a quota system during the summer months: Between July 1 and September 30, check in at the Sol Duc Ranger Station before setting off on these trails. If the area is too crowded, the rangers will suggest alternative trails in quieter, but no less spectacular, regions of the park. To avoid being turned away, skip Sol Duc and head to the Dosewallips or Staircase ranger stations for information on crossing the park along the Dosewallips River in the southeastern corner of Olympic.

OTHER ACTIVITIES **Back-Road Driving.** Because no roads penetrate more than a few miles into the park, Olympic offers limited opportunities for back-road driving. No vehicles of any kind are allowed off the park roads.

Biking. Mountain bikes are only allowed on two trails at Olympic: Spruce Railroad Trail (north shore of Lake Crescent) and Olympic Hotsprings Trail (in Elwha Valley). Bikes are not allowed off the trails. Roads in and around the park offer limited opportunities for cyclists; many are narrow, winding, steep, and, particularly in the summer, crowded with automobile traffic. There are no bike rental facilities inside the park. **Coast to Coast** (218 Sims Way, tel. 206/385–5900) and **P.T. Cyclery** (215 Taylor, tel. 206/385–6470), both in Port Townsend, rent bikes by the day and the hour.

Bird-Watching. With its proximity to both shoreline and mountains, Olympic is one of the truly outstanding national parks for bird-watchers. Bald eagles are found throughout the coastal reaches of the park; look for them soaring on the offshore breeze or nesting in the branches of Sitka spruce. Graceful great blue herons stalk the coastal estuaries on stiltlike legs, watching keenly for fishy morsels. In the forests, look for the large rectangular holes carved by red-headed pileated woodpeckers in standing dead trees called snags. Wild ducks, particularly mergansers and harlequins, bob along on calm stretches of forest streams; the charming water ouzel floats and dives, then walks along the stream bed searching for its meals. Higher up, in the alpine meadows, the gray-crowned rosy finch flits about in search of insects. Hurricane Ridge is the best place to observe blue grouse, whose booming calls attract females during the mating season. In early April, thousands of hawks congregate at the tip of Cape Flattery (at the northwestern end of the peninsula) on their way to their breeding grounds to the north.

Boating. Lake Crescent, one of the largest of Olympic's lakes, is the prime spot for boaters. Paddleboats, rowboats, and canoes are available for rent at the **Log Cabin Resort** (tel. 206/928–3245) at the lake's northeast end. The resort is open from mid-May through early October. The **Fairholm General Store** (tel. 206/928–3020) at the western end of the lake, rents boats May 1 to September 30; it's open 8 to 7 from Memorial Day to Labor Day and 9 to 6 the rest of the season. A U.S. Coast Guard courtesy inspection is required for any boat on the lake.

Fishing. The many streams and lakes at Olympic contain rainbow, brook, and sea-run cutthroat trout. A unique and beautiful race of trout, the crescenti, is found only in Lake Crescent. No license is required to fish for these species. Most prized of all are the huge and belligerent steelhead that spawn in the coastal streams each fall. Anglers need a State of Washington punch card, available from any general store or sporting goods outlet in the vicinity, to fish for them, or for the coho and chinook salmon that throng the ocean and the sound.

Horseback Riding. Horses are available for rental at **Quarter Moon Ranch** (tel. 206/683–5863), which can be reached by following the signs on Highway 101 near Sequim to Carlsborg; the ranch is located a half mile west of the Carlsborg Store on Spath Road.

Rock Climbing. Although the tallest of the park's peaks, Mt. Olympus, is only 7,965 feet high, many of the Olympic Mountains offer climbing challenges that far exceed their diminutive stature. Each year avid climbers converge here to try their skills on these jagged walls of rock. Mt. Olympus, with its crevassed glaciers and vertical rock walls, offers excellent snow and ice climbing. Mt. Storm King (4,534 feet), Mt. Ellinor (5,944 feet), and The Brothers (6,866 feet) are popular but less demanding. Mt. Constance (7,743 feet) and Mt. Anderson (7,365 feet) offer more exciting challenges to top-notch climbers. Climbing parties must register at the ranger station nearest their route. One tour operator—**Mountain Madness** (*see* Guided Tours, *above*)—offers climbing instruction, equipment rentals, and guided climbing excursions.

Snowshoeing and Ski Touring. Ski and snowshoe rentals and instruction are available at the Hurricane Ridge Visitor Center as long as the snow lasts, but the best conditions are from mid-December through late March. The most popular route for day-mushers is the 1¹/₂-mile Hurricane Hill Road, just west of the parking area. A marked snow-play area with trails and gentle hills has been set aside near the center for cross-country skiers, snowshoers, inner tubers, and children.

Swimming. The Pacific is a dangerous playground this far north: Even in summer, ocean temperatures seldom exceed 50°F, and ocean currents are vicious. The park's best swimming areas are at Lake Crescent, whose cool and inviting green water is distilled from the glaciated peaks that surround it. At Fairholm Campground, on the lake's west end, there is a small sandy beach with a roped-off swimming area. At the opposite end of the lake, East Beach Picnic Area sports a larger beach and, often, warmer air and water temperatures.

CHILDREN'S PROGRAMS Olympic offers few programs geared to children. In the summer, the park's regular naturalist programs begin. Children may find them interesting, but they're geared to all ages. Consult the bulletin boards at the visitor centers and campgrounds for information on location, subject matter, and scheduling.

EVENING ACTIVITIES On summer nights after the sun goes down, park naturalists give fireside lectures, illustrated with slides and movies, at the park's main campgrounds: Fairholm (Thursday to Saturday), Heart O' the Hills, Hoh, Mora, Sol Duc, and Kalaloch. Consult park bulletin boards for scheduling and subject information.

DINING

Surrounded by the fruitful waters of the Pacific and protected, island-flecked Puget Sound, the Olympic peninsula is a place for seafood. Tiny, delicate Quilcene oysters, rich chinook salmon, and, best of all, sweet, heavy-clawed Dungeness crab dominate menus. A bowl of creamy clam chowder is the perfect antidote to the chill of a hike through the cool, damp woods. One local specialty, the geoduck (pronounced *goo-ey duck*) clam, looks like something from a science-fiction movie when first plucked from the brine, its lank, leathery neck dangling a foot or more from the shell. But don't be scared off: The geoduck's flesh, pounded tender and quick-fried, is a famous local delicacy that every visitor should try.

Within the park, dining options are extremely limited. You'll have better luck in the peninsula's more sophisticated communities, particularly Port Angeles, Port Townsend, and Sequim (pronounced *squim*). A 7½% Washington sales tax is added to the bill.

INSIDE THE PARK **Kalaloch Lodge.** The dining room of this popular seaside resort, located just within the southern boundary of the park's coastal strip, is a reliable source of fresh seafood and well-aged beef. The menu changes seasonally, but it's hard to go wrong with the local oysters, crab, and salmon, often served baked or broiled with a simple lemon-butter sauce. Although the preparations are generally ordinary, the blufftop ocean view, through picture windows, is anything but. Try the seafood salad, a generous bowl of fresh greens mounded with smoked salmon, bay shrimp, and crabmeat. Avoid the chowder. *Hwy. 101, Kalaloch, tel. 206/962–2271. Reservations advised. Dress: casual. AE, MC, V. Moderate.*

NEAR THE PARK **C'est Si Bon.** You'd have to cross the sound to Seattle to find more elegant food than that offered at this classic French restaurant. The decor is French Provençal, with white linen and original art. The window tables overlook a modest rose garden and, beyond, the Olympic Mountains. Sumptuous oysters in beurre blanc and *fruits de mer au gratin* top the list of appetizers. Salmon in parchment, beef tournedos royale crowned with fresh crab and an intensely reduced shallot sauce, and any of the fresh nightly specials are the stars of the limited dinner menu. The wine list is ample, but a little overpriced. *2300 Hwy. 101E (4 mi east of Port Angeles), tel. 206/452–8888. Reservations advised. Dress: casual. AE, DC, MC, V. Closed Mon. No lunch. Expensive.*

Fountain Café. Port Townsend, home of the late science-fiction guru Frank Herbert, is a laid-back arts colony with the finest collection of Victorian homes and buildings north of San Francisco. With its intimate dining room filled with the work of local artists and its sophisticated, European-flavored treatments of exquisite local seafood, the Fountain is the quintessential Port Townsend restaurant. Try the impeccably fresh tiny oysters, available baked, sautéed, or any other way you want them. The pasta selections, which change frequently to reflect seasonal catches, are equally esteemed. *920 Washington St., Port Townsend, tel. 206/385–1364. Reservations required. Dress: casual. MC, V. Moderate–Expensive.*

Casoni's. Mama Casoni, the kindly matriarch of this local favorite, packs them in nightly with her traditional Italian specialties: veal marsala, spaghetti with local butter clams,

and quick-fried calamari served with a squeeze of lemon. Desserts are extravagantly rich. *104 Hooker Rd. (1¹/₂ mi west of Sequim on Hwy. 101), tel. 206/683–2415. Reservations advised. Dress: casual. AE, DC, MC, V. Closed Mon.–Tues. Labor Day–Memorial Day. No lunch. Moderate.*

The Greenery. Fresh, healthy salads, thick deli sandwiches, and a flair for homemade pasta have long made this a favorite with locals. Preparations are simple and unpretentious; try the cheesy open-face Dungeness crab sandwich at lunch and the fettuccine with smoked salmon, fresh tomato, mushrooms, garlic, and cream. The staff is friendly and attentive. *117-B E. 1st St., Port Angeles, tel. 206/457–4112. Reservations accepted. Dress: casual. AE, MC, V. Closed Sun. Dec.–Mar. Moderate.*

The Three Crabs. This former crab shack, where fishermen brought their catches to be cooked in the 1950s, is a crowd pleaser, consistently ranked as one of the region's favorite restaurants. Its secret: fresh local seafood, reasonably priced, simply prepared, and served in huge portions. Try the lightly breaded geoduck clam steaks, or, if you've worked up a real Olympic wilderness appetite, the massive seafood plate, heaped with fried shrimp, scallops, salmon, halibut, and crabmeat. Best of all is the whole steamed Dungeness crab, available in season (from October to April). The ambience is vaguely nautical, with knotty-pine walls and views of New Dungeness Bay. *11 Three Crabs Rd. (5 mi north of Sequim, on the bay), tel. 206/683–4264. Reservations advised. Dress: casual. MC, V. Closed Thanksgiving and Dec. 24–25. Moderate.*

Timber House. Quilcene is famous for its oysters, and this friendly, rustic restaurant is the place to get them—plump, sweet, and delicate. Try them raw on the half-shell, with a squeeze of lemon and a dollop of horseradishy cocktail sauce, or baked in the shell with drawn butter. Local Dungeness crabmeat, sautéed with butter, garlic, and wine, is outstanding. *¹/₂-mi south of Quilcene, on Hwy. 101, tel. 206/765–3339. Reservations ac-*

cepted. Dress: casual. MC, V. Closed Tues. Moderate.

Coffee House Restaurant and Gallery. This urban anomaly jump starts its daily horde of loyal customers with espresso drinks, home-made pastries, and sprouty vegetarian fare. It is cheery, eclectic, and cheap. *118 E. 1st St., Port Angeles, tel. 206/452–1459. Reservations accepted. Dress: casual. No credit cards. Inexpensive.*

Hungry Harry's Drive-In. Delicious logger-size burgers, fried chicken platters, crispy fries, and ludicrously low prices make this clean, friendly fast-food place a favorite with locals. It gets busy at lunch, but there's plenty of seating and a drive-through window as well. *Forks Ave. and A St., Forks, tel. 206/374–6612. No reservations. Dress: casual. No credit cards. Inexpensive.*

La Casita. This family-run Mexican restaurant overlooking Port Angeles harbor leans heavily on old standbys and combination plates. What sets it apart is its artful use of local fish. The seafood chimichanga is a crisp-fried burrito filled with Dungeness crab, bay shrimp, fresh cod, Monterey jack cheese, tomato, and chiles. The Dungeness crab enchilada is rich and delicate; the crab-stuffed cod Veracruz, poached in salsa and topped with gooey jack cheese, is a triumph. Don't overlook the *pollo asado* (boneless chicken breasts marinated in tequila and orange juice and charbroiled). *203 E. Front St., Port Angeles, tel. 206/452–2289. Reservations accepted. Dress: casual. AE, D, MC, V. Inexpensive.*

Shanghai Restaurant. This temple of Far Eastern gastronomy serves the best Chinese food on the peninsula. The huge menu features specialties from Szechuan and Hunan, most ranging from spicy to volcanic. The kimchilike Shanghai cabbage is enough to bring tears to your eyes, and the seafood items are masterfully done—tender, fragrant, and delicately sauced. The gingery kung pao shrimp is especially good. *Point Hudson Resort, at eastern tip of Port Townsend, tel. 206/385–4810. Reservations accepted. Dress: casual. D, DC, MC, V. Inexpensive.*

PICNIC SPOTS Olympic abounds with congenial spots for alfresco dining. So long as you pack out everything you brought in, any of the park's beaches, forested areas, and mountain meadows are suitable. But remember, *don't* feed the bears. Among Olympic's many official picnic areas, **Rialto Beach** is the best on the coast, **North Shore** is the most beautiful and least crowded on Lake Crescent, and **Hurricane Ridge** offers the most tables and best views in the mountains.

LODGING

Although there are a few national and regional chain properties on the Olympic Peninsula, most of the lodgings are independently owned. For a rustic, woodsy atmosphere try the historic lodges at Kalaloch, Lake Quinault, and Lake Crescent. If it's pampering you want, an ever-growing population of Northwest-flavor bed-and-breakfasts cater to romantics. And families seeking practicality will find numerous small, clean, budget hotels and cabin resorts.

As in most national parks, the busy season at Olympic runs from mid-June to early September, and the best lodgings are booked months in advance. In the off-season, particularly during the stormy "monsoon" season from December through March, there are some lodging bargains to be had: Expect to pay 20% to 25% less per night during the winter and early spring months. Bear in mind, however, that several of the charming old lodges inside the park—Lake Crescent Lodge, the Log Cabin Resort, and Sol Duc Hot Springs Resort—are closed from October or November through early May.

INSIDE THE PARK **Kalaloch Lodge.** This cedar-sided two-story lodge, built in 1953, sits on a low bluff overlooking the Pacific, just inside the southern boundary of Olympic's coastal strip. The lodge itself has only eight rooms, but 40 small cabins and a modern 10-room minimotel, Sea Crest House, straggle southward along the crest. The cabins are small but well appointed, each with kitchenette, deck, and fireplace or woodstove. One drawback: Most of the wood supplied by the management is wet and refuses to burn. Decor tends toward knotty pine and earth tones, with deep comfortable couches looking seaward out picture windows. At night, fat raccoons waddle from the shore pines to press their noses against the windows. There are no phones or TVs in the rooms, but there is a reading/TV room off the lounge. Cabins 1–16, and Macy and Overly, have the best ocean views. *Hwy. 101, HC 80, Box 1100, Forks, WA 98331, tel. 206/962–2271. 18 rooms, 40 cabins. Facilities: restaurant, coffee shop, lounge, general store, gas station. AE, MC, V. Expensive.*

Lake Crescent Lodge. Nestled deep in the forest at the foot of Mt. Storm King, its broad veranda and picture windows framing a view of its brilliant aquamarine namesake, historic Lake Crescent Lodge has been beguiling visitors to the peninsula since 1916. The former playground of pioneer gentility added a 10-room addition to supplement its 20 existing motel rooms, 17 modern cabins, and 5 lodge rooms, all but the latter with private bath. The grand old, two-story cedar-shingle lodge has an acceptable restaurant and a lively lounge; room decor is clean, functional, and heavy on the hand-rubbed wood. There are no phones or TVs in the rooms. Four of the cabins have fireplaces; all have small, private porches. *Barnes Point, south side of Lake Crescent (follow signs from Hwy. 101), HC 62, Box 11, Port Angeles, WA 98362, tel. 206/928–3211. 35 rooms and 17 cabins (5 rooms share 2 baths). Facilities: restaurant, lounge, boat rentals. AE, DC, MC, V. Closed Oct. 31–Apr. 25. Moderate.*

Sol Duc Hot Springs Resort. This 32-unit cabin resort lies deep in the brooding forest along the Sol Duc River, surrounded by 5,000-foot mountains. The bubbling, steaming sulfur springs fill three large outdoor pools, ranging from 98°F to 104°F. Nearby is a swimming pool, filled with slightly warmed glacial runoff. The resort was built in 1910; a 1988 renovation added fresh paint and bathrooms to each unit. Room decor is still functional, even spartan, but after a day's hiking in the rugged Seven Lakes Basin nearby, a dip in the pool, and dinner at the surprisingly sophisti-

cated restaurant in the lodge, you won't notice. *Sol Duc River Rd. (follow signs from Hwy. 101 between Forks and Port Angeles), Box 2169, Port Angeles, WA 98362, tel. 206/327–3583. 32 rooms, 6 cabins with kitchens. Facilities: restaurant, lounge, snack bar, hot spring, pool, general store/gift shop. AE, D, MC, V. Closed Oct.–mid-May. Moderate.*

NEAR THE PARK **Lake Quinault Lodge.** In a region known for scenic hostelries, few can match the splendid setting of Lake Quinault Lodge, just across the lake from the national park. Mountains loom all around, and a verdant swath of manicured lawn sweeps down to the lake from the crescent-shape veranda. There is an atmosphere of gentle antiquity about the place; the sprawling cedar-shingle lodge, built in 1926, once hosted President Franklin Roosevelt. Now it houses well-to-do couples and families from California, British Columbia, and the Puget Sound area. There are 92 rooms in all: 33 in the main lodge, 16 fireplace units attached to the lodge, and 43 units in the lakeside addition, ¹/₂ block away on the lake. Only about half the rooms have lake views, so be sure to specify. *South Shore Rd. (follow signs from Hwy. 101), Box 7, Quinault, WA 98575, tel. 206/288–2571. 92 rooms. Facilities: restaurant, lounge, game room, pool, sauna, Jacuzzi, canoes and rowboats. AE, MC, V. Expensive.*

Red Lion Bayshore Inn. This Washington-based chain is a regional favorite, charging a little more than most motels in this area but offering additional amenities. With 187 renovated units, this is the largest motor inn on the peninsula. Most of the spacious, modern rooms overlook the Strait of Juan de Fuca or the bay. Earth tones have replaced the gaudy blues, greens, and purples that formerly startled guests. There's a lively bar and a surprisingly good restaurant next door. *221 N. Lincoln, Port Angeles, WA 98362, tel. 206/452–9215 or 800/547–8010. 187 rooms. Facilities: restaurant, lounge, outdoor pool, cable TV. AE, D, DC, MC, V. Moderate–Expensive.*

Best Western Sequim Bay Lodge. This sparkling new addition to the peninsula lodging scene provides comfort in a quiet, wooded setting off Highway 101, just west of South Bay State Park, outside Sequim. The smallish rooms have the Best Western standards, plus some unexpected touches: There are hot tubs and fireplaces in nine of the suites. Good access to the national park, exquisite Dungeness National Wildlife Refuge, and Buckhorn Wilderness make Sequim a popular base for visitor operations. There's a steady but unspectacular restaurant off the lobby. *286522 Hwy. 101, Sequim, WA 98382, tel. 206/683–0691 or 800/528–1234. 54 rooms. Facilities: restaurant, lounge, 9-hole putting course, cable TV, pool. AE, D, DC, MC, V. Moderate.*

Ft. Worden. The 330-acre Ft. Worden was built as a turn-of-the-century gun emplacement to guard the mouth of Puget Sound. Its mighty cannons are long gone, and enterprising souls have now turned its beautiful Victorian officers' row into one of the more memorable lodgings on the Olympic Peninsula. The 23 spacious old houses overlooking the now-silent parade ground have been furnished with genuine and reproduction antiques. There are no phones, no TVs, no restaurant, and no lounge, but each house has a kitchen. Travelers can rent space ranging from a single-bedroom house all the way up to the entire complex through the Ft. Worden State Park Conference Center. The houses have a spare charm, and the old fort is a magical place for children. The abandoned gun emplacements echo eerily; there's an artillery museum, a bronze foundry, a marine science center, a dirigible hangar, and a graceful old lighthouse. The film *An Officer and a Gentleman* was shot here. Make reservations well in advance (a year or more). *Ft. Worden State Park Conference Center (1 mi north of Port Townsend), 200 Battery Way, Port Townsend, WA 98368, tel. 206/385–4730. 2 single-bedroom houses, 4 two-bedroom houses, 17 larger houses, 80 campsites with full hookup. No credit cards. Moderate.*

Manitou Lodge. A fat, shaggy dog named Eagle greets guests at this remote and unusual forest lodge. The towering A-frame common room, complete with 30-foot stone fireplace, is larger than all five guest rooms put together.

Room furnishings are a little austere, but the warmth of the inn's central areas makes up for it. There's a broad porch and comfortable chairs for sunset-watching. The coast is nearby, as are the trouty Sol Duc and Bogachiel rivers. This small, popular inn fills up quickly, so book well ahead for summer and weekends. *Kilmer Rd. (follow La Push Rd. west from Hwy. 101, then follow signs toward Mora and signs for lodge), Box 600, Forks, WA 98331, tel. 206/374–6295. 5 rooms. MC, V. Moderate.*

Aggie's Inn. Aggie's isn't exactly the Ritz. More of a cracker box, really. Its 114 rooms look like they were decorated out of the 1972 Sears catalog; there's hardly a square inch of wall covering or upholstery that's not petroleum-derived. To top it off, the swimming pool is shaped like an internal organ. But Aggie's is clean, friendly, and near the waterfront in downtown Port Angeles. The inn has room service and horse racing via satellite—the nearest thing to a casino in this neck of the woods. *602 E. Front St., Port Angeles, WA 98362, tel. 206/457–0471. 114 rooms. Facilities: restaurant, lounge, indoor pool, sauna. AE, D, DC, MC, V. Inexpensive.*

Bed-and-Breakfasts. With its laid-back charm; proximity to Seattle, Victoria, and the national park; and its wealth of well-preserved Victorian structures, **Port Townsend** is the peninsula's B&B capital, a haven of ornate guest houses and charming small hotels. Rates run from under $50 to $125 per night, but most rooms are in the $60–$85 range. Among the most esteemed: the five-room, 70-acre **Arcadia Country Inn** (1891 S. Jacob Miller Rd., 98368, tel. 206/385–5245), owned by the world-famous juggling troupe the Flying Karamazov Brothers; the 13-room **Bishop Victorian** (714 Washington St., 98368, tel. 206/385–6122 or 800/824–4738); fanciful, towered eight-room **F.W. Hastings House Old Consulate Inn** (313 Walker St., 98368, tel. 206/385–6753); immaculate, six-room **Heritage House** (305 Pierce St., 98368, tel. 206/385–6800); four-room **Holly Hill House** (611 Polk, 98368, tel. 206/385–5619); three-room **Lincoln House** (538 Lincoln St., 98368, tel. 206/385–6677 or, in WA, 800/477–4667), with its private, guests-only restaurant; ornate, friendly **Lizzie's** (731 Pierce St., 98368, tel. 206/385–4168), with eight rooms; the 15-room **Palace Hotel** (1004 Water St., 98368, tel. 206/385–0773); refreshingly modern, eight-unit **Ravenscroft Inn** (533 Quincy St., 98368, tel. 206/385–2784); and beautiful 10-room **Starrett House Inn** (744 Clay St., 98368, tel. 206/385–3205), almost baroque in its extravagance.

Most famous of all is the 12-room **James House** (1238 Washington St., 98368, tel. 206/385–1238), considered by many to be the state's—and maybe the region's—premier B&B. The beauty of the century-old house, its unrivaled views of the sound and sumptuous furnishings, and the impeccable hospitality of its owners harmonize into a memorable B&B experience.

Hard-working **Port Angeles,** at the park's northern gateway, has nearly as many B&Bs as Port Townsend but lacks that town's Victorian charm. Port Angeles's inns are a disparate group, smaller and less ornate than their Port Townsend counterparts. One exception to that rule is the **Tudor Inn** (1108 S. Oak St., 98362, tel. 206/452–3138), a sprawling half-timbered mansion built by Dr. Harold Butler, a colorful English dentist who moved to the peninsula in 1902. Beautifully furnished with antiques collected during the owners' eight years in Europe, the inn has six smallish rooms and a venerable Elizabethan feel. Dark wood, vibrant colors, leaded-glass windows, mirrored armoires, and distinctive touches, such as the 1848 vintage Broadwood & Sons grand piano, make every room of the house come alive. There's a well-stocked library off the dining room, and a good selection of videocassettes. Owners Jerry and Jane Glass, born in Houston but Anglophiles to the core, spent years understudying at top-quality European inns. From the furnishings to the sumptuous afternoon tea, the influence shows.

For a free listing of accommodations in Port Angeles, contact the **Port Angeles Chamber of Commerce** (tel. 206/452–2363).

CAMPING

The best and most popular accommodations at Olympic are the 17 campgrounds, which range from primitive backcountry sites reached only after grueling hikes to paved handicapped-accessible trailer parks with toilets and nightly naturalist programs. There are no showers at park campgrounds, and some are open in summer only. More intrepid hikers camp on the park's wilderness beaches or virtually anywhere in the mountain and forest areas of the park. The only requirements: You must have a backcountry use permit (*see* Visitor Information, *above*), and you must choose a site that is at least 1/2-mile inside the park.

Altogether there are about 925 formal sites in Olympic's campgrounds. Not surprisingly, the park's drive-in facilities are the most heavily used, particularly those at **Altaire** (30 sites, flush toilets, drinking water, fire grates) **Elwha** (41 sites, flush toilets, drinking water, fire grates, boat access, ranger station, public phone), **Fairholm** (87 sites, flush toilets, drinking water, fire grates, swimming, boat access, disposal station, public phone), **Heart O' the Hills** (105 sites, flush toilets, drinking water, fire grates, ranger station, public phone), **Hoh** (89 sites, flush toilets, drinking water, fire grates, disposal station, ranger station, public phone), **Kalaloch** (177 sites, flush toilets, drinking water, fire grates, disposal station, ranger station, public phone), **Mora** (94 sites, flush toilets, drinking water, fire grates, boat access, disposal station, ranger station, public phone), **Sol Duc** (80 sites, flush toilets, drinking water, fire grates, swimming, disposal station, ranger station, public phone), and **Staircase** (59 sites, flush toilets, drinking water, fire grates, ranger station, public phone). Not coincidentally, those campgrounds are the only ones that charge for sites ($8 per night). No reservations are accepted at any of the campgrounds; all space is allocated strictly on a first-come, first-served basis. On summer weekends, plan to arrive by Thursday night if possible.

Olympic's wilderness beaches provide a camping experience unmatched at other national parks. There is nothing quite like watching a Pacific sunset through a beach-log fire out of sight of another human being. Hikers can camp anywhere they like, provided it's well above the high-tide mark. Remote **Queets Campground** (20 sites, pit toilets, fire grates, ranger station, no water) lies deep in the lush old-growth forests in the southwestern corner of the park, hard by the park's largest Douglas fir tree. **July Creek Campground** (29 sites, pit toilets, drinking water, fire grates, swimming) offers gorgeous views of Quinault Lake and the rugged mountains beyond; nearby **North Fork** (7 sites, pit toilets, fire grates, ranger station, no water) and **Graves Creek** (30 sites, flush toilets,

drinking water, fire grates, ranger station) campgrounds lie deep in the forested foothills of the mountains themselves.

There are also thousands of isolated sites in the park's interior. It can be argued that the most beautiful of all are those located in **Enchanted Valley,** accessible via a 13-mile hike along the Enchanted Valley Trail, in the southeastern section of the park. This valley is known as Olympic's mountain-girded miniature Yosemite and is often called the Valley of a Thousand Waterfalls, because as the snow melts in late spring and early summer, hundreds of seasonal cascades appear on the valley walls.

Point Reyes National Seashore
California
By Pam Earing

Point Reyes National Seashore doesn't feel like a large national park such as Yellowstone. Instead, it's private, almost deserted most of the time, and you may think that *you* discovered it, happened upon it while driving up Highway 1 from San Francisco. Chances are, if you are not from the West Coast, you have never seen anything quite like it.

This is rugged coastal wilderness, where the waves pound the shoreline and the winds on the Great Beach are so strong you sometimes can't open the door to your car. This is a place where you want to snuggle up in the belly of a sand dune, listening to the surf and the wind and the gulls, offering your face to the sun or, more likely, the misty fog.

It is also a quiet place. Twisting, two-lane roads ride the undulating hills past grazing sheep and cattle, ranches with hitching posts, and springtime meadows splashed with color. There are shaded trails surrounded by sweet-smelling Douglas fir and Bishop pine, and open paths through tall grasses on the edge of salty *esteros.*

It was at Drakes Estero that Sir Francis Drake landed in 1579. There he encountered the Coast Miwok Indians, a group of hunters and gatherers who lived well on the area's bounty of acorns, berries, game, and fish. After Drake's short visit, other explorers came and went. In 1603 the Spanish explorer Don Sebastian Vizcaino named the area La Punta de Los Reyes for the Feast of the Three Kings, but it wasn't until almost 200 years after Drake's visit that settlers began to arrive.

Following periods of both Spanish and Mexican rule, California was acquired by the United States in 1848 (it became a state in 1850), and the land of Point Reyes became home to a number of dairy farms. (Dairy farms still operate on almost 18,000 acres of the park's land, through long-term lease arrangements.) In 1962, President John F. Kennedy signed legislation authorizing the establishment of Point Reyes National Seashore.

ESSENTIAL INFORMATION

VISITOR INFORMATION Information about the park can be obtained by writing to: Park Superintendent, **Point Reyes National Seashore,** Point Reyes, CA 94956.

Bear Valley Visitor Center (tel. 415/663–1092), located at the main entrance, is the largest visitor center in the park and is open weekdays 9 to 5 and weekends 8 to 5. The **Kenneth C. Patrick Visitor Center** (tel. 415/669–1250) on Drakes Bay is open weekends and holidays 10 to 5; the **Point Reyes Lighthouse Visitor Center** (tel. 415/669–1534) is open Thursday through Monday 10 to 5. The park's beach areas are open from 9 AM until one hour after sunset. Recorded information and weather can be obtained by calling 415/663–9029. For the hearing and visually impaired, the park provides audio programs and hands-on exhibits, as well as large-type interpretative handouts. Each visitor center provides a wheelchair for temporary use, free of charge.

Permits are required for the four hike-in camps and are available free by calling the Bear Valley Visitor Center, weekdays 9 to noon. The park administration accepts both individual and group reservations but recommends that they be made over the telephone rather than in writing. Camping is limited to a total of four nights per visit, with a maximum of 30 nights per year. There are no drive-in sites in the park.

FEES There are no entrance or permit fees at the park.

PUBLICATIONS An assortment of one-page fact sheets covering a variety of topics, from fishing regulations to trail riding, is available at the visitor centers. Point Reyes National Seashore publishes a newsletter three times a year listing interpretive programs and special events. You can also pick up the brochure, "Point Reyes Official Map and Guide," and detailed maps of the roads and trails in the park's North and South districts. The fact sheets, newsletter, maps, and brochure are free and are available at the visitor centers or by writing to the Park Superintendent (*see* Visitor Information, *above*).

The Bear Valley Visitor Center has a bookstore that sells publications about the park. Three helpful guides are:

Exploring Point Reyes (Wide World Publishing/Tetra, 1989), by Phil Arnot and Elvira Monroe, a book that is geared for hikers and provides detailed trail information; *Point Reyes* (Wilderness Press, 1988), by Dorothy L. Whitnah, the best general guide to the park and surrounding area; and *Natural History of Point Reyes* (Point Reyes National Seashore Association), by Jules Evens, which takes a comprehensive look at the park's diverse flora and fauna.

The best map of the Point Reyes National Seashore is published by the **United States Geological Survey** (USGS Map Sales, Box 25286, Denver, CO 80225, tel. 303/236–7477) and costs $4.

GEOLOGY AND TERRAIN Point Reyes National Seashore comprises 66,435 acres, or approximately 100 square miles, and has more than 140 miles of trails. It is distinguished by a hammerhead-shape peninsula that extends 10 miles from the coastline.

The San Andreas Fault is responsible for the park's diverse topography. Two tectonic plates, the North American and the Pacific, come together in a dramatic meeting, forming a rift zone that runs straight through the park. The entire Point Reyes peninsula rides on the eastern edge of the Pacific Plate, which moves steadily northwestward at a rate of about 2 inches a year. The San Francisco earthquake of 1906, whose epicenter was here, thrust the peninsula almost 20 feet northwestward.

The bedrock of 80-million-year-old granite lying west of the fault is completely different from the 100-million to 150-million-year-old Franciscan Formation rock lying to the east. Consequently, the soil is different, and it affects the types of plants found on either side of the Inverness Ridge.

The ridge forms a spine that runs parallel to the fault, and its eastern slopes are covered with dense forests of Douglas fir and Bishop pine that descend sharply into the pastures of the Olema Valley. On the seaward side of the ridge, the hills are covered with more than 20 species of shrub and chaparral-type growth, and they slope gently down to rolling pastures, finally ending at Limantour and Drakes beaches. Large, fingerlike estuaries indent the coastline here, creating muddy marshes teeming with bird life. (The *esteros*, or estuaries, are places where fresh and salt water mix.) Sweeping pastureland lies to the northwest, between the Pacific Ocean and Tomales Bay. At the tip of the peninsula, the promontory of Point Reyes rises above the sea. Miles of sandy beaches with rough, hazardous surf line the western coast above the point, and the more sheltered Drakes Bay forms a curving coastline below the point.

FLORA AND FAUNA Each season the park offers a wide range of activities that correspond to the presence of the varied plant and animal life found within its borders. Visitors can attend talks and guided tours given by naturalists or rangers every weekend. There are usually between five and seven programs from which to choose, and they are free of charge. Call any of the visitor centers for information.

The diversity of habitats has made Point Reyes a haven for birds. More than 430 species have been observed here—that represents about 45% of the recorded species in North America. Because the peninsula extends 10 miles out into the ocean it attracts many winter migrants. Seabirds include gulls, cormorants, herons, brown pelicans, and ducks. Land birds include pigeons, kites, wrens, woodpeckers, and turkey vultures. Hawks are common in the pasturelands. During the fall and winter, Limantour and Drakes esteros are feeding grounds for many species of waterfowl and shorebirds. Other great viewing spots are Five Brooks Pond, Olema Marsh, Tomales Bay, Bolinas Lagoon, and

Abbotts Lagoon. A bird checklist is available for $1 at the visitor centers.

The observation platform at Point Reyes Lighthouse (about 23 miles from the Bear Valley Visitor Center) is the best place to see gray whales on their 12,000-mile round-trip migration along the coast. In mid-December and January the whales travel south from the cold Alaskan waters to the west coast of Baja, where they calve and breed. Then in mid-February, March, and April they begin the return trip north to their nutrient-rich feeding grounds in Alaska. During the peak months of January and March it is not uncommon to see up to 100 whales a day, and they are often swimming surprisingly close to shore. Other good viewing spots are Chimney Rock and Tomales Point. Because parking at the lighthouse is limited, the park service runs a shuttle bus from the Kenneth C. Patrick Visitor Center on Drake's Bay to the point on weekends and holidays during whale-watching season.

The Sea Lion Overlook, near the lighthouse, is an excellent spot any time of year for viewing harbor seals and sea lions, which do not migrate. These creatures cannot maintain their body temperature by remaining in cold water all the time, so they "haul out" on land. Their preference is for sandy beaches, mud flats, and reefs. Pupping season occurs from March through May. Do not disturb lone pups on the beach—the mother is usually a short way off feeding in the water. If seals and sea lions even sense your presence, there is a chance they will abandon their hauling areas. Visitors are advised to stay completely clear of them at all times.

The tule elk was once abundant in the grassy habitats of this coast, but by 1860, hunting had killed off nearly the entire herd. In 1875, a single pair was discovered. From these two animals, the herd has slowly been expanded and transplanted to other locations. Tomales Point was selected as a reintroduction site for 10 members of the herd in 1978. There are now about 220 tule elk contained on 2,600 acres of grassland and scrub.

Deer are a common sight within the park—so common that park officials have had to initiate a deer management program. There are three wild and reproducing species living here. Native black-tailed deer, numbering about 2,500, are spotted mostly in open pastures feeding in early evening. Native to India and Ceylon, the axis deer, or chital, was introduced into the park in 1947 and 1948, and it is now estimated that the population has grown from the original eight to more than 400. Axis deer can be seen in large herds, usually in areas of coastal scrub or open grassland. Fallow deer, native to the Mediterranean region, were introduced into the park between 1942 and 1954, and there are now about 500 of them. Their colors range from white or buff to charcoal or brown with white spots. The white deer are especially beautiful. Fallow deer can be seen in most areas of the park.

Skunks, foxes, bobcats, gophers, weasels, rabbits, and raccoons are among the more common small mammals in the park.

During the spring and early summer you may find small, jellyfishlike Velella, or "by-the-wind-sailors," washed up on the sand. These blue or clear off-shore animals live on the water's surface and differ from true jellyfish in that they can change the direction in which they travel by extending or retracting their tentacles.

Tidepooling is a favorite activity at Point Reyes. The best tidepools occur during a minus low tide (when the water recedes farther than usual) and can be found at Palomarin Beach, Sculptured Beach, and at Chimney Rock. Depending on the intertidal zone, you can encounter such diverse organisms as purple sea urchins, ochre stars, ribbed limpets, and lined shore crabs.

Note: The Western black-legged tick carries the spirochete that causes Lyme disease. Cases are becoming more common in California. Avoid ticks by applying insect repellent and tucking pant legs into socks and shirttails into pants, since the ticks climb upward. Wear light-colored clothing on which they are easily spotted. A detailed pamphlet on Lyme disease is available at visitor centers.

There are 860 species of plants within the park, which account for 17% of all plant species in California. The low hills facing the sea are covered with grasses. Exotics, such as blue gum eucalyptus and Monterey cypress, can be found in the pastoral areas, and lupines and European dune grass are prevalent at the beaches. The freshwater and saltwater marshes are characterized by pickelweed and sea-blite. In addition to the Douglas fir and Bishop pine forests, mixed evergreen trees that are native to central California, such as bay laurel, buckeye, and coast live oak, are common.

Wildflowers can be found from February through June, with April and May being the peak months. Look for them in coastal areas where winds have prevented the growth of large conifers that would block the sun. The most common wildflowers are California poppy; checkerbloom (a wild cousin of hollyhock); Douglas iris, especially along the coast, or in the Bishop pine or Douglas fir forests; yellow composites, such as gumplant and tidytips; lupines, along the bluffs and dunes, and in the coastal hill; and wild radish, a member of the mustard family, in the fields and along the roadsides. Some of the best places in the park to view wildflowers are Chimney Rock, Abbotts Lagoon, and Tomales Point trails, as well as the Limantour Beach/Muddy Hollow area.

Note: Poison oak, identified by leaves in groups of three that are glossy green in summer and bright red in late summer and fall, is common on the peninsula. It is especially prevalent on the old, unmaintained trails in the southern portion of the park. When traveling cross country or on narrow or unmaintained trails, wear long pants and long sleeves.

WHEN TO GO The park's climate is similar to that of the Mediterranean, characterized by warm, dry summers and cool, rainy winters. However, the weather may vary dramatically—not only from one side of the fault to the other, but also from hour to hour. Summer days on the eastern side of the Inverness Ridge may be warm and sunny, differing in temperature by as much as 20 degrees from the ocean side, which is often blanketed in thick, chilly fog.

Expect constant, moderate to strong winds on the exposed headlands and beaches. Winds are generally northwesterly, with an average maximum velocity of 43 mph, although winds up to 130 mph have been clocked. They are strongest in November and December and tend to be lighter on the eastern side of the ridge.

The peninsula is the second-foggiest place on the continent, after Nantucket Island, and up to 2,700 hours of fog have been recorded annually. July, August, and September are the foggiest months, so a windbreaker or light jacket is advised.

Annual rainfall averages 11¹/₂ inches at the Point Reyes Lighthouse. A few miles inland, at the Bear Valley headquarters, the rainfall is much greater, averaging 36 inches a year. The heaviest rains are from December through March, and although there is scarcely any rain from mid-April through October, fog keeps the land damp.

The moderating effect of the Pacific Ocean creates an even climate with no great extremes in temperature from month to month. In midsummer the average temperature at the coast is 55°F, while the average midwinter temperature is 50°F. Still, there can be notable temperature differences on the same day in different areas of the park.

From February to July, mild weather creates good conditions for hiking and viewing wildflowers. Summer is an excellent time to explore the cool forests of the Inverness Ridge. The beaches are best in fall, when the foggy season has ended. The wet winter is a good time to see whales, seals, and migratory birds along the coast.

SEASONAL EVENTS The exact dates of the following festivals and events vary from year to year. Call the visitor centers for details (*see* Visitor Information, *above*).

May: Dairy Day at Historic Pierce Point Ranch celebrates early farming on the peninsula with demonstrations of milking, butter making, hauling, and other activities. **July: Native American Celebration at Kule Loklo** offers a modern-day look at Native American life with dancing, demonstrations of traditional skills, and items available for purchase. **August: Morgan Horse Ranch Festival** features demonstrations on grooming, training, blacksmithing, and shoeing, and includes a jumping exhibition. **October: Acorn Festival at Kule Loklo** celebrates the annual acorn harvest of the Coast Miwoks. Visitors can sample acorn mush, the staple food of these Native Americans.

Point Reyes Field Seminars conducts seasonal programs and events, including seminars with well-known wildlife photographers. Write or call for a brochure and listings: Point Reyes Field Seminars, Point Reyes National Seashore Association, Point Reyes Station, CA 94956, tel. 415/663–1200.

WHAT TO PACK There is only one food concession in the park, so you'll probably want to pack a lunch. Most people hike for one day at a time, so they need only a knapsack and a water bottle or canteen (in some areas the water is not potable, so bring your own to be safe). Heavy boots are unnecessary for trail-hiking in Point Reyes—a lightweight trail boot or hiking shoe is recommended. Binoculars and a camera are worth carrying.

It's advisable to pack a jacket or windbreaker at all times of the year because of the unpredictable fog and winds. If it's warm enough, bring along a swimsuit and towel for the beach. You may also want to bring long pants and long sleeves to avoid poison oak and ticks.

GENERAL STORES Just 5 miles from park headquarters is the **Inverness Store** (tel. 415/669–1041), which sells sandwiches, deli items, beer, wine, and liquor. It is open Monday through Saturday 9 to 7 and Sunday 8:30 to 7.

Perry's Delicatessen (tel. 415/663–1491) in Inverness Park sells sandwiches, cold meats, and beach and picnic supplies. Summer hours are 7 AM to 10 PM; winter hours, weekdays 7 AM to 9 PM, weekends 7 AM to 10 PM.

Three miles from the park is Point Reyes Station, where you can get sandwiches, deli items, beer, and wine from **Becker's Whale of a Deli** (tel. 415/663–1495), open year-round, daily 7:30 to 7:30, or the **Palace Market** (tel. 415/663–1016), which also sells liquor and is open year-round, daily 8:30 to 8.

Sandwiches, deli items, beer, and wine are also sold at the **Olema Store** (tel. 415/663–1479), just 1 mile from the park. Daily summer hours are 10:30 to 7:30; winter hours, 10:30 to 7.

ARRIVING AND DEPARTING There are four roads that enter the park, but it is best to use Bear Valley Road so that you can stop at the main visitor center, which serves as an excellent introduction to the park and from which several short nature walks begin. There are no visitor centers at the other road entrances.

By Plane. San Francisco International Airport and Oakland International Airport are both roughly 70 miles (1¹/₂ hours by car) from the park. Car rentals are available at both airports.

By Car and RV. Point Reyes National Seashore is an hour's drive north of San Francisco. The quickest route is north on Highway 101, then west on Sir Francis Drake Boulevard, which turns into Sir Francis Drake Highway. Take this road to Olema, where signs point the way to park headquarters, ¹/₂ mile farther west.

If you're feeling adventurous, opt for Highway 1, a sometimes-harrowing drive along the coastal cliffs north out of San Francisco to Olema. This route will take you longer, and you might want to avoid it at night or in bad weather, but it will make getting there a memorable part of your trip. On sunny weekends from spring through fall, southbound traffic to the Golden Gate Bridge can be backed up between 3:30 and 7.

By Train. Amtrak (tel. 800/872–7245) service from Chicago, Seattle, and Los Angeles terminates in Oakland. At press time, a new station was under construction and was scheduled to open in 1994 or 1995. Call Amtrak for an update on service. It is uncertain whether car rentals will be available at the new station, but for now you can rent a car at the Oakland International Airport, 12 miles away from the current station by cab.

By Bus. The No. 65 bus runs on weekends and holidays from San Rafael to Olema, and from Olema to park headquarters. The bus leaves San Rafael in the morning and returns in late afternoon. San Rafael is a major transfer point for buses from San Francisco and Marin County. You can take the No. 80 bus from San Francisco at 7th and Market streets and ask for a transfer to the No. 65 bus. The trip costs about $4 one way. Because schedules and fares vary, call **Golden Gate Transit** (tel. 415/453–2100) for information.

EXPLORING

The park's managers and conservationists and the people who live in the Point Reyes area would like to see the use of automobiles in the park reduced, so they continue to press for more public transportation. The townspeople are against widening the roads and building more parking lots to alleviate congestion. But as it stands, the shuttle bus to the lighthouse runs only from Drakes Bay and only on weekends during whale-watching season, from January through early March; without a car, bike, horse, or strong legs, you will be limited to the small area of trails around the Bear Valley Visitor Center.

Some park sites, such as Alamere Falls and Crystal Lake, can be reached only on foot or by horseback. These are part of a large section of the park, 24,200 acres, that has been designated wilderness and is off-limits to bicycles and motorized vehicles. The best way to explore the Point Reyes backcountry is to park at one of the four major trailheads and proceed on foot. For campers, this is a necessity: None of the four camping areas is accessible by car. Cyclists and horseback riders can make use of many backcountry trails in the park, but not all of them. Check at the visitor

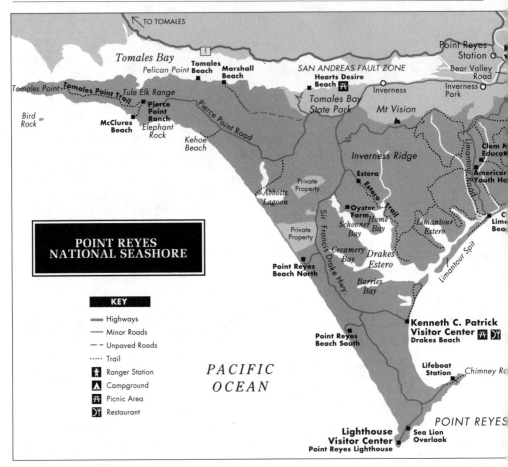

POINT REYES NATIONAL SEASHORE

KEY

- ▨▨▨ Highways
- —— Minor Roads
- – – Unpaved Roads
- ···· Trail
- 👤 Ranger Station
- ⛺ Campground
- ⛱ Picnic Area
- 🍴 Restaurant

centers to see which trails you can use (some are restricted on weekends, some are always restricted).

The park is small, and visitors traveling by car can easily get a good sense of the varied terrain within a day. The three major roads—Limantour, Pierce Point, and Sir Francis Drake—run by beaches, wooded area, and pastureland, but trying to cover all three roads in a day would not make for a very relaxing visit. Plan on a leisurely two-day stay, with an overnight at one of the campgrounds, the hostel, or a nearby inn.

THE BEST IN ONE DAY Day-trippers to Point Reyes should begin by getting an overview of the park at the Bear Valley Visitor Center. Take an hour or two to hike the short Earth-

quake Trail (*see* Nature Trails and Short Walks, *below*) and visit the Kule Loklo village (*see* Historic Buildings and Sites, *below*) and the Morgan Horse Ranch (*see* Historic Buildings and Sites, *below*). Families might opt to follow the scenic 4-mile Bear Valley Trail (*see* Longer Hikes, *below*) out to the ocean at Arch Rock, stopping en route for a picnic at Divide Meadow.

If you return to the trailhead by mid-afternoon, by all means take the 23-mile drive to the lighthouse, especially if it's whale-watching season. At other times, a good option is to drive to Chimney Rock to observe marine life in the tidepools (check tide schedules first). If you have less time, head for Drakes Beach, where high white cliffs meet the shore; in the

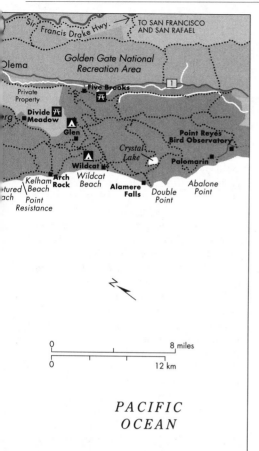

PACIFIC
OCEAN

fascinating features of the center is its seismograph station, which records the movement of the earth's plates throughout the world.

A 20-minute closed-captioned film, *Something Special,* shown on request, gives a review of the natural and cultural history of the park, and includes a re-creation of Drake's landing. Rangers are available to answer questions.

The Ken Patrick Visitor Center at Drakes Beach offers educational exhibits of the Drakes Beach area, including the unique whale fossil beds of the estero.

The Lighthouse Visitor Center, situated on the Point Reyes Headlands, features exhibits about the maritime history of the area, whales and sea lions, and headland wildflowers. The historic lighthouse is 300 steps down from the visitor center.

GUIDED TOURS The park service offers an extensive series of walks, talks, and educational programs on weekends and holidays. Rangers and naturalists give tours that focus on specific aspects of the park's wildlife, plant life, and history. These are open to the public free of charge.

A number of independent groups, such as the **Golden Gate Audubon Society** (2530 San Pablo Ave., Suite G, Berkeley, CA 94702, tel. 510/843–2222 or 415/383–1770) and the **California Native Plant Society** (1722 J St., Suite 17, Sacramento, CA 95814, tel. 916/447–2677), conduct field trips to the park, but these are scheduled on an infrequent, irregular basis. The Native Plant Society usually gives tours from February through June.

There are, however, some specialized tours:

Camelid Capers (Box 330, Inverness, CA 94937, tel. 415/669–1523) provides pack llamas for half- or full-day guided hikes at the national seashore. Led by owner Jerry Lunsford, these begin at $35 per person. On full-day trips you have the option of bringing your own lunch or enjoying gourmet picnics

nearby estero, shorebirds are plentiful. Wading and bird-watching are also favorite pastimes at Limantour beach and estero. Cap off your visit with a drive to Mt. Vision Overlook (*see* Scenic Drives and Views, *below*) for a dramatic sunset view of the entire seashore. This area is particularly beautiful during wildflower season.

ORIENTATION PROGRAMS The three visitor centers provide information on local weather, safety, and tide conditions. They also feature exhibits and post information about park programs.

The main center at Bear Valley has an auditorium, library, office, and exhibit area, as well as a bookstore with an excellent selection of books and trail maps. One of the most provided by the company at an extra charge. Reservations are required.

Sierra Club, Marin Group conducts field trips to the park (usually on a monthly basis) that are open to the public and free of charge. Featured topics and routes vary. Contact Jim Bonsey, tel. 510/526–8969.

Oceanic Society Expeditions (Fort Mason Center, Bldg. E, San Francisco, CA 94123, tel. 415/474–3385) runs a whale-watching boat tour between San Francisco Marina and Point Reyes every weekend, weather permitting, from the end of December through the end of April. Two naturalists specializing in marine life are on board. The trip takes about seven hours and costs $48 for adults, and $46 for senior citizens and children ages 10 to 15. Children under 10 are not permitted.

SCENIC DRIVES AND VIEWS There are few roads at Point Reyes, and these vary considerably in length and terrain. Limantour Road and several sections of Sir Francis Drake Highway are noted for their jagged, twisting turns, while travelers on Pierce Point Road will be treated to the pastoral scenes of California cattle grazing. Some of the park's best views of Drakes Estero, Tomales Bay, and the Pacific Ocean are seen while buzzing down the tarmac.

The paved, two-lane **Limantour Road** is the most direct route from Bear Valley to the ocean. Start on Bear Valley Road proceeding north for 1¹/₃ miles, then turn left onto Limantour Road. As it climbs tortuously over Mt. Wittenberg certain stretches of this road are extremely steep and narrow. It follows sharp curves for 8 miles down to Limantour Beach, a wide expanse of extremely fine, white-sand coastline. This is a windy spot, but many consider the beach's relatively calm but very cold waters excellent for an invigorating ocean dip. From the beach, you can amble along a trail that follows along the Limantour Spit, a finger of sand separating the ocean from the estuary. Usually foggy during the summer, the spit is still a fine place to view the egrets, blue heron, snowy plovers, and other shore and low-wading birds inhabiting the waters that surround it. Visitors should

proceed with caution beyond the 1-mile trail's end: Harbor seals and sea lions make their home near the tip of the spit, and park goers must not invade their privacy.

To get a feel for the park's varied geography, take the trip out to the **Tule Elk Range** and **Tomales Point**. Start on Bear Valley Road and travel north along the eastern edge of the peninsula through the Scottish-looking town of Inverness. This relatively straight drive provides fine views of the ocean to your left and slender Tomales Bay to your right. In about 8 miles the road will intersect with several beach roads, at which point you must make a choice. If you want to get a closer look at the bay, pick one of two roads bearing right that lead to Tomales Bay State Park's popular, sheltered beaches, **Hearts Desire** and **Marshall Beach.** You can even swim at these beaches. Wildlife lovers may opt to turn left and drive the 6¹/₂ miles through serene dairy and beef cattle country out to where **Pierce Point Road** divides a fenced-off tule elk preserve. Along this route there are parking lots where trails lead to Abbotts Lagoon, popular for bird-watching, and Kehoe beach, where you can explore tidepools. The road ends at the beginning of the elk sanctuary, but continue on foot for 3 miles to Tomales Point, the northernmost part of the peninsula (*see* Longer Hikes, *below*).

The 12-mile drive to **Mt. Vision Overlook** is a roller coaster of bumpy, twisting road. From Bear Valley take Sir Francis Drake Highway toward the lighthouse; the turnoff to Mt. Vision (1,282 feet high) will be on your left, 8³/₄ miles from the visitor center. At one point on this sharply inclined road you'll be treated to one of the park's most expansive views of North Beach and Drakes Estero. From the top of the mountain you can see the curving coastline of Drakes and Limantour beaches, the rocky hammer-shape promontory of Point Reyes, and the long stretch of coast from the lighthouse to Tomales Point.

The longest and most popular drive at the national seashore is the 23-mile stretch out to the **Point Reyes Lighthouse.** It is especially busy during the winter whale-watching season. Take Sir Francis Drake Highway south from Bear Valley Road and follow it to the end, stopping at various sites along the way. About 8¹/₂ miles from the Bear Valley Visitor Center, past the Mt. Vision turnoff and less than a mile west of the Estero trailhead turnoff, a ¹/₂-mile road on your left leads to **Johnson's Oyster Farm.** At this family-run business, oysters are farmed using an unusual Japanese method. In the retail sales room you can purchase oysters and pick up recipes and brochures that explain the growing method. Farther along Drake Highway on the right is **Point Reyes Beach,** a windy, exposed section of coast that is divided into two areas. At the 13¹/₄-mile marker is North Beach and at 15³/₄ miles is South Beach. Both are good places to picnic and beachcomb, but the surf is too strong for swimming or wading. Between the South and North beach turnoffs, a road on the left leads to Drakes Beach, a protected part of the coast where you can swim, wade, and picnic. The only food concession in the park is located here. As you continue southwest down Drake Highway the road sweeps back away from the ocean, passing several historic ranches and a few miles of coastal grass and bush. Reaching the end of the hammerhead, it splits. Take the right fork 1 mile to the lighthouse, which is about a 5- to 10-minute walk from the parking lot, followed by a long descent of 300 steps. En route, stop at Sea Lion Overlook, a popular spot for sea lions and harbor seals, and watch for them as well as common murres on the rocks on and off shore. The left fork dead-ends after 1 mile at the head of a short trail leading to Chimney Rock. On clear days, visitors have reported catching glimpses of the distant Golden Gate Bridge.

HISTORIC BUILDINGS AND SITES   A half-mile from the Bear Valley Visitor Center is Kule Loklo, a replica of a typical Coast Miwok village. It is estimated that the Miwoks, who were hunters and gatherers, lived in more than 100 small village communities in Marin and southern Sonoma counties at the time of Sir Francis Drake's visit in 1579. Among the buildings in the village are redwood-bark kotcas, in which Miwok families lived; an underground sweat lodge; and a ceremonial

dance house. Great care was taken to construct the buildings to resemble as closely as possible those built by the Miwoks. Follow the ¹/₄-mile trail and read the signs to learn about the life and culture of Coast Miwok villagers. It is not uncommon on Saturday to find volunteers offering demonstrations on arrowhead making or Miwok crafts. Entry to the village is free and it is always open to the public during daylight hours, but it is not regularly staffed. Schedules of cultural programs vary; call the Bear Valley Visitor Center (tel. 415/663–1092) before your visit.

Established in 1858, the newly restored **Pierce Point Ranch,** at the end of Pierce Point Road, is one of the park's historic ranches. Visitors can take a self-guided tour among the nine outbuildings, where exhibits describe butter churning and hay collecting while providing glimpses of the ranch's history. Once a year in May, the ranch sponsors Dairy Day, with demonstrations of farm activities and an exhibition of farm animals. The site is open seven days a week, dawn to dusk.

The **Morgan Horse Ranch** (tel. 415/663–1763), located behind the Bear Valley Visitor Center, is home to its namesake, America's first purebred. Dating back to 1789, the Morgan horse was originally bred in Vermont and is renowned for its strength, speed, and endurance. This horse farm provides mounts for rangers; it is the only operational horse breeding ranch in the national park system. Visitors can learn about the history of the ranch by reading the signs posted throughout the property. They may have the opportunity to watch the blacksmith at work or observe the horses on the outdoor obstacle course. The farm is staffed on most days from 8 to 4:30, but visitors are generally left to peruse the grounds on their own. Individual tours and demonstrations can be arranged, free of charge, by calling for an appointment.

The historic **Point Reyes Lighthouse** (tel. 415/669–1534), built in 1870, is located at the end of Drake Highway, 23 miles from the main visitor center. The point is a notorious navigational hazard, and the surrounding water is a graveyard of ships—46 shipwrecks were recorded in the first 60 years after the lighthouse was built. It is the windiest point on the west coast and the second-foggiest place on the continent. The beacon was retired from service in 1975, when the U.S. Coast Guard installed an automated light, but it is still maintained in excellent working condition. This is a prime whale-watching site, and a free bus shuttles passengers from Drakes Beach to the lighthouse on weekends and holidays during the January and February season. It runs from 10 to 4:30. You must make a reservation to witness the lighthouse lighting, which occurs the second and last Saturdays of the month, from April through December, shortly after the sun sets. Free 10- to 15-minute programs explaining how the lighthouse works are offered all year but not on a regular schedule. If you're curious, ask a ranger. At least one is on duty Thursday through Monday between 10 and 5. If wind velocity is more than 40 mph, the lighthouse is closed.

Because of the dangers at the point, a lifesaving station equipped with surfboats was established on the Great Beach just north of the lighthouse in 1889. Men kept vigil in four-hour shifts, looking for people who needed rescuing. Many lives and millions of dollars in cargo were saved. The historic **Lifeboat Station** (tel. 415/669–1534) was later moved to Drakes Bay, near Chimney Rock, before it finally closed its doors in 1969. The defunct station is now open to the public only on the second and last Sunday of some months. Call the Bear Valley Visitor Center for scheduled openings. Large cuts in federal funding have forced the park to cut back on many programs and hours of operation.

NATURE TRAILS AND SHORT WALKS Beginning at the Bear Valley Visitors Center, the **Earthquake Trail** is a very easy, paved, 1/2-mile self-guided trail that is completely wheelchair accessible. Traversing the area along the San Andreas Fault Zone where the land dislocated during the 1906 earthquake, the trail crosses Bear Valley Creek and passes through groves of willow and oak. Explanatory signposts along the way point out interesting geological features, and you can often spot

black-tailed deer and the beautiful white fallow deer.

Woodpecker Trail also starts at Bear Valley. An easy 3/4-mile self-guided trail, it runs uphill toward the forest. Woodpeckers are attracted to the coast live oaks and Douglas firs, and you'll find plenty of evidence along this trail, which crosses a meadow and ends at the red Morgan Horse barn (see Historic Buildings and Sites, above).

Completely flat, the **Kule Loklo (Coast Miwok) Trail** runs alongside eucalyptus groves for about 1/2 mile before it reaches the Coast Miwok replica village, where there is a lovely native plant garden. Also note that many of the tree trunks are pocked with holes made by woodpeckers, which store acorns in them.

LONGER HIKES Trail maps are available at the visitor centers. The principal trailheads are Bear Valley, Palomarin, Five Brooks, and Estero, all of which have parking. Many of the trails in the park were formerly old ranch roads that the park service has mapped and marked. There are many more old roads and trails that are not marked or maintained and are not found on the trail maps. Bring a compass and topographic map if you plan to hike these.

The most popular trail at the park with both hikers and cyclists is the **Bear Valley Trail,** a fairly easy, level walk of just over 4 miles along streams, under tall trees, through a meadow, and out to the sea. Unfortunately, this trail can be crowded with as many as 300 people on a good-weather weekend. No drinking water is available on the trail, but a picnic spot and toilets are located mid-route.

The 4 1/2-mile **Estero Trail** passes over undulating grassland and shrubbery, along the shore of Home Bay to Drakes Estero. This is a treeless route, but one on which you can find plenty of wildlife. The mudflats of the estero are a haven for birds. Since much of the area is still devoted to farming, you'll come upon cattle, but you'll see deer and harbor seals as well.

Rift Zone Trail runs for almost 5 level miles between the Bear Valley and Five Brooks Stable parking lots, along the top edge of the park, parallel to the San Andreas Fault. The trail begins south of the Bear Valley parking lot, traverses Bear Valley Creek, then continues to a wooded area of bay laurels and coast live oaks. Groves of eucalyptus and Monterey cypress also line the route. The next 3 miles travel through land that belongs to the Vedanta Society, a religious organization, and hikers must observe the society's rules: You can pass through only from 8 AM until two hours before sunset, and wheeled vehicles, camping, and picnicking are prohibited. Along the way, you'll see the old Shafter mansion, built in 1869 and now headquarters for the Vedanta Society Retreat. Next, the trail moves through forests alternating with meadows and marshes. It descends to a horse camp and ultimately comes out to the main road headed for the Five Brooks parking lot, from which it is usually easy enough to hitch a ride back to the visitor center.

Many consider the **Tomales Point Trail** one of the best trails in the Bay Area. It begins at Pierce Ranch and covers 5 easy miles along level ground, with scenic views of Tomales Bay. Come prepared for foggy or windy conditions—this is exposed terrain. The trail starts out on a gentle incline and gradually descends, passing Bird Rock, a favorite resting spot for cormorants. The last mile is over sand, leading to a bluff that overlooks the entrance to Tomales Bay. Most of the trail runs through the Tule Elk Range. You'll have to walk the 5 miles back to the trailhead.

Sky Trail requires a higher level of fitness than the other trails mentioned here. It is a steep 2¹/₂-mile hike that brings you to the highest point in the park—1,407-foot Mt. Wittenberg. It is also the most direct route to Sky Camp. Start on the Bear Valley Trail; about ¹/₄ mile along, Sky Trail branches off to the right. It is heavily forested with Douglas fir and California bay, and carpeted with ferns. An occasional meadow provides a rest stop. From the summit of Mt. Wittenberg, the peninsula, the ocean, and the valleys and mountains lying beyond the park's boundaries will take your breath away.

OTHER ACTIVITIES **Biking.** The park's paved roads are not recommended for cycling, especially on weekends, when traffic can be heavy, but there are 38 miles of dirt trails open to cyclists. It is best to have a mountain bike to negotiate the rough terrain. Check at the visitor centers for information on trail use and restrictions. You must stay on the trails, peddling at a maximum speed of 15 mph, and bicycles are prohibited on the 24,200 acres designated as wilderness areas.

Some of the more popular trails follow (distances are one-way): Miwok Village/Morgan Horse Loop, is an easy mile. Bear Valley Trail is a moderate-to-easy 3¹/₄ miles; the final ³/₄ mile of the trail is off-limits to bikes because it's in a designated wilderness area. Coast Trail is a moderate-to-easy 3 miles on a fire road with some beach access; park at the American Youth Hostel off Limantour Road. Stewart Trail, a mostly difficult trail starting at the Five Brooks Trailhead, branches off to Glen Camp (total 6 miles) or Wildcat Beach Camp (total 7 miles). Estero Trail is a moderate-to-difficult route that starts at the Estero Trailhead; the first 3 miles are fire road, and in the 1¹/₂ miles after that the trail becomes less marked.

If you need to rent a bike, try **Trail Head Rentals** (Hwy. 1 and Bear Valley Rd., Olema, tel. 415/663–1958), which has 18-speed mountain bikes for $24 a day on weekends and holidays, $20 on weekdays. In the afternoon, you can rent bikes for $7 an hour on weekends and $6 an hour on weekdays, with a two-hour minimum. Trail Head is open Thursday to Tuesday 10 to 6.

Bird-Watching. The park attracts serious bird-watchers from throughout the United States, and many educational walks and seminars are offered. During fall and winter, the wetlands of Limantour Estero and the mudflats at Drakes Estero are a haven for migrating shorebirds and waterfowl. Ring-necked ducks and green-winged teals can be observed. In winter, hooded mergansers and wood ducks can be spotted in the secluded

Five Brooks Pond. Abbotts Lagoon is a prime nesting area for many birds, including the endangered snowy plover. The pasturelands of Pierce Point Road are good for viewing land birds and birds of prey.

The **Point Reyes Bird Observatory** (tel. 415/868–1221 or 415/868–0655) is an independent, nonprofit study and conservation organization that has a field station on Mesa Road, 1/2 mile south of Palomarin Trailhead. Visitors can observe bird banding (the tagging of birds in order to monitor the area's species and population patterns) starting at sunrise through the following six hours, on Wednesday and weekends from Thanksgiving through April, and then daily from May through the end of November. The station is open to the public year-round from dawn to dusk; there is no fee.

Fishing. Persons 16 and older must have a valid California fishing license to take any fish, mollusks, or crustaceans in the park. A license can be obtained at many of the local stores for $24. Regulations for fishing hours, limits, and methods are found in the pamphlet "California Sport Fishing Regulations," available at stores selling licenses, bait, and equipment. These regulations are very specific to certain areas in the park and are strictly enforced. From May 1 through October 31, the State Department of Health places an annual quarantine on mussels because of algae-associated toxins. Point Reyes Headlands Reserve and Estero de Limantour Reserve are off-limits—all marine life is protected within their boundaries. Extreme caution should be observed at ocean beaches, where the heavy surf is dangerous. Many fishing areas can be reached only by foot trails, and some beaches only by boat.

Surf casters can catch flounder, surfperch, and sea trout. Along the shore, you'll find clams, cockles, mussels, and crabs.

Horseback Riding. More than 100 miles of trail are open to horseback riders, as are all beaches except Drakes. A trail map and information on restrictions is available at the visitor centers. Horses must be kept on trails. The shortest trails to the coast generally require two hours of riding time. It is a good idea to consult a topographic map, because some trails are quite steep. Plenty of drinking water for the horses can be found in streams, and hitching racks are provided at the four camps and at Kelham Beach. If camping overnight, bring your own feed.

Among the more popular trails are Bear Valley Trail (open to horses only on weekdays) and Greenpicker Trail.

You can rent a horse at **Five Brooks Stables** (Hwy. 1, 4 mi south of Olema, tel. 415/663–1570). Guided two-hour rides cost $35 a person, and guided half- and full-day trips cost $65 and $80 per person, with a four-person minimum.

Swimming. Some of the best swimming in the area is at the adjacent **Tomales Bay State Park** (tel. 415/669–1140), approximately a 20-minute drive from park headquarters. Its five small beaches are much less windy than the exposed beaches on the rest of the peninsula, and the water is warmer, calmer, and shallower than that of Drakes Bay. There is no lifeguard here, but there is a dressing room. Day visitors must pay a $5 entrance fee to the park.

If you don't mind cold water—average temperatures run from 48°F to 61°F—you can swim at **Drakes** and **Limantour** beaches. There are no lifeguards on duty, and only Drakes Beach has a bathhouse.

Don't consider swimming, or even wading, at the ocean beaches that run from the lighthouse up to Tomales Point. Powerful surf and undertow make these beaches extremely dangerous; lives have been lost here.

CHILDREN'S PROGRAMS Visitors with children will probably want to spend most of their time around the Bear Valley area seeing the educational exhibits at the visitor center, the Morgan Horse farm, and the Kule Loklo settlement; children also enjoy hiking the short, self-guided Earthquake and Woodpecker trails. There are also shady picnic grounds, but you must bring your own food since there is no concession.

All of the naturalist programs offered by the park are open to children, who may especially enjoy talks that focus on the local wildlife, such as "Sharks in Our Waters" and "Encounters with a Screech Owl." Programs change seasonally, so contact the Bear Valley Visitor Center for information (*see* Visitor Information, *above*).

Point Reyes Field Seminars (Point Reyes National Seashore Association, Bear Valley Rd., Point Reyes Station, CA 94956, tel. 415/663–1200) conducts one- and two-day nature and crafts programs about three times per season. Geared toward both families and individuals, some of these are set up like college-extension courses and cover such activities as basket weaving, photography, bird-watching, and local crafts. Prices vary slightly but are generally about $45 for three family members, $15 for each additional family member.

The **Point Reyes National Seashore Association** (*see above*) also runs a summer camp for boys and girls ages 7–12. The camp offers such activities as canoeing and hiking, but there is a strong emphasis on environmental studies. Five-day sessions are scheduled six times each summer and cost $260. At the six-day Adventure Camp, 13- to 16-year-olds backpack and camp out while learning new ways to protect the environment. This camp costs $330 and may include a canoe voyage and horseback riding.

EVENING ACTIVITIES Included in the park's regular nature series are a number of events that take place in the evening because of the nocturnal habits of certain animal species. In programs such as **Night Owls** and **Bats of Point Reyes,** visitors explore the behavior and habitats of these night-loving creatures. The popular **Evening Lighthouse Tour** is offered at sunset the second and last Saturday of the month during the summer; reservations are required, so call the Lighthouse Visitor Center (tel. 415/669–1534) the day of the tour. The giant lens is lighted at dusk just as it was by the lighthouse keepers until 1975. Occasionally, visitors are given the chance to explore the coastal forest at dusk and in the early evening on a mildly strenuous three-

hour guided hike to **Mt. Wittenberg.** Like other naturalist programs in the park, these evening events are free. Contact the Bear Valley Visitor Center for details.

Point Reyes Field Seminars offers a few evening events each season, including the **Hunter's Moon at Abbotts Lagoon,** an autumn moonlit hike on the Estero Trail, and **Moonlight Lyrics and Legend,** a wonderful family-style evening of storytelling and singing on Limantour Beach. For information about dates, fees, and other related events, call 415/663–1200.

DINING

Considering the wealth of marine life at the ocean and in Tomales Bay, it comes as no surprise that fresh seafood and shellfish are a dominant feature of the local cuisine. Whether it's served simply or embellished, a wide variety of Northern California seafood is offered at most restaurants. Since there is only one concession in the park (which closes at 6 PM), those who plan on having dinner in the area will have to eat at nearby restaurants, most of which are located within 5 miles of the park's main entrance. The towns in the Point Reyes area are fiercely opposed to overdevelopment, so don't expect to find fastfood eateries nearby. There are a number of coffee shops and local bakeries for those who prefer a light snack.

INSIDE THE PARK **Drakes Beach Café.** This is the park's only concession, and it comes highly recommended. The café seats 30 indoors, but if it is not too windy, you can enjoy your meal on the outdoor deck looking out at the ocean at Drakes Beach. The simple allwood structure has a very basic interior, with a woodstove providing warmth on chilly days. The homestyle cooking focuses on seafood—oyster stew, clam chowder, fish and chips—but the chicken tamales are a good choice, too. The barbecued oysters, served only on weekends, are rated as the best oysters in the Bay Area by local food critics. Bring your own alcoholic beverages. *Drakes Beach, Point Reyes National Seashore, tel.*

415/669–1297. Dress: casual. No credit cards. Inexpensive–Moderate.

NEAR THE PARK **Manka's.** Many locals consider this former hunting lodge to be the finest restaurant in the area. The chef comes from Greens, the best vegetarian restaurant in San Francisco, but the fare at Manka's reflects its hunting-lodge past, with hearty American dishes featuring local game, fowl, and fresh whole fish. Set atop a ridge overlooking Tomales Bay, the romantic dining room is elegantly rustic, with large windows, white linen tablecloths, and a huge centerpiece of garden flowers. The ever-changing specials include venison with wild blackcurrants and swordfish grilled in the fireplace. There are fresh fruit pies for dessert. *Argyle and Callendar Way, Inverness, tel. 415/669–1034. Reservations advised. Dress: casual but neat. MC, V. Closed Tues., Wed. Moderate–Expensive.*

Barnaby's. This popular seafood restaurant is located 1 mile north of the Inverness town center. Its spectacular view of Tomales Bay makes up for its rather bland furnishings, which are as casual as the dress code. Sit outside if the weather permits. Cooking is homestyle Californian with an Asian accent. Try the fresh local seafood and shellfish, or the ribs and chicken smoked with applewood. *12938 Sir Francis Drake Blvd., Inverness, tel. 415/669–1114. Reservations advised. Dress: casual. MC, V. Moderate.*

Vladimir's. This authentic Czechoslovak restaurant serves up hearty meals to those who need replenishment after a hard day's hiking. Located 4 miles from the park, in the center of Inverness, Vladimir's is designed to look like an Old World hunting lodge, with a dark wood interior and a burning hearth. The owner wears a Czechoslovak folkloric costume. House specialties include roast duck in lingonberry or plum sauce, chicken paprikas, and cabbage rolls. *12785 Sir Francis Drake Blvd., Inverness, tel. 415/669–1021. Weekend reservations required. Dress: casual but neat. No credit cards. Closed Mon. Moderate.*

Station House Café. At one time the Station House provided the best dining in the area, but when it moved to larger quarters its repu-

tation for excellent service and dynamic cooking was left behind. Nonetheless, the homestyle California cuisine here is still extremely popular with locals and visitors. Located in the center of Point Reyes Station, the bright spacious café is simply decorated with wood chairs and tables and the work of local photographers. A counter faces the open kitchen, and there are 10 tables in the new outdoor garden. Among the favorite dishes are those made with oysters, which come from Johnson's Farm in the park. Other specialties are mussels fettuccine and salmon with dill-and-baby-shrimp butter sauce. *Main St., Point Reyes Station, tel. 415/663–1515. Dinner reservations advised. Dress: casual. MC, V. Closed Thanksgiving and Dec. 24–25. Inexpensive–Moderate.*

Taqueria La Quinta. Families and hikers on a budget have made this colorful taqueria a popular choice for quick and healthy dining. The room is decorated with fruit-patterned wainscotting and Mexican folk art. A free salsa bar features three types of salsa for dipping chips or topping entrées. The menu includes such authentic Mexican fare as chile rellenos as well as vegetarian dishes. *Main St., Point Reyes Station, tel. 415/663–8868. Dress: casual. Closed Tues. No breakfast. No credit cards. Inexpensive.*

PICNIC SPOTS Point Reyes has three designated picnic areas, two of which have picnic tables and/or braziers. The only food concession in the park is at Drakes Beach, so you must bring your own picnic basket. The most accessible and largest area is set in a picturesque grove of trees near the **Bear Valley Visitor Center.** An equally popular spot at **Drakes Beach** has fewer tables and sits unassumingly on the grass beside the parking lot. To avoid the crowds, tote your basket for 1^1/$_2$ miles along Bear Valley Trail to the **Divide Meadow** picnic area—a placid heath without tables. All four hike-in camps also have picnic tables and braziers. In addition, at the adjacent Tomales Bay State Park's **Hearts Desire Beach** you can picnic in a tree-shaded area with sweeping views of the bay, then stroll down to the beach for a swim.

LODGING

There are few hotels and motels in the Point Reyes area, and the American Youth Hostel in the park fills up quickly, especially on weekends. If you don't want to stay at the park's hike-in camps, you can choose a nearby car campground or one of the many bed-and-breakfasts or inns. These tend to be small, and many establishments use the terms *inn* and *bed-and-breakfast* interchangeably. The inns, however, are more likely to offer complimentary hot tubs, and the more popular B&Bs require a two-night minimum stay on weekends. This is not an area where you can expect to find much in the way of budget accommodations. Expect to pay upwards of $65 for a double room.

INSIDE THE PARK **Point Reyes American Youth Hostel.** Originally a ranch house, the youth hostel provides dormitory-style lodging in a secluded valley 2 miles from Limantour Beach. It is accessible by car, foot, and bicycle, and has limited wheelchair access. A group of 20 or more is guaranteed exclusive use of a private redwood bunkhouse, with a large common room and fireplace. There are hot showers in both buildings and a fully equipped kitchen is accessible to the entire hostel. Bring your own soap, towels, sleeping bag, and food, but leave your pets at home. Prepaid reservations are recommended at least two to three weeks in advance. Office hours are daily 7:30 AM to 9:30 AM, and 4:30 PM to 9:30 PM. There is a maximum stay of three nights. *Box 247, Point Reyes Station, CA 94956, tel. 415/663–8811. 44 beds. MC, V. Adults $9 per night, children under 18 accompanied by a parent or guardian $4.50.*

NEAR THE PARK **Bear Valley Inn.** This classic Victorian two-story ranch-house built in 1899 is the closest inn to the park's main entrance. Although it is not as polished as Ten Inverness Way or the Blackthorne Inn—and not as expensive—the small, simple establishment emphasizes comfort and old-fashioned charm, from its lovely garden of herbs and flowers to its full home-cooked breakfasts made mostly from organic ingredients.

The parlor has a fireplace and is decorated with period pieces, including overstuffed velveteen sofas and handmade rugs. Each room has a different look: Choose either country comfort with handmade quilts and rustic antiques or Victorian elegance with velvet, lace, and a brass bed. There are no TVs. *88 Bear Valley Rd., Olema, CA 94950, tel. 415/663–1777. 3 rooms share bath. AE, MC, V. Expensive.*

Blackthorne Inn. The imaginative design of this inn, with its free-form layout, embodies the California Craftsman style. Constructed from native woods—cedar, redwood, and Douglas fir—and set in a secluded canyon 3 miles from park headquarters, the inn resembles a giant four-level treehouse. The main level is surrounded by a 3,500-foot deck, and a large A-frame sitting room features a stone fireplace. Rooms are decorated with an eclectic mix of wicker, antiques, and country-style furnishings and do not have TVs. The Overlook is the most spacious and comfortable room, but for sheer fantasy try the Eagle's Nest, an octagonal, glass-enclosed room reached by a spiral staircase. A buffet breakfast and use of the inn's hot tub is included in the price of a night's stay, but there is a two-night minimum on weekends. *266 Vallejo Ave., Inverness Park, Box 712, Inverness, CA 94937, tel. 415/663–8621. 3 rooms with bath, 2 share bath. Facilities: hot tub. MC, V. Expensive.*

Golden Hinde Inn and Marina. One of the largest accommodations in the area, this inn was built in the early '60s and reflects the style of that era—there are even lava lamps in some of the guest rooms. Set up like a motel, the Golden Hinde has a small registration office, no lobby or sitting room, and outside entry to each room. Eight units in an adjacent two-story building share four kitchenettes and offer more privacy and a view of Tomales Bay. Eighteen rooms have fireplaces, and there is an outdoor swimming pool. *12938 Sir Francis Drake Blvd., Box 295, Inverness, CA 94937, tel. 415/669–1389. 35 rooms with bath, 2 suites. Facilities: pool, cable TV. MC, V. Expensive.*

Manka's Inverness Lodge. This former hunting lodge, perched on a hill overlooking Tomales Bay, has the ambience of a rustic Adirondack retreat. Eight rooms (four in the main house, four in an annex) and two fishing cabins are simply decorated with Pendleton plaids, Beacon and Yukon blankets, and beds made of unpeeled Oregon fir. Rooms are small, but some have a large redwood deck that overlooks the bay. The sitting room is furnished with original furniture from the Arts and Crafts period, and has a stone fireplace that doubles as a cooking grill for the lodge's top-rated restaurant (*see* Dining, *above*). *Argyle and Callendar Way, Inverness, CA 94937, tel. 415/669–1034. 8 rooms, 2 cabins. Facilities: restaurant. MC, V. Expensive.*

Point Reyes Seashore Lodge. Located ¹/₂ mile from park headquarters, this recently built cedarwood lodge is one of the largest accommodations in the area with 18 rooms and three suites. Although not as secluded or private as many of the small inns, it offers such amenities as a library and a game room with an antique pool table, making it a good choice for families. All rooms face onto the park, and most have balconies or patios. None has a TV. A breakfast room with a fireplace and French doors opening onto a patio is decorated with fir furniture designed and made by the owners. Some rooms have a fireplace and/or Jacuzzi. A buffet breakfast is served. *10021 Hwy. 1, Box 39, Olema, CA 94950, tel. 415/663–9000. 18 rooms with bath, 3 suites. AE, D, MC, V. Expensive.*

Ten Inverness Way. Built in 1904, this romantic B&B is located in the village of Inverness, one block from Tomales Bay and an easy walk to shops and restaurants. The large sitting room is paneled in Douglas fir and boasts a player piano, several comfortable couches, and an immense stone fireplace. Antiques, fresh flowers, handmade quilts, and Oriental rugs give guest rooms a casual elegance. The back rooms overlook a garden, but Room 2, with its view of Tomales Bay, is a favorite. A full homemade breakfast features the house specialty, banana-buttermilk-buckwheat pancakes and chicken-apple sausages. Guests have use of a hot tub located in an adjacent cottage, but don't expect to watch TV. There is a two-night minimum stay on weekends. *10 Inverness Way, Box 63, Inverness, CA 94937, tel. 415/669–1648. 4 rooms with bath, 1 suite. Facilities: hot tub. MC, V. Expensive.*

Contact the following organizations for more information on accommodations in the Point Reyes area: **Inns of Point Reyes** (tel. 415/663–1420), **Bed & Breakfast Cottages of Point Reyes** (tel. 415/663–9445), **West Marin Chamber of Commerce** (tel. 415/663–9232), and **Coastal Lodging of Point Reyes National Seashore** (tel. 415/663–1351).

CAMPING

INSIDE THE PARK The fog makes it necessary for campers to have cover for the night—a lightweight tent or a tarp. Since the humidity can run high, it is better to have a fiberfill sleeping bag than a down one. Coast and Wildcat camps are especially damp. In addition to food supplies, you will need matches, a flashlight, lightweight cooking and eating equipment, and a sponge and scouring pad.

You must have a permit (they are free) to camp at Point Reyes National Seashore, where there are only four hike-in camping areas, which accommodate a limited number of people. Reservations for sites may be made up to 60 days in advance by calling the Bear Valley Visitor Center (tel. 415/663–1092) 9 to noon, weekdays only. You can camp for only four consecutive nights.

Sites fill up quickly on weekends and holidays, especially those set aside for groups. Reservations for Saturday will not be held past 10 AM. Visitors who arrive after 5 on any evening must make advance arrangements over the phone to pick up their camping permit after hours.

All campgrounds have pit toilets, drinking water, and a hitching rail for horses, but there are no troughs provided. Individual sites can accommodate up to eight people and are equipped with a space for a tent, a table, and a charcoal grill. Most group sites accommodate up to 25 people; at Wildcat the maximum group size is 40.

Wood fires are prohibited in campgrounds—only charcoal, gas stoves, or canned heat may be used—but you are allowed to make driftwood fires on sandy beaches below the high-tide mark. Sleeping on beaches, however, is prohibited and dangerous because of the rough surf and tides. Raccoons and skunks are numerous and aggressive, so food should be stored in the footlockers provided at the sites. Littering has been a problem at the sites: You are responsible for hiking out with every piece of trash you produce. Quiet hours are from sunset to sunrise.

There are nine walk-in sites, including one group site, at **Sky Camp,** on the western side of Mt. Wittenberg. The camp's 1,025-foot elevation offers you terrific views of Drakes Bay and the surrounding hills of Point Reyes. It's not as crowded here as it is in the two coastal camps, but it does require a somewhat hilly 1³/₄-mile hike from the Sky Trailhead, on Limantour Road.

There are no trees to provide protection from the wind at **Coast Camp,** located on an open, grassy bluff about 200 yards above the beach. This heavily trafficked area has 14 sites, including two group sites, and is an easy hike from the swimming area at Limantour Beach. From the Limantour Beach parking lot, it's a flat 2-mile hike down the beach or along Coast Trail via the dunes. From the Bear Valley Trailhead you will have to hike 6¹/₂ miles.

Those in need of a sound night's sleep will cherish the tranquility of **Glen Camp**'s 12 secluded sites in a wooded valley protected from ocean breezes (groups are not allowed here). From Bear Valley Trailhead, it's 4¹/₂ miles of relatively flat walking.

Wildcat Camp is in a green meadow a short walk from the beach. Nearby a small stream flows down into the sea. There are three hard-to-get individual sites, but the camp is much better known for its four, often noisy,

group sites. From Bear Valley Trailhead it's an ambitious 6¹/₃-mile hike traversing meadows and hills; from Five Brooks Trailhead, via Stewart Trail, expect a steeper 6¹/₃-mile hike.

NEAR THE PARK Just a few hundreds yards from the Bear Valley Visitor Center, **Olema Ranch Campground** (Hwy. 1, Olema, CA 94950, tel. 415/663–8001) has 60 tent sites, two large group sites, and 70 RV sites on 32 acres of grassy meadow, with trees, flowerbeds, and a creek. Children will enjoy the playground, and during summer weekends, campfire sing-alongs and free movies are provided. The privately owned ranch has flush toilets, hot showers, fire grates, a disposal station, and a new general store. Rates are $16 per night for up to two persons seeking a basic site for tent or RV ($2.50 per each additional person, $2 per extra vehicle); $23 for water, electricity, and sewage hookup. The charge for dogs is $1 per night. Visitors are welcome year-round.

Probably a better choice is the campground at **Samuel P. Taylor State Park** (Lagunitas, CA 94938, tel. 415/488–9897 for information only; 800/444–7275, 24 hours, for reservations), where there are 60 tent sites roughly half of which can accommodate RVs (although there are no hookups). The grounds, located on Sir Francis Drake Highway, 7 miles east of the Bear Valley Visitor Center, are heavily shaded by towering redwoods along with a number of slightly less daunting Douglas firs and oak trees. Flush toilets, drinking water, fire grates, and hot showers (for a nominal fee) are available. A disposal station, a public telephone, and a ranger station are also present. Rates are $14 per night April through October, $12 per night the rest of the year for up to eight people; and for dogs, which must be on a leash, the charge is $1 each. Reservations are required between May and October. Two of the sites are equipped for visitors with disabilities.

Redwood National Park
California

By Anita Marks
Updated by Susan Prockop

nyone who has forgotten what it feels like to be a child should visit the redwoods of northern California. Standing beside their massive trunks, following their graceful lines as they soar toward the heavens, a grownup will be reminded of what it felt like to be very small in a very big world. There are many places in Redwood National Park that can make even the most stuffy adult feel like a kid again. Tall Trees Grove, Fern Canyon, Lady Bird Johnson Grove, Stout Grove—who can remain pompous in the presence of these regal, 1,000-year-old giants?

Redwood National Park was created in 1968 along a thin strip of California coastline surrounding three state parks and stretching for 50 miles toward the border of Oregon. Ten years later it was further expanded in order to provide a "buffer" forest to protect the redwoods. Today the park incorporates Prairie Creek Redwoods State Park, Jedediah Smith Redwoods State Park, Del Norte Coast Redwoods State Park, and former timberlands that were privately owned. Although the national park now surrounds the state parks entirely, the state parks, where most of the older and more impressive trees can be found, are completely independent and have full jurisdiction within their borders.

The area has been the focus of environmental concerns since 1918, when the Save-the-Redwoods League was formed. The group began the push toward national-park status for the area, and it remains active in the redwoods' preservation. At present, work continues to protect the area against erosion by replacing trees taken through logging and eliminating unneeded roads.

Jedediah Smith was the first explorer to travel overland to this then-virgin forest. He came in 1828, but the area remained relatively unpopulated until gold-hungry fortune hunters began to fill the woods in the early 1850s. Plentiful and just as valuable, the real fortune in this area soon proved to be "red" gold— redwood lumber. The logging industry that sprang up in northern California remains healthy almost 150 years later, even though the 110,000 acres of parkland cannot be cut.

The area's logging and fishing industries are, in fact, older than the park. And so, a number of small towns are located within the park, although they are not parkland. The largest of these is Crescent City (population 3,200), which is home to one of the three Redwood National Park visitor centers. There is also one in Hiouchi and one in Orick.

ESSENTIAL INFORMATION

VISITOR INFORMATION Contact the **Redwood National Park Headquarters** (1111 2nd St., Crescent City, CA 95531, tel. 707/464–6101) for general information about those areas located outside the state parks. For information on the three state parks, contact the offices for **California State Parks at Camp Lincoln** (4241 Kings Valley Rd., Crescent City, CA 95531, tel. 707/464–9533), or contact **Prairie Creek Redwoods State Park** (Orick, CA 95555, tel. 707/488–2171) directly for detailed information on that park.

Visitors can request information about lodging, transportation, and local facilities by contacting either the **Crescent City/Del Norte Chamber of Commerce** (1001 Front St., Crescent City, CA 95531, tel. 800/343-8300) or the **Eureka/Humboldt Convention and Visitors Bureau** (1034 2nd St., Eureka, CA 95501-0541, tel. 707/443–5097). Those interested in finding out more about redwood preservation can contact the **Save-the-Redwoods League** (114 Sansome St., Room 605, San Francisco, CA 94104, tel. 415/362–2352).

FEES Admission to Redwood National Park is free. The state parks charge a fee of $6 per carload per day if you use any of the park facilities, such as the beach or the picnic areas. This fee covers the use of all the state parks for a period of 24 hours.

PUBLICATIONS The **Redwood Natural History Association** (1111 2nd St., Crescent City, CA 95531, tel. 707/464–9150) sells more than 160 books, posters, maps, coloring books, laminated field-identification cards, videos, and audiotapes on the park and on natural history in general. These materials are available at the park-information stations in Crescent City, Hiouchi, and Orick. You can also order a catalog and place your order by mail.

The more worthwhile books and pamphlets, which provide a good introduction to the area, include Joseph Brown's *Monarchs of the Mist,* a brief and readable history of the coast redwood and Redwood National Park, and Richard Rasp's *Redwood: The Story Behind the Scenery,* a photo essay on the forest and man's relation to it. The authoritative *Redwoods: The World's Largest Trees,* by Jeremy Hewes, is a fascinating compilation of historic and modern photos, line drawings, and prose that gives in-depth background on the park's history. Bill Schneider uses simple text and enchanting watercolors to describe big trees to small readers in *The Tree Giants.* Caranco and Labbe's *Logging the Redwoods,* slanted more toward the loggers-as-hardy-pioneers than the save-the-trees set, provides valuable historic information and photos detailing early logging practices in the area.

If you plan to hike even a single trail, order the Redwood Natural History Association's *Redwood National Park Trail Map* in advance of your trip. It lists all of the area's trails, with mileage, and elaborates on each trail's best and worst features. Nature buffs might appreciate *Northwest Waterbirds* and *Northwest Invertebrates,* double-sided laminated boards, by Macs Field Guides, which provide illustrations of local fauna.

GEOLOGY AND TERRAIN Ocean, rainforest, and rugged mountains crowd each other here, where in as few as 10 miles from the Pacific's beaches, sea-level elevations can give way to 6,000-foot mountains. The redwoods found in abundance within 30 miles of the coast disappear in the higher and drier areas, replaced by Douglas fir, oak, and red alder. Such rapid changes occurring within just a few miles lead to the dramatic differences that make the park so interesting.

This variety is the result of centuries of shifting in the earth's crust. Geologists theorize that the north coast was created from rocks that were pushed up from below the Pacific Ocean about 170 million years ago. These were eventually shifted toward the coast, shoving tons of ocean sediment ahead of them. When the sediment collided with the North American continent, the folding and faulting of earth created the coastal mountains and left an inland strip of sedimentary earth between the Coast Range mountains and the volcanoes of the Sierra Nevada range.

All this geological gyration has led to an amazing array of stone for rock hounds. The northern California coast holds everything from the sea-foam green serpentine that covers so many area beaches to the flecks of gold that brought the California Gold Rush of the mid-1800s. But it is the rich earth from the former ocean sediment that is probably most geologically crucial to the region, since it is part of the precise equation that helps nurture the prehistoric redwoods.

Since sediment is the product of settling rather than heat, such ground is prone to erosion. Given the rainforestlike climate on the coastal side of the mountains—where between 63 and 122 inches of rain falls annually—and the cobweb of rivers and streams that pass through here on their way to the Pacific, erosion is a nagging problem in the park. As a result, many more acres of trees have been protected along the park's boundaries to form a stabilizing watershed area.

FLORA AND FAUNA A common adage on the northern California coast says that everything here will either rust, root, or rot—bad news for everyone except the coast redwoods. The moisture-loving giants thrive in this area precisely because of the moderate temperature, excessive rainfall, and omnipresent fog.

Although the sand verbena and evening primrose that grow along local beaches are charming, the area really gained its national-park status because of the unique and magnificent local trees. The coast redwood, more properly known as *sequoia sempervirens,* is a botanical kissing cousin to the giant sequoia

of drier central California's Sierra Nevada mountains. Most coast redwoods are between 500 and 700 years of age, though they may live as long as 2,000 years—still only about half the life span of the older giant sequoias. But although they may be younger, the redwoods are definitely taller: It is a coast redwood that holds the title of world's tallest tree—nearly 368 feet, with a circumference of 44 feet. This particular beauty, which is more than 600 years old, can be found in the Tall Trees Grove at the south end of Redwood National Park.

The coast redwood is not only taller than the giant sequoia, it is also more popular—at least in everyday use. The giant sequoia is cursed (or blessed?) with brittle wood that is unsuitable for lumber, but the durable coastal redwood is favored by consumers for backyard picnic tables and garden trellises. The redwood is a tough tree. It suffers from no known mortal diseases, is virtually impervious to insects, and routinely survives lightning strikes. It exhibits amazingly tenacious growth habits, too: Cutting down a single redwood can cause a small grove to sprout. Stumps commonly send up several new shoots, and minor damage to a limb may result in an entirely new tree shooting up from a horizontal branch. A wind-toppled trunk will routinely put out new skyward shoots like a row of soldiers standing at attention along the massive log.

The north coast redwoods have developed over many centuries into what botanists call a climax forest, a mature and unchanging mix of plants and animals, all of which thrive in the dense shade the tall trees provide and the moist air of the region. As a result, plants here grow to a size that is much larger than would be common in other parts of the country. Humidity-loving fuchsias, the wild ancestor of the familiar garden plant, grow in lengthy, tangled vines. Native sword ferns form groves beneath the trees, thrusting their sawtooth fronds 6 to 8 feet high. Redwood sorrel, a cousin of the tiny clover that grows in northern lawns, forms 10-inch-high clumps with shamrock leaves that are 2 to 4 inches across.

A few plants grow to more traditional dimensions but are no less distinctive. Native rhododendron enjoys an extended blooming season under the forest canopy and can still be found in full flower in late July. Petite woodland iris, no taller than the oxalis, decorates the woods in shades ranging from off-white through purple, nearly all with a splash of yellow in the center. The curious-looking tanoak is another habitué of the woods. Although its mature foliage is leathery and dark green, new growth is tan. Also look for thimbleberries, blackberries, and huckleberries.

As the elevations become higher and drier—coast redwoods do not typically grow above 3,000 feet in elevation—the forest turns to Douglas fir, alder, and oak. Another common sight is the madrone tree, which ranges in height from shrub size to nearly 100 feet and is distinctive for its peeling reddish or orange bark. Keep an eye out for poison oak—you can spot it by its T-shape, jagged-edge, three-part leaf. It's very common in both the redwood lowlands and higher altitudes, and the itchy rash it bestows can be a nightmare.

Wildlife is nearly as plentiful as plant life in the park but may not be as visible. Backcountry hikers will usually have much more luck than drive-through park visitors in spotting local animals, though Roosevelt elk are readily visible along the stretch of U.S. 101 where the woods are temporarily replaced by prairie.

Backcountry campers may also observe mountain lions, black bears, and blacktail deer. Near the water, look for smaller animals such as the river otter, beaver, and mink. Local rivers and streams are a fisherman's paradise, filled with a plentiful supply of silver and king salmon, and rainbow, coast cutthroat, and steelhead trout.

Along the coastline you'll be able to see plenty of the ocean's mammals, including gray whales and porpoises. Seals and sea lions are often spotted playing in the surf.

Bird-watchers can enjoy a front-row seat for the Pacific Flyway, one of North America's four major bird-migration routes. Due to the diversity of environments in such a small area, an amazing 370 species of bird have been sighted in the park. These include rare and unusual species such as great blue herons, brown pelicans, pileated woodpeckers, spotted owls, and marbled murrelet. Many more-common birds also inhabit the park, including kingfishers, three species of warbler, wood ducks, ravens, and hawks.

WHEN TO GO Campers and hikers flock to the park during the summer, because it is the driest season; as a result, July and August are typically the park's busiest months. Birdwatchers prefer the spring and fall, in order to take advantage of the migratory seasons, and some of the best whale-watching goes on in December and January, when the giant mammals are slowly returning to northern waters, their young being "mentally imprinted" with the migration route. Freshwater fishermen chart their visits according to the timetable of the trout and salmon runs.

Temperatures vary widely throughout the park, with marked differences between the foggy coastal lowland and the interior's higher altitude. During the summer months temperatures along the coast usually remain in the mid-60s, though they can rise into the 70s on occasion. Much higher summer temperatures can be found in the interior, with highs ranging from 80°F to 100°F. Winter temperatures throughout the park hover between 30°F and 50°F. The weather here is fickle, so be prepared for the unexpected.

SEASONAL EVENTS **February:** For more than 20 years competitors from California and Oregon have gathered for the **World Championship Crab Races** (tel. 800/343–8300) held in Crescent City, where they race locally caught crabs and chow down at the accompanying crab feast. **April:** Crescent City is also the site of the **Redwood Country Open Fiddlers Contest** (tel. 707/464–2487), a three-day jam session that draws fiddlers from all over the West. **July 4:** The large **Fourth of July Celebration** (tel. 800/343–8300) held in Crescent City features fireworks, logging shows, food stalls, and a parade. Also in July is the **Tall Trees Rendezvous** (Del Norte County, tel.

707/464–4091), at which a local group reenacts snippets of the area's history. **August:** Of interest to foodies are the Klamath Salmon Festival (Klamath, tel. 707/482–7165) and the **Del Norte County Fair** (Crescent City, tel. 707/464–9556), a four-day festival that includes a carnival. The most unusual event in August, however, is certainly the **Banana Slug Derby** (tel. 707/488–2171) held in Prairie Creek Redwoods State Park, where competitors race large, yellow slugs—that's right, slugs. They also elect a banana slug queen to lead the banana slug parade. **December:** Visitors might like to see the **Illinois Valley Christmas Parade** (Cave Junction, tel. 503/592–3625).

WHAT TO PACK Temperatures in the park can be unpredictable (*see* When to Go, *above*), so try to dress in layers that can be removed as needed. When hiking in the woods, wear long pants, regardless of the season, to avoid contact with poison oak. Be sure to bring rain gear as well as sunscreen—the skies here are often overcast, but you've still got a good chance of getting a sunburn.

GENERAL STORES Although there are no general stores inside the park, more than two dozen grocery stores dot the map in the small towns surrounding it. Most of the better prospects are in Crescent City. On Highway 101 in Crescent City you can find grocery supplies at **Safeway** (tel. 707/465–3353) or across the highway at **Sentry** (tel. 707/465–4045). Both of these stores are open daily 24 hours and have a deli and bakery; Safeway has a florist, liquor store, and pharmacy as well. For general merchandise, including cosmetics, hardware, auto parts, sports equipment, and camera supplies, try **Payless** (tel. 707/465–3412), also on Highway 101 and open daily 9 to 9. If you are in the southern half of the park, visit the **Orick Market** (tel. 707/488–3225) in Orick. This well-stocked general store is open daily 8 to 7:30 and is also situated on U.S. 101. If you are traveling south, you'll see it on your left next to the post office.

ARRIVING AND DEPARTING Since access to Redwood National Park by public transportation is extremely limited, visitors will find that driving their own car or RV into the park is easiest. Redwood National Park is about 450 miles from San Francisco and 350 miles from Portland, Oregon. Crater Lake National Park is 175 miles north of Redwood, and Point Reyes National Seashore is about 400 miles to the south.

By Plane. Commercial air service to Crescent City and to Eureka/Arcata airport, 32 miles south of Orick, is provided daily by **United Express** (tel. 800/241–6522) from San Francisco.

Car-rental services in Eureka include: **Avis** (tel.707/839–1579), **Hertz** (tel.707/839–2172), and **National** (tel. 707/839–3229). In Crescent City, try **Enterprise** (tel. 707/464–2146) and **U-Save Auto Rental** (tel. 707/464–7813).

By Car and RV. Most drivers approach the park from San Francisco in the south via U.S. 101. This eight-hour drive is a pleasant one, past numerous stands of redwoods and through many lovely small towns.

Travelers arriving from Seattle or Portland, to the north, can follow either I–5 or U.S. 101 south into the park. Those who travel on I–5 should exit at Grants Pass, Oregon, onto U.S. 199. Follow U.S. 199 to its termination at U.S. 101 just north of Crescent City. This route allows for a side trip off U.S. 199 at Cave Junction to the Oregon Caves National Monument, but allow at least an extra half-day to visit the caves. Drivers, particularly those in RVs, should be aware that U.S. 199 is very narrow, especially on the southbound drive. Catching the coastal U.S. 101 requires some ingenuity at the northern end of the route, but has the advantage of leading straight into the park at the southern terminus. Those coming from the direction of Seattle should head south on I–5 to Olympia, then take U.S. 12 west to the coast, where it meets U.S. 101. Those driving from the Portland area should take Highway 99W southwest to Highway 18, which climbs the Coast Range mountains and joins U.S. 101 just north of Lincoln City.

Although traveling by car or RV is the easiest way to reach and explore the park, drivers should be aware that some of the roads off the main highways are not paved. Unpaved roads are often steep but are usually passable by any type of vehicle in the dry summer season. RVers should also be aware that RVs and trailers are not advised or not permitted at various places within the park, limiting the number of routes from which you can choose. Be sure to check your route with a ranger in advance to avoid aggravation later.

By Bus. Crescent City is served by **Greyhound** (tel. 707/464–2807), which operates two buses per day to San Francisco and two per day to Portland. The bus also makes stops at Orick and at the Redwood youth hostel on U.S. 101 in Klamath. The only local bus service is called **Dial-A-Ride** (tel. 707/464–9314 or 707/464–4314); it is an on-call bus service that operates inside the Crescent City limits.

By Taxi. Del Norte Taxi Service (tel. 707/464–6030) is the area's one taxi service. It is based in Crescent City but provides out-of-town and tour services.

EXPLORING

Driving along U.S. 101, you will pass through Redwood National Park for an hour or so and will see many of the famed redwood trees. But these monarchs, towering taller than 35-story skyscrapers, are not the only wonders in the park. There are also sandy beaches, pillared-rock seastacks, cliffs and coves, oak-lined prairie, and crystal-clear streams and rivers. Give yourself at least a full day at Redwood; it will be a gift you won't forget.

THE BEST IN ONE DAY If time is short, don't give in to the temptation to simply rubberneck while passing through. Tree-hugging is essential to the traveler's sense of wonder here. For a good, hands-on overview of what the park has to offer, with minimal hiking, explore Howland Hill Road in the morning and Gold Bluffs Beach in the afternoon.

Start the day by taking U.S. 101 south from Crescent City, making a left on Elk Valley Road and a right onto Howland Hill Road in

the Jedediah Smith Redwoods State Park. The narrow gravel road can be negotiated by most vehicles, but the park service does not recommend this trip for RVs and trailers. Although Howland Hill Road is only 8 miles long, you should allow at least 40 minutes for the trip so that you'll have time to wander into the forest. At Stout Grove, 2 miles west from South Fork Road, you'll find the Stout Tree, one of the largest redwoods in the park.

Return to U.S. 101 and head south for about 35 miles through the Del Norte Coast Redwoods State Park into Prairie Creek Redwoods State Park, and turn right onto Davison Road. Follow this winding, gravel road (no trailers or RVs over 20 feet in length) for another 6 miles or so until you reach Gold Bluffs Beach and Campground for a leisurely picnic lunch and a short hike. There is a state-park day-use fee of $6 per vehicle.

The lovely beach here is frequently visited by Roosevelt elk. Follow the trail at the north end of the beach, and, after wading across a shallow creek several times, you will arrive at Fern Canyon (*see* Nature Trails and Short Walks, *below*). Try to time your visit for late afternoon, when the lighting is particularly dramatic.

ORIENTATION PROGRAMS From Memorial Day through Labor Day the National Park Service and the three state parks sponsor a variety of free, ranger-led walks. Topics for these programs include the redwoods, tide pooling, geology, and local Native American culture. The topics vary according to available staff, so consult the information desk at the visitor centers located throughout the parks for a schedule of events.

GUIDED TOURS Two annual activities that occur on a predictable basis are the summer kayak trip on Smith River (*see* Other Activities, *below*) and the shuttle-bus tours to the remote Tall Trees Grove in the southern end of the park (*see* Longer Hikes, *below*).

SCENIC DRIVES AND VIEWS Five paved roads provide scenic routes through the park. To reach 2½-mile **Endert's Beach Road,** follow U.S. 101 south from Crescent City for 3 miles,

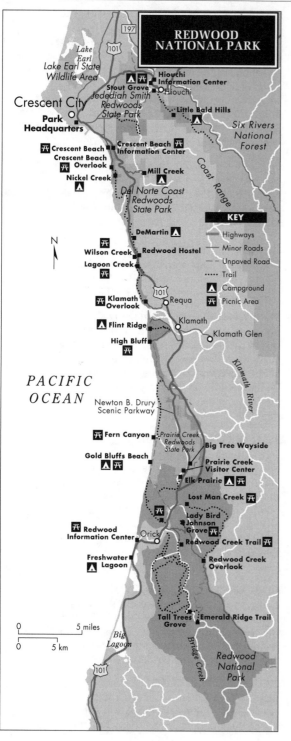

REDWOOD NATIONAL PARK

KEY

— Highways
— Minor Roads
— Unpaved Road
····· Trail
⛺ Campground
🏕 Picnic Area

then make a right. This route offers access to several beaches and a number of hiking opportunities. **Requa Road,** off U.S. 101 some 16 miles south of Crescent City, north of the Klamath River, is another good choice for hikers, picnickers, and whale-watchers; it is 5 miles long. **Bald Hills Road,** just 1 mile north of Orick, allows access to Lady Bird Johnson Grove, Tall Trees Grove, and plenty of elk, but, because of its steep grade, the 35-mile road is not recommended for trailers. You can pick up **Coastal Drive** from two points on U.S. 101, north of Prairie Creek Redwoods State Park. This 8-mile drive, parts of which are unpaved and not recommended for trailers, offers still more hiking, picnicking, and whale-watching opportunities. Formerly part of U.S. 101, the flat, well-graded **Newton B. Drury Scenic Parkway** is an excellent option for bicyclists and RVers. This redwood-lined, 10-mile route, offering access to camping and hiking, is located between Klamath and Orick; take the Prairie Crescent Street exit from U.S. 101.

The park also has four unpaved but well-graveled scenic routes. The 8-mile **Howland Hill Road,** northeast of Crescent City, passes through Stout Grove and has potential for light hiking and great photo opportunities. **Cal Barrel Road** is a 3-mile tour through Prairie Creek Redwoods State Park, 6 miles north of Orick. There is no turnaround for RVs. The 1-mile **Lost Man Creek Road,** 5 miles north of Orick, leads to the Lost Man Creek picnic area and serves as the terminus for the Holter Ridge Mountain Bike Trail. **Davison Road** is a 9-mile route through a mixed redwood and spruce forest that leads to Gold Bluffs Beach. From this beach, you can walk to Fern Canyon.

NATURE TRAILS AND SHORT WALKS Allow one hour to explore the 1½-mile round-trip **Fern Canyon Trail.** Carved away by erosion from Home Creek, the ¾-mile canyon has 60-foot walls covered with sword, maidenhair, and five-finger ferns. The trail ends at an abandoned mining town left over from the gold-rush days. From Gold Bluffs Beach it's an easy walk, although you do have to wade across a small stream several times. **Lady**

Bird Johnson Grove Nature Loop is a 1-mile round-trip trail that begins on Bald Hills Road about 2³/₄ miles from U.S. 101. The trail follows an old logging road through a mature redwood forest. Allow 45 minutes to complete the loop; the trail is, with assistance, wheelchair accessible. **Yurok Loop Trail** is also a 1-mile round-trip nature trail, with good bird-watching opportunities. Visit in the spring to enjoy a riot of wildflowers. You'll need about 45 minutes here.

LONGER HIKES There are six classifications of difficulty by which the almost 60 miles of trails in Redwood National Park are rated. A trail's difficulty is determined according to the steepness of the grade, the number of switchbacks, and the length of the trail. For a complete review of the park's trails, pick up a copy of the trail guide at any visitor center.

Although the **Coastal Trail** runs the entire 50-mile length of the park, smaller sections are accessible by frequent, well-marked trailheads. The difficulty of each section varies, depending on which part of the trail you decide to tackle. The 4-mile-long **Hidden Beach** section connects the Lagoon Creek picnic area with Klamath Overlook and provides a view of the coast as well as whale-watching opportunities. The somewhat more difficult **DeMartin** section, which you can pick up at milepost 15.6 on U.S. 101, leads past 5 miles of mature redwoods and through prairie. Those who feel up to a real workout will be well rewarded for hiking the brutal but stunning **Flint Ridge** section. This 4¹/₂-mile stretch of steep grades and numerous switchbacks starts at the Douglas Bridge parking area at the north end of Coastal Drive and leads past redwoods and Marshall Pond.

Another worthwhile hike is the **Tall Trees Trail,** leading to the Tall Trees Grove. Access to this area of the park is severely restricted: A maximum of 35 cars are allowed to drive to the trailhead daily, and those cars must have a free permit, which is available at the Redwood Information Center in Orick (RVs and trailers are not permitted). From Memorial Day through mid-September, you can take a shuttle bus from the Redwood Informa-

tion Center to the Tall Trees Trailhead for $7 per person (requested donation). The 3-mile round-trip trail is somewhat difficult on the return, climbing 650 feet in 1¹/₄ miles. The views of the park's—and the world's—tallest trees certainly are worth the trip.

OTHER ACTIVITIES **Bird-Watching.** Welcome to some of the best and most varied bird-watching possible. Some of nature's rarest and most striking winged specimens inhabit the area, including brown pelicans, great blue herons, pileated woodpeckers, spotted owls, and marbled murletts. Bird-watching walks led by park rangers are conducted throughout the summer season—check with the visitors center for information.

Fishing. Both deep-sea fishing and freshwater fishing are popular sports here. For information on the local companies that offer charter and/or guide service, contact the Crescent City/Del Norte County Chamber of Commerce (tel. 800/343–8300).

Kayaking. With the many miles of often shallow rivers and streams in the area, kayaking is a popular pastime. Park naturalists host two kayaking trips per day, Thursday to Monday, from mid-June to mid-July. The trip is a four-hour float on the Smith River, starting at the Hiouchi Information Center (tel. 707/458–3134). Participants must be at least 10 years of age and be able to swim. Reservations can be made in person at the Hiouchi Information Center no more than two days in advance. A donation of $6 is requested.

Swimming. The park is located on the shore of the Pacific Ocean and contains many bodies of water, so it's no surprise that swimming is popular. Remember, however, that most locations have little or no lifeguard service, and the water is extremely cold, even on the warmest days. The pounding surf and rip currents are treacherous. Swim only in protected, calm areas.

Whale-Watching. There are several good vantage points for whale-watching, including Crescent Beach Overlook, Klamath Overlook, and points along the Coastal Drive. Although most gray whales feed in Alaskan waters from

May through November, some spend the summer months off the coast here. To watch the migration, visit in December and January.

CHILDREN'S PROGRAMS All three state parks run a Junior Ranger program, in which rangers instruct children ages 7–12 on bird identification, outdoor survival skills, and more. The program runs daily at 3 PM during the summer: Check with Park Headquarters (tel. 707/464–6101) for specific location.

EVENING ACTIVITIES Inquire at a visitor center or check campground bulletin boards during the summer to find out what evening programs are scheduled. All three state parks have campfire programs in addition to talks and demonstrations covering such topics as local plants and wildlife, geology, forestry practices, and local Native American culture.

DINING

The small towns surrounding the park provide a handful of surprisingly good dining choices, but the biggest selection of eateries is in Crescent City. Most menus feature simply prepared dishes leaning heavily toward the region's plentiful seafood. Good food comes at reasonable prices here, and servings are sized to big appetites. Dress is casual.

Beachcomber Restaurant. Fresh seafood and ribs or chicken grilled over an open-pit barbecue are the house specialties at this local favorite. The decor is unmistakably nautical— diver's helmets, portholes, and brass ship's bells. *1400 U.S. 101S, Crescent City, tel. 707/464–2205. Reservations advised during summer. No credit cards. Closed Wed. and Dec. 15–Feb. 1. No lunch. Moderate.*

Harbor View Grotto. Don't let the tacky plastic salad bowls and amateurish oil paintings put you off: The Grotto offers some of the north coast's best fresh seafood. Portions are so immense that light eaters should consider ordering from the children's or senior's menus. An order of fillet of sole consists of six full-size fillets; scallops come in heaps of a dozen or more to a plate. *155 Citizens Dock Rd., Crescent City, tel. 707/464–3815. MC, V.*

Closed Thanksgiving, Dec. 24 and 25, Jan. 1. No lunch. Moderate.

Jim's Bistro. The closest thing to trendy among area restaurants, Jim's specializes in mesquite-grilled seafood from around the world. Try the grilled sirloin, or treat yourself to the best panfried oysters you're ever likely to taste. Jim's also has an extensive California wine list. *200 U.S. 101N, Crescent City, tel. 707/464–4878. Reservations accepted for large groups. No credit cards. Closed Sun., Mon., major holidays. No lunch. Moderate.*

Requa Inn. A hidden treasure overlooking the mouth of the Klamath River, this former stagecoach inn is well worth seeking out. Specialties include grilled ocean salmon and charbroiled filet mignon smothered in mushroom sauce. *451 Requa Rd., Klamath, tel. 707/482–8205. Reservations advised. AE, MC, V. Closed Jan. and Mon. Sept.–May. Moderate.*

Lino's Ristorante Italiano. At Lino's you'll find classic Italian cuisine and a respectable wine list. Try the antipasto, and don't miss the pastas and breads, all homemade daily. This is one of the few places in Crescent City with fabric tablecloths and napkins. *383 M St., Crescent City, tel. 707/464–2662. Reservations advised on weekends. AE, D, MC, V. Inexpensive.*

Northwoods Restaurant. Skip the Northwoods' predictable surf-and-turf dinner menu, but don't miss the hearty, worthwhile breakfast. They pile the buttermilk pancakes high, cook eggs the way you order them, and serve up mouth-watering platters of French toast. *675 U.S. 101S, Crescent City, tel. 707/465–5656. AE, D, MC, V. Inexpensive.*

Palm Café. Stop by this funky diner in Orick, where specialties of the house include such ubiquitous choices as meat loaf, lasagna, and Swiss steak. *121130 U.S. 101S, Orick, tel. 707/488–3381. Reservations advised for groups. AE, DC, MC, V. Inexpensive.*

PICNIC SPOTS A brief glance at a park-service map will tell you Redwood boasts more than a dozen picnic grounds, some of which can be quite small. Among the best are: **Jedediah Smith,** located 10 miles east of Crescent City on Highway 199; **Crescent Beach/Crescent Beach Overlook,** just 2 miles south of Crescent City off Enderts Beach Road; **Lagoon Creek,** where you can also beachcomb, fish the freshwater lagoon, or choose from several area hiking trails; **Highbluff,** on the Coastal Drive, where the sunsets and whale-watching are unequaled; **Lost Man Creek,** where you can sit in the shade of towering, 300-foot-tall redwoods; **Gold Bluffs Beach,** where Roosevelt elk stroll the beach (Fern Canyon is nearby); and **Elk Prairie,** where you'll also find a campground, nature trail, ranger station, and many, many elk. All grounds have tables and chemical toilets.

LODGING

If you think plush accommodations are a necessary part of travel, make your visit to Redwood National Park a day trip. There are no hotels, motels, or lodges inside the park, and you won't find anything too fancy in the towns around the park. Among the offerings, however, are three historic properties: a bed-and-breakfast inn, a former-stagecoach-stop-turned-rustic-lodge, and a youth hostel. The approach of all area lodgings is generally no-frills, but if good service and genuine friendliness are important to you, you'll appreciate the just-plain-folks ambience. Lobbies are usually only the size of a living room, but it's a common local custom to serve free coffee there each morning—along with plenty of friendly conversation and advice on local attractions for travelers.

Best Western Northwoods Inn. Modern and tastefully furnished in neutral colors, this motel is located in the center of town, across from the harbor. Avoid the units near the restaurant: it opens at 6:30 AM and attracts steady traffic. *655 U.S. 101S, Crescent City, CA 95531, tel. 707/464–9771 or 800/528–1234, fax 707/464–9461. 89 rooms. Facilities: restaurant, spa. AE, D, DC, MC, V. Expensive.*

American Best Motel. The natural redwood siding and modern furnishings at this rela-

tively new property will appeal to many travelers, as will its city-center location and proximity to four restaurants. While most of the units have a combination bath and shower, ask for one of the eight upstairs units that have only a shower and you can watch the fog roll through the harbor as the fishing boats putt in and out. *685 U.S. 101S, Crescent City, CA 95531, tel. 707/464–4111 or 800/ 622–9923. 48 rooms. AE, D, MC, V. Moderate.*

Best Western Ship Ashore. Notable if only for the vintage 1940s yacht moored next to it on the Smith River, this 50-room motel perched on the riverbank is probably the closest thing to a luxury facility the area has to offer. However, the 200 RV parking sites take the edge off the peace and quiet. The yacht, by the way, was the original hotel and now serves as a gift shop and local museum of sorts. *12370 U.S. 101N, Smith River, CA 95567, tel. 707/487–3141 or 800/528–1234, fax 707/487–7070. 50 rooms. Facilities: Jacuzzi in 15 units, 2 honeymoon suites with hot tubs, RV parking, gift shop/museum, restaurant. AE, D, DC, MC, V. Moderate.*

Curly Redwood Lodge. A visit to Curly Redwood Lodge is like staying at your favorite Aunt Hattie's, where you always got the biggest room and the comfiest bed. The motel's official claim to fame is that the redwood paneling and doors were cut from a single tree, but the real reason that it's so popular is the unobtrusive, yet always present, service staff. These are the sort of folks who go the extra mile and then respectfully decline a tip. *701 U.S. 101S, Crescent City, CA 95531, tel. 707/464–2137. 36 rooms. AE, MC, V. Moderate.*

Hiouchi Motel. This spartan but reliable sportsman's motel makes plain its purpose by proudly advertising plenty of freezer space for your catch. Still, it's not a bad little place for a nonfishing family to use as a modestly priced home base while exploring the surrounding redwoods. *2097 U.S. 199, Crescent City, CA 95531, tel. 707/458–3041. 17 rooms. MC, V. Moderate.*

Pacific Motor Hotel. In that only-in-California tradition, half of the lobby here is a retail liquor store. The rooms were all recently remodeled in mauve and beige, and some now have microwaves and minirefrigerators. *440 U.S. 101N, Box 595, Crescent City, CA 95531, tel. 707/464–4141 or 800/323–7917, fax 707/465–3274. 62 rooms. Facilities: restaurant, liquor store, complimentary use of health club next door. AE, D, DC, MC, V. Moderate.*

Palm Café & Motel. This tacky/chic little roadside motel is most notable for its namesake palm tree, a funky mural on the outside of the building that integrates the real windows with the trompe l'oeil. The generic hotel furniture and decor are nothing special, but the place does have an outdoor swimming pool. *121130 U.S. 101S, Orick, CA 95555, tel. 707/488–3381. 18 rooms. Facilities: restaurant, pool. AE, D, MC, V. Moderate.*

Patrick's Creek Resort. Getting away from it all is easy at this rustic (some might say primitive) former stagecoach inn, built in 1926 and located 30 miles from Crescent City. This is a true backcountry fishermen's lodge with fishing 100 feet from the resort. *13950 U.S. 199, Gasquet, CA 95543, tel. 707/457–3323. 14 rooms. Facilities: restaurant, pool. AE, MC, V. Moderate.*

Requa Inn. This bed-and-breakfast in a restored 1914 house features 10 individually decorated rooms with redwood wainscoting and Craftsman furniture that mirrors the building's architectural style. Seven rooms are still equipped with claw-foot bathtubs; the other three have modern showers. The rooms have neither televisions nor telephones, and no smoking is permitted. *451 Requa Rd., Klamath, CA 95548, tel. 707/482–8205. 10 rooms. Facilities: restaurant. Closed Jan., Mon. except during summer. AE, MC, V. Moderate.*

Royal Inn Motel. This centrally located facility has easy access to shopping and restaurants; is across the street from the Crescent City Chamber of Commerce and Redwood National Park Headquarters; and is just up the road from the harbor. It's a good choice for families on a budget: nine of the 36 units have kitchenettes, and another eight offer a micro-

wave oven and minirefrigerator. *102 L St., Crescent City, CA 95531, tel. 707/464–4113 or 800/752–9610. 36 rooms. AE, D, MC, V. Moderate.*

Redwood AYH Hostel. Travelers of all ages are welcome to stay in this vintage 1907 two-story Edwardian building. The guided nature walks led by employees (and praised by the national park staff) manage to impart a good dose of local pioneer and Native American history along with talk of the flora and fauna. There are a few beds in each room. Kitchen facilities are available. *14480 U.S. 101, Klamath, CA 95548, tel. 707/482–8265. 30 beds, 3 shared showers. MC, V. Inexpensive.*

CAMPING

The north coast offers an array of camping opportunities, ranging from primitive to well-equipped. One of the great aspects of the region is its temperate winter climate, which makes it possible to camp year-round. In the vicinity of Redwood National Park (within a 30-minute drive) there are nearly 60 public and private camping facilities with tent, RV, and trailer sites. In addition, there are backcountry sites for those wishing to immerse themselves in the magnificent wilderness. Be aware that the waters off the northern California coast are cold and rough and generally not suitable for swimming.

Disposal stations are available at three state-park campgrounds—Jedediah Smith, Mill Creek, and Elk Prairie—as well as at private campgrounds. None of the national-park, state-park, or national-forest campgrounds has RV hookups.

INSIDE THE PARK Redwood National Park operates five primitive camping areas. Four of these—Little Bald Hills, Nickle Creek, De-Martin, and Flint Ridge—are backcountry sites that can be reached only by hiking in. A backcountry permit, available at any of the park's visitor centers, is required for use of any backcountry site, but the permit is free, and there is no camping fee. The fifth site, Freshwater Lagoon, is a drive-in campground, and a donation is requested.

REDWOOD CAMPGROUNDS

Campground groups: **INSIDE THE PARK** (Little Bald Hills, Nickel Creek, DeMartin, Flint Ridge, Freshwater Lagoon) · **IN NEARBY STATE PARKS** (Mill Creek, Elk Prairie, Gold Bluffs Beach, Jedediah Smith) · **IN NEARBY NATIONAL FOREST** (Panther Flat, Grassy Flat, Patrick Creek, Big Flat)

	Big Flat	Patrick Creek	Grassy Flat	Panther Flat	Jedediah Smith	Gold Bluffs Beach	Elk Prairie	Mill Creek	Freshwater Lagoon	Flint Ridge	DeMartin	Nickel Creek	Little Bald Hills
Total number of sites	30	12	19	41	106	25	75	145	N.A.	10	10	5	5
Sites suitable for RVs	30	12	19	41	106	0	75	145	N.A.	0	0	0	0
Number of hookups	0	0	0	0	0	0	0	0		0	0	0	0
Drive to sites	•	•	•	•	•	•	•	•	•				
Hike to sites										•	•	•	•
Flush toilets		•			•	•	•	•					
Pit/chemical toilets	•			•						•	•	•	•
Drinking water		•	•	•	•	•	•	•		•	•		•
Showers				•	•		•	•					
Fire grates	•	•	•	•	•	•	•	•	•	•	•	•	•
Swimming	•	•		•	•								
Boat access					•	•							
Playground													
Disposal station					•		•		•				
Ranger station					•		•						
Public telephone		•			•		•		•				
Reservation possible		•	•	•	•¹		•¹		•¹				
Daily fee per site	free	$8**	$8**	$8**	$14*	$14*	$14*	$14*	$14*	free	free	Donation	free
Dates open	year-round	mid-May–early Sept.	mid-May–early Sept.	year-round	year-round	year-round	year-round	mid-May–early Sept.	year-round	year-round	year-round	year-round	year-round

¹Reservation fee charged. *$12 off-season. **$4 off-season.

The **Little Bald Hills** area, which is located 4 1/2 miles from its trailhead on the east end of Howland Hill Road, offers amazing ridgetop vistas from its five sites. There are chemical toilets, picnic tables, potable water, and fire rings here. **Nickel Creek** has five sites just 1/2 mile from the end of Enderts Beach Road on the Coastal Trail. The campground is near tide pools and has great ocean views. Facilities include a composting toilet, picnic tables, and fire rings; there is no potable water. Two and a half miles from the Coastal Trail trailhead, near DeMartin Hostel, is the **De-Martin** camping area, which has 10 sites in a grassy prairie that opens to a panoramic view of the ocean. DeMartin has a composting toilet, picnic tables, potable water, and fire rings. **Flint Ridge,** with 10 campsites under towering redwoods, is located approximately 1/4 mile from the Flintridge-trailhead parking area on the Coastal Drive. There's a composting toilet here, as well as potable water and fire rings.

Freshwater Lagoon, 1 1/2 miles south of Orick, offers unlimited primitive camping sites along the west shoulder of U.S. 101, with the ocean on one side of the road and a lake on the other side. RVs, trailers, and tents are permitted here, but most sites are taken by RVs and trailers. There is a 15-day maximum stay. Facilities are limited to chemical toilets, fire rings, and tables. There are no hookups and no water. A ranger station and a public phone are located just 1/4 mile north of here.

NEAR THE PARK The four campgrounds run by the state of California are the most posh, most expensive, and most likely to fill up first during the high season. All are developed campgrounds with flush toilets, drinking water, and fire grates. All but Gold Bluffs Beach have disposal stations and hot showers, and at all but Gold Bluffs Beach you can make reservations, from Memorial Day to Labor Day only, through Mistix (tel. 800/444–7275). There is a $6.75 reservation fee.

Mill Creek, in Del Norte Coast Redwoods State Park, has 145 sites, and is located 5 miles south of Crescent City on U.S. 101. In Prairie Creek Redwoods State Park, **Elk Prai-**

rie, with 75 sites, has a ranger station and a public phone, and is 5 miles north of Orick on U.S. 101; and **Gold Bluffs Beach,** with 25 sites, is accessed by traveling 8 miles on unpaved Davison Road south of Prairie Creek. *Note:* Trailers are prohibited on Davison Road, as are any vehicles more than 24 feet long and 8 feet wide. The beautiful **Jedediah Smith** campground in Jedediah Smith Redwoods State Park has 106 sites in groves of mature redwoods 8 miles northeast of Crescent City on U.S. 199. There's a ranger station and public phone here as well as a boat ramp, available only November to March (nonmotorized boats only). Jedediah Smith is on the Smith River, where it *is* possible to swim. All state-park campgrounds charge $14 in season ($12 off-season) for overnight use and $5 for day use only.

The **U.S. Forest Service** (tel. 707/457–3131 or 800/280–2267 for reservations) runs four campgrounds on national-forest lands surrounding the park, all located in prime fishing areas. These campgrounds have either flush or pit toilets and fire grates. None has a disposal station, and only Panther Flat has a shower. All but Big Flat have potable water, and you can swim at every campground but Grassy Flat. Three campgrounds are strung along U.S. 199, northeast of Redwood National Park, on the popular Smith River. These charge $8 per site per night in season ($4 off-season). Closest to the park is **Panther Flat,** with 41 sites 2 miles east of Gasquet on U.S. 199. Two miles farther along U.S. 199 you will come to **Grassy Flat,** which has 19 sites and is closed during winter. **Patrick Creek,** with 12 sites, is 3 miles farther east on U.S. 199, and is also closed during the winter. On the South Fork of the Smith River, 13 miles southeast of U.S. 199 on South Fork Road, is **Big Flat,** which has 30 sites, where you can camp free.

For an up-to-date listing of the many tent, RV, and trailer parks in the area, contact the **Crescent City/Del Norte County Chamber of Commerce,** the **Eureka/Humboldt Convention and Visitors Bureau,** or **Redwood National Park** (see Visitor Information, *above*).

Rocky Mountain National Park
Colorado

By Stephen Singular
Updated by Sandra Widener

Within a single hour's drive, you ascend from 7,800 feet at park headquarters to 12,183 feet at the apex of Trail Ridge Road, the highest continuous paved road in the United States. From this vantage, sweeping vistas take in high-country lakes, meadows flushed with wildflowers, rushing mountain streams, and cool dense forests of lodgepole pine and Engelmann spruce. Above, snow-dusted peaks dotted with small glaciers and patches of blue Colorado columbine seem to float in the sky. The fragile, treeless ecosystem of alpine tundra is seldom found outside the Arctic, but it makes up one-third of the park's terrain. Rocky Mountain National Park isn't a pretty passage; it is a moment of grandeur.

More than 2¹/₂ million people experience that grandeur annually, 80% of them in summer. That's roughly the same number of people that visit Yellowstone, which is nine times Rocky Mountain's size. They come for the 355 miles of hiking trails, as well as saddle rides, bus tours, rock-climbing, fishing, bicycle routes, seminars, and more. And, with all the extra people, from Memorial Day to Labor Day there are traffic jams in the small town of Estes Park, at the park's eastern entrance.

But even though Rocky Mountain is far more crowded than it once was, there are places in the backcountry that look and feel as wild as they did in the days when Native Americans roamed these woods. If you choose to come in early fall, after the crush of people and cars has gone and before the cold weather sets in, you'll enjoy brilliant autumn foliage and a better chance of spotting wildlife, which begin moving down from the higher elevations at this time. In winter, the backcountry snow can be 4 feet deep and the wind brutal at high elevations, but there's ski touring, snowshoeing, and ice fishing for the cold-weather adventurer.

Of course there is one very good reason to put up with the summer crowds: Only from Memorial Day to mid-October can you make that special drive over Trail Ridge Road, a ride that carries you high into the Rockies and makes you breathe deeply and shake your head in wonder. Just steps from your car you'll discover the park's oldest rocks and traces of volcanic ash. And way up there at the top of the world, you won't feel like you are simply looking at the mountains; you'll feel like you are part of them. That's a sensation you can take back home.

Rocky Mountain National Park comprises lands that were part of the Louisiana Purchase, acquired by the U.S. government in 1803. Fifty-six years later, the first white settler, Joel Estes, moved his family into a cabin in what would become Estes Park, and by 1909 a naturalist named Enos Mills had moved here and begun the campaign to save the area. In 1915 President Woodrow Wilson set aside 358 1/2 square miles of this land, near the heart of Colorado, to be preserved and protected as a national park. Since then, Rocky, as the locals call it, has been welcoming people from around the globe.

ESSENTIAL INFORMATION

VISITOR INFORMATION For general information on the park contact: Superintendent, Park Headquarters, **Rocky Mountain National Park,** Estes Park, CO 80517–8397, tel. 303/586–2371. For information on the area surrounding the park contact **Estes Park Chamber of Commerce** (tel. 800/443–7837) or the **Grand Lake Chamber of Commerce** (tel. 303/627–3402).

If you are planning an overnight trek into the backcountry, you must have a permit. It is free and can be picked up at any of four locations: just east of headquarters at the park's Backcountry Office, at the Kawuneeche Visitor Center, and at the Wild Basin or Longs Peak ranger stations. Permits can be obtained in advance by writing the above address or calling 303/586–4459. Phone reservations for summer must be made before June 1.

FEES Entrance fees are $5 per week per vehicle in the summer. Visitors entering the park on bicycles, mopeds, motorcycles, or on foot pay $3 for a weekly pass. Passengers on bus tours also pay $3. Access to the park is free in winter, except on weekends and holidays. The park's Annual Area Pass, which lets you come and go for a calendar year, costs $15.

PUBLICATIONS The **Rocky Mountain Nature Association** (Rocky Mountain National Park, Estes Park, CO 80517, tel. 303/586–2371, ext. 265; those with touch-tone service should call 303/586–3565, ext. 289), a nonprofit organization that works with the National Park Service, offers an outstanding selection of books, guides, postcards, and videos on the park. Books range from historical accounts of *Magnificent Mountain Women,* by Jane Robertson, to *Rocky Mountain Wildflowers,* by Kent and Donna Dannen, to the *Rocky Mountain National Park Coloring Book,* by Helen Henkel Larson.

The association also sells geologic maps of Rocky Mountain National Park and the more detailed United States Geological Survey (U.S.G.S.) maps. Detailed maps of the area can also be bought from **Trails Illustrated** (tel. 303/670–3457), which is based in Evergreen, Colorado.

The park itself sells numerous guides, maps, and books in the visitor center at the eastern entrance. The most useful of these are *Rocky Mountain National Park Hiking Trails; Rocky Mountain Splendor,* by Doris B. Osterwald (recommended for those who want to see the park by car); and *A Roadside Guide to Rocky Mountain National Park,* by Beatrice Elizabeth Willard and Susan Quimby Foster. The *High Country Headlines,* a free local publication available at the visitor centers, entrances, and ranger stations, has a schedule of ranger programs.

A good reference book for the park's flora is *Grassland to Glacier,* by Cornelia Fleischer and John C. Emerick. Another source is *Rocky Mountain Flora,* by William A. Weber. Look for *Rocky Mountain Mammals,* by David M.

Armstrong, if you want to be educated in the ways of the local wildlife.

GEOLOGY AND TERRAIN Rocky Mountain National Park comprises 415 square miles and has 78 named peaks over 12,000 feet. For 40 miles it strides the Continental Divide, the range of high peaks that determines whether a stream will flow east toward the Atlantic Ocean or west to the Pacific. The park's east side is dominated by deep valleys, cirque lakes (small bodies of water cut out by glaciers) and harsh mountain faces. The weather here is unpredictable, offering up thunderstorms on many summer afternoons. The western side of the park is softer, with pine forests and a gentler slope to the land. In wintertime, more snow falls here, but winds are diminished, which is an important fact: At these heights a breeze can knock you down.

Today, the visitor can see evidence of the park's long (1³/₄ billion years) and varied past. Scientists estimate that 530 million years ago the park was covered by water, but a highland was created when the earth's internal forces pushed the land under the sea upward. Consequently, the water receded over time and left tropical plains inhabited by dinosaurs. Continued uplift and faulting raised the Rockies above the surrounding terrain. Finally, glaciers from the Ice Age left the park as it looks now, full of scooped-out valleys and peaks carved by ice.

The park is divided into three ecosystems, which correspond to elevation. The Montane ecosystem, from 7,000 to 9,000 feet above sea level, features slopes, valleys, and stands of ponderosa pines. The subalpine ecosystem, which is found from 9,000 to 11,500 feet, straddles the tree line and supports forests of Engelmann spruce and subalpine fir along with a plethora of wildflowers. Finally, the alpine tundra—over 11,500 feet—features arctic temperatures, nasty winds, and barren stretches. Trees vanish and a meadowland of flowering grasses, mosses, and lichens appears briefly in the summer then changes color with the onset of autumn.

FLORA AND FAUNA The park's ecosystems hold great variety: 66 species of mammal, 260 species of bird, and 900 species of plant. Montane vegetation includes ponderosa pine in the drier regions and Douglas fir on the damp north slopes; willow and birch thrive in meadows fed by underground streams. Wildflowers, including the wood-lily and the yellow lady's slipper orchid, are found here.

The subalpine ecosystem supports lodgepole pine, Engelmann spruce, aspen, huckleberry, and subalpine fir. Some of these trees have been sculpted into bizarre shapes by the wind. Stunted trunks and branches, known as krummholz trees, live in this zone, often surviving for several centuries. A member of the orchid family called fairy slipper grows in the lower range of this area.

The plants that can survive at the elevation of the alpine tundra are few. They generally resemble mossy clumps with long roots, although a few startlingly beautiful wildflowers such as alpine avens, dwarf clover, and the alpine forget-me-not bloom briefly in late June or early July.

Birds and animals add color to Rocky's land, trees, and sky. The broad-tailed and the rufous hummingbirds are summer favorites at the park, along with woodpeckers, peregrine falcons, mountain and Steller's jays, mountain bluebirds, and Clark's nutcracker. The white-tailed ptarmigan—utterly white in its winter plumage—spends the cold months on the alpine tundra. Park authorities ask that visitors not feed any animals; abundant forage grows in the park throughout the year. Rangers will tell you about the best sites for bird-watching.

In the early part of the century black bears were few in number in the park, and today they hide in the backcountry, rarely spotted by hikers. Mountain lions and bobcats are, likewise, seldom seen. Bighorn sheep, however, are a more common sight, especially along Big Thompson Canyon in Horseshoe Park, near the Fall River Entrance Station. If you're lucky, you might spot moose in the willows of the Kawuneeche Valley, but you're more likely to see mule deer wandering along the main roads of the park, and you can often hear the soulful sound of coyotes baying at the moon at night. In autumn, herds of American elk (or wapiti, as the Shawnee people called them) roam down to lower elevations and are frequently visible near the park's eastern entrance during early morning or evening hours. Beaver are present near ponds and streams, although they usually work after dark. Squirrels, chipmunks, and marmots are common, but beware: They sometimes carry such serious diseases as bubonic plague and rabies and should not be approached or fed.

WHEN TO GO Only in summer can you drive across 45-mile Trail Ridge Road, for many the highlight of a trip here. The road closes with the first heavy snowfall—typically around mid-October—and usually reopens by Memorial Day. The other great advantage of traveling to Rocky in the summertime is that the climate is tame, making it possible to hike through much more of the 265,726 acres. Moreover, summer activities far outnumber winter ones. In summer you'll find biking, fishing, backpacking, horseback riding, llama trekking, river floating, and a number of local celebrations and festivals in the Estes Park area. The only problem with summer touring are the people and their cars, trucks, and RVs. Some drives through Rocky remain crowded well into September and even later into the leaf-gazing season.

Although the higher elevations are somewhat inaccessible in winter, there are still many trails where snowfall is minimal, and many hikers choose to take advantage of the solitude of cold-weather hiking. You can also snowmobile on the roads (on the west side only), snowshoe, and cross-country ski in the park, but be prepared for fierce winds and icy conditions. If you're a beginner you may have some trouble, especially if you are not acclimated to the high elevations.

Always keep in mind that, due to the altitude and shape of the landscape, weather in the park, even in summer, can vary in a big way. On summer days, temperatures reach into the 70s or 80s but drop into the 40s at night. Fortunately, all of the drive-in campgrounds

are below 9,400 feet, and the weather there is usually better than at higher elevations. On Trail Ridge Road it can snow in July.

The year-round weather patterns look like this: January and February are the coldest months and may leave 25 inches of snow at Bear Lake or the Hidden Valley area. Temperatures run from 15°F to 45°F in the daytime and 20°F to -10°F at night. March and April bring moisture and high winds with temperatures of 30°F to 55°F in the daytime and 5°F to 30°F at night. In April, trails are still covered with snow, but by May, snow is rarely found at lower elevations even though it still falls in the high country; however, there are frequent short afternoon showers. Temperatures are 45°F to 70°F in the daytime and 20°F to 40°F at night. June is warmer and July checks in as the warmest month, with more late-day showers. The temperature may reach 85°F in the daytime and fall to as low as 35°F at night. The wettest time of the year is August, whose last days are marked by cold fronts. Mixed rain and snow fall in September, with temperatures rising to 75°F in the daytime and slipping to 30°F at night. October is colder and snowier, particularly on the west side, but November's snowfall is usually light, and skiing conditions are not yet satisfactory. December is also light on snow, but the month registers high winds and even colder temperatures, the average being anywhere between 20°F to 50°F in the daytime and 30°F to -5°F at night. In winter, be mindful that the wind-chill factor is severe at higher elevations. Beware: At any time the climate can suddenly turn harsh, and roads may become slick, snow-packed, icy, and potentially dangerous.

SEASONAL EVENTS **Summer:** The town of Grand Lake, located just outside the southwestern boundary of Rocky Mountain National Park, hosts a **fishing derby** in which tagged trout are caught from Grand Lake and the tags redeemed for local merchandise. Contact the Chamber of Commerce (tel. 303/627-3402) for details. **July 4:** The **Fourth of July Celebration** (tel. 303/586-4431) in Estes Park features fireworks, an outdoor barbecue, a John Philip Sousa concert at the

Stanley Hotel, and an Arabian horse show. **Mid-July: Rooftop Rodeo and Western Week** (tel. 303/586–6104) in Estes Park includes an arts-and-crafts fair, a parade, and a rodeo full of cowboys. Grand Lake has **Buffalo Barbeque Weekend** (tel. 303/627–3402) featuring a lighted boat parade on the lake, fireworks, another parade downtown, and barbecued buffalo. **Early August:** The **Lipton Cup Regatta** (tel. 303/627–3402) takes place on Grand Lake. The story goes that when the Grand Lake Yacht Club was founded in 1905, several of its members persuaded Sir Thomas Lipton, the English tea baron, to donate a trophy for their annual regatta. Thus, a mountain tradition was born. The solid sterling silver cup is now worth $500,000. **Mid-September:** Estes Park holds a **Scottish/Irish Highland Festival** (tel. 303/586–2132), a weekend affair alive with highland dancing, sheepdog contests, and bagpipe and drum-major competitions. Estes Park also holds an **arts-and-crafts festival** (tel. 800/443–7837) in Bond Park, one of the largest such juried shows in the state of Colorado.

More than 70 seminars, conducted by the **Rocky Mountain Nature Association** (*see* Publications, *above*), are held each summer, with topics ranging from "Rocky Mountain Bird-watching" to "Opaque Watercolor Technique" to "Introduction to Mushrooming." Hidden Valley Lodge, located 10 miles west of Estes Park along Trail Ridge Road, is the center of this activity on the park's east side. Seminars west of the Continental Divide are held at Camp Kawuneeche, 8 miles north of Grand Lake. College credit is given for most of the sessions, which can last anywhere from three to six days; tuition varies from $34 to $84.

WHAT TO PACK Two general rules are (1) never go into the park without provisions for cold and wet weather and (2) always take along a high-energy snack and water. Even in summertime, be prepared for wet chilly interludes. If you go camping, take rain gear, extra blankets, and a first-aid kit. Park rangers suggest wearing layered clothing, especially in the spring and fall. For serious hikes, sturdy boots with ankle supports are a must—

tennis shoes are not suitable. Finally, the park's air is thin and dry, and many people find it helpful to put cream or lotion on their skin. Sunglasses and sun block are de rigueur.

GENERAL STORES Within the park, there is only one snack bar and souvenir shop, the **Trail Ridge Store** (tel. 303/222–3097), and it's been around for 50-odd years. Located near the Alpine Visitor Center, the store stocks sweatshirts and jackets, postcards, and assorted crafts items, and offers light meals, including chili, burgers, soup, and sandwiches. Picnic supplies can be bought at the **Safeway** (tel. 303/586–4447) supermarket in Estes Park. For camping and outdoors supplies you can try **Colorado Wilderness Sports** (tel. 303/586–6548), **The Hiking Hut** (tel. 303/586–0708), or **Outdoor World** (tel. 303/586–2114), all in Estes Park.

ARRIVING AND DEPARTING **By Plane.** The nearest major airport is **Stapleton International** in Denver, 65 miles southeast of the park.

By Car and RV. The best way to reach the east side of the park by car or RV is on Highway 34 or 36. The 65-mile ride from Denver to Estes Park should take about 1¹/₂ hours. Inside the park, Highway 34 becomes the touted Trail Ridge Road, which carries you across the Continental Divide and into Grand Lake.

If you want to enter the park's western boundary at Grand Lake, count on a two-hour drive from Denver: Take I–70 west to Highway 40 and turn north. Just past Granby go north on Highway 34 toward the park. Although Grand Lake is about 85 miles northwest of Denver, this western route, through Winter Park, Granby, and Grand Lake, is the more scenic.

By Train. Amtrak (tel. 800/872–7245) trains from around the country arrive and depart from Union Station in Denver.

By Bus. Charles Limousine (Box 4373, Estes Park, CO 80517, tel. 303/586–5151) offers year-round van service between Denver and Estes Park. The 10- to 14-seat vans make six daily trips June through August, four trips daily in September, and three trips daily October through May. It's a 1½-hour ride, and tickets cost $42 round-trip, $24 one-way. The company also runs tours of the park (*see* Guided Tours, *below*).

EXPLORING

You can certainly get a good enough feeling for Rocky Mountain National Park when you explore it by car, bus, or bicycle, but if you really want to *experience* the park you are going to have to use your own two feet. Trails take off in every direction, and if you hike upcountry for an hour or two you can enjoy some quiet isolation, even during the summer season. Although backpacking is still popular in America, in the 1990s only half as many backpackers have been coming to Rocky annually as they did at the height of the craze, in the mid-1970s.

It will take longer to explore the park on foot, but the added time and effort are well worth it. Start on an easy trail, perhaps around Bear Lake, and let your body acclimate to the altitude for a day or two (people with heart ailments or respiratory problems need to be particularly aware of the effects of this elevation on the body). After several days, you'll be ready for a more strenuous trail. Within a week you'll know parts of Rocky well and feel stronger than when you arrived.

To help visitors get out on the trail faster—without the hassles of driving in traffic and finding a parking space—the park runs a free shuttle bus daily in summer from the Glacier Basin parking lot to Bear Lake. Buses leave every half-hour from 8 AM to 9:30 AM and approximately every 12 to 15 minutes between 9:30 and 5:30. After Labor Day to the end of September, the shuttle runs only on weekends.

THE BEST IN ONE DAY If you are just passing through the Colorado Rockies and don't have much time, don't resist the temptation to drop in at Rocky Mountain National Park. A single day here is sure to be memorable—enough time to make you want to come back.

Start your day from Estes Park, driving west on Highway 36 into Rocky and stopping for an hour at the visitor center. Watch the 22-minute film and peruse the exhibits to get acquainted with the park. You can also pick up a map and various informative booklets.

Passing through the Beaver Meadows Entrance Station, you must continue driving northwest on Highway 36, past the juncture with the Trail Ridge Road (bear right at the fork), until you reach Fall River Road. Turn left, and drive straight through, toward Endovalley, to Old Fall River Road, which begins where the paved road ends. This 9-mile gravel route, with plentiful switchbacks and a 10-mile-per-hour speed limit, runs one-way uphill to the Alpine Visitor Center, where you'll find the Trail Ridge Store, the park's only gift store and snack bar; if you didn't bring a picnic lunch, you would do well to grab a bit to eat. While you're here, attend one of the ranger-led programs at the center.

Afterward, take Trail Ridge Road back toward Estes Park, stopping at various overlooks along the way, until you get to Highway 36 (about 19½ miles from the Alpine Visitor Center), which you must take south to the 10-mile Bear Lake Road. Follow Bear Lake Road south, stopping at Sprague Lake to walk the ½-mile trail around it (*see* Nature Trails and Short Walks, *below*). Another 3 miles down the road will bring you to Bear Lake, where you can relax quietly by the water or stretch your legs on a stroll to Nymph Lake (*see* Nature Trails and Short Walks, *below*). At this point you'll be ready to head back to your camp or hotel.

ORIENTATION PROGRAMS If you enter the park from the east, through Estes Park on Highway 36, a stop at the Visitor Center/Park Headquarters will help you get acquainted with Rocky. The center has a relief model of the park and shows a 22-minute film. You can also pick up informational booklets and maps here. Entering from the west, through Grand Lake, you will find exhibits on hiking, wildlife, and history at the Kawuneeche Visitor Center. The same film is shown here, but you'll have to request a viewing. At the Al-

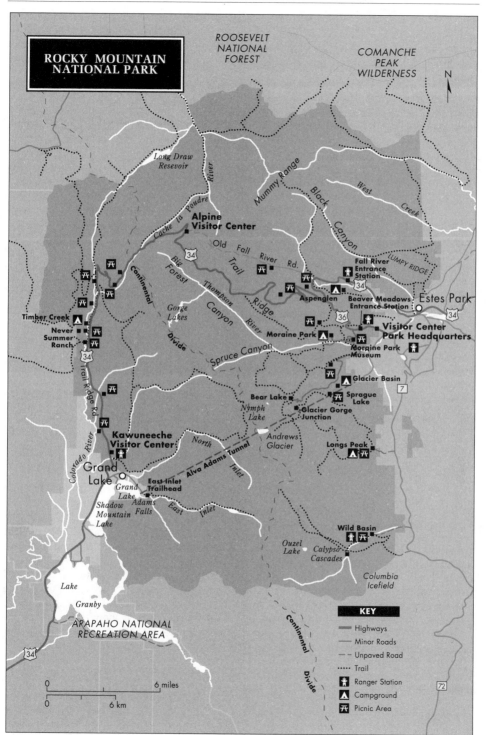

ROCKY MOUNTAIN NATIONAL PARK

ROOSEVELT
NATIONAL
FOREST

COMANCHE
PEAK
WILDERNESS

N

Long Draw
Resevoir

Cache la Poudre River

Mummy Range

Black Canyon

West Creek

LUMPY RIDGE

Alpine Visitor Center

Old Fall River Rd.

Big Forest

Trail Ridge

Thompson River

Fall River Entrance Station

Aspenglen

Beaver Meadows Entrance Station

Estes Park

Gorge Lakes

Spruce Canyon

Continental

Divide

Timber Creek

Never Summer Ranch

Moraine Park

Visitor Center Park Headquarters

Moraine Park Museum

Trail Ridge Rd.

Colorado River

Glacier Basin

Kawuneeche Visitor Center

North Inlet

Andrews Glacier

Bear Lake

Nymph Lake

Sprague Lake

Glacier Gorge Junction

7

Grand Lake

Grand Lake

Adams Falls

East Inlet

Alva Adams Tunnel

East Inlet Trailhead

Shadow Mountain Lake

Longs Peak

Ouzel Lake

Wild Basin

Calypso Cascades

Columbia Icefield

Lake Granby

ARAPAHO NATIONAL RECREATION AREA

Continental Divide

34

72

0 ————— 6 miles

0 ————— 6 km

KEY

— Highways

— Minor Roads

– – – Unpaved Road

· · · · Trail

🚹 Ranger Station

⛺ Campground

🍴 Picnic Area

pine Visitor Center, on Trail Ridge Road, you will learn about the ecology of the alpine tundra through exhibits on geology, harsh weather, and the adaptations of plants and animals.

GUIDED TOURS All-day outings in Rocky originating in Denver are offered year-round by **Scenic Mountain Tours** (2450 S. Spring-wood Court, Lafayette, CO 80026, tel. 303/665–7625). **Best Mountain Tours** (3003 S. Macon, Aurora, CO 80014, tel. 303/750–5200) runs a sightseeing-van service when at least four passengers sign up for its 15-seat loads. A 10-hour comprehensive trip through Rocky, starting in Denver, is available through **Gray Line Tours** (Box 17527, Denver, CO 80217, tel. 303/289–2841), in summer only. If you take a **Colorado Bug Tour** (3812 E. 17th Ave., No. 3, Denver, CO, 80206, tel. 303/399–6467) you'll ride in a classic car and munch on seasonal treats as you pass spec-tacular scenery. The driver is a former Colo-rado history teacher who narrates regular and customized tours year-round. **Charles Limousine** (Box 4373, Estes Park, CO 80517, tel. 303/586–5151) also runs year-round van tours in the park.

Don't miss the park's ranger-led walks and talks. More than 25 are given on both the east and west sides of the park, with topics cover-ing every aspect of local wildlife, geology, and vegetation. You can take a 1½-hour lake-shore stroll, for example, or a rigorous all-day hike to Lawn Lake covering about 12 miles round-trip. You can learn about everything from elk mating behavior to the lives of the early mountain men and women to things that go bump in the night. Some disabled-ac-cessible activities include simply meeting with a park ranger for a cup of coffee at 8 AM around a campfire: Satisfy your curiosity by unloading the myriad of questions you've accumulated about the fruits, flowers, ani-mals, and insects you've spied during your travels. Look for the program schedule in *High Country Headlines (see* Publications, *above).*

The visitor centers also provide guides for many of the park's most popular trails, rang-ing from easy ½-mile strolls to more invigo-rating nature walks above the tree line. The tundra walks are recommended but rigorous: Two to three hours of hiking at high altitudes is coupled with discussions of alpine plants, climate, and the process of adaptation to high elevations by living organisms.

SCENIC DRIVES AND VIEWS Since there are only two paved roads in the park, the options for driving are limited in number but spec-tacular in quality of view. In normal summer traffic 45-mile **Trail Ridge Road** is about a two-hour drive from the east side of the park to the west, but it's best to give yourself three to four hours to allow for leisurely stops at the numerous overlooks. From the road's top-most points you will get a glimpse of all 415 square miles of Rocky and discover arctic-like conditions in a world more than 11,000 feet above sea level. The road climbs gradu-ally, so its grade never exceeds 7%. Of the many turnoffs, don't miss Never Summer Ranch (tel. 303/627–3652), near the park's west boundary. This was a working ranch in the 1880s. From the road it's a short walk to the ranch, which has the only historic build-ings within the park. Free daily self-guided tours take place throughout the summer.

Ten-mile **Bear Lake Road** travels from High-way 36 to a high mountain basin very popular with tourists. The road dead-ends at Bear Lake and the Bear Lake Trailhead. Count on full parking lots between 10 and 3 in the summer. If you can't avoid traveling at those times, park your car at Glacier Basin and take the park's free summer shuttle bus to Bear Lake *(see* Exploring, *above).* Along Bear Lake Road, adjacent to the Moraine Park Museum, is the William Allen White Cabin, named after the famous Kansas journalist who wrote at Rocky in the summer. Visiting artists use the cabin in the warm months, so it's not open to the public. Schedule an hour for the full round-trip ride on Bear Lake Road.

The park's other driving option, **Old Fall River Road,** is 9 miles long. It's one-way and uphill, with a gravel surface and many switchbacks. The first road leading to the high country, it begins at the Endovalley picnic area and stays open from July to September, weather permitting. A multitude of visual pleasures unfold on its passage—see avalanche areas, waterfalls, flower-strewn meadows, alpine tundra, and wapiti.

NATURE TRAILS AND SHORT WALKS Starting at Bear Lake (9,475 feet), try the ¹/₂-mile one-way walk to **Nymph Lake,** an elevation gain of 225 feet. Another walk begins at the East Inlet Trailhead (8,391 feet) on the western boundary of the park; the ¹/₃-mile one-way trail climbs 79 feet in elevation to **Adams Falls,** an excellent spot for a picnic. The self-guided **Sprague Lake Nature Trail** begins at the Sprague Lake Picnic area and loops around the lake for about ¹/₂ mile. The trail is easily accessible to the disabled, and there are picnic tables, livery stables, and rest rooms at the trailhead. If you have an hour, the paved ¹/₂-mile one-way **Tundra Nature Trail** is a good bet. Signs along the way will teach you about the fragile ecosystem above the tree line. The trailhead is on Trail Ridge Road, about 4 miles south of the Alpine Visitor Center.

LONGER HIKES Follow Bear Lake Road for 1 mile, and, just past the Moraine Park Museum, turn right onto the spur road that leads to the **Cub Lake Trailhead.** The moderate 2¹/₃-mile one-way trek to Cub Lake climbs only 540 feet in elevation; it will take you about three hours to hike in and out. A moderately difficult hike with steep terrain and brilliant views of the Rockies is from the **Wild Basin Ranger Station** (8,500 feet), in the southeast corner of the park, to **Calypso Cascades.** It is 1³/₄ miles one-way and an elevation gain of 700 feet. A more strenuous trek, starting from the same point, is up to **Ouzel Lake,** a trip of 5 miles one-way and a gain of 1,510 feet in elevation. Another rigorous outing, where you can see firsthand how the park was carved by ice, is from **Glacier Gorge Junction** (9,240 feet), at the south end of Bear Lake Road, **to Andrews Glacier,** a 5-mile one-way journey and a gain of 2,460 feet in elevation.

The **Keyhole Route,** from Longs Peak Ranger Station, located 11 miles south of Estes Park off Highway 7, to Longs Peak (14,255 feet) requires ice axes and crampons for all but a few weeks (usually in August) of the year. The peak lies 8 miles from the trailhead, but, due to the difficulty of the last 2-mile leg of the trek, be advised that this is a 12- to 15-hour endeavor. The hale and hardy are advised to set off by 3 AM in order to approach the summit by noon and thereby escape afternoon lightning storms. Anyone who tackles this route should be in good condition and be able to maneuver ledges and steep ascents. Printed advice on what to expect on the climb is available at the ranger station and should be scrutinized before your trip.

OTHER ACTIVITIES **Back-Road Driving.** Vehicles are not allowed off-road anywhere in the park, but there are rugged routes in the surrounding national-forest lands. For information, call 303/887–3331.

Biking. There are no bike paths in the park, and bikes are not allowed on trails. Trail Ridge Road offers spectacular views but is too strenuous for the average person. Remember, although the grade of this road doesn't exceed 7%, it *begins* at an altitude most people will have trouble with, and going from east to west there's a 15-mile uphill stretch. At the top, you'll have to contend with winds that can reach 70 miles per hour. If you want to cycle, it's probably best to stay around the campgrounds. Rentals are available at **Colorado Bicycling Adventures** (tel. 303/586–4241).

Bird-Watching. The best time for bird-watching at Rocky is early in the morning, before the crowds arrive. Spring and summer are the best seasons. Lawn Lake, along the Roaring River, is an excellent place for viewing a variety of birds, including broad-tailed hummingbirds, hairy woodpeckers, robins, the occasional raptor, and ouzels, which frequent rapid streams and rivers. McGregor Ranch, along Black Canyon, and Adams Falls, due east of Grand Lake, are also prime spots for seeing wildfowl and flowers.

Boating and Rafting. No motorized boating is allowed inside the park. Nearly all of the lakes within Rocky are accessible only by hiking in, so you must carry your inflatable boat with you. For those willing to do this, **Sprague Lake** is an easy walk and a rewarding destination—it is directly accessed off Bear Lake Road and is equipped with a nature trail for the mobility-impaired. **Fan Lake,** though smaller (some will think too small), is also recommended for its easy access off Fall River Road. The park's rivers are generally too shallow for rafting.

The main location for water sports is not inside the park itself but at **Grand Lake** and in the **Arapaho National Recreation Area** (Sulphur Range District, Box 10, Hwy. 40, Granby, CO 80446, tel. 303/887–3331), which is just outside the southwest corner of the park.

Estes Park has Lake Estes, featuring a marina for those who want to rent a boat, but the action here is limited. This is primarily a "wakeless" body of water—waterskiing is permitted only on Tuesday and Thursday from 5 PM until dark. Call the marina at 303/586–2011.

If you're interested in rafting outside the park, **Rapid Transit Rafting** (Box 4095, Estes Park, CO 80517, tel. 303/586–8852 or 800/367–8523) of Grand Lake offers trips of moderate difficulty, good for the beginner. **Colorado Wilderness Sports** (358 E. Elkhorn Ave., Estes Park, CO 80517, tel. 303/586–6548) runs raft trips on the Cache la Poudre River, north of Estes Park, and other trips that last up to five days. Reservations are advised.

Fishing. Rocky is known as a wonderful setting in which to fish—home to brown, brook, rainbow, Colorado River cutthroat, and greenback cutthroat trout—but not the best place to catch something. Special regulations for fishing within Rocky Mountain National Park apply: Each person is allowed to have only one rod, and only artificial flies and lures are permitted, with exceptions made for children under 12. In some areas you are required to release the fish you have caught, and some waters are closed because native greenback cutthroat trout are being reintroduced in them. Rangers recommend the more remote backcountry lakes, since they are less rigidly regulated. If you fish, be patient and

enjoy the scenery. You'll need a Colorado fishing license, which costs from $5.25, for a one-day license, to $40.25, for a yearly non-resident license. These can be obtained at local sporting-goods stores.

Outside the park your chances are better. Lake Estes, on the east side of town, is frequently stocked with foot-long rainbow trout. The **Lake Estes Marina** (1170 E. Big Thompson Ave., tel. 303/586–2011) sells fishing licenses and tackle and rents boats. Head a few miles downstream from Lake Estes, and you'll discover fine fishing on the Big Thompson River. One hot spot, 8 miles from the lake, is called Grandpa's Retreat.

Known for its fishing, the town of Grand Lake boasts big brown trout, 20-pound Mackinaw, and kokanee salmon. In fact, between Grand Lake, Lake Granby, Shadow Mountain Lake, and the nearby Colorado River, an angler can stay pretty busy. Remember that rainbow and brown trout are more active in the spring and early summer, while kokanee bite later in the season. When the water freezes, think about trying your hand at ice fishing on Grand Lake or Shadow Mountain Lake.

Horseback Riding. Within the park, **High Country Stables** owns two operations. One is Glacier Creek Stables (tel. 303/586–3244), near Sprague Lake, and the other, Moraine Park Stables (tel. 303/586–2327), just beyond Moraine Park. Two-hour rides from these stables run about $25, but visitors are hardly confined to a single program. If you want to ride for as long as eight hours or even venture out on an overnight excursion, the choice is yours. Outside the park try one of two **Sombrero Stables** locations (Box 1735AC, Estes Park, CO 80517, tel. 303/586–4577, or 304 W. Portal Rd., Grand Lake, CO 80447, tel. 303/627–3514). Reservations are necessary for the four-hour and breakfast rides at Sombrero.

A special riding treat outside the park is llama trekking, which is offered by the **Keno Ranch** (Box 2385, Estes Park, CO 80517, tel. 303/586–2827 or 303/586–5994). The llamas carry all the food and supplies, while as many as 10 or 12 participants walk through mountainous areas about 4 miles outside of Estes

Park for a day-long adventure that includes a lunch cookout. Reservations are a good idea.

Rock Climbing. There are hundreds of classic climbs here for the novice or the hard-core technical rock-climber. **Longs Peak** and the 2-mile-long **Lumpy Ridge** provide every level of challenge, from basic to highly advanced. Many first-timers learn the art of technical climbing at Lumpy Ridge, 1½ miles north of Estes Park, although many routes there are closed from March to June because of nesting birds. Its rock outcroppings rise stalwartly behind the Stanley Hotel and can be seen from the town itself. If you're interested in a spectacular setting, sample **Petite Grepon,** an internationally famous spire that attracts groups from all over the world keen on a highly technical rock climb.

The **Colorado Mountain School** (Box 2062, 351 Moraine Ave., Estes Park, CO 80517, tel. 303/586–5758) holds classes for those who want to learn more about climbing before taking on the Rockies. They are the exclusive climbing concessionaires in the park and are an invaluable resource. Sixteen full-time guides work throughout the summer, leading everything from one-day introductory courses to day-long climbs to international expeditions. Equipment rentals and guided hikes are available. During the summer peak season, make reservations as far as six weeks in advance for climbs.

Ski Touring. On Rocky's east side the **Bear Lake Trailhead** is the point of departure for many winter activities. It is a fairly easy ½-mile one-way climb of several hundred feet to Nymph Lake. A half-mile beyond the west shore of Nymph Lake is Dream Lake, and 1 mile beyond that is Emerald Lake, but to reach these lakes you must be an experienced skier. These routes run through densely forested areas and offer breathtaking views of the high peaks. It's a one- to three-hour intermediate trek from Glacier Gorge Junction to Sprague Lake. The ski route follows the summer trail on the south side of Glacier Creek. All ski trails can be icy and windswept.

On the west side of the park is the **Tonahutu Creek Trail**—a gently sloping route that traverses broad expanses of meadowland. Leave your car at the Kawuneeche Visitor Center and ski east, away from the parking lot, then cruise the easy 2-mile trip down to Grand Lake. Warning: Skiers should beware of high winds and avalanches.

There are no ski rentals available within the park; however, **Never Summer Mountain Sports** (tel. 303/627–3642), in Grand Lake, rents backcountry skis for $12 per day. **Grand Lake Ski Shop** (tel. 303/627–8008) maintains groomed trails that you can use for a $6 trail fee ($2 for children under 16). The shop rents skis for use on its trails only; the cost is $8 for a half-day, $1 for children under 16.

Snowmobiling. Only on the west side of the park are you permitted to think snowmobile. When **Trail Ridge Road** is closed to other traffic, snowmobilers can leave from the Kawuneeche Visitor Center and use the first 15 miles of this road. Snowmobiling is also common on the streets of Grand Lake, and drivers have the same rights (and responsibilities) as vehicular traffic. For rental information, call the **Grand Lake Ski Shop** (*see above*).

Snowshoeing. The snowshoeing is good on any of the park's hiking trails, especially those around Bear Lake, off Old Fall River Road, and at Longs Peak. **Colorado Wilderness Sports** (358 E. Elkhorn Ave., Estes Park, tel. 303/586–6548) rents equipment for $10 per day, and the **Colorado Mountain School** (351 Moraine Ave., Estes Park, tel. 303/586–5758) charges $9 for one day or $7 per day for multiple days, but one of the best deals in town is found at the **YMCA** (just outside Estes Park, tel. 303/586–3341), which charges non-members $2 per day for a pass that lets you borrow snowshoes by putting down a $10 deposit (if you're a member, you don't even pay the $2).

Swimming. Within the park, streams and lakes are fed by melting snow and ice, and they stay cold. You can swim in Lake Estes, but be advised that it's a chilly dunk. You might spare yourself some agony by calling the **Lake Estes Marina** (tel. 303/586–2011) to rent a wet suit.

For those who prefer more civilized waters, the **YMCA** (tel. 303/586–3341) just outside of Estes Park has an indoor pool, as does the **Estes Park Aquatic Center** (660 Community Dr., tel. 303/586–2340), just south of Lake Estes.

CHILDREN'S PROGRAMS Children ages 6 to 12 will find many educational programs at Rocky, including puppet shows, bird walks, photo talks, and numerous safety seminars. Parents must accompany their children to these free gatherings.

One popular guided tour for children is titled "Beaver Tales." During the program called "A Child's View," children are encouraged to take part in hands-on projects that teach them the ways of the park ecosystem and how people affect it. Consult *High Country Headlines* for current listings (*see* Publications, *above*).

EVENING ACTIVITIES In the evening, from mid-June to Labor Day, nature programs are held at park headquarters, Aspenglen Campground, Glacier Basin Campground, Moraine Park Campground, and Timber Creek Campground. During the summer, evening slide shows and lectures take place at campgrounds throughout the park and at the visitor centers. Consult the free *High Country Headlines* (*see* Publications, *above*) for times and details. From September through May, programs are held at park headquarters on Saturday night only.

In Estes Park during the summer, all ages will enjoy the **Barleen Family Country Music Dinner Theatre** (tel. 303/586–5749) and the **Stanley Hotel Theatre/Fine Arts Series** (tel. 303/586–3371). There are a number of bars on Elkhorn Avenue that feature live music, including **Lonigan's** (110 W. Elkhorn Ave., tel. 303/586–4346). During the summer, the **Lazy B Ranch** (Dry Gulch Rd., tel. 303/586–5371 or 800/228–2116) hosts a chuck-wagon supper and Western show appropriate for the whole family.

Grand Lake has the rustic **Stagecoach Inn** (tel. 303/627–8079), with a dance floor and live country and western music on the weekends,

and **The Lariat Saloon** (tel. 303/627–9965), a watering hole for local cowbovs.

DINING

Inside the park there is only a lonely snack bar to feed the hungry hordes. But don't despair: Right outside the park, nearly 100 dining options in and around Estes Park and Grand Lake lay at your feet, with everything from Mexican to Cajun to French to Chinese fare. Many restaurants offer not only fine cuisine but also great views of Rocky. The majority of local cafés are modest, but the few that are a little pricey are worth it.

Dunraven Grille at the Stanley Hotel. When you enter the lobby of the Stanley Hotel, you feel as if you are attending a ball or coronation. Everything is fresh, white, and elegant. The space has retained its original turn-of-the-century fixtures, including glass-etched, globe chandeliers. The dimly lit, wood-paneled room features such specialties as grilled trout with wild rice, prime rib, and fillet of salmon and crab. Consider the Sunday champagne brunch at the McGregor Room—a local favorite served between 9 and 2. *333 Wonderview, Estes Park, tel. 303/586–3371. Reservations advised. Dress: casual but neat. AE, D, DC, MC, V. Moderate–Expensive.*

Corner Cupboard Inn. This historic landmark was built in Grand Lake in 1881, and its decor reflects its origins. Specialties of the house include Alaskan salmon steak and prime rib of beef, along with an overflowing salad bar. Ask for a look at the children's menu if the whole family comes along. If you're here to meet and mingle, wander into the adjoining Pub Room for some local nightlife. *1028 Grand Ave., Grand Lake, tel. 303/627–3813. Reservations advised. Dress: casual. MC, V. Moderate.*

Dunraven Inn. This is a favorite for both locals and out-of-towners. Homemade Italian cooking, a dark interior, and walls pasted with signed dollar bills from playful clientele entertain scads of repeat customers. The most popular dishes are lasagna, scampi, and veal parmigiana. In summertime the Dunraven is jammed, so be prepared for a wait. It's not so bad when you sit back and order a glass of wine from their large selection. *Hwy. 66, 4 mi southwest of Estes Park, tel. 303/586–6409. Reservations recommended. Dress: casual. DC, MC, V. No lunch. Moderate.*

Grand Lake Lodge Restaurant. Built circa 1925, this restaurant has very large, high, timber-vaulted ceilings, and boasts one specialty to please the eye rather than the palate: the view of Grand Lake. Other delights include the Sunday champagne brunch and numerous mesquite-grilled dishes. Between courses, the waiters and waitresses perform songs at your table. The restaurant serves breakfast, lunch, and dinner and has a children's menu. *Off Hwy. 34, 1/4 mi north of Grand Lake, tel. 303/627–3967. Reservations advised. Dress: casual. MC, V. Closed late Sept.–early June. Moderate.*

La Chaumière. This small French restaurant is located not in Estes Park but southeast of the town, a pretty drive down Highway 36 on a summer's evening. The exterior is rustic, with a setting that may seem unlikely for a fine dining experience, but the food is country French and a delight. The menu changes weekly but certain entrées are standard: poached salmon with herbed hollandaise, and sweetbreads with piñon nuts. *12 mi southeast of Estes Park on Hwy. 36, tel. 303/823–6521. Reservations advised. Dress: casual. AE, MC, V. Closed Mon. Moderate.*

Donuthaus. No trip to Rocky is complete without a stop at this small take-out donut shop. The coffee is hot, the price is right, and the sheer goodness and variety of donuts will cause you to loosen your everything-in-moderation standards, not to mention your belt. Try to leave room for the long johns and cake donuts. What's more, the atmosphere—it's downright neighborly—makes you feel as if you've lived in town for years. On the way out of Estes Park, head west on Highway 36 going toward the park. *Hwy. 36, tel. 303/586–2988. No reservations. Dress: casual. No credit cards. Closed Wed. Inexpensive.*

Johnson's Café. Estes Park is full of good breakfast spots, but Johnson's is unique. Lo-cated in a shopping-center complex a block from downtown, the restaurant has a simple and homey atmosphere. The service here is amiable, and, most important, the food is outstanding. "We don't use mixes," says owner Mary Johnson, who runs the café with her husband, Milt. Made-from-scratch best-sellers include Swedish pancakes, Milt's Wonderful Waffles, and Swedish potato pancakes. Lunch is of equally high caliber, especially some of the demonic desserts that ought to come with danger warnings: French Silk Pie, Mystery Pecan Pie, and Peanut Butter Fudge Pie. The kids' menu is handy for scaled-down portions. *Stanley Village Shopping Center, Estes Park, tel. 303/586–6624. No reservations. Dress: casual. No credit cards. Closed Sun. No dinner. Inexpensive.*

La Casa. This Mexican/Cajun restaurant on the main street of Estes Park has indoor dining as well as tables out back, where you can take in the sunshine, sip a margarita (they're on tap), and listen to a bubbling stream near the outdoor garden. The decor is south-of-the-border, and the menu is as interesting as it sounds—voodoo chicken, spicy blackened shrimp, and the specialty of the house, Estorito, a glorified Estes Park burrito with everything you can imagine on it. This place is laid back and casual, so don't dress up or call ahead. Live music is offered nightly. *222 E. Elkhorn Ave., Estes Park, tel. 303/586–2807. No reservations. Dress: casual. AE, D, DC, MC, V. Inexpensive.*

PICNIC SPOTS Most picnic areas within the park consist of widely spaced single tables and are not for large parties. One such spot, **Endovalley,** on the east side of Rocky, is found at the start of Old Fall River Road. The views here include beautiful Fan Lake, Fall River Pass, and aspen groves. Picnic tables, fire grates, and rest rooms allow comfortable outdoor eating. On the west side of the park, near the Continental Divide, is **Lake Irene**, which also has fire grates, tables, and rest-rooms.

LODGING

No hotels exist within Rocky Mountain National Park itself, but in the surrounding area you can check in at an expensive hotel, a bed-and-breakfast, a cabin, or a guest ranch. The **Estes Park Chamber of Commerce Lodging Referral Service** (tel. 303/586–4431 or 800/443–7837) has information on them all.

Riversong Bed and Breakfast. The living room of this romantic retreat holds an impressive library, where guests are known to settle down with a book by the fireplace and not emerge for hours. It's that relaxing. The bedrooms feature antique furniture and fireplaces, and some even have a big sunken bathtub. The showpiece is Cowboy's Delight: a large room with a queen-size four-poster bed and wood-burning stove located in the Carriage House. A fishing stream and private hiking trails run through the spacious grounds. Join a staff member on one of the property's guided tours. *Box 1910, Estes Park, CO 80517, tel. 303/586–4666. 7 rooms. Facilities: fishing stream, hiking trails. MC, V. Expensive.*

Stanley Hotel. The Stanley Hotel was built in 1909 by F. O. Stanley, who invented the Stanley Steamer automobile. It was built to compete with other hotels of its size throughout the world, and it is now on the National Register of Historic Places. Although somewhat frayed around the edges, the hotel has a history, and its elegance has been maintained with dignity and style. The white-painted wood exterior is complemented by exquisite public rooms. The guest rooms vary. Some are beautifully furnished with antiques; others are rather shabby, with worn carpeting and furniture that can only be characterized as old. Some rooms have modern, renovated bathrooms; others still have claw-foot tubs (but are available at reduced rates). There are brass beds and four-poster beds with lace canopies. Two suites have nonworking fireplaces. The views from the corner rooms make them some of the best. In addition to fine cuisine in the Dunraven Grille (*see* Dining, *above*), the hotel offers theater and concerts. Summer reservations must be made at least two months in advance. *333 Wonderview, Box 1767, Estes Park, CO 80517, tel. 303/586–3371 or 800/762–5437, fax 303/586–3673. 92 rooms. Facilities: restaurant, heated pool with Jacuzzi, conference facilities; golf courses, hiking trails, and stables nearby. AE, D, MC, V. Expensive.*

Hi Country Haus. This condominium is located in the town of Winter Park, about two hours from Estes Park if you drive through Rocky over Trail Ridge Road. It offers luxury studio rooms, plus one-, two-, and three-bedroom condos with linens, fireplace, and a complete kitchen. You'll find whirlpools, a swimming pool, a sauna, and a stocked trout pond on the property complex. During the cold months, Winter Park is one of Colorado's favorite ski resorts; summer highlights include rafting, alpine sliding, rodeos, golf, tennis, and a jazz festival. *Box 3095EP, Winter Park, CO 80482, tel. 303/726–9421 or 800/228–1025. 195 condominiums. Facilities: whirlpools, swimming pool, sauna, trout-stocked pond. AE, D, MC, V. Moderate–Expensive.*

Wind River Ranch. This is a taste of the Old West, a ranch suitably graced with collections of antiques and Native American artifacts. Occupying 112 acres outside Estes Park, Wind River offers views of Longs Peak and Mt. Meeker. The cabins are rustic, but the heated swimming pool is thoroughly modern. On-the-ranch activities include hiking, horseback riding, spa treatments, children's programs, movies, and bingo, as well as fishing in a pond stocked with trout. On top of that, meals (buffets, steak dinners, and pastries) are included in the rates. No pets are allowed, however, and a three-day minimum stay is requested. Drive 7¼ miles south of Estes Park on Highway 7 to reach this tasteful retreat. *Box 3410AC, Estes Park, CO 80517, tel. 303/586–4212 or 800/523–4212. 10 cabins, 4 rooms in ranch house. Facilities: restaurant, spa, stocked pond, pool. D, MC, V. Closed Labor Day–May. Moderate–Expensive.*

Aspen Lodge. The "ultimate family resort" has your pick of family-reunion packages. The lobby, made of log and stone and featuring a vast fireplace, sets the tone for this Western-style guest ranch located 8 miles south of Estes Park. You can choose between a room in the main lodge or a cabin. During summer, meals are included in the cost of a room, and there's a two-night minimum stay on weekends. *6120 Hwy. 7, Estes Park, CO 80517, tel. 303/586–8133 or 800/332–6867. 36 rooms and 20 cabins. Facilities: tennis, horseback riding, sauna, hot tub, outdoor pool, fishing, racquetball, volleyball, hay rides, private cross-country skiing, sleigh rides, snowmobiling, ice skating, tobogganing. D, DC, MC, V. Moderate.*

Grand Lake Lodge. Built of lodgepole pine in 1920, this accommodation is known as "Colorado's favorite front porch." With both Grand and Shadow Mountain lakes below, the lodge is a gathering place for guests who wish to observe the calming vista at their leisure or who amble over to the in-house restaurant (*see* Dining, *above*) for breakfast. For those who crave peace and quiet, two-unit cabins (with bath) grant secluded sanctuary in the hills, away from the summer crowds. The entrance to the lodge is ¹/₄ mile north of the Grand Lake turnoff on Highway 34. *Box 569, Grand Lake, CO 80447, tel. 303/627–3967 (summer) or 4155 E. Jewel, Suite 104, Denver, CO 80222, tel. 303/759–5848 (off-season). 66 units. Facilities: restaurant, heated pool, horses, playground, recreation room, gift shop. AE, D, MC, V. Closed mid-Sept.–early June. Moderate.*

Lemmon Lodge. Located on the banks of Grand Lake, this hideaway has 22 cabins that are usually booked at least a year in advance. Each one is distinctive, and all but one have kitchens. The lodge offers seclusion, a sandy beach, and a private dock for those who bring along a boat. During the summer, a minimum stay of four days is required. *Box 514, Grand Lake, CO 80447, tel. 303/627-3314 (summer) or 303/725-3511 (winter). 22 cabins. Facilities: private beach, and dock. MC, V. Closed mid-Sept.–late May. Moderate.*

Telemark Resort. At night, as you lie in bed in your cabin, you can hear the Big Thompson River rushing down from the mountains. Deer graze nearby. In summer, guests can let their children loose to enjoy the grounds-picnic tables, horseshoe pits, and a play area for youngsters allow young and old to relax and take pleasure in their surroundings. Trout fishing in the river is an option. In winter, the Telemark caters primarily to skiers. Some of the cabins have color TV, fireplaces, and screened porches. Located just outside Estes Park, Telemark can be found on Highway 36 as you drive west toward Rocky. *Box 100AC, Estes Park, CO 80517, tel. 303/586-4343 or 800/669-0650. 26 cottages. Facilities: picnic areas, fire grates, children's play area. AE, MC, V. Moderate.*

Estes Park Center/YMCA of the Rockies. This is not exactly a typical Y. Many people consider it the ideal resort for those traveling with children. Throughout the summer, lots of activities are planned for the kids—horseback riding and hayrides, basketball and tennis, roller-skating and swimming. In wintertime, the Y offers cross-country skiing on adjacent park acreage, plus ice-skating and snowshoeing. Equipment can be rented on the premises. The 860-acre resort has 200 cabins, a restaurant, a library, a grocery store, and a museum. Cabins feature fireplaces, full bedrooms, and kitchens. Large groups and conferences are welcome. The Y is 3 miles west of Estes Park. *Estes Park Center/YMCA, 2515 Tunnel Rd., Estes Park, CO 80511–2550, tel. 303/586-3341 or 303/623-9215. 200 cabins with bath. Facilities: restaurant, library, grocery store, museum. No credit cards. Inexpensive–Moderate.*

CAMPING

There are five designated drive-in campgrounds at Rocky Mountain National Park and numerous opportunities for backcountry camping. In addition, visitors can choose from the many sites in the Arapaho National Recreation Area, near Grand Lake; in the surrounding Arapaho National Forest; and in private campgrounds in Estes Park.

ROCKY MOUNTAIN CAMPGROUNDS

	INSIDE THE PARK					NEAR THE PARK				
	Moraine Park	Glacier Basin	Longs Peak	Timber Creek	Aspenglen	Arapaho National Recreation Area	Arapaho National Forest	Estes Park Campground	KOA	Spruce Lake RV Park
Total number of sites	247	150	26	100	54	439	93	62	90	110
Sites suitable for RVs	91	70	0	70	NA	200	93	12	70	110
Number of hookups	0	0	0	0		0	0	0	70	110
Drive to sites	•	•	•	•	•	•	•	•	•	•
Hike to sites			•							
Flush toilets	•	•		•	•	•		•	•	•
Pit/chemical toilets			•	•		•	•			
Drinking water	•*	•*	•*	•*	•*	•	•*	•	•	•
Showers								•	•	•
Fire grates	•	•	•	•	•	•	•	•	•	
Swimming										•
Boat access						•				
Playground								•	•	•
Disposal station	•	•		•		•			•	•
Ranger station	•	•	•	•	•	•				
Public telephone	•	•	•	•		•		•	•	•
Reservation possible	•	•				•		•	•	•
Daily fee per site	$10**	$10**	$7**	$7**	$7	$7–$9	$7	$14	$13–$16	$15–$23
Dates open	year-round	late May–Labor Day	year-round	year-round	late May–late Sept.	Memorial Day–Labor Day	year-round	Apr.–Nov.	year-round

*In summer only. **Fee charged only when water is available.

INSIDE THE PARK Three of the drive-in campgrounds at Rocky (Timber Creek, Aspenglen, and Longs Peak) assign sites on a first-come, first-served basis; at the other two (Moraine Park and Glacier Basin) reservations are required from late May through the first week in September and can be made through Mistix (tel. 800/365–2267). It costs $7 or $10 per night for individual sites, as long as the water is turned on (it is shut off around October 1 at most campgrounds). When there is no water, there is no camping fee. The 14 group sites at Glacier Basin each cost $20 to $50 per night and can accommodate 10 to 50 people, depending on the site. From June through September, camping within the park is limited to seven days, three days at Longs Peak. During the summer, most campgrounds offer nightly campfire programs.

RVs are welcome at all campgrounds except Longs Peak. RV spaces are standard width and 30 feet long, and most of the RV sites in the park are paved. There are no hookups or showers in the park. Disposal stations are located at Moraine Park, Glacier Basin, and Timber Creek.

Closest to Estes Park, 1 mile down Bear Lake Road, on the Cub Lake Trailhead turnoff, is **Moraine Park Campground,** which is open year-round. This campground has 247 sites, with flush and pit toilets, drinking water in summer, fire grates, a ranger station, and a public phone. This is the most open campground setting, in a ponderosa-pine woodland on a bluff overlooking the Big Thompson River and Moraine Park.

If you drive 3 miles farther down Bear Lake Road, you will reach the 150-site **Glacier Basin Campground,** which closes from Labor Day to the end of May. Here you'll find flush toilets, drinking water in summer, fire grates, a ranger station, and a public phone. The campground is located near Sprague Lake and is 300 feet higher in elevation than Moraine Park Campground. It is in a denser, lodgepole-pine forest and has a vista that includes the Continental Divide and three glaciers.

The 26-site **Longs Peak Campground** is about 10 miles from Estes Park, off Highway 7, and a long way from Trail Ridge Road. It is open year-round, but RVs are not allowed here—a rule that contributes to the campground's sense of quiet and isolation. Facilities include flush and pit toilets, drinking water in summer, fire grates, and a ranger station.

Also open year-round is the **Timber Creek Campground,** which is located off Trail Ridge Road, 8 miles inside the west entrance of the park, just north of Never Summer Ranch. This 100-site campground has flush and pit toilets, drinking water in summer, fire grates, a ranger station, and a public phone. It is beside the Colorado River, which makes it an angler's paradise.

The small, 54-site **Aspenglen Campground** is closed from late September to late May. Set in open pine woodland by Fall River, it does not have the views of Moraine Park or Glacier Basin, but it is the first campground to fill up on the east side of the park in summer. Just 1/2 mile into the park and 5 miles from Estes Park, off Highway 34, Aspenglen has some excellent walk-in sites for those who want to pitch a tent away from the crowds but still close to the car. There are flush toilets, drinking water in summer, fire grates, a ranger station, and a public phone.

In order to camp in the **Rocky Mountain backcountry,** you must obtain a free backcountry permit from park headquarters, the West Unit Office, or a ranger station. Call ahead (tel. 303/586–4459) to get your permit in advance, or pick one up when you arrive.

There are designated campsites with fire rings even in the backcountry but very few of them. If you want still-more-primitive conditions, ask the rangers about camping in cross-country zones, which are farther back into the wilderness and have no designated sites. Be aware that special regulations apply to cross-country zones; the rangers will tell you what you need to know. At any backcountry campsite, you should follow basic camping rules: bury human waste, do not dump soapy water or food scraps into streams and lakes, and carry out any garbage you may accumulate.

Wood fires are restricted to specific areas; you are encouraged to use a portable stove. Remember, pets are not allowed in the backcountry—it is dangerous for them, for you, and for the wildlife.

NEAR THE PARK There are many campgrounds and backcountry sites in the area surrounding Rocky Mountain National Park. Call the **Arapaho National Recreation Area** (tel. 303/887–3331) and the **Arapaho National Forest** (tel. 303/887–3331) to find out about public facilities. Among the numerous privately owned campgrounds are: **Estes Park Campground** (tel. 303/586–4188), **KOA** (tel. 303/586–2888), and **Spruce Lake RV Park** (tel. 303/586–2889), which is one of the few private campgrounds to stay open year-round.

Sequoia and Kings Canyon National Parks

California

By Matt Peters

Updated by Mimi Kmet

Famed naturalist John Muir once wrote: "Climb the mountains and get their good tidings. Nature's peace will flow into you as sunshine flows into trees. The winds will blow their own freshness into you, and the storms their energy, while cares will drop off like autumn leaves."

Contemporary visitors to Sequoia and Kings Canyon National Parks can hear the mountains' inspirational greetings. And they can walk, as Muir did, awestruck among the silent giants, marveling at the deep granite canyons and the snowcapped peaks.

The two parks share a boundary and are administered as one park. They now encompass more than 1,300 square miles that are rivaled only by Yosemite National Park, to the north, in terms of rugged Sierra beauty. The topography runs from foothill chaparral, at an elevation of 1,500 feet, in the west, to the Giant Sequoia belt at 5,000 to 7,000 feet, to the towering peaks of the Great Western Divide and the Sierra Crest; 14,494-foot Mt. Whitney, the highest point in the contiguous United States, is the crown jewel of the east side.

Many of the major attractions in both parks can be reached by automobile, but the majority of acreage is without roads. If you expect to simply drive through, you may be disappointed: The panoramic views and striking geological features found in other national parks exist here, but they are less accessible. If you want to explore these parks, you will have to hike. And you'll have more than 700 miles of trails from which to choose.

Today 2 million people visit the parks annually. They come to while away peaceful hours on uncrowded trails through meadows and conifer groves, or to head into the rugged grandeur of the backcountry. But there was a time, beginning in the 1860s, when people came to these timberlands to cut trees, and in some places the scars are still evident. By 1890, however, the area's beauty was officially recognized, as was its value as a watershed, and the destruction was put in check by the establishment of a 50,000-acre Sequoia National Park, the country's second national park. This was followed by the designation of the tiny 2,560-acre General Grant National Park a week later. At this time, additional acreage was granted to Sequoia; although this nearly tripled its size, Sequoia remained small by national park standards. Years of prodding by environmentally minded people resulted in further growth of Sequoia. It wasn't until 1940 that the General Grant Park was expanded to include the high country around the South Fork Kings River and renamed Kings Canyon National Park, and it wasn't until 1965 that Cedar Grove and Tehipite Valley were protected within the Kings Canyon domain.

ESSENTIAL INFORMATION

VISITOR INFORMATION Information about the two parks is available by contacting the Superintendent, **Sequoia and Kings Canyon National Parks,** Three Rivers, CA 93271, tel. 209/565–3341 (listen to the recorded message and stay on the line for additional park information). **Guest Services,** the concessionaire that manages accommodations in the parks, can be reached at 209/561–3381, or by fax at 209/561–3135. Call 209/565–3351 for a recorded message, updated about 9 AM daily, that relates road and weather information 24 hours a day.

Free wilderness permits are required for all overnight trips into the backcountry (tel. 209/565–3708). Reservations are accepted only by mail, beginning with March 1 postmarks. You have the best chance of getting a permit on the dates you request if you choose to travel on weekdays rather than weekends; also avoid holidays. Without a reservation, you may still get a permit, but arrive early: They are distributed on a first-come, first-served basis. If you plan to travel with horses, burros, or llamas, find out in advance about the regulations for trails and forage areas.

FEES The $5 per vehicle fee allows you to enter both parks for one week; those on foot, bicycle, bus, or other form of transportation pay $3 for a pass that is good for seven days. U.S. citizens who are 62 or older and those U.S. citizens who are permanently disabled can enter free with proper identification. An annual pass to the two parks is $15 for the calendar year.

PUBLICATIONS The **Sequoia Natural History Association** (Ash Mountain, Box 10, Three Rivers, CA 93271, tel. 209/565–3758) will send you a brochure listing the numerous maps, books, pamphlets, and video- and audiocassettes that it sells. Among the best offerings are the *Sequoia and Kings Canyon Official National Park Handbook.* The 212-page book includes numerous color photos and discusses how to get around the parks, the area's climate, plant and animal adaptations, the sequoias and their relationship with fire, how man has endangered the park, and the park today. One section is devoted to the high country. *Wildflowers of Sequoia–Kings Canyon National Parks* divides the parks' flowers by color to help neophyte botanists in identifying species. It has 48 pages with 90 color photos, covering wildflowers from the foothills to the high country. With 229 pages and many color plates, *Discovering Sierra Birds,* by Edward Beedy and Stephen Granholm, can help both novice and expert birders to learn more about the parks' winged creatures. A picture book that might do well on your coffee table is *Sequoia Yesterdays,* which features black-and-white historical photographs chronicling the parks from 1890 to the present. It documents the power of the timber industry, congressional acts, the Sierra Club's work at the parks, and the early park service years. Not for the casual reader is *Challenge of the Big Trees,* Larry Dilsaver and William Tweed's 379-page history of the parks, covering the natural world, Native Americans, explorers and exploiters, the forests, and the selling of the sequoias. A topographic map of Sequoia and Kings Canyon, printed on tear-proof, waterproof fabric, is a fine companion for all hikers.

GEOLOGY AND TERRAIN About 225 million years ago, this area of California was at the ocean's edge and the meeting point of two tectonic plates: The heavier plate formed an ocean basin, and the lighter plate was that of the North American Continent. These two plates collided, and slowly the heavier one slipped beneath the continent, a process called subduction. This collision created heat and pressure that eventually melted the lower rocks and pushed them toward the surface. A string of volcanoes venting magma formed along the coast, and the eruptions left beds of sediment, both marine and terrestrial, that in turn were covered and cracked by subsequent eruptions.

Much of the magma, however, never made it to the surface. Instead, it began to cool and harden, and after tens of millions of years masses of this igneous material accumulated on the edge of the continental plate. The angle of collision between the two plates changed, and the line of igneous rock moved to the east. This igneous, or "fire-caused," rock is the granitic rock at the surface of today's Sierra.

Eighty million years ago this granite was mostly covered by sedimentary and metamorphic rock. But when the forces pushing the two plates together shifted, about 25 million years ago, and continental stretching and uplift began, the once-molten rock began to move toward the surface. The overlying layers of rock weathered away and exposed the granite. For 10 million years now the granite rock that forms the Sierra Nevada has been rising.

The two parks are comprised of more than 860,000 acres on the western flank of the Sierra and can be divided into three distinct zones cut by stream and river canyons. In the west are the lower elevation foothills—rolling hills covered with shrubby chaparral vegetation or golden grasslands dotted with oaks. At the middle elevation, from about 5,000 feet to 9,000 feet, there are rock formations mixed with meadows and huge stands of conifers. The Giant Sequoia belt is here. The high alpine section of the parks is extremely rugged, a land of harsh rock forma-

tions in a string of peaks reaching above 13,000 feet and towered over by Mt. Whitney.

To the north, the Kings River cuts a swath through the backcountry and over the years has formed a granite canyon that, at places, towers nearly 4,000 vertical feet above the canyon floor. From Junction Overlook, located on the drive to Cedar Grove, visitors can observe the drop from 10,051-foot Spanish Mountain to the Kings River, a distance of 8,200 feet. Spanish Mountain sits approximately 2½ miles north of the river. The confluence of the Middle and South Forks of the Kings River also can be seen from the overlook.

FLORA AND FAUNA As the elevation of these parks changes, so do the wildlife and plants that inhabit the different ecological zones. Spring usually arrives in the foothills in early March, its telltale signs moving like a shadow of light up the Sierra's side, so that by mid-July the wildflowers blossom in the higher elevations.

The gently rolling foothills, ranging in elevation from 1,500 feet to 4,500 feet, are primarily oak woodland and chaparral, where you will find chamise and the red-barked manzanita. An occasional yucca plant, a veritable vegetative porcupine, is also found here. The amount of groundwater determines the density of the oak groves, which, in early spring, are carpeted with knee-high grass. Fields of white popcorn flower also cover hillsides, and the yellow fiddleneck appears. As summer enters, the intense heat and absence of rain cause the hills to turn brown. Small creatures stalk these lands, including the bushy-tailed California ground squirrel, which scours the countryside for berries, acorns, and grasses. Coyotes, skunks, and gray fox are also present, as is the noisy and sassy scrub jay, a blue and gray bird that seems to delight in scolding anyone who crosses its path.

It is the parks' mid-zone forests, home to the sequoias, that draw the crowds. But in addition to these giant trees, there are such evergreens as red and white fir, western juniper, incense-cedar, and the pines—Jeffrey, lodgepole, sugar, and ponderosa. Wildflowers include the yellow blazing star and the red Indian paintbrush. Here there are golden-mantled ground squirrels, Steller's jays, chipmunks, gray squirrels, mule deer, and, of course, black bears. One of the most obvious inhabitants is the Douglas squirrel, or chickaree, who spends most of his days policing his territory in noisy fashion, all the while clipping cones from the tops of the firs, pines, and sequoias.

The high country, with its fierce weather and scarcity of soil, is sparsely vegetated. Foxtail and whitebark pines have gnarled and twisted trunks, the result of years of high wind, heavy snowfall, and freezing temperatures. Life is smaller here than at lower elevations, and in summer, you will see yellow-bellied marmots, pikas, weasels, mountain chickadees, and Clark's nutcrackers. Leopard lilies and shooting stars grow near streams and meadows.

WHEN TO GO During the summer months, daytime highs usually run in the 70s in the middle elevations, where the parks' most popular attractions are located. Overnight lows average 50°F. The lower elevations often experience temperatures above 100°F, with overnight lows averaging in the mid 60s. Visitors should bear in mind that summer thundershowers are not uncommon, and that the weather can change quickly in the mountains.

In winter, mid-elevation temperatures usually range from the low 20s to mid-40s, with overnight lows down into single digits, and low-hanging clouds can move in and obscure the countryside for days. Most of the 40 to 50 inches of precipitation this elevation receives falls during the winter, which means that much of the area is covered deep in snow from December to May. Highway 198 to Giant Forest and Highway 180 to Grant Grove are open year-round but are subject to closures or chain restrictions due to snowfall. The Generals Highway, which connects the two areas, is usually open year-round, but it, too, is often closed in winter.

The best times to visit the parks are during late spring and early fall, when the temperatures are still moderate and the crowds thin. The parks draw their heaviest crowds during the month of August and over holiday weekends. Summer visitors should remember that they will be approaching the parks from the west, across the San Joaquin Valley, where temperatures often exceed 100°F from late May through early September. From November through April lodging rates within the park are reduced by more than 20%.

SEASONAL EVENTS **April:** The **Jazzaffair,** held in the town of Three Rivers, is a festival of mostly swing jazz held at several locations, with shuttle buses between sites. **Early May:** The **Redbud Festival,** in Three Rivers, is a two-day arts and crafts festival; the **Woodlake Rodeo,** in Woodlake, is a weekend event that draws large crowds. **Early December: Carolers** gather at the base of the General Grant tree, the nation's official Christmas tree. (For more information on these and other events, contact the **Visalia Chamber of Commerce,** tel. 209/734–5876.)

WHAT TO PACK Because summer nights and early mornings are cool, it is best to wear layered clothing. A warm jacket and long pants are essential, and a waterproof hat and coat are recommended any time of the year. In winter, pack long underwear, gloves, wool socks, and a heavy jacket. Hikers will need sturdy shoes, and waterproof boots are advisable in winter. The sun's rays are intense, so sunscreen and sunglasses are a must. Motoring tourists should bring tire chains in anticipation of snow, which may be encountered at any time between fall and spring. Formal attire is not required at any of the restaurants within the parks.

GENERAL STORES Small stores carrying most essential items and foods are located in the lodging centers at **Giant Forest, Grant Grove, Cedar Grove,** and **Stony Creek.** There is also a store in the **Lodgepole** area. In summer the stores are open 8 AM to 9 PM. Winter hours are 8 to 7. The stores at Lodgepole, Cedar Grove, and Stony Creek are closed in winter. Specific information about the stores is available by contacting **Guest Services** (Box 789, Three Rivers, CA 93271). All stores may be reached by calling 209/565–3381.

ARRIVING AND DEPARTING There is no public transportation to the parks, and public tours are limited (see Guided Tours, below), so you will probably be driving. San Francisco is 280 miles from the parks, a drive that will take you six hours; Los Angeles is 240 miles and five hours away. Fresno, the largest city near the parks, is 55 miles from Grant Grove; Visalia, 35 miles away from the southern entrance of the parks on Highway 198, is also used as a base for exploring the area. Many people stay in Three Rivers, just outside Sequoia, on Highway 198. Other National Park Service areas that are fairly close by western standards are Death Valley, an eight-hour, 345-mile haul, and Yosemite, a five-hour, 185-mile drive.

By Plane. Sequoia and Kings Canyon National Parks are serviced by the **Fresno Airport** (tel. 209/498–4700), located 5 miles from downtown Fresno and 55 miles from the parks. At the **Visalia Airport** (tel. 209/738–3201) commercial passengers may arrive on **American Eagle** (tel. 800/433–7300), which makes connections with Los Angeles and San Jose airports. Rental car companies at the Visalia airport are **Budget** (tel. 209/625–5446) and **Hertz** (tel. 209/651–1300). The larger hotels in Fresno provide free airport shuttles, but both **Budget** (tel. 209/251–5616) and **Hertz** (tel. 209/251–5055) offer rentals at the airport.

By Car and RV. Only two roads lead into the parks, and both approach from the west: Highway 180 from Fresno passes through the peninsulalike Grant Grove in the southwestern section of Kings Canyon National Park, travels north then east through the national forest, reenters the park as the Kings Canyon Highway, then dead-ends in Cedar Grove; it takes about two hours to make the round-trip drive from Grant Grove. Highway 198 travels 36 miles from Visalia, entering Sequoia National Park from the southwest at Ash Mountain. The road turns into the Generals Highway, a winding 56-mile road that con-

nects with Highway 180, thus linking the two parks. No roads enter the parks from the east, but there are three spur roads off U.S. 395 that come within 3 to 5 miles of the east boundary. These head west from Lone Pine, in the south; Independence, near the middle; and Big Pine, in the north. Highway 168, which stems off U.S. 395 at Bishop, travels 19 miles south to the lakes just north of Kings Canyon's northernmost boundary. All of these spur roads have campgrounds.

If you are traveling in an RV or with a trailer, study a map of the park and the restrictions on these vehicles. Between Potwisha Campground and Giant Forest on the Generals Highway, the advised length limit for trailers is 22 feet, and 35 feet is the absolute maximum limit for trailers; single vehicles may not exceed 40 feet; combination vehicles may not exceed 50 feet. The width limit is 8 feet. Large RVs and autos pulling trailers are advised to use Highway 180 from Fresno to the park, a straighter, easier route than Highway 198. From Highway 198 to Giant Forest, the Generals Highway is extremely narrow and climbs 5,000 feet in 17 miles. From June 15 to September 15, trailers longer than 15 feet should not go beyond Potwisha Campground between 9 AM and 5 PM on weekends and holidays. Steep grades (5%–8%) and heavy traffic may cause vehicles to overheat; overheated brakes are common. The National Park Service is in the midst of a long-term road-improvement program, and motorists are likely to encounter sporadic delays over the next several years.

By Train. Amtrak (tel. 800/872–7245) has stations in Fresno and Hanford, which is located 15 miles from Visalia. A shuttle bus (included with the fare) takes train passengers from Hanford to Visalia. Amtrak also works with private companies that offer overnight tour packages from train and bus stations; for more information, call 800/321–8684.

From Los Angeles, a late-night bus carries train passengers from downtown to the train station at Bakersfield, where they can board the train for **Hanford** and take the shuttle to

Visalia (the fare is $33 one-way, $40 round-trip, and includes both bus transfers). Near the Hanford train station, car rental agencies are **Budget** (tel. 209/583–6123) and **Ford** (tel. 209/584–5531). In Visalia, the nearest car rental agency is **Standard** (tel. 209/732–4716).

From the Transbay Terminal in downtown San Francisco, a bus takes train passengers to the Oakland station, where they can catch the train to **Fresno** ($38 one-way, $45 round-trip, including the bus). In Fresno, car rentals are available from **Standard** (tel. 209/442–0902) and **Budget** (tel. 209/224–2066), both of which offer free shuttles from the train station to their offices, and **Hertz** (tel. 209/251–5055), which will reimburse customers for their cab fare from the train station.

By Bus. Both Fresno and Visalia have **Greyhound Lines** (tel. in Fresno, 209/268–1829; in Visalia, 209/734–3507) depots, with buses that come from San Francisco and Los Angeles. Typically, it costs $44 for a round-trip ticket from Los Angeles to Visalia and about $55 from San Francisco.

EXPLORING

There are three main centers of interest in the two parks: In Kings Canyon, there is the eponymous river and its surrounding Cedar Grove, as well as Grant Grove; and in Sequoia most people flock to the Giant Forest. From early May through October all the roads in the parks are open, providing access to some spectacular scenery. But the nature of these parks is best appreciated by including at least a few short walks in your tour. If you have only one or two days and want to see all three of these areas, it is best to stay in Grant Grove, which is a one-hour drive from both Cedar Grove and Giant Forest (along the Generals Highway). If you do not plan on extensive hikes, two to three days is ample time for these two parks to introduce themselves.

THE BEST IN ONE DAY From late spring through early fall you will probably be able to drive the major roads within the parks in four to five hours. Start out on Highway 198

and enter Giant Forest in the early morning, heading straight for the visitor center at Lodgepole. A half hour spent here will give you a good overview of the area and an idea of what you might want to see in your limited time at the parks. During the summer, an hourly shuttle van makes the roundtrip journey from Lodgepole Campground through Giant Forest Village to Moro Rock and Crescent Meadow.

From the visitor center, backtrack on Generals Highway 2½ miles to reach the General Sherman Tree, the world's largest living thing. It is just a short walk from the parking area; signs clearly mark the way. This giant is between 2,300 and 2,700 years old, 275 feet high, and has a diameter at its base of 36½ feet. Its trunk weighs about 1,385 tons. First-time visitors with time to spare should stroll down the Congress Trail, an easy 2-mile loop through the heart of the sequoia forest that takes one to two hours to complete (see Nature Trails and Short Hikes, below).

Next, head farther south still and turn off on the Moro Rock–Crescent Meadow Road (see Scenic Drives and Views, below). Make the effort to climb the steep ¼-mile staircase leading to the summit of Moro Rock, a large granite dome from which you can gaze out over the western end of Sequoia National Park. Even if you go just a short distance up you'll get a wonderful view. Nearby Crescent Meadow gives an excellent midsummer wildflower show, and a 1-mile round-trip hike from the meadow leads to Tharp's Log, the summer home of Hale Tharp, built inside a fallen sequoia (see Historic Buildings and Sites, below).

Back on Generals Highway, head north to Grant Grove, where the General Grant Tree has been standing for 1,800 to 2,000 years. You can reach the tree, which President Calvin Coolidge ordained as the Nation's Christmas Tree in 1926, via a half-mile loop trail. Nearby, a 2⅓-mile (one-way) spur road (not recommended for trailers and RVs) leads to Panoramic Point, from which the jagged shards of granite peaks loom some 20 miles

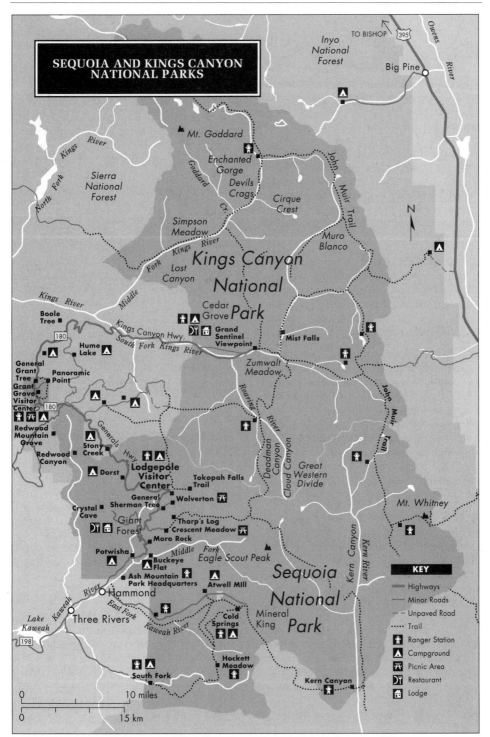

SEQUOIA AND KINGS CANYON
NATIONAL PARKS

TO BISHOP

Inyo
National
Forest

Big Pine

Owens River

Mt. Goddard

Enchanted
Gorge

Devils
Crags

Cirque
Crest

John Muir Trail

Muro
Blanco

Goddard Cr.

Simpson
Meadow

Kings River

North Fork Kings River

Sierra
National
Forest

Lost
Canyon

Kings Canyon
National
Park

Middle Fork Kings River

Cedar
Grove

Grand
Sentinel
Viewpoint

Mist Falls

Kings Canyon Hwy.

South Fork Kings River

Zumwalt
Meadow

Kings River

Boole
Tree

Hume
Lake

General
Grant
Tree

Panoramic
Point

Grant
Grove
Visitor
Center

Redwood
Mountain
Grove

Redwood
Canyon

Stony
Creek

Generals Hwy.

Roaring River

Deadman Canyon

Cloud Canyon

Great
Western
Divide

John Muir Trail

Dorst

Lodgepole
Visitor
Center

Tokopah Falls
Trail

General
Sherman Tree

Wolverton

Mt. Whitney

Crystal
Cave

Giant
Forest

Tharp's Log

Crescent Meadow

Moro Rock

Middle Fork

Eagle Scout Peak

Kern Canyon

Kern River

Potwisha

Buckeye
Flat

Ash Mountain
Park Headquarters

Atwell Mill

Sequoia
National
Park

Hammond

East Fork

Cold
Springs

Mineral
King

Kaweah River

Three Rivers

Lake
Kaweah

Kaweah River

Hockett
Meadow

South Fork

Kern Canyon

KEY

Highways
Minor Roads
Unpaved Road
Trail
Ranger Station
Campground
Picnic Area
Restaurant
Lodge

0   10 miles

0   15 km

in the distance (*see* Nature Trails and Short Walks, *below*).

From Grant Grove take Highway 180 east. You will drive along the scenic Kings River Canyon, and in an hour's time you'll descend to Cedar Grove, which is situated at the upper end of a yosemite valley (*yosemite* is the generic term given to glacial U-shape valleys). While this valley lacks the towering waterfalls of the Yosemite Valley in Yosemite National Park, it does offer views of huge granite cliffs similar to those in the famous park. Cedar Grove is a good place to sit on a rock next to the Kings River and watch the sinking sun cover the granite faces in a golden wash.

ORIENTATION PROGRAMS A number of slide shows are presented year-round at the visitor centers. They usually begin every hour on the hour and last about 20 minutes. A variety of topics is covered, including the creation of the parks, both geologically and politically.

GUIDED TOURS Guided tours of the parks are available through private tour companies: Park Headquarters (tel. 209/565–3164) can provide a complete listing. **Guest Services** (tel. 209/561–3314 or 209/565–3381) runs summer tours to Giant Forest twice daily. Adults pay $9.95, senior citizens pay $8.50, and children 12 and under pay $4.75 for these trips. The company also has an all-day tour of Kings Canyon that costs $22 for adults, $20 for senior citizens, and $11 for children.

SCENIC DRIVES AND VIEWS The **Kings Canyon Highway** winds alongside the powerful Kings River, below the towering granite cliffs and past the tumbling waterfalls of a canyon John Muir called "a rival to Yosemite." One mile past the Cedar Grove Village turnoff, the U-shape canyon becomes broader, and you can witness its glacial past. In the granite walls you can see the work of glaciers, wind, rain, and river. Four miles farther along is the Grand Sentinel Viewpoint, where you will see the 3,500-foot tall granite monolith and some of the most interesting rock formations in the canyon. The drive takes about one hour each way. Take Highway 180 east from Grant Grove.

The **Moro Rock–Crescent Meadow Road** is a 3-mile paved spur road that begins at Giant Forest Village and explores the southwest portion of this sequoia grove. It is not a steep road, but it has many sharp curves and is closed in winter, when it may be used as a ski trail. It is not recommended for RVs or trailers any time of year. Among the odd attractions on this road are the Auto Log and the Tunnel Log (*see* Historic Buildings and Sites, *below*). For excellent views of the Great Western Divide and the western half of Sequoia National Park, you will have to climb a steep 1/4-mile staircase to the summit of Moro Rock. About 100 yards from the end of the road is Crescent Meadow, John Muir's "gem of the Sierra," where brilliant wildflowers bloom in mid-summer. Many trails begin here, including the 1-mile route to Tharp's Log (*see* Historic Buildings and Sites, *below*) and the High Sierra Trail, which runs 71 miles to the summit of Mt. Whitney.

Generals Highway connects Grant Grove with Giant Forest to the south. It is a narrow, twisting road that runs past Stony Creek, the Lost Grove, Little Baldy, and the General Sherman Tree. Under normal driving conditions it takes approximately one hour to complete the drive, but during the summer months, this is the most heavily traveled road in the park and traffic can slow you down. Several trailheads are located off the Generals Highway, including the Congress Trail (*see* Nature Trails and Short Walks, *below*), the Trail For All People at Round Meadow, and the Hazelwood Nature Trail. Also on this road is the Lodgepole Visitor Center, located 4 1/2 miles north of Giant Forest Village, which features excellent exhibits and audiovisual programs describing the Sierra Nevada and sequoia natural history.

HISTORIC BUILDINGS AND SITES During the Roaring '20s, wealthy Santa Barbara businessman George Knapp commissioned extravagant fishing expeditions into Kings Canyon. In order to store quantities of gear he built a small cabin, which still stands. **Knapp's Cabin** is a short walk from a turnout about 2 miles east of the Cedar Grove Village turnoff.

You can drive your car onto the top of the **Auto Log,** a fallen giant sequoia that is located about 1 mile from Giant Forest on the Moro Rock–Crescent Meadow Road, and you can actually drive through **Tunnel Log,** a giant fallen sequoia located 2³/₄ miles from the Giant Forest Village on the same road. A bypass is available for larger vehicles.

A 2-mile trail that begins at Crescent Meadow in Giant Forest clearly marks the way to **Tharp's Log,** which is named for Hale Tharp, the first non–Native American resident in the sequoia forest. Tharp ran cattle there in the 1860s, and he built a cabin onto the end of this giant sequoia log, which was hollowed out by fire.

During the 1920s and 1930s Shorty Lovelace trapped in what is now the southern section of Kings Canyon National Park, and later moved his operation into Sequoia National Forest. He erected a series of **cabins** along his trapline, each a day's walk apart. Some of his weather-beaten cabins have been preserved, though none can be reached within a day's hike from the road. They sit far into the backcountry and are seen only by the occasional backpacker.

Even tall people can walk through the entire 100-foot length of the **Fallen Monarch,** a hollowed-out, fallen sequoia, which is located near the General Grant Tree. Early explorers, cattle ranchers, and Native Americans used the log for shelter, as did the soldiers who began patrolling the area during the late 1880s.

A walk up the General Grant Trail will lead you to the **Gamlin Cabin,** built by brothers Thomas and Israel Gamlin as a summer cabin in 1867. The brothers used it primarily for storage as they moved their cattle through the area or logged sugar pines; they operated in the area until the 1880s. The cabin, which is listed on the National Register of Historic Places, was returned to an area close to its original site in 1931 and was rehabilitated in 1981. The roof and lower timber are giant sequoia.

Built as a mill pond, **Hume Lake** supplied water for a flume that floated rough-cut sequoia lumber to the planing mill at Sanger, 54 miles below in the San Joaquin Valley. The lake is in Sequoia National Forest and offers swimming, fishing, boat rentals, and a campground. It is located 8 miles north of Grant Grove on Highway 180, then 3 miles south on Hume Lake Road.

NATURE TRAILS AND SHORT WALKS Sequoia **National Park.** Two miles north of the Giant Forest Village is the 1,385-ton General Sherman Tree, the biggest of the big trees; those who take the time to read the text at the nearby sequoia slab will learn how these big trees depend on fire for their existence. The easy 2-mile **Congress Trail** is a largely paved loop that starts out near the General Sherman Tree and winds through the heart of the sequoia forest. In the one to two hours it takes to complete the loop you will pass groups of trees known as the House and Senate, and individual trees called the President and McKinley.

Crystal Cave (tel. 209/565–3134), a marble cavern with stalactites, cave pearls, and flowstone, is at least a 45-minute drive from Giant Forest Village. The cave, closed at press time, is slated to reopen in summer 1994 (call ahead to confirm).

Kings Canyon National Park. One of the shortest trails in the parks is the one that leads to the **General Grant Tree,** the third-largest living tree in the world. President Calvin Coolidge designated the tree the Nation's Christmas Tree (not to be confused with the national Christmas tree, which appears on the Capitol mall each winter). President Eisenhower designated the tree a national shrine, making it the nation's only living memorial to American soldiers who have died while fighting for the United States in its wars. The trail is only ¹/₃ mile, but it passes the Gamlin Cabin and the Fallen Monarch (*see* Historic Buildings and Sites, *above*). Paved and fairly level, it begins 1 mile northwest of the Grant Grove Visitor Center.

While in Grant Grove take the time to walk out to **Panoramic Point,** which you can reach via a spur road that heads east through the visitor center parking lot, curves left around a meadow, then splits; you should bear right at the intersection, marked Panoramic Point, which is 2¹/₃ miles farther along. (Trailers and RVs are not recommended on the steep and narrow road.) A ¹/₄-mile walk from the parking lot leads to a viewpoint from which you can see the High Sierra, from Mt. Goddard in northern Kings Canyon Park to Eagle Scout Peak in Sequoia Park. Mt. Whitney can't be seen from the west side of the park because of the height of the Great Western Divide. The Park Ridge Trail, a 4-mile round-trip, begins here (*see* Longer Hikes, *below*).

LONGER HIKES **Sequoia National Park.** The moderately strenuous **Tokopah Falls Trail** follows the Marble Fork of the Kaweah River for 1³/₄ miles one way and dead-ends below the impressive granite cliffs and cascading waterfall of Tokopah Canyon. It will take you 2¹/₂ to 4 hours to make the 3¹/₂-mile round-trip journey. The trail starts in Lodgepole Campground, located 4¹/₂ miles north of the Giant Forest Village, and passes through a lodgepole pine forest.

Little Baldy Trail climbs 700 vertical feet in 1³/₄ switchbacking miles and ends at a mountain summit with a great view of the peaks of the Mineral King area and the Great Western Divide. The trail begins at Little Baldy Saddle, 11 miles north of the Giant Forest Village on the Generals Highway, and it will take three to four hours to walk to the summit and back.

Kings Canyon National Park. The **Don Cecil Trail** climbs the cool north-facing slope of Kings Canyon, passing Sheep Creek Cascade and offering several good views of the canyon and the 11,000-foot Monarch Divide. The trail leads to Lookout Peak, from which there is an incredible panorama of the park's backcountry. It is a strenuous, all-day hike of 13 miles (round-trip) that climbs to a 4,000-foot summit.

From the canyon floor at Cedar Grove take the **Hotel Creek Trail** up a series of switchbacks until it splits. Follow the route left through chaparral to the forested ridge and rocky outcrop known as Cedar Grove Overlook, from which you'll see Kings Canyon stretched out below. This strenuous 5-mile round-trip hike gains 1,200 feet and takes three to four hours to complete. If you take the right fork of the Hotel Creek Trail, you will descend to the **Lewis Creek Trail,** about 1¹/₄ miles past the overlook junction. Turn left onto this trail, which passes through a huge area that was burned in 1980. From the beginning of the Hotel Creek Trail to the end (really the trailhead) of the Lewis Creek Trail, 2 miles west of the Cedar Grove Village turnoff, you will cover 8 miles with a 1,200-foot elevation gain and loss; it will take about five hours to hike this route.

The sandy **Mist Falls Trail** follows the glaciated South Fork Canyon through forest and chaparral, past several rapids and cascades, to one of the largest waterfalls in the two parks. This 8-mile round-trip hike is relatively flat, but climbs 600 feet in the last mile. It takes four to five hours to complete. The trailhead is at Road's End, 5¹/₂ miles east of the Cedar Grove Village turnoff.

Hikers may want to explore the area in Sequoia National Forest called **Converse Basin,** once the largest grove of sequoias in the world. Early in the century practically every mature tree in this area was cut down, and today it is still barren, with only a small amount of brush growing among the granite boulders. The Boole Tree was one of the few giants to be spared, and the oldest-known giant sequoia, the Muir Snag, is found here. It was more than 3,000 years old when it died. The basin is reached by a graded dirt road off Highway 180, 6 miles north of Grant Grove. Maps of the area are available at the visitor center.

The **Park Ridge Trail** begins at the end of the road to Panoramic Point, in Grant Grove. It is a fairly flat 4-mile hike to the Park Ridge fire lookout and back. If you are lucky enough to make this hike on one of the few days when western views are not smoggy, you will be able to see the San Joaquin Valley. It is more likely, however, that you'll look to the east and the great peaks of Kings Canyon.

About 8 miles southeast of Grant Grove on Generals Highway, there is a turnoff onto a bumpy dirt road that dead-ends after about 2 miles at Redwood Saddle. Here is the trailhead to **Redwood Canyon,** where there are miles of trails leading through the world's largest grove of the world's largest trees. Take in the cascades and quiet pools of Redwood Creek on a short walk, day hike, or overnight backpacking trip. This area is a mixed conifer forest, with meadows and shrubland.

OTHER ACTIVITIES There is no off-road driving allowed in the parks; and no boating, rafting, or snowmobiling.

Biking. Those who would rather travel by bicycle than by car may be disappointed at Sequoia and Kings Canyon. Bicycles are allowed only on the paved roads, and the steep highways have such narrow shoulders that bicyclists are discouraged from riding on them.

Bird-Watching. Not seen in most parts of the United States, the white-headed woodpecker and the pileated woodpecker are common in most mid-elevation areas here. There are also a large number of hawks and owls in these two parks, including the renowned spotted owl. Ranger-led bird-watching tours are held on a sporadic basis. Visitors should call the parks' information number (tel. 209/565–3134) or check the listing found in the *Sequoia Bark,* the biweekly newspaper that everyone receives as they enter the parks.

Fishing. There is a limited amount of trout fishing in the parks' creeks and rivers—primarily in the Kings and Kaweah rivers—from late April through mid-November. Those venturing into the backcountry on multiday trips will find some good fishing in some of the parks' secluded lakes. A California fishing license ($24) is required for persons 16 and older; anglers should check state and park fishing regulations for special closures and restrictions. Licenses and fishing tackle are usually available in Lodgepole, Stony Creek, Grant Grove, and Cedar Grove. Only Grant Grove is open year-round.

Horseback Riding. Four private operators offer everything from one-hour jaunts to full-service, multiday pack trips into the backcounty. Popular one-day destinations out of Cedar Grove include Mist Falls and Upper Bubb's Creek. In the backcountry, many equestrians head for Volcanic Lakes or Granite Basin, ascending trails that reach elevations of 10,000 feet. Costs per person range from $15 for a one-hour guided ride to $200 per day for fully guided trips on which the packers do all the cooking and camp chores, leaving the riders to spend their nonriding time at their own leisure. Contact **Cedar Grove Pack Station** (Box 295, Three Rivers, CA 93271, tel. 209/565–3464); **Grant Grove Stables** (c/o Postmaster, Kings Canyon NP, CA 93633, tel. 209/335–2482); **Mineral King Pack Station** (Box 61, Three Rivers, CA 93271, tel. 209/561–4142); or **Wolverton Pack Station** (Box 641, Woodlake, CA 93286, tel. 209/565–3445).

Ski Touring. There are cross-country touring centers and marked trails at **Wolverton** (tel. 209/565–3435), near Giant Forest, and **Grant Grove** (tel. 209/335–2314). Qualified instructors give two-hour group lessons that cost $25 per person, and rentals are available for $15 per day (children $11). The centers operate 9 to 5 weekdays and 8 to 6 weekends and holidays, from Thanksgiving through April, depending on the amount of snowfall.

Sledding. The Wolverton area near Giant Forest, and the Big Stump and Azalea areas in Grant Grove allow sleds, inner tubes, and platters.

Snowshoeing. Free naturalist-guided snowshoe walks are offered on weekends and holidays, as conditions permit (usually mid-December to mid-March). It is recommended that you make reservations through the visitor centers (tel. in Grant Grove 209/335–2315; in Giant Forest/Lodgepole 209/565–3782). Snowshoes may be rented at the Wolverton and Grant Grove ski touring centers for $8.50 per day.

Swimming. The scenic, sometimes raging rivers in the area are not conducive to swimming or wading, because of swift currents, cold waters, and treacherous footing. **Lake Kaweah** (tel. 209/561–3155 or 209/597–2301), which is located about 10 miles outside the park's southern entrance, is a lower elevation lake where boating, swimming, and fishing are enjoyed. There are bathrooms and a campground at the lake. Another option for swimming is **Hume Lake** (tel. 209/338–2251), located in Sequoia National Forest, 8 miles north of Grant Grove on Highway 180, then 3 miles south on Hume Lake Road. You can also fish in Hume Lake, and boat rentals are available.

CHILDREN'S PROGRAMS A variety of programs for kids are offered in July and August in Grant Grove, Cedar Grove, and Giant Forest. Among the most popular is the Patch Program, where kids (and adults) earn patches by participating in a variety of free ranger-led activities, including nature walks. Don't expect to earn a patch in one afternoon—it takes several days. The activity schedule is listed in the free newspaper *Sequoia Bark.*

EVENING ACTIVITIES During the summer months, evening campfire programs are held at many of the parks' campgrounds. In winter, programs are held at the Lodgepole Visitor Center or the Beetle Rock Center, and the Grant Grove Visitor Center on Friday or Saturday. Additional programs are sometimes offered during holidays. During summer a full schedule of programs is published in the *Sequoia Bark.* Year-round the program schedules are posted on bulletin boards.

DINING

The major areas within the parks have only one or two restaurants, serving breakfast, lunch, and dinner. These are simple, no-frills eateries where basic American meals—steak, hamburgers, pancakes, and eggs—are served and prices are moderate. Health-conscious eaters will find a limited selection of foods, including salads, fruit platters, and frozen fish (primarily salmon and halibut). All of the restaurants within the parks are managed by **Guest Services** (Giant Forest, Box A, Sequoia National Park, CA 93262, tel. 209/565–3381).

The Giant Forest Cafeteria and the Grant Grove Restaurant are open year-round. Stony Creek closes Labor Day, Cedar Grove and the Giant Forest Lodge Dining Room close at the end of September, and Lodgepole closes in mid-October. The restaurants are open 7 AM to 9 PM in summer and 7 AM to 8 PM in winter.

INSIDE THE PARKS **Giant Forest Lodge Dining Room.** This is the fanciest restaurant in the two parks, with cloth tablecloths, soft lighting, and a quiet atmosphere. The dinner menu features soups, salads, fried or grilled chicken, a variety of ocean fish, and prime rib; the Sunday morning buffet brunch includes waffles, pancakes, eggs, omelets, toast, sausage, juice, and fruit. *MC, V. No lunch. Moderate.*

Cedar Grove Restaurant. As in many fast-food restaurants, patrons here order their food at a counter and then carry it themselves to a table. The limited menu includes hamburgers, hot dogs, and sandwiches for lunch and dinner; eggs, bacon, and toast for breakfast. *MC, V. Inexpensive.*

Giant Forest Cafeteria. Fish, chicken, and a veggie stir-fry are served in a cafeteria-style setting. Open for breakfast, lunch, and dinner, this is the place to feed a family on a budget without suffering from heartburn. *MC, V. Inexpensive.*

Grant Grove Restaurant. This spacious family-style restaurant, with wood tables and chairs and a long counter, serves American standards for breakfast, lunch, and dinner: eggs, burgers, and steak. Among the tasty specials is a delicious red snapper in lemon-mushroom sauce. Chef's salads, fruit platters, and seasonal fish specials are also offered. *MC, V. Inexpensive.*

Lodgepole Delicatessen. For a quick lunch or dinner try this tiled deli for hot and cold sandwiches, hamburgers, pizza, and other short-order items. One favorite: the Sequoia Sub, made with several meats and cheeses on a choice of breads. Indoor and outdoor tables seat about 60. *MC, V. Inexpensive.*

Stony Creek Smokehouse. At this medium-size sit-down coffee shop you can have eggs and hash browns in the morning, broiled burgers for lunch, and steak and potatoes for dinner. It is located midway between Grant Grove and Giant Forest. *MC, V. Inexpensive.*

NEAR THE PARKS **White Horse Inn.** Locals consider this the finest dining in town. Filled with antiques and bedecked with draperies and mirrors, the White Horse exudes an English air. The restaurant is known for its salads, which are prepared tableside. You will get one if you order the house special, a succulent prime rib served with baked potato. Other good choices are teriyaki chicken and duck à la Montmorency, which is half a roasted duck in a cherry sauce. For dessert, try the mousses and tarts. *42975 Sierra Dr., Three Rivers, tel. 209/561–4185. AE, D, MC, V. Closed Mon. and Tues. Moderate.*

Clingan's Junction Restaurant. If you're anywhere near this place when you get hungry, make the drive. For breakfast you'll be treated to omelets or strawberry waffles with gobs of potatoes; at lunch try the turkey breast sandwich with hot peppers and mushrooms. A chicken-fried steak dinner might start with homemade soup and include fresh-baked breads and pies. There is a dieter's special, and if you don't see what you want on the menu, just ask. *35591 E. Kings Canyon Hwy. (Hwy. 180), Clingan's Junction, tel. 209/338–2559. AE, MC, V. Inexpensive.*

The Noisy Water. Yet another family-style establishment, The Noisy Water is named for the Kaweah River, which flows within view of the restaurant's numerous windows. Try the eggs, pancakes, or french toast for breakfast, French-grilled sourdough burger at lunch, and the 16-ounce T-bone or 10-ounce lobster for dinner. Several menu selections are offered for vegetarians and health-conscious diners. Wine and beer are available with meals. On warm days sit out on the veranda. *41775 Sierra Dr., Three Rivers, tel. 209/561–4517. AE, MC, V. Inexpensive.*

Staff of Life. The sunny atmosphere in this local hangout allows the many indoor plants to flourish. Lunch, served from 11 to 4, includes soups, salads, and sandwiches, ranging from roast beef to a vegetarian sandwich of avocado, tomato, cucumber, lettuce, and red onion. Try the yogurt smoothies or any of the cakes and mousses. *41651 Sierra Dr., Three Rivers, tel. 209/561–4937. AE, D, MC, V. Inexpensive.*

PICNIC SPOTS The picnicking options in these two parks are unlimited. Numerous creeks and streams and countless stands of pine and sequoia provide thousands of peaceful and scenic places to take a midday meal. Food and beverages can be purchased at any of the general stores located in the park villages.

There are two designated picnic areas in Kings Canyon and five in Sequoia. All are spacious, with picnic tables, grills, and rest rooms. The **Columbine** area is located in Kings Canyon's Grant Grove, roughly 1 mile north of the visitor center on the road to the Grant Tree. It is shaded by pines. Less than a half-mile inside the park entrance on Highway 180 is the **Big Stump** picnic area, which is more open than Columbine. Near Sequoia's Giant Forest, 2 miles north of the General Sherman Tree on the Generals Highway and another 2 miles along the Wolverton Road, the **Wolverton** picnic area sits among white and red firs and a variety of pines. There is also a very popular picnic area at the edge of **Crescent Meadow,** and another at **Halstead Meadow** on the Generals Highway. Near the parks' southern entrance, just before the road to the Buckeye Flat campground, is the **Hospital Rock** picnic area, which is in a foothills setting. Another occupies the lawn near the **Foothills Visitor Center.**

LODGING

All of the parks' lodges and cabins are open during the summer months, but in winter only some of those in Giant Forest and Grant Grove remain open. A variety of accommodations is offered at Giant Forest and Grant Grove, from rustic cabins without baths to deluxe motels. From November through April, excluding holiday periods, low-season rates are in effect, resulting in savings of 20%

to 30%. The room tax in California is 10%, and the sales tax is 7¹/₄%.

Lodging facilities within the parks are operated by Sequoia Guest Services, an authorized concessionaire of the National Park Service, and each of the areas has a simple, inexpensive restaurant. *For information and reservations, contact Sequoia Guest Services, Box 789, Three Rivers, CA 93271, tel. 209/561–3381, fax 209/561–3135. MC, V.*

INSIDE THE PARKS **Giant Forest.** There are seven different types of accommodation in this area of Sequoia National Park, including rustic cabins without bathrooms, family cabins that sleep six, and a deluxe motel. Facilities and decor vary in a big way: Some cabins have only kerosene lamps and propane heat; motel rooms have carpeted floors and double and queen-size beds. The prices for these range accordingly — from $28.50 to $97.50. The lowest-price cabins are not available in winter.

Grant Grove. The most luxurious accommodations here are carpeted cabins with a private bath, electric wall heaters, and double beds. Most of these units, however, are in twos, and the adjoining walls are a little thin. Other cabins are even simpler, with wood stoves providing heat, and kerosene lamps providing light. A central rest room and shower facility is nearby. Rates here range from $23 in low season to $51.50 in high season.

Cedar Grove. At the bottom of Kings Canyon, in one of the prettiest areas of the parks, this is a good location for those who plan on staying a few days and doing a lot of day-hiking. Although accommodations are close to the road and there is quite a bit of nonguest traffic here, Cedar Grove manages to retain a quiet atmosphere. Those who don't want to camp will have to book a room well in advance — the motel/lodge has only 18. Each room is air-conditioned and carpeted and has a private shower and two queen-size beds. Open late May through September, the lodge charges $72 per night.

Stony Creek. Open from late May to September, the 11-room motel here is actually on national forest land between Grant Grove and Giant Forest. It sits at 6,800 feet among the peaceful pines. The nearby creek is stocked with trout. The rooms, at $72 per night, are carpeted and have private showers.

NEAR THE PARKS The only nearby lodging outside the parks is in Three Rivers, where there are several motels that charge from $45 to $65 per night. Reservations there can usually be made with only a week's advance notice. Staying inside the parks' boundaries, however, will save driving time and provide a better feel for the area. As a last resort, you can get a room in either Visalia or Fresno, which are located 60 and 90 minutes from the park entrances, respectively.

In Three Rivers the best choices are: **Best Western** (40105 Sierra Dr., Three Rivers, CA 93271, tel. 209/561–4119. 44 rooms. Facilities: pool, spa. AE, D, DC, MC, V); **Buckeye Tree Lodge** (46000 Sierra Dr., Three Rivers, CA 93271, tel. 209/561–5900. 12 rooms. AE, D, DC, MC, V), and **Lazy J Ranch** (39625 Sierra Dr., Three Rivers, CA 93271, tel. 209/561–4449. 18 cabins, some with kitchenettes. Facilities: pool, river access. Recommended for families. AE, D, DC, MC, V).

CAMPING

Campgrounds are by far the most economical accommodations in Sequoia and Kings Canyon National Parks, and they are probably the most fun. Located near each of the major tourist centers, the parks' campgrounds are equipped with tables, fire grills, drinking water (except for South Fork), garbage cans, and either flush or pit toilets. The only campground that takes reservations is Lodgepole in Sequoia National Park (contact Mistix, tel. 800/365–2267). All others assign sites on a first-come, first-served basis, and for weekends in July and August they are often filled up by Friday afternoon. Most campgrounds permit a maximum of one vehicle and six persons per site.

SEQUOIA AND KINGS CANYON CAMPGROUNDS

	South Fork	Potwisha	Buckeye Flat	Lodgepole	Dorst	Atwell Mill	Cold Springs	Azalea	Sunset	Crystal Springs	Sentinel	Moraine	Sheep Creek
	INSIDE SEQUOIA							**INSIDE KINGS CANYON**					
Total number of sites	13	44	28	260	218	23	37	118	184	67	83	120	111
Sites suitable for RVs	0	44	0	149	200	0	0	88	154	41	83	120	111
Number of hookups	0	0	0	0	0	0	0	0	0	0	0	0	0
Drive to sites	•	•	•	•	•	•	•	•	•	•	•	•	•
Hike to sites													
Flush toilets		•	•	•	•			•	•	•	•	•	•
Pit/chemical toilets	•					•	•						
Drinking water	•	•	•	•	•	•	•	•	•	•	•	•	•
Showers				•*		•	•	•*	•*	•*	•*	•*	•*
Fire grates	•	•	•	•	•	•	•	•	•	•	•	•	•
Swimming													
Boat access													
Playground													
Disposal station		•		•	•			•					•
Ranger station		•		•			•	•			•		
Public telephone		•		•	•	•	•	•		•	•	•	
Reservation possible				•									
Daily fee per site	$5	$10	$10	$12**	$10	$5	$5	$10**	$10	$10	$10	$10	$10
Dates open	mid-May–Oct.	year-round	mid-Apr.–mid-Oct.	year-round	Memorial Day–Labor Day	Memorial Day–mid-Oct.	Memorial Day–mid-Oct.	year-round	Memorial Day–mid-Sept.	Memorial Day–mid-Sept.	mid-May–mid-Oct.	mid-May–mid-Oct.	mid-May–mid-Oct.

*Pay showers nearby. **Free after heavy snowfall.

335

Potwisha, Grant Grove, Lodgepole, Dorst, and Cedar Grove campgrounds are the only areas where trailers and RVs are permitted. Sanitary disposal stations are available year-round in the Potwisha and Azalea (snow permitting) areas; from Memorial Day to mid-October in Lodgepole; from Memorial Day to Labor Day in Dorst; and from May to mid-October in Sheep Creek. There are no hookups in the parks, and only a limited number of campsites can accommodate vehicles longer than 30 feet.

Lodgepole, Potwisha, and Azalea campgrounds stay open all year. Other campgrounds open some time from mid-April to Memorial Day and close either after Labor Day or later in September or October. Campers should be aware that the nights, and even the days, can be chilly into early June.

In the foothills area of Sequoia, the **South Fork Campground** (13 sites, pit toilets, ranger station) tends to draw an older crowd, and remains fairly quiet, largely because of its isolated location. Sites cost $5 per night. **Potwisha** (44 sites, flush toilets, disposal station, public phone) and **Buckeye Flat** (28 sites, flush toilets) are located at 2,100 feet and 2,800 feet, respectively. There are more families with children here than at South Fork. Both charge $10 per site, per night.

The two largest campgrounds in the parks are near the Giant Forest: **Lodgepole** (260 sites, flush toilets, pay showers nearby, launderette, disposal station, ranger station, public phone) and **Dorst** (218 sites, flush toilets, disposal station, public phone). Sites cost $12 per night at Lodgepole and $10 per night at Dorst. Lodgepole is located within 1/2-mile walk of the visitor center, restaurants, and service station, and is a 10-minute drive from Giant Forest. With so many campers, Lodgepole tends to be among the noisiest campgrounds in the parks, but even here, the noise dies down at night.

The most isolated campgrounds in the two parks are **Atwell Mill** (23 sites, pit toilets, public phone) and **Cold Springs** (37 sites, pit toilets, ranger station, public phone), in the Mineral King area of Sequoia. Both are for tent campers only and are favored by those making day hikes to the area's lakes, streams, and peaks. To get here you must travel on a steep, tightly curved road not recommended for RVs. Nearby is Silver City, a private community where pay showers are available. Atwell Mill is at 6,540 feet in a second-growth sequoia forest. Cold Springs, at 7,800 feet elevation, is in a subalpine area. Sites at both campgrounds are $5 per night.

The campgrounds in Grant Grove—**Azalea** (118 sites, flush toilets, disposal station, ranger station, public phone), **Sunset** (184 sites, flush toilets, public phone), and **Crystal Springs** (67 sites, flush toilets, public phone)—are similar to Lodgepole and Dorst, in that they are situated near the giant sequoias and close to restaurants, stores, and other facilities. Sites cost $10 at all of them. There are pay showers nearby. But these campgrounds are not quite as big and don't get as much traffic.

They do draw a lot of families, so those seeking solitude would do well to make the one-hour drive to Cedar Grove, where there are four adjacent campgrounds: **Sentinel** (83 sites, flush toilets, ranger station, public phone), **Moraine** (120 sites, flush toilets), **Sheep Creek** (111 sites, flush toilets, disposal station), and **Canyon View** (groups only). These campgrounds are located near the far end of Kings Canyon and have nearly vertical views of the granite walls and outcroppings through a forest of firs and pines. The Kings River runs nearby. Only 3 miles away are a number of trailheads leading into the backcountry. There is usually a more active crowd camping here—those who take long day hikes. Pay showers, store, small restaurant, service station, and motel are located in the nearby village. All four of these campgrounds charge $10 per site, per night.

Waterton/Glacier International Peace Park

Alberta/Montana

By Bud Journey

lacier National Park embodies the essence of the Rocky Mountains. The massive peaks of the Continental Divide constitute its backbone, where ribbons of pure, clear streams, the result of melting snow and alpine glaciers, form the headwaters of the Columbia River to the west and the Mississippi to the east. Coniferous forests, rocky mountaintops, thickly vegetated stream bottoms, and green-carpeted meadows and basins provide homes and sustenance for a wide variety of wildlife. Flora is profuse. Raw nature dominates.

The northern boundary of Glacier National Park coincides with the international border, where it meets Canada's Waterton Lakes National Park. Together, the two parks are called Waterton/Glacier International Peace Park.

Motorized access is limited in both parks, but the few roads can take the traveler through a range of settings—from densely forested lowlands to craggy heights. The Going-to-the-Sun Road, which snakes through the precipitous center of Glacier National Park, is one of the most dizzying rides on the North American continent. Navigating the narrow, curving highway, built from 1922 to 1932, you will understand why access to it is restricted. Vehicles more than 20 feet long and 7½ feet wide (including mirrors) are not allowed to drive over Logan Pass—a restriction that is enforced at checkpoints at the east and west entrances.

Motoring through Waterton/Glacier park allows you to see much of what both parks have to offer. You can't miss the spectacular scenery. And the wildlife, large and small, often appear along roads, especially in the early morning and late afternoon. The hiking routes through various sections of the parks present a chance to delve deep into the area's natural richness. At times, exploring Waterton/Glacier is like stepping into the past for a glimpse of what the frontier was like.

Most development and services in these two parks are concentrated around St. Mary Lake, on the east side of Glacier; Lake McDonald, on the west side of Glacier; and the Waterton townsite at about the center of the Canadian park. However, other islands of development occur in such locations as Many Glacier, in the northeastern part of Glacier; Logan Pass Visitor Center, at the summit of Going-to-the-Sun Road, on the Continental Divide; and Apgar Village, at the foot of Lake McDonald. At Waterton there's a golf course and a riding stable within a few miles of town.

The Peace Park offers all kinds of accommodations, from tent camping to castlelike hotels, and food services from the most basic to gourmet. But the focus of a trip here remains the region's natural wonders, and the opportunities to see those wonders up close are many.

Waterton Lakes National Park was established in 1895; its main proponent was Frederick William Godsal. Glacier National Park was established on May 11, 1910, largely through the efforts of George Bird Grinnell, editor of *Forest and Stream* magazine. During the early years Glacier was essentially roadless, and a saddle-horse concession transported about 10,000 yearly visitors around the park on more than 1,000 horses. In 1932 the Going-to-the-Sun Road was completed, and motor vehicles took over as the primary mode of transportation in the park, giving today's more than 2 million annual visitors a far easier passage. Through the efforts of the U.S. and Canadian Rotarians, the two parks joined to form the first International Peace Park in 1932.

ESSENTIAL INFORMATION

VISITOR INFORMATION For information on the park contact Glacier Park Headquarters, **Glacier National Park,** West Glacier, MT 59936, tel. 406/888–5441; or the Superintendent, **Waterton Lakes National Park,** Waterton Park, AB, Canada T0K 2M0, tel. 403/859–2224.

Additional information on Waterton is available through the **Waterton Park Townsite Chamber of Commerce,** Box 55-6, Waterton Lakes National Park, AB, Canada T0K 2M0, tel. 403/859–2203.

Backcountry hikers who plan to stay overnight or have a campfire must obtain a Backcountry Use Permit. This is available at park headquarters and all ranger stations and information centers within the parks.

FEES A seven-day vehicle pass to Glacier is $5. Those entering on foot, motorcycle, or bicycle pay $3. A park pass, good for one calendar year, costs $15. A day pass to Waterton costs $5, a four-day pass costs $10, and an annual pass is $20 ($30 gives you annual entry to all Canadian national parks). All fees at Waterton are quoted in Canadian dollars. You must pay to enter each park; fees are not transferable.

PUBLICATIONS Park headquarters at both Waterton and Glacier have a variety of pamphlets and maps about the region, some of them free. Let park employees at headquarters know your areas of interest, and they will send you the appropriate publications.

Probably the best device for familiarizing yourself with Waterton/Glacier International Peace Park is the newspaper *Waterton/Glacier Guide.* Produced jointly by the two parks, it contains articles on the many activities available in the parks, including special events, wildlife-interpretative programs, religious services, suggestions for excursions, warnings about park hazards, and camping information. The newspaper is available at park entrances and visitors centers, and by mail from Park Headquarters (*see* Visitor Information, *above*).

Be sure to get a free copy of the catalog of books, maps, and videos about the Glacier area sold by the **Glacier National History Association** (West Glacier, MT 59936, tel. 406/888–5756), and about the Waterton area sold by the **Waterton Natural History Association** (Box 145, Waterton Park, AB T0K 2M0, tel. 403/859–2624).

Free printed works distributed by the parks include: "Ski Trails of Glacier National Park," "Nature With a Naturalist," "Backcountry, Glacier National Park," "Glacier National Park," "Waterton/Glacier International Peace Park Map," "Waterton/Glacier Guide," "Fishing Regulations" (for both parks), "The Trees and Forests of Waterton Lakes National Park," "You Are in Bear Country," "Checklist of Birds Found in Water Lakes National Park," and "Waterton Lakes National Parks Visitors Guide."

These short publications may provide all the information you'll need prior to visiting the park, but for those who want more in-depth data, here is a list of some larger publications sold by the natural-history associations.

Geology Along Going-to-the-Sun Road: Glacier National Park—A Self-Guided Tour for Motorists, which is applicable to both parks; *Hiker's Guide to Glacier National Park; Short Hikes and Strolls in Glacier National Park; The Grizzlies of Glacier* (Mountain Press), by Walter L. Hanna; *A Climber's Guide to Glacier National Park* (Mountain Press), by Gordon J. Edwards; *Glacier—The Story Behind the Scenery* (KC Publications), by Kathleen E. Ahlenslager; *The Story of the Highway Across Glacier National Park: Going-to-the-Sun Road* (Woodland Press), by Rose Houk; *Waterton and Northern Glacier Trails,* by Charles Russell, Beth Russell, Valerie Haig-Brown, and John Russell, an excellent description of hiking routes in Waterton, updated in 1991; *Montana's Continental Divide,* by Bill Cunningham, from Montana Geographic Series #12, published by *Montana Magazine,* Inc.; and *Waterton Lakes National Park,* by Heather Pringle, a sightseeing-tour guide with trail descriptions, history, and background on flora and fauna.

GEOLOGY AND TERRAIN The Continental Divide cuts through Waterton/Glacier from north to south, forming the western boundary of Waterton. Glacier's western boundary is marked by the meandering, clear waters of the North Fork of the Flathead River, and to the north and east only a brief transition of rolling hills separates the high Rockies from the expansive Great Plains. In Waterton that transition does not exist; the change is sudden and dramatic, giving the park its claim to fame as the place where "the mountains meet the prairie." To the south of Glacier lies the vast 1¹/₂-million-acre Bob Marshall Wilderness Area and to the northwest of both parks the Rockies continue to Canada's Banff and Jasper national parks.

Glacier is the fourth-largest national park in the contiguous 48 states, at just over 1,600 square miles. It's about 40 miles wide at the international boundary and about 53 miles long from north to south. The highest point, just south of the international boundary, in the northeast part of the park, is 10,448-foot Mt. Cleveland. The lowest point is at the confluence of the North and Middle forks of the Flathead River, at an elevation of 3,150 feet along the western border of the park.

Glacier's partner to the north, Waterton, contains about 202 square miles; it is about 23 miles wide and 14 miles long. The highest point is 9,600-foot Mt. Blakiston, located in the northwestern part of the park, and the lowest point, at an elevation of 4,050 feet, is at Waterton River, which runs south to north through the park.

Glacier National Park has 50 glaciers, 200 lakes, and 1,000 miles of streams, most of which contain native trout. Lake McDonald, located near the west entrance to the park, is the largest lake in the park, at 10 miles long and 1 mile wide. The slightly smaller St. Mary Lake is located near the east entrance. Other sizable lakes include Kintla, Bowman, Quartz, and Logging along the west slope of the park and Two Medicine, Sherburne, Glenns, and Cosley along the east slope.

Upper Waterton Lake is the largest lake in Waterton Lakes park, nearly 7 miles long and 1 mile wide. It's also the deepest lake in the Canadian Rockies and once yielded a huge 51-pound, 12-ounce lake trout to an angler from nearby Lethbridge. The other large lakes in the park include Middle and Lower Waterton lakes to the north and east of Upper Waterton, and Cameron Lake in the extreme southwestern part of the park. Rivers and streams also abound in the park.

FLORA AND FAUNA With the great differences in elevation in the park comes a variety of plant species. Among the trees, conifers are most prevalent, with 15 species at various elevations: western white pine, lodgepole pine, whitebark pine, ponderosa pine, western larch, subalpine larch, Engelmann spruce, subalpine fir, grand fir, Douglas fir, western red cedar, Pacific yew, western hemlock, Rocky Mountain juniper, and common juniper.

Lodgepole pine grows in old burns at all elevations. Cedar, yew, and hemlock form dense thickets in low, dark, wet areas on the western side of the Continental Divide. Western white pine and ponderosa pine are also found only on the west side of the divide; they are low- to mid-elevation trees that can grow to great sizes, often with no branches for the first 20 to 30 feet. Mature ponderosa, found only in the North Fork area of Glacier, often have a yellowish-brown tinge and are sometimes called yellow pine. One of the most interesting trees is the larch, the only conifer that is deciduous; its needles turn golden in the fall before falling off. The whitebark pine is an often stunted tree that grows at high elevations, usually on the dry, east side of the divide.

At least 10 broadleaf species are also present in the park, most found at lower elevations. They are black cottonwood, quaking aspen (so named for the quaking appearance of its leaves in the breeze), willow, paper birch, chokecherry, pin cherry, black hawthorn, alder, and Douglas maple.

From early spring to late summer, Waterton/Glacier is covered with more than 1,000 species of flowers, including glacier lilies, pale-blue forget-me-nots, false dandelions, red paintbrush, and red-purple fireweed. At times, whole basins are virtually ablaze. One of the most unusual wildflowers is beargrass, which is not grass and is not eaten by bears. Beargrass is actually a variety of lily with tough grasslike leaves that were sometimes used by Native Americans for weaving baskets. It is sometimes called squaw grass.

In spite of the breadth of plant life in the parks, animals often steal the show. Among the animals, none draws more attention than the bear. Waterton/Glacier has many black bears, and it's one of the few parks with a substantial number of grizzlies. Visitors should be aware of a few bear-related precautions when exploring the park. Backcountry hikers should be out only during the day, and they should make lots of noise as they walk through bear country by singing loudly, carrying on a loud conversation, or performing some other noisy activity that will warn away bears. People who camp in the backcountry must wash their utensils after every meal and hang their food in a tree, well away from sleeping areas. Campers who use drive-in campgrounds must store their food in a closed, hard-side vehicle. Visitors should *never* approach a bear, no matter how cute, cuddly, and harmless it may appear.

Bears are not the only animals in the park. Park officials warn visitors not to feed any of the park wildlife. Feeding animals is not only a hazard to humans, who may become the victims of aggressive animals that have lost their fear of people, but it is also a hazard to the animals: When it becomes necessary to keep wildlife away from humans, rangers must either move the animal, in which case it may be injured, or kill it. The animals here are sometimes visible and approachable, but they are best observed from a distance.

Another high-profile animal that is making a comeback in Waterton/Glacier is the gray wolf. Wolves were almost totally absent from the U.S. side of the border for about 50 years. Then, a little more than 10 years ago, a female wolf linked up with a male along the international boundary. These two animals produced a litter that researchers dubbed the Magic Pack because of their ability to disappear and reappear. From that original pack, several others have formed, denning in Glacier park. Wolf numbers have sporadically increased in recent years, and one pack has ranged as far south as Dixon, only 40 miles northwest of Missoula, Montana.

Mountain goats are also found in generous numbers in Glacier National Park and can often be seen along the Going-to-the-Sun Road and Highway 2 at the park's southern boundary. The Goat Lick (a natural exposure of mineral salts) at the extreme southern tip of Glacier almost always provides opportunities to view goats and other wildlife.

Bighorn sheep and mule deer are usually present in and around the Waterton townsite. Elk are a common sight on the prairie in fall, winter, and spring, but they are never seen in or near town. Whitetail deer, moose, and coyotes are also found in Waterton. Other large animals that live in the park are bobcats, lynx, mountain lions, foxes, and wolverines. Smaller animals include ground squirrels, pikas, snowshoe hares, porcupines, martens, beavers, marmots, and chipmunks.

At least 250 species of birds, including songbirds and raptors, live in both parks. Bald eagles and osprey are among the raptors. Franklin, ruffed, and blue grouse have also been spotted here, as have Canadian jays and kingfishers. The parks are well known for the large numbers of migratory waterfowl on lakes and rivers in autumn.

Among the fish inhabiting the park's waters are burbot (ling), northern pike, whitefish, kokanee salmon, grayling, sculpin, and a few varieties of trout, including cutthroat, bull, brook, rainbow, and lake (Mackinaw). All except sculpin are considered sport fish and can be caught with angling equipment.

Visitors should be prepared to deal with ticks and mosquitoes. Ticks are most common in spring, and although Lyme disease has not been reported in the immediate area, it's always a good idea to check for them after walking through shrubs and high grasses. Mosquitoes, on the other hand, can be quite a nuisance. The mosquito problem is worse in early and midsummer than it is in late summer and early fall. To get away from them, stay away from dark, damp places, where they tend to congregate. If you have a choice of campsites, try to pick one in a dry, open spot, where a breeze may blow the mosquitoes away. A good insect repellent will help.

WHEN TO GO Snow removal on the Going-to-the-Sun Road is usually completed by mid-June. That event opens Glacier National Park to summer activities, and by July 1 all naturalist programs are operating. Canada's Victoria Day, celebrated with a long weekend in late May, marks the beginning of summer activities in Waterton. Most people prefer traveling to this part of the country in summer, when the snow has substantially receded. The wildflower displays begin on the prairie in spring, and by early summer (late June and July) there are flowers blooming all through the parks. In late summer and autumn you'll catch the highest alpine blooms.

Summer is the time that wildlife redistributes itself throughout the parks after spending the long winter in dens and lowland winter ranges. It's when a profusion of flora covers the landscape with new grasses, flowers, and budding trees. The moisture that's been trapped in snowfields and glaciers is released into lakes by ribbons of water splashing down rocky mountainsides, accentuating the rugged scenery.

More and more people, however, are taking advantage of the parks in winter. Some facilities remain open throughout the cold season, and a variety of skiing and other cold-weather recreational opportunities abound.

Temperatures can reach into the 90s in the summer and dip as low as -40°F in the winter (primarily east of the Continental Divide). But if there is one constant, it is that the weather is unpredictable: It can vary considerably, even within a single day. In Waterton, another weather constant is the wind, which is often fierce.

The weather is usually most consistent in early September, and since by then the crowds have substantially decreased, this is a favored month to visit Waterton/Glacier.

SEASONAL EVENTS Late April to early May: One of the biggest events of the year at Glacier is Show Me Day, when visitors get a chance to watch the plowing of the Going-to-the-Sun Road. Spectators park downhill from the work site, then are shuttled up the hill to a spot across the canyon from the plowing. From there, visitors can watch road crews plow tons of packed snow from this mountaintop road, creating man-made avalanches in the process. Park-service employees provide spotting scopes and disperse information to the people watching the show. Unfortunately, this event is governed by so many uncontrollable variables that it has actually occurred only three times in the past eight years. **July 1 (Canadian Independence Day) to July 4:** The Days of Peace and Friendship focus on the International Peace Park theme, with special programs and interpretative walks. Due to budget constraints, however, this has become a very low-key celebration. **August:** The annual **Beargrass Festival** (tel. 403/859–2203) in Waterton is sponsored by the private sector in the Waterton townsite. The event may include Native American dancers, a story-telling contest, a fiddling competition, cowboy poetry, a golf tournament, and a chili cook-off.

Every summer the Waterton Natural History Association (*see* Publications, *above*) offers the **Heritage Education Program,** in which qualified instructors teach courses on a variety of topics, including archaeology, bears, flora, and birds. Photography workshops are also offered. Prices range from $35 to $100 per course. The number of participants is limited.

WHAT TO PACK Bring clothes for all kinds of weather. In summer you may find yourself in shorts and a T-shirt one day and donning heavily insulated foul-weather gear the next. Layered clothing is a good idea, as is sound footwear suitable for walking over wet, uneven terrain. Rain gear is also a must. Thunderstorms can develop at any time. Don't forget to bring insect repellent. Once in the park, you'll be glad you brought binoculars, as well as your good camera with lots of film.

GENERAL STORES In Glacier and Waterton, general stores are small and have limited inventories. Most sell fishing and camping supplies as well as food and drink.

For information on Glacier's camp stores, contact the concessionaire **Glacier Park, Inc.** (Box 147, East Glacier Park, MT 59434–0147, tel. 406/226–5551 mid-May to late Sept.; and Dial Tower, Station 1210, Phoenix, AZ 85077, tel. 602/207–6000 Oct. to mid-May). These small stores are located in several commercial areas of Glacier, such as Apgar Village, Lake McDonald, Rising Sun, Swiftcurrent, and Two Medicine.

There are also stores just outside the park at West Glacier, East Glacier, and St. Mary.

The best place to pick up food supplies in the Waterton townsite is the **Rocky Mountain Food Mart** (tel. 403/859–2526), which is open daily 8 AM to 10 PM in July and August, with hours varying in other months. Camping equipment is sold at **Waterton Sports and Leisure** (tel. 403/859–2612).

ARRIVING AND DEPARTING Glacier National Park is in northern Montana, just off the northernmost federal highway, U.S. 2. It has an east entrance and a west entrance, but the direction from which you enter probably will depend on the direction in which you're traveling; there is no particular advantage to entering at either entrance. Provincial Roads 5 and 6 enter Canada's Waterton Lakes National Park, but only Provincial Road 5 travels into the interior.

You can reach Glacier National Park by plane and train, but you'll want to rent a car or take the new shuttle service to see the Going-to-the-Sun Road.

Waterton/Glacier is 230 miles south of Banff and 350 miles south of Jasper. It is about 400 miles north of Yellowstone.

By Plane. Glacier Park International Airport (tel. 406/257–5994), about 30 miles southwest of the park, between Kalispell and Whitefish, serves Glacier Park. **Delta** (tel. 800/221–1212) and **Horizon** (tel. 800/223–9437) offer daily flights to and from the airport. Rental cars are available at the airport through **Hertz** (tel. 406/257–1266 or 800/654–3131), **National** (tel. 406/257–7144 or 800/328–4567), **Avis** (tel. 406/257–2727 or 800/331–1212), and **Budget** (tel. 406/755–7500 or 800/527–0700).

Flathead/Glacier Transportation Company (tel. 406/862–7733) runs eight-passenger vans from the airport to the park. To get to West Glacier, just outside the west entrance of the park, it costs $32 for the first passenger and $2 for each additional passenger. To the town of East Glacier, on the southeast side of the park, it costs $100 for the first passenger and $2 for each additional person. To Many Glacier, a developed area on the northeast side of the park, the rate is $140 plus $2 for each additional rider.

The nearest commercial Canadian airport is at **Lethbridge** (tel. 403/382–3165), about 70 miles northeast of Waterton, about a 1¹/₂-hour drive. It is served by **Time Air** (tel. 800/426–7000), a subsidiary of Canadian Airlines, and **B.C. Air** (tel. 800/776–3000).

By Car and RV. U.S. 2 skirts the south end of the park, and the west entrance is directly off this highway at West Glacier. The east entrance is just off U.S. 89 at St. Mary. U.S. 89 connects with U.S. 2 at Browning, about 30 miles south of St. Mary.

U.S. 2, the northernmost federal highway, is a two-lane road that runs across northern Montana. If you're coming from the south on I–90, the best roads to take to U.S. 2 are U.S. 15, beginning near Butte, Montana, and U.S. 93, starting 9 miles west of Missoula. U.S. 2 is an uncrowded road that offers a good look at rural Montana and a high probability of seeing wildlife.

Waterton is approachable from the east by Provincial Road 5 and from the north by Provincial Road 6. These roads come together on the north end of the park, and Provincial 5 leads to the interior of the park. The best approach to Waterton from the United States is U.S. 89 to State/Provincial 17, known as the Chief Mountain International Highway. This road closes when the customs station closes, from mid-September to mid-May. When it is closed, take U.S. 89 north to the border, where the customs station remains open. The road becomes Provincial Road 2 and runs north to Cardston, where you can pick up Provincial Road 5 west to the park.

By Train. Amtrak (tel. 800/872–7245) stops at West Glacier regularly and at East Glacier during busy seasons. There is no train to Waterton.

By Shuttle. Rocky Mountains Transportation (1410 E. Edgewood Dr., Whitefish, MT 59937, tel. 406/862–2539) operates a shuttle service along the Going-to-the-Sun Road between July 1 and August 31. Buses, which make stops at major trailheads, campgrounds, and other developed areas between West Glacier and St. Mary, run approximately every 1¹/₂ hours between 7:50 AM and 8 PM; riders can take the entire route round-trip, or use the bus for short hops along the way. Unlimited ridership for one day costs $28, for two days, $35; an unlimited one-day family pass runs $50. The price for a round-trip without stops is $24; rates between stops depend on the distance traveled, but can be as low as $2.

EXPLORING

You can explore Waterton/Glacier by touring in a car or RV or by boating, horseback riding, or walking. Those who prefer an urban setting might choose to view the scenery and observe the wildlife while playing the Waterton golf course or walking the streets of Waterton. Just about everyone will want to head out on a car, shuttle, or bus tour of the precipitous Going-to-the-Sun Road, but those with more time and a bent for adventure might try a more vigorous activity such as exploring on horseback or on foot.

The visitor here has a vast expanse of land to explore. An exhaustive one-day trip can take you through both parks, but it's a shame to hurry. Take your time, and spend several days traveling and nosing around the parks. There's plenty to hold your interest.

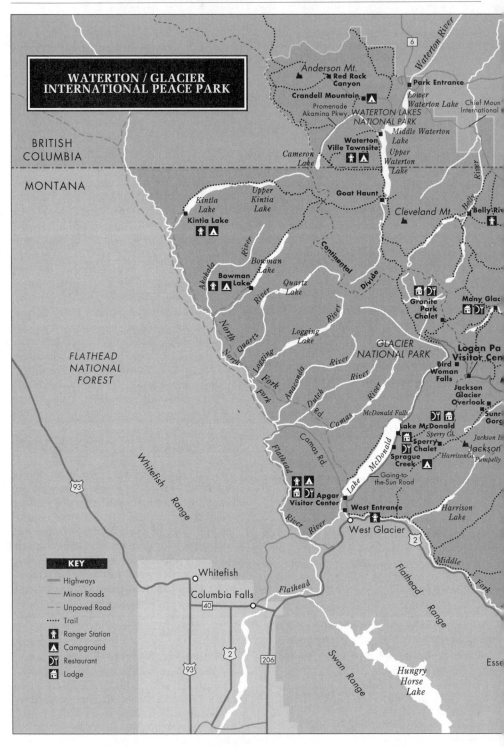

WATERTON / GLACIER
INTERNATIONAL PEACE PARK

BRITISH
COLUMBIA

MONTANA

FLATHEAD
NATIONAL
FOREST

Anderson Mt.
Red Rock
Canyon
Crandell Mountain
Promenade
Akamina Pkwy
WATERTON LAKES
NATIONAL PARK

Park Entrance
Lower
Waterton Lake
Chief Moun
International

Middle Waterton
Lake
Upper
Waterton
Lake

Waterton
Ville Townsite

Cameron
Lake

Goat Haunt

Cleveland Mt.

Belly Riv

Kintla
Lake
Kintla Lake

Upper
Kintia
Lake

Bowman
Lake
Bowman Lake

Quartz
Lake

Continental

Divide

Granite
Park
Chalet

Many Glac

Logan Pa
Visitor Cen

Logging
Lake

GLACIER
NATIONAL PARK

Bird
Woman
Falls

Jackson
Glacier
Overlook

Sunr
Gorg

McDonald Falls

Lake McDonald
Sperry Gl.
Sperry
Chalet

Jackson Gl.
Jackson
Harrison Gl. Pompelly

Sprague
Creek

Going-to-
the-Sun Road

Apgar
Visitor Center

West Entrance

Harrison
Lake

West Glacier

Whitefish
Range

Middle

Flathead
Range

Whitefish

Columbia Falls

Flathead

Swan Range

Hungry
Horse
Lake

Esse

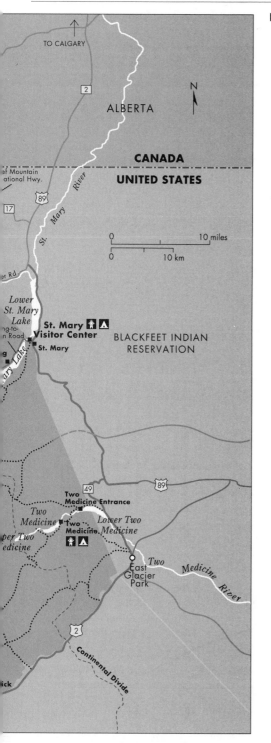

THE BEST IN ONE DAY It's hard to beat the Going-to-the-Sun Road (GTTS) for a one-day trip in Glacier National Park (*see* Scenic Drives and Views, *below*).
Although the road passes through a fraction of what the park has to offer, it does travel from the lowest elevations to the summit of the Continental Divide. Many species of flora and fauna appear along the road, and numerous turnoffs scattered along the way provide stops for viewing, resting, or photographing the scenery. The trip is short enough to allow brief excursions on some of the many trails, along with a visit to the Logan Pass Visitor Center, located about halfway through the park at the highest point of road.

The GTTS Road is a narrow, winding route flanked by precipitous mountainsides. Visitors who feel uneasy about driving on such a road can take a tour in a charming, old-fashion tour bus with a removable top. These tours are run by Glacier Park, Inc. (*see* Guided Tours, *below*), the same people who run the lodging and food services in Glacier. Another option is to take the Rocky Mountains Transportation shuttle (*see* Arriving and Departing, *above*).

Waterton is a much smaller park than Glacier, so a one-day excursion allows time for more than one driving route. The Chief Mountain International Highway is the longest road, and from it you will see the Rocky Mountain Front, the area where the mountains meet the prairies. The Akamina Parkway goes to Cameron Lake, at the base of the Continental Divide, just below the ridge where Alberta, British Columbia, and Montana meet. The Red Rock Parkway takes you from the prairie up a major valley to Red Rock Canyon, where water has cut through the earth, exposing red sedimentary rock. Wildlife viewing is also a highlight on this drive. You can easily cover all three routes in a single day. There are numerous picnic areas, pullouts, and exhibits along these roads and at Cameron Lake and Red Rock Canyon, which both serve as major trailheads for a variety of short and long hikes.

GUIDED TOURS A bus or shuttle tour of Going-to-the-Sun Road can be exciting, and taking one of the cruises offered on Waterton Lake, St. Mary Lake, Lake McDonald, Two Medicine Lake, or Many Glacier can provide a visitor with a close-up look at the great natural attributes of the Peace Park.

Glacier Park, Inc. (East Glacier, MT 59434, tel. 406/226–5551 or, in winter, 602/207–6000) provides a variety of guided tours in vintage 1936 Scarlet Buses, with roll-back tops. These driver-narrated tours cover just about every part of Glacier National Park accessible by road. They cost 34¢ per mile; some trips are as short as 15 minutes, while others run nearly the entire day. Children under 12 pay half-price, and babies who don't occupy their own seats ride free.

An international guided boat tour starts in the town of Waterton and cruises Upper Waterton Lake across the border into Goat Haunt, Montana. Run by **Waterton Shoreline Cruises** (Box 125, Waterton, Alberta, Canada T0K 2M0, tel. 403/859–2362 in summer; R. R. 6, Calgary, AB T2M 4L5, tel. 403/285–0341 in winter), this narrated tour makes short stops at several points in Canada and the United States. Adults pay $14 and children ages 6–12 pay $7; those under 6 ride free.

Glacier National Park SceniCruise (Box 5262, Kalispell, MT 59903, tel. 406/888–5727 or 406/732–4430) offers summer cruises on Lake McDonald and Many Glacier, Two Medicine, and St. Mary lakes. Cruises last from 45 minutes to 1 1/2 hours. Rates range from $6.50 to $8 for adults and from $3 to $4 for children ages four to eight. Small-boat rentals are also available: Nonmotorized boats cost $5 per hour or $25 per 10-hour day; motorboats cost $10 per hour or $50 per day. You can rent a canoe for $5 an hour.

SCENIC DRIVES AND VIEWS Entering Glacier National Park at the west entrance, you come to a stop sign about a mile inside the park. If you turn left, you will reach Apgar Village, on the southwest end of Lake McDonald. Apgar is a tiny community that's the hub of activity for the west side of the park. It has lodging, food, gift shops, a campground, a picnic area, rest rooms, swimming, boating, and a visitor center. Just about a mile north of the village, make a right onto the 43-mile **North Fork Road,** which follows the west boundary of the park and parallels the North Fork Flathead River. This winding dirt road runs through an area that is among the lowest in elevation in the park. It consists of river-bottom terrain and is marked by lodgepole-pine flats. Glimpses of the Whitefish Range appear to the west. The road continues north to Bowman Creek, where a spur road leads to Bowman Lake, then on to Kintla Lake, where it dead-ends. Both Bowman and Kintla lakes have campgrounds and good trout fishing. Allow four to six hours for the round-trip drive to Kintla Lake.

Back at the stop sign just inside the west entrance, turn right to get on the **Going-to-the-Sun Road**—probably the biggest single attraction in Glacier National Park. This road travels along the southwestern side of Lake McDonald, past the Lake McDonald Lodge, where you need a room reservation about six months in advance. The Lake McDonald Coffee Shop and the lodge dining room, however, are fine places to stop for breakfast or lunch. (If you're not in a hurry, rent a small boat or canoe here or take a guided cruise on the lake.)

As you leave Lake McDonald behind and begin the long, winding climb to Logan Pass, stop to view McDonald Falls, which can be reached via a short trail on the left side of the road. In this same area you can see the treeless avalanche chutes on the mountainsides, where bears are often visible, especially during late spring.

At the first big switchback on GTTS Road, you can park your car and make the 4-mile climb on foot to the Granite Park Chalet. It is currently closed for repairs but may reopen after 1995.

When you resume your trip to the summit, you'll find ample turnoffs where you can stop to enjoy the colors and shapes of the high country. You'll probably want to photograph Bird Woman Falls across the canyon.

At the Logan Pass summit, stop at the Logan Pass Visitor Center to listen to a talk about the alpine environment, pick up a book on the local flora and fauna, or enjoy the newly remodeled exhibits. Then take a short hike along the Highline Trail for a look at the scenery. Have a friend take your picture as you follow this trail, which has been cut out of a sheer cliff. At this point, you can also choose a 3-mile round-trip guided hike to Hidden Lake Overlook.

The trip down the east side of the Continental Divide is shorter than the drive up the west side. The terrain here, where the road was carved out of the mountain, is slightly more friendly than the terrain on the west side of the divide, where the road was blasted out of solid rock.

Among the attractions on this stretch of GTTS Road is the East Side Tunnel, which is just over the hump from Logan Pass. The tunnel cuts through a rock point, and the road passes by the bald, 9,642-foot Going-to-the-Sun Mountain, before descending to St. Mary Lake. Along the way, flowers color the grassy basins, with beargrass dominating from mid- to late summer.

Just as the GTTS Road descends into the trees, you will pass Jackson Glacier looming in a rocky pass across the canyon. According to a roadside marker, the glacier is shrinking and may disappear in another 200 years (a guess).

Traveling another 2 miles down the road, you will see Virginia Falls, which empties into St. Mary Falls, which in turn runs into the upper end of St. Mary Lake. It's a fairly short walk from the road to the falls. Drive another 3/4 mile, where a 25-yard walk will take you up to Sunrift Gorge.

At Rising Sun, on St. Mary Lake, you may choose to take advantage of the first rest room since the summit, stop for something to eat at the coffee shop, or take a boat tour. The St. Mary Visitor Center is just up the road. If you're tired, you can stay overnight at the Rising Sun campground or, if you've made reservations, at St. Mary Lodge (*see* Lodging,

below). It will take you about two hours to drive back to the west entrance.

The best time to drive the GTTS Road is the last two or three hours before dark; that's when the lighting is best for photos, the wildlife is most likely to appear, and the crowds have left the road.

The **Many Glacier Road** enters the northeast side of the park, west of Babb, Montana, and travels along Sherburne Lake for almost 5 miles, penetrating a glacially carved valley surrounded by mountains. As the road moves toward the mountains, it passes through a scrubby forest of lodgepole pines, aspen, and cottonwood, with meadows that are covered with grass and flowers during the summer. (The road is often closed by snow during the winter, usually from October to May). The farther you travel up the valley, the more clearly you can see Grinnell and Salamander glaciers. Formed only about 4,000 years ago, these two glaciers were one ice mass until 1926, and they continue to shrink.

After driving 12 miles you will arrive at Swiftcurrent, the end of the road. Here you can camp, fish, ride horseback, hike, take a boat cruise, or stop for a meal at the coffee shop. If you camp or stay at the motel, you can attend the rangers' campfire talks. Swiftcurrent is also the starting point for a number of long and short hikes, including one to Grinnel Glacier. The high basin on the north side of the valley, visible from the Swiftcurrent parking lot, is a good place to spot bears, mountain goats, and sheep.

The **Chief Mountain International Highway** leads northwestward from the U.S. side of the international boundary toward the town of Waterton. It starts in the rolling hills at the edge of the prairie and climbs through open fields and patches of cottonwood and aspen trees. As the road climbs, the surrounding forest thickens, and deciduous trees begin to give way to mixed conifers, mostly lodgepole pine and spruce. This road passes through the extreme northeastern corner of Glacier before it enters Canada's Waterton Lakes National Park, heading down toward Waterton Lakes and passing through a similar succession of vegetation in reverse. (The road closes in the fall, when the customs station closes, and reopens in late spring.) The Lewis Overthrust becomes visible on the left, and a roadside marker tells you that you're looking at 1.6-billion-year-old rock that has been thrust over 100-million-year-old rock by movement in the earth's crust. If you have a good pair of binoculars, you might spot grizzly bears, mountain goats, or other wildlife on the grassy, parklike hills of the Lewis Overthrust. On the final descent into the valley, Waterton unfolds before you in one of the most comprehensive views of the park. This road is 22 miles long and takes about an hour to drive one-way.

NATURE TRAILS AND SHORT WALKS In Glacier, one of the most popular hiking areas is **Logan Pass,** at the summit of the Going-to-the-Sun Road on the Continental Divide. The easy 1^1/$_2$-mile one-way self-guided Hidden Lake Nature Trail runs southwest from Logan Pass Visitor Center to Hidden Lake Overlook, from which you can see the lake and McDonald Valley.

Trail of the Cedars starts a few miles northeast of Lake McDonald on the GTTS Road. It is a ^{1}/$_2$-mile boardwalk loop trail through an ancient cedar-and-hemlock forest. At the end of the trail, there's a view of Avalanche Gorge. It's very popular with families with small children, senior citizens, and the disabled.

The **Bear's Hump Trail** is a ^{3}/$_4$-mile trail that starts at the Waterton Information Centre. It is a fairly steep climb, but it provides a great view of the town, the chain of Waterton Lakes, and surrounding mountains.

LONGER HIKES The **Highline Trail** goes north from the Logan Pass Visitor Center to the Granite Park Chalet and beyond, starting out in spectacular fashion. Cut out of a sheer rock cliff, it winds along for 7^1/$_2$ miles and overlooks a vast portion of the southwest side of the park.

Many Glacier Hotel is the starting point for several trails running south, west, and north. A day hike can take you within viewing distance of glaciated canyons, steep mountains,

and profuse flora, as well as a variety of wildlife. This can also be the starting point for overnight hiking to the interior of the park.

Two Medicine is the access point for hiking the southeastern part of Glacier. From there, visitors can get to Appistoki Falls, Paradise Point, and Rockwell Falls, as well as backcountry sites in the southern part of the park.

Backcountry lakes that can be accessed by trails from the North Fork Road on the west side of Glacier National Park include Logging (about 8 miles round-trip), Quartz (about 15 miles), Rogers (10 miles), and Trout (12 miles) lakes. On the northeast side of the park, trails are the only way to Cosley (15 miles), Glenns (18 miles), Helen (25 miles), and Elizabeth (16 miles) lakes.

The **Lakeshore Trail** begins at the Waterton Townsite and parallels the west side of Upper Waterton Lake, passing Boundary Bay and the international boundary before reaching Goat Haunt in Glacier National Park. It's about 3^1/$_2$ miles one way to Boundary Bay and about 6^1/$_2$ miles one-way to Goat Haunt, where you may see goats grazing. A Canadian park interpreter and a U.S. ranger lead the International Peace Park Hike along this trail on Saturday during July and August.

The **Snowshoe** and **Blakiston Valley** trails skirt the north and south sides of Anderson Mountain in the northwest part of Waterton. These trails are major access routes for several backcountry destinations. While walking along you are sure to see wildflowers and wildlife. The two trails form a 15-mile loop around the mountain, starting from the Red Rock Canyon Trailhead, at the end of the Red Rock Parkway.

OTHER ACTIVITIES Biking. Pedaling is as good a way as any to see both parks. Cyclists in Glacier National Park should stay on the main roads, but even they tend to be narrow and steep. Many Glacier Road and the roads around Lake McDonald have mild slopes and are not difficult to bike. The Two Medicine Road is an intermediate route, with a mild grade at the beginning, becoming steeper as you approach Two Medicine. Restrictions

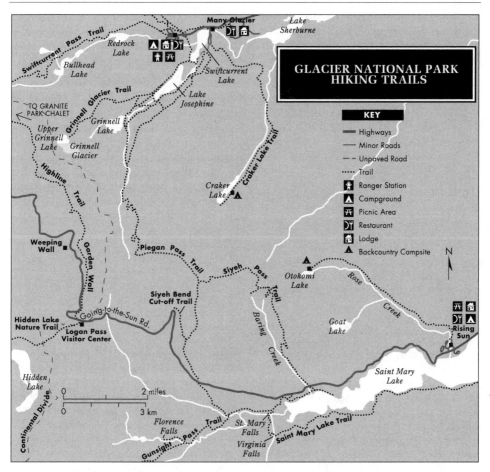

GLACIER NATIONAL PARK
HIKING TRAILS

KEY

━━━ Highways
── Minor Roads
- - Unpaved Road
····· Trail
🛉 Ranger Station
🔺 Campground
🔺 Picnic Area
🍴 Restaurant
🏠 Lodge
🔺 Backcountry Campsite

apply during peak traffic periods. GTTS road is closed to bikes from 10 to 4. Mountain biking is not allowed on park trails.

Waterton National Park allows bikes on some designated trails: Check with park headquarters for updated information. Red Rock Canyon Road has a mild slope, making it a relatively easy ride. The Cameron Lake Road is an intermediate route.

Bird-Watching. The Peace Park is home to at least 250 avian species, from songbirds to raptors. Among the species that get the most attention are birds of prey, including ospreys and bald eagles. Waterfowl are numerous along the parks' waterways, particularly in fall; look for Canada geese and the rare harlequin duck.

Fishing. Both parks have a number of lakes and rivers where the fishing is good. The sport-fishing species include burbot (ling), northern pike, whitefish, kokanee salmon, grayling, and cutthroat, rainbow, lake (Mackinaw), and brook trout. In Waterton, a license costs $13 for the year or $6 for seven days. In Glacier, a license is not required. Special restrictions apply in several areas, so visitors should read the regulations before fishing. A catch-and-release policy is encouraged in both parks.

You can fish in most waters of the parks, but the best fishing is generally in the least accessible spots.

Golf. It costs $23.50 a day to play the 18 holes at the **Waterton golf course** (tel. 403/859–

2383), just outside town. Don't be surprised if you see moose, elk, deer, bighorn sheep, and other wildlife on the greens and from the greens while playing.

Glacier Park Lodge (tel. 406/226–9311), in East Glacier, has a nine-hole course, which you can play for $9 (nine holes) or $15 (18 holes). **Glacier View Golf Course** (tel. 406/888–5471), in West Glacier, is an 18-hole course. The greens fees are $10 for nine holes and $18 for 18 holes.

Horseback Riding. Trail-riding is available in Waterton, but at press time the concessionaire for Glacier had lost its contract and a new concessionaire had not been chosen. Call Glacier Park Headquarters for an update. For Waterton, the rates per person run from $12.50 per hour to $64 per day. Contact **Alpine Stables** (tel. 403/859–2462).

Rafting. You can either bring your own boat or choose from four outfitters that offer guided white-water rafting in the pristine waters of the Flathead River drainages: **Glacier Raft Company** (Box 218, West Glacier, MT 59936, tel. 406/888–5454 or 800/332–9995; or Box 945D, Polson, MT 59860, tel. 406/883–5838 or 800/654–4359), **Glacier Wilderness Guides and Montana Raft Company** (Box 535, West Glacier, MT 59936, tel. 406/888–5466 or 800/521–RAFT), **Great Northern Whitewater** (Box 278, West Glacier, MT 59936, tel. 406/387–5340 or 800/735–7897), and **Wild River Adventures** (Box 272B, West Glacier, MT 59936, tel. 406/387–9453 or 800/826–2724).

Ski Touring. Cross-country skiing is increasingly popular in the Peace Park, especially on the U.S. side. It's a good way to observe wildlife, but be careful not to chase the animals; it causes unnecessary stress that could hamper their ability to survive the winter. Glacier National Park distributes a free pamphlet entitled "Ski Trails of Glacier National Park," which describes 14 ski trails that have been identified by the park.

Skiing opportunities in Waterton Lakes National Park are concentrated along the Aka-mina Parkway, especially near Cameron Lake. Don't expect to ski around the Waterton townsite; the wind usually blows the snow away. The free pamplet "Winter Activities" has additional information.

Swimming. You can swim in some of the lakes in both parks, but good judgment should be exercised when swimming in the very cold, and sometimes rough, waters of these mountain lakes. The best choices are Apgar Village beach on Lake McDonald and the Waterton town beach on Upper Waterton Lake, which is often windy and cold. There is a swimming pool at the Waterton townsite.

Tennis. There are public tennis courts at the Waterton townsite, adjacent to the campground. These are available on a first-come, first-served basis, and there is no fee. There is usually not a long wait. The courts are open year-round, although the nets are taken down for winter at the end of September.

CHILDREN'S PROGRAMS There are many children's programs at Glacier, but they vary from year to year. In one program a ranger leads kids in a role-playing skit about bears. During the skit, the youngsters discover how difficult it can be for injured bears to survive and build up enough fat reserves to get them through the winter. This program is designed to make children look at animals in the wild in a different light.

In Waterton the many children's programs include puppet shows on Sunday afternoon at the townsite. Call 403/859–2224 for information. Both parks sponsor the International Junior Naturalist Program, in which kids can earn a certificate by participating in programs in either park.

EVENING ACTIVITIES Waterton Lakes National Park offers interpretative-theater programs every evening in the summer, from 8:30 to 9:30, and there's a summer camp fire program at Belly River. At the Waterton townsite there are lounges and a summer cinema.

Many campgrounds at Glacier also host evening campfire programs, and adults can settle in for the night at one of the lounges in the park's hotels and lodges.

DINING

Dining generally takes a back seat to other attractions in and around Waterton/Glacier; however, prepared foods ranging from ice cream to complete dinners can be found in small, commercially developed areas. Health foods are not a priority in the Peace Park, but at least one dining room (at Waterton's Kilmorey Lodge) has "Heart Smart" entrées, and most eating places will custom cook your food to cut down on fat and sodium, if you request it.

INSIDE WATERTON **Bayshore Dining Room.** This modern dining room and coffee shop has a view of the lake and mountains from the dining room and serves beef, chicken, trout, salads, and other Western fare. *Waterton Ave., downtown Waterton, tel. 403/859–2291. AE, MC, V. Moderate.*

Kilmorey Lodge (Lamp Post Dining Room). This full-service, sit-down diner offers Western food, and you can order standard fare or the "Heart Smart" entrées. *Next to lake on left as you enter town of Waterton, tel. 403/859–2334. AE, DC, MC, V. Moderate.*

Prince of Wales Lodge Dining Room. Here enjoy fine dining on Western foods in a spectacular Swiss-chalet setting. *On hill overlooking Upper Waterton Lake, on north side of Waterton, tel. 403/859–2231. D, MC, V. Moderate.*

Zum-M-M's. This triple-service Western-food eatery offers a fast-food counter, a sit-down café, and a dining room. *Waterton Ave. in downtown Waterton, tel. 403/859–2388. AE, MC, V. Inexpensive–Moderate.*

New Frank's Restaurant. The only restaurant in the Peace Park serving both Western and Chinese food. *Waterton Ave. in downtown Waterton, tel. 403/859–2240. AE, MC, V. Inexpensive.*

Pearl's. A squeaky-clean sandwich/pasta shop that exhibits sandwich ingredients in a glass display case, from which customers can make their choices. *Windflower Ave. (1 street west of Waterton Ave. in Waterton), tel. 403/859–2284. MC, V. Inexpensive.*

Waterton Park Cafe. This small, renovated café serves Western food. There is also a children's menu. *Waterton Ave. in downtown Waterton, tel. 403/859-2393. V. Inexpensive.*

INSIDE GLACIER **Lake McDonald Lodge Dining Room.** Here you'll find Western fare with an Old West atmosphere. *Off GTTS Road about halfway along south side of Lake McDonald, tel. 406/888–5431. D, MC, V. Moderate.*

Many Glacier Dining Room. This restaurant offers fine dining in an early 1900s chalet environment, with Western foods on the menu. *Near end of Many Glacier Rd., on south side just before Swiftcurrent Campground, tel. 406/732–4411. D, MC, V. Moderate.*

Cedar Tree Deli. Order sandwiches, ice cream, and yogurt from the counter. There is no sit-down dining. *Going-to-the-Sun Rd. in Apgar Village, tel. 406/888–5232. No credit cards. Inexpensive.*

Eddie's Cafe. Sit-down restaurant with beef, chicken, rainbow trout, salads, and other Western foods. *Going-to-the-Sun Rd. in Apgar Village, tel. 406/888–5361. MC, V. Inexpensive.*

Lake McDonald Coffee Shop. A modern coffee shop that looks out of place sitting in Glacier Park. It offers sit-down dining on Western food ranging from sandwiches to steaks. *Next to Lake McDonald Lodge on south side of Lake McDonald, tel. 406/888–5431. D, MC, V. Inexpensive.*

Rising Sun Coffee Shop. This modern coffee shop overlooking St. Mary Lake serves the same Western foods found at Lake McDonald Coffee Shop and Swiftcurrent Coffee Shop. *North side of St. Mary Lake, about 5 mi inside east entrance, tel. 406/732–5523. D, MC, V. Inexpensive.*

Swiftcurrent Coffee Shop. Another dining room that serves Western food identical to that of Rising Sun Coffee Shop and Lake McDonald Coffee Shop. *End of Many Glacier Rd., next to Swiftcurrent Campground, tel. 406/732–5531. D, MC, V. Inexpensive.*

NEAR GLACIER **Glacier Park Lodge.** Here you'll enjoy fine dining in a natural megalog structure, with all the amenities of a top dining room. Western food is served. *Hwy 49, next to railroad station in East Glacier, tel. 406/226–9311. D, MC, V. Moderate.*

St. Mary Lodge Dining Room (Snow Goose Grill). This restaurant offers fine dining in a Western setting that is an alternative to dining in the park. Steaks and pasta are specialties, as is whitefish caught from nearby St. Mary Lake. *Just outside the east entrance of Glacier Park at St. Mary, tel. 406/732–4431. AE, MC, V. Moderate.*

PICNIC SPOTS All campgrounds within the Peace Park have picnic areas, with tables, water, and cooking grills that can double as barbecue pits. However, if you don't need these amenities for your picnics, there are dozens of turnoffs along the park's roads where you can snack while enjoying the scenery. The Lake McDonald area is especially scenic, as are many of the turnouts between the Rising Sun Campground and the East Side Tunnel. Remember, it's important that you don't feed the animals and that you take your garbage with you.

LODGING

Lodgings in the Peace Park tend to be fairly rustic and simple, though there are a few grand lodges and some modern accommodations. The emphasis here is on what's outside the rooms: A number of places offer lovely settings and magnificent views. Despite the great demand for a limited number of rooms in and around the Peace Park, the rates are surprisingly reasonable. However, it's best to reserve your rooms from six months to a year in advance to insure yourself a place to stay— especially for the busy months of July and August. A few rooms become available al-

most daily due to cancellations, but don't count on it.

Two popular historic lodgings in Glacier Park, the Granite Park Chalet and Sperry Chalet, have been closed for major repairs. Congress has appropriated $1 million for the renovations, but the chalets are not likely to reopen until 1995 or later.

INSIDE WATERTON **Prince of Wales Hotel.** This grand hotel in downtown Waterton is designed like a Swiss chalet and is somewhat old-fashion, but the view is great, especially from the rooms facing south toward the lake. *Glacier Park, Inc., East Glacier, MT 59434, tel. 403/236–3400. 82 units. Facilities: restaurant, tea room, cocktail lounge, gift shop, evening entertainment. D, MC, V. Closed mid-Sept.–mid-May. Expensive.*

Bayshore Inn. This is probably the most modern motel in the Peace Park. Its "L" shape matches the shoreline of Upper Waterton Lake and parallels a gravel beach. *Box 38, Waterton Townsite, AB T0K 2M0, tel. 403/859–2211. 70 units. Facilities: restaurant, coffee shop, cocktail lounge, gift shop, hot tub, laundromat, room service, evening entertainment. AE, MC, V (no credit-card guarantees). Moderate–Expensive.*

Aspen-Windflower Motel. This motel-style one- and two-story structure located in the middle of Waterton has a good view. It's plain but clean. *Box 100, Waterton Townsite, AB T0K 2M0, tel. 403/859–2255. 50 units (18 cabins), 14 kitchenettes. Facilities: Jacuzzi. AE, MC, V. Closed late Oct.–early May. Moderate.*

Crandell Mountain Lodge. This is an old, two-story chalet-design building in a tree-covered niche in Waterton. *Box 114, Waterton, AB T0K 2M0, tel. 403/859–2288. 13 units, 8 kitchenettes. AE, DC, MC, V. Moderate.*

El Cortez Motel. This motel-style, decaying brick building in downtown Waterton has a good view. *Box 67, Waterton Townsite, AB T0K 2M0, tel. 403/859–2366. 35 units. AE, DC, MC, V. Closed Nov.–Apr. Moderate.*

Kilmorey Lodge. The only year-round, full-service lodge in Waterton, this is an old-style two-story structure that faces the lake and is surrounded by trees. *Box 100, Waterton Townsite, AB T0K 2M0, tel. 403/859–2334. 25 units. Facilities: restaurant, coffee shop, cocktail lounge, room service. AE, DC, MC, V. Moderate.*

INSIDE GLACIER **Many Glacier Hotel.** The most isolated of the grand hotels, located along Swiftcurrent Lake on the northeast side of the park, it is also considered by many the most scenic. *Glacier Park, Inc., East Glacier, MT 59434, tel. 406/226–5551 or 602/207–6000. 210 rooms. Facilities: restaurant, snack bar, cocktail lounge, evening entertainment, gift shop, gas station. D, MC, V. Closed mid-Sept.–May. Expensive.*

Lake McDonald Lodge. This lodge located on the west side of Glacier at Lake McDonald has an Old West look to it. The lobby is decorated with mounts of wild animals. *Glacier Park, Inc., East Glacier, MT 59434. tel. 406/226–5551 or 602/207–6000. 100 rooms. Facilities: restaurant, coffee shop, cocktail lounge, store, evening entertainment, gas station. D, MC, V. Closed Oct.–May. Moderate–Expensive.*

Apgar Village Inn. This two-story motel-style wood structure with balconies faces Lake McDonald and has a beach. There is a spectacular view of the lake and mountains. *Glacier Park, Inc., East Glacier, MT 59434, tel. 406/226–5551 or 602/207–6000. 36 units, 12 kitchenettes. D, MC, V. Closed Oct.–early May. Moderate.*

Rising Sun Motor Inn. This motel resembles a barracks from the outside, but it overlooks St. Mary Lake and it's clean and neat. *Glacier Park, Inc., East Glacier, MT 59434, tel. 406/226–5551 or 602/207–6000. 72 units (25 cabins) rooms and cabins. Facilities: coffee shop, camp store. D, MC, V. Closed Oct.–early June. Moderate.*

Swiftcurrent Motor Inn. These plain but practical motel and cabin units, sitting at the end of the Many Glacier Road, have a good view. *Glacier Park, Inc., East Glacier, MT 59434, tel. 406/226–5551 or 602/207–6000. 88 units (26 cabins, some without bathrooms). Facilities: restaurant, camp store, laundromat. D, MC, V. Closed Sept. 4–June 19. Moderate.*

Village Motor Inn. Located in a lovely, woodsy setting, this historic hotel, built in the early years of this century, is the only lodging in Glacier Park not run by Glacier Park, Inc. The units are plain but meticulously clean. *Box 398, West Glacier, MT 59936, tel. 406/888–5484. 48 units (25 cabins), 23 kitchenettes. D, MC, V. Closed Oct.–Apr. Moderate.*

NEAR GLACIER **Glacier Park Lodge.** Located at East Glacier, just off Highway 2, this impressive full-service lodge was built in the second decade of this century, using 500- to 800-year-old fir and cedar logs 3 feet in diameter as the main supports. *Glacier Park, Inc., East Glacier, MT 59434, tel. 406/226–5551 or 602/207–6000. 155 rooms. Facilities: restaurant, snack bar, cocktail lounge, evening entertainment, heated pool, gift shop, 9-hole golf course. D, MC, V. Closed mid-Sept.–mid-May. Expensive.*

Glacier Motel. These small, clean contemporary motel units and cabins are in East Glacier. *Box 93, East Glacier, MT 59434, tel. 406/226–5593. 16 units (9 motel, 7 cabins), 11 kitchenettes. MC, V. Closed late Sept.–early May. Moderate.*

River Bend Motel. This small, no-frills, clean motel sits in a wooded setting on the edge of West Glacier, across the Middle Fork of the Flathead River from Glacier Park. *Box 398, West Glacier, MT 59936, tel. 406/888–5662. 32 units (5 cabins), 4 kitchenettes. Facilities: restaurant, camp store, laundromat within 100 yards. D, MC, V. Closed Oct.–mid-May. Moderate.*

St. Mary Lodge Motel. Located just outside the east entrance of Glacier Park, this large motel has a variety of comfortable room options. *St. Mary, MT 59417, tel. 406/732–4431 or 208/726–6279. 70 units (13 cabins), 12 kitchenettes. Facilities: restaurant, cocktail* *lounge, laundromat. AE, MC, V. Closed Oct. 2–Mother's Day. Moderate.*

Vista Motel. Located about a mile outside the west entrance, this small, modern motel has comfortable rooms and a great view of Glacier Park. *Box 98, West Glacier, MT 59936, tel. 406/888–5311 or 800/831–7101. 25 units, 6 kitchenettes. Facilities: heated pool. AE, D, MC, V. Closed Sept. 24–May 30. Moderate.*

Glacier Highland Motel. Located about 1/2 mile outside Glacier Park, this motel is old but clean. It is sprawled out into three buildings, all fairly close to one another. There are 13 units open during the winter. *Box 397, West Glacier, MT 59936, tel. 406/888–5427. 33 units, 5 kitchenettes. MC, V. Inexpensive.*

Jacobson's Cottages. Located outside Glacier Park in East Glacier, these individual cottages are among trees. *Box 216, East Glacier, MT 59434, tel. 406/226–4422. 12 cabins. Facilities: kitchen. D, MC, V. Closed Oct. 2–May 14. Inexpensive.*

Mountain Pine Motel. This small, modern, clean, one-story motel is in East Glacier. *Box 260, East Glacier, MT 59434, tel. 406/226–4403. 26 units. AE, D, DC, V. Closed Oct. 2–Apr. Inexpensive.*

Sears Motel and Campground. This bare-bones motel in East Glacier looks better on the inside than the outside, and it is clean. *Box 275, East Glacier, MT 59434, tel. 406/226–4432. 16 rooms, 19 camping units, 12 RV hookups. Facilities: Rent-a-Wreck car rentals. D, MC, V. Closed Oct.–early May. Inexpensive.*

CAMPING

INSIDE GLACIER All Glacier Park campgrounds are operated on a first-come, first-served basis, and during the busy months of July and August they usually fill up in the early afternoon. Fees are $8 or $10, depending on the services available, and are only charged when water is available. No utility hookups or showers are provided in park campgrounds, but showers are available at Rising Sun and Swiftcurrent Motor Inns for a nominal fee. Drinking water and cement-and-metal fireplaces, which can double as barbecue pits, are found in all campground and picnic areas. Questions about any Glacier National Park campgrounds should be directed to Park Headquarters, Glacier National Park, West Glacier, MT 59936, tel. 406/888–5441.

Apgar Campground (196 sites, flush toilets, disposal station, swimming, boat access, ranger station, public phone) is at Lake McDonald, near the west entrance. It's large, busy, and close to many activities and services. It's located within a short walking distance of Apgar Village. Cost: $10.

Rising Sun Campground (83 sites, flush toilets, disposal station, boat access) is another large, busy campground, near food and such water sports as fishing, cruising, and paddling. It's on the north side of St. Mary Lake, 5 miles west of the east entrance. Cost: $10.

Two Medicine Campground (99 sites, flush toilets, disposal station, ranger station, public phone, boat access) at Two Medicine Lake, on the southeast side of the park, is not near a town and its facilities, as are Apgar and Rising Sun, but Two Medicine is scenic and usually fills up later than the other campgrounds. It's located at the end of Two Medicine road, next to Two Medicine Store, 11 miles northwest of East Glacier. Some hardy campers swim in the lake. Cost: $10.

Bowman Lake Campground (48 sites, pit toilets, ranger station, boat access), on the northwest side of the park near Polebridge, is where you give up convenience for less-crowded camping. It's located at the end of Bowman Lake Road on the west end of Bowman Lake. Cost: $8.

Many Glacier Campground (114 sites, flush toilets, disposal station, ranger station, public phone, boat access) is another large busy campground with lots of activities and facilities. It is located in a scenic valley and is the hopping-off place for hiking into the northern part of the park. It's located at the end of Many Glacier Road, adjacent to Swiftcurrent. Cost: $10.

WATERTON/GLACIER CAMPGROUNDS

	INSIDE GLACIER					INSIDE WATERTON		
	Apgar	Rising Sun	Two Medicine	Bowman Lake	Many Glacier	Waterton Townsite	Belly River	Crandell Mountain
Total number of sites	196	83	99	48	114	238	24	129
Sites suitable for RVs	196	83	99	48	114	95	0	60
Number of hookups	0	0	0	0	0	95	0	0
Drive to sites	•	•	•	•	•	•	•	•
Hike to sites							•	
Flush toilets	•	•	•		•	•		•
Pit/chemical toilets				•			•	
Drinking water	•	•	•	•	•	•	•	•
Showers						•		
Fire grates	•	•	•	•	•		•	•
Swimming	•							
Boat access	•	•	•	•	•			
Playground						•	•	•
Disposal station	•	•	•		•	•		•
Ranger station	•		•	•	•	•		•
Public telephone	•		•		•	•		
Reservation possible								
Daily fee per site	$10*	$10	$10	$8	$10	$13–$17.50**	$7.25**	$10.50**
Dates open	year-round	early June–early Sept.	late June–early Sept.	mid-May–early Sept.	early June–early Sept.	mid-May–late Sept.	late May–mid-Oct.	late May–early Sept.

*Free in winter, no running water. **Canadian dollars.

There are six other campgrounds scattered along the roadways of the park: **Fish Creek** (180 sites, $10), **Avalanche** (87 sites, $10), **St. Mary** (156 sites, $10), **Cut Bank** (19 sites, $8), **Kintla Lake** (13 sites, $8), and **Sprague Creek** (25 sites, $10).

INSIDE WATERTON Waterton's campgrounds are also available only on a first-come, first-served basis. The townsite campground operates a waiting-list service in which campers must report to the campground with valid permits. If there is not a campsite available, a waiting-list ticket will be issued. Tickets for those sites that become available are listed daily from 10 AM to 11 AM and 12 PM to 1 PM. For more information contact Waterton Lakes National Park, Waterton Park, Alberta, Canada T0K 2M0, tel. 403/859–2224.

Waterton Townsite Campground is a large, busy campground with all the facilities of the town within walking distance. It has lots of conveniences but can also get crowded and noisy at times. It's on the south end of Waterton and has 95 full-service sites (power, water, sewer), $17.50; 113 multi-use sites (kitchen shelters with stoves, drinking water, flush toilets, tables), $13; 30 walk-in sites (flush toilets and tables), $13. The campground has washrooms, showers, sewage disposal, and picnic tables, as well as a public telephone, information kiosk, and a playground.

Belly River (24 sites, kitchen shelters with stoves, fireplaces, drinking water, tables, dry toilets, washroom, playground) is a small, tree-covered campground well away from heavy commercial activity. It's located off Chief Mountain Highway, 18 miles east of Waterton, near Belly River. Cost: $7.25. Group camping available by reservation.

Crandell Mountain (129 tent and trailer sites, kitchen shelters with stoves, drinking water, flush toilets, tables, fire pits, washrooms, playground, disposal station) is a heavily treed area without commercial development. It's located off Red Rock Parkway, 11 miles from Waterton, at about the center of the park. There is an information kiosk at the campground. Cost: $10.50.

Yellowstone National Park
Wyoming
By Andrew Giarelli
Updated by Candy Moulton

Where else but Yellowstone can you pull off an empty highway at dawn to see two bison bulls shaking the earth as they collide in battle before the herd, and an hour later be caught in an RV traffic jam? For more than 120 years the grandmother of national parks has been full of such contradictions, which usually stem from its twin goals: to remain America's preeminent wildlife preserve as well as its most accessible one.

The most recent contradiction in the park is the result of the great fires of the summer of 1988. Above the South entrance, along dizzying Lewis River canyon, a landscape of charred trees to the west seems to suggest a disaster that will alter the park's appearance for generations. Yet below the North entrance, the multicolored mosaic of burned, untouched, and regenerating areas along the Gallatin Range reinforces the idea that fire is essential to Yellowstone's natural cycle. The fires sweep out deadwood on the forest floor

and release nutritious ash into the watershed. They open the forest canopy to more light, allowing for more grasses and sprouts, which feed mammals ranging from rodents to bison and elk. In the process, meadows of brilliant wildflowers form. The chain of benefits goes on and on. The newly opened canopy makes the smaller rodents more vulnerable to hawks and eagles, thereby increasing the latter's population. Browsers, such as moose and deer, flourish with the new array of plant life—and they will surely be followed by more predators, such as grizzly bears, and scavengers, such as coyotes.

The abundance of wildlife in the park has been known to Native Americans for thousands of years. Blackfoot, Crow, Bannock, Flatheads, Nez Percé, and Northern Shoshone hunters frequented the area, although only one small Shoshone band named Sheepeaters lived in what is now the park. Mountain man John Colter became the first white man to explore Yellowstone in 1807–

08, and his stories about geysers and boiling rivers prompted some mapmakers to dub the uncharted region Colter's Hell. It is popularly believed that a Sioux description of the yellow rock varieties in the Grand Canyon of Yellowstone gave the park its name, adapted by early 19th-century French trappers. Unverified reports of outlandish natural phenomena continued filtering out of Yellowstone from the 1820s through the 1860s. In 1870, a government expedition encamped where the Firehole and Gibbon rivers join to form the Madison and agreed that this remarkable land should become a national park. In 1872, Congress declared Yellowstone the world's first national park.

ESSENTIAL INFORMATION

VISITOR INFORMATION For information on the park contact the National Park Service (**Yellowstone National Park,** WY 82190, tel. 307/344–7381). Information and reservations for lodging, dining, and activities are available from **TW Recreational Services, Inc.** (Yellowstone National Park, WY 82190–9989, tel. 307/344–7311). To find out more about the surrounding towns contact the **Wyoming Division of Tourism** (I–25 at College Dr., Cheyenne, WY 82002, tel. 307/777–7777 or 800/225–5996) or **Travel Montana** (Dept. of Commerce, Helena, MT 59620, tel. 406/444–2654 or 800/541–1447).

Information on facilities and services in Cody, Wyoming, and outside the East entrance can be obtained from the **Cody Visitors and Conventions Council** (Box 2777, Cody, WY 82414, tel. 307/587–2297). If you plan to travel through Jackson, contact the **Jackson Hole Visitors Council** (Box 982, Dept. 41, Jackson Hole, WY 83001, tel. 307/733–7606 or 800/782–0011, ext. 41).

All overnight backcountry activity requires a Backcountry Use Permit, which must be obtained in person no more than 48 hours before the planned trip. For information, call the Backcountry Office (tel. 307/344–2160). In summer you can get these free permits seven days a week, 8 to 4:30, at Mammoth Ranger Station/Visitor Center, Canyon Ranger Sta-

tion/Visitor Center, Grant Village Visitor Center, South entrance Ranger Station, Bechler Ranger Station, and Old Faithful Ranger Station. Hours vary in spring, fall, and winter. Backcountry camping is allowed only in the park's designated campsites, with exceptions during winter season (October 15 to May 15). All backcountry campsites have restrictions on group size, stock use, boating, fires, and length of stay.

FEES Entrance fees give visitors a seven-day pass to Yellowstone and Grand Teton national parks. The cost is $10 per automobile and $4 per visitor entering by snowmobile, motorcycle, bus, bicycle, or on foot; children under 17 enter free. You can buy a calendar-year pass to the two parks for $15.

PUBLICATIONS The National Park Service (*see* Visitor Information, *above*) distributes its yearly "Official Map and Guide" and its seasonal newspaper, *Yellowstone Today,* at park entrances and by mail. It will also send specific seasonal information and activity information as requested.

If you plan to hike in the backcountry, get a topographical map. A good one, printed on waterproof and tearproof plastic, is available from **Trails Illustrated** (Box 3610, Evergreen, CO 80439, tel. 800/962–1643). The **Yellowstone Association** (Box 117, Yellowstone National Park, WY 82190, tel. 307/344–2293) sells a "Trip Planner Package," which includes roadside, wildlife, hiking, bird, and geological guides, as well as detailed maps of the park's northern and southern halves. Many other Yellowstone books, posters, and videos are available from this association and are sold at the park's visitor centers.

One of the best historical references is Lee Whittlesey's *Yellowstone Place Names* (Montana Historical Society, 1988), a detailed, fascinating narrative about the park's many sights and sites. The handiest trail guide is Tom Carter's *Day Hiking Yellowstone* (Minuteman Press, 1990), which, despite its title, also details popular overnight trips. The classic geological, ecological, and human history of the park is *The Yellowstone Story,* two volumes by Aubrey L. Haines. For more information on geology, read William R. Keefer's *The Geologic Story of Yellowstone National Park.* A much more critical history is Alston Chase's controversial *Playing God in Yellowstone* (1986), which chronicles a century's worth of government mismanagement. This book foreshadowed the controversy over the 1988 Yellowstone fires; the park service at first refused to sell it at visitor centers. The best and most beautiful mile-by-mile roadside guide to the park is *National Parkways: Yellowstone National Park,* part of a series on national parks by **Worldwide Research and Publishing Company** (Box 3073, Casper, WY 82602).

Just as striking as its natural wonders are Yellowstone's man-made structures: the elegant Lake Yellowstone Hotel and the magnificently rustic Old Faithful Inn. The two best books on the history, architecture, and trivia surrounding these buildings are Barbara Dittle and Joanne Mallmann's *Plain to Fancy: Story of the Lake Hotel* (Roberts Rinehart Press, 1987) and Susan C. Scofield's *The Inn at Old Faithful* (Crown's Nest Associates, 1979).

GEOLOGY AND TERRAIN Yellowstone is a high plateau ringed by even higher mountains. Roadside elevations range from 5,314 feet at the North entrance to 8,859 feet at Dunraven Pass. The Gallatin Range to the west and north, the Absaroka and Beartooth ranges to the north and east, and the Tetons to the south all have peaks higher than 10,000 feet. Scenery ranges from near-high desert around the North entrance to lodgepole pine forests around the South entrance, and otherworldly landscapes of stunted pine and shrub around thermal areas.

With some 10,000 geysers, hot springs, fumaroles, and mud pots, Yellowstone's 3,472 square miles comprise the world's largest thermal area. Cataclysmic volcanoes "blew" 2 million years ago, then again 1.2 million and 600,000 years ago. The last one deposited 240 cubic miles of hot gas, ash, pumice, and rock debris, collapsing a 28- by 47-mile caldera, or basin, now in the park's center. Magmatic (molten rock) heat under the

Yellowstone Caldera continues to fuel the park's five most famous geyser basins—West Thumb, Old Faithful (or Upper), Midway, Lower, and Norris—which contain most of Yellowstone's 200 to 250 active geysers. Geysers occur when surface water seeping down through the porous rock is superheated and, as it rises to the surface and the pressure decreases, turns into steam. When that water is not superheated or under pressure, it rises to the surface to form hot springs, such as those at Mammoth. Fumaroles, visible at geyser basins and elsewhere along the caldera (try the Washburn Hot Springs Overlook, south of Dunraven Pass), result when the water is present in such small quantities that rather than flowing out it is continually released as steam. Fumaroles become mud pots, such as the stinking, simmering Mud Volcano, between Canyon and Fishing Bridge, when the acidic gases decompose rocks around the fumarole into mud and clay.

Although much of the Yellowstone caldera is hard to see, some major park sites mark its boundaries. The road from Madison to Norris follows the caldera's northwest rim; along the way, Gibbon Falls cascades over the caldera wall. From Washburn Hot Springs Overlook you can see a 35-mile northeastern stretch of the caldera boundary from Mt. Washburn south to the Red Mountains. From Lake Butte Overlook, you can see the caldera boundary 4 miles to the east.

After the volcanic eruptions came at least three glacial periods, the last one ending 8,500 years ago. Yellowstone Lake, North America's largest mountain lake, was formed by glaciers. So was Hayden Valley. There the glaciers left behind clay soil and fine silt that doesn't allow trees to grow but does allow for rich shrubland coveted by wildlife. Glacial debris blocked the Yellowstone River above the Upper Falls, creating a large lake in Hayden Valley. When this natural dam broke, its waters scoured out the Grand Canyon of the Yellowstone. Rounded boulders strewn along the Northeast entrance road are also testament to glaciers.

FLORA AND FAUNA The park's most common tree is the lodgepole pine, soaring tall and straight in dense stands with few branches on its lower trunk. Although lodgepole accounts for 80% of all park forests, six other conifers—most notably Engelmann spruce and subalpine fir—are interspersed with it. Sagebrush and rabbitbrush are common around Mammoth Hot Springs, while willows grow in moist sections of the Hayden and Lamar valleys.

Wildflowers abound in July and August in alpine meadows. Most common are Indian paintbrush, lupine, yellow monkey-flower, mountain bluebell, fireweed, and Rocky Mountain fringed gentian (the official park flower).

Yellowstone contains the biggest concentration of mammal species in the lower 48 states: seven ungulates (hooved animals), two bears, and 49 other mammals. There are also 279 bird species, five reptile species, and four species of amphibian. Elk, moose, mule deer, and bison are Yellowstone's most commonly seen large mammals. The best times to see these and other wildlife in summer are early morning and late evening. About 30,000 elk, or Wapiti, roam meadows, especially around the Midway and Upper geyser basins, the Lewis River area near the South entrance, and Mammoth Hot Springs. Some 500 to 700 moose feed throughout lowland marshy areas in summer, especially in the Hayden Valley and at Pelican Creek east of Fishing Bride. Mule deer, also called blacktail deer, frequent Old Faithful, Lake, Canyon, and the area between the North entrance and Tower. Bison, the park's largest animals at around 2,000 pounds, move to upland meadows in the Lamar and Hayden valleys in summer, although lone bison are often seen by roadsides. Despite their ponderous appearance, bison are unpredictable and can sprint at 30 miles per hour, three times faster than an average person can run. Almost every year, several visitors who approach bison too closely are seriously injured.

Bears are Yellowstone's most famous animals. From the 1930s through the 1960s, they frequented roadsides, begging food from obliging tourists. Increasing injuries and property damage forced the park service to wean bears from their human dependence in the early 1970s. Today there are far fewer roadside bears and fewer people injured by bears. Black bears (actually black, brown, or cinnamon) are the most commonly seen. Although they may seem clownish and are disinclined to attack people, black bears are still dangerous. Never approach one, especially a female with cubs.

Yellowstone is home to 200 to 300 of the fewer than 1,000 threatened grizzly bears surviving in Montana, Wyoming, and Idaho. They are bigger than black bears (3½ feet high at the shoulders, as opposed to 3 feet) and have dish-faced profiles and a pronounced hump between the shoulders. They come in a range of colors, from almost-black to light cream. Several park service brochures available at all entrances detail precautions you should take to avoid grizzly encounters; however, the park can offer no guarantee of absolute safety. Grizzlies may attack without warning and for no apparent reason; the last person to lose his life to a Yellowstone grizzly lost it in 1986. Grizzlies are solitary animals and prefer the park's deepest backcountry. Most roadside sightings of black bears and occasional grizzlies occur in early morning or evening near tree cover along open areas.

Bighorn sheep, males with massive curved horns, mostly stay above timberline among rocky crags. In summer they often appear around Mt. Washburn, 15 to 30 to a flock. Coyotes, which inhabit caves and burrows, appear often in Hayden Valley and the park's northern ranges. Count yourself lucky if you see a bobcat in the backcountry; count yourself blessed if you see a fleeting mountain lion. Badgers, beavers, foxes, marmots, minks, muskrats, otters, and wolverines also inhabit the park. Yellowstone has occasional unverified sightings of Rocky Mountain wolf, an endangered species. The possibility of reintroducing wolves into the park has been debated for years: Environmentalists say the predators are essential to the Yellowstone ecosystem, and ranchers outside the park are fearful of losing stock.

Backcountry lakes and rivers are especially rich in bird life: black and white ospreys hover over surfaces, while Canada geese bob and white pelicans dive for fish.

The park service will send you a "Birds of Yellowstone National Park" checklist of the park's 279 bird species and a "Wildlife" checklist, and the Yellowstone Association sells several Yellowstone mammal and bird guides (*see* Visitor Information, *above*).

WHEN TO GO   Most people visit Yellowstone in summer. In any given year, more than 3 million visitors will come to the park during summer and only 120,000 in winter. Those winter visitors, however, are the ones who see the park at its most magical—with steam billowing from geyser basins to wreath trees in ice, while bison and elk forage close to roads turned into ski and snow vehicle trails. All Yellowstone roads except the Northeast entrance to Cooke City, Montana, are closed to wheeled vehicles from early November to early May; they are open to oversnow vehicles from mid-December to mid-March. Spring road openings usually follow this pattern: Mammoth–Norris, mid- to late March; West entrance, mid-April; East and South entrances, early May; Old Faithful–West Thumb, late May; Beartooth Highway (Northeast entrance) end of May; Tower–Canyon, beginning of June.

The average maximum temperature at Mammoth in July is 80.3°F and the minimum is 45.5°F, with extremes from 96°F to 25°F. August temperatures are similar. When hiking, be prepared for cold rain dropping temperatures by up to 20 degrees. January average highs and lows are 28.7°F and 9°F, with extremes from 50°F to -41°F. Old Faithful is often 5 to 15 degrees colder than Mammoth. January snowfall at Mammoth averages 17$^{1}/_{2}$ inches, although it has reached 77 inches. Snow is possible year-round at such high elevations as Mt. Washburn. June and September are often wet and cloudy throughout the park's lower elevations, but in September, and to a lesser extent October, there

are some delightfully sunny days—albeit 5 to 20 degrees cooler than in midsummer. April and May are the best months for viewing baby bison, moose, and other new arrivals, but many park roads are closed for snowplowing, and few services are available outside Mammoth.

SEASONAL EVENTS   **Mid-March:** The **Rendezvous Ski Race** (tel. 406/646–7701) in West Yellowstone, Montana, is one of eight segments in the cross-country Great American Ski Chase. **Early May to early October:** Students in grades 5–12 show off their park-related artwork at **Imagine Yellowstone** (tel. 307/344–2265), an annual exhibit at Canyon and Mammoth visitor centers. **Late May to late October:** The **Yellowstone Institute** (tel. 307/344–2294) sponsors dozens of short, mostly in-the-field courses on park flora, fauna, geology, and outdoor skills. **Mid-June:** **College National Finals Rodeo** (tel. 406/587–2637) in Bozeman, Montana, is the leading event on the national college rodeo circuit. **Late June to early July:** The **Plains Indian Pow-Wow** (tel. 307/587–4771) and **Cody Stampede** (tel. 307/587–2297), both in Cody, Wyoming, celebrate the Native American and cowboy heritages of the Northern Plains. **Mid-August:** The **Festival of Nations** (tel. 406/446–1718) in Red Lodge is a nine-day extravaganza of free food, dancing, music, and exhibits celebrating the ethnic groups who settled this mining town at the foot of the spectacular Beartooth Highway, 69 miles from Yellowstone's Northeast entrance.

WHAT TO PACK   In summer expect intense dry heat, bone-chilling drizzle, and much in between—sometimes on the same day. Layering is the best solution: Try a short-sleeved shirt, sweatshirt, and a hooded windbreaker. Even if it's warm, carry long pants. Gloves and raingear are also a good idea; you can carry them in a small knapsack. Walking shoes are essential, but hiking shoes are recommended for trails.

Yellowstone's extreme winters make attention to proper clothing critical, even if you plan to stay inside a car or snowcoach. You should have thermal underwear, wool socks and outerwear, waterproof boots, a lined coat, and warm headgear. If you're planning on skiing or snowmobiling, consider polypropylene underwear and socks: It resists moisture from outside and wicks away your body's own moisture. Sunscreen, sunglasses, and binoculars for viewing wildlife are worth bringing in any season.

GENERAL STORES The oldest national park concessionaire, **Hamilton Stores, Inc.** (Box 250, West Yellowstone, MT 59758) has been serving Yellowstone since 1915. Today, it runs 14 park stores, some of which are interesting destinations themselves. The Old Faithful Lower Store, for example, has a knotty pine porch with benches that beckon tired hikers, as well as an inexpensive lunch counter. All stores sell souvenirs ranging from the tacky (cowboy joke items and rubber tom-toms) to the authentic ($60 buffalo-hide moccasins and $200 cowboy coats). Stores are generally open from May through September; Mammoth is open year-round. The following stores are located in the park and are listed with their summer hours. Hours vary during the shoulder seasons.

Old Faithful Lower General Store (tel. 307/545–7282) 7:45 AM to 9:45 PM, **Old Faithful Upper General Store** (tel. 307/545–7237) 7:45 AM to 9:30 PM, **Old Faithful Photo Shop** (307/545–7258) 7:30 AM to 10 PM, **Grant Village General Store** (307/242–7266) 7 AM to 10 PM and **Mini Store** (tel. 307/242–7390) 8 to 6, **Bridge Bay Marina Tackle Shop** (tel. 307/242–7326) 8 AM to 9 PM, **Lake General Store** (tel. 307/242–7563) 8 AM to 9:30 PM, **Fishing Bridge General Store** (tel. 307/242–7200) 7:45 AM to 9:30 PM, **Canyon General Store** (tel. 307/242–7377) 7:45 AM to 9:30 PM and **Photo Shop** (tel. 307/344–7757) 7 AM to 10 PM, **Tower Store** (tel. 307/344–7786) 8 AM to 9 PM, **Roosevelt Store** (tel. 307/344–7779) 7:45 AM to 9 PM, **Mammoth General Store** (tel. 307/344–7702) 7:30 AM to 9 PM, and **Christmas-Photo Shop** (tel. 307/344–7757) 9 to 8.

Outside the park, 2 miles below the South entrance, **Flagg Ranch Village** (Box 187, Moran, WY 83013, tel. 307/733–8761 or 800/443–2311) has a grocery store, gift shop,

and tackle shop that are open from mid-May to mid-October and mid-December to mid-March. Summer hours for the gift shop are 8 AM to 10 PM, for the grocery store 7 AM to 10 PM, and for the tackle shop 8 to 5. Winter hours vary.

In Gardiner, Montana, 5 miles north of Mammoth Hot Springs, the **Conoco Travel Shoppe** (tel. 406/848–7681) is open daily 5:30 AM to 11 PM, the **Exxon Convenience Store** (tel. 406/848–7742) is open Monday to Saturday 6 AM to 11 PM and Sunday 6 AM to 10 PM, and the **North Entrance Food Farm** (tel. 406/848–7524) is open Monday to Saturday 8 to 8, Sunday 9 to 7. All are on U.S. 89 and all sell groceries and outdoor supplies year-round.

ARRIVING AND DEPARTING The park has five entrances, all of which join the Grand Loop Road. The most breathtaking entry is from the northeast on U.S. 212, the Beartooth Highway. U.S. 89 from Livingston, Montana, is an easier drive, and it is the only entrance open to wheeled vehicles in winter. Those coming from Grand Teton will use the South entrance (U.S. 89–191–287). This route, along with U.S. 20 through West Yellowstone to the West entrance and U.S. 14–16–20 from Cody to the East entrance, are the most heavily trafficked.

By Plane. The two most convenient airports are **Jackson Hole Airport** (tel. 307/733–7682), outside Jackson, Wyoming, and 50 miles from the South entrance; and **Yellowstone Regional Airport** (tel. 307/587–5096), outside Cody, Wyoming, and 52 miles from the East entrance. Jackson has daily flights connecting through Denver or Salt Lake City on several national and commuter airlines; Cody is served by **Continental** (tel. 800/525–0280) year-round.

Bozeman's **Gallatin Field** (tel. 406/388–6632), 90 miles from the West entrance, also has daily flights on national airlines connecting through Minneapolis and Denver. **West Yellowstone Airport** is closest to the park and served daily by **Skywest** (tel. 406/646–7351 or 800/453-9417) from June through October, but closed to everything but ski-planes the rest of the year.

During the summer, none of these airports offers public transportation to the park or even into their respective towns, but some lodgings in each town supply free airport shuttles. Taxi service from Yellowstone Regional Airport is through **Cody Connection Taxi** (tel. 307/587–9292), which charges $5 for the first person and $1 for each additional person to get into town. **West Yellowstone Taxi** (tel. 406/646–7359) charges about the same from West Yellowstone Airport into town. One-way taxi fares from Gallatin Field into Bozeman and from Jackson Hole Airport into Jackson average $12 for a carload of people.

Car rentals are available at each of these airports. At Cody's Yellowstone Regional Airport, you can rent cars from **Avis** (tel. 800/331–1212) or **Hertz** (tel. 800/654–3131). Bozeman's Gallatin Field has Avis, Hertz, **Budget** (tel. 800/527–0700), **Payless** (tel. 800/548–9551), and **Rent-A-Wreck** (tel. 406/587–4551). You can also rent RVs in Bozeman from **C&T Trailer Supply** (2000 N. 7th Ave., Bozeman, MT 59715, tel. 406/587–8610). West Yellowstone Airport has a Hertz desk, and Budget (tel. 406/646–7634) and Payless (tel. 406/646–9332) have offices in town with free airport shuttle service. Avis (tel. 307/733–3422), Budget (tel. 307/733–2206), Hertz (tel. 307/733–2272), and **National** (tel. 307/733–4132 or 800/328–4567) all operate at Jackson Hole Airport. In the town of Jackson, cars are also available at **Dollar** (tel. 307/733–0935), **Jackson Hole Car Rental** (tel. 307/733–6868), **Resort** (tel. 307/733–1656), and **Rent-A-Wreck** (tel. 307/733–5014).

By Car and RV. The 69 miles from Red Lodge, Montana, to the Northeast entrance traverse the 11,000-foot-high Beartooth Pass, whose dizzying switchbacks were cut in the 1930s. The drive from Red Lodge takes about two hours and is best avoided at night, in bad weather, and when traveling by RV. The easier, all-season approach is from the north on U.S. 89, which exits I–90 in Livingston, Montana, and enters the park at the North entrance. This road traverses about 60 miles of the appropriately named Paradise Valley,

with the Yellowstone River flanked by the gentle Gallatin Range on the west and the towering Absaroka Range on the east, until it reaches the original 1903 stone entry arch in the funky old tourist town of Gardiner, Montana. Also good for RVs is the West entrance, 60 miles from Ashton, Idaho, on U.S. 20; the West entrance is also 90 miles from Bozeman, Montana, through winding Gallatin Canyon on U.S. 191. It is 53 miles from Cody, Wyoming, to the East entrance on U.S. 14–16–20 through the Shoshone National Forest; just past the entrance is a climb up 8,530-foot Sylvan Pass. From Jackson, Wyoming, U.S. 89–191–287 travels 64 miles through Grand Teton National Park to the South entrance; this route is fairly easy on RVs. Grand Teton Park, 6 miles from the South entrance, is often visited in conjunction with Yellowstone. Utah's Arches and Canyonlands national parks and Zion National Park are almost 700 miles from Old Faithful. Grand Canyon Village in Arizona is more than 950 miles away, and Colorado's Rocky Mountain National Park is 548 miles from Old Faithful.

By Train. The nearest **Amtrak** (tel. 208/234–2150 or 800/872–7245) station is in Pocatello, Idaho, 196 miles from Old Faithful. Only two trains call at this station: one from Seattle, which arrives at 3:10 AM; and one from Chicago, which comes in at 11:40 PM. The ticket office is open daily, but only from 10 PM to 5 AM; it's also open Tuesday to Thursday 6 AM to 1:30 PM. The nearest car rental office is at the Pocatello airport, so you may be able to arrange to have a car waiting for you, but then again you may not.

By Bus. Greyhound Lines (tel. 800/231–2222) serves West Yellowstone, Montana (depot at Menzel's Travel Agency, 127 Yellowstone Ave.), twice daily year-round, with one bus northbound from Salt Lake City, Utah (depot at 160 W. South Temple St.), and one southbound from Bozeman, Montana (depot at 625 N. 7th Ave.). Three daily east–west buses pass through Bozeman, as does one southbound to West Yellowstone. Greyhound does not serve Cody or Jackson, Wyoming. **Cody Bus Lines** (tel. 800/733–2304) provides daily service from Billings.

From mid-May to mid-September, several bus lines outside the park shuttle visitors to Old Faithful, where they can make noon connections to TW Services tour buses. From Bozeman, **Karst Stage** (tel. 406/586–8567) runs one bus every day but Sunday. On Monday, Wednesday, and Friday, the bus leaves at appoximately 7 AM, with pickups at all Bozeman motels, and goes to the North entrance. Tuesday, Thursday, and Saturday it departs at 9 AM for the West entrance. Round-trip fare is $49.50; Bozeman–Old Faithful is $34 one way, and Bozeman–Mammoth is $20 one way. Fares do not include park entrance fees.

From early December to early March, Karst Stage operates daily park shuttles from Gallatin Field in Bozeman to Mammoth and West Yellowstone ($36–$38 round-trip). At West Yellowstone, Mammoth, and Flagg Ranch, TW Services offers snowcoach tours into the park (*see* Guided Tours, *below*).

EXPLORING

Although the plane and bus connections to Yellowstone are adequate, the park, like so many others, remains car country. The Grand Loop Road and five entrance roads pass nearly every major park sight and region, with interpretative displays, overlooks, and/or short trails at each. Actual driving times along the 142-mile Grand Loop Road are difficult to estimate because the maximum speed is 45 mph or lower where posted, roads are narrow and winding, surfaces may be rutted, and traffic may be heavy. If you're nervous about driving steep roads with sharp and sometimes unprotected drop-offs, consider TW Services' tour buses (*see* Guided Tours, *below*).

You can drive the Grand Loop Road in a day—but don't do it unless you must. In order to make full stops at all of Yellowstone's major roadside attractions, you'll need at least three days.

THE BEST IN ONE DAY If you have just one day in Yellowstone, it is best to explore a single area. A good choice would be the five major geyser basins, which all occupy the

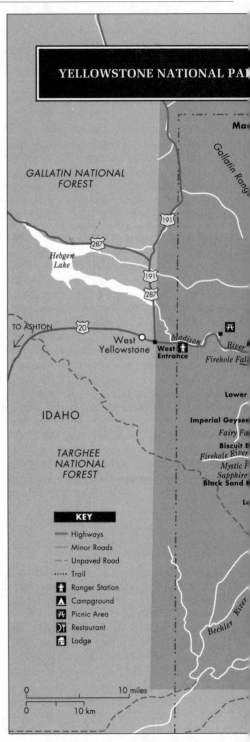

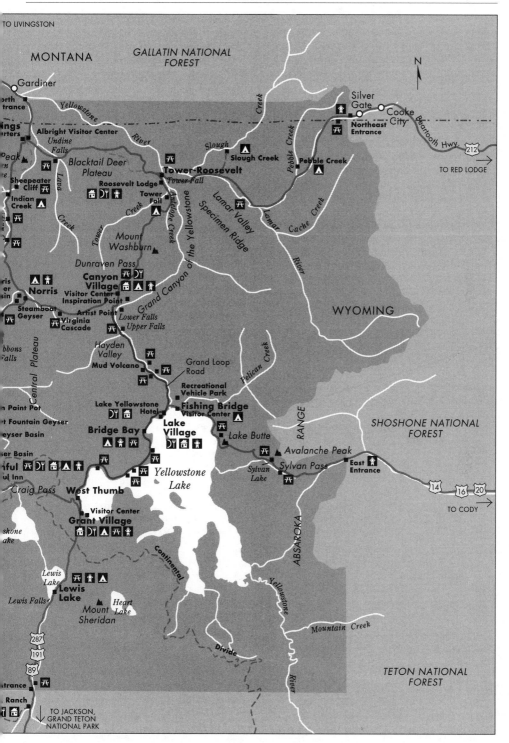

TO LIVINGSTON

MONTANA   GALLATIN NATIONAL
           FOREST

N

Gardiner

orth
trance

Yellowstone

ings
rters

Albright Visitor Center

Undine
Falls

eak

Blacktail Deer
Plateau

Sheepeater
Cliff

Lava

Indian
Creek

Slough

Creek

Silver
Gate

Cooke
City

Northeast
Entrance

Beartooth

Hwy.

212

TO RED LODGE

Slough Creek

Tower-Roosevelt

Roosevelt Lodge

Tower
Fall

Tower Fall

Antelope Creek

Lamar Valley

Specimen Ridge

Pebble Creek

Pebble Creek

Cache Creek

Lamar

River

WYOMING

River

Creek

Mount
Washburn

Tower

Creek

Dunraven Pass

Canyon
Village

Visitor Center
Inspiration Point

Grand Canyon of the Yellowstone

Norris

ris
er
sin

Steamboat
Geyser

Virginia
Cascade

Artist Point

Lower Falls

Upper Falls

bbons
alls

Central Plateau

Hayden
Valley

Mud Volcano

Grand Loop
Road

Recreational
Vehicle Park

Pelican Creek

SHOSHONE NATIONAL
FOREST

n Paint Pot

t Fountain Geyser

eyser Basin

Lake Yellowstone
Hotel

Fishing Bridge

Visitor Center

r Basin

Bridge Bay

Lake
Village

Lake Butte

RANGE

ful

ul Inn

Craig Pass

West Thumb

Yellowstone
Lake

Avalanche Peak

Sylvan Pass

Sylvan
Lake

East
Entrance

14

16

20

TO CODY

Visitor Center

Grant Village

ABSAROKA

Continental

shone
ake

Lewis
Lake

Lewis
Lake

Lewis Falls

Mount
Sheridan

Heart
Lake

Yellowstone

Mountain Creek

287

191

89

trance

Divide

River

TETON NATIONAL
FOREST

Ranch

TO JACKSON,
GRAND TETON
NATIONAL PARK

southwest end of the Grand Loop. At each you can take short interpretative trails out to major features. You might choose to concentrate on the Grand Canyon of Yellowstone, taking time to walk either Uncle Tom's Trail or the Lookout Point Trail for close views of the Upper and Lower Falls (*see* Nature Trails and Short Walks, *below*).

From the North and Northeast. If you are entering the park from the north or northeast, begin at dawn, with wildlife viewing in Lamar Valley. Drive south over Dunraven Pass and spend the morning sightseeing at Canyon. Follow the North Rim Drive (*see* Scenic Drives and Views, *below*) stopping to take the very short paved walks out to Inspiration, Grandview, and Lookout points. You can leave the car at either the Inspiration Point or Brink of Upper Falls parking areas and walk all or part of the North Rim Trail (*see* Nature Trails and Short Walks, *below*), from which there are views of the river and both the Lower (308-foot) and Upper (109-foot) falls. Return to your car and take Artist Point Drive to Artist Point and the best view of the Lower Falls and much of the Canyon (*see* Scenic Drives and Views, *below*). Unwrap a picnic lunch at Chittenden Bridge, where Artist Point Drive connects with the Grand Loop Road.

Continue clockwise around the Grand Loop's north half to Norris. At this point you will have to decide whether you want to veer south for an afternoon around Old Faithful or north to Mammoth Hot Springs. Both areas offer many easy walks past outstanding thermal features. At Old Faithful, you can place the famous geyser into context by walking the 1 1/3-mile Geyser Hill Loop (*see* Nature Trails and Short Walks, *below*) or a variety of other Upper Geyser Basin trails. Since you have come such a long way, you will probably want to join the throngs of visitors waiting for the next eruption: Do it from the deck of the Old Faithful Inn, a building that certainly deserves a bit of your exploring time (*see* Historic Buildings and Sites, *below*).

If you choose Mammoth, park at the base of the Lower Terrace and hike the Lower Terrace

Interpretive Trail (*see* Nature Trails and Short Walks, *below*) past Liberty Cap and other strange, brightly colored limestone formations. If you drive 1 1/2 miles south of the visitor center you will reach the Upper Terrace Drive, from which there are more closeups of hot springs and an overview of both terraces. The road is narrow and not suited for large RVs or trailers. Later, you can poke around Mammoth's old red-roof Army buildings and finish the day with dinner at Mammoth's Terrace Restaurant.

From the South and West. If you enter the park from the south or west, it's best to focus on the geyser basins around Old Faithful, Norris Geyser Basin, Canyon, and Yellowstone Lake. Start with the geysers: Old Faithful's trails are frequently visited by elk in the early morning. After exploring the Upper Geyser Basin around Old Faithful, head north toward Norris Geyser Basin, detouring onto the 3-mile Firehole Lake Drive (*see* Scenic Drives and Views, *below*). When you reach Norris walk the 1/4 mile out to Steamboat, the world's tallest active geyser (although it seldom erupts), and look around the Norris Museum's geyseriana. It should be about time for lunch. You can drive the 12 miles east to Canyon and eat in Canyon Village, or stop at the Virginia Cascade picnic area, about 5 miles east of Norris.

When you're through exploring Canyon (follow the tour described above), head south through Hayden Valley with an eye out for bison and other wildlife. It's 16 miles to Bridge Bay at Yellowstone Lake's northern end. From here take a Scenicruise boat tour (*see* Guided Tours, *below*) of the northern lake, and then have an elegant dinner at Lake Yellowstone Hotel. Drive the 10 miles east to Lake Butte Overlook for spectacular sunset views.

From the East. If you are arriving from the east, start with sunrise at Lake Butte and early morning wildlife viewing in Hayden Valley, moving counterclockwise around the Grand Loop's southern half to morning sightseeing at Canyon, early afternoon at Old Faithful, and back to Yellowstone Lake at West Thumb (*see tours described above*). From here follow the lake's western shore back up to Bridge Bay for a late afternoon boat ride and dinner at Lake Yellowstone Hotel.

ORIENTATION PROGRAMS Ranger naturalists give talks on natural history at all of the park's visitor centers in summer. They also lead wildlife field trips (*see* Guided Tours, *below*). Park visitor centers offer free films, talks, slide shows, skills workshops, walking tours, campfire programs, and living history demonstrations geared to each area. Check *Discover Yellowstone,* a seasonal newspaper available at all visitor centers, for details on this season's schedule. Note that visitor center hours vary depending on the time of year.

Mammoth's Albright Visitor Center (tel. 307/344–2263) alternates the historical film *The Challenge of Yellowstone* with a slide show titled "Winter in Yellowstone" all day. It is open 8 to 7 mid-June to mid-August; 9 to 5 the rest of the year.

Throughout the day the **Old Faithful Visitor Center** (tel. 307/545–2750) shows the nine-minute film *Yellowstone: A Living Sculpture,* which explains the park's geothermal activity. It is open 8 to 8 early June to early September, 9 to 4:30 December to mid-March. Spring and fall hours vary but are generally shorter than summer and winter hours.

Canyon Visitor Center (tel. 307/242–2550) focuses on the Grand Canyon of the Yellowstone. It has a geology exhibit and shows an audiovisual program called "Faces of Yellowstone." This center is typically open 8 to 7 mid-June to mid-August; and 9 to 5 mid-May to mid-June and mid-August to late September.

All of the following areas host ranger-led programs and some show films and videos: **Norris Museum** (tel. 307/344–2812) 9 to 5 mid-May to early June, 8 AM to 9 PM early June to early September, 9 to 5 early September to mid-September; **Tower-Roosevelt** area (tel. 307/344–7746); **Fishing Bridge Visitor Center** (tel. 307/242–2450) 9 to 5 late May to mid-June, 8 to 6 mid-June to late August, 9 to 6 late August to early September; and **Grant**

Village Visitor Center (tel. 307/424–2650) 9 to 5 mid-May to mid-June, 8 to 8 mid-June to late August, 9 to 6 late August to early September.

GUIDED TOURS Ranger-led programs are offered at all visitor centers from mid-June to mid-August and include one- to three-hour geyser basin hikes at major thermal areas, backcountry orienteering sessions, hawk-watching on the Canyon's north rim, bird-watching and fire of '88 field trips at West Thumb, a six-hour strenuous hike up Specimen Ridge at Mammoth Hot Springs, and photography skills workshops and walks throughout the park. For information call 307/344–7381.

TW Recreational Services (Yellowstone National Park, WY 82190–9989, tel. 307/344–7311) schedules a range of full-day bus tours from various park locations from mid-May to mid-September along the Lower Loop ($24 adults, $12 ages 5–11, not including lunch). Lower Loop tours leave from Old Faithful and Grant Village; Upper Loop tours leave from Lake, Fishing Bridge, Canyon, and Mammoth. The buses stop frequently, and the guides, mostly college students, are usually knowledgeable and enthusiastic. From early June to late September the company also offers **Scenicruise Rides,** one-hour boat tours around the northern part of Yellowstone Lake, from which you can view the Absaroka Mountains and the Lake Yellowstone Hotel. The trip is narrated by the captain ($7.09 adults, $3.94 ages 2–11). In winter, TW Services offers **snowcoach tours** (about $65 round-trip adults, children half-price) to Old Faithful and Canyon, half-day snowmobile tours ($85 per machine) from Mammoth to Norris Geyser Basin on Thursday, various cross-country ski tours ($25–$85), and winter wildlife bus tours through Lamar Valley ($12.50 adults, $6.25 children).

Karst Stage (*see* Arriving and Departing, *above*) includes an informal narrative on its trips into the park, but these tours are not as detailed as those given by TW Recreational Services. **National Park Tours** (tel. 307/733–

4325) offers tours from Jackson, Wyoming, into the park.

If you plan to make a self-guided driving tour of the park, be sure to rent a **TourGuide,** a compact-disc player that uses Sony Data Discman CD-ROM technology to teach you about the park. TourGuide has five hours of well-presented audio, covering history, geology, wildlife, ecology, and park services, as well as a few visuals. Blocks of information are numerically coded, and you can easily select what you want to hear by punching the appropriate numbers on the keypad. The unit, which plugs into your car's cigarette lighter and broadcasts over your FM radio, rents for $24.95 and is available at nine locations—four just outside the park's entrances and five at hotels within the park. For more information, call 800/247–1213.

SCENIC DRIVES AND VIEWS There are 370 miles of paved roadway within Yellowstone, and the figure eight pattern of the main road, the Grand Loop Road, makes all areas of the park accessible. Hardly a segment of road is dull, but the following tour points out various highlights.

In the northwest section of the park, south of Mammoth Hot Springs, the Grand Loop Road passes the inactive hot spring cone called Liberty Cap, which is visible from the Mammoth Hot Springs parking area. Two miles south of Mammoth off the Grand Loop Road is the narrow and tortuous **Upper Terrace Loop Drive,** a 1 1/2-mile tour past 500- year-old limber pine trees and mosses growing through white travertine, which is composed of lime deposited when Mammoth's hot, acidic springs come in contact with open air. This eerie landscape is further delineated by brilliant orange, yellow, green, and brown algae growing atop the travertine. Farther down the Grand Loop Road, about 5 miles south of Mammoth, the one-way dirt **Bunsen Peak Road** circles 8,564-foot Bunsen Peak; it will take about 25 minutes to make the 8-mile drive. This area displays the full range of the effects of the Yellowstone fires, from mosaic burns to completely charred landscapes. RVs and trailers are not allowed on either road.

If you travel the Grand Loop Road east toward Roosevelt, you will pass the one-way **Blacktail Plateau Drive,** a dirt road that traverses sagebrush hills and pine forests. The 45-minute excursion may reward you with a coyote sighting in early evening.

In the 19 miles from Roosevelt south to Canyon, the **northeastern Grand Loop** passes some of the park's finest scenery. The road twists beneath a series of leaning basalt towers 40 to 50 feet high, to the Tower store. Take the short path from the parking lot to view 132-foot Tower Fall, which is best seen in morning. Ascending through arid sagebrush fields dotted with stands of aspen and heavily burned areas, the road passes 10,243-foot Mt. Washburn. The rough, unpaved **Chittenden Road** leaves the main road for a 2-mile bounce up a north flank of the mountain to a sweeping overlook. Just 5 miles past Chittenden Road you'll pass the Grand Loop's highest point, Dunraven Pass (8,859 feet), covered in wildflowers and subalpine fir.

At Canyon Village, the paved 2 1/2-mile one-way **North Rim Drive** leads first to Inspiration Point, where the Yellowstone River plunges 900 feet below. The often-crowded overlook is a two-minute trek uphill then down about a dozen steps. Next stop on this detour is Grandview Point, where another short paved trail leads to a view of the 308-foot Lower Falls in the distance. A little farther along is Lookout Point. From here a difficult 1/2-mile switchback trail descends 600 feet to the Brink of the Lower Falls; this trail is best taken in morning, when sunlight often creates a misty rainbow.

Return to Grand Loop Road and less than 1/2 mile along, turn left into Upper Falls Parking Area. From there you can hike the 500-foot trail to a platform hanging over the 109-foot Upper Falls. Drive another 1/2 mile south on the Grand Loop, turn left onto the Chittenden Bridge, and follow **Artist Point Drive,** which leads to the best Canyon views. The five-minute walk from the parking area ends at a platform perched 700 feet above the canyon's gray, pink, orange, and yellow rhyolite rock;

you will understand why this is one of the park's most photographed scenes.

Moving south out of Canyon, the 16 miles to Fishing Bridge (you must turn left onto East Entrance Road to reach it) crosses the Hayden Valley, one of Yellowstone's best roadside wildlife viewing areas. Fishing Bridge, once famous for postcards showing fishermen lining its banks, is now reserved for cutthroat trout spawning and the waterfowl activity that attends it. You can watch from a viewing area on the bridge. Ten miles east, a 1-mile spur road leads to **Lake Butte,** a wooded promontory rising 615 feet above Yellowstone Lake and a prime sunset-watching spot. The **East Entrance Road** continues for 16 miles to the park boundary; it winds through the Absarokas, the most beautiful alpine setting of any park road.

If you travel west from Fishing Bridge to West Thumb, the Grand Loop Road follows Yellowstone Lake for about 23 miles, with numerous turnoffs and picnic areas. About 12 miles south of West Thumb, the **South Entrance Road** tops the sheer black lava walls of Lewis River Canyon, another place that was heavily burned. Turn into the parking area just before the bridge here for a close-up of Lewis River Falls.

Going northwest 17 miles from West Thumb on the Grand Loop Road, you'll reach **Old Faithful Road,** on your right. Park at the visitor center, and walk the few hundred feet to benches surrounding Old Faithful Geyser. Although not the park's biggest geyser, Old Faithful has been the world's most famous geyser since its discovery in 1870; each of the 18 to 22 daily eruptions is predicted at the visitor center.

About 8 miles north of Old Faithful, on the right, the 3-mile, one-way **Firehole Lake Drive** passes Great Fountain Geyser, which explodes between 75 and 150 feet into the air, and on occasion reaches as high as 200 feet. If you're touring the park by snowcoach in winter, watch for the large bison herd here. Just before crossing the Firehole River, you will come to the entrance to the paved 2-mile, one-way **Firehole Canyon Drive,** on your left.

This road twists through a 700- to 800-foot-deep canyon past 40-foot Firehole Falls.

At this point you have reached Madison. Traveling east, the Grand Loop enters 1,000-foot deep Gibbon Canyon, whose black lava walls contrast sharply with its riverbed reddened by iron deposits. Gibbon Falls drops 84 feet in this canyon; it is actually cascading over a piece of the Yellowstone caldera's northwest rim. An adjacent picnic area overlooks the canyon. West of Madison, the **West Entrance Road** hugs the Madison River for 14 miles: This is a fine sunset drive, with views of National Park Mountain (at whose foot the encamped 1870 Washburn expedition hit upon the idea of making Yellowstone a national park) and the heavily fished Madison River.

Norris Junction, site of Norris Geyser Basin, is 14 miles northeast of Madison on Grand Loop Road. Though oddly not as renowned as Old Faithful's Upper Geyser Basin, Norris is richer in superlatives: North America's hottest geyser basin (highest underground recording 459°F); Yellowstone's oldest geyser basin (over 115,000 years old); and the world's tallest individual geyser (Steamboat Geyser, with rare eruptions over 300 feet—three in 1989, one in 1990, and one in 1991). Norris is divided into the open, concentrated geysers of Porcelain Basin on the east and the forested, scattered geysers of Back Basin on the west, with the quaint 1930 log and stone Norris Museum in the middle (*see* Nature Trails and Short Walks, *below*).

Mammoth Hot Springs is 21 miles north of Norris. Eight miles into this stretch on the right you pass Obsidian Cliff, whose volcanic glass was prized by the region's Native American tribes for projectile points. About 5 miles farther north on the right is a 1/2-mile turnoff to Sheepeater Cliff, where the park's only known year-round Native American inhabitants—a couple of hundred Shoshones mockingly nicknamed "Sheepeaters" by other tribes—lived until the 1870s. A small display here describes their meager existence. Immediately north of here the main road opens onto Swan Lake Flats, a prime elk habitat, and then continues to Mammoth.

HISTORIC BUILDINGS AND SITES Among the stern, gray stone buildings at Mammoth is the **Albright Visitor Center,** which was an Army Bachelor Officers' Quarters from 1886 to 1918. Also dating from the time when Mammoth was Fort Yellowstone are the former **Surveyor's Headquarters,** now park offices (next to the hotel), and the former **parade grounds,** now an empty field below the Terrace Restaurant.

Completed in 1891 and restored for its 1991 centennial, the **Lake Yellowstone Hotel** is the oldest surviving lodging in any national park. It is listed on the National Register of Historic Places. The hotel was quite plain until a 1903 renovation, when architect Robert Reamer added the columns, gables, and decorative moldings that give it its distinctive neo-Colonial air. In 1923–24 and 1927–28 Reamer completed the hotel's transformation from railroad hostelry to elegant resort with lobby and dining room renovations (*see* Lodging, *below*).

It is hard to imagine that any work could be done in Yellowstone during the long, cold winter, but the **Old Faithful Inn** was built during the winter of 1903–04, also under the direction of Robert Reamer. The inn is as massively rustic as the Lake Yellowstone Hotel is elegant, and other than two flat-roof wings added in 1913 and 1927, it looks much as it did in 1904. A foundation of volcanic rhyolite and giant lodgepole pillars support the 79-foot-high structure, one of the world's tallest log buildings. From its steeply pitched roof looms an uneven array of dormer windows with crisscrossed lodgepole decorations. During the summer, an employee dressed as a 1915 chambermaid gives living history tours of the property. Another 500 tons of rhyolite form the 40-foot high lobby chimney, replete with a gargantuan popcorn popper and 14-foot-long clock (*see* Lodging, *below*).

NATURE TRAILS AND SHORT WALKS There are 1,210 miles of trails and 85 trailheads in Yellowstone. Because of space limitations, it

is impossible to describe all of the trails here, so a sampling is given. Don't be surprised to find some trails closed temporarily due to weather conditions or bear activity. For more information on specific areas of the park, contact the visitor center in that area (*see* Visitor Information, *above*).

From parking areas at the south end of Mammoth village, the **Lower Terrace Interpretive Trail** leads past the most outstanding features of the multicolored, steaming Mammoth Hot Springs. Start at Liberty Cap, at the area's north end, named for its resemblance to Revolutionary War patriots' caps. Head uphill on the boardwalks past bright and ornately terraced Minerva Spring. Or else drive up to the Lower Terrace Overlook on Upper Terrace Drive (*see* Scenic Drives, *above*) and take the boardwalks down past New Blue Springs (which, inexplicably, is no longer blue) to the Lower Terrace. This route works especially well if you can park a second vehicle at the foot of Lower Terrace. Either route should take about an hour.

From Tower Fall Overlook (*see* Scenic Drives, *above*), the 1/2-mile, round-trip **Tower Fall Trail** switchbacks down through pine trees matted with luminous green wolf lichen to the base of the waterfall. There, you are actually standing at the northern end of the Grand Canyon of the Yellowstone, whose more famous section lies 18 miles upriver (south).

At Canyon, the 1³/₄-mile (one-way) **North Rim Trail** from Grandview Point to Chittenden Bridge and the 2-mile (one-way) **South Rim Trail** from Chittenden Bridge to Artist Point connect to all major turnoffs from the North Rim and Artist Point drives. Thus you can take small sections of these trails or combine the two into a three-hour (one-way) Grand Canyon experience far more intimate than you get just scurrying to and from your car along the way (it is, however, helpful to have a car parked at either end). The 1/2-mile one-way section of the North Rim Trail from Brink of Upper Falls Parking Area to Chittenden Bridge hugs the rushing Yellowstone as it approaches the Canyon. Both trails are partly paved and fairly level, and throughout

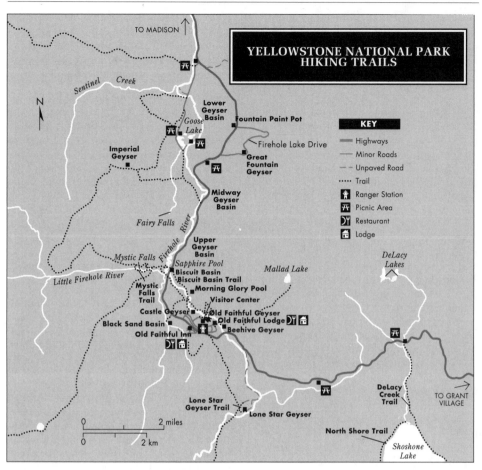

YELLOWSTONE NATIONAL PARK HIKING TRAILS

TO MADISON

Sentinel Creek

N

Lower Geyser Basin
Fountain Paint Pot

Goose Lake

Firehole Lake Drive

Imperial Geyser

Great Fountain Geyser

KEY

Highways
Minor Roads
Unpaved Road
Trail
Ranger Station
Picnic Area
Restaurant
Lodge

Midway Geyser Basin

Fairy Falls

Firehole River

Upper Geyser Basin

DeLacy Lakes

Mystic Falls
Sapphire Pool
Biscuit Basin
Biscuit Basin Trail
Morning Glory Pool

Mallad Lake

Little Firehole River

Mystic Falls Trail

Visitor Center

Castle Geyser
Old Faithful Geyser
Black Sand Basin
Old Faithful Lodge
Beehive Geyser
Old Faithful Inn

Lone Star Geyser Trail
Lone Star Geyser

DeLacy Creek Trail

TO GRANT VILLAGE

0   2 miles
0   2 km

North Shore Trail

Shoshone Lake

these walks you'll get spectacular views of the canyon, which is up to 1,200 feet deep and has sheer walls of yellow, red, brown, and white rock; the silvery thread of foam is the river below. To hear and feel the Yellowstone's power, take on the much steeper side trails into the canyon: The **Brink of Lower Falls Trail** switchbacks 1/2 mile one-way from the parking area of that name (it's 1 3/4 miles south of Inspiration Point on the North Rim Trail) 600 feet down to the brink of Lower Falls. Even more spectacular—and very strenuous—is the 700-step **Uncle Tom's Trail,** which descends 500 feet from the parking area of that name off Artist Point Drive or from a turnoff at South Rim Trail (both about 1/2 mile north of Chittenden Bridge) to the roaring base of Lower Falls. Much of this walk

is on steel sheeting, which can have a film of ice in early morning or in spring and fall.

At the Mud Volcano parking area, some 10 miles south of Canyon, the 3/4-mile round-trip **Mud Volcano Interpretive Trail** loops gently around seething, sulfuric mud pots with such names as Sizzling Basin and Black Dragon's Cauldron, and Mud Volcano itself.

Drive another 6 miles south to Lake Junction and 3 miles east on the East Entrance Road to reach the well-marked and mostly flat 1 1/2-mile loop of **Storm Point Trail,** which leaves the south side of the road for a perfect beginner's hike out to Yellowstone Lake. The trail rounds the western edge of Indian Pond, then passes moose habitat on its way to Yellowstone Lake's Storm Point, named for its frequent afternoon wind storms and crashing waves. Heading west along the shore, you're likely to hear the shrill chirping of yellow-bellied marmots, rodents that grow as long as 2 feet. Also look for ducks, pelicans, and trumpeter swans.

Old Faithful and its environs in the Upper Geyser Basin are rich in short walking options, starting with three connected loops that depart from Old Faithful Visitor Center. The ³/₄-mile **Old Faithful Geyser Loop** simply circles the benches around Old Faithful, filled nearly all day long in summer with tourists. Currently erupting approximately every 75 minutes, Yellowstone's most frequently erupting big geyser—although not its largest or most regular—reaches heights of 100 to 180 feet. Head counterclockwise around the Old Faithful boardwalk ¹/₃ mile from the visitor center crossing the bubbling Firehole River to the turnoff for **Geyser Hill Loop,** a 1¹/₃-mile round-trip from the visitor center. The first attraction is on your left: violent but infrequent Giantess Geyser. Giantess is active only two or three times a year, but when it does erupt, it spouts 100 to 250 feet high for five to eight minutes once or twice hourly for 12 to 43 hours; the ground shakes from its underground explosions. A bit farther on your left is Doublet Pool, whose complex ledges and deep blue waters are highly photogenic. Near the loop's end on your right, Anemone Geyser starts as a gentle pool, overflows, bubbles, and finally erupts, 10 feet or more, repeating the cycle every three to eight minutes. **Observation Point Loop,** a 2-mile round-trip from the visitor center, leaves Geyser Hill Loop boardwalk and becomes a trail shortly after the latter crosses the Firehole River; it circles a picturesque overview of Geyser Hill with Old Faithful Inn as a backdrop. A longer but still easy boardwalk trek is the **Morning Glory Pool Trail,** 1¹/₂ miles one-way from the visitor center. Along the way you pass stately Castle Geyser, possessing the biggest cone of any park geyser and currently erupting every 9 to 10 hours, reaching heights of 90 feet for up to an hour. Morning Glory Pool, named for its resemblance in shape and color to the flower, is a testament to human ignorance: Tons of

coins and trash tossed into it over the years clogged its vent, cooling it and allowing algae to turn it a dull and listless brownish green. Happily, a thorough cleaning in 1991 returned the pool to its original blue color.

Three miles north of Old Faithful off the Grand Loop Road, the Biscuit Basin Parking Area accesses the 2¹/₂-mile round-trip **Biscuit Basin Trail,** a boardwalk across the Firehole River to colorful Sapphire Pool. From the boardwalk's west end, the **Mystic Falls Trail** (a trail, not a boardwalk) gently climbs 1 mile (3¹/₂ miles round-trip from Biscuit Basin Parking Area) through heavily burned forest to the lava-rock base of 70-foot Mystic Falls, then switchbacks up Madison Plateau to a lookout offering the park's least crowded view of Old Faithful and Upper Geyser Basin.

Directly across Grand Loop Road from the end of Firehole Lake Drive, the **Fountain Paint Pot Nature Trail** is an easy ¹/₂-mile loop boardwalk past hot springs, colorful mud pots, and dry fumaroles at its highest point.

At Norris Geyser Basin, **Porcelain Basin Trail** is a ³/₄-mile partially boardwalked loop from the north end of Norris Museum through whitish geyserite stone and past extremely active Whirligig and other small geysers. **Back Basin Trail** is a 1¹/₂-mile loop from the museum's south end past Emerald Spring, Steamboat Geyser, Cistern Spring (which drains when Steamboat erupts), and Echinus Geyser. The latter erupts 50 to 100 feet every 35 to 75 minutes, making it Norris's most dependable big geyser.

LONGER HIKES Again, space allows for only a sampling of Yellowstone's many longer hikes. Always check at a ranger station for trail and wildlife conditions, sign the trailhead register, and carry a topographical map when backcountry hiking.

At Mammoth, the 2¹/₂-hour, 5-mile round-trip **Beaver Ponds Loop Trail** starts between Liberty Cap and Mammoth Photo Shop, climbing 350 feet through 2¹/₂ miles of spruce, fir, and open meadows. Moose, antelope, and occasionally bear may be sighted. This steady, moderate climb to extensive beaver ponds (look for their dams) offers spectacular views of the Mammoth Terraces on the way down.

South of Mammoth on the left side of Bunsen Peak Road, just past the entrance to the road, the moderately difficult 4-mile, three-hour round-trip **Bunsen Peak Trail** climbs 1,300 feet to Bunsen Peak for a panoramic view of Blacktail Plateau, Swan Lake Flats, the Gallatin Mountains, and the Yellowstone River Valley (use a topographical map to locate these landmarks). The easier 4-mile, two-hour round-trip **Osprey Falls Trail** starts 3 miles from the entrance of Bunsen Peak Road at a small parking area on the right. A series of switchbacks drops 800 feet to the bottom of Sheepeater Canyon and the base of the Gardner River's 151-foot Osprey Falls. As at Tower Fall (*see* Nature Trails and Short Walks, *above*), the canyon walls are basalt columns formed by ancient lava flow. Look to see if this trail's once abundant raspberry and strawberry plants have recovered from the 1988 fires. At press time this trail was closed for repairs; call ahead to find out if it has reopened.

Starting at Slough Creek Campground some 7 miles east of Tower-Roosevelt Junction off the Northeast Entrance Road, the **Slough Creek Trail** climbs steeply for the first 1 1/2 miles before reaching expansive meadows and prime fishing spots, where moose are common and grizzlies occasionally wander. From this point the trail, now mostly level, meanders another 9 1/2 miles to the park's northern boundary.

Nineteen miles east of Lake Junction on the north side of East Entrance Road and across from a parking area, the difficult 4-mile, four-hour round-trip **Avalanche Peak Trail** climbs 2,150 feet to the peak's 10,566-foot summit, from which you'll see the rugged Absaroka Mountains running north and south. Some of these peaks have patches of snow year-round. Look around the talus and tundra near the top of Avalanche Peak for alpine wildflowers and butterflies. Below you, Yellowstone Lake spreads magnificently; use your topo map to distinguish its various arms. Don't try this trail before late June or after early September—it may be covered in snow. At any time of year, carry a jacket: The winds at the top are strong.

Starting 1 mile north of Lewis Lake on the east side of South Entrance Road, the very difficult 24-mile, 13-hour round-trip **Heart Lake–Mt. Sheridan Trail** provides one of the park's premier overnight backcountry experiences. After traversing 4 miles of partly burned lodgepole pine forest, the trail descends into Heart Lake Geyser Basin and reaches Heart Lake itself at the 8-mile mark. This is one of Yellowstone's most active backcountry thermal areas (the biggest geyser here is Rustic Geyser, which erupts 25 to 30 feet about every 15 minutes). Circle 1/2 mile counterclockwise around the northern tip of Heart Lake and camp at one of five designated backcountry sites on the western shore (remember to get your permit beforehand); enjoy the hazy sunrise over the lake next morning. Leave all but essentials here (you'll return by the same route) for the 3-mile, 2,700-foot climb to the top of 10,308-foot Mt. Sheridan. Heart Lake is directly below you, and Shoshone and Lewis lakes, along with part of Yellowstone Lake, unfold in the distance. To the south, looking very close, you'll see the Tetons.

The **Shoshone Lake–Shoshone Geyser Basin Trail** is a 22-mile, 11-hour moderately difficult overnight trip combining several shorter trails. It can be abridged into a simple day hike out to Shoshone Lake. The trail starts as DeLacy Creek Trail 9 1/2 miles east of Old Faithful on Grand Loop Road's north side, gently descending for 3 miles to Shoshone Lake's north shore. On the way, look for sandhill cranes and browsing moose. At the lake turn right and follow the North Shore Trail 8 miles, first along the beach and then through lodgepole forest. Make sure you've reserved one of the several good backcountry campsites along this trail. Also take about an hour to explore the Shoshone Geyser Basin, reached by turning left at the fork at the end of the trail and walking about 1/4 mile. Next morning turn right at the fork, follow Shoshone Creek for 2 miles, and make the gradual climb over Grant's Pass. At the 17-

mile mark the trail crosses the Firehole River and divides; take a right onto Lone Star Geyser Trail and continue past this fine coned geyser through Upper Geyser Basin backcountry to Lone Star Geyser Trailhead, 2 miles east of Old Faithful on the Grand Loop Road.

In the park's far northwest, starting on the east side of U.S. 191, 25 miles north of West Yellowstone, the extremely difficult 16$\frac{1}{2}$-mile, 10-hour **Skyline Trail** is another combination trail that climbs up and over numerous peaks whose ridgelines mark the park's northwest boundary before looping sharply back down to U.S. 191 via Black Butte Creek. Starting at Specimen Creek Trailhead, follow Specimen Creek Trail 2$\frac{1}{2}$ miles and turn left at the junction, passing petrified trees to your left past the junction. At the 6$\frac{1}{2}$-mile mark, turn left again at the fork and start climbing 1,400 feet for 2 miles up to Shelf Lake, one of the park's highest bodies of water at 9,200 feet altitude. The lake has two designated backcountry campsites; your night here will be cold even in the heart of summer. Just past the lake begins Skyline Trail proper, following the ridge with steep drop-offs on either side and craggy Bighorn Peak looming ahead. Watch for bighorn sheep and marvel at the spectacular vistas all around you as you approach Bighorn Peak's summit. The trail's most treacherous section is just past the summit, dropping 2,300 feet in the first 2$\frac{1}{2}$ miles of descent; make sure you take a left where the trail forks at the big meadow just past the summit (otherwise you'll keep following Skyline Trail) to reach Black Butte Creek Trail, which hits U.S. 191 just 2 miles north of your starting point. Moose and elk can be seen along this last 2$\frac{1}{2}$-mile stretch.

OTHER ACTIVITIES **Back-Road Driving.** All-terrain vehicles are not allowed on any trails, and all other vehicles are restricted to designated roads.

Biking. More visitors tour parts of the park by bicycle every year, despite the fact that Yellowstone's roads are typically narrow, rough, and have no shoulder. Some 300 miles of roadway are available to bicyclists, but bikes are prohibited on trails and in the backcoun-

try. Bunsen Peak and Blacktail Deer Plateau roads, near Mammoth, allow two-way bike and one-way auto traffic. Bicyclists face stiff climbs at Craig Pass, between Old Faithful and West Thumb; Sylvan Pass, between the East entrance and Fishing Bridge; and Dunraven Pass, north of Canyon.

Some roads restricted to bicycle and foot travel are: the abandoned railroad bed paralleling the Yellowstone River near Mammoth (5 miles); Riverside Trail starting at the West entrance (1 mile); the paved trail from Old Faithful's Hamilton Store to Morning Glory Pool (2 miles); and Natural Bridge Road near Bridge Bay (1 mile).

Bikes can be rented and repaired in West Yellowstone, Gardiner, Livingston, and Bozeman, Montana, as well as in Cody and Jackson, Wyoming. In Gardiner, try **Trailhead Sporting Goods** (tel. 406/848–7712). A big selection of mountain bikes is available from **Mountain Bike Outfitters** (tel. 307/733–3314) in Moose, Wyoming, north of Jackson, for $6 per hour and $24 per day.

Boating. Boating is allowed on Yellowstone and other lakes, but you must have a permit ($10 motorized, $5 nonmotorized), which must be obtained in person at the South entrance, Lewis Lake Campground, Grant Village Visitor Center, Bridge Bay Marina, Lake Ranger Station, or Mammoth Visitor Center. Be aware that Yellowstone Lake is subject to sudden high winds, and its waters are extremely cold. Boating is not allowed on rivers and streams, nor on Sylvan, Eleanor, and Twin lakes.

TW Recreational Services rents boats at Bridge Bay Marina from mid-June through mid-September (*see* Visitor Information, *above*). Rowboats cost $4.50 per hour or $20 per eight-hour day; 18-foot outboards cost $19.75 per hour; 22- and 34-foot cabin cruisers with fishing tackle included cost $34 and $48 per hour (minimum two hours); docking slips for private boats cost $5 to $6.50 per night.

Fishing. The season starts Memorial Day weekend and ends the first Sunday in November. Cutthroat, brook, lake, and rainbow trout, along with grayling and mountain whitefish, inhabit Yellowstone's waters. Everyone 12 and older must have a fishing permit, which can be obtained free of charge from any ranger station, visitor center, or Hamilton store. Catch and release is the general policy, but there are exceptions: Get a copy of the fishing regulations at any visitor center. No live bait is allowed. Prime areas include: Yellowstone River north of Canyon; Madison River between Madison and the West entrance; Yellowstone, Sylvan, and Shoshone lakes. Fishing supplies are available at all Hamilton stores; the biggest selection is at Bridge Bay.

Horseback Riding. Many of the horses that are used on guided tours have been ridden by too many people, so the animals are often unresponsive. TW Recreational Services runs one- and two-hour guided rides that leave Mammoth from late May through mid-September, Roosevelt and Canyon from early June to early September; the trips cost about $12 and $22, respectively.

Better than the above guided tours is the nightly trail ride to the Old West Cookout, which leaves from Roosevelt Lodge at 4:30 and 5:15, depending on how long a ride you want to take. This trip is available between early June and early September and costs about $30 for a one-hour ride and $37 for a two-hour ride. Children ages 8–11 pay about $22 and $29, respectively (height restrictions apply). Advance reservations are required. Check at lodging activities desks, or contact TW Services (*see* Visitor Information, *above*).

About 50 area outfitters also lead horsepacking trips and trail rides into Yellowstone. Expect to pay about $650 for a five-day/four-night backcountry trip, $1,200 for nine days/eight nights, including meals, horses, tents, and guides. Try **Thorofare-Yellowstone Outfitting** (Box 604, Cody, WY 82424, tel. 307/587–5929 or 800/326–5928), or contact the park (tel. 307/344–7381) for a complete listing. You cannot rent a horse without a guide.

Skiing and Snowshoeing. You can rent touring and telemark skis and snowshoes from TW Services at Mammoth Hot Springs Hotel and Old Faithful Snow Lodge. It costs $12.50 per day for touring skis, $10 for telemark skis and snowshoes. Skier shuttles run from Mammoth Hotel to Mammoth Terraces (free), Mammoth Hotel to Tower ($8.60 round-trip), and Snow Lodge to Fairy Falls ($6.50, drop-offs only). Canyon, West Thumb, and Madison have intermittently staffed warming huts; huts at Indian Creek, Fishing Bridge, and Old Faithful are unstaffed. All are open 24 hours. At Old Faithful, the easy Lone Star Geyser Trail passes thermal features and links to several other trails ranging from easy to difficult. The Riverside Trail starting at the West entrance follows the Madison River and involves one traverse up a short, steep hill. The Canyon area has trails for beginner to intermediate skiers with some awesome rimside views, as well as dangerous switchbacks for advanced skiers only. Detailed maps are available at the visitor center.

Downhill skiers can head to the **Sleeping Giant** (tel. 307/587–4044) ski area, 4 miles west of the East entrance.

Snowmobiling. This is one of the most exhilarating ways to see the park and its wildlife. Most of the Grand Loop as well as the West, South, and East entrance roads are open to snowmobiles from mid-December to mid-March. You must drive on the right and in single file. You must be 16 or older to ride a snowmobile alone in the park; those who are 12 to 15 years old may drive if they are supervised by someone 21 or older.

TW Services (*see* Visitor Information, *above*) rents snowmobiles at Mammoth Hotel and Old Faithful Snow Lodge for $110 per day. In West Yellowstone try **Ranch Snowmobile Rentals** (tel. 406/646–7388 or 800/234–4083) or **Rendezvous Snowmobile Rentals** (tel. 406/646–9564 or 800/426–7669); at the East entrance, **Pahaska Teepee** (tel. 307/527–7701 or 800/628–7791) rents machines, as well as cabins.

CHILDREN'S PROGRAMS Ranger-led activities at all visitor centers (*see* Orientation Programs and Guided Tours, *above*) include children's programs. Some topics: 19th-century stagecoach robberies, geyser discovery walks, nature games, bears, and animal tracking. Most are free and aimed at ages 6–12, and many are accessible to people using wheelchairs. Some require reservations at visitor centers; baby-sitting is not available.

EVENING ACTIVITIES Mammoth, Canyon, Grant Village, and Bridge Bay amphitheaters hold free ranger-led campfire programs during summer. Family programs for those with young children are held at 7 to 7:30; normal campfire programs start at 9 to 9:30. Topics include Yellowstone's food chain, Native American and mountain-man legends, animal bones, bison, and 19th-century photographers.

DINING

The Northern Rockies have come a long way since the days when roadside signs advised "This is cow country—eat beef!" You'll still find excellent steaks and prime rib, cut from sage-fed beef, but new eating habits have also taken hold. Among the offerings are grilled chicken and fish, vegetarian dishes, and light sauces. Expect less formality than you'd find elsewhere, even in the fanciest restaurants.

INSIDE THE PARK **Lake Yellowstone Hotel Dining Room.** This double-colonnaded dining room adjoining the hotel lobby has wine and green carpeting, peach walls, wicker chairs, and linen napkins—as well as great wildlife-viewing out its big square windows overlooking the lake. The clientele tends to be older and quieter than that at other park restaurants. Specialties include prime rib prepared in a dry marinade of thyme, rosemary, and garlic; fettuccine with smoked salmon and asparagus spears, combined with a light dill cream sauce; and Tuscan shrimp, with Tuscan peppers, sautéed mushrooms, and roasted tomatoes, finished with wine and fresh basil. Baked acorn squash filled with cheeses, raisins, and apples is a popular entrée. *Lake Yellowstone Hotel, Lake Village Rd., tel. 307/344–7901, ext. 4229. Dinner reservations required. Dress: casual but neat. AE, D, DC, MC, V. Closed late Sept.–late May. Moderate–Expensive.*

Grant Village Restaurant. The floor-to-ceiling windows of this lakeshore restaurant provide grand views, but the green director-style chairs are uncomfortable. The most contemporary of the park's restaurants, Grant Village has pine-beam high ceilings and cedar-shake walls. Order the 10-ounce New York strip steak topped with sautéed mushrooms or the fettuccine primavera. *Next to post office on Grant Village Rd., tel. 307/344–7901, ext. 3449. Dinner reservations required. Dress: casual. AE, D, DC, MC, V. Closed late Sept.– early June. Moderate.*

Mammoth Hot Springs Dining Room. A windowed wall in this dining room overlooks what was once the Army's parade and drill field at Mammoth Hot Springs. The airy art deco–style restaurant is decorated in gray, deep green, and maroon, with bentwood chairs upholstered in burgundy. The two best entrées here are the nearly boneless panfried Idaho trout topped with slivered almonds, and the fettuccine in pesto sauce with shrimp and scallops. *Across street from Mammoth Hot Springs Hotel, tel. 307/344–7901, ext. 5314. Dinner reservations required. Dress: casual. AE, D, DC, MC, V. Closed mid-Sept.- mid-Dec., mid-Mar.–mid-May. Moderate.*

Old Faithful Inn Dining Room. Lodgepole walls and ceiling beams, a giant volcanic rock fireplace, and green-tinted windows etched with scenes from the 1920s set the mood here. Soaked in history, the restaurant remains a big, friendly place where servers somehow find time amid the bustle to chat with diners about their home states and the park. Specialties include grilled ahi tuna finished with Arizona chili butter, and grilled chicken breast glazed with honey-lemon butter. Don't pass up the mud pie—coffee ice cream in Oreo cookie crust, smothered in melted fudge, and topped with pecans. The buffet breakfast is daunting. *Old Faithful Inn, tel. 307/344–7901, ext. 4999. Dinner reservations* required. *Dress: casual but neat. AE, D, DC, MC, V. Closed mid-Oct.–early May. Moderate.*

Roosevelt Lodge Dining Room. The pine chairs and tables in this rustic eatery are often filled with locals from the towns surrounding the park. Many come to indulge in the restaurant's "family menu," in which each entrée is served with separate bowls of cole slaw, mashed potatoes, corn, baked beans, and cornbread muffins with honey. Other good choices are barbecued baby-back pork ribs and fried chicken. *Roosevelt Lodge, tel. 307/344–7311. Reservations not accepted. Dress: casual. AE, D, DC, MC, V. Closed early Sept.–early June. Moderate.*

Old Faithful Snow Lodge Restaurant. Next to the Old Faithful Inn, this unimposing little restaurant has fake wood paneling and oilcloth tablecloths. Its low prices attract families. The menu is the same for lunch and dinner, with hearty soups, hamburgers, and seafood lasagna as top choices. *Snow Lodge, Old Faithful Bypass Rd., tel. 307/344–7311. Reservations not accepted. Dress: casual. AE, D, DC, MC, V. Closed late Oct.–mid-Dec., mid-Mar.–mid-May; no lunch early Sept.–late Oct. Inexpensive.*

A number of park cafeterias serve standard burgers, meat loaf, and sandwiches. These are usually large, bustling places frequented by families, and the volume can be quite loud. They all accept AE, D, DC, MC, and V. Brief reviews follow:

Canyon Lodge Cafeteria. This is the park's busiest lunch spot, serving chili, soups, and such traditional American fare as meat loaf and hot turkey sandwiches. It has a full breakfast menu. *Off North Rim Dr., tel. 307/344–7311. Closed early Sept.–mid-June. Inexpensive.*

Lake Lodge Cafeteria. Choose from a full breakfast menu as well as hearty lunches and suppers. *Far end of Lake Village Rd., tel. 307/344–7311. Closed mid-Sept.–early June. Inexpensive.*

Old Faithful Lodge Cafeteria. This cafeteria has the best tableside view of Old Faithful. It serves meat loaf, lasagna, individual pizzas, and more, all day long. *South end of Old Faithful Bypass Rd., tel. 307/344–7311. Closed mid-Sept.–late May. Inexpensive.*

Pony Express Snack Shop. You can get fast-food burgers, sandwiches, and french fries here all day. *Off Old Faithful Inn lobby, tel. 307/344–7311. Closed late Sept.–late May. Inexpensive.*

Terrace Grill. Although the exterior here is elegant, only fast food is served. *Side entrance to Mammoth Hot Springs Hotel, tel. 307/344–7311. Closed late Sept.–mid-May. Inexpensive.*

NEAR THE PARK **Chico Hot Springs Restaurant.** A long, low room in a resort dating to the turn of the century, this is one of Montana's best restaurants. Pine tables, upturned barrels as server stations, and informal young servers give Chico its ranch atmosphere. The clientele is a mix of Yellowstone-bound tourists, local ranchers, and trendy Montanans from as far away as Helena. Especially good are the beef Wellington and the filet mignon cut from sage-fed Montana beef. Outlandish desserts include a chocolate oblivion torte. The all-you-can-eat Sunday brunch features custom-made omelets and muffins and breads baked on the premises. Behind the restaurant is one of the region's most rollicking saloons, with live country or rock 'n' roll music on weekends. *25 miles south of park on E. River Rd., Pray, MT, tel. 406/333–4933. Dinner reservations required. Dress: casual. D, MC, V. Expensive.*

Livingston Bar and Grill. This spot is popular with Paradise Valley locals, who often come to socialize at its mahogany bar. Grilled Rocky Mountain trout, rib-eye steaks, and buffalo burgers are the best entrées; appetizers include groaning platters of onion rings and nachos. The brave might try Rocky Mountain oysters—breaded and fried testicles of young bulls. *130 N. Main St., Livingston, MT, tel. 406/222–7909. Dinner reservations advised. Dress: casual. MC, V. Moderate.*

Proud Cut. Some of the best prime rib in northwest Wyoming is served in this cowboy-style restaurant and bar, where historic Western photographs add to the atmosphere. The full menu includes steak, shrimp, crab legs, 1/2-pound cheeseburgers, homemade soups, and desserts. *1227 Sheridan Ave., Cody, WY, tel. 307/527–6905. Reservations suggested. Dress: casual. AE, D, DC, MC, V. Moderate.*

Bacchus Pub and Rocky Mtn. Pasta Co. The pub, actually a café with tables and a counter, is in the restored lobby of the former Baxter Hotel. It serves burgers, whole-wheat sandwiches, and hearty soups. The French dip roast beef and meatball subs are especially good. The Pasta Co. is a dinner restaurant set into one of the lobby's darker recesses. It does creditable versions of such regional Italian specialties as baked pasta primavera and fettucini alfredo, along with poultry, veal, seafood, and beef entrées. *105 W. Main, Bozeman, MT, tel. 406/586–1314. Reservations advised. Dress: casual but neat. AE, MC, V. No lunch at Pasta Co. Inexpensive–Moderate.*

La Comida. With indoor country Mexican decor and shaded sidewalk tables in downtown Cody, this tourist and lunch-crowd favorite offers better-than-average combination plates of chicken, spinach, pork, and beef enchiladas, burritos, and tacos. *1385 Sheridan Ave., Cody, WY, tel. 307/587–9556. Reservations accepted. Dress: casual. AE, D, DC, MC, V. Inexpensive–Moderate.*

Trapper's Inn. This popular restaurant recalls the days of the mountain men with a menu featuring sourdough pancakes, biscuits, and rolls accompanying massive breakfasts; thick soups; and steak dinners. The decor runs to pine furniture and mountain-man memorabilia. Trout with eggs is one of the best breakfast offerings; lunch standouts include buffalo burgers on sourdough bread, and onion soup. *315 Madison Ave., West Yellowstone, MT, tel. 406/646–9375. Reservations advised. Dress: casual. AE, MC, V. Inexpensive–Moderate.*

Book Peddler. More suited to San Francisco than to West Yellowstone, perhaps, but a refreshing change of pace, this crowded book-shop's back room is a café featuring cappuccino, gourmet coffee specials, hot spiced cider in winter, and muffins baked on the premises. During the summer you can while away some time at one of the outdoor tables. *106 Canyon St., West Yellowstone, MT, tel. 406/646–9358. Reservations not accepted. Dress: casual. No credit cards. Inexpensive.*

Casa Sanchez. The best Mexican food in Yellowstone country is served up in two downstairs rooms of a converted house on a Bozeman side street. Casa Sanchez is decorated in turn-of-the-century style, and the hands-on attention from its owner results in superb *chile verde* (green chili with pork) and *colorado* (red chili with beef), carne asada burritos, and pork or chicken enchiladas. The hot sauce here is extremely hot. Enjoy your meal on the redwood deck in summer. *719 South 9th St., Bozeman, MT, tel. 406/586–4516. Reservations accepted. Dress: casual. MC, V. No Sun. lunch. Inexpensive.*

PICNIC SPOTS The park's approximately 50 picnic areas all have tables, but only seven have fire grates: Lava Creek, Snake River, Grant Village, Spring Creek, Nez Percé, Old Faithful East parking lot, and Yellowstone River. Only LP gas stoves may be used in the other areas. None of the picnic areas has running water; most have pit toilets.

About 5 miles east of Mammoth on the Grand Loop Road, the **Undine Falls** picnic site is set along Lava Creek, a short walk to the 60-foot falls. On the Northeast Entrance Road, about 4 miles east of Slough Creek Campground Road, a picnic site offers superb views of wildlife-rich Lamar Valley. The **Dunraven Pass** picnic area sits at 8,800 feet, with eastward views of Washburn Hot Springs and the Yellowstone caldera border. At **Canyon,** try the picnic area off Artist Point Drive just after it crosses the Yellowstone River. Eight picnic areas line the north and west shores of **Yellowstone Lake,** all with excellent views. Halfway out to the West entrance from Madison, a pretty site sits on the banks of the Madison River. **Gibbon Falls** picnic site east of Madison is the most scenic in this section of the park. The area near **Obsidian Cliff,** about 8 miles north of Norris, occupies prime elk and moose viewing terrain.

LODGING

Park lodgings are all run by TW Recreational Services. They range from two of the national park system's magnificent old hotels to bland modern motels to simple cabins. Old Faithful and Lake Yellowstone have lodgings in all categories and are the most convenient for visiting major sights; they are, however, the most crowded areas. Old Faithful Snow Lodge and Mammoth Hot Springs Hotel are the only accommodations open in winter; rates are the same as in summer. Cabins in the park fall under the following categories: Western and Frontier (shower or tub); Family (tub and sink); Budget (sink only); Rough Rider and Rustic (no facilities, but showers and toilets nearby). Make reservations at least two months in advance for July and August for all park lodgings. TW Services must receive a deposit covering the first night's lodging within 14 days of the date you make your reservation, but reservations made within 14 days of arrival can be guaranteed with a credit card. No park lodgings have room TVs or phones. For all park lodgings, contact: Reservations Dept., **TW Recreational Services, Inc.,** Yellowstone National Park, WY 82190–9989, tel. 307/344–7311.

Outside the park, West Yellowstone remains the most popular gateway lodging area, with about 50 hotels, motels, and cabin clusters. Cooke City and Silver City, at the Northeast entrance, look as if they were lifted from the 1950s, with funky old log-cabin motels, neon grizzly bear signs, and a rugged high country atmosphere. Gardiner, at the North entrance, has about 15 mostly uninspiring motels. Jackson, Wyoming, at the South entrance, and Cody, Wyoming, at the East entrance, both have a full range of hotels and motels, as do Bozeman, Livingston, and Red Lodge, Montana.

INSIDE THE PARK **Lake Yellowstone Hotel and Cabins.** Fresh from its eight-year restoration, the dowager of national park hotels once more exudes 1920s elegance. Fewer families congregate here than at other park lodgings. Older visitors come to relax in the lake-facing Sun Room while a string quartet plays in late afternoon, to shop behind the etched green windows of the expensive Crystal Palace Gift Shop, or to warm themselves on chilly days before the tile-mantel fireplace in the colonnaded lobby. Off mauve-carpeted hallways, the rooms have peach carpeting, pine furniture, and brass beds. All have bathrooms. Although the east wing is newer (1923) than the west (1903), both wings have lake-facing rooms; the hotel's cheapest rooms are smaller and don't face the lake. You will have to climb the stairs to get to the first floor of both wings, but elevators access the second and third floors. Set unobtrusively in back of the hotel, the newly renovated cabins are all Western or Frontier class and have pine beds and paneling. *184 rooms, 1 suite, 102 cabins. Facilities: restaurant, lobby bar, activities desk, gift shop. AE, D, DC, MC, V. Closed late Sept.–late May. Moderate–Expensive.*

Canyon Lodge. With plain pine-frame cabin clusters and a main lodge building, this is one of Yellowstone's more mundane lodgings. Cabins are furnished with modern, inexpensive chairs and sofas. The main lodge is heavily trafficked at lunchtime. This is the park's biggest lodging, and the one you're most likely to end up in if you arrive without reservations. *At first turn into parking lot on North Rim Dr. 580 cabins. Facilities: 3 restaurants, lounge, gift shop, activities desk. AE, D, DC, MC, V. Closed late Aug.–mid-June. Moderate.*

Grant Village Motel. Yellowstone's newest and least attractive lodging was finished in 1984 amid controversy over whether it detracted from the park's atmosphere. It certainly helps relieve the park's room crunch. Cedar shingle siding covers the check-in and restaurant buildings, and six lodge buildings have rough pine exteriors painted gray and rust. Rooms are undistinguished, with standard motel decor. *At end of Grant Village Rd. 299 rooms. Facilities: 2 restaurants, lounge, activities desk, gift shop. AE, D, DC, MC, V. Closed late Sept.–late May. Moderate.*

Lake Lodge. The cabin clusters here are similar to those at Canyon Lodge, but there is a much nicer main lodge nestled in the trees overlooking Lake Yellowstone. Parts of the main lodge date to 1920, providing a fine example of earlier park architecture. *At far end of Lake Village Rd. 186 cabins. Facilities: restaurant, lounge, gift shop. AE, D, DC, MC, V. Closed mid-Sept.–mid-June. Moderate.*

Mammoth Hot Springs Hotel and Cabins. Built in 1937, with one wing surviving from 1911, this hotel has a spacious art deco lobby and small motel-style rooms; there are cabins in back. The rooms here aren't as nice as those at the other two historic park hotels, but Mammoth is generally less crowded. *94 rooms (67 with bath), 2 suites, 126 cabins (73 with bath). Facilities: 2 restaurants, cocktail lounge, gift shop, activities desk. AE, D, DC, MC, V. Closed mid-Sept.–mid-Dec., mid-Mar.–late May. Inexpensive–Moderate.*

Old Faithful Inn. Past its steep rhyolite and lodgepole log exterior, through the massive veranda and iron-latched red lobby door, you enter a log-pillared lobby that is as national park lodgings were originally meant to be. Thick leather chairs, rockers, and big wool Navajo rugs form three distinct sitting areas in the main lobby, one of which centers around the three-story fireplace. Two balconies above the lobby allow guests to watch the action below from more cozy leather chairs and sofas; pine writing desks are interspersed among the sitting furniture. You can watch Old Faithful erupt from chairs on the veranda deck. Guests range from leather-clad bikers to long-robed Russian Orthodox priests, with families (from all over the country) predominating. Rooms in the 1904 "old house" section have brass beds, and some have deep, brass-foot tubs. Newer upper-range rooms in the 1913 east and 1927 west wings contain Victorian cherrywood furniture. The east wing was completely renovated in 1993 and rooms now have Stickley furniture; four-poster, queen-size beds; and bathrooms. Renovation of the west wing began in fall 1993 and is slated for completion in early 1994. An elevator serves the upper floors. First-floor old house rooms are the hotel's noisiest. Rooms facing Old Faithful geyser cost more, but rear-facing rooms are much quieter. *First left turn off Old Faithful Bypass Rd. 327 rooms (97 with bath). Facilities: 2 restaurants, cocktail lounge/bar, activities desk, gift shop. AE, D, DC, MC, V. Closed mid-Oct.–early May. Inexpensive–Moderate.*

Old Faithful Snow Lodge. This is a nondescript brown motel-style building that was the only lodging damaged by the 1988 fires; as a result, its Western cabins are the park's newest. A small lobby with modern stone fireplace is heavily used in winter (this is one of only two park lodgings open). *Off Old Faithful Bypass Rd., next to visitor center. 31 lodge rooms (1 with bath), 34 cabins. Facilities: restaurant, gift shop. AE, D, DC, MC, V. Closed mid-Oct.–mid-Dec., mid-Mar.–mid-May. Inexpensive–Moderate.*

Roosevelt Lodge. Another budget choice that surpasses more expensive park options, this lodgepole log lodge, with sleeping accommodations in nearby cabins, was built in 1920. Its long, log-rail front porch lined with rocking chairs is a favorite hangout of tired hikers and horseback riders. Inside, half of the single big room features a sitting area with large fireplace, rockers, and pine tables; the other half is a restaurant. *At Tower–Roosevelt Junction on Grand Loop Rd. 80 cabins (8 with bath). Facilities: restaurant, lounge, gift shop. AE, D, DC, MC, V. Closed early Sept.–early June. Inexpensive–Moderate.*

Old Faithful Lodge. Not to be confused with the Snow Lodge, this budget choice is actually nicer than some of the park's mid-range options. Built in 1927, the lodge itself boasts a lodgepole log-and-panel combination exterior and interior. The lobby features a giant (although infrequently used) stone fireplace, wood wildlife carvings by regional artists, rustic pine furniture, and a commanding view of Old Faithful. Lodging is in cabins nearby. *At far end of Old Faithful Bypass Rd. 132 cabins (83 with bath). Facilities: cafeteria, 2 snack shops, gift shop. AE, D, DC, MC, V. Closed mid-Sept.–late May. Inexpensive.*

NEAR THE PARK **Lone Mountain Guest Ranch.** At the foot of the awesome Spanish

Peaks and near the Big Sky resort village, some 40 miles north of the West entrance, this is one of the Northern Rockies' premier guest ranches, and it is open year-round. Luxurious log cabins each have a wood stove, enclosed front porch with rocking chairs, pine beds, and thick wool blankets to ward off chilly nights. Activities center around horseback riding. Although the ranch will sometimes accept two- or three-night bookings, one-week stays are standard. *Off Big Sky Rd. at U.S. 191, Box 145, Big Sky, MT 59716, tel. 406/995–4644. 17 cabins. Facilities: restaurant, bar, outdoor Jacuzzi, gift shop. MC, V. Expensive.*

Gallatin Gateway Inn. Restored and re-opened in 1987, this two-story neoclassical Spanish-style hotel 12 miles south of Bozeman was built by the Chicago–Milwaukee Railroad for Yellowstone-bound passengers in 1927. Behind a facade of stucco and rounded windows lies a large checkerboard-tile lobby and a huge lounge/ballroom with mahogany ceiling beams. An entire wall of arched windows and a walk-in fireplace, topped by an original railroad clock, make this hotel nearly as compelling as the historic hostelries within the park. Rooms have been repainted white and stripped of any distinguishing character, but the bathrooms retain their original brass fixtures. *Hwy. 191, Box 376, Gallatin Gateway, MT 59730, tel. 406/763–4672. 35 rooms (32 with bath). Facilities: restaurant, 2 lounges, pool, Jacuzzi, tennis court, concierge, fly-fish casting pond. AE, D, MC, V. Moderate–Expensive.*

Huntley Lodge. Actually a full-service hotel in a ski resort 56 miles north of the West entrance, this modern building has a long sleek lobby, slate and pine walls, and spacious modern rooms. It usually has vacancies in summer. *Mountain Village at end of Big Sky Rd., off U.S. 191, Box 1, Big Sky, MT 59716, tel. 406/995–4211, 800/548–4486, or, in MT, 800/824–7767. 200 rooms. Facilities: 2 restaurants, lounge, health club, pool, sauna, tennis court and 18-hole golf course nearby, concierge, convention center, gift shop. AE, D, DC, MC, V. Moderate–Expensive.*

Irma Hotel. Open year-round, this cowboy-elegant pine and sandstone hotel in downtown Cody was built by legendary Indian scout and Wild West showman Buffalo Bill Cody in 1902 and named after his daughter. The hotel is decorated with mounted buffalo, moose and bighorn sheep heads; its pièce de résistance is a long cherrywood bar in the saloon, a gift from Queen Victoria. Renovated motel-style rooms still contain some original Victorian furniture, washbowls, and Western art. Ask for a room in the old hotel itself, rather than in the annex. *1192 Sheridan Ave., Cody, WY 82414, tel. 307/587–4221. 40 rooms. Facilities: restaurant, airport shuttle. AE, D, DC, MC, V. Moderate–Expensive.*

Chico Hot Springs Resort. This white-frame property dates to 1900 and is a well-established favorite with locals, who come to soak in its two-temperature, naturally heated mineral pool. Accommodations range from lodge rooms with a wide variety of antique ranch pine furniture and some brass beds to modern motel units, cabins, and chalets. Only the lodge rooms offer the full Chico experience. The lobby, with its big game heads and antique piano, exudes informality. *2 mi east of U.S. 89, 35 mi north of the North entrance (follow signs on U.S. 89), Pray, MT 59065, tel. 406/333–4933 or 800/HOT–WADA, fax 406/333–4694. 82 rooms (25 with bath), 5 cabins, 5 chalets. Facilities: 2 restaurants, 2 bars, hot-spring pool, hot tub, gift shop. D, MC, V. Inexpensive–Expensive.*

Pahaska Teepee Resort. Buffalo Bill Cody built his hunting lodge here in the Shoshone National Forest in 1901; it's now a National Historic Site. The resort's main log building, decorated with big-game heads, is complemented by a lively saloon. Guests stay in small, basic log cabins, which do not have TVs, phones, or air-conditioning but are heated in winter. This is one of a half-dozen lodges along the road to the East entrance; it is the closest one to the park. In winter Pahaska grooms a network of cross-country ski trails and rents skis and snowmobiles. Families and larger groups should ask about renting out the Big House. *183 Yellowstone Hwy., Cody, WY 84214, tel. 307/527–7701 or*

800/628–3391. 52 cabins. Facilities: restaurant, airport shuttle in winter, bar, gift shop, hot tub. AE, MC, V. Closed Nov., Apr. Moderate.

Lockhart Bed and Breakfast Inn. Once the home of western author Caroline Lockhart, this freshly renovated 1890 Victorian on the west side of Cody is furnished in antiques and offers an all-you-can-eat country breakfast. Smoking is not allowed. *109 W. Yellowstone Rd., Cody, WY 82414, tel. 307/587–6074 or 800/377–7255. 7 rooms with bath in inn, 6 rooms with bath in motel, 1 family cabin. Facilities: 5 RV hookups, airport shuttle. MC, V. Inexpensive–Moderate.*

Sportsman's High. Near downtown West Yellowstone, this bed-and-breakfast has antiques-filled rooms and a wraparound porch with an outdoor hot tub. No smoking. *750 Deer St., West Yellowstone, MT 59758, tel. 406/646–7865. 5 rooms with bath. MC, V. Inexpensive–Moderate.*

Sun House. This modern B&B outside Bozeman has passive solar heating and features a large solarium and indoor garden. *9986 Happy Acres W, Bozeman, MT 59715, tel. 406/587–3651. 3 rooms, 1 with bath. MC, V. Inexpensive–Moderate.*

CAMPING

Yellowstone has 11 National Park Service–operated campgrounds and one RV park operated by TW Recreational Services. It also has about 300 designated backcountry campsites, most with food storage poles. Camping in anything other than a designated campsite within Yellowstone is strictly prohibited, but if you can't find a site in the park there are dozens to choose from in the surrounding area. Besides the commercial campgrounds near every town and city outside the park, there are over four dozen National Forest Service campgrounds set off roads that pass through the nearby Shoshone, Gallatin, Custer, and Targhee national forests.

INSIDE THE PARK All NPS campgrounds have combination tent-trailer sites. Only TW Services's Fishing Bridge RV Park has hook-ups. All campsites in the park are available only on a first-come, first-served basis, except for those at Bridge Bay and Fishing Bridge (*see below*). From late June to mid-August, all park campgrounds may fill by noon. Pets are not allowed in the backcountry, but they may stay at roadside campgrounds as long as they are on leashes.

Bridge Bay. With 420 sites set back from Yellowstone Lake in a wooded grove 3 miles southwest of Lake Village, this is the largest park campground. It has flush toilets, hot water, drinking water, fire grates, a disposal station, a ranger station, and a public phone. Bridge Bay also features a marina, rental boats, fishing, campfire talks, and guided walks. Don't expect solitude. Hot showers ($1.50) are 4 miles away at Fishing Bridge. This campground is open from late May to late September, and reservations may be made from early June to Labor Day, no more than eight weeks in advance, through Mistix (tel. 800/365–2267). Cost: $10 per site.

Canyon. A quarter mile east of Canyon Village, near laundry and the visitor center, this 280-site campground is popular with families and accessible to Canyon's many short trails. Hot showers are available for $1.50. Canyon has flush toilets, hot water, drinking water, fire grates, a disposal station, a ranger station, and a public phone. The campground is open from early June to early September. Cost: $8 per site.

Fishing Bridge RV Park. Located at Fishing Bridge Junction, this is the only full RV facility in the park, with 345 sites. Trailers must be under 40 feet, with no canvas; sites are mostly gravel. Liquid propane is available, and laundry facilities are nearby. There are flush toilets, drinking water, hot water, pay showers, a disposal station, a ranger station, and a public phone. Reservations may be made through TW Services (*see* Visitor Information, *above*). Although Fishing Bridge is on Yellowstone Lake, there is no boat access here. The campground is open from late May to early September. Cost: $19 per site.

Grant Village. The second-largest campground, with 403 tent-trailer sites, flush toi-

YELLOWSTONE CAMPGROUNDS

	Bridge Bay	Canyon	Fishing Bridge RV Park	Grant Village	Indian Creek	Lewis Lake	Madison	Mammoth Hot Springs	Norris	Pebble Creek	Slough Creek	Tower Fall
Total number of sites	420	280	345	403	75	85	292	85	116	36	29	32
Sites suitable for RVs	420	280	345	403	75	85	292	85	116	36	29	32
Number of hookups	0	0	345	0	0	0	0	0	0	0	0	0
Drive to sites	•	•	•	•	•	•	•	•	•	•	•	•
Hike to sites												
Flush toilets	•	•	•	•			•	•	•			
Pit/chemical toilets					•	•				•	•	•
Drinking water	•	•	•	•	•	•	•	•		•	•	•
Showers		•	•	•								
Fire grates	•	•		•	•	•	•			•	•	•
Swimming												
Boat access	•			•		•						
Playground												
Disposal station	•	•	•	•			•					
Ranger station	•	•	•	•		•	•	•	•			
Public telephone	•	•	•	•			•	•				
Reservation possible	•*		•									
Daily fee per site	$10	$8	$19	$8	$6	$6	$8	$8	$8	$6	$6	$6
Dates open	late May–late-Sept.	early June–early Sept.	late May–early Sept.	late June–early Oct.	mid-June–mid-Sept.	early June–Nov.	early May–Nov.	year-round	mid-May–late Sept.	mid-June–early Sept.	late May–Nov.	late May–mid-Sept.

*June to Labor Day only.

lets, drinking water, showers ($1.50), fire grates, disposal station, ranger station, and public phone, Grant Village is another of Yellowstone's not-so-rough places to rough it. Near the lake, it has a boat launch but no dock. Maximum trailer size is 45 feet. Try for a site to the right of the far end of the campground road for the best lake views. Open from late June to early October. Cost: $8 per site.

Indian Creek. This creekside campground about 8 miles south of Mammoth is near Swan Lake Flats, a prime wildlife-viewing area. It has 75 combination sites (maximum trailer size is 45 feet), with pit toilets, fire grates, and drinking water, but no showers, disposal station, or ranger station. Indian Creek is open from early June to mid-September. Cost: $6 per site.

Lewis Lake. This is the park's nicest midsize campground for views and quiet, set somewhat away from the main tourism action, off the South Entrance Road. It has fewer amenities than Mammoth, but it's the only campground besides huge Bridge Bay and Grant Village with a boat launch. Try for a site to the right of the campground loop road for the best lake views. Lewis Lake has 85 tent-trailer sites, with pit toilets, drinking water, fire grates, and a ranger station. It's open from mid-June to November. Cost: $6 per site.

Madison. About the size of Canyon campground but with 292 combination sites (maximum trailer size 45 feet), Madison is quieter and a little more rugged. Sites near the river are nicest. There are flush toilets, drinking water, a disposal station, a ranger station, and a public phone, but no showers. It's open from early May to November. Cost: $8 per site.

Mammoth Hot Springs. These 85 combination sites are on a sagebrush hillside also popular with elk and mule deer. It is more exposed than most campgrounds and gets quite hot on summer days. The Mammoth complex is just above; its amphitheater, where rangers hold evening talks, is nearby. This campground has flush toilets, drinking water, fire grates, a ranger station, and a pub-

lic phone. Mammoth is open all year. Cost: $8 per site.

Norris. This is a medium-size park campground, with 116 combination sites (maximum trailer size 45 feet) adjoining the Gibbon River; it's a fishermen's favorite. There are flush toilets and a ranger station, but no showers or disposal station. Lately, the drinking water here has not been potable, due to geyser activity. Norris is open from mid-May to late September. Cost: $8 per site.

Pebble Creek. This cramped little campground right off the Northeast Entrance Road, about 12 miles into the park, isn't as nice as Slough Creek farther down the road, but it does offer a view of the 10,554-foot peak called The Thunderer. It has 36 combination sites (maximum trailer size 45 feet), with pit toilets, drinking water, and fire grates, but no showers, hot water, disposal station, or ranger station. Pebble Creek is open mid-June to early September. Cost: $6 per site.

Slough Creek. A small, creekside campground 10 miles northeast of Tower junction, off a spur road, this is about as far from Yellowstone's beaten path as you can get without actually camping in the backcountry. There are just 29 combination sites, with pit toilets, drinking water, and fire grates. This campground is open from late May to November. Cost: $6 per site.

Tower Fall. Three miles southeast of Tower–Roosevelt junction, this small campground is heavily trafficked and within a short hiking distance of the roaring waterfall. It has 32 combination sites (maximum trailer size 25 feet), with pit toilets, drinking water, and fire grates; hot water and flush toilets are at Tower Store rest rooms nearby. There are no showers, boat access, or disposal station. There's a ranger station 3 miles north. The campground is open from late May to mid-September. Cost: $6 per site.

If you plan on camping in Yellowstone's backcountry, you will have to choose one of the 300 marked campsites. Each has a cleared area for a tent and most have food storage poles. You will need a free permit, which can be picked up at any visitor center or ranger station (*see* Visitor Information, *above*).

Lower/Midway Geyser Basins. Five of the most accessible backcountry camping sites are short hikes away from the Biscuit, Midway, and Lower geyser basins parking areas. From Biscuit Basin, a trail leads to campsites at Firehole Meadows and Falls. Both are extremely popular. Fairy and Imperial Meadows campsites are just a few miles from the Midway turnoff, and two small campsites are 2 to 3 miles in from the Sentinel Meadows Trailhead at Lower Geyser Basin. This area is open from early June to mid-March.

Shoshone Lake. The north and east shores of this fairly accessible, lovely backcountry lake are lined with 12 campsites, accessible by foot, canoe, or both. Get permits at Grant Village or South entrance ranger stations. There is also a ranger station at the campground, which is open year-round.

Upper Geyser Basin. The Lone Star Geyser area, 2 1/2 miles southeast of Old Faithful, and Mallard Lake, 3 1/2 miles to the northeast, have three campsites each. The one right at Lone Star is one of the park's few handicapped- accessible backcountry sites. Both are open year-round.

Yellowstone Lake. The big lake's east shore has nine backcountry sites, accessible either from the Nine Mile Post Trailhead or Sedge Bay Trailhead, both located where the East Entrance Road meets the lake. Some have restrictions on travel away from campsites. Get permits at Lake, Bridge Bay, or Grant Village ranger stations. Some of these sites are available year-round.

NEAR THE PARK **Flagg Ranch Village.** This sprawling complex 2 miles from the South entrance also has a motel and cabins, two restaurants, a saloon with satellite TV, a grocery store, gift and tackle shops, gas station, hot tubs, interdenominational church service, and guided float and horseback trips. Flagg Ranch has 75 tent sites and 96 grassy RV sites with full hookups. There are flush toilets, hot water, showers, drinking water, laundry facilities, raft access, and disposal station, but no swimming. Pets are allowed. Liquid propane is sold. Extra long (45 feet) spaces are scattered through the campground. *Box 187, Moran, WY 83013, tel. 307/733–8761 or 800/443–2311, fax 307/543–2356. Cost: $21 RV sites with hookups, $16 tent sites. Closed mid-Oct.–mid-Dec., mid-Mar.–mid-May.*

Hitching Post Campground & RV Park. This medium-size commercial facility 29 miles from the East entrance has a trout pond, pony rides, paddleboats, trail rides, fishing on the Shoshone River, and miniature golf. There are 35 tent sites and 65 grassy trailer sites (maximum size 35 feet), with flush toilets, hot water, showers, drinking water, fire grates, playground, pool, and disposal station. Pets are allowed. *3256 N. Fork Hwy., Cody, WY 82414, tel. 307/587–4149. Cost: $11–$16 for tent and RV sites, $20–$50 for camper and full cabins. Closed Dec.–Mar.*

Yellowstone Park KOA. A huge facility 6 miles outside the West entrance on U.S. 20, this KOA also has cabins, a game room, a hot tub, and miniature golf. There are 50 tent sites and 200 grassy RV sites, with full hookups (maximum size 42 feet), flush toilets, hot water, showers, drinking water, fire grates, playground, indoor pool, and disposal station. Pets are allowed; liquid propane is sold. *Box 327, West Yellowstone, MT 59758, tel. 406/646–7606. Cost: $23–$26 for RVs. Closed Oct.–Apr.*

Yosemite National Park
California

By Pamela Hegarty
Updated by Andres Puhvel

s early as 1919, visitors from around the world entered Yosemite from the south near Mariposa, gleefully riding a stagecoach through a tunnel bored into the trunk of a single sequoia. At the top of the rise to the south of Yosemite Valley, they came upon an incomparable sight—a deep, green canyon with walls of flawless gray granite rising 3,000 feet into the clouds and graceful waterfalls plummeting down from their angelic heights. It's the same vista that you will see today.

In this one compact valley are two of the world's 10 highest waterfalls (Upper Yosemite and Ribbon), the largest single granite rock on earth (El Capitan), and one of the Americas' most recognized peaks (Half Dome). But the 7-mile-long, 1-mile-wide Yosemite Valley is just a small slice of the 750,000-acre national park. In Yosemite's southern tip, for example, is the Mariposa Grove of Big Trees. These giant sequoias are the largest living things on earth, towering 20 stories above the forest floor. One branch of the Grizzly Giant is wider in girth than the trunk of many trees in the forest.

Then there's the high country—take Tioga Road as it rises up from the valley to elevations of 6,000 to 10,000 feet, where an untamed expanse of rolling meadows, pristine forest, hidden lakes, and rocky domes unfolds. Here backpackers usually begin their journeys into Yosemite's wilderness area, which makes up an impressive 95% of the park land.

A four- to five-hour drive from San Francisco and six hours from Los Angeles, Yosemite is now one of the most easily accessible of the West's national parks. It is also one of the most popular. With over 750 miles of trails, Yosemite offers its nearly 4 million annual visitors countless means of exploration and retreat.

In 1864 Abraham Lincoln took time off from the Civil War to make Yosemite Valley and the Mariposa Grove of Big Trees a state reserve. At the urging of conservationist John Muir and many like him, the area surrounding the valley and the grove was designated a national park in 1890 by President Benjamin Harrison. It wasn't until 1906 that the state of California returned Yosemite Valley and the Mariposa Grove to the federal government, which incorporated these areas in Yosemite National Park.

ESSENTIAL INFORMATION

VISITOR INFORMATION For general information, contact the National Park Service, Information Office, Box 577, **Yosemite National Park,** CA 95389, tel. 209/372–0200 or 209/372–0264 for a 24-hour recorded message. Dialing 209/372–1000 will give touch-tone callers access to all visitor-information lines in Yosemite, including those at park-operated hotels, camping offices, and ranger stations. You can also call the **Valley Visitor Center** (tel. 209/372–0299); the **Tuolumne Meadows Visitor Center** (tel. 209/372–0263), which is only open in summer; the **Big Oak Flat Information Center** (tel. 209/372–0615), which is open daily in summer and weekends in winter; and the **Wawona Ranger Office** (tel. 209/372–0564).

Wilderness permits are required for all overnights in Yosemite's backcountry. Permits are free and are available at the visitor centers and ranger stations. Reservations for overnight trail use are accepted by mail only between March 1 and May 31. Send a brief itinerary to the Wilderness Office at the National Park Service office (*see above*). Fifty percent of the capacity for each trailhead is available by reservation. The balance is on a first-come, first-served basis 24 hours prior to trailhead departure. Trailhead quotas, especially for those leaving the valley, are usually met early, so plan ahead.

FEES Admission to the park is $5 per car for a week's stay, or $3 per person if you don't arrive in a car. For $15, you can purchase a one-year pass to Yosemite.

PUBLICATIONS A plethora of publications on Yosemite ranges from simple maps to extravagant picture books; a variety is sold at visitor centers or is available via catalog from the **Yosemite Association** (Box 230, El Portal, CA 95318, tel. 209/379–2646).

The official National Park Service handbook *Yosemite* is an informative, 143-page guide with color photos. A foldout *Map & Guide to Yosemite Valley* describes trails, bike paths, flora, fauna, and vista points and gives a brief history of the park; it has color photos of major landmarks. For those who like driving, the 77-page *Yosemite Road Guide* tells about the history of each road marker in Yosemite, but the book needs updating. The *Yosemite Magazine*, complimentary to all hotel guests, and the *Yosemite* brochure, included with park admission, are both excellent sources of information and include color photographs. The *Yosemite Guide* newspaper, available free at entrance gates and all public buildings, is an indispensable resource for current activities and operating hours.

GEOLOGY AND TERRAIN Yosemite National Park encompasses 1,170 square miles, from the popular Yosemite Valley, at a 4,000-foot elevation; east to the nearly deserted backcountry, which rises as high as 13,000 feet at the Sierra crest; south to the Mariposa Grove of Big Trees; and north to the Hetch Hetchy Reservoir and the mountain wilderness beyond.

The area that is now the Sierra Nevada and the Great Valley of California was once a vast sea. Sand, silt, and mud eroded from ancient mountain ranges bordering the waters and settled to the sea floor, eventually becoming rock. Geologic forces warped the rock layers, lifting them up and forming a mountain range. Eighty to 250 million years ago, molten rock cooled and crystallized beneath the mountains. Ten to 80 million years ago, this cooled rock uplifted and became the Sierra Nevada. The top layers of the original sedimentary rock from the sea bottom eroded away.

Immense ruptures and cracks in the mountain range birthed canyons and valleys. Several million years ago, during the Ice Age, glaciers deepened and widened the canyons. What is now Half Dome was a tower of rock. A vertical joint cracked, forcing a portion of this immense rock to crumble; some of the rubble was partially carried away by glaciers. But when the last glacier left Yosemite Valley 10,000 to 15,000 years ago, Half Dome was still not a dome. Although some of Yosemite's domes were helped along by glacial erosion, most were formed by exfoliation. In this process, layers of rock crack apart and fall off, like the skin of a snake, leaving behind a rounded surface.

Geologists believe that for around 20,000 years following the Ice Age, a lake filled the valley bottom. The waterfalls that pour into the valley brought in silt and sediment that eventually transformed the lake into today's level meadow surrounded by pines and oaks.

FLORA AND FAUNA Yosemite is home to approximately 37 types of trees, 1,400 flowering plants, 77 species of mammals, 242 varieties of birds, and 29 different types of amphibians and reptiles.

The most visible animals are the coyote, often seen along valley roads in the evening, and the mule deer, the only kind of deer in Yosemite. These large-eared deer are especially prevalent in the valley during the winter months, when snow forces them down from higher elevations. Deer graze the lawns of the historic estate at Wawona and of the golf course across the road. Remember that these graceful "Bambis" are wild animals with sharp hooves and antlers. More people in the park are harmed by deer every year than by bears or any other animals. Do not approach or feed them.

Bighorn sheep are spotted occasionally in Inyo National Forest, but sightings are infrequent in the park itself.

The American black bear, which often has a brown coat, is the only species of bear in Yosemite (the California grizzlies were hunted to extinction by the turn of the century). Some are active year-round at any time of day or night, but only a lucky minority of

visitors actually see one. Those who encounter a bear are advised to make loud noises, bang pots, and wave arms to scare the animal away. If it doesn't scare, retreat. Bears will go after coolers (breaking car windows to get at them) and any food, even cans of soda, so be sure all food and cooking utensils are properly stored. If backpacking, string all food in a bag from a high tree branch—no matter what the season.

The most commonly seen bird is the blue Steller's jay, delighting visitors along trails, in campgrounds, and around public buildings. Dedicated birders may catch a glimpse of the rare and endangered great gray owl, which makes its home at the mid-elevations (6,000 to 8,000 feet). The golden eagle is sometimes seen soaring above the valley. Three known pairs of the endangered peregrine falcon nest in the park and are carefully protected by the park service.

The Mariposa Grove of Big Trees is the most famous of the three sequoia forests in Yosemite. Sequoias naturally grow only along the west slope of the Sierra Nevada between 4,500 and 7,000 feet in elevation. Starting from a seed the size of an oat flake, each of these ancient monuments knows remarkable proportions in adulthood. You might want to take a rough measure of some of the bases— Grizzly Giant takes more than 15 people holding hands to form a human chain around its base. Fires, incidentally, are integral to their existence, releasing seeds from the cones and clearing the forest soil for new growth, and are started by the park service under carefully controlled conditions.

In late May the valley's dogwood trees bloom with white, starlike flowers. Wildflowers, such as black-eyed Susan, bull thistle, cow parsnip, lupine, and meadow goldenrod, peak in June in the valley and in July at the higher elevations.

WHEN TO GO Without a doubt, summer is Yosemite's most crowded season, especially in the valley. The weather is warm and dry— with an average 90°F high and 50°F low in the valley and a 70°F high and 30°F low at Tuolumne—and many activities are offered, but you will have to contend with traffic jams, noxious tour buses, and fully booked accommodations. This is, however, the only time of year when the Tioga Road into the high country is sure to be open.

In autumn, the waterfalls may not be the torrents of spring and tourist activities are curtailed, but visitors will find solitude even in the valley, crisp fall air, and bargains on lodging. Daytime temperatures in the valley remain warm (60°F to 70°F) until November.

Outdoors enthusiasts will enjoy winter, when visitors are few, deer flock to the valley from the snowed-in higher elevations, and fires warm the restaurants and lounges. Daytime temperatures are mild (40°F), but nights are chilly (20°F to 30°F). Snow on the valley floor is minimal. Cross-country and alpine skiing, as well as free ranger-led snowshoe walks, are available at Yosemite's Badger Pass Ski Area. Many winter visitors come expressly for the annual Vintners' and Chefs' Holidays (see Seasonal Events, below).

In spring, the mighty waterfalls reach their peak with the snowmelt from the higher elevations. May greets the white dogwood blossoms suspended in the valley forest. White and pink Western azaleas bloom in late May and early June. The days become warmer, with temperatures ranging from 60°F to 70°F, and nights are crisp at 30°F to 40°F.

Consult Yosemite Area Road and Weather Conditions (tel. 209/372–0200) for current information on temperatures and precipitation.

SEASONAL EVENTS November 7th to mid-December: Vintners' Holidays (Holidays Hotline, tel. 209/454–2020) are held midweek in the grand parlor of the Ahwahnee Hotel. Free seminars by California's most prestigious vintners culminate in an elegant, albeit pricey, banquet dinner ($80). **January:** At Chefs' Holidays (Holidays Hotline, tel. 209/454–2020), similar to the Vintners' Holidays, enjoy free cooking demonstrations by celebrated chefs—creations are as diverse as exotic mushroom dishes and chocolate pastry. There is also a banquet dinner, which

costs $75, not including wine. **December 23: Yosemite Pioneer Christmas** (tel. 209/372–0564), at the Pioneer Yosemite History Center, is an old-fashioned program of caroling, candlelight tours, and stagecoach rides at the Wawona area of the park. **Early May to late October:** One of Yosemite's best-loved evening activities is Lee Stetson's portrayal of naturalist John Muir in a celebrated one-man show. Performances of *Conversation with a Tramp* and *Stickeen* are held on Tuesday and Friday, early May through summer, at the Yosemite Theater. Tickets are $5 for adults, and $2 for children under 13.

WHAT TO PACK The key to packing for Yosemite is to bring layers, especially if you're visiting between seasons. Sierra weather is unpredictable: sunny one day, cold and rainy the next. A sweater will come in handy no matter what the season. Warm jackets, hats, and mittens are recommended for winter. Sturdy hiking boots with good traction are advisable for hikers; trails can be steep and rocky.

GENERAL STORES You can get almost anything you need in Yosemite Valley's stores, but you'll have to pay the price. You may want to stock up on fruits, trail mix, and other nonperishable picnic goodies before coming into the park. Many of the valley stores are open year-round, 9 to 9 daily during the warmer months and 9 to 7 during the cooler months (November through March).

The Village Store (Yosemite Village, tel. 209/372–1253) is the largest store in the park, offering groceries, magazines, books, film, photo processing, clothing, camping supplies, postcards, gifts, and souvenirs.

Nearby is **Degnan's Delicatessen** (Yosemite Village, tel. 209/372–1454), with made-to-order sandwiches, salads, and gourmet foods, and **Degnan's Nature Crafts** (Yosemite Village, tel. 209/372–1453), a gift shop. The **Ansel Adams Gallery** (Yosemite Village, tel. 209/372–4413) is the most elegant store in the park, with Ansel Adams prints, fine artwork, and top-quality Native American crafts.

At the Ahwahnee Hotel, the **Sweet Shop** (tel. 209/372–1271) in the lobby sells Ahwahnee-logo merchandise, candy, and sundries, while the **Gift Shop** (tel. 209/372–1409) specializes in fine gifts, Native American jewelry, and handicrafts.

At the Yosemite Lodge, the **Gift/Apparel Store** (tel. 209/372–1297) offers Yosemite souvenirs, picnic supplies, and film. Also at the lodge, the **Indian Shop** (tel. 209/372–1438) features Native American artwork and moccasins.

Curry Village has a year-round **Mountain Shop** (tel. 209/372–1296), with rock-climbing and backpacking supplies, and a **Gift Shop** (tel. 209/372–1291). Wawona has a small year-round grocery store, **Wawona Store** (tel. 209/375–6574), which is open 8 to 8 in summer and 9 to 6 the rest of the year. Badger Pass Ski Area offers a winter-only **Sport Shop** (tel. 209/373–1333) with ski clothing, sunglasses, and sun lotions. Tuolumne Meadows offers a summer-only **Grocery Store** (tel. 209/372–1328), which is open 9 to 6, and a rock-climbers' **Mountain Shop** (tel. 209/372–1335).

Operating hours for all stores vary according to season and are listed in the *Yosemite Guide,* which is available free at the park entrances and public buildings.

ARRIVING AND DEPARTING The most convenient way to travel to Yosemite is by car, but once in the valley you won't need an automobile. An excellent, free shuttle bus circles continually (7:30 AM to 10 PM in summer, 9 AM to 10 PM the rest of the year) stopping at all valley destinations. In winter, a free bus carries skiers from the valley to Badger Pass. In summer, there is one daily bus to the high country that costs less than $20. This is especially useful for backpackers, who can take the bus up to Tuolumne Meadows, then hike back down into the valley, thus avoiding a grueling 4,000-foot climb on foot *(see Longer Hikes, below)*. For hiker-bus reservations, call 209/372–1240 or ask at any hotel tour desk.

By Plane. If you're coming in from out of state, you will most likely fly into San Fran-cisco or Los Angeles, then drive. An alternative is to fly into Fresno, which is 97 miles southwest of the park. In addition, **United Express Airlines** (tel. 800/241–6522) offers less frequent service from San Francisco to Merced. Bus transportation is available from Fresno and Merced to Yosemite *(see By Bus, below)*; car-rental companies include **Avis** (tel. 800/331–1212), **Hertz** (tel. 800/654–3131), **Dollar** (tel. 800/800–4000), and **Budget** (tel. 800/527–0700).

By Car and RV. Yosemite is a four- to five-hour drive from San Francisco and a six-hour drive from Los Angeles. From the west, three highways come to Yosemite; all intersect with Highway 99, which runs north–south through the central valley. Highway 120 is the northernmost and most direct route from San Francisco, but it crosses a longer portion of foothills and rises higher into the mountains, which can be snowy in winter. Highway 140 from Merced allows for more highway driving. Highway 41 from Fresno is the shortest route from Los Angeles and offers the most dramatic first look at Yosemite Valley, just as you emerge from the Wawona Tunnel.

If you're coming from the east, Highway 120, the Tioga Road, will take you over the Sierra crest, past Tuolumne Meadows and down the west slope of the mountains into the valley. It's scenic, but the mountain driving may be stressful for some, and it's only open in the summer, due to heavy snow in the upper elevations.

Carry chains no matter what your approach to Yosemite. They are often mandatory on Sierra roads during snowstorms. Sierra weather is unpredictable and driving can be treacherous. If you get caught in the valley and need to buy chains there, you'll pay twice the normal price.

For the most up-to-date information on traffic and highway conditions outside the park, consult California Road Conditions (tel. 800/427–ROAD).

Yosemite Valley is 229 miles from Sequoia National Park, 180 miles from Kings Canyon National Park, and about 300 miles from

Death Valley National Monument via the Tioga Pass (open only in summer).

By Bus. Yosemite Grey Line (tel. 209/443–5240; in CA, 800/640–6306) runs buses from Fresno ($40 round-trip) and Merced (north of Fresno on Highway 99, $30 round-trip) to Yosemite Valley. **Yosemite Via** (tel. 209/722–0366) runs buses from Merced to Yosemite ($30 plus $3 entrance fee round-trip, 2¹/₂ hours one-way). The Greyhound and Amtrak stations and the Fresno and Merced airports are regular stops, but call ahead to let the bus company know when you plan to arrive.

By Train. Amtrak (tel. 800/872–7245) has train service to Merced, where you can connect with public bus transportation (*see* By Bus, *above*). **Hertz** (tel. 800/654–3131) rents cars from the station in Merced.

EXPLORING

The magnificent sites of Yosemite Valley are easily accessible by auto or free shuttle bus, with short, handicapped-accessible trails to the bases of the powerful waterfalls. An alternative is to take a guided tour of the highlights (*see* Guided Tours, *below*). To truly experience the incomparable beauty of this national treasure, however, you should allow time for longer hikes off the well-beaten tourist paths, up the canyons, through the Big Trees, into the high country.

THE BEST IN ONE DAY A woman once asked Carl Sharsmith, longtime Yosemite ranger-naturalist, "What would you do if you had only one day in Yosemite National Park?" "Madam," he replied, "I'd go sit by the Merced River and cry!"

Many visitors schedule only one day in Yosemite. It is enough for a whirlwind tour of the highlights, but it leaves little time for lingering or enjoying the many trails and activities. Still, if that's all the time you have, you'll want to spend most of it in Yosemite Valley.

You will be entering the valley from the west. You may want to orient yourself at the Valley Visitor Center. A brief audiovisual program,

available in five languages, suggests an itinerary for those with only one day in the park, and rangers are extremely helpful in recommending the best short hikes for the season. But if you're really pressed for time, it's best to stop at the vista points as you come to them. The circle road around the valley is one-way, which means you'll have to double back to individual sites you passed on the way to the visitor center.

Your first stop should be the **Bridalveil Fall**. The parking lot is about 20 yards up Highway 41 from the valley road (Southside Drive). A short paved trail with a slight rise will take you to the base of this graceful 620-foot cascade. The Ahwahneechee people called it Pohono, or "spirit of the puffing wind," as breezes blow this lacy waterfall sideways along the cliff face.

As you head farther into the valley, **El Capitan** will loom to your left. Turnouts along the road provide unbeatable vistas of this largest single granite rock on earth, rising 3,593 feet—more than 350 stories—above you. Shadows of clouds set off ever-changing patterns of light on its vertical striations. Those with keen eyes and a pair of binoculars may spot tiny rock climbers as they slowly ascend "El Cap's" vertical surface.

Take a left over Sentinel Bridge and park. Walk to the center of the bridge for the best view of **Half Dome** and its reflection in the Merced River. Photographers take note: this scene is best just before sunset, when the river is still and Half Dome glows with a rosy gold.

Drive back over the bridge and continue on Southside Drive. Hardy hikers may want to go straight to the Curry Village day-use lot, walk to the end of the shuttle-bus road and climb the moderately steep trail to the footbridge overlooking the 317-foot **Vernal Fall** (1¹/₂ miles round-trip; allow 1¹/₂ hours). Beyond Vernal Fall, the trail climbs to the 594-foot **Nevada Fall** (*see* Longer Hikes, *below*).

The road turns left across the Merced River. Take the short side-road, which dead-ends at the **Ahwahnee Hotel.** Even if you aren't staying in this elegant lodge, it's worth a visit.

Reminiscent of a grand hunting lodge, the Ahwahnee has immense common rooms showcasing museum-quality, antique Native American rugs and baskets (*see* Historic Buildings and Sites; Dining; and Lodging, *below*).

Looping back toward the west, follow the signs for **Yosemite Village.** A large parking lot lends access to the gift stores, fast-food restaurants, and, most importantly, the **Valley Visitor Center** (*see* Visitor Information, *above*), with its exhibits on park geology and an excellent selection of books on Yosemite. Behind the center is a small, **re-created Ahwahneechee village.** For more Native American lore, take a quick peek at the **Indian Cultural Museum** next door and its impressive collection of baskets.

From here it's a short walk or drive to **Yosemite Falls.** This is the highest waterfall in North America and the fifth-highest in the world. Though it looks like one cascade, Yosemite Falls is actually three waterfalls, a powerful chain of water twice the height of the Empire State Building. From the granite ridge high above you, Upper Fall drops 1,430 feet straight down. The Cascades, or Middle Fall, tumbles over another 675 feet, pouring into the steep 320-foot drop of the Lower Fall. This is an excellent spot to fit in a short hike by following the mile-long loop trail through the forest back to the parking lot (*see* Nature Trails and Short Walks, *below*).

Those with more time in Yosemite should drive up Highway 41 to **Tunnel View.** The parking lots for this vista point are on either side of the road just before the tunnel. Below, tucked into 5 miles of pure inspiration is Yosemite Valley, with Bridalveil Fall on the right, El Capitan on the left, and Half Dome forming the backdrop to this deep, green canyon.

Farther up Highway 41 is the turnoff for the road to **Glacier Point** (closed in winter), which provides another spectacular panorama of Yosemite, taking in the valley below and high country peaks on the horizon (*see* Scenic Drives and Views, *below*).

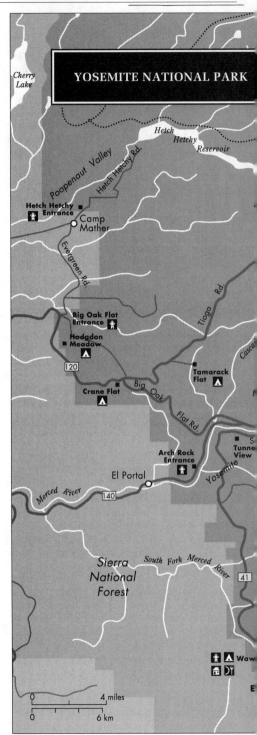

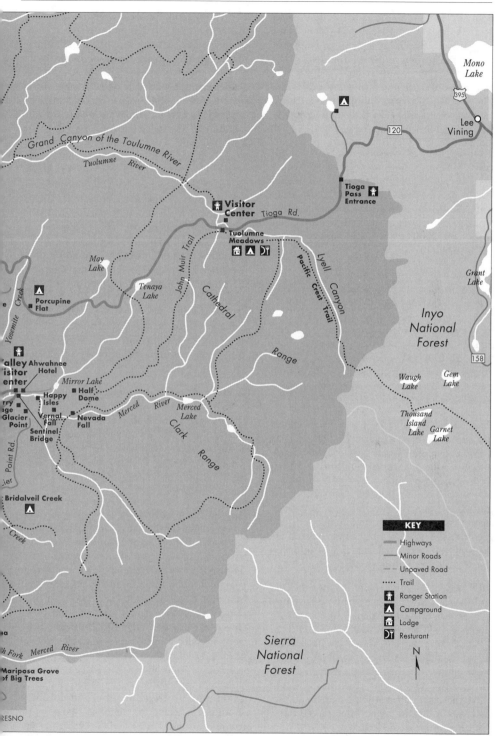

Mono
Lake

395

Lee
Vining

120

Tioga
Pass
Entrance

Grand Canyon of the Toulumne River

Tuolumne River

Visitor
Center

Tioga Rd.

Tuolumne
Meadows

Grant
Lake

May
Lake

Porcupine
Flat

Tenaya
Lake

John Muir Trail

Cathedral

Range

Lyell Canyon

Pacific Crest Trail

Inyo
National
Forest

158

Yosemite Creek

Valley
Visitor
enter

Ahwahnee
Hotel

Mirror Lake

Half
Dome

Waugh
Lake

Gem
Lake

rry
age
Glacier
Point

Happy
Isles

Vernal
Fall

Nevada
Fall

Merced River

Merced
Lake

Clark

Range

Thousand
Island
Lake

Garnet
Lake

Sentinel
Bridge

Point Rd.

Bridalveil Creek

Creek

KEY

Highways

Minor Roads

Unpaved Road

Trail

Ranger Station

Campground

Lodge

Resturant

N

Sierra
National
Forest

h Fork Merced River

Mariposa Grove
of Big Trees

RESNO

Highway 41 curves through the mountains south to the **Pioneer Yosemite History Center** (*see* Historic Buildings and Sites, *below*) at Wawona (30 miles; allow 45 minutes). Cross the New England–style covered bridge to this collection of Yosemite's first log buildings. The nearby **Wawona Hotel** (*see* Historic Buildings and Sites; Dining; and Lodging, *below*) is a pleasant stop for lunch.

Six miles south is the **Mariposa Grove of Big Trees**. More than 20 giant sequoias are visible from the parking lot, but to get a true feeling for the size of these trees, take the ³/₄-mile walk along the self-guided nature trail to **Grizzly Giant**. This gargantuan tree is 32 feet in diameter, 209 feet tall, and believed to be 2,700 years old.

In the summer, the high country is accessible by driving east out of Yosemite Valley along Highway 120. **Tuolumne Meadows** (55 miles from the valley) is the most extensive meadow system in the Sierra Nevada. Picnickers and day hikers enjoy the crystalline lakes, rolling fields, and rounded granite domes. Many backpackers begin their journeys from here, but you'll need to get acclimated to the 8,575-foot altitude.

ORIENTATION PROGRAMS For an overview of the beauty, diversity, and history that is Yosemite, see the 20-minute audiovisual presentation shown at the Yosemite Valley Visitor Center every hour. The rangers here are extremely helpful; they can tell you about trail conditions, the best hikes in any given season, park activities, and more. Exhibits illustrate the geology and unique natural aspects of the park. The Big Oak Flat Information Station has a slide show.

GUIDED TOURS Tours to fit every schedule and a variety of interests are run by **Yosemite Concession Services Corporation** (5410 E. Home Ave., Fresno, CA 93727, tel. 209/372–1240). Tickets may be purchased at tour desks in valley hotels. Advance reservations are recommended. Tours are offered spring through fall, conditions permitting, unless otherwise stated. Prices quoted are for adults. Children under 13 pay half the quoted rates. Children under 5 ride free.

The **Valley Floor Tour** is a 26-mile, two-hour tour of the valley's highlights, with narration of the history, geology, and plant and animal life. It operates all year with open-air trams or enclosed motor coaches, depending on conditions. The price is $13.75. The **Mariposa Grove of Big Trees** is a six-hour trip costing $29 from Yosemite Valley to the giant sequoias in Mariposa Grove. A half-day trip from Yosemite Valley hotels to the vista at **Glacier Point**, 3,200 feet above the valley, operates approximately from June 1 through Thanksgiving and costs $17.75. For a full-day combination of the Big Trees and Glacier Point tours, with lunch at the historic Wawona Hotel (meal not included in tour price), try the **Grand Tour.** It is available from approximately June 1 through Thanksgiving at the price of $38. The **Big Trees Tram Tour** ($6) is a one-hour, open-air tram tour of the Mariposa Grove of Big Trees. The **Moonlight Tour,** a late-evening version of the Valley Floor Tour, is offered on full-moon nights and the three nights prior, from April through September, depending on weather conditions, for $13.75.

If you want a full day's outing across Tioga Road to Mono Lake, with photo stops at highlights, opt for the **Tuolumne Meadows Tour.** Hikers and backpackers can also take this bus to high-country trailheads. It operates July through Labor Day, and the price varies with the drop-off point. The round-trip to Tuolumne Meadows is $18.

Saddle Trips leave from the valley stables (open Easter through mid-October) and Wawona, White Wolf, and Tuolumne Meadows (summer only). All saddle and pack animals require guides. Riders must be at least seven years old and 44 inches tall. A full-day tour runs $60, a half-day $40, and a two-hour ride costs $30. Reservations are required. The **Overnight Cross-country Ski Tours** are a variety of winter-only tours ranging from a weekend overnight to Glacier Point ($90) to a six-day Trans-Sierra Expedition ($350). Prices include breakfast, dinner, lodging, guide, and instruction. Photo enthusiasts shouldn't miss the free daily 1¹/₂-hour tours called **Camera Walks** led by professional photographers. Sign up in advance at hotel desks.

In addition to these commercial tours, park rangers lead a variety of free walks. How about snowshoeing at Badger Pass in the wintertime? Check the visitor center or your *Yosemite Guide* for trips and schedules.

SCENIC DRIVES AND VIEWS If you didn't enter Yosemite Valley via **Highway 41 from Fresno,** it's worth the drive up this curvy road just to enjoy the vista from **Tunnel View.** Pull into the parking area on either side of the road immediately before the entrance to the tunnel. This is the most popular view in Yosemite, overlooking the valley, with El Capitan on the left, Bridalveil Fall on the right, and Half Dome as a backdrop.

From here, you may want to continue through the tunnel and head up to **Glacier Point** (open summer only) for another awe-inspiring view of the valley. A short walk from the parking lot brings you to the top of a sheer rock cliff, where you can peer straight down at the valley about 3,200 feet below. Across the valley, you can see the entire 2,425-foot plummet of Yosemite Falls. Altogether, allow about an hour for this 32-mile drive from the valley.

Highway 41 is also the road from the valley to the **Mariposa Grove of Big Trees.** If you're planning to include a visit to the sequoias, get an early morning start from the valley. This road winds up through both open and wooded areas, some charred from recent forest fires, and has panoramic views of forested hills. It then curves back down to Wawona and back up to the grove.

You may want to stop for lunch at the 1879 **Wawona Hotel** and its delightful Victorian-style parlor and dining room (*see* Historic Buildings and Sites; Dining; and Lodging, *below*). Nearby, you can explore the **Pioneer Yosemite History Center,** a collection of authentic, century-old buildings that have been relocated here from throughout the park (*see* Historic Buildings and Sites, *below*).

In the summer, take a drive up through the high country toward Tioga Pass on Highway 120 East to the alpine scenery of **Tuolumne Meadows.** Highlights include crystal-blue lakes, grassy meadows, and rounded peaks. Keep a sharp eye out for the neon colors of rock climbers, who seem to defy gravity on the cliffs.

HISTORIC BUILDINGS AND SITES The Yosemite Valley's 1927 **Ahwahnee Hotel** is a stately lodge of granite and concrete beams, stained to look like redwood, that is a perfect man-made complement to Yosemite's natural majesty. Even if you aren't a guest, take time to visit the immense parlors with their walk-in hearths and priceless, antique Native American rugs and baskets. The dining room is extraordinary, its high ceiling interlaced with massive sugar-pine beams. Guest rooms are expensive and are sometimes reserved up to a year in advance (*see* Dining and Lodging, *below*).

The **Wawona Hotel,** in the southern tip of Yosemite National Park, was the park's first lodge, built in 1879. With a whitewashed exterior and wraparound verandas, this is a fine example of Victorian resort architecture, a blend of rusticity and elegance. It is now a National Historic Landmark. The hotel annexes on this estate are also turn-of-the-century, the last built in 1918. Meals and lodging are available here (*see* Dining and Lodging, *below*).

Near the Wawona Hotel is the **Pioneer Yosemite History Center,** a collection of Yosemite's first log buildings, relocated here from around the park. A covered bridge that welcomed the park's first tourists leads to a villagelike setting. Century-old structures include a homesteader's house, a blacksmith's shop, a bakery, and a mountaineer's cabin. In the summer, costumed docents play the roles of the pioneers. Accessible year-round, the buildings are open Wednesday through Sunday, 10 to 5, from late June to Labor Day. Donations are accepted.

NATURE TRAILS AND SHORT WALKS There are several short trails that will get you out of the car and into the park in quick order. For an

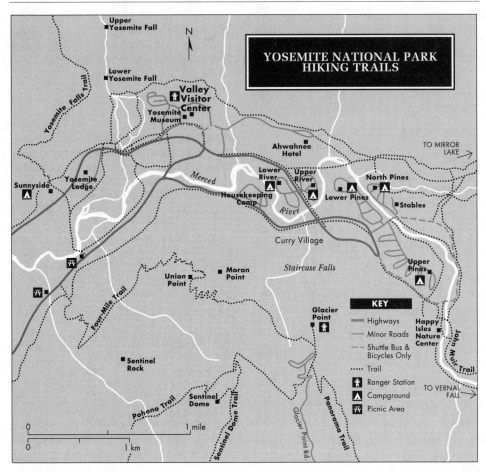

excellent map and description of many valley hikes, invest in the colorful *Map & Guide to Yosemite Valley* ($2.50) available at the Yosemite Valley Visitor Center.

Tucked behind the Valley Visitor Center, a short loop trail (about 100 yards) circles through a recreation of an **Ahwahneechee village** as it might have appeared in 1872, 20 years after the Native Americans' first contact with Europeans. Markers explain the lifestyle of Yosemite's first residents through the eyes of a young child. Allow 30 minutes.

A Changing Yosemite is a self-guided nature trail (pick up a pamphlet at the trailhead) that begins about 75 yards in front of the Valley Visitor Center. This level walk follows the road, then circles through Cook's Meadow.

The informative pamphlet explains the continually changing geology of the valley. Allow at least 45 minutes for this 1-mile paved loop trail, which is wheelchair-accessible.

You can see the dizzying height of **Yosemite Falls** from the parking lot but can only experience its power by following the 1/4-mile one-way paved trail to its base. The path leads to a footbridge, often showered with the mist of the mighty falls, that crosses the rushing waters with Lower Yosemite Fall towering above you. Many return to the parking lot at this point, but the intrepid walker can continue across the bridge to a surprisingly little-traveled route. This level, wooded 1-mile path winds through the cool forest, meandering several times over creeks via footbridges. In a secluded spot, you'll discover the site of John Muir's cabin, with Yosemite Falls as a backdrop. The trail circles back to the Lower Fall parking lot.

The base of **Bridalveil Fall** is also just ¼ mile from its parking lot. The trail follows a rocky creek up to a patio often sprayed with the mist of this wind-blown falls. You might get wet while peering straight up at the 620-foot waterfall. The paved trail has a slight, 100-foot rise but is wheelchair-accessible.

A popular, easy trail leads from Shuttle Bus Stop No. 17 (near the valley stables) 2 miles round-trip to **Mirror Lake**. But don't expect to find a blue expanse reflecting the surrounding cliffs. In a natural process called succession, Mirror Lake is changing from lake to meadow. In fact, by summer's end, it is often completely dry. Allow one hour for this hike, but if you want to go farther you can continue on the 3-mile **Mirror Lake Loop** for an added hour of pleasant hiking.

For a more strenuous short hike, follow the **John Muir Trail** from Happy Isles (Shuttle Bus Stop No. 16) to a vista of Vernal Fall and its 317-foot drop. This 1½-mile round-trip trail is a little steep in places, rising 400 feet altogether, but you'll be rewarded with an outstanding view of Vernal Fall from the footbridge crossing the river. Allow about one hour for this hike. The famous John Muir Trail continues south for 200 miles over the Sierra crest to Mt. Whitney, the highest peak in the contiguous United States (*see* Longer Hikes, *below*).

LONGER HIKES Before heading out on any long hike, it's a good idea to check trail conditions with the rangers. The following trails climb to higher elevations and are closed during winter snows. In warmer seasons, these trails may be muddy and slippery because of their proximity to waterfalls.

The **John Muir Trail,** from Happy Isles to the Vernal Fall vista (*see* Nature Trails and Short Walks, *above*), is the first stretch of a steep but spectacular hike to the top of Vernal Fall. After crossing the river, leave the John Muir Trail for the **Mist Trail,** which borders the cascading river and its spraying foam, hence its name. Allow about three hours for the 1,050-foot elevation gain on this 3-mile round-trip hike from Happy Isles.

From the top of Vernal Fall you can continue to climb the Mist Trail to the top of **Nevada Fall**, passing the shimmering Emerald Pool on the way. You can walk to the brink of this fall (there's a vista point with guardrails) for a dizzying view of the water plummeting 594 feet straight down. Do not try to edge out over the open rock where the falls begin or you may be plummeting straight down with them. From here, you'll view the panorama of Yosemite's rounded domes. The placid Emerald Pool is an inviting spot for a picnic. Allow six to eight hours for this 7-mile round-trip hike from Happy Isles to the top of Nevada Fall and back. The trail climbs almost 2,000 feet in elevation from Happy Isles.

Ardent and courageous trekkers can continue on the **John Muir Trail** from the top of Nevada Fall to the top of Half Dome. Some visitors try to do this entire 10- to 12-hour, 16¾-mile round-trip trek from Happy Isles in one day. If you're planning to do this, remember that the 4,900-foot elevation gain and the altitude of 8,842 feet will cause shortness of breath. Backpackers can hike to a campground near the top of Nevada Fall the first day, then climb to the top of Half Dome and hike out the next day. In any case, wear shoes with excellent traction and bring gloves. The last pitch up the back of Half Dome is very steep. The only way to climb this sheer rock face is to pull yourself up using the steel cable handrails, which are only in place from late spring to early fall. Those who are squeamish about heights, and even some who aren't, choose not to attempt this last portion of the climb. Those who brave the ascent will be rewarded with an unbeatable view of Yosemite Valley below and the high country beyond. They'll get that top-of-the-world feeling enjoyed by rock climbers.

Steep but rewarding, the **Yosemite Falls Trail** climbs from the valley to the top of the tallest waterfall in North America. Once you see the

2,425-foot drop of this waterfall from the base and picture yourself on top, you'll know that the trail is for hardy hikers only. A narrow path with a railing leads to the actual brink of Upper Yosemite Fall. The six- to eight-hour trail, with a 2,700-foot elevation gain, is 7 miles round-trip from the trailhead at Sunnyside campground (Shuttle Bus Stop No. 8).

There are several options for those who don't want an uphill hump. You can take a bus to Glacier Point ($9.25) and one of the valley's best views, then hike back down to the valley from there. **Four-Mile Trail** descends from Glacier Point, zigzagging through forest to the valley floor, where, with a relatively short walk, you can catch a free shuttle bus back to your starting point. If you decide to hike up the Four-Mile Trail and hike back down again, allow about six hours for the 9¹/₂-mile round-trip (the trail was lengthened to make it less steep, but its name was not changed), with a 3,220-foot elevation gain.

Another trail starting at Glacier Point is the **Panorama Trail,** which circles 8¹/₂ miles through forest, past the secluded Illilouette Falls, to the top of Nevada Fall, where it connects with either the Mist Trail or the John Muir Trail to follow first Nevada then Vernal fall to the valley floor. Arrange for an early morning bus ride to Glacier Point, and allow a full day for this hike, even though it has an overall 3,200-foot elevation loss.

Backpackers can utilize the Tuolumne Meadows bus to reach the high country (available July through Labor Day), then backpack down to the valley. This is one way to enjoy the views and trails emanating from the valley without an uphill struggle with full pack. You can also take a bus up, enjoy your backpacking trek in the high country, then take the bus back down to your valley starting point. The bus leaves the valley daily at 8 AM, traveling east on Tioga Road to Lee Vining, then turning around and, after a two-hour stop at Tuolumne Meadows, returning to the valley at 4 PM. Arrange in advance with the bus driver to be picked up in the high country so that you don't miss the bus. Bus prices vary according to drop-off point. One-way fare to Tuolumne Meadows from the valley is $12.

In the Wawona area, the **Chilnualna Falls Trail** runs 4 miles one-way to the top of the falls, then leads into the backcountry, connecting with miles of other trails. This is one of the most inspiring and secluded trails, but it is easily accessible off Chilnualna Falls Road. Watch for the sign leading to a parking lot to your right, just before the paved road turns to dirt. This hike leads past a tumbling cascade, up through forests, and to a steep ascent, at the top of which there are panoramic vistas. Day hikers should plan on hiking to the waterfall, then returning via the same path.

OTHER ACTIVITIES **Art Workshops.** From late March through early October, professional artists offer free midday workshops in watercolor, etching, drawing, and other subjects. Classes are held outdoors at inspiring spots, depending on the weather. Bring your own materials or purchase the basics for about $10. Register at the **Art Activity Center** (Yosemite Village, tel. 209/372–1442), adjacent to the Ansel Adams Gallery.

Biking. Yosemite Valley is ideal for biking, especially for families. More than 8 miles of scenic, mostly level bike-ways in the valley offer a safe and pleasant alternative to the relatively narrow roads. Bike rentals, with helmets, are available through the **Lodge Bike Stand** at two locations: Yosemite Lodge (tel. 209/372–1208), which is open year-round, conditions permitting; and Curry Village (tel. 209/372–1200), open during the summer and fall and spring, weather permitting. Rentals cost $5 per hour or $16.25 per day. These are standard, one-speed bikes with foot brakes. Child-carriers are not available. You'll find a bike-way map on the back of the *Yosemite Guide* and at bike-rental stands. There is no mountain biking permitted on any Yosemite foot or horse trail.

Bird-Watching. Park rangers lead free bird-watching walks in Yosemite Valley during the summer months, usually one day each week. Binoculars are sometimes available for loan. Several intensive two- to four-day seminars for beginning and intermediate birders are offered May through July by the **Yosemite Association** (Box 230, El Portal, CA 95318, tel. 209/379–2646). Fees range from $95 to $130. More than 200 bird species have been spotted in the park, including the sage sparrow, pygmy owl, blue grouse, and mountain bluebird. Ask for a bird list at a visitor center.

Fishing. The waters in Yosemite are not currently stocked. Trout, mostly brown and rainbow, live here but are not plentiful. You will need a fishing license. State residents pay $23.90 for a year's license. Nonresidents must fork over $64.30. Residents and nonresidents may purchase a one-day license for about $8 at the **Yosemite Village Sportshop** (tel. 209/372–1286, summer only), next to the village store. For information, contact the Department of Fish and Game (3211 S St., Sacramento, CA 95816, tel. 916/227–2244).

Horseback Riding. If you want to take a horse or pack animal into the park, you must be accompanied by an authorized guide. Scenic trail rides range from two hours ($30) to half days ($40), and full days ($60), and six-day High Sierra saddle trips ($700). Participants in the six-day trips are chosen by lottery; those interested must apply at least a year and a day in advance. Stables are open late spring through early fall in **Yosemite Valley** (tel. 209/372–1248) and during the summer only in **Wawona** (tel. 209/375–6502), **White Wolf** (tel. 209/372–1323), and **Tuolumne Meadows** (tel. 209/372–1327). Reservations must be made in person at the stables or at the hotel tour desks.

Rock Climbing. The **Yosemite Mountaineering School** (tel. 209/372–1244, Sept.–May in the Valley; 209/372–1335, June–Aug. in Tuolumne Meadows) has a variety of lessons and seminars for the beginner as well as the advanced climber. The one-day basic lesson ($100 for one person, $70 each for two, $45 each for three or more) includes some bouldering and rappelling and a 60-foot climb. You must be at least 14 years old and be in reasonably good physical condition. Intermediate and advanced classes include instruction in belays, jamcrack techniques,

self-rescue, summer snow climbing, and free climbing. Classes are offered mid-April through early October. If you are already an experienced climber, ask at the mountaineer shop in Curry Village what areas would be best for your level of skill.

Skating. You can ice skate from late October through mid-March at the outdoor **Curry Village Ice Skating Rink** (Yosemite Village, tel. 209/372–1441). The admission price is $5 adults, $4.50 children. Skate rental costs $1.75.

Skiing. Yosemite offers cross-country and alpine skiing at **Badger Pass** (tel. 209/372–1330) in the winter months. A free shuttle bus carries skiers from Yosemite Valley to the ski area; it takes about 40 minutes. Badger Pass opened in 1935 and is the oldest operating ski area in California. It is a compact area with one base lodge and gentle terrain, factors that make it ideal for families and beginners. Four chair lifts and two surface lifts access nine runs. Lift tickets are $26 adults, $11.75 children 4 to 12 for all-day weekend pass; $21 adults, $10.50 children all-day mid-week. Senior citizens over 65 and everyone exactly 40 years old ski free every day. Ask about midweek packages. Alpine and cross-country ski schools and rentals are available.

Of Yosemite's 350 miles of skiable cross-country trails and roads, 90 begin at Badger Pass, but you can also ski at Crane Flat and the Mariposa Grove. The Glacier Point Road is not plowed but is groomed in winter. It's a 21-mile round-trip ski from Badger Pass to the vista at Glacier Point. Overnight trans-Sierra ski tours are also available.

Snowshoeing. Park rangers offer free snowshoe tours at Badger Pass during the winter months when the ski area is operating. These 2-hour walks include rest stops, during which the ranger explains animal behavior in winter.

Swimming. Several swimming holes with small sandy beaches can be found along the Merced River at the eastern end of Yosemite Valley. Find gentle waters to swim; currents are often stronger than they appear and temperatures are chilling. Do not attempt to swim above or near waterfalls or rapids. Fatalities have occurred. Outdoor swimming pools (summer only) are located at Curry Village (tel. 209/372–1405) and Yosemite Lodge (tel. 209/372–1250).

CHILDREN'S PROGRAMS Junior Rangers (ages 8–9) and Senior Rangers (ages 10–12) are scheduled activities led by a park ranger and offered during the summer. Parents are welcome to accompany children or drop them off for the day's activities. Children earn a certificate for each day they participate in these free naturalist activities. After three days, they earn a patch. Happy Isles Nature Center Children's Program (ages 5–7) is a free one-hour ranger-led program offered daily in the summer. A less formal Junior Snow Rangers program is offered during winter months.

Children also will enjoy the Family Discovery Walks led by park rangers; Wawona's Pioneer Yosemite History Center with its costumed docents in summer; biking; walk-and-lead ponies; guided saddle rides; and skiing and ice skating in winter.

A referral list of baby-sitters who have taken a certification course is available through the Ahwahnee Hotel and the Yosemite Lodge (*see* Lodging, *below*). Parents contract individually with each baby-sitter, but it's suggested that you pay at least minimum wage. Advance arrangements are recommended.

EVENING ACTIVITIES In the evenings, ranger talks, slide shows, and documentary films present unique perspectives on Yosemite. Programs vary according to season, but there is usually at least one activity per night in the valley. One of the best-loved presentations is Lee Stetson's portrayal of John Muir in *Conversation with a Tramp* and *Stickeen* (*see* Seasonal Events, *above*). Check the *Yosemite Guide* for location and time of the shows.

Adults can relax with a cocktail at the Yosemite Lodge lounge, with its large-screen television and central fireplace; at the Ahwahnee Hotel; and at the Wawona Hotel, which features a ragtime pianist and singer on weekends (*see* Lodging, *below*).

DINING

Yosemite is not known as a gourmet's delight. The food here is primarily basic American. Those on a budget should head for the cafeteria at Yosemite Lodge (open year-round) and the hamburger stand at Curry Village (open spring to fall).

Since nighttime activities are limited, many visitors choose to dine in one of the slower-paced restaurants. Dinner at the Ahwahnee Hotel, with its magnificent, candlelit dining room, and at the Wawona Hotel, with its nostalgic, Victorian ambience, are both romantic. Choose a restaurant for the setting, since the food is similar, with a few exceptions, in all of them. All restaurants in Yosemite are run by Yosemite Concession Services Corporation. Operating hours vary by season and are listed in the *Yosemite Guide* newspaper, which you will receive as you enter the park. All restaurants in Yosemite are casual, with the exception of the Ahwahnee, where most of the dinner patrons wear a sport coat and tie or evening dress.

INSIDE THE PARK **The Ahwahnee Dining Room.** This is the most romantic and elegant setting in Yosemite, if not California. In the evening, this massive room, with its floor-to-ceiling windows and soaring, 34-foot-high ceiling supported by immense sugar-pine beams, glows with candlelight. Specialties include lobster Newburg, prepared with saffron, sherry, and cream sauce; chicken piccata with fettuccine Alfredo; and prime rib. Most dinner patrons wear jacket and tie or evening dress. *Ahwahnee Hotel, Yosemite Valley, tel. 209/372–1489. Reservations required for dinner. Jacket advised. AE, D, MC, V. Expensive.*

Four Seasons Restaurant. Next to the Mountain Room Broiler (*see below*), this large, casual restaurant is ideal for families looking for something less hectic than the cafeteria. Entrées include barbecued breast of chicken, grilled trout almandine (fresh when available), and New York strip steak. Vegetarian meals and a children's menu are available. Show up early for dinner or be prepared for a long wait in line in the busy seasons. *Yosemite Valley, tel. 209/372–1269. Reservations not accepted. Dress: casual. AE, D, MC, V. Moderate.*

The Loft. On the second floor of the large A-frame building that also houses Degnan's Deli and Degnan's Fast Food (*see below*), The Loft is the only sit-down restaurant in Yosemite Village. At lunchtime, you can glimpse Glacier Point and Yosemite Falls from large dormer windows as you enjoy a corned beef sandwich, soft taco, or salad. The dinner menu includes prime rib, grilled trout, Cajun-style catfish, and meatless lasagna. The food is good and reasonably priced, and the setting is superb. *Yosemite Village, tel. 209/372–1081. Reservations not accepted. Dress: casual. AE, D, MC, V. Moderate.*

Mountain Room Broiler. Choose this restaurant if you're looking for casual fine dining away from the noise and crowds of other Yosemite Valley dining areas but not as formal or expensive as the Ahwahnee. Knicker-clad waiters and life-size photographs depicting rock climbers give the Broiler a robust atmosphere. It is conveniently located at Yosemite Lodge. The focus here is on simply prepared steaks and fish, including filet mignon, salmon, and trout. *Yosemite Valley, tel. 209/372–1281. Reservations not accepted. Dress: casual. AE, D, MC, V. Moderate.*

Wawona Hotel Dining Room. This is a romantic, nostalgic setting dating back to the late 1800s, with white-linen cloths, tabletop candles in hurricane lamps, and friendly service. Along with the prime rib, trout, and daily chicken specials, selections include a Szechuan vegetable platter and roast pork with plum sauce. A children's menu and Sunday brunch also are offered. *Wawona Hotel, tel. 209/375–6556. Reservations required for dinner. Dress: casual. AE, D, MC, V. Moderate.*

There are several year-round fast-food options near the Valley Visitor Center. In an alpine-style building with fireplaces, **Degnan's Deli** offers sandwiches, salads, and gourmet cheeses, while **Degnan's Fast Food** serves pizza and ice cream. Nearby, the **Village Grill,** open spring to fall, serves hamburgers, croissant sandwiches, and ice cream frosties. Summer-only restaurants are located in the **Tuolumne Meadows Lodge** (tel. 209/372–1313) and **White Wolf Lodge** (tel. 209/ 372–1316).

NEAR THE PARK **Erna's Elderberry House.** Many repeat visitors to Yosemite plan on stopping here on the way to or from the park. Erna's boasts four dining rooms with a French provincial flair and an outside terrace overlooking the Sierra. Prix-fixe, six-course dinners change nightly but may include fresh mountain trout filled with a red-pepper mousseline; a smoked-duck-and-chanterelle-mushroom double consommé with foie gras dumplings; a nectarine-and-Campari sorbet; roast quails filled with green-lentil puree and fresh figs; six seasonal vegetables; and caramelized blood oranges with bitter-chocolate ice. *48688 Victoria La., Oakhurst, tel. 209/683–6800. Reservations advised. Jacket advised. MC, V. No lunch Sat.–Tues., no dinner Mon. and Tues. Expensive.*

Coffee Express. If you're coming into Yosemite via Highway 120, you'll pass this cozy, casual lunch spot with friendly service. Try the chicken salad with apples and alfalfa sprouts and at least one piece of the irresistible pies. If time allows, check out the Iron Door Saloon, which claims to be the oldest operating saloon in California, across the street. *Hwy. 120, Groveland, tel. 209/962–7393. No reservations. Dress: casual. No credit cards. Closed Thurs. No dinner. Inexpensive.*

PICNIC SPOTS You can find everything you need for a delicious picnic in Yosemite Valley. Try **Degnan's Deli** (tel. 209/372–1454) for sandwiches and cheeses and the **Village Store** (tel. 209/372–1253) for all your grocery needs. Ready-made picnic lunches are available through Yosemite hotels with advance notice. There are seven picnic areas located along the main roads in the western end of Yosemite Valley: Cathedral Beach, Yellow Pine, Sentinel Beach, Happy Isles, Bridalveil Fall, Devil's Elbow, and Swinging Bridge. All of these areas have picnic tables, rest rooms, and garbage receptacles, and all except Happy Isles and Bridalveil Fall have fire rings. There are no grills in the valley picnic areas and no water spigots. Outside the valley, there are picnic areas with tables at Glacier Point (rest rooms, garbage receptacles, water), Mariposa Grove (rest rooms, garbage receptacles, water), Wawona (grills, water nearby), Tenaya Lake (rest rooms, garbage receptacles, fire rings, some grills), and Lembert Dome (garbage receptacles, fire rings). Many picnickers prefer to hike along one of the many scenic trails and choose an impromptu spot or vista point for a picnic.

LODGING

Lodging in Yosemite ranges from the elegant Ahwahnee Hotel to spartan tent-cabins, but all exhibit an air of rusticity complementary to their natural setting. In the valley, Yosemite Village is the most densely populated area, with several two-story, hotel-style buildings and a large community of one-room wood cabins. This area also offers the most food, shopping, and restaurant services and is within easy walking distance of Yosemite Falls and the Valley Visitor Center. The Ahwahnee Hotel is in a more secluded, quiet setting, away from the valley crowds; it is the only hotel in Yosemite that offers color television, room service, and minibars. Curry Village, another community of wood cabins and tent cabins, is within walking distance of the trails emanating from Happy Isles. In the summer, you can find rustic lodges at Tuolumne Meadows and White Wolf.

Reserve your room or cabin in Yosemite Valley as soon as possible. You can make a reservation up to 366 days before your arrival date. Hotel rooms and cabins with private bath are particularly popular. The Ahwahnee, Yosemite Lodge, and Wawona Hotel are often sold out on weekends, holiday periods, and all days between May and September within minutes after the reservation office opens. All reservations for lodging in Yosemite are made through **Yosemite Concession Services Corporation** (Central Reservations, 5410 E. Home Ave., Fresno, CA 93727, tel. 209/252–4848).

If you visit in November through March, especially midweek, you'll have a much easier time getting a reservation, and you'll pay a discounted room rate. If you must visit in the busy season and can't get a reservation, try asking for the less popular tent cabins at Curry Village. You may be able to upgrade after you arrive. Call 30 days, 15 days, or seven days in advance of your arrival. These are common dates when rooms held by previous reservations are canceled. Join a group tour, which often books blocks of rooms in advance. Though risky, you also can put your name on a wait list the day you arrive at Yosemite. Reservations without deposit are held only until 4 PM without a confirmation. If you're very lucky, a room may become available. Otherwise, plan on a long drive (sometimes one to two hours) to the nearest open hotel outside the park.

INSIDE THE PARK **Ahwahnee Hotel.** This grand, 1920s hotel, with its exterior of granite and concrete painted to look like redwood, is the perfect complement to Yosemite. Now a National Historic Landmark, it has dramatic common areas warmed by walk-in hearths, decorated with Native American rugs and baskets, and graced with views of Yosemite through towering windows. The guest rooms are standard, highlighted with a Native American motif. *123 rooms. Facilities: restaurant, lounge, pool, tennis. AE, D, MC, V. Expensive.*

Wawona Hotel. This circa-1879 National Historic Landmark is located in the southern end of Yosemite National Park, near the Mariposa Grove of Big Trees. It's an old-fashioned Victorian estate of whitewashed buildings with wraparound verandas. The rooms reflect their turn-of-the-century origin—most are small and do not have a private bath. The Victorian parlor in the main hotel is fun and romantic, with a fireplace, board games, and a pianist who sings Cole Porter tunes on weekend evenings. *104 rooms. Facilities: restaurant, lounge, pool, tennis, stables, golf course adjacent. AE, D, MC, V. Open daily*

Easter week through Thanksgiving, during Christmas week and weekends year-round. Moderate.

Yosemite Lodge. This property encompasses a variety of lodging alternatives, from rustic cabins to deluxe hotel rooms. The least expensive cabins are one room, with electric heater, and share a camp-style, indoor bathroom with flush toilets in a separate building. For those who don't need luxury, these cabins can be delightful, especially if you can get one by the river. Guest rooms in the hotel range from simple motel-style digs to deluxe rooms with cathedral ceilings and balconies overlooking Yosemite Falls. *495 rooms. Facilities: 2 restaurants, cafeteria, lounge, pool, 2 gift shops. AE, D, MC, V. Moderate.*

Curry Village. This is a large community of cabins and tent cabins in a woodland setting on the eastern end of Yosemite Valley. The one-room cabins, spartan but adequately furnished, are a lower-cost alternative to Yosemite's hotels. Tent cabins have wood frames and canvas walls and roof. Those without bath share campground-style community showers and toilets. Linen service is provided, but cooking is not allowed in the cabin area. *183 cabins, 427 tent cabins, 18 hotel rooms. Facilities: fast-food restaurant, pool, skating rink, stables. AE, D, MC, V. Inexpensive–Moderate.*

NEAR THE PARK Additional lodging is available in Yosemite's gateway cities, but the nearest town, El Portal, is still 14 slow mountain miles from the Valley Visitor Center. The next nearest town, Midpines, is 36 miles away, and Mariposa, with the most lodging options, is 43 miles away. The Mariposa County Chamber of Commerce (Box 425, Mariposa, CA 95338, tel. 209/966–2456) covering Mariposa, El Portal, and Fish Camp, offers a free brochure listing all county hotels, motels, bed-and-breakfasts, restaurants, and sights. For a free comprehensive guide to lodging and sightseeing options to the south of Yosemite, contact the Southern Yosemite Visitors Bureau (Box 1404, Oakhurst, CA 93644, tel. 209/683–4636). For hotels in Groveland, ask for the lodging guide from

Tuolumne County Visitors Bureau (Box 4020, Sonora, CA 95370, tel. 209/533–4420 or 800/446–1333).

A number of inns and motels are located within a 25-mile (1- to 1½-hour) drive of Yosemite Park. Consider the following: **Cedar Lodge** (9966 Hwy. 140, El Portal, CA 95318, tel. 209/379–2612; 206 rooms; restaurant, pool, gift shop; AE, MC, V; Moderate–Expensive); **Berkshire Inn** (19950 Hwy. 120, Groveland, CA 95321, tel. 209/962–6744; 10 rooms; Jacuzzi, TV in common room, Continental breakfast; no credit cards; Moderate); **Best Western Yosemite Gateway Inn** (40530 Hwy. 41, Oakhurst, CA 93644, tel. 209/683–2378 or 800/528–1234; 118 rooms; heated indoor/outdoor pool, sauna, whirlpools, exercise room; AE, D, DC, MC, V; Moderate); **Best Western Yosemite Way Station** (4999 Hwy. 140, Box 1989, Mariposa, CA 95338, tel. 209/966–7545 or 800/528–1234; 78 rooms; heated pool, spa, Continental breakfast; AE, D, DC, MC, V; Moderate); **Shilo Inn** (40644 Hwy. 41, Oakhurst, CA 93644, tel. 209/683–3555 or 800/222–2244; 80 rooms; pool, sauna, whirlpool, steam room, exercise room; AE, D, DC, MC, V; Moderate); **Yosemite Gold Rush Inn** (4994 Bullion St., Box 1989, Mariposa, CA 95338, tel. 209/966–4344 or 800/321–5261; 61 rooms; small pool, whirlpool, gift shop, Continental breakfast; AE, MC, V; Moderate); and **Miners Inn** (Rte. 140 at Rte. 49N, Box 246, Mariposa, CA 95338, tel. 209/742–7777; 64 rooms; pool, whirlpool, movies; AE, D, MC, V. Inexpensive–Moderate).

CAMPING

There are more than 1,900 campsites in the 14 drive-in and two walk-in campgrounds at Yosemite National Park. In addition, backpackers can hike to numerous backcountry areas where they can pitch a tent away from the crowds. Free wilderness permits are required for overnights in the backcountry; you can get these at visitor centers and ranger stations or by contacting the Wilderness Office in advance of your trip (*see* Visitor Information, *above*). When camping in the backcountry, you must be at least 4 miles from any developed area and at least 1 mile from roads and trailheads. Fires are permitted only in existing fire rings at specified elevations; ask a ranger before you head out.

All valley campgrounds, with the exception of Sunnyside Walk-in, can be reserved through **Mistix** (tel. 800/365–2267). In addition, Mistix takes reservations for Hodgdon Meadow from May to October and for Crane Flat and half the sites at Tuolumne Meadows for as long as those campgrounds remain open. You can reserve campsites no sooner than eight weeks before your arrival. Yosemite campgrounds consistently sell out within minutes of the time they become available during the high season. Call Mistix as soon as the office opens exactly eight weeks in advance of your visit to ensure a campsite. Mail-in reservations are processed at the same time as phone reservations. Weather regulates the opening day of the seasonal campgrounds; dates given here are approximate. When you make a reservation it is for a particular campground but not a particular site; arrive early for the best selection. Sites at all other campgrounds are available on a first-come, first-served basis.

RVs longer than 35 feet may not be accommodated in campgrounds. There are no hookups in the park, but LP gas is available at the service stations. Generators are permitted sparingly and only during daylight hours. Gravel and dirt RV sites are available in all park campgrounds except the valley's Upper River and the walk-in campgrounds. Larger sites are generally given to big RVs. Tamarack Flat and Yosemite Creek are accessible only by an access road that is not recommended for large RVs or trailers.

Yosemite Valley campgrounds are located along the Merced River on the relatively flat valley floor, at an elevation of about 4,000 feet. They are in forested areas, with pines, firs, and incense cedars. Campgrounds in the valley are well maintained but crowded, especially in summer. Lack of undergrowth between tent sites means there's not much privacy. Showers are available for a nominal fee at Curry Village and at valley swimming pools in season.

The **North Pines** campground (85 sites, flush toilets, drinking water, fire grates, swimming, ranger station, public phone, laundry and showers nearby) is located in the valley. Some of the sites are too close to the stables' horsey odor. North Pines is open from May to October; sites cost $12 per night.

Upper Pines (238 sites, flush toilets, drinking water, fire grates, swimming, disposal station, ranger station, public phone) is the only valley campground to allow pets. It is open from April to November; sites cost $12 per night. The valley's **Lower Pines** (172 sites, flush toilets, drinking water, fire grates, swimming, ranger station, public phone) is open year-round; sites cost $12 per night. Both have laundry and showers nearby.

Upper River (124 sites, flush toilets, drinking water, fire grates, swimming, ranger station, public phone) is a tents-only valley campground and is open from April to October. Sites cost $12 per night. **Lower River** (138 sites, flush toilets, drinking water, fire grates, swimming, disposal station, ranger station, public phone) is open from April to October; sites cost $12 per night. Both have laundry and showers nearby.

Sunnyside Walk-in (35 sites, flush toilets, drinking water, fire grates, ranger station, public phone) is the only valley campground available on a first-come, first-served basis and the only one west of Yosemite Lodge. It is a favorite for rock climbers and solo campers, so it fills quickly and is typically sold out every day from spring through fall. Sunnyside is open year-round; sites cost $2 per person per night. Those with wilderness permits and those without a motorized vehicle may be placed by rangers in an overflow area called the **Backpacker's Walk-in** (25 sites, flush toilets, drinking water, fire grates, swimming), which has a two-night limit. It's open from May to October; sites cost $2 per person per night.

In the southwestern section of the park, near the Mariposa Grove of Tall Trees, there are

YOSEMITE CAMPGROUNDS

	North Pines	Upper Pines	Lower Pines	Upper River	Lower River	Wawona	Bridalveil Creek	Hodgdon Meadow	Crane Flat	Tamarack Flat	White Wolf	Yosemite Creek	Porcupine Flat	Tuolumne Meadows
Total number of sites	85	238	172	124	138	100	110	105	166	52	87	75	52	314
Sites suitable for RVs	85	238	172	0	138	100	110	105	166	52	87	75	52	314
Number of hookups	0	0	0	0	0	0	0	0	0	0	0	0	0	0
Drive to sites	•	•	•	•	•	•	•	•	•	•	•	•	•	•
Hike to sites														
Flush toilets	•	•	•	•	•	•	•	•			•			•
Pit/chemical toilets										•		•	•	
Drinking water	•	•	•	•	•	•	•	•	•		•			•
Showers														
Fire grates	•	•	•	•	•	•	•	•	•	•	•	•	•	•
Swimming	•	•	•	•	•	•								
Boat access														
Playground														
Disposal station		•			•	•								•
Ranger station	•	•	•	•	•	•	•		•					•
Public telephone	•	•	•	•	•	•					•	•		•
Reservation possible	•	•	•	•	•	•	•							•
Daily fee per site	$12	$12	$12	$12	$12	$7	$7	$10	$10	$4	$7	$4	$4	$10
Dates open	May–Oct.	Apr.–Nov.	year-round	Apr.–Oct.	Apr.–Oct.	year-round	June–Sept.	year-round	May–Oct.	June–mid-Oct.	June–mid-Sept.	June–Sept.	June–mid-Oct.	June–mid-Oct.

100 sites located along the river at **Wawona** (flush toilets, drinking water, fire grates, swimming, disposal station, ranger station, public phone). At an elevation of about 4,000 feet, these are open year-round and cost $7 per night.

On Glacier Point Road, past the Badger Pass Ski Area, there is a campground at **Bridalveil Creek** (110 sites, flush toilets, drinking water, fire grates, public phone). It sits higher than 7,000 feet, in an area forested with lodgepole pines, and can be quite brisk in the fall. It is open from June to September; sites cost $7 per night.

Hodgdon Meadow (105 sites, flush toilets, drinking water, fire grates, ranger station, public phone) is located on the park's western boundary, near the Big Oak Flat Entrance. At an elevation of 4,800 feet, it has vegetation similar to that in the valley, but there is no river and no development here. It is open year-round, and sites cost $10 per night.

At 6,200 feet, the **Crane Flat** campground (166 sites, flush toilets, drinking water, fire grates, public phone) is also on the western boundary, south of Hodgdon Meadow, off Big Oak Flat Road. It is just 17 miles from the valley but far from the valley's bustle. A small grove of sequoias is nearby. Crane Flat is open from May to October; sites cost $10 per night.

A spur road off the western end of Tioga Road brings you to **Tamarack Flat** (52 sites, pit toilets, fire grates), which is in a forested area with lodgepole pines, red firs, and some cedars. This is a more primitive campground, one without water. Only small RVs can be accommodated here. It is open from June to mid-October; sites cost $4 per night.

In the high country (8,000 feet), off Tioga Road, is **White Wolf** (87 sites, flush toilets, drinking water, fire grates, public phone), situated among lodgepole pines. It is open from June to mid-September, and sites cost $7 per night. Farther east on Tioga Road, a spur road leads to **Yosemite Creek** (75 sites, pit toilets, fire grates, public phone), which is open from June to September and charges $4 per site per night. Neither of these campgrounds is suitable for large RVs.

The primitive **Porcupine Flat** campground (52 sites, pit toilets, fire grates) is at 8,100 feet. It's located on Tioga Road, at about the center of the park, and is open from June to mid-October; sites cost $4 per night.

The most developed high-country campground is at **Tuolumne Meadows** (314 sites, flush toilets, drinking water, fire grates, disposal station, ranger station, public phone). The campground is in a wooded area just south of a subalpine meadow, and it affords easy access to high peaks with spectacular views. Campers here can use the showers at the Tuolumne Meadows Lodge. Tuolumne is open from June to mid-October. Half the sites can be reserved in advance through Mistix (*see above*). Sites cost $10 per night.

Zion National Park
Utah
By Tom Wharton

I n 1863 a Mormon settler named Isaac Behunin moved to southern Utah and built himself a cabin in the heart of this great canyon. Having fled religious persecution, Behunin called his new home Zion; it was, he felt, the promised land, a place of refuge and peace.

Today, Behunin's sanctuary is Utah's most developed and busiest national park, with more than 2¹/₂ million annual visitors, who crowd its lodge and two large campgrounds. Close to a major interstate that connects Las Vegas with Salt Lake City, the park is easy to reach, and its 30 miles of paved roads and easy hiking trails make it a cinch to explore.

Still, don't be fooled into thinking that Zion is too tame for a national park. Anyone who ventures away from the canyon roads will discover rugged trails, sandstone walls reaching 2,000 feet or more into the sky, and a fascinating and complex desert ecology.

The Virgin River, a muddy little stream that can turn into a violent red torrent during the spring runoff or after a summer thunderstorm, shaped Zion's mighty canyons. Under a bright sky, a hiker in Zion National Park can enter a side canyon barely 20 feet across and be sandwiched between towering sandstone walls, which are washed in shades of crimson, vermilion, tan, and orange, and often stained with dark patches of carbon residue.

The names given to Zion's mountains and canyons reflect the awe with which early visitors greeted them. When first declared a national monument in 1909, the park was called Mukuntuweap, a name given to it by the local Native American Paiute people. The Mormons, however, wanted the area to be called Zion, and they pressured President Wilson into naming it just that when Mukuntuweap became Zion National Monument in 1918, and, subsequently, Zion National Park in 1919. Many of the other place-names in the park—Kolob Canyons and Mt. Moroni, for example—are taken from Mormon theology. (Kolob is the star closest to God's residence, and Moroni is a principal figure in the Book of Mormon.) It was a Methodist minister, Frederick Vining Fisher, passing through Zion on a day trip in 1916, who gave the park some of its most evocative names: Angels Landing, the Great White Throne, and the Three Patriarchs.

To learn about local culture and get a feel for small-town life in predominantly Mormon Utah, visit the hamlet of Springdale, at the park's South entrance. Although a few garish motel signs mar an otherwise attractive setting, the town possesses a charm not often seen in gateway communities to national parks. Small shops, simple restaurants, and old pioneer homes dot the landscape.

ESSENTIAL INFORMATION

VISITOR INFORMATION Contact Superintendent, **Zion National Park**, Springdale, UT 84767, tel. 801/772–3256. If you plan on camping in the backcountry or hiking through the Narrows, you must have a backcountry permit, which you can pick up at no charge at either the Zion Canyon Visitor Center, near the park's South entrance, or the Kolob Canyons Visitor Center, in the northwest corner of the park just off I–15. In the winter months, the visitor centers open at 8 and close at 5, but hours are extended until as late as 8 during the busy summer months.

FEES A seven-day entrance pass to the park for a passenger vehicle costs $5. The entry fee for bus passengers, pedestrians, and bicyclists is $3 per week. A $10 fee is charged to escort oversize RVs wider than 7 feet 10 inches or higher than 11 feet 4 inches through the long, narrow tunnel on the Zion–Mt. Carmel Highway (Route 9).

PUBLICATIONS The **Zion Natural History Association** (Springdale, UT 84767, tel. 800/635–3959) sells a wide variety of maps and guides at its bookstores in both visitor centers. A list of publications is available, and credit card orders are accepted by phone.

The best general guidebook to the park is J.L. Crawford's *Zion National Park, Towers of Stone*. The free brochure and newspaper given out at park entrances outline the major hikes, but visitors seeking a more detailed description of the trails should consider buying *Hiking in Zion National Park, The Trails*, by Bob Lineback, and *Exploring the Backcountry of Zion National Park, Off-Trail Routes*, by Thomas Brereton and James Dunaway. Hikers may also want to purchase the waterproof, tear-resistant *Trails Illustrated Topo Map of Zion National Park*. If you want to *see* the park's offerings, pick up one of the four different videos available from the Zion Natural History Association.

GEOLOGY AND TERRAIN The proclamation President Taft signed in 1909 setting aside Zion Canyon as a national monument justifies its preservation by stating that it is an "extraordinary example of canyon erosion." Zion does indeed seem like an experiment in geology—a powerful testament to the abrasive effects of wind and water on a landscape. About 13 million years ago, the Virgin River and its tributaries began carving out all the canyons of Zion park and sculpting the steep cliffs that today rise 2,000 feet from the Zion Canyon floor.

But the story of Zion goes back much further in time—as far back as 280 million years. Sandstone, shale, and limestone sedimentary layers can be seen on the cliffs. At the bottom is the Moenkopi layer of the early Triassic period, and as your eyes skim up the rock face you will see Shinarump, Chinle, Moenave, Kayenta, Navajo, Temple Cap, Carmel, and Dakota, the most recent layer, which was laid down in the Cretaceous period. It is Navajo sandstone—the remains of ancient sand dunes—that dominates the scenery. These layers are held together by calcium carbonate and iron oxide; the iron oxide results in the red color.

Those expecting to find a bleak desert landscape will be astounded by Zion's brilliant palette and odd geologic formations. The cliffs range in color from white and pastels to tan, orange, and vibrant crimson. The

147,035-acre park comprises areas of rock that can resemble fairy castles and goblins. Part of the fun of visiting Zion is challenging your vocabulary to find just the right words to describe this fanciful world.

Spanning 310 feet, Kolob Arch, one of the world's largest natural arches, is here at Zion. In the hanging gardens of Weeping Rock, water seeps out of the sandstone allowing wildflowers, moss, and ferns to grow. On the eastern edge of the park is a huge petrified sand dune, aptly named Checkerboard Mesa for the grid that is etched onto its surface. The grid's horizontal lines are remnants of the rock's original sedimentation; the vertical lines are shallow cracks resulting from weathering—freezing, thawing, and heating—as well as expansion and water.

The interpretative displays in the visitor center and signs near turnoffs and trailheads explain Zion geology in great detail, but car travelers should buy *The Sculpturing of Zion*, by Wayne Hamilton.

FLORA AND FAUNA Zion National Park has a greatly varied terrain and elevation; the park ranges from Sonoran desert to alpine forest. At times it resembles a huge, red rock garden, with a variety of plants and flowers, and ponderosa pines that seem to grow right out of the hard rock. Zion is especially colorful in the fall and spring, when wildflowers bloom. In winter, the remaining brown oak leaves, practically the same color as the canyon walls, cling to the trees, and after a rainstorm, droplets of water form on the exposed branches of leafless trees. Cottonwood trees grow along the banks of the Virgin River, providing picnickers on the canyon bottom with shade from the scorching summer heat.

Red rocks, greenery, and purple, red, and yellow wildflowers make the hanging gardens one of the most interesting areas to see in the spring and summer months. Golden and cliff columbine, scarlet monkey-flower, and maidenhair fern hang from the sides of the sandstone cliffs along the Gateway to the Narrows Trail (*see* Nature Trails and Short Walks, *below*). The lush growth makes this part of Zion seem more like a tropical rainforest than a desert.

Typical desert plants do, however, thrive in Zion. Yuccas, buffalo berry, hedgehog cactus, and prickly pear are prevalent in the dry exposed areas of the park.

Call the Red Butte Gardens and Arboretum of Utah's "wildflower hotline" (tel. 801/581–4747) from April to late September for a recording that tells you which flowers are blooming in Zion and throughout the state. Once you reach the park, use the Zion Natural History Association's *Wildflowers of Zion National Park* to identify the specimens you find.

Along with the wildflowers, there is an abundance of wildlife. Expect to see mule deer in the main Zion Canyon, especially in the late fall and winter months, when the leaves drop from the cottonwood trees and the canyon bottoms and meadows are more exposed. Although mountain lions roam the park, a person could spend a lifetime here without ever seeing one of these shy, elusive cats. Small lizards are often spotted sunning themselves on the hot sandstone along the trails, and squirrels are common. Some 270 different birds have been identified here. Birds as large as golden eagles and as small as canyon wrens or Gambel's quail reside in the park, as do roadrunners.

Note: You may be tempted to feed the park's animals, especially the deer, but this practice is illegal and can result in fines. It is also detrimental to the well being of the animals and potentially dangerous to you. Despite their docile appearance, these animals are wild and may attack if approached. Deer have been known to kick people and on rare occasions have gored people. Also, don't pick flowers or plants, no matter how pretty they appear. Wildflowers quickly wilt and die when picked; leave them to be enjoyed by others.

WHEN TO GO As is the case in many of Utah's national parks, spring and fall are the best times to visit Zion. Temperatures then are moderate, and the crowds are smaller. Adding to the park's already colorful setting are wildflowers, which reach their peak in May, and the autumn leaves of maple, cottonwood, aspen, ash, and oak, which hit their peak in late October and early November.

Summer is high season at Zion, and with the greening of the meadows comes congestion at the visitor centers and main parking lots, as well as on the more popular trails. If you're driving the Zion–Mt. Carmel Highway, prepare for traffic delays near the long tunnel as rangers block off traffic to escort large RVs through. Although the climate is dry, temperatures can top 105°F in summer, and thunderstorms and flash floods are common. On the bright side, there is nothing quite like being in Zion right after a summer thunderstorm, when waterfalls seem to form everywhere. Summer also brings a greater choice of interpretative and evening programs.

Relatively mild winter temperatures make Zion a pleasant place for a December sojourn and the easiest Utah park to visit year-round. In winter park roads are regularly plowed, and they remain open all year, as do Zion Lodge and the Watchman campground. Check with rangers before going hiking in the winter. Some trails become extremely slick and icy, and snow can block trails at higher elevations, although it usually melts quickly.

Temperatures in all areas of Zion may fluctuate greatly within the course of a single day, but typically, it is warm at the bottom of the canyon and much cooler at the top. Even in July, however, a hike through the waters of the Narrows can be a chilling experience, and in February the temperature often rises to 60°F only a few days after a winter storm. January highs can range from 39°F to 60°F, lows from 15°F to 27°F. In April, highs are between 62°F and 80°F, lows 37°F and 59°F. The average highs for July run 93°F to 103°F, and lows are fairly constant, between 64°F and 73°F. In October, highs range from 70°F to 88°F and lows from 42°F to 62°F.

SEASONAL EVENTS **Thursday to Saturday after Labor Day:** Held annually in or near Zion is the **Southern Utah Folklife Festival** (tel. 801/772–3434), a commemoration of Na-

tive American and early Mormon settler life, with displays of foods and crafts, stories from local residents, horse-drawn wagon rides, and square dances. **July 1 to September 7:** The **Utah Shakespearean Festival** (tel. 801/586–7880) at Southern Utah University in Cedar City (59 miles north of Zion), includes three Shakespeare productions each summer, as well as three modern plays. Performances are in three theaters, including an outdoor replica of the Globe Theatre. There are matinees and evening performances; tickets are usually available the day of the show, but reservations are suggested.

WHAT TO PACK If you plan to hike the Zion Narrows, which involves wading through the deep waters of the Virgin River, bring waterproof bags to protect your equipment and an old pair of hiking boots or sneakers that you don't mind getting wet. On the steeper trails, a walking staff and good hiking boots are recommended—Zion's sheer cliffs can be dangerous.

The desert sun is brutal during summer. Bring water on all hikes and wear wide-brim hats and sunscreen. Rain gear is useful even in summer, when sudden thunderstorms and flash floods occur.

GENERAL STORES The supermarkets in and around Zion National Park are small convenience stores that also carry curios and souvenirs. The store nearest the park is in Springdale: the **Canyon Supermarket** (652 Zion Park Blvd., tel. 801/772–3402), open from 8 to 6 in winter and 8 AM to 9 PM in summer. **Zion Park Market** (855 Zion Park Blvd., tel. 801/772–3902) is open 9 to 6:30 in winter and 8:30 to 7:30 in summer. **Zion Canyon Campground Store** (962 Zion Park Blvd., tel. 801/772–3237) is open 8 to 6:30 in winter and 8 AM to 9 PM in summer. There is another branch in Springdale. Two miles from the park's East Entrance is **Zican** (no phone), which is open 8 AM to 6 PM

ARRIVING AND DEPARTING Most visitors arrive in Zion by car or on a tour bus. Airports and bus stations in Cedar City and St. George are a good distance away from the park, as are Amtrak stations in Salt Lake City and Las

Vegas. There are three main entrances to Zion National Park: the South and East entrances, which are linked by Route 9 (Zion–Mt. Carmel Highway), and the less-used Kolob Canyons entrance, in the northwest corner of the park.

By Plane. SkyWest Airlines (The Delta Connection) (tel. 800/453–9417) has regular flights from Salt Lake City and Las Vegas to St. George (43 miles from Zion) and Cedar City (60 miles from Zion). Rental cars and limousine services are available in both cities, but St. George has more agencies (*see* By Car and RV, *below*). You can also arrange to take a tour bus to the park (*see* Guided Tours, *below*).

By Car and RV. Interstate 15 (I–15) runs from Salt Lake City, northeast of Zion, to Las Vegas, to the southwest, and connects to Zion's Kolob Canyons Road. The park's South and East entrances are located on Route 9, which branches off I–15 near St. George. A more scenic, although slower, alternative from Salt Lake City to the East and South entrances is U.S. 89, which also links Zion to Bryce Canyon National Park and the Grand Canyon.

It is a 5½-hour, 309-mile drive from Salt Lake City to Zion; a 2½-hour, 119-mile drive from the Grand Canyon's North Rim; a 5-hour, 253-mile drive from the South Rim; a 3-hour, 158-mile drive from Las Vegas; and about a 2-hour, 86-mile drive from Bryce Canyon National Park.

You can measure the length of your RV at the South and East entrances. RVs wider than 7 feet 10 inches, higher than 11 feet 4 inches, or longer than 40 feet (50 feet including a trailer) require an escort through the narrow tunnel on Route 9, which is the only road that bisects the park. The $10 escort fee can be paid at either park entrance and is good for two trips for the same vehicle over a seven-day period. In summer, no appointment is needed. Rangers are stationed at both tunnel entrances from 8 AM until 8 PM to coordinate the escort. In the off-season, escorts must be arranged either in advance at the South or East entrances or by phoning the visitor center (tel. 801/772–3256).

RVs longer than 21 feet may not enter or park at the Weeping Rock parking area at any time, or at the Temple of Sinawava parking lot, at the end of the Zion Canyon, from 9 to 5. Passengers may be dropped off at a designated area at Temple of Sinawava. A shuttle service between Zion Lodge, where parking is allowed, and the Temple of Sinawava takes 50 minutes and costs $2.75 round-trip for adults and $1.75 for children 12 and under. Check with the lodge for additional tours that are offered occasionally.

You can rent a car in St. George from **A–1 Car Rental** (590 E. St. George Blvd., tel. 801/673–8811), **Avis** (St. George Municipal Airport, tel. 801/673–3686), **Budget** (1275 N. Highland Dr., tel. 801/673–6825), **Dollar Rent-A-Car** (1175 South 150 East, tel. 801/628–6549), and **National** (St. George Municipal Airport, tel. 801/673–5098).

Cedar City car rentals include **Avis** (Municipal Airport, tel. 801/586–3033), **Hertz** (943 S. Main St., tel. 801/586–6096), **National** (Municipal Airport, tel. 801/586–7059), and **Speedy Rental** (650 N. Main St., tel. 801/586–7368).

To rent a car in Las Vegas or Salt Lake City, call **Hertz** (tel. 800/654–3131), **Avis** (tel. 800/331–1212), or any other major rental agency.

By Train. Amtrak (tel. 800/872–7245) services both Salt Lake City and Las Vegas, where car rentals (*see* By Car and RV, *above*) and bus tours (*see* Guided Tours, *below*) are available.

By Bus. Greyhound Lines (tel. 801/355–4684) goes from Salt Lake City and Las Vegas to St. George and Cedar City, where you'll need to rent a car or take a taxi or limo (*see* By Car and RV, *above*). You can also arrange for a bus tour (*see* Guided Tours, *below*).

EXPLORING

Although most people only view the wonder of Zion from the windows of their car as they drive the mere 30 miles of road that cross the park, Zion is a place for walkers. Hiking trails are many, ranging from flat, paved half-mile walks to strenuous eight-hour climbs and multi-day backpacking excursions. If you are seeking southern Utah's famed white-water rafting, mountain biking, or four-wheel-drive adventures, head east to Canyonlands National Park.

There are two distinct sections at Zion: the Zion Canyon area in the south, which contains some of the park's most spectacular scenery and receives the great majority of its visitors, and the Kolob Canyons region in the north, which attracts people who put a premium on solitude. You can see the southern sector in two or three hours by driving the 7 miles up the Zion Canyon Scenic Drive, stopping at a few major turnouts, then backtracking to Route 9 and heading out of the park. Such a trip would, however, be tiresome, and you'll probably feel like getting out of the car.

Plan on spending at least two or three days here. Take the one-hour horseback ride from the lodge, schedule a half-day in the remote Kolob Canyons, strap on a backpack and sleep under the backcountry stars. And don't miss nearby Springdale's famed bumbleberry pie.

THE BEST IN ONE DAY There is much to see in the Four Corners area of Utah, Colorado, Arizona, and New Mexico, and travelers often try to fit in as many parks as they can in a short amount of time. Those with only one day to spend in Zion should eat breakfast at the Zion Lodge in the early morning. In summer you can sit out on the patio overlooking the canyon and watch the sun rise and the colors change. You'll have to backtrack 3¹/₂ miles to reach the Zion Canyon Visitor Center, near the park's South entrance, but it is the best place to get oriented. You can pick up park literature, books, and posters, and bombard the rangers with questions. The short slide show and small museum are informative introductions to the park.

The 7-mile Zion Canyon Scenic Drive, from the Zion Canyon Visitor Center to the Temple of Sinawava, ranks as one of the premier drives in Utah (*see* Scenic Drives and Views, *below*). At the Temple of Sinawava, change into your hiking shoes and head out on the

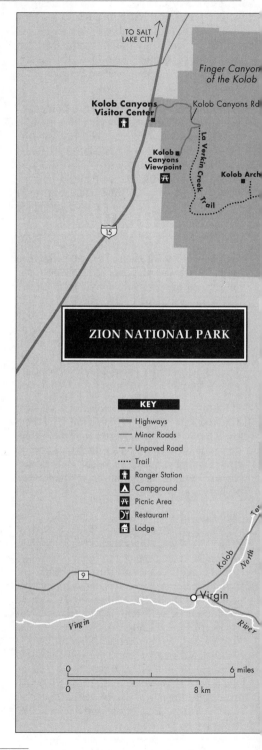

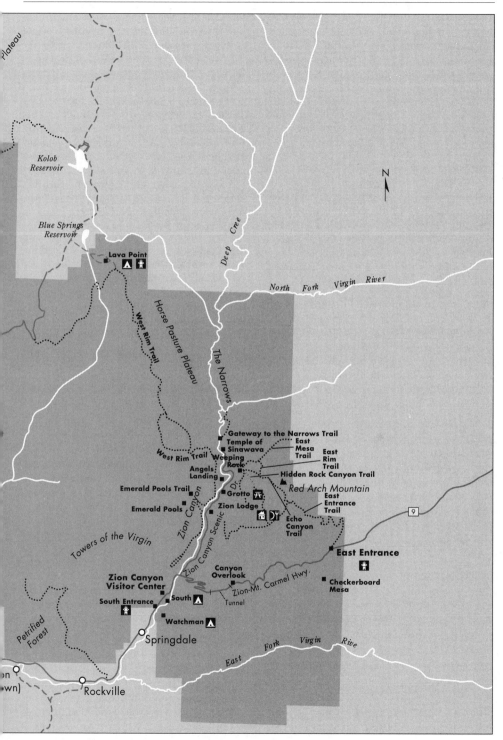

Plateau

Kolob
Reservoir

Blue Springs
Reservoir

N

Deep Creek

Lava Point

Horse Pasture Plateau

West Rim Trail

West Rim Trail

The Narrows

North Fork Virgin River

Gateway to the Narrows Trail
Temple of
Sinawava
East
Mesa
Trail
East
Rim
Trail
Weeping
Rock
Angels
Landing
Hidden Rock Canyon Trail
Red Arch Mountain
Emerald Pools Trail
Grotto
East
Entrance
Trail
9
Emerald Pools
Zion Lodge

Zion Canyon

Zion Canyon Scenic Dr.

Echo
Canyon
Trail

Towers of the Virgin

East Entrance

Canyon
Overlook

Checkerboard
Mesa

**Zion Canyon
Visitor Center**

Zion-Mt. Carmel Hwy.

South Entrance
South
Tunnel

Petrified
Forest

Watchman

on
wn)

Springdale

Rockville

East Fork Virgin River

Gateway to the Narrows Trail. The 2-mile, two-hour round-trip course passes through the hanging gardens. After this hike return to the Zion Canyon Scenic Drive and travel south for 1¹/₂ miles, until you reach the trail-head for the easy ¹/₂-mile round-trip walk out to Weeping Rock, one of Zion's many unusual geological formations. (For details of both hikes, *see* Nature Trails and Short Walks, *below.*)

At this point you will be ready for lunch, and the Grotto picnic area, 1 mile farther south, is just the spot for an impromptu canyon picnic. At Zion Lodge, ¹/₂ mile south of the Grotto, take the 1¹/₄-mile trail to Emerald Pools (*see* Nature Trails and Short Walks, *below*). On a hot summer's day watching the waterfall here is refreshing, although swimming is prohibited.

Finish off your afternoon by driving east for 11 miles along the Zion–Mt. Carmel Highway past the Checkerboard Mesa to the park's East entrance (*see* Scenic Drives and Views, *below*). Photo opportunities abound as the light of dusk plays over the canyons. Backtrack to the South entrance and exit the park; dinner or a drink in Springdale will help you wind down.

ORIENTATION PROGRAMS Audiovisual presentations at park visitor centers can be stale and boring, but the short multimedia program at the Zion Canyon Visitor Center is an exception. Slides covering every season and time of day are narrated by people who have lived and worked at Zion. The show is informative and suggests some of the best ways to see the park.

GUIDED TOURS Many tour bus operators offer packages to Bryce, Zion, and the Grand Canyon, as well as to Las Vegas and Lake Powell. The **Utah Travel Council** (Council Hall/Capitol Hill, Salt Lake City, UT 84114, tel. 801/538–1030) compiles an annual list of motorcoach tours, which runs close to 75 pages and includes tours into Utah from all over the United States and Canada.

Grayline Motor Tours of Salt Lake City (tel. 801/521–7060) offers a three-day package trip for $290 to Bryce, Zion, and the Grand Canyon from mid-June through the first week of September. **Scenic West Tours** of Salt Lake City (tel. 800/723–6249) offers package tours from May through October; a three-day, two-night excursion to Bryce, Zion, and the Grand Canyon costs $350 (double occupancy). **Toraco Enterprises** of St. George (tel. 801/628–8687) sells Zion tours leaving from the St. George airport and the airports and bus stations in Las Vegas and Salt Lake City. Other operators are **R & R Tours** (tel. 801/628–7710), in St. George, and **Western Leisure** (tel. 800/532–2113), in Salt Lake City. These tours last from two hours to a full day and range in price from $25 to $60 per person.

The National Park Service organizes daily hikes through the park except during the off-season. Check at the visitor centers for times and places. There are also guided tours on horseback (*see* Other Activities, *below*), and a few bicycle touring companies offer trips into Zion (*see* Other Activities, *below*).

SCENIC DRIVES AND VIEWS The best times to take a drive through Zion National Park are at sunrise and sunset, when the low light accentuates the colors of the surrounding cliffs. There are only four drives in Zion, one of which does not stay entirely within the bounds of the park.

Everyone who comes to Zion should drive the 13-mile round-trip route of **Zion Canyon Scenic Drive,** which begins 1 mile north of the South entrance and ends at the Temple of Sinawava parking area. There are several pullouts along the way that are ideal for picture-taking. Satisfying short walks for those with limited time are the easy Gateway to the Narrows Trail, which starts at the Temple of Sinawava, and the Weeping Rock Trail, which you can pick up along the scenic drive, 1¹/₂ miles south of Sinawava.

The segment of Route 9 that passes through the park is called the **Zion–Mt. Carmel Highway;** it climbs from the bottom of the canyon at the South entrance 13 miles up winding switchbacks and through tunnels carved out of the rock. It passes the petrified sand dunes of the Checkerboard Mesa before reaching the

East entrance. This is the road that connects Zion to Bryce Canyon and the Grand Canyon; it is particularly popular with kids, who love the tunnels. The Canyon Overlook Trail (*see* Nature Trails and Short Walks, *below*), just east of the long tunnel, is one of the most attractive hikes off this road. Drivers of over-size RVs must follow special regulations on this drive (*see* Arriving and Departing, *above*).

There are two drives in more remote areas of Zion: the 11-mile round-trip journey along **Kolob Canyons Road,** from the Kolob Canyons Visitor Center to the Kolob Canyons Viewpoint, and the 50-mile round-trip drive from the town of Virgin north along the **Kolob Terrace Road** to Lava Point and Kolob Reservoir. Kolob Canyons Road climbs more than 1,000 feet in 5 miles and ends at a viewpoint from which you can look out at the narrow finger canyons below. The latter route runs along the western edge of the park, passing farmhouses and bright green fields that form a striking contrast with the red slickrock. A good way to escape the crowds, this drive allows you to enjoy spectacular views from the top of the canyon without having to take a long hike.

HISTORIC BUILDINGS AND SITES A few examples of Mormon architecture can be found in such tiny towns as Toquerville, Rockville, and Springdale on the outskirts of Zion National Park, but the only truly historic building within the park is the **Zion Lodge**—and it has been rebuilt. The Union Pacific Railroad constructed the first Zion Lodge in 1925; some of the old cabins still in use date back to that time. A 1966 fire during a renovation project completely destroyed the lodge, but it was rebuilt in 1986 in keeping with the original design by architect Stanley Underwood (lodges at Bryce Canyon and Yosemite were also designed by Underwood). The lodge is open year-round and has a restaurant, snack bar, curio shop, and auditorium (*see* Lodging, *below*).

NATURE TRAILS AND SHORT WALKS The easiest trails at Zion are in many cases the most interesting. This is especially true of the 1¹/₄-mile round-trip hike to the **Lower Emerald Pool,** where three waterfalls cascade off the red cliffs. Another mile up a steady, rocky incline will take you to the larger **Upper Emerald Pool,** which is at the base of several 1,000-foot sheer sandstone cliffs. The lower pool is accessible by wheelchair, but some assistance may be needed on the last part of the trail.

To see just how imposing Zion Canyon can be, park your car at the Temple of Sinawava and take the easy, relatively flat 2-mile round-trip **Gateway to the Narrows Trail.** This is an especially beautiful route in spring and summer, when colorful wildflowers hang from the canyon walls. It will take about 90 minutes to complete the walk, but the way is shaded and the Virgin River keeps it cool. Interpretive signs tell the natural history of the canyon. The trail is accessible to the disabled, although some assistance may be needed higher into the canyon.

The ¹/₂-mile round-trip **Weeping Rock Trail,** in Zion Canyon, leads to a spring that issues from a rock and creates hanging gardens in the spring and summer. The 1-mile round-trip **Canyon Overlook Trail** begins just east of the long tunnel on the Zion–Mt. Carmel Highway and ends at a viewpoint overlooking lower Zion Canyon, Pine Creek Canyon, and the Zion–Mt. Carmel Highway switchbacks.

LONGER HIKES Perhaps the most famous trail in the park is the 16-mile one-way path through the **Zion Narrows,** an aptly-named slit of a canyon. Some hikers start outside the park and hike their way in. Most of their time is spent wading through the icy waters of the Virgin River. Because of the danger of flash flooding, it is necessary to get a free permit from the visitor center the afternoon before you make this long trip. Because the area has been overused, the park now issues only 80 permits for those hiking the entire length of the Narrows. It can take two days to cover the 16 miles, although strong hikers can make it in 12 hours. Those who spend the night must camp in one of the 12 group sites, each of which is limited to 12 campers. Most people, however, simply hike in from the Temple of Sinawava for a mile or two and then come back (no permit is required to do this). It is best to check at the visitor center for information on the Narrow Canyon Danger Level—a measure of current depth, temperature, river current, and weather conditions in the Narrows. Even in the summer months, have alternative hiking plans; rangers close this trail at the slightest hint of a thunderstorm.

Another challenging hike is the 5-mile round-trip climb to **Angels Landing,** a large ridge on the west side of Zion Canyon (you can see it from the road below). Plan on four hours for this strenuous hike, which starts at the Grotto Picnic Area and climbs 1,488 feet. The last half-mile follows a vertiginous ridge with a drop-off of 1,500 feet. In places where the trail gets narrow, chains are provided. This is a hike you won't forget.

The trail to Angels Landing stems off the popular **West Rim Trail,** which is 26½ miles round-trip. This trail begins at the Grotto Picnic area and ends at Lava Point, a 3,593-foot climb that takes at least 20 hours to negotiate. Hikers should plan on spending the night in the primitive campsite at Lava Point before heading back to the Grotto. If you only have time to hike part way, you will still be rewarded with views of some fine slickrock canyons not visible from the road.

The **East Rim Trail** travels 8 miles round-trip along the east rim to Observation Point, where there is a panoramic view of the valley below. Beginning at the Weeping Rock parking lot, the trail climbs 2,148 feet in a series of paved switchbacks cut into the rock. It passes through a twisting canyon so narrow the sky is often hidden from view. A side trip worth exploring is the **Hidden Canyon Trail,** which originates at the Weeping Rock parking lot and travels 2 miles round-trip through a pretty little canyon and ends at a small natural arch.

Venture into the more remote Kolob Canyons area in the northwest corner of the park and consider spending a day making the 14-mile round-trip journey to **Kolob Arch,** which, with a 310-foot span, is one of the world's largest freestanding arches. This trek begins at Lee Pass, on the Kolob Canyons Road, and involves a 699-foot descent into the canyon (that's an ascent on the return). Plan on hiking for 10 hours or, better yet, backpack and spend the night. There is a good, year-round spring at the bottom of the canyon.

OTHER ACTIVITIES **Back-Road Driving.** There are good all-terrain vehicle play areas in the nearby town of Hurricane, but none in Zion. For more information contact the Bureau of Land Management Cedar City District (176 East D.L. Sargent Dr., Cedar City, UT 84720, tel. 801/586–2041).

Biking. Zion is not a great place to cycle, largely because bicycles are limited to paved roads, which tend to be narrow and congested. No bikes are allowed on any hiking trail or in the 1-mile Zion–Mt. Carmel tunnel. Since bicycles must be carried through the tunnel, cyclists should check at the entrance station or call ahead to make arrangements. Rentals are not available in the park, but are available in Springdale at **Zion Canyon Cycling Co.** (Box 272, Springdale, UT 84767, tel. 801/772–3929). Write to park headquarters (*see* Visitor Information, *above*) for a free brochure on bicycling in Zion.

Cycling aficionados will find some excellent mountain biking trails outside of Zion. Companies operating tours that pass through the park and cover trails outside the park are **Backcountry Bicycle Tours** (Box 4029, Bozeman, MT 59772, tel. 406/586–3556) and **Backroads Bicycle Touring, Inc.** (1516 5th St., Suite Q333, Berkeley, CA 94710, tel. 800/245–3874).

Bird-Watching. More than 270 bird species have been identified in Zion National Park, including American dippers, black-headed grosbeaks, American kestrels, turkey vultures, canyon wrens, roadrunners, and even golden eagles. Rarer species are nesting peregrine falcons, Mexican spotted owls, and pygmy nuthatches. You will see the largest variety of birds in May and June. Good places to look for them are near the sewage lagoons or in the cemetery in Springdale, along the Virgin River, and on the uplands, near such plateaus as Checkerboard Mesa and Lava Point. Ask a park naturalist at the visitor center for a bird list.

Boating and Tubing. There is no boating inside the park, but you can put in at nearby Quail Creek Reservoir (tel. 801/635–9412). Rentals, however, are not available. Despite the danger, many people take inner tubes down the Virgin River. Concessionaires operating from a trailer parked outside the park's South entrance rent tubes for $5 a day, 10–7, late spring through Labor Day weekend.

Fishing. Fishing is poor inside the park, but Kolob Reservoir, roughly 5 miles north of Lava Point and accessible only by dirt road, provides good trout angling. Largemouth bass and trout are found in Quail Creek Reservoir, 30 miles from the park. A Utah fishing license is required both inside and outside the park; you can buy one in local grocery and outdoor stores or from the Division of Wildlife Resources in Cedar City (622 N. Main St., tel. 801/586–2455). A license, good from the date of purchase to the end of the calendar year, costs $40 for nonresidents and $18 for residents; it will cost you $15 for a five-day license and $5 for a single day.

Flight-Seeing. Make reservations at least two days in advance to fly over the park with **Cedar City Air Service** (2281 W. Kitty Hawk Dr., Box 458, Cedar City, UT 84720, tel. 801/586–3881). During summer, it's best to plan an early morning or late-evening flight, because midday rides tend to be bumpy and uncomfortable when it's warm outside. In 25 minutes you'll fly from Cedar City over Kolob and Zion canyons and back, a trip that costs $46 per person (a 35-minute look at the same area costs $65). There is a two-person minimum on all flights.

Horseback Riding. Those bothered by elevations and heat should try exploring Zion on horseback. Guided rides along several picturesque trails are available from **Bryce–Zion–Grand Canyon Trail Rides** (tel. 801/772–3967 in season; tel. 801/679–8665 off-season), located near the Zion Lodge. One-hour ($10) and half-day ($30) rides are offered from mid-March through October. Experi-

ence is not necessary, but children must be at least five years old. Make advance reservations.

Rock Climbing. Rangers recommend Zion's cliffs for experienced rock climbers only, largely because sandstone is more difficult to negotiate than granite. No permits are required unless you plan to spend the night. You should, however, check in with the rangers to find out if there are restrictions on any routes; many climbing areas are closed in spring and summer to protect nesting peregrine falcons. Fall and spring are ideal times to climb; summers are often too hot. For free literature, stop in at the visitor centers or write to park headquarters (*see* Visitor Information, *above*). You must provide your own climbing equipment.

Snowmobiling. Snowmobiles are permitted only on unplowed roads, which are few in Zion, but there are good routes just outside the park. Contact the Utah Division of Parks and Recreation (1636 W. North Temple St., Salt Lake City, UT 84116, tel. 801/538–7220) for snowmobiling information.

Snowshoeing and Ski Touring. Some snowshoeing and cross-country skiing is available on the higher plateau areas of the park; Wildcat Canyon and the upper West Rim Trail have the best conditions.

Swimming. Although a few visitors wade in the Virgin River or more remote streams, swimming at Zion is limited. Some motels in Mt. Carmel and Springdale have pools, but no public facilities exist. The Pah Tempe Hot Springs (tel. 801/635–2879), near La Verkin (27 miles from Zion), and Quail Creek Reservoir are your best bets for a swim in the area.

CHILDREN'S PROGRAMS The Zion Nature Center's **Junior Ranger Program** (tel. 801/772–3256), for kids six to 12 years old, ranks among the best children's programs in all the national parks. The center is within walking distance of both campgrounds and operates from June through Labor Day, with registration each morning and afternoon. Rangers offer instruction on such topics as wildlife protection and conservation. There is a $1 fee per child.

EVENING ACTIVITIES Evening programs at Zion's campgrounds vary from year to year; they often include slide shows, night hikes, and historical reenactments. Other evening entertainment can be had at **O. C. Tanner Amphitheater** (tel. 801/673–4811), a block outside the park's South entrance, which hosts concerts, slide shows, and ethnic dances. "The Grand Circle," a multimedia show depicting national parks in the area, is presented nightly June to September on a huge screen. For the finale, the cliffs of Zion are illuminated. Tickets to this hour-long show cost $4 for adults, $10 for families, and $3 for students, and may be purchased at the door.

DINING

Dining around Zion tends to be a down-home American affair. The restaurants in this corner of Utah are neither fancy nor expensive, but the food they prepare is wholesome, filling—and definitely Western. Expect barbecue and a lot of red meat, although vegetarian selections can be found, too. The Zion Lodge is the only restaurant inside the park; the others reviewed here are in Springdale, Utah, near the park's South entrance. Most of these have picture windows and patios with canyon views, allowing you to enjoy the scenery even though you are outside the park. Unless otherwise stated, the restaurants below have a state liquor license, allow casual dress, and require no reservations.

INSIDE THE PARK **Zion Lodge.** This is the quintessence of Western family dining, one of the classier places to eat in the area. A wall of windows overlooks the maws of the great canyon, and a wood-beam ceiling and historic photos lend the room the requisite pioneer atmosphere. White tablecloths and candles add a formal touch. As busy as it is, the restaurant is surprisingly low-key and serves high-quality food. The specialty here is the Pioneer's Pride Dinner, usually either pork chops marinated in apple cider, or apple sausage–stuffed chicken breasts. In summer,

consider a table on the patio. Other than a small snack bar nearby, this is the only dining area inside the park. *Zion National Park, tel. 801/772–3213. Reservations strongly advised. AE, DC, MC, V. Moderate.*

NEAR THE PARK **Flanigans.** Flanigans' Santa Fe pastels create a soothing, intimate atmosphere. With its southwestern decor and walls covered with photographs of Utah, this is one of the more refined restaurants in Springdale. The menu features a southwestern game plate consisting of medallions of venison, pheasant, and game sausage of elk or buffalo meat, served over wild rice. Only wine and beer are served in the dining room. *428 Zion Park Blvd., Springdale, tel. 801/772–3244. Reservations advised. AE, D, DC, MC, V. Closed occasionally in December at the owner's discretion. Moderate–Expensive.*

Bit and Spur. A bit on the pricey side, this extremely popular Springdale restaurant is one of the best Mexican restaurants in Utah. In addition to standard Mexican dishes, expect such offbeat entrées as seafood enchiladas and Zuni stew, a variation of a Zuni-Hopi dish that combines lamb, rabbit, juniper berries, New Mexican and Ancho chilis, baby corn, potatoes, and a dash of gin. Live rock and country-western music are sometimes featured on weekends. *1212 Zion Park Blvd., Springdale, tel. 801/772–3498. Reservations advised. MC, V. No lunch. Closed 2 weeks in Dec. Moderate.*

Bumbleberry Inn. One mile south of the park boundary is this venerable family restaurant, which is known for its patented bumbleberry pie. What's a bumbleberry? The waitress will be more than happy to tell you. The inn is also known for its country-fried steaks, chicken, and spaghetti. No alcohol is served or allowed on the premises. *897 Zion Park Blvd., Springdale, tel. 801/772–3224. AE, D, MC, V. Closed Sun. Moderate.*

Driftwood Lodge. This restaurant, like many in the area, has a rustic ranch decor and picture windows framing a pasture and red cliffs. Trout, large portions of prime rib, moist roasted chicken, and steaks are served; the chicken is your best bet. Pastries and bread are homemade. *1515 Zion Park Blvd., Springdale, tel. 801/772–3262. AE, D, DC, MC, V. Moderate.*

Pioneer Lodge and Restaurant. Generically prepared American food—steak, liver, trout, halibut, and spaghetti dinners—comes with a full salad bar. An old fireplace and heavy wood beams add a rustic touch. Don't miss the homemade ice cream pie. *828 Zion Park Blvd., Springdale, tel. 801/772–3009. AE, D, MC, V. Closed Dec.–Mar. Inexpensive–Moderate.*

Electric Jims. This fast-food hamburger stop is the last restaurant you'll see before reaching the park's South entrance. Electric Jims has the look of a '50s diner with a southwestern touch—and some of Utah's best fast food. The broiled chicken breast is served with sprouts, Swiss cheese, and an Ortega chili; a vegetarian sandwich called the Moonlight Express is heaped with bean sprouts, pickles, tomatoes, cucumbers, and Ortega chili. But happiness is the Virgin Burger (the Virgin River runs nearby) and a fresh fruit shake. The lemonade is good, too. Outdoor tables are available. *Zion Park Blvd., Springdale, tel. 801/772–3838. No credit cards. Closed during the winter months at discretion of owner. Inexpensive.*

Zion Pizza and Noodle Company. You can eat inside or on the porch of this old church, which has been transformed into a pizza and pasta restaurant. Each night brings a different pasta special, but among the regular dishes not to miss is the manicotti marinaro. There's a trading shop located downstairs and a bookstore next door, so you can shop when you're through with dinner. *868 Zion Park Blvd., Springdale, tel. 801/772–3815. No credit cards. Inexpensive.*

PICNIC SPOTS Of the two picnic spots inside the park, the Grotto Picnic Area is the largest and most developed. Situated in the heart of Zion Canyon and not far from the lodge, this area is equipped with fire grates, picnic tables, water, rest rooms, and even grass. The other, a small primitive area with tables and pit toilets, is at the end of the Kolob Canyons Road, in the northwest corner of the park. Picnic supplies are available at the small general stores in Springdale or just outside the East entrance. The best place to pick up supplies in the Kolob Canyons area is in Cedar City.

LODGING

Finding a room or campsite in summer or during holiday weekends isn't easy, even in Cedar City or St. George. Plan to arrive early in the day or make reservations well in advance. The most convenient places to stay outside the park are in Springdale, just outside the South entrance, or in neighboring Rockville, both of which border the park and allow overnight visitors to enjoy the park scenery even though they're staying in town.

Those looking for an authentic brush with rural Utah will do their best to stay at a bed-and-breakfast, where fluffy towels and good home cooking make you feel as though you're visiting friends. Many of the inexpensive lodgings listed below are no more than places to put your head at night, but if a swimming pool or hot tub beckon after a day of hiking, a motel in Springdale might be your ticket.

INSIDE THE PARK **Zion Lodge.** Being the only lodging available within the park, the motel-like units and cabins of this property are booked up every night during the summer and early fall. The 1920s lodge burned in 1966 but was quickly rebuilt that year, and its exterior was recently restored to resemble the original. Stone columns hold up the large terrace off the dining room, which was rebuilt using native timber. The modern motel units are spacious, and all have porches or private balconies that open onto splendid canyon views. The 40 private cabins are more rustic—dark and sometimes even musty—but with large stone fireplaces (gas-burning) and porches off each one, they are more desirable than the motel units, even though they cost more. The noticeable absence of a 20th-century crutch—the TV—forces guests into the great outdoors. Reservations should be made well in advance, although in winter, rooms can usually be booked on arrival. *Zion National Park, Box 400, Cedar City, UT, 84720, tel. 801/586–7686 for reservations, 801/772–3213 to reach the lodge, fax 801/586–3157. 121 rooms and cabins with bath. Facilities: restaurant. AE, DC, MC, V. Moderate–Expensive.*

NEAR THE PARK **Best Western Driftwood Lodge.** On well-manicured grounds, this standard motel has perhaps the best swimming pool in Springdale. *1515 Zion Park Blvd., Box 98, Springdale, UT 84767, tel. 801/772–3702. 47 rooms with bath. Facilities: restaurant, swimming pool, hot tub. AE, D, DC, MC, V. Moderate–Expensive.*

Cliffrose Lodge and Gardens. A quarter mile from the park's South entrance and surrounded by botanical gardens and acres of lawn and trees, this new hotel guarantees a quiet night's sleep. Rooms are spacious and have balconies that provide great views of Zion Canyon and Watchman Mountain. *281 Zion Park Blvd., Springdale, UT 84767 tel. 801/772–3234 or 800/243–8824. 36 rooms with bath. Facilities: swimming pool, hot tub. AE, D, MC, V. Moderate–Expensive.*

Thunderbird Best Western. Just what you would expect from a Best Western: clean, comfortable but nondescript rooms. There is a golf course nearby. *Mt. Carmel Junction of U.S. 89 and Rte. 9, Box 36, Mt. Carmel, UT 84755, tel. 801/648–2203 or 800/528–1234. 65 rooms with bath. Facilities: swimming pool, hot tub. AE, D, DC, MC, V. Moderate–Expensive.*

Under the Eaves Guest House. Built of sandstone blocks cut from the canyon walls in 1935, this antiques-filled B&B has served at various times as the Springdale post office, school, and library. A full breakfast is served. *980 Zion Park Blvd., Box 29, Springdale, UT 84767, tel. 801/772–3457. 3 rooms with bath, 2 rooms share 1 bath. MC, V. Pets allowed by arrangement. Moderate–Expensive.*

Zion House Bed-and-Breakfast. Well-known in town for its gracious hospitality, the Zion House has spacious modern bedrooms decorated in gray and pink with views of the park. Guests are treated like family; they eat a huge

breakfast together and enjoy the comforts of the downstairs common room. *801 Zion Park Blvd., Box 323, Springdale, UT 84767, tel. 801/772–3281. 2 rooms with bath, 2 rooms share 1 bath. Moderate–Expensive.*

Bumbleberry Inn. The newly decorated rooms at this motel have patios or balconies. *897 Zion Park Blvd., Springdale, UT 84767, tel. 801/772–3224. 24 rooms with bath. Facilities: pool. AE, D, MC, V. Moderate.*

Canyon Ranch Motel. With both cabins and motel rooms, this is a great place for families even though the units are unremarkable. Many visitors choose those with kitchenettes. There are shade trees and picnic tables, and the location, just ½ mile from the park, cuts driving time substantially. *668 Zion Park Blvd., Box 175, Springdale, UT 84767, tel. 801/772–3357. 21 units with bath; 5 with kitchenettes. Facilities: swimming pool, Jacuzzi. D, MC, V. Moderate.*

Flanigans. Kelly-green carpets and pastel southwestern furnishings contribute to the appeal of this property, which resembles a big log cabin from the outside. Tranquil paths lead to the pool area. *428 Zion Park Blvd., Box 100, Springdale, UT 84767, tel. 801/772–3244 or 800/765–7787. 36 rooms with bath. Facilities: pool. AE, D, DC, MC, V. Moderate.*

Handcart House Bed-and-Breakfast. This new stucco home, filled with antiques, was built in the Mormon pioneer style in honor of the owners' ancestors, who pulled handcarts across the country. Breakfast is generous and served with a local prickly-pear jelly. *244 W. Main St., Box 146, Rockville, UT 84763, tel. 801/772–3867. 3 rooms with bath. AE, MC, V. Moderate.*

Harvest House Bed-and-Breakfast. Barbara and Steven Cooper came to Zion for a visit and just couldn't leave. Barbara, the former co-owner and head chef of the Boston-based Harvest Catering Company, delights visitors with fresh homemade pastries, preserves, and other treats: cheese blintzes, almond French toast, and carmelized bananas. *29 Canyon View Dr., Box 125, Springdale, UT*

84767, tel. 801/772–3880. 4 rooms with bath. Facilities: hot tub. MC, V. Moderate.

Pioneer Lodge. A mile from the park entrance, this large, Western-style motel has wood-trimmed railings and a restaurant with old wagon wheels hanging above the front doors. The 42 rooms were all completely remodeled in 1989. *838 Zion Park Blvd., Box 480, Springdale, UT 84767, tel. 801/772–3233. 42 rooms with bath. Facilities: swimming pool, Jacuzzi. AE, D, MC, V. Moderate.*

Zion Canyon Campground Cabins. These cabins are on the grounds of a private RV park, near the Virgin River—a great place to be on a hot summer day. Two people can sleep in each cabin, and one family unit accommodates five. *479 Zion Park Blvd., Box 99, Springdale, UT 84767, tel. 801/772–3237. 12 cabins with bath. Facilities: laundromat, game room, convenience store, pizza parlor. MC, V. Moderate.*

Zion Park Motel. Set in the center of downtown Springdale, this motel has its own adjacent general market. It is convenient to everything but a bit lacking in personality. *855 Zion Park Blvd., Box 365, Springdale, UT 84767, tel. 801/772–3251. 23 rooms. Facilities: swimming pool, laundry, market. AE, D, MC, V. Moderate.*

Blue House Bed-and-Breakfast. Here, you can watch sunrise break over the jagged sentinels at the entrance to Zion or contemplate an orchard framed by red cliffs. This new blue frame house with white trim is decorated with plush carpets, floral bedspreads, wicker, and oak. The ample breakfast, complete with homemade preserves, makes a night here a steal. *125 E. Main St., Box 176, Rockville, UT 84763, tel. 801/772–3912. 2 rooms share bath, 1 with bath. MC, V. Inexpensive–Moderate.*

Terrace Brook Lodge. This lodge is situated on two grassy acres, and roughly half of its rooms offer panoramic views of the canyon. Tall trees provide much-needed shade after a day of touring. *990 Zion Park Blvd., Box 217, Springdale, UT 84767, tel. 801/772–3932 or 800/342–6779. 23 rooms. Facilities: swim-*

ming pool, picnic/barbecue area. AE, D, MC, V. Inexpensive–Moderate.

El Rio Lodge. This is a small property where all the rooms have balconies over the roof of the motel's office. *995 Zion Park Blvd., Box 326, Springdale, UT 84767 tel. 801/772–3205. 10 rooms. MC, V. Inexpensive.*

CAMPING

INSIDE THE PARK In high season, Zion's two large campgrounds, the 140-site **South Campground** and the 270-site **Watchman,** fill almost every night. Located near the park's South entrance, these facilities resemble those in other national parks: They have spacious sites and well-maintained rest rooms with only cold running water. Both campgrounds have flush toilets, drinking water, fire grates, a disposal station, and a public phone. Although both areas have sites that are large enough for RVs, neither offers hookups or showers. Only Watchman is open year-round; South Campground is open from mid-April to mid-October. These campgrounds are set beneath cottonwood trees near the Virgin River; the best sites are closest to the river—and farthest from the road. Both charge $7 per site per night.

The only other campground in the park is the small, primitive **Lava Point,** with only six sites for tents or RVs. These sites have fire grates, but there is no water at Lava Point. This free campground is located off the beaten track, on the northern edge of the park, so before you head out there, ask at the visitor center if space is available. Lava Point is open from early June to mid-October. Reservations are not accepted for any park campground.

NEAR THE PARK Some of the best camping facilities, especially for tenters, are in the nearby **Coral Pink Sand Dunes State Park** (tel. 801/874–2408). The 22-site campground here tends to be less crowded than those at Zion. Coral Pink's campground has flush toilets, hot showers, drinking water, fire grates, a disposal station, and a ranger station. It is open year-round. All sites cost $9 per night Sunday–Thursday, $10 Friday and Saturday,

ZION CAMPGROUNDS

	INSIDE THE PARK			NEAR THE PARK				
	South	Watchman	Lava Point	Coral Pink Sand Dunes State Park	Snow Canyon State Park	Zion Canyon	East Zion RV Park	Bryce/Zion KOA
Total number of sites	140	270	6	22	36	150	15	80
Sites suitable for RVs	140	270	6	22	36	100	15	60
Number of hookups	0	0	0	0	14	100	15	50
Drive to sites	•	•	•	•	•	•	•	•
Hike to sites								
Flush toilets	•	•		•	•	•	•	•
Pit/chemical toilets			•					
Drinking water	•	•		•	•	•	•	•
Showers				•	•	•		•
Fire grates	•	•		•	•	•	•	•
Swimming						•		•
Boat access								
Playground				•	•	•		•
Disposal station	•	•		•	•	•	•	•
Ranger station				•	•			
Public telephone	•	•			•	•	•	•
Reservation possible				•*	•*	•	•	•
Daily fee per site	$7	$7	free	$9–$10	$9–$11	$12–$14	$11	$15–$18.50
Dates open	mid-Apr.–mid-Oct.	year-round	early June–mid-Oct.	year-round	year-round	year-round	year-round	early May–mid-Oct.

*Reservation fee charged.

but there are no hookups. The one group site at Coral Pink does have electricity and can accommodate up to 40 people or five vehicles (call ahead to inquire about the availability of this site). Be aware that 80% of Coral Pink's visitors come to use their off-road vehicles (ATVs and dune buggies) on the 5-mile stretch of sand dunes. Evening quiet hours are strictly enforced, however, so families can still enjoy a quiet night of sleep. Coral Pink is roughly 10 miles south of Mt. Carmel Junction on U.S. 89 (25 miles from Zion) and a natural place to break during a journey between Zion and the Grand Canyon's North Rim.

Sixty miles southwest of Zion, on the way to Las Vegas and Death Valley, is **Snow Canyon State Park** (tel. 801/628–2255), which has a 36-site campground set in striking sandstone coves, surrounded by juniper trees. This campground also has flush toilets, hot showers, drinking water, fire grates, a disposal station, a ranger station, and a public phone. It is open year-round. Snow Canyon has 14 electricity and water hookups for RVs as well as a playground. Tent sites cost $9, and RV sites cost $11 per night.

Reservations are recommended at all Utah State Parks, especially in summer. Call 800/322–3770 Monday through Friday, 8–5, or write to the Utah Department of Natural Resources (1636 W. N. Temple St., Suite 116, Salt Lake City, UT 84116). There is a reservation service charge of $5 per site in addition to the camp fee.

Several good private facilities near the park offer RV hookups. The closest is the **Zion Canyon Campground** (Box 99, Springdale UT 84767, tel. 801/772–3237), located about a half-mile south of the South entrance and open year-round. This campground has 150 sites, 100 of which are gravel and have full hookups. It is surrounded on three sides by the park's rock formations, and many of the sites are on the river. Facilities include flush toilets, showers, drinking water, fire grates, a disposal station, a public phone, a laundry

room, a playground, a game room, and a restaurant. There is swimming in the Virgin River. A site with a hookup costs $14 for two people; without a hookup it's $12 for two. Reservations are requested by mail one month in advance.

In Mt. Carmel Junction, 15 miles east of the East entrance, at the junction of Route 9 and U.S. 89, the 15-site **East Zion RV Park** (tel. 801/648–2326) offers most of what the Zion RV Park offers, but it doesn't have hot water, fire grates, or a swimming pool. There is, however, a golf course and two restaurants across the street. Sites cost $11 per night, and reservations, though generally not necessary, can be made by phone. It's open year-round.

Those headed to or from Bryce Canyon National Park might want to stop over at the **Bryce/Zion KOA,** on U.S. 89, about 50 miles from both Bryce and Zion and 90 minutes from the Grand Canyon. This secluded campground is set amid juniper and oak trees at the base of majestic pink cliffs. It has 60 RV (30 water/electric and 20 full hookups) and 20 tent sites as well as two large group sites that can each accommodate up to 40 people. There are flush toilets, hot showers, drinking water, fire grates, a disposal station, and a public phone here. Laundry facilities and a general store are convenient additions, and the playground, swimming pool, hiking trails, and guided horse tours will keep campers busy. The KOA is closed from October 15 to May 1. Sites cost $15 to $18.50 and should be reserved in advance. Contact Glendale KOA, Box 186, Glendale, UT 84729, tel. 801/648–2490.

Huge campgrounds and trailer parks in the towns of Hurricane (29 miles away) and St. George (43 miles away) cater primarily to the area's growing retirement community. Some have golf courses and most have swimming pools. Since they tend to attract "snowbirds," summer rates here generally range from $9 to $11 for two people, and are as much as $20 for full hookups. There is almost always space.

Fodor's Travel Guides

Available at bookstores everywhere, or call 1–800–533–6478, 24 hours a day.

U.S. Guides

Alaska

Arizona

Boston

California

Cape Cod, Martha's Vineyard, Nantucket

The Carolinas & the Georgia Coast

Chicago

Colorado

Florida

Hawaii

Las Vegas, Reno, Tahoe

Los Angeles

Maine, Vermont, New Hampshire

Maui

Miami & the Keys

New England

New Orleans

New York City

Pacific North Coast

Philadelphia & the Pennsylvania Dutch Country

The Rockies

San Diego

San Francisco

Santa Fe, Taos, Albuquerque

Seattle & Vancouver

The South

The U.S. & British Virgin Islands

The Upper Great Lakes Region

USA

Vacations in New York State

Vacations on the Jersey Shore

Virginia & Maryland

Waikiki

Walt Disney World and the Orlando Area

Washington, D.C.

Foreign Guides

Acapulco, Ixtapa, Zihuatanejo

Australia & New Zealand

Austria

The Bahamas

Baja & Mexico's Pacific Coast Resorts

Barbados

Berlin

Bermuda

Brazil

Brittany & Normandy

Budapest

Canada

Cancun, Cozumel, Yucatan Peninsula

Caribbean

China

Costa Rica, Belize, Guatemala

The Czech Republic & Slovakia

Eastern Europe

Egypt

Euro Disney

Europe

Europe's Great Cities

Florence & Tuscany

France

Germany

Great Britain

Greece

The Himalayan Countries

Hong Kong

India

Ireland

Israel

Italy

Japan

Kenya & Tanzania

Korea

London

Madrid & Barcelona

Mexico

Montreal & Quebec City

Morocco

Moscow & St. Petersburg

The Netherlands, Belgium & Luxembourg

New Zealand

Norway

Nova Scotia, Prince Edward Island & New Brunswick

Paris

Portugal

Provence & the Riviera

Rome

Russia & the Baltic Countries

Scandinavia

Scotland

Singapore

South America

Southeast Asia

Spain

Sweden

Switzerland

Thailand

Tokyo

Toronto

Turkey

Vienna & the Danube Valley

Yugoslavia